Economic Issues, Problems and Perspectives

Finance of Renewable Energy in a Sustainable World
Faruk Dayi, PhD (Editor)
ISBN: 979-8-89530-541-6
eBook ISBN: 979-8-89530-593-5

Economic Integration: Strategies, Challenges and Global Implications
Alina Hyz, PhD
and Panagiotis E. Kaldis, PhD (Editors)
ISBN: 979-8-89530-338-2
eBook ISBN: 979-8-89530-404-4

The New Geography in the Global Automotive Industry
Marcelo José do Carmo, PhD,
Mário Sacomano Neto, PhD,
Júlio César Donadone, PhD,
Aditya Kuthar and Shreya Gupta
ISBN: 979-8-89530-029-9
eBook ISBN: 979-8-89530-077-0

Sprawl and the City: Realizing a Sustainable Mediterranean Urbanization
Ioannis Vardopoulos, Alessia D'Agata,
Francisco Escrivà Saneugenio
and Luca Salvati, PhD (Editors)
ISBN: 979-8-89530-006-0
eBook ISBN: 979-8-89530-044-2

Navigating Sustainability: A Comparative Analysis of Micro vs. Macro Strategies in Least Developed Countries
Medani P. Bhandari, PhD
and Medani Adhikari
ISBN: 979-8-89113-771-4
eBook ISBN: 979-8-89113-822-3

Financial Sector Development and Pandemics in an Era of Sustainable Development Goals
Paul Adjei Kwakwa, PhD (Editor)
ISBN: 979-8-89530-548-5
eBook ISBN: 979-8-89530-617-8

Diabetes: Research, Economic Impact, and New Programs
Lisa Primitiva (Editor)
ISBN: 979-8-89113-545-1
eBook ISBN: 979-8-89113-620-5

Stablecoins: Background, Risks and Legislation
Olivier Bullock (Editor)
ISBN: 979-8-89113-502-4
eBook ISBN: 979-8-89113-549-9

More information about this series can be found at
https://novapublishers.com/product-category/series/economic-issues-problems-and-perspectives/

Economic Issues, Problems and Perspectives

snova
New York

Liam Moore
Editor

Healthcare:
Costs, Competition and Transparency

snova
New York

Additional color graphics may be available in the e-book version of this book.

Library of Congress Cataloging-in-Publication Data

ISBN: 979-8-89530-633-8 (Hardcover)
ISBN: 979-8-89530-648-2 (eBook)

Published by Nova Science Publishers, Inc. † New York

Contents

Preface

The rising costs of care for individuals is one of the single greatest threats to the overall economic security of Americans. Over the past 30 years, the cost of healthcare has steadily risen by almost 5 percent, annually. Rising costs have coincided with a sharp rise in consolidation within the healthcare industry. Lowering these costs can be achieved through greater price transparency in the healthcare system. This book discusses the need to improve price transparency in health care as well as improve competition amongst payers and providers of health care to help lower costs for patients.

Chapter 1

Lowering Unaffordable Costs: Examining Transparency and Competition in Healthcare*

Committee on Energy and Commerce

Tuesday, March 28, 2023
House of Representatives, Subcommittee on Health,
Committee on Energy and Commerce,
Washington, DC.

The subcommittee met, pursuant to call, at 1:02 p.m., in the John D. Dingell Room 2123 of the Rayburn House Office Building, Hon. Brett Guthrie (chairman of the subcommittee) presiding.

Members present: Representatives Guthrie, Burgess, Latta, Griffith, Bilirakis, Johnson, Bucshon, Hudson, Carter, Dunn, Pence, Crenshaw, Joyce, Harshbarger, Miller-Meeks, Obernolte, Rodgers (ex officio), Eshoo (subcommittee ranking member), Sarbanes, Ca´ rdenas, Ruiz, Dingell, Kuster, Blunt Rochester, Craig, Schrier, Trahan, and Pallone (ex officio).

Also present: Representatives Allen, Balderson, and Matsui.

Staff present: Alec Aramanda, Professional Staff Member, Health; Jolie Brochin, Clerk, Health; Seth Gold, Professional Staff Member, Health; Grace Graham, Chief Counsel, Health; Jack Heretik, Press Secretary; Nate Hodson, Staff Director; Peter Kielty, General Counsel; Emily King, Member Services Director; Carla Rafael, Staff Assistant; Lydia Abma, Minority Policy Analyst; Waverly Gordon, Minority Deputy Staff Director and General Counsel; Saha Khaterzai, Minority Professional Staff Member; Una Lee, Minority Chief Health Counsel; Greg Pugh, Minority Staff Assistant; and C.J. Young, Minority Deputy Communications Director.

Mr. GUTHRIE. The subcommittee will come to order. The Chair recognizes himself for an opening statement.

---

* This is an edited, reformatted and augmented version of Hearing Before the Subcommittee on Health of the Committee on Energy and Commerce House of Representatives, Serial No. 118–16, dated March 28, 2023.

In: Healthcare: Costs, Competition and Transparency
Editor: Liam Moore
ISBN: 979-8-89530-633-8

Opening Statement of Hon. Brett Guthrie, a Representative in Congress from the Commonwealth of Kentucky

Today we are holding a bipartisan hearing to examine the rising cost of healthcare for patients and their families. Rising costs of care for individuals is one of the single greatest threats to the overall economic security of Americans. Over the past 30 years, the cost of healthcare has steadily risen by almost 5 percent, annually. In 2021 costs eclipsed 4 trillion annually, amounting to roughly $13,000 per person.

Rising costs have coincided with a sharp rise in consolidation within the healthcare industry. There have been almost 1,800 hospital mergers between 1998 and 2021, leading to about 2,000 fewer hospitals throughout the country. Larger health systems are also buying physician practices at record rates. More than 80,000 physician practices were acquired in 2018, a marked increase over the more than 35,000 acquired in 2012.

The three largest pharmacy benefit managers represent over 80 percent of the marketplace, and many have merged with insurance companies, specialty pharmacies, retail pharmacies, and even drug distribution.

Today we spend 31 percent of all healthcare expenditures on hospital services, 20 percent on physician services, and 9 percent on prescription medications. It is important to note that these are just recent trends. The point of today's hearing is to better understand these trends, which I believe can be achieved through greater price transparency in the healthcare system.

Despite having all this aggregate expenditure information widely available to the public, patients and employers are unable to access an upfront price for giving an item or service. They cannot make informed decisions about how and where to spend their money as they can in virtually every other industry. Consequentially, this leads to high, unexpected costs, a lack of trust with the healthcare system, and a reluctance to seek critical healthcare services.

Not long ago, a constituent called me. He was frustrated because he could not find the price to get a simple healthcare procedure done. He had health insurance, but was trying to find high-quality care at the best price within his budget. Unfortunately, this was a—is a frustration shared by millions of Americans.

I hope today that—I hope that today can be a start on finding bipartisan solutions to make healthcare pricing more transparent and the healthcare system easier to navigate for patients. We should start with any improvements necessary to the Centers for Medicare and Medicare Services' Hospital Price Transparency Rule and the multidepartment Transparency in Coverage Rule.

These rules require hospitals to publicly post prices of hundreds of common procedures on their website in a user-friendly format and require private health plans to disclose information about pricing and what patients are obligated to pay. All of this information gives patients and employers that pay for health insurance for their employees more information and some peace of mind to know how much their healthcare procedures or services would cost ahead of ahead of receiving the care.

It is imperative for the Biden administration to conduct greater enforcement efforts on these rules to better serve patients with clear and actionable price information.

It is also crucial for Congress to codify and strengthen these important transparency rules to support a more efficient price transparency regulatory environment.

Congress should also consider solutions to make other parts of the healthcare system more transparent. We should build on our bipartisan work to make the pharmacy benefit managers more transparent and ensure patients as well as employers are getting the best possible deal on their prescription drug benefits. This could also lead to greater access to biosimilars and generics when they come to market.

Shining a light on middlemen who are making prescriptions more expensive is one important step to bolster competition and lower prices.

Further, patients, especially seniors, are unnecessarily paying more money for the same service because of the location where it was delivered, which requires further discussion.

It is well past time to carefully examine the root causes of these inefficiencies that are plaguing patients with higher costs and more confusion. By working together across the aisle, I am hoping we can make important strides to make the healthcare system easier for patients to navigate, so they can get the healthcare they need. To that end, I look forward to today's discussion.

I really appreciate working with the ranking member and our staffs together to put this wonderful panel together. Every witness is a bipartisan witness and was—is brought together, and we really appreciate it.

[The prepared statement of Mr. Guthrie follows:]

Chair Brett Guthrie Opener
Health Hearing Entitled, "Lowering Unaffordable Costs: Examining Transparency and Competition in Health Care"

As Prepared for Delivery Today, we will hold a bipartisan hearing to examine the rising costs of health care for patients and their families. The rising costs of care for individuals is one of the single-greatest threats to the overall economic security of Americans and their households. Over the past thirty years, the cost of health care has steadily risen by almost 5% annually, eclipsing $4 trillion annually, or roughly $13,000 per person. Over this same period, the United States has also seen a sharp rise in consolidation within the health care industry. There have been almost 1,800 hospital mergers between 1998 and 2021, leading to about 2,000 fewer hospitals throughout the country. Larger health systems are also buying physician practices at record rates as more than 80,000 physician practices were acquired in 2018, a marked increase over the more than 35,000 acquired in 2012. The three largest pharmacy benefit managers represent over 80% of the marketplace and many have merged with insurance companies, specialty pharmacies, retail pharmacies, and even drug distribution. Today, we spend thirty one percent of all health care expenditures on hospital services, twenty percent on physician services, and nine percent on prescription medications. However, despite having all this aggregate expenditure information widely available to the public, patients and employers are unable to access an up-front price for a given item or service. They cannot make informed decisions about how and where to spend their money like they can in virtually every other industry. This not only leads to high unexpected costs, but more consequentially a lack of trust with the health care system and a reluctance to critical seek health care services. I hope today can be a start on finding bipartisan solutions to make health care pricing more transparent and the health care system easier to navigate for patients, starting with any improvements necessary to the Centers for Medicare and Medicare Services' hospital price transparency rule and the multi-Department transparency in coverage rule. These rules require hospitals to publicly post the prices of hundreds of common procedures on their website in a user-friendly format and require private health plans to disclose information about pricing and what patients are obligated to pay. All of this information gives patients and employers that pay for health insurance for their employees more information and some peace of mind to know how much their health procedure or services would cost ahead of receiving care. It is imperative for the Biden Administration to conduct greater enforcement efforts on these rules in order to better serve patients with clear and actionable price information. It is also crucial for Congress to strengthen these important transparency rules to support more efficient price transparency regulatory environment.

Congress should also consider solutions to make other parts of the health care system less opaque. We should build on our bipartisan work to make Pharmacy Benefit Managers be more transparent. Shining a light on middlemen who are making prescriptions more expensive is one important step to bolster competition and lower prices for patients. Further, patients, especially seniors, are unnecessarily paying more money for the same service simply because of the location where it was delivered.

It's time to carefully examine the root causes of these inefficiencies that are plaguing patients with higher costs and more confusion. And just maybe, by working together across the aisle on "first downs," we can make the health care system easier for patients to navigate and ultimately get the health care they need. To that end, I look forward to today's discussion and I yield back.

Mr. GUTHRIE. I appreciate your hard work, and I yield back, and I will now recognize my good friend, the gentlelady from California, Representative Eshoo, for 5 minutes for an opening statement.

Opening Statement of Hon. Anna G. Eshoo, a Representative in Congress from the State of California

Ms. ESHOO. Thank you, Mr. Chairman, for holding this important hearing, and welcome to all the witnesses. We can't wait to start asking you questions.

The late Uwe Reinhardt—he was a prestigious health economist who often appeared before this subcommittee—famously said "It's the prices, stupid" when critiquing why the U.S. spends so much on healthcare. Twenty years since Dr. Reinhardt's seminal analysis, our Nation's inflated healthcare prices are still the primary reason why the U.S. spends significantly more on healthcare than any other country in the world.

A quick comparison to other large, wealthy nations shows the U.S. is an outlier. We spend two to three times more on prescription drugs and medical devices. We spend $10,000 more, on average, per hospital discharge. We spend seven times more per capita on health insurance administrative costs. Despite spending nearly 18 percent of GDP on healthcare, we have fewer practicing doctors and nurses, fewer hospital beds per capita, and a lower life expectancy than other wealthy nations. We also have the highest avoidable death rates and maternal and infant mortality, and an obesity rate nearly two times more than the average of our peer nations. None of this, none of these points are bragging rights, for sure.

In other words, we spend more, but we get much less. So that is why I am pleased that we are holding this important hearing on healthcare transparency today. I am fully supportive of the efforts to shine a light on the fraud and the waste and the abuse percolating in our healthcare industry. But we need to do more than shine a light. Fortunately, over the past 2 years, we have made some major strides.

First, we finally gave Medicare the ability to directly negotiate prescription drug prices, which will save taxpayers more than $300 billion over 10 years. The Biden administration has implemented price transparency regulations, which require hospitals to publicly post prices for all their services on their websites in a user-friendly format.

Now, the hospitals, I would say, have been slow to comply. But CMS recently found that 70—at least 70 percent of hospitals are in compliance with the rules over 2 years after they were finalized. But this has to be 100 percent participation. CMS is now stepping up enforcement measures against the 30 percent of hospitals who remain noncompliant. And I would just put out a call today: Don't fall into the CMS enforcement lane. Do it yourselves. You have had time, do this.

Third, we are finally wrangling the abuses by Medicare Advantage programs. The administration has taken steps to recover improper payments to private plans and return this money to the Medicare Trust Fund. This is going to put money back into the pockets of American taxpayers and protect the long-term solvency of Medicare for future generations.

Looking forward, we have to examine reforms to pharmacy benefit managers, PBMs, the secretive middlemen in the prescription drug industry that drive up prices and keep out affordable drugs. And, Mr. Chairman, I was glad to hear in your opening statement that you view this the same way.

Mr. GUTHRIE. Absolutely.

Ms. ESHOO. Count me in with you to do something about this. We really have to start spending smart. This means spending money on preventive care, public health, and biosecurity. So again, I am glad that we are having this hearing today.

But I am disappointed that we didn't receive the witness testimony until 1:00 yesterday, even though the hearing was noticed 3 weeks ago. But let's have a good hearing.

I want to acknowledge—and I saw them out in the hall—the patients—the patient rights advocates. They all have patient gowns on. I don't see them in the hearing room. I guess they will come in shortly. But I want to acknowledge their advocacy, because advocacy is always highly instructive to Congress.

[The prepared statement of Ms. Eshoo follows:]

Committee on Energy and Commerce
Opening Statement as Prepared for Delivery of Subcommittee on Health Ranking Member Anna Eshoo
Hearing on "Lowering Unaffordable Costs: Examining Transparency and Competition in Health Care"
March 28, 2023

The late Uwe Reinhardt, a prestigious health economist who often appeared before this Subcommittee, famously said "it's the prices, stupid" when critiquing why the U.S. spends so much on health care.

Twenty years since Dr. Reinhardt's seminal analysis, our nation's inflated health care prices are still the primary reason why the U.S. spends significantly more on health care than any other country in the world.

A quick comparison to other large, wealthy nations shows the U.S. is an outlier:

- The U.S. spends two to three times more on prescription drugs and medical devices.
- The U.S. spends $10,000 more on average per hospital discharge.
- The U.S. spends seven times more per capita on health insurance administrative costs.

Despite spending nearly 18 percent of GDP on health care, we have fewer practicing doctors and nurses, fewer hospital beds per capita, and a lower life expectancy than other wealthy nations.

We also have the highest avoidable death rates and maternal and infant mortality, and an obesity rate nearly two times more than the average of our peer nations.

None of these points are bragging rights for sure.

In other words: we spend more, but get less. Much less.

And that's why I'm pleased we are holding this important hearing on health care transparency today. I'm fully supportive of efforts to shine a light on the fraud, waste, and abuse percolating in our health care industry.

But we need to do more than shine a light. Fortunately, over the past two years, we've made major strides. First, we finally gave Medicare the ability to directly negotiate prescription drug prices, which will save taxpayers more than $300 billion over ten years.

Second, the Biden Administration implemented price transparency regulations which require hospitals to publicly post prices for all their services on their websites in a user-friendly format.

While hospitals were slow to comply, CMS recently found that at least 70 percent of hospitals are in compliance with the rules over two years after they were finalized.

But this has to be 100% participation.

CMS is now stepping up enforcement measures against the 30 percent of hospitals who remain non-compliant.

I would just put out a call today to not fall into the CMS enforcement lane. Do it yourselves. You've had time, do this.

Third, we're finally wrangling the abuses by Medicare Advantage programs. The Administration has taken steps to recover improper payments to private plans and return this money to the Medicare Trust Fund. This will put money back into the pockets of American taxpayers and protect the long-term solvency of Medicare for future generations.

Looking forward, we have to examine reforms to pharmacy benefit managers (PBMs), the secretive middlemen in the prescription drug industry that drive up prices and keep out affordable drugs.

Mr. Chairman, I was glad to hear in your opening statement that you view this the same way. Count me in with you to do something about this.

We have to start spending ‘smart.’ This means spending money on preventive care, public health, and biosecurity.

I’m very glad we’re having this hearing today, but I’m disappointed that we didn’t receive the witness testimony until 1PM yesterday even though this hearing was noticed three weeks ago.

I want to acknowledge, and I saw them out in the hall, the Patient Rights Advocates.

I want to acknowledge their advocacy because advocacy is always highly instructive to Congress.

I look forward to the productive testimony from our expert witnesses to highlight the ways we can address the tremendous waste in our healthcare system and improve the lives of all Americans.

Ms. ESHOO. So with that, Mr. Chairman, I yield back.

Mr. GUTHRIE. Thank you. The gentlelady yields back. I now recognize the chair of the full committee, Chair Rodgers, for 5 minutes for an opening statement.

Ms. ESHOO. There they are.

Opening Statement of Hon. Cathy Mcmorris Rodgers, a Representative in Congress from the State of Washington

Mrs. RODGERS. Yes. Thank you, Mr. Chairman. There they are, the patient rights advocates.

Welcome, thank you for being here. [Applause.]

Mrs. RODGERS. Yes, welcome to the Energy and Commerce Committee and a very important hearing today. And it is an issue that we are addressing with bipartisan support. I really appreciate the comments of the chairman, the ranking member, as we are focused on driving down the cost of healthcare.

It is a top concern, as cost of living has surged. More than 60 percent of Americans are living paycheck to paycheck. It means they are just one medical bill away from a financial emergency, one doctor visit away from not being able to pay the rent for their groceries or gas.

A recent poll of Americans with health insurance found more than half ranked reducing healthcare costs as their top healthcare policy priority. For a more secure and healthier future, people need to have certainty and stability.

As the ranking member just mentioned, the United States spends more on healthcare as a percentage of our economy than any other developed nation, and CBO projects that the Federal healthcare costs per person are expected to grow faster than the economy, meaning the U.S. will continue to spend more as a percentage of our economy. So I am pleased that we are working together in a bipartisan way to hold this hearing on what the Federal Government can do about the high cost of healthcare.

Improving price transparency in our healthcare system is one of the ways that we can drive down costs. It is fundamental to restoring the doctor-patient relationship. Right now it is nearly impossible for patients or their employers to shop for the best and most affordable care they or their employees need. It is nearly impossible for people to plan ahead and budget their healthcare costs.

Take, for example, Dani Yuengling from South Carolina. She needed a biopsy and had a $6,000 deductible. Her hospital's price tool estimated that she would pay $1,400. After receiving the bill, she found out that the true cost of the service was nearly 18,000, and she was on the hook for more than $5,000. Patients shouldn't be in the dark until after they receive care and their bills come. Now, the Trump administration finalized two rules on price transparency. The first rule requires hospitals to post standard charges and payer-specific rates for all items and services and a consumer-friendly display of at least 300 shoppable services like an MRI. The second rule requires insurers to post comprehensive rate information and provide patients personalized pricing information for 500 items and services. That includes a wide spectrum of services, from routine doctor visits and imaging services to more complex care like knee replacements, or even delivering a baby.

Unfortunately, independent evaluators broadly agree that most hospitals have not complied fully with the rules. We need stronger enforcement at CMS, which to date has only leveled—levied two penalties against hospitals for not posting accurate information for patients.

We will hear from a hospital in my district that is transparent and in compliance with the rules about their experience, and why we should have reasonable expectations that other hospitals should comply with these rules. Eastern Washington employers have also been on the forefront of utilizing price transparency for good. Schweitzer Engineering Laboratories in my district, one of the largest private employers in eastern Washington, has been a leader in utilizing price transparency to deliver better quality care at lower prices.

We know from stories like these, if fully implemented, these rules help Americans. A recent economic analysis found that, together, both rules could reduce spending for privately insured individuals by tens of billions through 2025 alone, with low-income Americans seeing the most significant benefits. Ranking Member Pallone and I have worked together on oversight for these rules for the past 2 years, and I look forward to continuing that bipartisan work today.

Additionally, we will also examine how more competition can help lower healthcare costs. Hospital physician and health insurance markets have become increasingly consolidated. Consolidation hasn't just been limited to hospitals buying other hospitals or physician groups buying other physician groups, also known as horizontal integration. We have seen a rise in vertical integration, where purchases occur across different sectors within the healthcare system.

For example, this could mean hospitals acquiring physician groups or insurers buying PBMs. For patients, this could mean their insurance company may own their doctor's practice, their pharmacy, and the PBM that decides what they pay for medicine. These—are these arrangements in the best interests of patients? It remains to be seen, and one of the reasons why we are having this hearing today.

So thank you. Thank you to the witnesses. We are grateful for your expertise and work, and looking forward to having this bipartisan conversation.

[The prepared statement of Mrs. Rodgers follows:]

Cathy McMorris Rodgers Opening Statement Health Hearing entitled, "Lowering Unaffordable Costs: Examining Transparency and Competition in Health Care" as Prepared for Delivery

Opening Statement INTRO

Today we are examining in a bipartisan way how to drive down the costs of health care.

This is a top concern as the cost of living as surged across the board.

More than 60 percent of Americans are living paycheck to paycheck.

It means they are just one medical bill away from a financial emergency.

One doctor visit away from not being able to pay their rent... for their groceries... or gas.

A recent poll of Americans with health insurance found more than half ranked "reducing health care costs" as their top health care policy priority.

For a more secure and healthier future, people need more certainty and stability.

The United States spends more on health care as a percentage of our economy than any other developed nation.

And CBO projects that federal health care costs per person are expected to grow faster than the economy, meaning the U.S. will continue to spend more as a percentage of the economy.

So I am pleased that we've worked in a bipartisan way to hold this hearing on what the federal government can do about the high costs of health care.

Transparency

Improving price transparency in our health care system is one way we can drive down costs. It's foundational to restoring the doctor-patient relationship.

Right now, it is nearly impossible for patients or their employers to shop for the best and most affordable care they or their employees need.

It is nearly impossible for people to plan ahead and budget for their health care costs.

Take the example of Dani Yuengling, from South Carolina. She needed a biopsy and had a $6,000 deductible. Her hospital's price tool estimated she would pay $1,400.

After receiving the bill, she found out the true price of the service was nearly $18,000. She was on the hook for more than $5,000.

Patients shouldn't be in the dark until after they receive care and after their bills come.

The Trump Administration finalized two rules on price transparency.

The first rule requires hospitals to post standard charges and payer-specific rates for all items and services and a consumer- friendly display of at least three-hundred shoppable services like an MRI.

The second rule requires insurers to post comprehensive rate information and provide patients personalized pricing information for five-hundred items and services.

That includes a wide spectrum of services – from routine doctor visits and imaging services, to more complex care, like knee replacements or even delivering a baby.

Unfortunately, independent evaluators broadly agree that most hospitals have not complied fully with the rules.

We need stronger enforcement from CMS, which to date has only levied two penalties against hospitals for not posting accurate information for patients.

We will hear from a hospital in my district – *that is transparent and in compliance with the rules* – about their experience and why we should have reasonable expectations that other hospitals should be able to comply with these rules.

Eastern Washington employers have also been on the forefront of utilizing price transparency for good.

Schweitzer Engineering Labs in my district, one of the largest private employers in Eastern Washington, has been a leader in utilizing price transparency to deliver better quality care at lower prices.

We know from stories like these that, if fully implemented, these rules will help Americans.

A recent economic analysis found that together, both rules could reduce spending for privately-insured individuals by tens of billions through 2025 alone, with low-income Americans seeing the most significant benefits.

Ranking Member Pallone and I have worked together on oversight of these rules over the past two years, and I look forward to continuing that bipartisan work today.

Competition

Additionally, we will also examine how more competition can help lower health care costs.

Hospital, physician, and health insurer markets have become increasingly consolidated.

Consolidation hasn't been just limited to hospitals buying other hospitals or physician groups buying other physician groups – also known as horizontal integration.

We have seen a rise in vertical integration, where purchases occur across different sectors within the health care system.

For example, this could mean hospitals acquiring physician groups or insurers buying PBMs.

For patients, this could mean their insurance company may own:

- Their doctor's practice
- Their pharmacy; and
- The PBM that decides what they pay for medicine Are these arrangements in the best interest of patients?

It remains to be seen, and it is one reason we need to have this hearing today.

Closing

Thank you again to everyone on our witness panel today.

We're grateful for your expertise and work to help inform how this committee will lead to lower health care costs and improve the quality of life for all Americans.

I am glad we are having this bipartisan conversation and I look forward to working productively together.

Mrs. RODGERS. I yield back.

Mr. GUTHRIE. Thank you. I thank the Chair for yielding. The Chair now recognizes the gentleman from New Jersey, the ranking member of the full committee, Mr.—Representative Pallone for 5 minutes for an opening statement.

Opening Statement of Hon. Frank Pallone, Jr., A Representative in Congress from the State of New Jersey

Mr. PALLONE. Thank you, Chairman Guthrie.

Today's bipartisan hearing builds on this subcommittee's critical efforts to lower healthcare costs and make coverage more affordable. More Americans have health coverage today than ever before, thanks to the Affordable Care Act and the expansion subsidies included in the American Rescue Plan and the Inflation Reduction Act.

A record-breaking 40 million people have gained coverage, and a record high 16.5 million Americans have coverage through the ACA marketplace. Millions of families have seen the cost of their monthly insurance premiums go down by more than 20 percent. The average family is saving $2,400 in premiums a year, thanks to the ACA enhancements we made over the last 2 years. And the Inflation Reduction Act will also lower prescription drug prices for America's seniors.

We are making significant progress, but high healthcare costs and affordability continue to be a challenge and a financial burden for American families. Our healthcare system is complex and challenging. Too many patients are forced to wait until after they receive care and have the medical bill to fully understand how much they owe.

Patients deserve greater transparency in the prices they pay for healthcare. Today consumers are not able to easily obtain price information in advance. Sometimes the price information that is provided is inaccurate and misleading, making it difficult to determine the true value of the care. And patients also face wide price variations. The lack of transparency makes it difficult to compare across providers in advance of receiving care.

Prices for healthcare services also vary widely across different geographic areas, but also across providers in the same geographic area. According to an analysis by the New York Times, a single hospital can have up to a 300 percent price difference for the same service, depending on the insurer. Another analysis by the Peterson Center and the Kaiser Family Foundation found the price of a joint replacement for knee or hip surgery varied widely across the 20 largest metropolitan areas, ranging from less than 20,000 to more than 70,000.

So a lack of transparency into these prices makes it difficult for both consumers and employers to make informed decisions. Employers have difficulty accessing data that could help them negotiate competitive prices and design high-value plans.

The contracts of pharmacy benefit managers are also opaque. This makes it difficult for employers and plan sponsors to understand drivers of cost and negotiate savings. We also need greater oversight and enforcement of pharmacy benefit managers.

We must also build on the Hospital Price Transparency Final Rule and the Transparency in Coverage Final Rule requirements. The Hospital Price Transparency Rule is meant to bring more transparency to healthcare by requiring hospitals to display charges for the most-used services in a consumer-friendly way. However, I am concerned by reports that many hospitals are either acting slowly or not yet complying with the final rule.

I am also troubled by reports that some hospitals are making it more difficult for consumers to access the information. I understand that some hospitals are requiring consumers to input personally identifiable information in order to access information that should be easily available, or burying the information deep in their websites.

All this is inexcusable, so I look forward to hearing from the witnesses on what reforms are necessary, and what more Congress can do to further strengthen those regulations.

While greater price transparency is important, I don't believe it is sufficient in and of itself to expand coverage or to improve affordability. Today 43 percent of U.S. adults are inadequately insured, and half of uninsured or underinsured Americans face problems paying their medical bills. More than 40 percent of adults have delayed or forgone medical care because of the cost. And more than 100 million Americans have medical debt. So transparency alone will not help lower out-of-pocket costs for families.

We need to couple greater transparency with real solutions that will lower costs, and that is why we must continue to build on the historic progress we have made over the last 2 years. We need to continue to expand coverage and make healthcare more affordable and accessible for all Americans. It is critical that we make the ACA subsidy expansions permanent and build on the success of the Inflation Reduction Act to further lower drug prices for consumers. So today's hearing is an important bipartisan step in our continued effort to reduce healthcare costs. I look forward to the witnesses' testimony.

[The prepared statement of Mr. Pallone follows:]

Committee on Energy and Commerce
Opening Statement as Prepared for Delivery of Ranking Member Frank Pallone, Jr., Health Subcommittee Hearing on "Lowering Unaffordable Costs: Examining transparency and Competition in Health Care"
March 28, 2023

Today's bipartisan hearing builds on the Subcommittee's critical efforts to lower health care costs and make coverage more affordable.

More Americans have health coverage today than ever before, thanks to the Affordable Care Act and the expansion subsidies included in the American Rescue Plan and the Inflation Reduction Act. A record-breaking 40 million people have gained coverage, and a record high 16.5 million Americans have coverage through the ACA Marketplaces. Millions of families have seen the cost of their monthly insurance premiums go down by more than 20 percent. The average family is saving $2,400 in premiums a year thanks to the ACA enhancements we made over the last two years. The Inflation Reduction Act will also lower prescription drug prices for America's seniors.

We are making significant progress, but high health care costs and affordability continue to be a challenge and a financial burden for American families. Our health care system is complex and challenging. Too many patients are forced to wait until after they receive care and have the medical bill to fully understand how much they owe.

Patients deserve greater transparency in the prices they pay for health care. Today, consumers are not able to easily obtain price information in advance. Sometimes, the price information that is provided is inaccurate and misleading, making it difficult to determine the true value of the care.

Patients also face wide price variations. The lack of transparency makes it difficult to compare across providers in advance of receiving care. Prices for health care services also vary widely across different geographic areas but also across providers in the same geographic area. According to an analysis by the New York Times, a single hospital can have up to a 300 percent price difference for the same service, depending on the insurer. Another analysis by the Peterson Center and the Kaiser Family Foundation found the price of a joint replacement for knee or hip surgery varied widely across the 20 largest metropolitan areas, ranging from less than $20,000 to more than $70,000.

Lack of transparency into these prices makes it difficult for both consumers and employers to make informed decisions. Employers have difficulty accessing data that could help them negotiate competitive prices and design high value plans. The contracts of pharmacy benefit managers are also opaque. This makes it difficult for employers and plan sponsors to understand drivers of cost and negotiate savings. We also need greater oversight and enforcement of pharmacy benefit managers.

We must also build on the Hospital Price Transparency Final Rule and the Transparency in Coverage Final Rule requirements. The Hospital Price Transparency rule is meant to bring more transparency to health care by requiring hospitals to display charges for their most used services in a consumer-friendly way. However, I am concerned by reports that many hospitals are either acting slowly or not yet complying with the final rule. I am also troubled by reports that some hospitals are making it more difficult for consumers to access the information. I understand that some hospitals are requiring consumers to input personally identifiable information in order to access information that should be easily available or burying the information deep in their websites.

This is inexcusable. I look forward to hearing from the witnesses on what reforms are necessary and what more Congress can do to further strengthen those regulations.

While greater price transparency is important, I don't believe it is sufficient in and of itself to expand coverage or to improve affordability. Today, 43 percent of U.S. adults are inadequately insured, and half of uninsured or underinsured Americans face problems paying the ir medical bills. More than 40 percent of adults have delayed or foregone medical care because of the cost, and more than 100 million Americans have medical debt. Transparency alone will not help lower out-of-pocket costs for families. We need to couple greater transparency with real solutions that will lower costs.

That's why we must continue to build on the historic progress we have made over the last two years. We need to continue to expand coverage and make health care more affordable and accessible for all Americans. It is critical that we make the ACA subsidy expansions permanent and build on the success of the Inflation Reduction Act to further lower drug prices for consumers.

Today's hearing is an important bipartisan step in our continued effort to reduce health care costs. I look forward to the witnesses' testimony, and I yield back.

Mr. PALLONE. And with that, Mr. Chairman, I would yield back, Chairman Guthrie.

Mr. GUTHRIE. Thank you. I thank the ranking member for yielding back.

The Chair reminds Members that, pursuant to the committee rules, all Members' opening statements will be made part of the record.

Are there any further opening statements? Any opening statements on the Republican side, any on the Democrat? Any further opening statements?

Seeing none, I would like to introduce our witnesses. Our first witness today is Chris Severn, cofounder and CEO of Turquoise Health. Our second witness is Matthew Forge, CEO of Pullman Regional Hospital. Our third witness is Marilyn Bartlett, senior policy fellow with the National Association of State Health Policy. Our fourth witness will—is—witness is Sophia Tripoli, director of healthcare innovation at Families USA. And our final witness today is Ben Ippolito, senior fellow in economic policy studies with the American Enterprise Institute.

I thank you all for being here and the time that you put into being here today and preparing for—to be here today. I thank you. Some of you—most of you have testified. If you haven't, you have 5 minutes. You will see a green button, and—a yellow button means it is getting close to time to—yellow light, time to wrap up. And then—that is right, we get to push the buttons on our side— the lights will wrap up, and then red means that—to finish up, if possible.

So we will start with our first witness. Our witness will be Mr. Severn.

You are recognized for 5 minutes for an opening statement.

Statement of Chris Severn, Cofounder and Chief Executive Officer, Turquoise Health; Matthew Forge, Chief Executive Officer, Pullman Regional Hospital; Marilyn J. Bartlett, Senior Policy Fellow, National Academy for State Health Policy; Sophia Tripoli, Director, Center for Affordable Whole– Person Care, Families USA; and Benedic Ippolito, Ph.D., Senior Fellow, American Enterprise Institute

Statement of Chris Severn

Mr. SEVERN. Chairman Guthrie, Ranking Member Eshoo, members of the Health Subcommittee, thank you for the opportunity to testify at today's hearing.

We started Turquoise Health in 2020 as a direct response to the 2019 Executive orders on price transparency for hospitals and health insurers. In my 10-year background working with the secret contracts negotiated between providers and insurers, it was clear to me this sudden profusion of price transparency data would both spur healthcare price competition and reform the patient financial experience.

Prior to January of 2021, there was no accessible market data for patients to price shop. Perhaps equally important, there was no data to drive regional macroeconomic price competition. In late 2020, as we prepared to launch Turquoise, a platform that would allow patients to browse these new prices for free, bipartisan efforts in Congress passed the No Surprises Act. This new legislation detailed a much-needed workflow for communicating good-faith estimates for insured patients. Critically, it also outlined an avenue for patients to dispute inaccurate estimates after the fact.

These three laws each mandate essential data and system changes that will finally permit insured patients and their employers to know the cost of care. Any significant modification to these laws could lead to the overall dilution of the intended dual aims of creating competition and empowering savvy consumers of healthcare.

There are three main themes I aim to shed light on today: What is the state of compliance with existing transparency mandates? What impacts are we already observing on the economics of healthcare? And three, in what areas can additional government effort further the impact of these laws?

On the state of compliance, Turquoise is one of the few data companies that monitors all 6,000 hospital websites on a quarterly basis and all health insurance websites on a monthly basis. As of March 1st, we have seen over 5,100 hospitals publishing price information, compared to just 1,800 hospitals this time 2 years ago. Health insurers were required to publish pricing data 18 months after hospitals, starting July 1st of 2022. As of March 1st, we have discovered over 180 insurers with pricing data published, an increase from 69 in July of last year. We estimate these prices to represent 96 percent of covered commercially insured lives in the United States.

Notably, the new insurance disclosed data represents prices for all types of providers, not just hospitals. This creates a compelling new competitive dynamic around the site of care: When is it most cost effective to treat in a hospital or surgery center or at home? On the impact of the new transparency mandates, the sudden infusion of billions of healthcare prices into the system requires time for the industry and innovators like Turquoise to adjust. The initial setup time required for data ingestion, software development, and consumer adoption explains much of the gap in perception between the optimism felt by startups like Turquoise and the skepticism felt by—in the press, excuse me.

Turquoise has now nearly 50,000 website visitors browsing prices for free every month, a 400 percent increase from a year ago. This data also reaches patients and employers through 20 distribution partners working on care navigation. Critically, we are also beginning to see this data embedded into the clinician workflow at the time of the referral.

Will these new efforts to decrease the cost—will these new efforts decrease the cost of healthcare in the U.S.? There is existing literature to support that competition and consumer choice will lead to lower prices.

But these new laws also present a second massive opportunity to reduce the administrative costs of healthcare, which studies note to exceed 30 percent of every dollar spent in the U.S.—healthcare dollar spent in the U.S.—by standardizing the payment of medical claims and the reimbursement methods negotiated between providers and insurers.

That being said, we are still far from seeing the full impact of this new data on the industry. While dozens of academic researchers now use this data to monitor and publish on economic progress, we need continued government intervention to carry out price transparency's potential. Notably, hospitals and payers should be held accountable to publish transparency data. Enforcement has lagged, and this delays progress for patients.

The No Surprises Act needs enforcement dates for key outstanding critical measures such as the convening of good-faith estimates across multiple providers and the provision of the advanced explanation of benefits. These two requirements permit the vast majority of America's commercially insured patients to benefit from the consumer protections of the law.

Finally, hospitals should be required to publish data in a standard format. CMS introduced this format in November of 2022 as a recommendation, and this should be made a requirement as soon as possible in order to create cleaner data sets for patients.

Thank you for your time today and for your continued focus on healthcare price transparency in the U.S.

[The prepared statement of Mr. Severn follows:]

Chris Severn Written Statement

We started Turquoise Health in 2020 as a direct response to the 2019 executive orders on price transparency for hospitals and health insurers. In my 10-year background working with the secret contracts negotiated between providers and insurers, it was clear this sudden profusion of price transparency data would both spur healthcare price competition and reform the patient-financial experience. Prior to January of 2021, there was no accessible market data for patients to price shop. Perhaps equally important, there was no data to drive regional macroeconomic price competition.

In late 2020 as we prepared to launch Turquoise, a platform that would allow patients to browse these new prices for free, bipartisan efforts in Congress passed the No Surprises Act. This new legislation detailed a much needed workflow for communicating Good Faith Estimates for insured patients.

Critically, it also outlined an avenue for patients to dispute inaccurate estimates after the fact.

These three laws each mandate essential data and system changes that will finally permit insured patients and their employers to know the cost of care. Any significant modifications to these laws could lead to the overall dilution of the intended dual aims of creating competition and empowering savvy consumers of healthcare.

There are three main themes I aim to shed light on today:

- What is the state of compliance with existing transparency mandates?
- What impacts are we already observing on the economics of healthcare?
- In what areas can additional government effort further the impact of these laws?

On the state of compliance. Turquoise is one of the few data companies that monitors all 6,000 hospital websites on a quarterly basis, and all health insurance websites on a monthly basis. As of March 1st, we've seen over 5,100 hospitals publish pricing information, compared to just 1,800 hospitals this time in 2021.

Health insurers were required to publish pricing data 18 months after hospitals, starting July 1st of 2022. As of March 1st, we've discovered over 180 insurers with pricing data published, an increase from 69 in July of last year. We estimate these prices to represent 96% of covered commercially insured lives in the United States.

Notably, the new insurance-disclosed data represents prices for all types of providers, not just hospitals. This creates a compelling new competitive dynamic around the site of care: when is it most cost effective to treat in a hospital, surgery center, or at home?

On the impact of the new transparency mandates. The sudden infusion of billions of healthcare prices into the system requires time for the industry and innovators like Turquoise to adjust. The initial setup time required for data ingestion, software development, and consumer adoption explains much of the gap in perception between the optimism felt by startups like Turquoise and the skepticism felt in the press.

Turquoise now has nearly 50,000 website visitors browsing prices for free every month, a 400% increase from a year ago. This data also reaches patients and employers through 20 distribution partners working on care navigation. Critically, we're also beginning to see this data embedded into the clinician workflow at the time of referral.

Will these new efforts decrease the costs of healthcare in the US? There is existing literature to support that competition and consumer choice will lead to lower prices. But these new laws also present a second massive opportunity to reduce the administrative cost of healthcare, which studies note to exceed 30% of healthcare expenditure in the US, by standardizing the payment of medical claims and the reimbursement methods negotiated between providers and insurers.

That being said, we are still far from seeing the full impact of this new data on the industry. While dozens of academic researchers now use this new data to monitor and publish on economic progress, we need continued government intervention to carry out price transparency's potential. Notably:

1. Hospitals and payers should be held accountable to publish transparency data. Enforcement has lagged, and this delays progress for patients.
2. The No Surprises Act needs enforcement dates set for key outstanding critical measures, such as the convening of Good Faith Estimates across multiple providers, and the provision of the Advanced Explanation of Benefits. These requirements permit the vast majority of America's commercially insured patients to benefit from the consumer protections of the law.
3. Finally, hospitals should be required to publish data in a standard format. CMS introduced this format in November of 2022 as a recommendation, and this should be made a requirement as soon as possible in order to create cleaner data sets for patients.

Thank you for your time today and your continued focus on healthcare price transparency in the United States.

View associated reference information for monitoring the progress of price transparency

- Turquoise Health's March 2023 Price transparency progress report:
  - blog.turquoise.health/march-price-transparency-progress-report (releasing on 3/27)
- Select academic research power by the new price transparency data:
- blog.turquoise.health/price-transparency-research-studies-powered-by-turquoise-health

Mr. GUTHRIE. I thank you for your testimony.

The Chair now recognizes Mr. Forge for 5 minutes for your opening statement.

Statement of Matthew Forge

Mr. FORGE. All right, thank you. Good afternoon, Chairs Rodgers and Guthrie, Ranking Members Pallone and Eshoo, and members of the committee. Thanks so much for having me all the way from Pullman out to see you today.

Again, my name is Matt Forge, I am the chief executive officer for Pullman Regional Hospital. I have served as a leader in rural healthcare in Idaho, Washington, and Wisconsin over the past 8 years and certainly understand the importance of pricing transparency, especially as it relates to supporting effective healthcare decision making for individuals and families seeking healthcare.

You know, we really are here for the communities that we serve, everything that we do. Pullman Regional Hospital is a public hospital district, so everything that we do is in relation to their best interests. Transparency is really, really important to us. I want to give you kind of a—we have been compliant with the law since 2019, which we are really proud of. And so I want to give you kind of a ground-level observation and look into that.

So first of all, let's talk with—about the positives that we have experienced with the transparency in the law. You know, one, it is driving a greater understanding of a really complex environment, down to the ground level. So not just within our communities to patients—patients are having conversations that they have never had before—but also within our organization, as we are able to provide more thorough information that our patients can utilize in their decision making, which is fantastic.

I think the second one, which we are really, really excited about now, is it is creating a table that we can go with people like Schweitzer Engineering and other industries within our community—it is creating a table where we are looking at data and having conversations about how to lower cost and increase value of healthcare within our environment. Those are really, really important conversations to have, and I think for one of the—for the first time we are starting to have those in our community.

Three—and I think is a big reason why we are here today—is greater competition. Now, Pullman Regional Hospital is one of five hospitals in our region, so of course we are competing. And I think the important thing is that we are not just talking about cost. I think when we are having those conversations with our patient financial counselors and our patients about a joint replacement surgery, we are talking about quality as well. So we are talking about cost, but we are talking about quality. And it is really coming to the table and having those conversations together.

Now, we have been there since 2019. I have personally been working on this my entire career, trying to—you know, point-of- care cost reporting is something that people are really interested in. It is a challenging thing to accomplish.

So the first challenge that we face is making it accurate and meaningful. We all know healthcare is a complicated business. It changes all the time. It is a fingerprint business. That means every individual that comes in has a little bit different experience. They have a different employer. And so making sure that that information is accurate and meaningful is difficult. And especially in rural America, that is something that we are really struggling with. But there's a lot of people putting a lot of time and effort into that.

Managing constant changes. Health insurance plans change every single year. You know, our regulations are changing consistently. We are spread thin as leaders. So, of course, managing those constant changes, pricing strategies, payer contract tracking, changes in the marketplace are difficult. So managing that here.

And then a big one is competing priorities. We have to recruit physicians. We have to manage healthcare needs within our community. All these things come up against ensuring that we have great pricing transparency. So while it is one piece, it is a part of a bigger puzzle that will—that we are working hard to solve.

And then, as we look forward to opportunities and how we can get help from you all today, is continue to align incentives. I mentioned working with industries within our community. We are talking about data. That data is becoming transparent. We are talking about real-life things, real-life problems, and making progress there.

Continue to help us simplify. Our patients are asking for that. Our communities are asking for that. We are asking for that. It is not a simple process, and we need to continue to work with each other to simplify this.

And then how can we minimize distractions? You know, these programs are fantastic. I am a huge believer in all of them, and I work hard in doing that. Getting them to be operational is extremely challenging. And if we are managing multiple priorities through this, it makes it more and more difficult to handle these things, especially from a rural perspective. So help us minimize distractions.

Again, this is a really important topic, and I really appreciate you guys having me today. Thank you.

[The prepared statement of Mr. Forge follows:]

Testimony of Matthew W. Forge Pullman Regional Hospital CEO

Good afternoon Chairs Rodgers and Guthrie, Ranking Members Pallone and Eshoo and members of the Committee.

I am Matt Forge, Chief Executive Officer for Pullman Regional Hospital, installed November 2022. I have served as a leader in rural healthcare in the states of Idaho, Washington and Wisconsin for more than eight years and understand the importance of transparency in pricing, especially as it relates to supporting effective healthcare decision-making for individuals and families seeking healthcare. Thank you for the opportunity to share Pullman Regional's journey toward price transparency.

Pullman Regional Hospital is a 25-bed critical access hospital nestled in the wheat fields of Eastern Washington in Pullman, WA. Originally on the campus of Washington State University, Pullman Regional opened its doors to a new 95,000 square-foot-facility in 2004, about two miles away from campus.

Today we are a hospital with eleven clinics and offer healthcare services ranging from psychiatry, 3D digital mammography, robotic-assisted surgery to a family medicine residency center and a very busy emergency department serving two college towns.

We are an independent, public district hospital governed by an elected board of commissioners.

Our journey as a transparent organization started before federal requirements. As a community hospital close to two Universities we serve an educated population and value being a patient-focused provider of healthcare that helps our patients make educated decisions.

In 2019 we published a price estimation tool, list of patient prices and a charge description master portal on our transparency webpage.

Our goal was to make these tools simple enough to understand but comprehensive enough to be thorough. Keeping information up-to-date as rules and regulations change is a continual work in progress, but Pullman Regional Hospital is committed to helping our community make educated decisions about their healthcare.

Pulling together pricing information and comparing ourselves in the regional market identified several services that were priced much higher than our competitors; this gave us the opportunity investigate how we lower our costs for medical devices and components so that we could pass that savings to patients.

Pullman Regional Hospital is one of five hospitals within an hour's drive, and that environment has helped us remain competitive in pricing, quality and breadth of services.

Philanthropy through donations and grant awards have also helped us in our transparency journey. Most years our operating margin is 2% and any additional capital spend necessary to continue improvements to our hospital comes from philanthropy. Grants and donations for expansion projects and medical technology have helped us upgrade our spaces so that we can serve more patients and attract high quality physicians to practice rural medicine. Grant and donor stewardship is transparency in how funds were used.

While we were ahead of the federal regulations around pricing transparency this helped us broaden our efforts to have a pricing model that was consistent, fair and deliberate. We always want to focus on what is best for patients and help simplify the complexities of healthcare.

This journey of transparency hasn't been easy and it will continue to be a work in progress. It's a challenge to provide comprehensive healthcare and necessary services like behavioral health with the current reimbursement models. Providing comprehensive, accessible, affordable and quality healthcare as a public district hospital is a challenge. Maintaining staffing levels and recruiting and retaining quality providers in a rural environment is a challenge. Charity care requirements have doubled, adding to this challenge.

These are our challenges as we continue to prioritize patient care and help our patients know what to expect when they choose Pullman Regional Hospital. We do what we do because we want to elevate the health of our communities and be open and accessible to everyone as a community hospital. Our patients are our children's teachers, our neighbors, our mail carriers; this is our community to serve.

As we continue to work towards simplifying the healthcare experience for our patients and providing transparency in pricing we too seek simplification in keeping up with changing regulations for pricing transparency and look forward to working together on these goals.

Mr. GUTHRIE. Thank you for being here. I know that you traveled a long way. I know the Chair enjoys showing great things that are happening in her home State, so thanks for making the long trip. I appreciate it.

Next, Ms. Bartlett, you are the national policy—policy fellow for National Association of State Health Plans, but your State health plan was Montana. So please give our regards to your Governor. We miss him on the committee, and tell him hello for us.

You are now recognized for 5 minutes for an opening statement.

Statement of Marilyn J. Bartlett

Mr. BARTLETT. Thank you. Chair Rodgers, Ranker Pallone, Chairman Guthrie, and Ranking Member Eshoo. Thank you for this opportunity to testify this afternoon. I am a senior policy fellow with the National Academy of State Health Policy, but I am also a healthcare cost consultant. And today I am speaking as Marilyn Bartlett, a forensic accountant focused on following the money in the healthcare system to support policy, employer-sponsored health plans, and all with the goal of lowering healthcare costs.

I hope my testimony today will help the committee not only understand the challenges for healthcare purchasers, but the opportunities to make systemic and lasting change to benefit all Americans.

Let me begin by sharing a story about the Montana State employee health plan. It has been hailed as something revolutionary, but what we did was nothing more than demanding transparency, analyzing the data, and negotiating for fair prices. The fact that this is remarkable is indicative of a dysfunctional market that is our current model.

I was hired in late 2015 by the State of Montana to save the health plan from insolvency. It had just ended a year losing 28 million. By 2017 we had $112 million in reserves and had achieved a savings of $121 million.

How did we do it? We negotiated contracts with every Montana hospital to reimburse as a multiple of Medicare Cost Plus. No longer were we going to stand for a secret discount off of an unknown figure.

And we had contracts. There was no balance billing of members. We terminated our traditional PBM, we moved to a transparent passthrough model, and we also removed CVS from our pharmacy network because they would not accept our prices. We invested strongly in primary care.

So what happened? Employees have had enhanced benefits. They have had no raise to premium—last time was in 2016. And we were able to return over 50 million taxpayer dollars to Montana General Fund because we were over-funded.

The effort was bipartisan. The Democratic Governor and the Republican legislature worked together, and the State employees in the union were engaged throughout the process. We disrupted the status quo.

Since then, other States have successfully launched reference- based pricing. Oregon State employees have seen a savings of 33 percent in the first year. California's State employee plan saw savings between 12 and 18 percent for various surgical procedures. And imagine the tremendous savings you could have if the Federal Employee Health Benefits plan were to take a similar approach with your 8 million members.

Other employers and unions have effectuated meaningful change, but it is often against strong headwinds from the industry that profits from the status quo. The State of New Jersey and their unions achieved billions in savings by launching a payment integrity program and a PBM reverse auction. SEIU 32BJ used data to stop egregious billing, and a small Pennsylvania county has identified 4 million in savings by negotiating directly with hospitals.

The Hospital Transparency Rule was passed in order to allow plans and consumers to compare prices of services and supplies across hospitals. Patient Rights Advocate reports only 25 percent of the hospitals have published complete machine-readable files containing all of the required files which are needed for a consumer, and especially for an employer, providing benefits.

The Consolidated Appropriations Act mandates employers to have full access to their data, yet carriers are blocking them at every turn, evidenced by a string of lawsuits. Owens & Minor, a large, publicly traded company headquartered in Virginia, has been forced to sue Anthem to get their plan data after 18 months of demands. A recent survey found that 89 percent of the voters believe Congress should take action to reduce health—hospital prices, and 72 percent are in agreement that the prices should be limited to two times the Medicare rate.

We can and we must do better. The State of Montana plan did it, other employers are doing it, and the Federal employee health plan can do it. But we have to have price and cost transparency.

Thank you again for your bipartisan leadership. [The prepared statement of Ms. Bartlett follows:]

Marilyn J Bartlett, CPA, CMA, CFM, CGMA

Thank you, Chair Rodgers, Ranker Pallone, Chairman Guthrie, and Ranking Member Eshoo, for the opportunity to testify this afternoon.

I am a Senior Policy Fellow with the National Academy for State Health Policy and a Healthcare Cost Consultant. Today, I am speaking as Marilyn Bartlett, a forensic accountant focused on "following the money" in healthcare to support policy, employer sponsored health plans, with the goal of lower healthcare costs. I hope my testimony today will help the Committee understand not only the challenges for healthcare purchasers, but the opportunities to make systemic and lasting change to the benefit of all Americans.

Let me begin by sharing a story about my efforts with the Montana State Employee Health Plan. The story has been hailed as something revolutionary, but what we did was nothing more than demand transparency, analyze the data, and negotiate a fair deal. The fact that this is remarkable is indicative of the dysfunctional market that is our current model.

In late 2014, I was hired by the State of Montana to save the state employee health plan from financial failure, having lost $28 million for the year and on the brink of further insolvency. By 2017, we had $112 million in reserves, a savings of increase of $121 million. How did we do it?

- We negotiated contracts with Montana hospitals to pay a multiple of Medicare rate, rather than pay a secret discount off an unknown figure, with no balance billing to members.
- We terminated our traditional PBM contract and moved to a transparent, pass-through model, and also removed CVS from our network for not accepting our pricing demands.
- And, we invested in primary care.

The effort was bipartisan, with a Democratic Governor and a Republican Legislature; and the State employees and union were engaged throughout the process.

Other states have successfully launched reference-based hospital pricing plans. Oregon state employee health plan saw savings of 33% in 2021 after launching a plan similar to Montana. California's state employee plan saw reductions ranging from 12% to 18% for various surgeries using a reference-based pricing approach.

Imagine the tremendous savings opportunity if the FEHBP were take a similar approach. A conservative estimate of taxpayer savings would yield several billions of dollars over a 10-year period.

Other state and local governments, unions, and employers have also effectuated meaningful change in their healthcare purchasing – often against strong headwinds from the industry and the industry that profits from the status quo.

- The State of New Jersey's health plan, which covers about 800k lives, implemented a payment integrity program that leveraged transparency data and saved over $150M in just over one year on the medical plan, and engaged in a reverse auction for a pass-through PBM contract saving $2.5B over a 5 year term.
- The SEIU 32BJ Health Fund saved over $30M in 2022 by studying their data and removing a very prominent Manhattan hospital whose negotiated price with their carrier was egregious – even by New York standards, preserving $0 premium plans for their members.
- A small county in Pennsylvania saved their taxpayers $4 million dollars direct contracting with hospitals, after comparing their plan prices to Hospital Price Transparency files.

What do all of these initiatives have in common? Data and access to transparent pricing information. Transparency is vital in moving to a functional market and lowering healthcare prices – put simply, we must have the data. Despite a decade of transparency laws on the books, employers, unions, states, and other purchasers continue to face challenges with substantial non-compliance:

- The Hospital Price Transparency rule was passed in order to allow plans and consumers to compare prices of services and supplies across hospitals, Patient Rights Advocate reported only 25% of hospitals have published complete machine-readable files, containing all the required data fields prescribed by law.
- The Consolidated Appropriations Act, Transparency, Section 201 mandates employers have full access to all of their data, yet carriers are blocking them at every turn, as evidenced by a string of recent lawsuits. Owens & Minor, a large publicly traded company headquartered in Virginia, requested claims data to fulfill their ERISA fiduciary role, but after 18 months of requesting the data, sued Anthem to get their plan data.

A recent survey found that 89% of the voters believe Congress should take action to reduce hospital prices, with 72% in agreement that hospital prices should be limited to two times the Medicare rate. This is an important issue to all Americans at a moment in time when we are seeing life expectancy rates decline across every demographic faster than their counterparts in other wealthy nations.

The current healthcare industrial complex benefits from opacity and information asymmetry, in the hope that America will continue paying unchecked prices. We can and must do better. The State of Montana Employee Health Plan did it, other employers are doing it, the FEHBP can do it – but we must have price and cost transparency from the industry that is costing us so much.

Thank you again for your bipartisan leadership on this issue.

Mr. GUTHRIE. Thank you. The gentlelady yields back.

Now the Chair now recognizes Ms. Tripoli for 5 minutes for your opening statement.

Statement of Sophia Tripoli

Ms. TRIPOLI. Chair McMorris Rodgers, Ranking Member Pallone, Chair Guthrie, Ranking Member Eshoo, members of the committee, thank you for the opportunity to testify today. It is an honor to be with you this afternoon.

On behalf of Families USA, a leading national, nonpartisan voice for healthcare consumers working to ensure the best health and healthcare equally accessible and affordable to all, I want to thank you for this critical discussion on healthcare affordability, transparency, and competition.

Today's hearing is urgently needed. Our healthcare system is in a crisis, evidenced by lack of affordability and poor quality. It will take all of us working together across political parties from rural and urban communities alike to fix it.

Every person in the United States should have affordable, highquality healthcare that prevents illness, allows them to see a doctor when they need it, and helps to keep their families healthy. Yet almost half of all Americans report forgoing medical care due to the costs. A third say that the cost affects their ability to secure basic needs like food and housing. And over 40 percent of American adults, 100 million people, face medical debt. Unaffordable healthcare is a persistent problem for national and State governments and affects the economic vitality of middle-class and working families.

Despite this financial burden, our health is not better. Our moms and babies die at higher rates, and a quarter of a million people a year are killed by the healthcare system for medical errors, infections, and the like. Make no mistake: America's families are suffering, and swift action is needed.

At its core, this crisis is driven by a misalignment between the business interests of the healthcare sector and the health and financial security of our Nation's families. Healthcare industry consolidation has eliminated competition and allowed monopolistic pricing to push our Nation's families to the brink of financial ruin. Americans of all watched as their local hospitals have become health systems, and those systems were bought by large healthcare corporations to increase prices year after year. These higher prices are passed on to families as annual increases, and insurance premiums and cost sharing have become profit margins for large hospital corporations.

Since 2015, hospital prices have increased as much as 31 percent nationally, now accounting for nearly one-third of U.S. healthcare spending, and growing four times faster than workers' paychecks. And these prices are irrational, with a knee replacement costing three times as much in Sacramento, California, than in Tucson, Arizona, and an MRI at Mass General Hospital in Boston, Massachusetts, ranging from $800 to $4,200, just depending on the insurance carrier.

Particularly concerning is that healthcare is one of the only sectors in the U.S. economy where consumers are blinded to healthcare prices until after they have received a service and a subsequent bill. This lack of transparency is a major barrier to the healthcare sector competing based on fair prices and high-quality care.

But it doesn't have to be this way. We know what is driving the crisis, and we know how to fix it. Solutions can be deployed right away to end these pricing abuses, restore competition, and make healthcare more affordable.

We urge the committee to consider well-vetted, bipartisan solutions, including strengthening and codifying price transparency rules, addressing payment differentials that incentivize consolidation and drive up costs, and limiting anticompetitive behavior in provider and health plan contracts.

Ultimately, the healthcare sector's economics must change to align with the health and financial security of the American people. Congress has overwhelming public support to do this: 93 percent of Americans agree that we pay too much for the quality of care that we get, and 9 in 10 voters believe that Congress should act to reduce hospital prices.

I would like to finish my remarks with the story of Kynghee Lee from Ohio to illustrate just how anticompetitive these prices have become. Ms. Lee has arthritis, and once a year goes to a rheumatologist for a steroid injection in her hand to relieve her pain. Each round of injection costs her $30. But in 2021, when she arrived at her usual office to see her regular rheumatologist, she found they had moved up one floor in the building. She thought nothing of it until she received a bill for nearly $1,400. Ms. Lee's infusion clinic was moved from an office-based practice to a hospital-based setting, resulting in a price increase of more than 4,500 percent for the exact same service from the exact same provider. This is a national scandal. This committee has the power and responsibility to stand up for our Nation's families and stop pricing abuses driven by big healthcare corporations.

I thank the committee for your time and look forward to answering any questions you might have.

[The prepared statement of Ms. Tripoli follows:]

Testimony of Sophia Tripoli, MPH
Director of the Center for Affordable Whole-Person Care Families USA
Before the House Energy and Commerce Health Subcommittee
Lowering Unaffordable Costs:
Examining Transparency and Competition in Health Care
March 28, 2023

Chairman Guthrie, Ranking Member Eshoo, members of the Committee, thank you for the opportunity to testify today at this critical hearing focused on health care affordability, transparency, and competition. It is an honor to be with you this afternoon. My name is Sophia Tripoli, and I am the director of Families USA's Center on Affordable Whole Person Care. For more than 40 years, Families USA has been a leading national, non-partisan voice for health care consumers working to achieve our vision of a nation where the best health and health care are equally accessible and affordable to all. In October 2022, we launched the Center for Affordable Whole Person Care in affirmation of our commitment to revolutionize America's health care system to hold the health care industry accountable for delivering affordable, equitable, high- quality health care.

The U.S. Health System in Crisis

Today's hearing is urgently needed. Our health care system is in crisis, evidenced by a lack of affordability and poor quality.[1] And it is going to take all of us working together, across political party and health policy philosophy, from rural and urban communities alike, to fix it.

At its core, our nation's affordability crisis is driven by a fundamental misalignment between the business interests of the health care sector and the health and financial security of our nation's families – a business model that allows industry to set prices that have little to do with the quality of the care they offer. These high and irrational prices are largely due to trends in health care industry consolidation that have eliminated competition and allowed monopolistic pricing to push our nation's families to the brink of financial ruin.[2]

The good news is that you and your colleagues in Congress have the support of the American people in making needed changes. Ninety-three percent of Americans agree that our country is paying too much for the quality of health care we receive, and more than half of adults in that same poll said that their most recent health care experience was not worth the cost.[3] Brand new polling released just last week shows that almost 90% of voters say it is important for this Congress to take action to reduce hospital prices, including 95% of Biden voters and 85% of Trump voters.[4]

It is not surprising that Americans are united around the urgent need to address these issues. Almost half of all Americans have reported having to forgo medical care due to the cost, and almost a third have indicated that the high cost of medical care is interfering with their ability to secure basic needs like food and housing,[5] and over 40 percent of American adults – 100 million people – face medical debt.[6] High and rising health care costs are a critical problem for

---

[1] Emma Wager, Jared Ortaliza, and Cynthia Cox, *How Does Health Spending in the U.S. Compare to Other Countries?,* Peterson-KFF Health System Tracker, January 21, 2022, https://www.healthsystemtracker.org/. See also, Nisha Kurani, Emma Wager, *How does the quality of the U.S. health system compare to other countries?,* Peterson-KFF Health System Tracker, September 30, 2021. https://www.healthsystemtracker.org/.

[2] Robert A. Berenson et al., *Addressing Health Care Market Consolidation and High Prices*, The Urban Institute https://www.urban.org/sites/default/files/publication/101508/addressing_health_care_market_consolidation_and_high_prices_1. pdf. See also, Naomi N. Levey, "100 Million People in America are Saddled with Health Care Debt," Kaiser Health News, June 16, 2022, Health https://khn.org/news/article/diagnosis-debt-investigation-100-million-americans-hidden-medical-debt/.

[3] West Health, *West Health-Gallup 2021 Healthcare in America Report*, West Health-Gallup 2021 Healthcare in America Report - westhealth.org.

[4] Arnold Ventures, Arnold Foundation Survey (Study #14460), February 2023. https://www. arnoldventures.org/stories/new-poll-majority-of-voters-support-aggressive-congressional-action-to-lower-hospital-prices?x-craft-preview=FZfdMAYpOB&token=WENwOldeHSblx2pRQ6y01tk_BGY5flyX.

[5] NORC at the University of Chicago and West Health, *Americans' Views on Healthcare Costs, Coverage and Policy*, March 2018 https://www.norc.org/NewsEventsPublications/PressReleases/Pages/survey-finds-large-number-of-people-skipping-necessary- medical-care-because-cost.aspx.

[6] Naomi N. Levey, *100 Million People in America are Saddled with Health Care Debt*, Kaiser Health News, June 16, 2022, https://khn.org/news/article/diagnosis-debt-investigation-100-million-americans-hidden-medical-debt/.

national and state governments, and affect the economic vitality of middle-class and working families - crippling the ability of working people to earn a living wage. Today's real wages — wages after accounting for inflation — are roughly the same as four decades ago, while employer health insurance premiums have risen dramatically.[7] At the same time, nearly 90% of large employers say that rising health care costs will threaten their ability to provide health care benefits to employees over the next five to 10 years if costs are not lowered.[8]

Notably, the excessive cost of health care does not generally buy Americans higher-quality care or even higher volumes of care. In fact, the opposite is true. Despite spending two to three times more on health care than other industrialized countries, the United States has some of the worst health outcomes, including some of the lowest life expectancy and highest infant mortality rates.[9,10,11] These health outcomes are even worse for people of color who experience higher rates of illness and death across a range of health conditions compared with their white counterparts.[12]

These abysmal health outcomes and extraordinarily high prices are the product of broken financial incentives within the U.S. health care system. Our current system rewards building local monopolies and price gouging instead of rewarding success in promoting the health, well-being and financial security of the community.[13] And hospital prices in particular have become highly problematic as the role of hospitals in our economy has shifted over the last 60 years from charitable institutions to corporate entities, resulting in a fundamental misalignment between the business interests of the hospital sector and the interests of the patients they serve.[14]

---

[7] Drew DeSilver, "For Most U.S. Workers, Real Wages Have Barely Budged in Decades," Pew Research Center, August 7, 2018, https://www.pewresearch.org/fact-tank/2018/08/07/for-most-us-workers-real-wages-have-barely-budged-fordecade. See also, Gary Claxton et al., *Health Benefits in 2022: Premiums Remain Steady, Many Employers Report Limited Provider Networks for Behavioral Health*. Health Affairs, October 27, 2022. https://www.healthaffairs.org/stoken/tollfree/2022_11_CLAXTON/full.

[8] "*Vast Majority of Large Employers Surveyed Say Broader Government Role Will Be Necessary to Control Health Costs and Provide Coverage, Survey Finds*," Kaiser Family Foundation, April 29, 2021, Vast Majority of Large Employers Surveyed Say Broader Government Role Will Be Necessary to Control Health Costs and Provide Coverage, Survey Finds | KFF.

[9] Munira Z. Gunja et al., U.S. Health Care from a Global Perspective, 2022: Accelerating Spending, Worsening Outcomes, Commonwealth Fund (Jan. 31, 2023), https://www.commonwealthfund.org/publications/issue-briefs/2023/jan/us-health-care- global-perspective-2022.

[10] OECD (2023), Life expectancy at birth (indicator). doi: 10.1787/27e0fc9d-en (Accessed on 27 January 2023); *See also*, Peterson-KFF Health System Tracker: Health Consumption Expenditures Per Capita. https://www.healthsystemtracker.org/chart-collection/health-spending-u-s-compare-countries-2/#Health%20consumption%20expenditures%20per%20capita,%20U.S.%20dollars,%20PPP%20adjusted,%202020%20or%20nearest%20year (accessed 27 January 2023).

[11] Rabah Kamal, Julie Hudman, and Daniel McDermott, "What Do We Know About Infant Mortality in the U.S. and Comparable Countries?" Peterson-KFF Health System Tracker, October 18, 2019, https://www.healthsystemtracker.org/.

[12] "Racism and Health," Centers for Disease Control and Prevention, last reviewed November 24, 2021, https://www.cdc.gov/minorityhealth/racism-disparities/index.html.

[13] Robert A. Berenson et al., *Addressing Health Care Market Consolidation and High Prices*, The Urban Institute https://www.urban.org/sites/default/files/publication/101508/addressing_health_care_market_consolidation_and_high_prices_1. pdf. See also, Assessing Current and Expected Growth of Alternative Payment Models: A Look at the Bold New Goals for Downside Risk," Leavitt Partners, November 18, 2019, https://leavittpartners.com/assessing-current-and-expected-growth-of-alternative-payment-models-a-look-at-the-bold-new-goals-for-downside-risk/. See also MedPAC, *Report to Congress: Medicare Payment Policy,* March 2023. https://www.medpac.gov/wp-content/uploads/2023/03/Mar23_MedPAC_Report_To_Congress_SEC.pdf.

[14] From 1970 to 2019 the percentage of hospitals that were part of hospital systems rose substantially, from 10 percent to 67 percent, including a moderate increase from 58 percent to 67 percent between 2009 and 2019. For more information, see Fulton BD, Arnold DR, King JS, Montague AD, Greaney TL, Scheffler RM. The rise of cross-

These higher prices result in $240 billion annually coming out of workers' paychecks and instead becoming profits for large health care corporations.[15,16,17]

Health Industry Consolidation Driving High Prices

America's health care affordability crisis stems from high, rising, and variable prices across a wide range of health care goods and services, including prescription drugs and diagnostic tools such as MRIs and CT scans. For example, the price of Humira — a drug used to treat arthritis — is more than four times as expensive in our country as in the United Kingdom and almost twice as expensive as in Germany.[18] The average price of a hospital-based MRI in the United States is $1,475.[19] That same scan costs $503 in Switzerland and $215 in Australia.[20] These higher prices for an identical service are the main driver of the dramatic increase in per capita health care spending in our country, where health care accounted for nearly 20% of the nation's GDP in 2020, far exceeding health care spending by any other industrialized country.[21]

These irrational and unjustifiable prices are largely due to trends in health care industry consolidation that have eliminated competition and allowed monopolistic pricing to flourish.[22] This consolidation has taken place without meaningful regulatory oversight or intervention, and is becoming more acute.[23] In fact, there are few truly competitive health care markets left,

---

market hospital systems and their market power in the US. Health Aff (Millwood). 2022;41(11). https://doi.org/10.1377/hlthaff.2022.00337. See also, Bob Herman, The corporatization of hospital systems, Axios, June 21, 2019. https://www.axios.com/2019/06/21/the-corporatization-of-hospital- systems.

15 William H. Shrank, Teresa L. Rogstad, and Natasha Parekh, "Waste in the US Health Care System: Estimated Costs and Potential for Savings," JAMA 322, no. 15 (2019): 1501–1509, https://jamanetwork.com/journals/jama/articleabstract/2752664.

16 Ioana Marinescu and Herbert J. Hovenkamp, "Anticompetitive Mergers in Labor Markets," Indiana Law Journal 94 (2019): 1031–1063, https://scholarship.law.upenn.edu/cgi/viewcontent.cgi?article=2967&context=faculty_scho larship.

17 David I. Auerbach and Arthur L. Kellermann, "A Decade of Health Care Cost Growth Has Wiped Out Real Income Gains for an Average US Family," Health Affairs 30, no. 9 (2011): 1620–1636, https://www.rand.org/pubs/external_publications/EP201100172.html.

18 Nisha Kurani, Dustin Cotliar, and Cynthia Cox, "How Do Prescription Drug Costs in the United States Compare to Other Countries?" Peterson-KFF Health System Tracker, February 8, 2022, https://www.healthsystemtracker.org/.

19 Michael Chernew et al., Are Health Care Services Shoppable? Evidence from the Consumption of Lower-Limb MRI Scans, Working Paper 24869 (Cambridge, MA: National Bureau of Economic Research, July 2018, revised January 2019), https://www.nber.org/system/files/working_papers/w24869/w24869.pdf.

20 Sarah Kliff, "The Problem Is the Prices: Opaque and Sky High Bills Are Breaking Americans — and Our Health Care System," Vox, October 16, 2017, https://www.vox.com/policy-and-politics/2017/10/16/16357790/health-care-pricesproblem.

21 Emma Wager, Jared Ortaliza, and Cynthia Cox, "How Does Health Spending in the U.S. Compare to Other Countries?" Peterson- KFF Health System Tracker, January 21, 2022, https://www.healthsystemtracker.org/chart-collection/healthspending-u-s-compare-countries-2/#GDP%20per%20capita%20and%20health%20 consumption%20spending%20 per%20capita,%202020%20(U.S.%20dollars,%20PPP%20adjusted).

22 Robert A. Berenson et al., *Addressing Health Care Market Consolidation and High Prices*, The Urban Institute https://www.urban.org/sites/default/files/publication/101508/addressing_health_care_market_ consolidation_and_high_prices_1. pdf. See also, Congressional Budget Office, *Policy Approaches to Reduce What Commercial Insurers Pay for Hospitals' and Physicians' Services,* September 2022. https://www.cbo.gov/system/files/2022-09/58222-medical-prices.pdf/.

23 Gerard Anderson, Peter Hussey, and Varduhi Petrosyan, "It's Still the Prices, Stupid: Why the US Spends So Much on Health Care, and a Tribute to Uwe Reinhardt," Health Affairs 38, no. 1 (2019), https://www.healthaffairs.org/doi/10.1377/ hlthaff.2018.05144.

with 95% of metropolitan statistical areas (MSAs) having highly concentrated hospital markets, nearly 80% of MSAs having highly concentrated specialist physician markets, and 58% of MSAs having highly concentrated insurer markets.[24]

- Hospital consolidation: Hospital mergers are occurring more frequently both within and across health care markets, leading to higher prices in both cases. According to the American Hospital Association, there were 1,577 hospital mergers from 1998 to 2017.[25,26] An estimated 40% of those mergers took place from 2010 to 2015.[27]
- Insurance consolidation: Insurance markets are not as highly concentrated as providers, but there is evidence of markets with little competition between insurers. Between 2006 and 2014, the four-firm concentration ratio —the extent of market control held by the four largest firms, Aetna, Blue Cross Blue Shield, United and Anthem — for the sale of private insurance increased from 74% to 83%.[28]Vertical Integration: The number of hospital-acquired physician practices grew from 35,700 in 2012 to more than 80,000 in 2018.[29] Over this same time period, the percentage of physicians employed by a hospital or health system nearly doubled, from 25% to 44%.[30] Recent research found that over 55% of physicians are now employed in hospital-owned practices.[31] This trend was accelerated by the COVID-19 pandemic, which exacerbated the financial vulnerabilities of independent and smaller physician practices and threatened the near collapse of entire sectors of the health care system — particularly primary care.[32] Nearly 23,000 physicians left independent practice to work for a hospital or other corporate entity after the onset of the COVID-19 pandemic, while hospitals and other corporate entities acquired nearly 21,000 additional

---

24 Jaime S. King et al., Preventing Anticompetitive Healthcare Consolidation: Lessons from Five States (Source on Healthcare Price and Competition and Nicholas C. Petris Center on Health Care Markets and Consumer Welfare of the University of California.

Berkeley School of Public Health, June 2020), https://sourceonhealthcare.org/profile/preventing-anticompetitive-healthcare- consolidation-lessons-from-five-states/.

25 "Chart 2.9: Announced Hospital Mergers and Acquisitions, 1998–2015," TrendWatch Chartbook 2016: Trends Affecting Hospitals and Health Systems (Washington, DC: American Hospital Association, 2016).

26 Chart 2.9: Announced Hospital Mergers and Acquisitions, 2005–2017," TrendWatch Chartbook 2018: Trends Affecting Hospitals and Health Systems (Washington, DC: American Hospital Association, 2018).

27 Martin Gaynor, "Examining the Impact of Health Care Consolidation," statement before the U.S. House Committee on Energy and Commerce Oversight and Investigations Subcommittee, Washington, D.C., February 14, 2018.

28 Leemore S. Dafny, "Evaluating the Impact of Health Insurance Industry Consolidation: Learning from Experience," The Commonwealth Fund, November 2015, https://www.commonwealthfund.org/publications/issue-briefs/2015/nov/evaluatingimpact-health-insurance-industry-consolidation.

29 "Updated Physician Practice Acquisition Study: National and Regional Changes in Physician Employment, 2012-2018," Physicians Advocacy Institute (PAI), February 2019, http://www.physiciansadvocacyinstitute.org/Portals/0/assets/docs/021919-Avalere-PAI-Physician-Employment-Trends-Study-2018-Update.pdf?ver=2019-02-19-162735-117.

30 PAI, "Physician Practice Acquisition Study."

31 Venkatesh, Shruthi. 2019. "The Impact of Hospital Acquisition on Physician Referrals." Unpublished manuscript, Carnegie Mellon University, Pittsburgh, PA.

32 Avalere Health, "COVID-19's Impact on Acquisitions of Physician Practices and Physician Employment 2019-2020," Physicians Advocacy Institute, June 2021, http://www.physiciansadvocacyinstitute.org/Portals/0/assets/docs/Revised-6-8-21_PAI-PhysicianEmployment-Study-2021-FINAL.pdf?ver=K6dyoekRSC_c59U8QD1V-A%3D%3D.

physician practices from 2019 to 2020, representing a 25% increase in corporate-owned practices.[33]

Hospital Pricing Abuses

Nowhere is the negative impact of consolidation more evident than the rising cost of hospital stays and services, which have increased dramatically in the last decade and make up a large portion of increasing health care costs overall.[34],[35],[36] These cost increases have occurred despite lower hospital utilization and are largely due to escalating prices, which are the result of hospitals buying other hospitals and community doctors to eliminate competition and form big health care corporations and medical monopolies.[37,38]

Americans in many communities have watched as their local hospitals became health systems, and those health systems were bought by large health care corporations. What most in the public and policymaking community have not realized is how much this has destroyed any real competition in our health care sector; allowing hospitals to dramatically increase their prices every year.[39],[40] Between 1990 and 2023, hospital prices have increased 600% - and just since 2015, hospital prices have increased as much as 31% nationally, now accounting for nearly one-third of U.S. health care spending, and growing more than four times faster than workers' paychecks.[41,42,43,44]

---

[33] Ibid.

[34] Health Care Cost Institute, *2020 Health Care Cost and Utilization Report*, May 2022. https://healthcost institute.org/images//pdfs/HCCI_2020_Health_Care_Cost_and_Utilization_Report.pdf.

[35] Emily Gee, *The High Price of Hospital Care*, June 26, 2019. Center for American Progress. https://www.american progress.org/article/high-price-hospital-care/.

[36] Nisha Kurani and Cynthia Cox, "What drives health spending in the U.S. compared to other countries" Peterson-KFF Health System Tracker, September 25, 2020, https://www.healthsystemtracker.org/. See also, Zack Cooper, et al., *Hospital Prices Grew Substantially Faster Than Physician Prices for Hospital Based Care in 2007-14*. Health Affairs, February 2019. https://doi.org/10.1377/hlthaff.2018.05424.

[37] Health Care Cost Institute, *2020 Health Care Cost and Utilization Report*, May 2022. https://healthcost institute.org/images//pdfs/HCCI_2020_Health_Care_Cost_and_Utilization_Report.pdf.

[38] Robert A. Berenson et al., *Addressing Health Care Market Consolidation and High Prices*, The Urban Institute https://www.urban.org/sites/default/files/publication/101508/addressing_health_care_market_consolidation_and_high_prices_1. pdf.

[39] Martin Gaynor, What to Do About Health-Care Markets? Policies to Make Health-Care Markets Work (Washington, DC: The Hamilton Project, March 2020), https://www.brookings.edu/wp-content/uploads/ 2020/03/Gaynor_PP_FINAL.pdf.

[40] Robert A. Berenson et al., *Addressing Health Care Market Consolidation and High Prices*, The Urban Institute https://www.urban.org/sites/default/files/publication/101508/addressing_health_care_market_con solidation_and_high_prices_1. pdf.

[41] Nisha Kurani and Cynthia Cox, "What drives health spending in the U.S. compared to other countries" Peterson-KFF Health System Tracker, September 25, 2020, https://www.healthsystemtracker.org/.

[42] Drew DeSilver, "For Most U.S. Workers, Real Wages Have Barely Budged in Decades," Pew Research Center, August 7, 2018,
https://www.pewresearch.org/fact-tank/2018/08/07/for-most-us-workers-real-wages-have-barely-budged-fordecade.

[43] Health Care Cost Institute, *2020 Health Care Cost and Utilization Report*, May 2022.https://health costinstitute.org/images//pdfs/HCCI_2020_Health_Care_Cost_and_Utilization_Report.pdf.

[44] West Health, *The Healthcare Cost Crisis: An American Epidemic*. https://healthcostcrisis.org/, (ARC analysis of Healthcare Cost and Utilization Project, Agency for Healthcare Research and Quality).

These high prices, combined with intentionally opaque billing practices, often hit consumers at their most vulnerable moments. Consider the story of Nicki Pogue:

> In August 2018, Pogue ran a high-altitude trail race with a chest cold. After returning home she started having difficulty breathing, rapid pulse, tingling in her extremities, dizziness, and had difficulty walking. Her neighbor rushed her to the closest hospital where they ran multiple tests—an EKG, chest X-rays, and blood tests – but they could not pinpoint what was wrong with her. Luckily after four hours she stabilized and was sent home. A month later, a $13,000 bill arrived. When she reviewed her bill, she noticed that the biggest charge was a mysterious line item for "ER EX/TX RM LEVEL V," which came with a fee of more than $11,000. She had no idea what this charge was and did not get any transparency or explanation from the hospital. She spent the next five months working to decipher the bill on her own, only to discover the hospital had miscoded her Emergency Severity Index and severely over-charged her.[45]

High and Irrational Prices Fueled by a Lack of Transparency

Importantly, hospital prices are not only high, but have become essentially irrational:

- In 2020, across all hospital inpatient and outpatient services, employers and private insurers paid on average 224% of what Medicare pays for the same services.[46]
- Prices at hospitals in concentrated markets are 12% higher than those in markets with four or more rivals without any demonstrated improvement in the quality or access to care.[47,48,49] All the while, the workforce in these concentrated markets suffers - wages for nurses and other health care workers decrease significantly after mergers and acquisitions.[50]
- Prices for the exact same service vary widely, sometimes even within a single hospital system:
  - A colonoscopy at a single medical center in Mississippi can range from $782 to $2,144 depending on insurance.[51]

---

[45] Families USA, "Center for Affordable Whole Person Care Launch," Facebook, https://www.facebook.com/watch/live/?ref=watch_permalink&v=502440418144915. Accessed March 26, 2023.

[46] Whaley, C. et al. Prices Paid to Hospitals by Private Health Plans. RAND. 2022. https://www.rand.org/pubs/research_reports/RRA1144-1.html.

[47] Cooper, Z. et al. The Price Ain't Right? Hospital Prices and Health Spending on the Privately Insured. The Quarterly Journal of Economics. 2019. https://academic.oup.com/qje/article-abstract/134/1/51/5090426?Redirected From=fulltext&login=false.

[48] Gaynor, M. Diagnosing the Problem: Exploring the Effects of Consolidation and Anticompetitive Conduct in Health Care Markets. Statement before the Committee on the Judiciary Subcommittee on Antitrust, Commercial, and Administration Law. U.S. House of Representatives. 2019. https://www.congress.gov/116/meeting/house/109024/witnesses/HHRG-116-JU05-Bio-GaynorM- 20190307.pdf.

[49] *The Impact of Hospital Consolidation on Medical Costs.* NCCI Insights. 2018. https://www.ncci.com/Articles/Pages/II_Insights_QEB_Impact-of-Hospital-Consolidation-on-Medical-Costs.aspx.

[50] Prager, E. Schmitt, M. *Employer Consolidation and Wages: Evidence from Hospitals.* American Economic Association. 2021. https://www.aeaweb.org/articles?id=10.1257/aer.20190690.

[51] Kliff, S. Katz, J. *Hospitals and Insurers Didn't Want You to See These Prices. Here's Why.* The Upshot. The New York Times. 2021. https://www.nytimes.com/interactive/2021/08/22/upshot/hospital-prices.html.

- At one health system in Wisconsin, an MRI costs between $1,093 and $4,029 depending on level of insurance.[52]
- Across the country, the average price for a knee replacement ranges from $21,976 in Tucson, Arizona to $60,000 in Sacramento California.[53]
- The price of an MRI at Mass General Hospital in Boston Massachusetts ranged from $830 to $4,200 depending on the insurance carrier.[54]

What's more, consumers and employers, who are the ultimate purchasers of health care, have limited insight into what the prices of health care services are, until after they've received a bill. For the majority of Americans – 66%– who receive health care through private insurance,[55] health care prices are established in closed-door negotiations between large hospital corporations and health plans based on who has more market power.[56] These health care prices, often referred to as the negotiated rate, are buried in proprietary contracts without insight into or oversight over the price of health care services by the public and policymakers.[57] Health care is one of the only markets in the U.S. economy in which consumers are blinded to the price of a service until they receive a bill after the services is delivered.[58] It is the epitome of a broken market that threatens the financial security of American families and fails to serve their needs.

Congress has the Power to Fix our Broken System

It does not have to be this way. We know what the major drivers of high and irrational health prices are, and we know how to fix them. As federal lawmakers, you have an obligation to carefully steward our national health care resources and taxpayer dollars. We urge the Committee to consider well-vetted, bipartisan, and commonsense legislation that would remedy some of the most obvious health system failings, and to take on rising health industry consolidation among hospitals, insurers, and other health care organizations that enables anticompetitive behaviors, prevents healthy competition in markets and results in monopolies that set outrageous and unjustifiable prices. Policymakers should also ensure there is a great deal more transparency around both the cost of care and health care outcomes, including for

---

52 Ibid.

53 *National Chartbook of Health Care Prices.* The Health Care Cost Institute. 2016. https://healthcostinstitute.org/national- chartbook-health-care-prices-2015.

54 Kliff, S. Katz, J. *Hospitals and Insurers Didn't Want You to See These Prices. Here's Why.* The Upshot. The New York Times. 2021. https://www.nytimes.com/interactive/2021/08/22/upshot/hospital-prices.html.

55 US Census, Health Insurance Coverage in the United States: 2020, https://www.census.gov/library/publications/2021/demo/p60- 274.html.

56 Kliff, S. Katz, J. *Hospitals and Insurers Didn't Want You to See These Prices. Here's Why.* The Upshot. The New York Times. 2021. https://www.nytimes.com/interactive/2021/08/22/upshot/hospital-prices.html.

57 Jaime King, Testimony before the House Committee on Energy and Commerce and Subcommittee on Oversight and Investigations, (July 17, 2018), https://democrats- energycommerce.house.gov/sites/democrats.energycommerce.house.gov/files/documents/Testimony-King-OI-Hrg-on-Examining-State-Efforts-to-Improve-Transparency-of-Health-Care-Cost-2018-07-17.pdf.

58 Danielle Scheurer, *Lack of Transparency Plagues U.S. Health Care System*, The Hospitalist, May 1, 2013. https://www.the-hospitalist.org/hospitalist/article/125866/health-policy/lack-transparency-plagues-us-health-care-system.

vulnerable populations living in rural America, people of color and people living with disabilities.

One crucial way this Committee can address provider consolidation and encourage competition in the health care system is through price transparency. Unveiling prices is a critical step towards achieving truly affordable health care, improved health, and more competitive health care markets across the U.S. health care system. Price transparency pulls back the curtain on prices so that policymakers, researchers, employers, and consumers can see how irrational health care prices have become and take action to rein in pricing abuses.[59] Further, unveiling prices can specifically inform where the highest and most irrational prices are occurring in the health care system, so policymakers can implement more targeted policy solutions to bring down the cost of health care.[60]

Consumer advocates have long sought transparency in health care prices. Following years of consumer advocacy, the Center for Medicare and Medicaid Services (CMS) finalized the Hospital Price Transparency Rule, which requires hospitals to make public their standard charges for the care they provide including negotiated rates.[61] The rule requires hospitals to publish this information online in a machine-readable format (to allow third parties to analyze these data) and to provide a consumer-friendly online tool to allow consumers to compare prices for at least 300 "shoppable" services.[62] Additionally, in 2020 CMS also finalized another important price transparency regulation – the Transparency in Coverage Rule, which requires health insurers to make similar disclosures and to provide an online tool to allow consumers to estimate out-of- pocket costs.[63]

Yet, more than two years after the Hospital Price Transparency Rule took effect, most hospitals across the country remain out of compliance with the federal rules. Recent estimates suggest that no more than 55% of hospitals are in full compliance with the rule, while other estimates suggest that number is closer to one in five.[64,65] Clearly more work is needed to achieve meaningful transparency of health care price and quality data. We urge Congress to

---

[59] Robert A. Berenson et al., *Addressing Health Care Market Consolidation and High Prices*, The Urban Institute https://www.urban.org/sites/default/files/publication/101508/addressing_health_care_market_consolidation_and_high_prices_1. pdf. See also, Robert A. Berenson et al., *Addressing Health Care Market Consolidation and High Prices;* Jaime King, Testimony before the House Committee on Energy and Commerce and Subcommittee on Oversight and Investigations, (July 17, 2018), https://democrats-energycommerce.house.gov/sites/ democrats. energycommerce.house.gov/files/documents/Testimony-King-OI-Hrg-on-Examining-State-Efforts-to-Improve-Transparency-of-Health-Care-Cost-2018-07-17.pdf.

[60] Phillip Longman and Harris Meyer, *Why Hospitals Keep Their Prices Secret*, July 6, 2020. Washington Monthly. https://washingtonmonthly.com/2020/07/06/why-hospitals-keep-their-prices-secret/.

[61] 84 FR 65602 (Nov. 27, 2019) (codified at 45 C.F.R. §§ 180.10-.110).

[62] Ibid.

[63] 85 FR 72158 (Nov. 12, 2020) (codified at 26 C.F.R. §§ 54.9815-2715A1 to -2715A3, 29 C.F.R. §§ 2590.715-2715A1 to -2715A3, 45C.F.R. §§ 147.210-.212).

[64] Patient Rights Advocate, *Fourth Semi-Annual Hospital Price Transparency Report*, February 2023, https://www.patientrightsadvocate.org/february-semi-annual-compliance-report-2023. See also, Emefah C. Loccoh, et al., *Hospital Adherence to the Federal Price Transparency Mandate: Results from a Nationally Representative Sample*, January 17, 2023. Journal of General Internal Medicine. See also, Morgan Henderson and Morgane Mouslim, *Assessing Compliance with Hospital Price Transparency over Time*, Journal of General Internal Medicine. https://link.springer.com/article/10.1007/s11606-023-08039-0.

[65] Turquoise Health, *Price Transparency Impact Report: Q3 2022*. https://assets.turquoise.health/ impact_ reports/TQ_Price- Transparency-Impact-Report_2022_Q3.pdf. See also, Meena Seshamani (CMS) and Douglas Jacobs (CMS), *Hospital Price Transparency: Progress And Commitment to Achieving Its Potential*, February 14, 2023, Health Affairs. https://www.healthaffairs.org/content/forefront/hospital-price-transparency-progress-and-commitment-achieving-its-potential.

pass legislation to strengthen the Hospital Price Transparency Rule to push back on the industry gaming by sharpening data requirements and establishing standard formats, eliminating loopholes, and further increasing penalties to encourage greater compliance by hospitals.

We also encourage the Committee to address payment differentials across sites of service that incentivize further consolidation and are a major driver of unaffordable care for America's families. Market inefficiencies that come from site-specific payment rates are a significant problem and if addressed could save American families and payers billions of dollars.[66] These site payment differentials drive care delivery from physician offices to higher-cost hospital outpatient departments.[67] This shift is a major driver of higher spending on health care services which require lower resources such as office visits and minor procedures.[68] Additionally, these payment differentials create a financial incentive for hospitals to consolidate by buying physician offices and rebranding them as off-campus outpatient hospital departments (HOPDs) and facilities in order to receive higher payments.[69] This type of consolidation – vertical integration between hospitals and physicians – leads to a growingly anticompetitive market where hospitals increase market power to demand even higher prices from commercial payers.[70] These higher commercial prices are then passed on to American families and come directly out of workers' paychecks, typically as monthly health insurance premiums.[71]

Currently, hospitals that own doctors' offices that have been rebranded as off-campus HOPDs are allowed to charge a "facility fee" in addition to the higher fees they bill for the physician services they provide.[72] The result is that consumers not only receive a bill for the visit with the physician but also for the use of the hospital facility where the visit occurred.[73] These bills together (the physician fee and the facility fee) amount to a higher total cost for the consumer than if the service was just provided in the physician's office.[74]

To understand what this looks like for patients, here is the story of Kyunghee Lee:

> Kyunghee Lee has arthritis and once a year she would go to a rheumatologist for a steroid injection in her hand to relieve pain in her knuckles. For a few years, each round of injections cost her $30. In 2021, she arrived at her usual office and the rheumatologist she regularly saw had moved to a new floor of the building - just one floor up. She didn't think anything of it, as the rest of the appointment went as usual, until she received a bill for $1,394. The infusion clinic that Lee went to had been moved from an office-based practice to a hospital-based setting, and as a result the price of the same service she had been relying upon increased a staggering 4,546%. Lee's bill had a $1,262 facility fee attached, making up the majority of the increase in

[66] Committee for a Responsible Federal Budget, *Moving to Site Neutrality in Commercial Insurance Payments*, February 14, 2023. https://www.crfb.org/papers/moving-site-neutrality-commercial-insurance.

[67] Ibid.

[68] Ibid.

[69] Ibid.

[70] Hannah T. Neprash et al. "Association of Financial Integration Between Physicians and Hospitals With Commercial Health Care Prices." *JAMA Internal Medicine* 2015;175(12):1932-1939.

[71] Ibid. See also, David I. Auerbach and Arthur L. Kellerman, "A Decade of Health Care Cost Growth Has Wiped Out Real Income Gains for an Average US Family," Health Affairs 30, no. 9 (September 2011), https://www.rand.org/pubs/external_publications/ EP201100172.html.

[72] Committee for a Responsible Federal Budget, Moving to Site Neutrality in Commercial Insurance Payments, February 14, 2023. https://www.crfb.org/papers/moving-site-neutrality-commercial-insurance.

[73] Ibid.

[74] MedPAC, *Medicare and the Health Care Delivery System, Report to the Congress,* June 2022. https://www.medpac.gov/wp- content/uploads/2022/06/Jun22_MedPAC_Report_to_Congress_v2_SEC.pdf.

cost, even though she saw the same doctor and received the same treatment as the years prior. Lee and her family didn't know what they would do about the shot in the following year when the story was reported.[75]

This is patently ridiculous, and this kind of abusive pricing should not be allowed to continue. We urge the Committee to consider implementing site-neutral payment policies as recommended by MedPAC in 2022,[76] and to eliminate site-dependent reimbursement distortions that indirectly incentivize acquisition of non-hospital patient access points.[77] The Congressional Budget Office (CBO) estimates that this policy could save Medicare approximately $140 billion over the next decade.[78] And, the Committee for a Responsible Budget projects that these policies could reduce health care spending by $153 billion over the next decade including lowering premiums and cost- sharing for Medicare beneficiaries by $94 billion and for those in the commercial market by $140 -$466 billion.[79]

We also urge the Committee to take a close look at anticompetitive practices and clauses in health care contracting agreements, which occur in a variety of places including between providers and insurers and in clinician and health care worker employment arrangements.[80] In contracts between provider entities and insurers, large entities in highly consolidated markets have the upper hand in contract negotiations to build networks and set prices. As a result, many of these contracts include terms that limit access to higher-quality, lower-cost care. When anticompetitive terms are present in health care clinician and worker employment contracts, they can further stifle competition, lead to burnout exacerbating workforce shortages,[81] impede patient access to preferred providers and care, and lead to higher prices for health care services.[82]

Beyond these immediate steps, policymakers should focus on a broader redesign of the economic incentives of the health care sector to align with consumers and families. Ultimately, policy solutions should reorient health care payment and delivery to the goal that we all have

---

75 Lauren Weber, *Her Doctor's Office Moved One Floor Up. Her Bill Was 10 Times Higher,* March 26, 2021, Kaiser Health News. https://khn.org/news/article/bill-of-the-month-hospital-facility-fee-outpatient-arthritis-injections/.

76 MedPAC, *Medicare and the Health Care Delivery System, Report to the Congress,* June 2022. https://www.medpac.gov/wp-content/uploads/2022/06/Jun22_MedPAC_Report_to_Congress_v2_SEC.pdf.

77 Committee for a Responsible Federal Budget, *Moving to Site Neutrality in Commercial Insurance Payments*, February 14, 2023. https://www.crfb.org/papers/moving-site-neutrality-commercial-insurance.

78 Congressional Budget Office, *Proposals Affecting Medicare—CBO's Estimate of the President's Fiscal Year 2021 Budget*, March 25, 2020. https://www.cbo.gov/system/files?file=2020-03/56245-2020-03-medicare.pdf.

79 Committee for a Responsible Federal Budget, *Equalizing Medicare Payments Regardless of Site-of-Care,* February 23, 2021. https://www.crfb.org/papers/equalizing-medicare-payments-regardless-site-care.

80 A notable example of a hospital system allegedly employing anticompetitive contracting practices was in the case of Sutter Health, based in California. Health care prices in northern California, where Sutter Health operated, grew four times faster than prices across the rest of the state between 2004 and 2013. Glenn A. Melnick and Katya Fonkych, "Hospital Prices Increase in California, Especially Among Hospitals in the Largest Multi-Hospital Systems," Inquiry 53 (June 2016), https://www.researchgate.net/publication/303891826_Hospital_Prices_Increase_in_California_Especially_Among_Hospitals_in_the_Largest_Multi-hospital_Systems. See also, Jenny Gold, *Surprise Settlement In Sutter Health Antitrust Case*, October 16, 2019, Kaiser Health News. https://khn.org/news/surprise-settlement-in- sutter-health-antitrust-case/.

81 Erik B. Smith, *Ending Physician Noncompete Agreements—Time for a National Solution,* Journal of American Medical Association *(JAMA)*, December 3, 2021. https://jamanetwork.com/journals/jama-health-forum/fullarticle/2786894.

82 Prager, E. Schmitt, M. *Employer Consolidation and Wages: Evidence from Hospitals.* American Economic Association. 2021. https://www.aeaweb.org/articles?id=10.1257/aer.20190690.

— improved health for ourselves and our families that is affordable and economically sustainable.

Once again, the American people want action. Large majorities of voters support a range of policies to lower prices. Voters from both sides of the aisle broadly support:[83]

- Requiring hospitals to publicly disclose their prices (87%)
- Limiting outpatient fees to the same price charged by doctors in the community (85%)
- Preventing hospitals from engaging in business tactics that reduce competition (75%)
- Limiting mergers and acquisitions (74%)

Thank you again for holding this hearing today. Congress should seize this momentum to immediately implement commonsense policies that rein in abusive health care prices and make health care more affordable for everyone. The journey to fully transform our health care system is long, but Congress holds the power to take the next critical steps. Families USA stands ready to support you in this essential and urgently needed work.

Mr. GUTHRIE. I thank you for your testimony. I appreciate it.

I will note there is a vote on the floor. We still have 318 left to vote, so I know we are going to have time for the next—to finish our opening statements, and then we will—probably one or two people may be able to ask questions. We will see how it moves forward.

But now, Dr. Ippolito, I will recognize you for 5 minutes for an opening statement.

Statement of Benedic Ippolito, PhD

Dr. IPPOLITO. Well, thanks very much, Chairman Guthrie, Ranking Member Eshoo, and members of the subcommittee. My name is Benedic Ippolito. I am an economist at the American Enterprise Institute here in Washington, D.C.

You know, the high costs of healthcare underpin nearly every health policy debate that we have and, frankly, many nonhealth policy debates. Rising costs in programs like Medicare and Medicaid create budgetary pressures for the government, right? That stresses tax bases, and it crowds out other valuable uses for that fund—those funds. Whether it is lowering taxes, whether it is spending money on other programs you like, you can't do it if healthcare is taking all the money.

Within the employer-based market, rising insurance costs eat away at the wage growth of workers. And across all of those settings, it becomes more expensive to expand insurance, either to cover more people or to cover more services. Of course, all of that isn't necessarily a problem, per se, if we think that healthcare spending reflects the demands of consumers, their preferences, right, be it clinical quality, nonclinical value, convenience, whatever it might be.

However, at this point there is very ample evidence that much of our spending reflects market frictions and inefficiencies rather than consumer preferences. And I think this hearing today is highlighting two key sources of those frictions.

---

[83] Arnold Ventures, Arnold Foundation Survey (Study #14460), February 2023. https://www.arnoldventures.org/stories/new-poll-majority-of-voters-support-aggressive-congressional-action-to-lower-hospital-prices?x-craft- preview=FZfdMAYpOB&token=WENwOldeHSblx2pRQ6y01tk_BGY5flyX.

Markets require informed consumers who have meaningful choice. If purchasers—whether it is individuals, a State health plan, an employer—if they do not have any meaningful choice, then their decision reflects nothing about their preferences, it just reflects the fact that that was the only option they had. And the same goes for a purchaser who doesn't have any information. If you make a choice but you don't really know the full cost of that PBM, insurance plan, whatever it is, well, that choice doesn't really reflect your underlying preferences. And that really is the fundamental problem here.

So in both of those cases, we have high prices that can persist for reasons that are divorced from value. So economic theory and empirical evidence are very clear that improving competition within healthcare markets increases pressures on firms to improve quality and decrease costs. Increasing transparency in conjunction can help market actors make the best use of the choices that are made available to them and push markets to invest in the things they value by providing clear signals, by moving with their feet— voting with their feet, if you will.

In other words—and I do think this is the key point here—more competition and transparency doesn't just lower spending in some indiscriminate manner. Rather, it targets spending that does not reflect value to consumers. And that is the key point, I think, to this hearing.

Beyond this, policies that make progress along these dimensions, particularly transparency, are important for informing the policy- making process. We need an accurate understanding of how markets work and when they do not. That is key to redesigning incentives that, for example, may affect consolidation incentives that were brought up earlier, and understand when more active intervention is justified.

And I will just take a moment to highlight we are probably going to talk about a lot of policies that are informed by the last 10 or so years. There has been an explosion of understanding of the commercial healthcare market. We much better understand the prices and the spending in those markets, how important consolidation is, and that is a direct function of the fact that we have much better data today about commercial healthcare prices than we did, say, 10 or 15 years ago.

In my written testimony I emphasize a host of specific policy options that can help address high healthcare costs by increasing competition and transparency, with a particular emphasis on those that have attracted bipartisan interest in recent years. And I will just note that that was coauthored with Loren Adler of the Brookings Institution and was recently copublished by AEI and Brookings. I am not going to summarize that list now, but I will note that this is an issue that spans just about every part of healthcare. And so that is a long way of saying that this hearing is keying in not just on healthcare costs in general, but rather two of the most important underlying sources of inefficient spending in healthcare markets.

And I thank you for the invitation to be here today, and I look forward to your questions.

[The prepared statement of Mr. Ippolito follows:]

Statement before the House Committee on Energy and Commerce Health Subcommittee on "Lowering Unaffordable Costs: Examining Transparency and Competition in Health Care"

Improving Competition and Transparency in Health Care Markets

Benedic Ippolito, PhD
Senior Fellow
March 28, 2023

The American Enterprise Institute (AEI) is a nonpartisan, nonprofit, 501(c)(3) educational organization and does not take institutional positions on any issues. The views expressed in this testimony are those of the author.

Nearly every health policy challenge is magnified by the high underlying cost of health care in the United States. High expenditures in programs like Medicare or Medicaid create budgetary pressures for state and federal governments. This stresses tax bases and crowds out valuable spending in other programs. Meanwhile, the high cost of employer-sponsored insurance reduces wage growth of workers. Across all settings, this phenomenon makes it more costly to expand coverage to new services or people.

High health care costs are not necessarily problematic if they reflect preferences of individuals. However, there is ample evidence that some health spending reflects market imperfections, like a lack of information or choice. In some cases, these reflect natural features of health care markets (e.g., some care is purchased in urgent circumstances) while in others they reflect explicit policy decisions (e.g., policies that encourage consolidation or mute cost sensitivity). Regardless, these features can generate high expenditures that do not reflect value to consumers.

Increasing transparency and competition within health care will improve market functioning and can help target spending that does not reflect consumers' preferences. Congress has a number of policy options to do that across many settings within health care. In the rest of my testimony, I will outline specific areas where policy changes can improve transparency and competition within health care markets.[84]

Policy Options to Improve Competition and Transparency

Increasing Transparency and Oversight of Consolidation

Rising consolidation represents a major challenge to the functioning of health care markets. Economic theory predicts that less competition will reduce pressure for firms to lower costs and improve quality. As Adler and Ippolito (2023) note, empirical research has confirmed these predictions within health care markets.

---

[84] Throughout this testimony I rely heavily on material from Loren Adler and Benedic Ippolito "Procompetitive Health Care Reform Options for a Divided Congress," *American Enterprise Institute and The Brookings Institution* (March 16, 2023).

A large body of evidence finds that the merger of potential competitors within health care markets increases costs[85] to consumers and is suggestive that it also reduces the quality of care.[86] That is, when hospitals or physician groups in the same geographic market merge together (or one acquires the other) they are able to extract higher prices from private insurers and employers. Newer research suggests that similar effects also may arise from mergers that occur across different markets within the same state.[87] Higher costs are at least partially passed on to individuals in the form of higher premiums and cost-sharing[88] or to employees in the form or lower wages.[89] A growing body of evidence now also suggests that vertical consolidation between hospitals and physician groups leads to increased costs[90] (above and beyond the effects of any resulting horizontal consolidation in the physician specialties being acquired by hospitals) with unclear effects on quality.[91]

While the potential harm of anticompetitive mergers and acquisitions is relatively clear, many such transactions can still occur (of course, not all consolidation raises competitive concerns). In this section, I highlight reasons for this and discuss policies to improve oversight of consolidation. Later in this testimony I discuss related policy reforms that would decrease the incentives for health care firms to consolidate.

Firms are required to notify federal antitrust authorities if the value of their merger or acquisition exceeds a threshold—$111.4 million in 2023 (adjusted annually for inflation).[92] Many transactions within health care fall below this threshold, including most involving

---

[85] E.g., Zack Cooper et al., "The Price Ain't Right? Hospital Prices and Health Spending on the Privately Insured," *The Quarterly Journal of Economics* 134, no. 1 (February 1, 2019): 51–107, https://doi.org/10.1093/qje/qjy020; Leemore Dafny, Kate Ho, and Robin S. Lee, "The Price Effects of Cross-Market Mergers: Theory and Evidence from the Hospital Industry," *The RAND Journal of Economics* 50, no. 2 (2019): 286–325, https://doi.org/10.1111/1756-2171.12270.

[86] E.g., Nancy D. Beaulieu et al., "Changes in Quality of Care after Hospital Mergers and Acquisitions," *New England Journal of Medicine* 382, no. 1 (January 2, 2020): 51–59, https://doi.org/10.1056/NEJMsa1901383; Thomas Koch, Brett Wendling, and Nathan E. Wilson, "Physician Market Structure, Patient Outcomes, and Spending: An Examination of Medicare Beneficiaries," *Health Services Research* 53, no. 5 (October 2018): 3549–68, https://doi.org/10.1111/1475-6773.12825.

[87] Dafny, Ho, and Lee, "The Price Effects of Cross-Market Mergers: Theory and Evidence from the Hospital Industry," *RAND Journal of Economics* (April 10, 2019), https://doi.org/10.1111/1756-2171.12270.

[88] Daniel Arnold and Christopher M. Whaley, *Who Pays for Health Care Costs? The Effects of Health Care Prices on Wages* (Santa Monica, CA: RAND Corporation, 2020), https://doi.org/10.7249/WRA621-2.

[89] See Conor Lennon, "Employer-Sponsored Health Insurance and Labor Market Outcomes for Men in Same-Sex Couples: Evidence from the Advent of Pre-Exposure Prophylaxis," *Economics & Human Biology* 47 (December 2022): 101156, https://doi.org/10.1016/j.ehb.2022.101156; Gruber, Jonathan. "The incidence of mandated maternity benefits." The American economic review (1994): 622-641.

[90] E.g., Soroush Saghafian et al., "The Impact of Vertical Integration on Physician Behavior and Healthcare Delivery: Evidence from Gastroenterology Practices" (Cambridge, MA: National Bureau of Economic Research, February 2023), https://doi.org/10.3386/w30928; James Godwin et al., "The Association between Hospital-Physician Vertical Integration and Outpatient Physician Prices Paid by Commercial Insurers: New Evidence," *INQUIRY: The Journal of Health Care Organization, Provision, and Financing* 58 (January 2021), https://doi.org/10.1177/00469580211991276; Brady Post, Tom Buchmueller, and Andrew M. Ryan, "Vertical Integration of Hospitals and Physicians: Economic Theory and Empirical Evidence on Spending and Quality," *Medical Care Research and Review* 75, no. 4 (August 2018): 399–433, https://doi.org/10.1177/1077558717727834.

[91] See Thomas G. Koch, Brett W. Wendling, and Nathan E. Wilson, "The Effects of Physician and Hospital Integration on Medicare Beneficiaries' Health Outcomes," *The Review of Economics and Statistics* (August 16, 2021), 1–15, https://doi.org/10.1162/rest_a_00924.

[92] Federal Trade Commission, "FTC Announces 2023 Update of Size of Transaction Thresholds for Premerger Notification Filings and Interlocking Directorates," January 23, 2023.

physician practices, which greatly decreases the odds of a transaction being challenged.[93] These smaller mergers can still have important implications for competition, particularly if a single owner assembles a large market share through a series of smaller transactions. Private equity investors often follow this strategy.[94]

Congress can improve transparency and oversight of these transactions in a number of ways. First, it can lower the threshold for pre-merger notification. Second, it can require notification if the cumulative value of acquisitions in a given market by a single owner exceed the reporting threshold (even if a single transaction does not rise to that level). Third, it can task the antitrust agencies with tracking market concentration levels in health care markets. Together, these would give the agencies greater knowledge of transactions and help them better assess when smaller mergers, or a series of such mergers, present competitive concerns.

Relatedly, Congress can consider legislation that makes ownership structures more transparent making it easier to identify when one owner amasses a significant market share via smaller, less-salient acquisitions (proposals like HR 6885 or HR 5825 embody this idea).[95] In addition, they can expand the Transparency in Coverage rule to include information about the total volume of each service that was used by each plan's enrollees. Doing so would make it easier to calculate information about market shares and average prices.

Finally, some have suggested that Congress amend the Clayton Act to make it easier to challenge potentially anticompetitive mergers.[96] They could, for example, require regulators to demonstrate only that a merger "meaningfully" lessens competition rather than "substantially" so. It could also be modified to allow regulators to challenge a series of transactions that collectively have the same effect. These changes could be directed specifically at transactions within health care to reduce potential unintended consequences.

Discouraging Consolidation Through Site Neutral Payments

Congress can work to dissuade further consolidation by revisiting Medicare payment policies. Specifically, Medicare typically pays a higher price if a given service is performed at a hospital outpatient department (HOPD) than if it is delivered at a physician's office. This differential payment rate across sites of service provides an incentive[97] for hospitals to acquire physician's offices. A growing body of evidence[98] finds that this type of consolidation increases costs for

---

[93] E.g., Thomas Wollmann, "How to Get Away with Merger: Stealth Consolidation and Its Effects on US Healthcare" (Cambridge, MA: National Bureau of Economic Research, May 2020), https://doi.org/10.3386/w27274.

[94] See Erin C. Fuse Brown et al., "Private Equity Investment as a Divining Rod for Market Failure: Policy Responses to Harmful Physician Practice Acquisitions," *USC-Brookings Schaeffer Initiative for Health Policy* (October 5, 2021).

[95] For the complete text of HR 6885, see https://www.congress.gov/bill/117th-congress/house-bill/6885. For the complete text of HR 5825, see https://www.congress.gov/bill/116th-congress/house-bill/5825.

[96] E.g., Leemore S. Dafny, "How Health Care Consolidation Is Contributing to Higher Prices and Spending, and Reforms That Could Bolster Antitrust Enforcement and Preserve and Promote Competition in Health Care Markets," *Testimony Before the U.S. House Committee on the Judiciary Subcommittee on Antitrust, Commercial and Administrative Law*, April 29, 2021.

[97] See Brady Post et al., "Hospital physician Integration and Medicare's Site based Outpatient Payments," *Health Services Research* 56, no. 1 (February 2021): 7–15, https://doi.org/10.1111/1475-6773.13613.

[98] E.g., Marah Noel Short and Vivian Ho, "Weighing the Effects of Vertical Integration Versus Market Concentration on Hospital Quality," *Medical Care Research and Review* 77, no. 6 (December 2020): 538–48, https://doi.org/10.1177/1077558719828938; Cory Capps, David Dranove, and Christopher Ody, "The Effect of

both Medicare and commercial payers. In addition, it can directly increase costs to beneficiaries.[99]

In a market without these distortions, we would expect non-hospital-based providers to compete for patients as services become routine enough to be delivered outside of hospitals. Current payment models impede this. As Adler and Ippolito (2023) summarize, there have been recent efforts to address these incentives:

> In recent years, both Congress and the Trump Administration have taken steps to require site-neutral payments in limited circumstances.[100] As a result, clinic visits at off-campus HOPDs and any service delivered at an off-campus HOPD that was established after November 2, 2015 are reimbursed based on the physician fee schedule (PFS) rather than the more generous outpatient prospective payment system (OPPS). However, these provisions did not address services other than clinic visits at grandfathered off-campus HOPDs, services at on-campus HOPDs, or services performed at other types of facilities such as [Ambulatory Surgery Centers], freestanding emergency departments, and cancer hospitals.

Congress can further reduce consolidation incentives stemming from Medicare's payment policy. For example, a recent proposal from Representative Victoria Spartz would reimburse all off-campus HOPD services based on the PFS.[101] Congress could also reduce payments to all HOPDs for certain services that can be safely delivered outside of the hospital setting (MedPAC has identified a number of such procedures[102]).

Both the Obama and Trump administrations included similar proposals in their budget submissions.[103] Basing payments on the physician fee schedule for all off-campus HOPDs and certain services at on-campus HOPDs would lower deficits by about $140 billion over 10 years.[104]

Increasing Transparency into Pharmacy Benefit Managers

Policymakers have expressed concerns about the role of Pharmacy Benefit Managers (PBMs) and whether they contribute to high drug costs or other market distortions. PBMs, which manage drug benefits for insurers by negotiating with drug makers, designing formularies, and

Hospital Acquisitions of Physician Practices on Prices and Spending," *Journal of Health Economics* 59 (May 2018): 139–52, https://doi.org/10.1016/j.jhealeco.2018.04.001; Laurence C. Baker, M. Kate Bundorf, and Daniel P. Kessler, "Vertical Integration: Hospital Ownership Of Physician Practices Is Associated With Higher Prices And Spending," *Health Affairs* 33, no. 5 (May 2014): 756–63, https://doi.org/10.1377/hlthaff.2013.1279.

99 Patient liability is typically 20% coinsurance if patients do not have supplemental coverage. Even if beneficiaries do have supplemental coverage, this phenomenon can increase Medigap premiums or costs to Medicaid and former employers.

100 See Loren Adler et al., "CMS' positive step on site-neutral payments and the case for going further," *USC-Brookings Schaeffer Initiative for Health Policy*, (August 10, 2018).

101 For the complete text, see https://www.congress.gov/bill/117th-congress/house-bill/8133/.

102 MedPAC, "Medicare and the Health Care Delivery System," *Report to the Congress*, June 15, 2022.

103 See Department of Health & Human Services, "Budget in Brief: Fiscal Year 2016"; Department of Health & Human Services, "Budget in Brief: Fiscal Year 2021."

104 Congressional Budget Office, "Proposals Affecting Medicare—CBO's Estimate of the President's Fiscal Year 2021 Budget," March 25, 2020.

contracting with pharmacies, have attracted attention for a number of reasons. As Adler and Ippolito (2023) note:

> Concerns about PBMs are largely based on a few key facts. First, the PBM market has become relatively consolidated over time, with three firms—Caremark, Express Scripts, and OptumRx—controlling 80 percent of the market.[105] (The major PBMs are also now vertically integrated with insurance companies.) In addition, PBMs are also alleged to facilitate pricing structures that increase costs for some consumers. Notably, they may encourage drug makers to set very high list prices while selling to insurers or PBMs at much lower "net" prices. Because consumer out-of-pocket liability can be a percent of the list price, this increases costs to sicker enrollees taking expensive medications. They may also affect competition within the pharmacy market by steering patients to use pharmacies that they own. Using selective contracting can lower costs to consumers but also may drive independent pharmacies out of business. Finally, PBM contracts are relatively opaque, which makes it harder to assess the harms or benefits of their behavior.

The opacity of these contracting arrangements makes it difficult for policymakers to assess their role in drug markets and for plan sponsors to make informed decisions when choosing a PBM. There are a number of ongoing efforts to improve policymakers' understanding of PBMs. The Federal Trade Commission recently announced an investigation[106] into PBMs while requests from the House Oversight Committee[107] will also elicit information on contracting practices.

In addition, legislative proposals like the Lower Health Care Costs Act of 2019 would require PBMs to disclose a host of information, including rebates, costs, and fees.[108] CBO estimated that this would lower deficits by $1.7 billion by helping plan sponsors to better evaluate contracts and triggering more competition between PBMs.[109]

Increasing Competition Through Contracting Reforms

Dominant firms in health care markets can reduce choice and impede entry of potential competitors by demanding certain provisions in their contracts. Congress is well-justified in considering restrictions on these clauses in an effort to encourage more cost competition, particularly in markets that are already relatively consolidated.[110]

For example, dominant health care providers can require that insurers agree to clauses which disallow them from incentivizing patients to seek care at potentially lower-cost providers (through "anti-tiering" or "anti- steering" clauses). A dominant hospital might also require an

---

[105] For coverage, see Adam J. Fein, "The Top Pharmacy Benefit Managers of 2021: The Big Get Even Bigger," April 5, 2022.

[106] For coverage, see Ed Silverman, "FTC will investigate pharmacy benefit managers and their role in prescription drug costs," June 8, 2022.

[107] Committee on Oversight, "Comer Launches Investigation into Pharmacy Benefit Managers' Role in Rising Health Care Costs, March 1, 2023.

[108] For the complete text, see https://www.congress.gov/bill/116th-congress/senate-bill/1895.

[109] Congressional Budget Office, "S. 1895, Lower Health Care Costs Act,' July 26, 2019.

[110] See Brent D. Fulton, "Health Care Market Concentration Trends In The United States: Evidence And Policy Responses," *Health Affairs* 36, no. 9 (September 2017): 1530–38, https://doi.org/10.1377/hlthaff.2017.0556.

insurer to include all affiliated providers in their network or none ("all-or-nothing" clause). This can effectively extend a provider's dominant position in one part of the market to others (these clauses can interact with network adequacy laws in ways to make them particularly powerful). These types of contract provisions directly undercut insurers' main tools for encouraging price competition.

Similarly, dominant insurers can stifle competition by demanding "most favored nations" clauses. These require that providers not give any other insurer a lower price than the dominant insurer. This makes it very challenging for other insurers to compete on price, even if they use tools like narrower networks.

These types of contracting provisions have less bite in competitive markets. In a market with many providers, for example, an insurer could simply avoid contracting with a hospital that demands an anti-tiering, anti-steering, or all-or-nothing clause (or negotiate price concessions in exchange). Thus, efforts to restrict the use of these contract provisions are likely to target markets with meaningful consolidation.

The Lower Health Care Cost Act[111] would have banned the use of these contracting terms, which CBO estimated would modestly reduce premiums in the private insurance market and increase federal revenues by $1.1 billion over the budget window.[112] The CBO recently indicated that cost savings would be larger in updated estimates.[113]

Addressing Consolidation Incentives in the 340B Program

The 340B drug discount program may have the unintended consequence of encouraging greater consolidation within provider markets. Policymakers should consider whether redesigning the program can reduce this incentive while achieving the program's stated goals.

The 340B program requires drug makers to give large discounts to qualified health care providers, which include disproportionate share hospitals, federally qualified health centers, hemophilia centers, and others. The discounts are large (estimated at 25-50 percent in 2011) and are largely designed to subsidize providers that treat large volumes of low-income patients.[114] The program has grown very rapidly over time.[115]

This design has the potential to increase consolidation incentives and overall costs, however. Adler and Ippolito (2023) summarize the key concerns:

> First, a 0B hospital has an incentive to acquire private physician practices since it can purchase drugs cheaper than the practice can, increasing consolidation in those fields. Second, these discounts could mean hospitals earn high margins on products that are more expensive for insurers, encouraging them to prescribe costlier medicines.

---

[111] See footnote 26.

[112] See footnote 27.

[113] Congressional Budget Office, "Policy Approached to Reduce What Commercial Insurers Pay for Hospitals' and Physicians' Services," p. 24, September 29, 2022.

[114] Government Accountability Office, "Manufacturer Discounts in the 340B Program Offer Benefits, but Federal Oversight Needs Improvement," September 23, 2011.

[115] See Karen Mulligan, "The 340B Drug Pricing Program: Background, Ongoing Challenges, and Recent Developments," *Schaeffer Center White Paper Series*, (October 14, 2021).

One paper found that hospitals have responded to these incentives by dispensing more drugs, acquiring more physicians in some drug-intensive specialties, and treating fewer patients on Medicaid.[116] However, it did not find evidence that hospitals provided more or better care to low-income patients. On average, 340B hospitals also have higher Part B spending per beneficiary, which is consistent with (but not proof of) them altering their prescribing behavior due to the program.[117]

As CBO notes,[118] "a policy change that applied drug discounts under the 340b program on a patient-level basis—that is, to patients with certain characteristics rather than to all patients at certain sites of care—might reduce hospitals' and physicians' incentives to consolidate." While we are not aware of a formal score for this kind of proposal, we expect cost savings to be small in the budget window, partly because of uncertainty and because it would take some time for this policy to play out. Still, this reform improves incentives, more effectively subsidizes providers treating many low-income individuals, and would potentially fit well within legislation that reformed other aspects of the program.

Beyond this type of program redesign, Congress could also reduce payments to 340B hospitals to reflect lower acquisition costs, which should lower consolidation incentives to some degree. This would also save Medicare money directly. For example, the Centers for Medicare and Medicaid Services estimates that Medicare would save $1.6 billion per year by lowering payments from the current 106% of ASP to 77.5% of ASP. HHS' recent attempt to implement a policy along these lines was overturned[119] in court because the agency did not complete the required survey of hospital acquisition costs. While the administration could revisit this, Congress could pass legislation along these lines instead.

Improving Upon Recent Transparency Rules

The federal government has recently made an effort to increase transparency in the commercial health care markets through two federal rules—the Hospital Price Transparency Rule and the Transparency in Coverage Rule. These efforts have the potential to fill in gaps in existing data and improve market functioning.[120] Congress has the opportunity to build on these policies by increasing compliance and, in some cases, the breadth of information provided.

The Hospital Price Transparency Rule, which took effect January 1, 2021, requires hospitals to disclose a variety of pricing information.[121] These data include information about gross charges, negotiated rates, and cash prices for all services, along with a consumer-friendly display for a set of shoppable services. The Transparency in Coverage Rule, which began to take effect in 2022, requires insurers to post in-network rates for covered services, allowed

---

[116] Sunita Desai and J. Michael McWilliams, "Consequences of the 340B Drug Pricing Program," *New England Journal of Medicine* 378, no. 6 (February 8, 2018): 539–48, https://doi.org/10.1056/NEJMsa1706475.

[117] Government Accountability Office, "Action Needed to Reduce Financial Incentives to Prescribe 340B Drugs at Participating Hospitals," June 5, 2015.

[118] See footnote 31.

[119] For coverage, see James Romoser, "In an opinion that shuns Chevron, the court rejects a Medicare cut for hospital drugs," June 15, 2022.

[120] For a discussion, see Yang Wang et al., "Insurer Price Transparency Rule: What Has Been Disclosed?" *Health Affairs Forefront* (February 2, 2023), https://doi.org/10.1377/forefront.20230127.553761.

[121] See https://www.ecfr.gov/current/title-45/subtitle-A/subchapter-E/part-180#180.40.

amounts and billed charges for out-of-network care, and price comparison tools to aid consumers.[122]

However, early evidence suggests that full compliance with transparency requirements among hospitals has been relatively low.[123] This may, in part, reflect the relatively modest penalties associated with noncompliance. Following an increase in 2022, penalties ranged from $300 to $5,500 per day based on hospital size. By comparison, the insurer rule comes with a penalty of $100 per day per impacted individual, which can increase substantially for large insurers.[124] Congress could consider increasing the penalties for hospitals that are out of compliance with the rule. For example, a bill introduced by Senator John Kennedy proposes doubling these fines.[125]

In addition, there are opportunities to improve the drug pricing information collected via the Transparency in Coverage Rule. Critically, researchers have noted that these data do not include information about the dosage for a physician-administered drug (essentially how much of the drug the price corresponds to).[126] This makes it very challenging to understand the price for a standard dose and to compare across insurers. In addition, the rule was meant to include information about pharmacy-dispensed medications, but that was delayed by CMS. Should Congress want to codify this rule, including these elements would make the data more useful to researchers and policymakers.[127]

Improving Competition in Medicare Advantage

By generating competition among insurers, Medicare Advantage (MA) has the potential to lower costs, improve plan design and, in turn, patient health. However, there is reason to believe that competition could both be more robust and better directed towards cost and quality.

MA plans are currently paid a capitated amount per enrollee that is based on beneficiary spending in Traditional Medicare (TM) in that area. These payments are risk adjusted to reflect the higher costs associated with enrolling sicker beneficiaries. Each MA plan submits a bid which reflects their estimated cost of providing Parts A and B coverage to a typical beneficiary. If they submit a bid below the local benchmark, they can keep part of the difference, allowing them to lower premiums or offer more services.

One of the primary concerns with MA is that the current structure encourages insurers to effectively compete on coding intensity—that is, making enrollees appear sicker—instead of

---

122 For the complete text, see https://www.ecfr.gov/current/title-45/subtitle-A/subchapter-B/part-147/section-147.210.

123 E.g., Maanasa Kona and Sabrina Corlette, "Hospital and Insurer Price Transparency Rules Now In Effect But Compliance Is Still Far Away," September 12, 2022, https://doi.org/10.1377/forefront.20220909.326193.; Turquoise Health, "Price Transparency Impact Report," October 18, 2022; Patient Rights Advocate.org, "Fourth Semi-Annual Hospital Price Transparency Report," February 2023.

124 See footnote 38.

125 For more information, see https://www.kennedy.senate.gov/public/press-releases?ID=8BEB2EF5-5C5F-45B4-BFE0- 0E27AE780E50.

126 See footnote 38.

127 See Centers for Medicare & Medicaid Services, "FAQs about Affordable Care Act and Consolidated Appropriations Act, 2021 Implementation Part 49," August 20, 2021.

other features that are more valuable to enrollees.[128] By doing this, insurers can generate higher risk-adjusted payments from the federal government, which allow them to offer more generous plans than their competitors. While MA plans do appear to generate cost savings,[129] they are paid more[130] than it costs to cover similar beneficiaries if they enroll in TM. Excess payments to MA plans are only partially passed through to enrollees.[131]

As Adler and Ippolito (2023) note, there are a number of options to improve competition within MA:[132]

> First, rather than the government collecting about 35% of the difference between plan bids and benchmarks, more of that difference could be paid to plans to fund extra benefits or reduce premiums. Limiting what is effectively a tax on lower bids would encourage greater price competition. On its own, this proposal would likely increase federal Medicare spending and the generosity of MA benefits, but it could be combined with a reduction to MA benchmarks. Empirical evidence suggests that the reduction to benchmarks would also enhance MA plan competition, causing plans to price more aggressively.[133] Federal savings or costs from this proposal will depend on the magnitude of reduction to benchmarks.
>
> Others have argued[134] that a clearer choice infrastructure could improve MA plan competition, for instance by more clearly communicating[135] premium reductions below the standard Part B premium to potential enrollees.
>
> Other policy reform proposals, including some from MedPAC, aim to limit the ability of MA plans to game the risk adjustment system in an effort to increase payments from the government.[136] Lessening this incentive would discourage insurers from focusing as many resources on coding intensity and, instead, encourage more competition over prices and quality. CBO estimates that increasing the adjustments for coding intensity such that MA plan payments better reflect the actual expected costs of enrollees would reduce deficits by about $50 billion

---

[128] See Michael Geruso and Timothy Layton, "Upcoding: Evidence from Medicare on Squishy Risk Adjustment," *Journal of Political Economy* 128, no. 3 (March 2020): 984–1026, https://doi.org/10.1086/704756.

[129] See Vilsa Curto et al., "Health Care Spending and Utilization in Public and Private Medicare," *American Economic Journal: Applied Economics* 11, no. 2 (April 1, 2019): 302–32, https://doi.org/10.1257/app.20170295.

[130] MedPAC, "Improving the Accuracy of Medicare Advantage Payments by Limiting the Influence of Outliers in CMS's Risk- adjustment Model," June 15, 2022.

[131] See Marika Cabral, Michael Geruso, and Neale Mahoney, "Do Larger Health Insurance Subsidies Benefit Patients or Producers? Evidence from Medicare Advantage," *American Economic Review* 108, no. 8 (August 1, 2018): 2048–87, https://doi.org/10.1257/aer.20151362; Mark Duggan, Amanda Starc, and Boris Vabson, "Who Benefits When the Government Pays More? Pass-Through in the Medicare Advantage Program" (Cambridge, MA: National Bureau of Economic Research, March 2014), https://doi.org/10.3386/w19989.

[132] In addition to those listed here, many policy experts argue in favor or a more fundamental shift towards a competitive bidding model for MA.

[133] See Mark Duggan, Amanda Starc, and Boris Vabson, "Who Benefits When the Government Pays More? Pass-through in the Medicare Advantage Program," *Journal of Public Economics* 141 (September 2016): 50–67, https://doi.org/10.1016/j.jpubeco.2016.07.003.; Daria Pelech and Zirui Song, "Pricing and Pass-Through in Response to Subsidies and Competition: Evidence from Medicare Advantage Before and After the Affordable Care Act," *Harvard Medical School Working Paper* (October 19, 2018), https://www.hcp.med.harvard.edu/sites/default/files/Pricing_Pass-through_MA_10-19-2018_HCP.pdf.

[134] E.g., John Bertko, et al., "Medicare Advantage: Better information tools, better beneficiary choices, better competition," *USC- Brookings Schaeffer Initiative for Health Policy* (November 27, 2017), https://www.brookings.edu/wp-content/uploads/2017/11/ma- consumer-reforms.pdf.

[135] For evidence, see Karen Stockley et al., "Premium Transparency in the Medicare Advantage Market: Implications for Premiums, Benefits, and Efficiency" (Cambridge, MA: National Bureau of Economic Research, June 2014), https://doi.org/10.3386/w20208.

[136] See footnote 48.

over the 10-year budget window (budgetary savings estimates would likely be substantially higher today).[137]

The current administration also recently expanded risk adjustment data validation (RADV) audits to reduce excess or inappropriate payments made to plans. However, there are arguments to allocate more funding through legislation to expand this further by auditing more contracts and potentially increasing penalties, which is likely to have a large return-on- investment for the federal government.[138]

Spurning More Competition Among Physician-Administered Drugs

By reforming the way Medicare pays for physician-administered drugs, Congress can increase competition between branded products and lower spending levels.

When providers administer certain drugs, Medicare reimburses them 106% of the drug's Average Sales Price (ASP), which is a measure of the average purchase price for the product.[139] (In addition, they are paid a fee to administer the product). Because the six percent "add on" payment scales with a drug's price, it gives providers an incentive to administer more expensive medications when there are multiple treatment options. Moreover, competitive pressures across drugs are further reduced because tools like formularies, step therapy, or prior authorization are not typically used in Part B. Evidence is consistent with these features affecting outcomes. Enrollees in Medicare Advantage plans, which are better able to influence choices, are more likely to receive lower-cost products in these situations.[140]

There are a number of proposed reforms aimed at improving these incentives to create more robust competition among these drugs, as Adler and Ippolito (2023) highlight:

> One method to improve price competition among drugs would involve shifting the direct drug purchasing decisions from providers to payers or third-party vendors. In Medicare, legislation could set up a vendor model similar to those proposed (but ultimately retracted) by the Obama and Trump Administrations.[141] Under such a model, large vendors with significant purchasing power would buy drugs and compete to provide them to physicians. Alternatively, Congress could shift the coverage of some drugs from the Part B benefit into Part D.[142] One study suggested that doing so could reduce spending on affected drugs by 7 to 18%.[143] Such savings should be

---

[137] Congressional Budget Office, "Modify Payments to Medicare Advantage Plans for Health Risk," *Options for Reducing the Deficit: 2019 to 2028*, December 13, 2018.

[138] E.g., Travis C. Williams et al., "Medicare Advantage Audit Changes Let Plans Keep Billions In Overpayments," (February 27, 2023), https://doi.org/10.1377/forefront.20230224.7772.

[139] Following the Budget Control Act of 2011, the effective payment rate became 104.3% of the ASP. See Cole Werble, "Medicare Part B, "Health Affairs Health Policy Brief, August 10, 2017.

[140] Anderson, Kelly E., Daniel Polsky, Sydney Dy, and Aditi P. Sen. "Prescribing of low-versus high-cost Part B drugs in Medicare Advantage and traditional Medicare." *Health services research* 57, no. 3 (2022): 537-547.

[141] Rachel Sachs, "Administration Outlines Plan to Lower Pharmaceutical Prices in Medicare Part B," *Health Affairs Forefront* (October 26, 2018), https://www.healthaffairs.org/do/10.1377/forefront.20181026.360332.

[142] Department of Health and Human Services, "American Patients First: The Trump Administration Blueprint to Lower Drug Prices and Reduce Out-of-Pocket Costs," May 16, 2018.

[143] Thomas J. Hwang et al., "Analysis of Proposed Medicare Part B to Part D Shift with Associated Changes in Total Spending and Patient Cost-Sharing for Prescription Drugs," *JAMA Internal Medicine* 179, no. 3 (March 1, 2019): 374, https://doi.org/10.1001/jamainternmed.2018.6417.

weighed against the difficulties imposed on patients by the tools such as formularies, step therapy, and prior authorization that are largely generating the savings.

Congress could also reduce providers' financial incentive to administer more costly drugs when there are therapeutic substitutes available. Both the Obama and Trump Administrations proposed doing so by shifting at least part of the 6% of ASP add-on into a flat dollar amount, which could also be done through legislation.[144] Alternatively, Medicare could generate price competition in these cases by paying the same amount for drugs that are substitutes for each other. This gives providers a strong incentive to choose the cheaper option. MedPAC has suggested doing so when biologic drugs have nearly-identical biosimilar competitors.[145]

Congress embraced a similar goal in the IRA by temporarily increasing the add-on payment for biosimilars to 8% of the reference biologic's price (instead of 6%) as long as the biosimilar had a lower ASP than the reference product.[146] This gives both products an incentive to compete on price while giving a leg up to the new competitor. Given that providers are generally averse to switching patients who are well managed by the originator biologic drug, it is not unreasonable to preference biosimilars in such a way. Congress could extend this policy beyond its 2027 expiration date.

Medicare could generate greater savings by extending this type of policy to classes with multiple clinically comparable branded products.[147] This type of policy would come with additional considerations, like accommodations for cases where products may not be interchangeable for some patients.

Mr. GUTHRIE. The gentleman yields back.

Like I said, there is a vote on the floor. There are two votes. And so we are going to recess the committee. And as soon as the second vote is cast, I am going to come straight back. So—and then I will be the first one recognized. So people, plan to get back accordingly. I appreciate it.

The committee will be in recess. [Recess.]

Mr. GUTHRIE. The committee will come back to order.

It is now time for Members' questions, and the Chair will recognize himself for the purpose of—5 minutes for the purpose of asking questions.

So, Ms. Bartlett, I know that you were in the Montana healthcare policy, and so my question is, what I—we want individuals out shopping for their healthcare. We want individuals to have access to that, and shop for their healthcare.

But I think what is going to drive the system more—I mean, it would be difficult if I was in your situation in Montana, and calling, trying to make a—negotiate with hospitals, whatever. But when you have 21,000 covered lives—I think that is what you had—it is more bargaining power, I would say, for you to move forward. And I think getting our big employer groups involved in this would be important to really—to make this work the way that we think it should work.

And so my questions were, what did you find—where did you find the most excess spending in Montana?

---

[144] See footnote 59.

[145] 62 See footnote 19.

[146] See Centers for Medicare & Medicaid Services, "Frequently Asked Questions: Inflation Reduction Act Biosimilars Temporary Payment Increase," October 1, 2022.

[147] Committee for a Responsible Federal Budget, "Injecting Price Competition into Medicare Part B Drugs," *The Health Savers Initiative*, July 26, 2021.

And then what were a couple of the biggest drivers in spending? And as you spent less, did your employees have less care, or did you spend less and they still had quality care? Because we all want to make sure we have quality as well.

So I would like to ask you that: What were the big costs, what were the big drivers of your costs, and as you spent less, did they have less care?

Mr. BARTLETT. Well, thank you, Chairman Guthrie.

Our biggest spend was in hospitals. And being an accountant and getting my data, I analyzed it, and 43 percent of our plan spend were in the Montana hospitals. So I knew I had to hit that first. And we didn't have price transparency. I would argue we still don't have it now, totally. But what I did was run my claims through an independent Medicare repricer to see what I was paying at different hospitals as a multiple of Medicare. And I found the highest was 611 percent. And I found a range that two of the hospitals were at that had high quality. And to me, they became the efficient hospitals, and I definitely negotiated to get them in the range. So we did separate contracts with each hospital to negotiate to get in the range.

I also implemented Health Care Blue Book, which would show prices as red, yellow, green and quality as red, yellow, green, so that employees could shop right now.

I do believe that at that point employees were looking for a full bit of information to make decisions, but I also feel, as an employer, I was a fiduciary. I had to make sure only reasonable costs were spent, and I was also a steward of taxpayer dollars. So I had to make sure everything was transparent. I knew the Medicare rate, and I could verify whether or not they were.

Now, you raise a really good question about the size of employer.

I had a total of 31,000 lives on the plan.

Mr. GUTHRIE. Oh, 31,000. I thought it was 21.

Mr. BARTLETT. And yes, that did give me bargaining power. I have worked with employer forums, employer groups that bring together employee plans to do that. They still are struggling to get their data from their carrier, and they also come up against a wall with the carriers and with the consultants, large brokerage firms, any brokerage firm who has a vested interest to keep them where they are because of commissions.

So transparency of the whole chain of middlemen and payers, I broke a lot of that out. I fired Aon, I did my own data analysis, and I fired our TPA, I fired our PBM, and contracted differently.

Mr. GUTHRIE. Well, so I guess my question—you know, I used to work in the automotive supply business. And I will tell you, if I had a 611 percent markup on a product that I was selling them, the CEO of said automotive company would have fired the buyer buying from me moving forward.

But the question is just how you know the price. So we want to get into transparency, where people know the price they are shopping for. I don't know if it is too high, too low, or whatever, but the market can determine that if people know what the price is. And so, as we develop transparency, what do you think are the one or two things that absolutely are musts for us to make sure that you have access to? Because you said you went to a lot of effort, and lot of people aren't going to have that kind of buying power. So what is an absolute must for you to know what the marketing——

Mr. BARTLETT. I think two things you need. In my world it was— hospital prices was the big thing, although I did save 23 percent on pharmacy. But you needed to make sure you have the price. And we are starting to see that in a few of the hospital price transparency files that are complete. I can see the prices by every plan, and I can see the cash price. And I have been surprised.

And STAT published an article showing that 55 percent of the charges are—cash price are lower than the insurance-negotiated rate.

Mr. GUTHRIE. Well, thank you. I am sorry I am out of time. I had some more questions. I had some for Mr. Severn, and I will submit those for the record.

The Chair now yields back to himself and will recognize the gentlelady from California, my friend Ms. Eshoo, for 5 minutes for questions.

Ms. ESHOO. Thank you, Mr. Chairman, for holding this hearing. And to each of the witnesses, I think you all are terrific. You are highly instructive, given your experience, where you come from, what you do.

This is about transparency and, like, who can be against transparency, right? Except there are some people that are. So this is an important hearing.

I have to say, though, that I am somewhat skeptical that patients pick hospitals based on price. I think we go to the hospital that our insurance network covers. Because people that—their out-of-pocket costs are what are foremost in their mind. I think that insurers need to negotiate prices to lower hospital costs. And in some areas, you know, there are health systems that have been bought up—that have bought up every practice in town, and they can demand insurers pay whatever price they set.

So I think that in this whole examination, Mr. Chairman, we need to bring the insurers in here and the PBMs. We really want to get at hidden costs and how they operate, and then how we should operate based on how they operate. I think that that would be an important examination for us. Great.

To Dr. Ippolito, it is nice to see you again. Thanks for coming back to the committee. Civica Rx is, as you know, it is a nonprofit drug company. They announced in August that it would offer an important generic drug to treat prostate cancer for $160 a month. This is about $3,000 a month less than the average cost for someone on a Medicare Part D plan. But many health plans are having trouble getting this lower cost to their members because of obstruction by PBMs.

So I think there is an evident answer to my question. Why do you think PBMs—what do you think they have to gain by keeping their costs so high for Medicare beneficiaries?

Dr. IPPOLITO. Well, I mean, PBMs are certainly at the—they have long been blamed for the phenomenon of very high-list prices for many brand drugs. And particularly in Medicare Part D——

Ms. ESHOO. Right.

Dr. IPPOLITO [continuing]. That can really——

Ms. ESHOO. But why do you think they are doing it?

Dr. IPPOLITO. It is because they get paid on the rebates, the differential——

Ms. ESHOO. It is all about money.

Dr. IPPOLITO [continuing]. Between the list and the net price.

Ms. ESHOO. Right, it is all about money.

What would you suggest to us that we do to get at how PBMs manipulate costs this way? That is a—I mean, this is a stunning difference right here.

Dr. IPPOLITO. Yes, I——

Ms. ESHOO. You know, $160 a month versus over 3,000 and over.

Dr. IPPOLITO. Yes, it is an enormous difference. And I think the central point, the big difference between list and net prices in the drug market represents one of the most dysfunctional parts of healthcare, at least in its current form. So anything you can do to try and align lists and net prices in the drug market aligns—it doesn't just lower the out-of-pocket for the senior taking that drug. What it does is it aligns the incentive. Suddenly, the insurer has the same incentive to negotiate for the same low net price that the consumer gets at the out-of-pocket—out-of-pocket, right?

So I think, in terms of conceptual approach, that is the key: aligning the list and the net price in the drug market.

Ms. ESHOO. Thank you.

To Ms. Tripoli, welcome back. I know Families USA has testified at our subcommittee many, many times to the betterment of the hearings and what we do.

Sutter Health has—is really dominant in my congressional district, and they have a new CEO that came in and met with me maybe a few weeks ago—3 weeks ago, something like that, very recently—and before he even asked me what I had on my mind, I told him. And at the top of my list was that they were turning away new patients with traditional Medicare but accepting patients who have Medicare Advantage and private insurance.

Obviously, I don't support that. I don't support that practice. And these complaints have come from my constituents. When I asked him about it, he said that as they moved to hire more doctors, that that would—that policy would not remain in place. But when we circled back with them, they had changed their mind about it. Not a good policy.

Is this—in your view or your understanding, is this a common practice of health systems nationwide?

Ms. TRIPOLI. Thank you for the question, and I would agree that is—it is outrageous. I think it is just another example of how broken the markets have become, where we have large systems like Sutter with dominant power, and they are able to make all kinds of decisions about prices, turning away patients because of the types of rates that they are getting. So it is completely, completely unacceptable, I would agree.

Ms. ESHOO. But what it is is that the privately insured are favored over the publicly insured. So how would you address that? What would you recommend this committee on a bipartisan basis to do?

Mr. GUTHRIE. You have got to sum up there, when——

Ms. ESHOO. Mm-hmm.

Ms. TRIPOLI. I think it is the very solutions that we are here——

Ms. ESHOO. Oh, it is way over.

Ms. TRIPOLI [continuing]. To talk about today.

Ms. ESHOO. You can respond in writing to me in length.

Mr. GUTHRIE. OK.

Ms. ESHOO. Thank you. Thank you, Mr. Chairman.

Mr. GUTHRIE. Yes, we want to hear your response.

Ms. TRIPOLI. Thank you for the question.

Ms. ESHOO. Yes, we need the response.

Mr. GUTHRIE. So the Chair now recognizes Chair Rodgers for 5 minutes for questions.

Mrs. RODGERS. Thank you, Mr. Chairman. I have long said that price transparency is foundational to restoring the doctor-patient relationship. And as I mentioned in my opening statement, we have studies that show billions in savings for the healthcare system.

I wanted to start by asking each one of you if you agree, yes or no, that robust price transparency will empower patients and help with the downward pressure on prices.

I will start——

Mr. SEVERN. Yes. Yes.

Mrs. RODGERS. I will just go across.

Mr. SEVERN. I will start real quick. I mean, there is a reason I dropped everything and started a business with a bunch of great people to work on this. It is a really big event that all these prices are now public.

In the first effort over these past 2 years, especially for innovators that jumped in, is get all the data and create market forces. I am not an economist, but——

Mrs. RODGERS. OK, thank you.

Mr. SEVERN [continuing]. Before——

Mrs. RODGERS. I want to keep this going.

Mr. SEVERN. Yes, oh, yes.

Mrs. RODGERS. OK, Mr. Forge, yes. Thank you.

Mr. FORGE. Yes, absolutely.

Mrs. RODGERS. Thank you.

Mr. FORGE. Yes.

Mr. BARTLETT. Yes, absolutely, too.

Mrs. RODGERS. Thank you.

Ms. TRIPOLI. Yes.

Mrs. RODGERS. Great.

Dr. IPPOLITO. Yes.

Mrs. RODGERS. Great. We are unified.

So coming back to Mr. Forge, I am just personally very proud of the work that you have done at Pullman Memorial Hospital, a critical access hospital in eastern Washington leading the charge on price transparency. And it is clear that you also believe that you are doing right by your patients. Hospitals around the Nation should look to Pullman as an example.

So do you believe that your experience is one that can be scaled and replicated nationwide?

Mr. FORGE. Well, I think, you know, first of all, I think transparency is always good. You know, we are all really smart people, and we can solve problems. If they are under the table, we are going to have a difficult time doing that. So I think, first and foremost, getting these challenges on the—you know, pricing and these things—on the table is how we are going to solve them.

I think it is a big challenge as you are looking across the country. We are going to have to prioritize it as a key strategy, because there are so many priorities in healthcare.

So absolutely, I think it can be scaled.

Mrs. RODGERS. Thank you. Would you speak to recommendations that you have for improving hospital transparency experience, while making sure that the data is available to patients and employers?

Mr. FORGE. Well, I think making—I think data is going to be the key to it. I think right now we are having to fight to get access to data. But once we do have access to data and we are sitting down with our partners like we are doing with the business community in Pullman, we are able to come up with solutions that make our communities a great place to receive care, a great place to live, and a great place to conduct business.

Mrs. RODGERS. Great. Thanks again for being here.

Mr. FORGE. Thanks for having me.

Mrs. RODGERS. Mr. Severn, I—you know, so we all agree on— that price transparency is important.

There's been a lot of issues with the hospital requirements. And unlike Pullman, not all the hospitals are in compliance with the CMS standards. And, you know, we need to have data quality completeness and user friendliness.

So I wanted to ask, Turquoise helps hospitals come into compliance with the Federal regulations. If we increase hospital standards for data quality and completeness, do you have advice on the biggest challenges hospitals face?

And are there ways that we can help mitigate those challenges while increasing the quality of the data and compliance?

Mr. SEVERN. Yes, there was—it is a great question. There was a big initial setup of publishing this data for hospitals in Pullman and a lot of others, and they had to guess on a format, because there was no standard format. With the payer rule, there was a prescribed format: the table looks like this, the columns are named this. And hospitals would have appreciated that and, you know, innovators and folks using the data would have appreciated that. And so, you know, we now have a suggested standard that came out, and I would suggest making that enforced. And I think that also helps hospitals know, if we follow this standard, we are in compliance, we are not guessing, and we don't have a question mark when CMS comes and looks at our file.

Mrs. RODGERS. And I would also like you to speak to how you believe this is going to improve patient care. So increased compliance, better data, how is that going to bolster the patient-facing transparency, and ultimately directly helping patients?

Mr. SEVERN. Yes, there was a great point earlier about will patients shop for care. And, you know, I hope they do, we are banking on it.

But, you know, when my primary care doctor says, "Hey, you need an MRI" and there are four health systems in San Diego, I want those prices in front of my primary care to say, "Hey, you could go to any of these four. You could save $1,000 if you go to Sharp instead of UCSD." And so, by making a standard, you speed up that data reaching the EHR in front of the doctor, so that they have that data in front of them.

Mrs. RODGERS. Well, again, it is just—thank you all for being here. I really appreciate your input on this important issue. And we are—we have more work to do.

Thank you, I yield back.

Mr. GUTHRIE. I thank the gentlelady for yielding back, the Chair for yielding back. The gentleman from California, Mr. Ca´ rdenas, is recognized for 5 minutes for questions.

Mr. CA´RDENAS. Thank you, Chair Guthrie and Ranking Member Eshoot, for holding this hearing, and thank you to our witnesses for being here to give us your expertise and your opinions.

Americans are getting crushed by skyrocketing healthcare costs. Medical debt is weighing down far too many people, preventing them from spending on basic necessities and causing deeper financial pain beyond their healthcare. It is shameful that an individual's health can completely derail them financially. And what is worse, in most cases there is no information about how to make the best decision about their care.

I am glad to see new rules being instituted to increase transparency about cost and coverage and in hospitals and healthcare settings. But there is still much to be done to make sure these rules are implemented in a way that is usable and easy to understand.

I apologize, I am having a hard time reading my notes because I have allergies. And I was talking to one of my doctor colleagues, and he goes, "Let's go walk outside. It is a beautiful day," right? I forgot that I am probably going to get hit with my allergies. By the time I got to this building, I can barely see, and my eyes are watering. And I was walking with a doctor. My point is he couldn't help me in the moment.

So access is real and different for every person. And in America, it appears, in my opinion, in districts like mine, which are a little bit lower-income than average, access and how we communicate with people really can make the difference as to whether or not they are going to get the care that they deserve and need, even though they might have insurance, even though they might have coverage. How to access that coverage is a real issue.

So, Dr. Ippolito, thank you for providing your remarks today, and I hope I said your name right. That is the way I used to call my uncle. His first name was Hipolito. You are the second person in my life I have met with the same name.

Part of having real transparency is ensuring that the information is accessible and understandable to everyone. To your knowledge, what efforts are being made to ensure that cost disclosures and comprehensible and easy, accessible—that are comprehensible, and easy, accessible for all, including for those with limited health literacy or reduced access to digital platforms?

Dr. IPPOLITO. Well, I think the answer to that is there is sort of twofold. The first is that making sure that the submitted forms come in some type of reasonable format that includes both the raw data that is submitted to places like Turquoise that they use, and the stuff that is put in the user-friendly format. But the second piece of this is places like Turquoise.

I mean, this is how markets work. Sometimes information is put out, and it is complicated. But Consumer Reports exists. You don't need to know everything about a car and everything about an engine to understand which one is better and which one is worse. And so there really is a role for places just like Turquoise, actually.

Mr. CA´RDENAS. Thank you.

In districts like mine, Spanish is the primary language for many, many families. And to your knowledge, what efforts are being made to ensure that non-English speakers can still have the same tools at their disposal to make informed decisions?

Dr. IPPOLITO. You know, I am not sure about the answer to that question right now. I would have to look it up after.

Mr. CA´RDENAS. OK, thank you very much. Does anybody have an answer to that question?

Please.

Ms. TRIPOLI. I think on the price transparency requirements in particular, my understanding is there is not a requirement for the information to be in any other language other than English.

Mr. CA´RDENAS. OK. Well, thank you for that. I think that in this very diverse country, we should make an effort to at least make sure that it is accessible to people, and that if there's language barriers, we have the technology and the ability to make it more accessible, which at the end of the day means better outcomes for individuals, for people. So thank you for that answer.

I also want to acknowledge the impact of the cost of medications on American families as well. I am thrilled that the Inflation Reduction Act was signed into law, and with it the many provisions to lower drug costs. But there are still several aspects of the drug-pricing pipeline that are unclear at best. As we turn our attention more to the role of pharmacy benefit managers, or PBMs, as they are called, in the cost of drugs, I am left wondering why there is so little transparency in this space.

Dr. Ippolito, how might greater public transparency around rebates and who they go to impact costs? Can you discuss some of the benefits that we could expect?

Dr. IPPOLITO. Yes. PBMs are extraordinarily—have extraordinarily complicated contractual relationships. And when you say PBMs, I would include things like PBM aggregators that are at a whole different level but affiliated with those entities as well.

The problem is it makes it extremely difficult if you are a plan sponsor, if you are an employer, to evaluate that contract and compare two PBMs to each other if the contracts are very complicated, there's 20 different fees, and you may or may not even be getting all the rebates passed through to you.

So the point about simplifying that information, making it clear to the person purchasing the plan how much this costs and what exactly I am getting suddenly makes it much, much easier to compare one PBM versus the other.

Mr. CA´RDENAS. Thank you very much.

With that, I will yield back the balance of my time.

Mr. GUTHRIE. I thank the gentleman for yielding back. The Chair now recognizes Dr. Burgess for 5 minutes for the purpose of asking questions.

Mr. BURGESS. I thank the chairman. Great panel today. I am glad we are doing it.

Transparency is something that is—a lot of us talk about. It has been very, very difficult to achieve. I would be remiss if I did not acknowledge the signing of the Executive order in June of 2019. I was down at the White House when that happened, and I could not believe the people in the audience that day and how genuinely excited they were that someone at some level had finally elevated this to the point where something was actually going to get done. I—you know, as a Member of the House, and Article 1 in the Constitution, I don't think Executive orders are the way to go, I think we should do it legislatively. But we had not been able to do it legislatively. So the President did it with an Executive order and, to my surprise, it did not disappear 21⁄2 years ago, when the presidency changed.

Well, Mr. Chairman, I would like to ask—it is a short document, but it is a phenomenal document, so I would ask unanimous consent to introduce into the record President Trump's Executive order on price transparency.

Mr. GUTHRIE. Any objection? Seeing none, so ordered.

[The information appears at the conclusion of the hearing.]

Mr. BURGESS. So, Dr. Ippolito, let me ask you. And one of the things I have worked on for a number of years—I never understood why in the Affordable Care Act they carved out and said physician-owned practices or physician-owned hospitals could not expand after the passage of the Affordable Care Act.

So I have a bill with Henry Cuellar of Laredo. It is a bipartisan bill to repeal the ban on physician-owned hospitals. Personal experience myself, owning an ambulatory surgery center, my dad, who was a general surgeon, actually had a physician-owned hospital when he was in practice—I think doctors understand what it takes to make a hospital run, and they want the best facility for their patient. They want their patients to go to a facility that meets their needs and is obviously of top notch in quality.

I have worked with a hospital in McAllen, Texas, Doctors Hospital Renaissance, for many years on these policies. They operate on the Texas-Mexico border, a 530-bed general acute physician- owned hospital. During the pandemic, Doctors Hospital Renaissance converted its rehabilitation hospital—rehabilitation unit into a 102-bed COVID hospital in a matter of 10 days. They had to get a waiver from CMS to do that because they weren't allowed to expand as a physician-owned hospital. But a phenomenal service they provided in a part of the world that really wasn't receiving much in the way of services.

And then, in addition to all of that, prior to COVID they received an accreditation for and opened several medical residency programs in primary care to bolster the physician workforce in what is a very underserved area of our State.

So I would just like to hear your thoughts on the value of physician-owned hospitals. If we are going to combat consolidation in the healthcare space, physician-owned hospitals, do they play a role in this?

Dr. IPPOLITO. Yes. I mean, I think one of the lessons over the last, say, 20 or 30 years is that we ought to take any competition where we can get it in healthcare markets. And, you know, the bar ought to be very high for impeding entry of new competitors. And so, yes, there is some concern about, you know, potential creamskimming with physician-owned hospitals. But to be completely honest, I don't really know that it is more acute in those settings than it is in, say, an environment where an insurer is vertically integrated with physicians. So that is a long way of saying——

Mr. BURGESS. Yes.

Dr. IPPOLITO [continuing]. It is a reasonable addition.

Mr. BURGESS. I would refer you to an article in Health Affairs of March of 2007 that I wrote that actually refuted that concept. Brilliant article.

[Laughter.]

Mr. BURGESS. So let me ask you this: Is there anything that— else we can be doing to support the smaller and independent practice of medicine?

Dr. IPPOLITO. Yes, I mean, there's a number of things. I guess there's two buckets. One is getting rid of barriers to entry for new competitors. So whether that is certificate of need laws in some States—I don't think Texas has one——

Mr. BURGESS. Not anymore.

Dr. IPPOLITO [continuing]. But I think a number of other States have them still. Whether it is scope of practice, trying to make sure that people can actually practice up until their training. And on the other end, you have got to think about other policies that really do make it difficult for physician practices to compete with hospitals. Getting paid much less to, for example, administer a drug compared to a hospital-based——

Mr. BURGESS. Right.

Dr. IPPOLITO [continuing]. Facility suddenly makes it very difficult for that kind of facility to——

Mr. BURGESS. So site neutrality is something this committee should focus on.

Let me just ask you one last question. Mark Cuban came into our Doctors Caucus a few weeks ago and talked about his company, Cost Plus Drugs. They offer generic drugs at a discount, transparent price by removing PBMs altogether. Do you see a future for that type of activity?

You talked about a line list of net prices. It seems like that is what is being accomplished there.

Dr. IPPOLITO. Yes, at least for some drugs it seems like there is a reasonable future for that kind of arrangement.

It is going to be challenging in the big-name brand drug market to do that. But on the plus side, it is another sort of effort to chip away at the current standard of very high list prices and low net prices. We have seen that in other places. We have seen insulin makers lower list prices. We have seen by biosimilar makers that are competing with Humira offer products at lower list price versions. And so I think the totality of evidence suggests there is at least an effort to move in that direction.

So that is a reasonable goal, and I think that is one way to do it.

Mr. BURGESS. Thank you, Mr. Chairman. I will yield back.

Mr. GUTHRIE. I thank the gentleman for yielding back. The Chair now recognizes Dr. Ruiz for 5 minutes for the purpose of asking questions.

Mr. RUIZ. Thank you all for being here today.

High healthcare costs continue to be a challenge for American families. About half of Americans have reported difficulty affording healthcare. Time and time again, my constituents tell me they ration or forgo medication or care because of the cost. In the emergency department, the first question I would get was, “Am I going to be OK?” And the second question was, “How much is this going to cost? Am I going to be able to afford it?”

So even in nonemergency healthcare settings, patients cannot see prices in advance and are forced to wait until after they receive medical care and get the bill to fully understand how much they owe.

Ms. Tripoli, can you discuss some of the challenges patients face in navigating the health system and how increasing transparency can help patients achieve savings?

Ms. TRIPOLI. Absolutely. Thank you for the question. I think there are two.

The big purpose of price transparency is that we have a system where we actually don’t know what the prices are until we get a service and we get a bill. Price transparency helps to crack that wide open. The most important pricing information that we need in price transparency is the negotiated rate. That is the rate that is being negotiated behind closed doors between dominant health systems, hospitals, and plans and then buried in proprietary contracts with no insight or oversight from the public.

Pulling out that information gives patients the ability to say, “I want to get my MRI for $80 at this facility, and not for $3,000 at the one half-mile down the road.” It has direct ability for consumers to be able to shop and also for policymakers to be able to intervene where prices have gotten too out of control.

Mr. RUIZ. Thank you. You know, and I agree, patients deserve greater transparency in the prices they pay for healthcare. But right now, despite the transparency rules that went into effect in January 2021, it is still difficult for consumers to access pricing.

So, Ms. Tripoli, in your testimony you discussed how some hospitals are failing to fully comply with the Hospital Price Transparency Final Rule. Can you briefly discuss how hospitals’ failure to fully comply with the provisions of the final rule is making it difficult for consumers to access critical information on pricing?

Ms. TRIPOLI. Absolutely. I think that it is just another example of the gaming of keeping pricing—prices hidden, how broken the markets are, that this pricing information is incredibly valuable for hospitals to keep hidden so they can increase prices year after year with no insight or oversight from the public.

So I think being able to pull down the pricing information is critical. We are seeing hospitals doing everything from not posting any pricing information to posting a price as a percentage of Medicare, for example, 120 percent of Medicare, which is meaningless for most consumers. They are publishing information in various formats that are not usable or machine readable. They are using a lot of "N/As" as examples, as well.

Mr. RUIZ. Yes, so what are some ways Congress can further strengthen the final rule?

Ms. TRIPOLI. Congress absolutely should be strengthening and codifying, increasing—including, as we have heard some of the testimony already today about creating more standards around the format, outright prohibiting hospitals from being able to price— post anything other than a dollar-and-cents amount. The actual price is what we need. More streamlining around the names of services, so we can actually compare and understand what the services are across hospitals.

And I would also say that increasing the fine for hospitals that don't comply. The $2 million max fine is not sufficient to incentivize most hospitals to comply.

Mr. RUIZ. I would also add the out-of-pocket costs for patients, as well, given the different health insurances that are out there. I continue to be concerned with reports of low hospital compliance, and I believe Congress needs to further strengthen the regulation. I believe we also need to couple transparency with policies that will further expand coverage and lower healthcare costs.

So, Ms. Tripoli, can you discuss how the subsidy expansions included in the Inflation Reduction Act are helping lower costs for families?

Ms. TRIPOLI. Absolutely. I mean, the bottom line is that our families are facing a healthcare affordability crisis. The extensions of the subsidies that were passed through the IRA were critical to be able to support families in a moment when 100 million people are facing medical debt because they can't actually afford the cost of care. So we absolutely should be extending those subsidies to continue to support families.

And we also have to address the root problem of what is driving our affordability crisis. It is prices, it is predominantly driven by prices by hospitals due to unchecked consolidation from the last several decades. And so it is really—it is critical that we are—it is both/and. We have to also look at the root causes to address the affordability crisis.

Mr. RUIZ. Well, thanks to the subsidy expansion in the Inflation Reduction Act, millions of families have seen the cost of their monthly insurance premiums go down, and the average family is saving $2,400 in premiums a year. More than 40 million Americans are enrolled in the health coverage through the Affordable Care Act, the highest total on record. It is imperative that we make permanent the enhanced premium tax credits.

So I thank you, and I yield back my time.

Mr. GUTHRIE. The gentleman yields back. The Chair now recognizes Mr. Griffith for 5 minutes for questions.

Mr. GRIFFITH. Thank you, Mr. Chairman.

Mr. Severn and Mr. Forge, we have been discussing the Hospital Price Transparency Rule, which obligates the hospitals, as you have been testifying about, to post the "discounted cash price" for services to their website. But it seems like some cash prices are not available at specific hospitals.

Are there any barriers in place prohibiting hospitals from complying and posting these cash prices?

Mr. FORGE. I mean, I think there's a lot of challenges that's associated with posting cash prices. Fundamentally, they are in there. They are—we are talking about lists of thousands. I know that we are looking at top 300s, but there is a lot in there. We have mentioned the negotiated prices, you know, that we are talking about. I think the part that we haven't talked enough about is transparency around payer strategies. You know, a lot of times in healthcare you are talking—in hospitals it is a 24-hour business, you know, that we are providing care. And, you know, you are looking at, potentially, three service lines that have a profit margin that helps support, you know, the other ones.

I think that, you know, sometimes hospitals have a, you know, have a difficulty, you know, sharing some of that. It is complicated, and it is difficult to manage. And so that is where we are with that.

Mr. GRIFFITH. And do you agree with that, Mr. Severn?

Mr. SEVERN. Yes, cash prices are interesting for hospitals, because when this law came out you had 6,000 hospitals—some of them didn't have a cash pricing policy. Some did, some didn't. And this law forced them to think about cash prices maybe for the first time formally.

And when we think about competition, if you have options, and you are uninsured or you have a high deductible and you want to cash pricing option, Pullman or a hospital can say, "Hey, we have a clear menu of cash prices, come on in." And to me, that is competition.

And so, if there is a hospital that hasn't come up with a clear cash pricing strategy or is late to the game, that is just market competition. And we—you know, we would hope to display sort of cash pricing certainty on the Turquoise website to reward forward-thinking hospitals doing that.

Mr. GRIFFITH. And let me continue, Mr. Severn. How can HHS strengthen the price transparency rules and improve compliance so that consumers and tech developers can access all prices system- wide and more meaningfully shop for the best care?

Mr. SEVERN. Is this a question about the hospital rule, or payer rule, or both combined?

Mr. GRIFFITH. Let's go with both.

Mr. SEVERN. OK. So on the hospital rule, you know, we have had 21⁄2 years with this. It is enforcing the standards. So adopting the standard as required, and enforcing it.

On the payer rule, you know, because it is all items and services for all providers, the data is just so much bigger. You know, I wish we had a scale replica of the comparison in size. And for that it is more course correction. There is a good process that CMS has going technically for technical specifications with the payer rule. I would say continue that process, continue iterating. It comes down to minor course corrections: adding a few fields, renaming a few fields, being more specific. And we will see more proliferation of these rates on the payer side.

Mr. GRIFFITH. Well, and having these rates out there is helpful. I recently met with a company that works in Ohio: Sidecar. I think they have actually worked with you some at Turquoise. And what they do is they figure out—based on the region that is set up by the ACA, they figure out what the average cost is for various procedures, and they cover you. They don't go through middlemen. They just say, "We are going to give you the money for the average cost. If you spend more, that is your choice. You can spend more, but it is out of your pocket. If you spend less, you can save that savings for future medical care." Or you can click a box that says "Send me the check." And I think that is an interesting, disruptor concept. We will see how it goes as it goes forward.

Last week, ProPublica published a report that found Cigna, which covers or administers healthcare for 18 million people, built a system to instantly reject claims for not being medically necessary without its doctors even opening or looking at the patient's file to make them go through extra steps.

Mr. Forge, based on your experience as a hospital CEO, what impact does this type of a system do when it automatically rejects medical claims? What does it do to the patients?

And I have got about 39 seconds.

Mr. FORGE. Sure. Well, I talked about it earlier in terms of distraction. You know, we have to train and get our people ready in denials management, you know, making denials management a priority. And so they are working hard, you know, to do that. That keeps us away from strategies to help, you know, support our patients, you know, up to the right speed.

So, you know, we have a lot of distractions out there—those are one of them—that is preventing us from helping our patients.

Mr. GRIFFITH. And in the last couple of seconds that I have I would just say that is what makes Sidecar—and I am not fully advocating it, I am just saying it makes it kind of interesting, because they get rid of all those middlemen and you, the consumer, get to help drive what is going to happen. And you can either spend more on a doctor if you particularly want that doctor, or find somebody who has a lower price or a hospital that has a lower price. And I think putting the consumers in charge—I understand there are some who may never use that, but there's a lot of us out there that would start doing it, and that creates the competition Mr. Severn has been talking about.

My time is up, I yield back.

Mr. GUTHRIE. The gentleman yields back. The Chair now recognizes Ms. Blunt Rochester for 5 minutes for questions.

Ms. BLUNT ROCHESTER. Thank you, Mr. Chairman, for the recognition, and thank you to our witnesses for your testimonies. I am grateful that we are having this hearing today that is focused on how the lack of price transparency is making healthcare unaffordable for countless Americans.

The Federal Government has recently made strides toward increasing transparency in the commercial healthcare market through two important Federal rules. But it is clear that more must be done to help Americans struggling with the crushing weight of healthcare costs.

Ms. Tripoli, in your testimony you note that almost half of Americans have reported having to forego medical care due to cost. Almost a third of Americans indicate that the high cost of medical care is interfering with their ability to secure basic needs like food and housing. And although 8.2 million fewer Americans are struggling with medical debt under the Biden-Harris administration, too many Americans continue to have problems paying their medical bills.

Can you give specific examples of how healthcare transparency can result in lower healthcare prices, and also let our constituents know why we should have faith in the policies that we are discussing, that they really will bring down cost?

Ms. TRIPOLI. Thank you for the question. I think there are two pieces to the price transparency rule that are really important. One is the negotiated rates and making sure we can actually see how irrational prices have become, and then we can make informed policy decisions that target where they have gone too far in the price gouging direction. The other part of that, as was also mentioned earlier, is around making sure that you can understand out-of-pocket costs. Those are the two most important pieces of information for consumers.

At the end of the day, price transparency is about disrupting the status quo in the hospital business model, which is keep prices hidden, buy up the local competition, price gouge year after year, all on the backs of the American people. So price transparency both for hospitals and for plans helps to disrupt that market and give policymakers, purchasers, employers the tools and consumers to be able to get a better deal in healthcare.

Ms. BLUNT ROCHESTER. Thank you.

The Hospital Price Transparency Rule requires that hospitals publish a consumer-friendly online tool that allows people to shop for services and make informed decisions. Yet some patients may not have the medical literacy necessary to navigate and take full advantage of the online tools.

Mr. Forge, it sounds like your hospital has been successful in developing a tool that is simple to navigate, yet comprehensive. What steps did you take to accomplish this, and how can other hospitals replicate your success?

Mr. FORGE. Well, a couple of things. We have a transparency website that went up in 2019. So we have a place, you know, right on our website that is directing patients right there. And I think that you hit on a good point that is something that we are really working on that I think benefits everybody, which is medical literacy.

You know, I mean, it is a very complicated system and difficult for patients to understand. And so we are just trying to give multiple methods: a website, but also in-person, you know, care conferences. Like I told you, the patient financial counselors are really helping to train patients on—right at the front end of service, to make sure that they are making the right decisions for themselves and their families.

Ms. BLUNT ROCHESTER. Thank you. You know, I am really concerned about this because I looked at a couple of these websites, and they are not equal. And some are still very hard to understand.

And so, Ms. Tripoli, I would also like to hear your perspective on how hospitals can make it easier for consumers and employers to compare prices for services and make informed decisions.

Ms. TRIPOLI. Absolutely. I think, first and foremost, we have got to get all the hospitals complying with the basic rules. And we know we have got a lot of work to do to be able to get there. I think part of that is making sure we have more standardization across what the required services are, so that when you are looking for an MRI in one hospital, that same MRI is showing up in another hospital. There is a little bit of variability right now.

And I think the other piece to point out is we also have to clean up the data files. Like, we have to actually have prices. We have to have the same standard way for how we are describing services, so that consumers can actually understand. You know, most folks don't know what a CPT code is.

Ms. BLUNT ROCHESTER. Right.

Ms. TRIPOLI. So we need a description to explain, well, what does that mean?

Ms. BLUNT ROCHESTER. Exactly.

Ms. TRIPOLI. And what price am I getting for that service?

Ms. BLUNT ROCHESTER. Thank you. I have, like, 30 seconds left, but Ms. Bartlett, I cochair the Primary Care Caucus, and so I was really pleased and interested to hear about your work with primary care. Can you tell us how you invested in primary care, and how that specifically helped save the plan from insolvency?

Mr. BARTLETT. Yes, thank you. We implemented five on-site or near-site primary care clinics. Employees and dependents could have an appointment online. They could schedule—all appointments were 20 minutes. You could do back-to-back appointments. We negotiated radiology, ultrasound lab contracts with independents that were wonderful. We also had health coaches for diabetic care clubs. And so we improved access, because the employees had no cost to go to these.

Ms. BLUNT ROCHESTER. That is so powerful. Thank you, Mr. Chairman, and I yield back.

Mr. GUTHRIE. Thank you. Ms. Blunt Rochester yields back. The Chair now recognizes Dr. Bucshon for 5 minutes for the purpose of asking questions.

Mr. BUCSHON. Thank you, Mr. Chairman, and I will start by expressing my appreciation to the members of this committee and the witnesses here today for what seems to be a shared commitment to lowering the costs of healthcare by increasing transparency and accountability in our healthcare system.

Many of you know about my long-time interest in a program known as 340B, named for a section of the Public Health Service Act in which it appears. The 340B drug-pricing program was created by Congress in 1992 to enable providers, and I quote, "to stretch scarce Federal resources as far as possible, reaching more eligible patients and providing more comprehensive services."

If you take away one thing from my comments today, let it be this: I support the 340B program, and I want to see it succeed. I want Federal resources to be put to good use. I want services to reach more patients, and I want patients to have access to more comprehensive services.340B operates by allowing certain entities—theoretically, those that serve our most vulnerable populations—to purchase prescription drugs from manufacturers at a discount. They are permitted to pocket that discount because we expect that they are providing disproportionate amounts of charity care for patients who are uninsured or underinsured. But because Congress failed in 1992 and in the last 30 years since to set clear guidelines and parameters for the program, we have no way of knowing when the program is being exploited, and we know that it is.

And that is not just my opinion. A GAO report and a report from this committee's Oversight Subcommittee a number of years ago said so very clearly.

Although I have heard rumors and have seen smaller-scale examples, for the last decade, at least, exploitation of the 340B program was clearly and strikingly demonstrated in a New York Times article published last September. I encourage all of my colleagues to read the article, which I will submit for the record.

I ask unanimous consent to submit that for the record.

Mr. GUTHRIE. Hearing no objection, so ordered.

[The information appears at the conclusion of the hearing.]

Mr. BUCSHON. The gist of this is—and I am quoting again— "Starting in the mid-2000s, big hospital chains figured out how to supercharge the program"—I am quoting from the article — "where patients with generous private insurance could receive expensive drugs but on paper make the clinic's extensions of poor hospitals to take advantage of 340B."

The article discusses how a large hospital system in Richmond, Virginia—not far from here, in the former district of our late friend and former committee member, Don McEachin—did just that. It purchased a 340B-eligible hospital in a poor, predominantly Black neighborhood, used the hospital's 340B status to purchase discounted drugs for use at points of care across the system, decreased services to patients at that 340B hospital, including closing its ICU, and profited to the tune of $100 million per year on the 340B program.

We also know from disclosures of Fortune 500 companies that 340B is seen for—by profit entities as a revenue generator for shareholders. For example, CVS Health, the fourth-largest company in the country, warned investors in its 2022 annual shareholder filing that changes to the 340B program could, and I quote, "materially and adversely affect the company." Information like this informs us exactly where the 340B discounts are likely not going to: the patients.

I hope to eventually work on broad, large-scale reforms to the program. But in the short term, consistent with this hearing, I am calling for Members of Congress to join me in advocating for more transparency on the discounts.

Can we not agree that entities benefiting from the discounts need to show the American people what they are doing with the savings, and for that matter, what the savings are? This wouldn't be difficult, because CMS already requires many types of providers, the grantees, to report similar data.

So Mr. Forge, does Pullman Hospital report its annual amounts of charity care and payer shortfall?

Mr. FORGE. Yes, we are required to share our charity care outlay——

Mr. BUCSHON. To CMS, correct. And if Congress asked Pullman to report how much savings in 340B they receive in the aggregate each year, would that be feasible?

Mr. FORGE. I think anything is feasible. I think we can share any information that is asked for us—you know, asked from us. Transparency in the spirit is what we are looking for.

I can say that it is a challenging program to manage. We have to get outside help to help us manage that.

Mr. BUCSHON. Right, a lot of smaller facilities like yours have to have third-party people to do——

Mr. FORGE. Correct.

Mr. BUCSHON [continuing]. That reporting. But it is being done, including in my district. And if a small critical-access hospital like yours has the ability to collect and submit data, I have no doubt that other entities do as well.

I don't think there is anything hospitals should be afraid of when it comes to 340B transparency, honestly. If an institution needs this benefit to continue helping patients, let them show us so we can support those efforts and make sure we have a strong program.

With that, Mr. Chairman, I yield back.

Mr. GUTHRIE. I thank the gentleman for yielding. The Chair now recognizes Mrs. Dingell from Michigan for 5 minutes for questions.

Mrs. DINGELL. Thank you, Mr. Chairman, and thank you, Ranking Member Eshoo, for convening this hearing.

Nobody—Democrat, Republican, independent, anybody—should be harmed by medical expenses. And as healthcare continues to rise, it is important that consumers have access to accurate pricing information about their healthcare.

You know, I think the current healthcare system is gobbledy- gook. I am healthy, but for—I have had an infection, and I have had three CAT scans at three different institutions in the last 3 months. They have all been between 6 and $8,000. Medicare covers a few hundred, my insurance covers another few hundred, but each of them has a different amount, and the rest of it goes into Never Never Land. And I am one of the lucky ones, because I have Medicare and insurance. People can't understand the system.

And talk to a pharmacist or a patient these days. Pharmacy benefit managers? I had a pharmacist ranting at me that a pill that cost them $10 for 30 pills, they were—the pharmacy benefit manager was charging the customer $700. It is wrong.

So the Hospital Price Transparency Final Rule is a step in the right direction to improve transparency in healthcare prices. It went into effect in January 2021. But since the hospital rule went into effect, studies have found that most hospitals are not meeting all the requirements of this final rule.

Ms. Tripoli, one concern we continue to hear is the difficulties with the erratic compliance, with some estimates being as little as 16 percent of hospitals being in full compliance of the regulations. What do you think the obstacles are to preventing this compliance?

Ms. TRIPOLI. Thank you for the question. I think, at the end of the day, it is just about the business model of the sector, which is to keep prices hidden so that they can continue to increase prices year after year on the backs of the American people. There is not a strong enough financial incentive or requirement to get prices — disclose prices, because that pricing information is the most valuable piece of information in the hospital business model.

So price transparency, unveiling prices, requiring the negotiated rate to be disclosed for the public is hugely powerful, disrupts the status quo, and it actually allows policymakers to make targeted decisions about how irrational prices have become, and it allows academics to understand where does high value occur—value care occurring, where is low-value care occurring, and then we can make targeted interventions to make sure all people living in this country have high-value care.

Mrs. DINGELL. So some of my colleagues were asking this question, but I am going to ask it again as, you know, what can we do to help encourage that compliance?

You said there's no incentives. Do we penalize? There is—what specifically would you recommend we do to start to increase this compliance number?

Ms. TRIPOLI. I think strengthening and codifying the rule into statute is a good step in terms of strengthening on top of the requirements that are already there.

I think specifically prohibiting hospitals from posting prices as a percentage of Medicare or a percentage of gross charges—so we actually need dollars and cents. Dollars——

Mrs. DINGELL. So talk in English.

Ms. TRIPOLI. Exactly, in English. To that point, we actually need to understand beyond a confusing code that most folks don't understand what that is, a description that puts things in layman's terms: What is this?

We need more standardization across the services that we can actually compare apples to apples, and not oranges to grapefruits. And I would say the other piece that has not been mentioned yet is we need quality information. The only way to assess high-value care is if we have price and quality together so we can determine is that a value product that—and are we getting our money's worth for that?

Mrs. DINGELL. Thank you. And I should have said Spanish or French or— "layman's language" is a much better word.

Ms. TRIPOLI. Absolutely.

Mrs. DINGELL. Mr. Severn, while the rule also requires hospitals to publish the prices of common health services, we have heard about challenging—the challenges of accessing the data. What kind of data are hospitals currently reporting, and how is a lack of standardization contributing to data inconsistencies?

Mr. SEVERN. Yes, thank you for the question. So with about 5,100 hospitals in our database now, which is much better than 2 years ago, we have had to written—we have had to write over 1,000 unique programs to bring that data in.

If you had a standard, not only is it easier to ingest all the data and enforce compliance, it also puts some pressure on the gobbledy- gook of the rates, because there is now a column and a suggested format that—it is a payment method column. And if the payment method is really simple—just cash, a full, inclusive rate—patients and referring physicians and employers will go towards the upfront price. And so, you know, the standard will beget competition on simplicity, as well.

Mrs. DINGELL. I am out of time, so I will yield back, Mr. Chairman.

Mr. BUCSHON [presiding]. I yield briefly to the gentleman from Texas for a unanimous consent request.

Mr. BURGESS. Thank you, Mr. Chairman. As a consequence of my excellent staff, they were able to dig up the excellent article that I referenced from Health Affairs from 15 years ago.

[Laughter.]

Mr. BURGESS. And I ask unanimous consent to put that in the record.

Mr. BUCSHON. Without objection.

[The information appears at the conclusion of the hearing.]

Mr. BUCSHON. I now yield to the gentleman from Florida for his 5 minutes for questioning, Mr. Bilirakis.

Mr. BILIRAKIS. Thank you. Thank you, Doctor. I appreciate it, and I want to thank the panel for their testimony.

Dr. Ippolito, as you know, Community Health Centers are required under law to have a sliding fee schedule for low-income patients based on their needs. One way they do this is by passing through the 340B rebates to their patients to lower their prescription drug costs. This allows health centers to meet the unique needs of their communities, and they do an outstanding job.

However, when they utilize contract pharmacies, we have seen instances where these pharmacies will take these rebates and not pass them on to patients. Do you think that is fair?

Dr. IPPOLITO. Well, I mean, I—it certainly seems to undermine the goals of that program. And I think it speaks to this broader question about the 340B program, which is, as it increases in size, are we comfortable with how the program is actually targeted? Are the right sort of institutions benefiting?

We heard earlier about—a question about, well, which hospitals are benefiting? Is it community access hospitals? Is it safety-net hospitals? Is it the Johns Hopkins and the elite academic medical centers of the world? I think this is a question that is along those same lines.

Mr. BILIRAKIS. Thank you. Should we be concerned by the consolidation incentives you mentioned in your testimony, your written testimony, that also allows for single entities to take 340B rebates that should instead be legally passed on to the patient?

How do we incorporate a policy that ensures consistent compliance and accountability in the program?

And that is the bottom line. So if you could comment on that, I would appreciate it.

Dr. IPPOLITO. Yes. I think, if you think about 340B, the two big questions are is it targeted well, and is it functioning just literally the way we think it is supposed to be functioning? Are the discounts going where they are on paper supposed to be going? Are there duplicate discounts between the Medicaid program and the 340B program?

When you talk about—you mentioned consolidation—I heard at the beginning of that. You know, one of the ramifications of this whole program is that it gives this enormous arbitrage opportunity to hospitals that have 340B status, that suddenly they have a big opportunity to propose to a physician that practices independently: "If you come affiliate with us, we have an enormous advantage on our acquisition costs for these medications, and we can basically share that with you." And so it is another contributor to this phenomenon of greater consolidation over time, and it goes back to that question about targeting.

Mr. BILIRAKIS. OK. Again, Dr. Ippolito, can you discuss if the way that Medicare reimburses for physician-administered drugs has contributed to the consolidation trend of hospitals purchasing local physician practice offices?

And how do we fix this problem without further squeezing small independent providers?

Dr. IPPOLITO. Well, yes. A Medicare payment policy is like a double whammy on top of a 340B. So 340B gives the hospital a big advantage on the acquisition cost, and then Medicare pays the hospital-affiliated facility more than it would an independent physician to administer that drug. And there certainly have been proposals to address that. I know H.R. 19, I believe, incorporated some site-neutral payments, even just for administration of drugs.

But that is part of this broader effort that places like MedPAC have highlighted. There are certain services that seem like they are basically the exact same service, and they don't really need access to the hospital. And so we ought to start thinking about whether we should reimburse those things in a way that is both saving Medicare money, but it doesn't disadvantage these independent physician practices quite as much.

Mr. BILIRAKIS. Thank you very much.

Finally, I am interested in implementation of the price transparency rules—and I know that my good friend Mrs. Dingell here on this.

Mr. Severn and Ms. Bartlett, how can HHS not only boost hospital compliance but ensure that compliant hospitals have prices that make sense and are easy to understand for the consumer— that is the bottom line for it to work—so that patients and websites can access more prices and more—meaningfully shop for the best care, please?

We will go ahead and start with Mr. Severn. I don't have a lot of time, though.

Mr. SEVERN. Thanks for the question. The first—and I have said this a few times—there is a standard that is suggested. And the moment that standard is enforced and there is an enforcement date, it makes it easier for all of us to see what is in these files. It shouldn't be just Turquoise, a company with the resources, that can go through and process all this data. It should be easier to access this. And so the first step to making compliance and enforcement easier is having a standard to look through these 6,000 files.

Mr. BILIRAKIS. Thank you. Ms. Bartlett?

Mr. BARTLETT. I would agree. I think having a standard, a template, as—would be the first big step to get those prices out, and standard descriptions and everything. But some standards would be great.

Mr. BILIRAKIS. Thank you.

I don't—I ran out of time, so I will yield back. Thank you, I appreciate it.

Mr. BUCSHON. The gentleman yields back. I now recognize the gentlelady from Washington, Dr. Schrier.

Ms. SCHRIER. Thank you, Mr. Chairman. Thank you to all the witnesses for being here today, and a big, special thank you to Mr. Forge for coming out from Spokane, from Pullman. Thank you for the work that you have done for rural patients.

You have all pointed out how transparency is critical in bringing down costs and for patients to know what they are paying for.

Dr. Ippolito, I was intrigued by the discussion in your testimony—and many people have commented on it now—about different Medicare reimbursement rates, depending on whether— what procedures take place in a hospital, a hospital-affiliated center, or a freestanding clinic, or an ambulatory center that is not associated. And, of course, this sets up all kinds of wrong incentives. And this is not pointing at the people doing the wrong thing for the wrong reason, it is just that when you have, say, an orthopedic surgeon who has to do a knee replacement, there may be pressure from all kinds of directions for that doctor to do a knee replacement in a hospital rather than an outpatient surgical center, even though for a low-risk patient doing that is the safer and better thing to do and even though, you know, in a hospital—a hospital is a very expensive place to stay for a night, when you can just as well go home and do your rehab and PT at home.

So, you know, I was just going to ask you to expand a little bit on all of this, what we should do about it, whether you are finding that hospitals are buying up ambulatory surgical centers to kind of run around this issue, and how you suggest fixing it.

Dr. IPPOLITO. Well, sure. I mean, the short answer to your last question there is "yes." There has certainly been a lot of consolidation of facilities that otherwise would have not been affiliated with a hospital into the hospital sphere, if you will.

I will just emphasize one thing that hasn't really come up is that, especially in the Medicare market, the site of service doesn't just affect, like, aggregate Medicare spend or something like that, which obviously matters for taxpayers and budgets and all those things, which are very real. But it matters for the person who is getting the care, because your out-of-pocket can be a 20 percent co-insurance. Well, if the bill is larger, 20 percent of a larger bill is a larger bill, you know.

Ms. SCHRIER. That is right.

Dr. IPPOLITO. And so I think we don't want to lose sight of that. It is one of the examples where consolidation issues sometimes sound abstract. They affect the medium and the long run. That is an example where, yes, you can affect the consolidation incentives in a meaningful way, like you point to, but in the short run it materially affects out-of-pocket spending for people. So it is one of the avenues through which we can really make a big difference in the relatively short term.

Ms. SCHRIER. And I think you brought up a really important— there about whether people feel that if you are paying 20 percent of the bill, then you actually feel—and you can have some power in making those decisions.

Mr. Severn, you were talking about MRIs costing vastly different amounts at different locations. And I was going to say that, with many insurance companies—for example, with mine—there is a copay. And so I don't feel it if there is a higher price or a lower price for the MRI, and the insurance company negotiates whatever price they want that has nothing to do with the list price.

I was wondering if you could talk a little bit about transparency there, but also how to give people more agency so that, when there is a higher or a lower price out there, it serves us to go for the place with the lower price. Give us some, like, good skin in the game, if I am explaining that——

Mr. SEVERN. Thanks for the question. So there's a couple ways to summit Transparency Mountain.

You mentioned one of them, which is just copay-based plans. And there's a lot of startups innovating to say, hey, no matter where you go, here is the copay.

You know, giving patients the skin in the game, there's a couple of different mechanisms. High-deductible plans is one. Having a percent, coinsurance, is one. And it is back to the issue of, hey, 20 percent of a bigger number is more money, right? And so the problem with saying patients need skin in the game but without giving them a variable that is necessary to calculate that skin in the game is what was so ludicrous before 2021.

Now we have this key negotiated rate variable, where if you have a high deductible plan or a percent coinsurance, you can do the math as a patient. But I think what I am advocating for is they shouldn't have to do the math. You know, companies like Turquoise should make it as simple as possible, like you are buying a toaster off Amazon, to say you will pay $50 if you go here.

Hopefully, that answers your question.

Ms. SCHRIER. Thank you. Yes, I appreciate it. And I know how much people are suffering from high prices.

I just wanted to lastly touch on PBMs. I use insulin. I have seen the price of insulin go up from about $40 a bottle to north of 300 now. We have talked about that before and the role of PBMs in those pricing changes. And just want to say to my colleagues I am happy and ready to work on combating some of these perverse incentives for pharmacy benefit managers, where they get compensated more for a higher negotiated medication price.

So thank you. I yield back.

Mr. BUCSHON. The gentlelady yields back. I now yield to the gentleman from Ohio, Mr. Johnson, for his 5 minutes.

Mr. JOHNSON. Thank you, Mr. Chairman, and thank you to our witnesses for being here today.

I think this is a crucial time for discussion on price transparency, and I thank the chairman for having this hearing. It comes as Congress is in the middle of debt limit discussions with the President, and healthcare costs are a really big part of what is driving the national deficit. The Medicare Trust Fund will be insolvent in less than 5 years, and our national debt is over $31 trillion, a major reason why healthcare costs are simply too high.

Runaway healthcare prices are bankrupting the country, often putting everyday Americans, our constituents, in financial distress. They are having to choose between paying for healthcare or paying for groceries, energy, and other necessities. Oftentimes, they go without the healthcare that they need because they can't afford to go to the doctor, and they can't afford the insurance premiums that would get them there.

Healthcare costs now make up nearly 20 percent of GDP. This is not sustainable. At a time when inflation is crushing families, it is our responsibility to scrutinize the contributors to these skyrocketing costs and either call for regulatory changes or make statutory changes when appropriate.

So my first question, Dr. Ippolito, how can increased healthcare price transparency and competition tamp down these costs and start to give families a little more wiggle room?

Will this help change the trajectory for healthcare costs?

Dr. IPPOLITO. Yes. Well, I mean, it is a necessity, to some degree. If an employer or an individual doesn't really have much in the way of choice, well, there is not much way for them to put any downward pressure on prices in their local market. And I think we have certainly heard about specific examples of that today.

You know, in terms of a high-level point, you know, it is easy to lose sight of the direct impact that competition in healthcare costs have on people. We forget you don't see that if you have employer-based coverage, that costs $20,000 a year. And economic theory and evidence is extremely clear: Employees pay for that, every cent of it. Every time we see healthcare costs go up, even if just for a sliver of workers, we see the wages adjust for that sliver of workers. And so we really need to hammer home that point. This is not some abstract budgetary issue that affects the government in some sense. It is an issue that directly affects people, both through wages and their tax bill and so many other things.

Mr. JOHNSON. OK. Better price transparency throughout the healthcare system will result in greater competition, lower costs, and create a better level of trust between patients, insurers, and providers. Congress has given the Biden administration the tools necessary to ensure compliance of the hospital price transparency regulations already on the books.

So my next question, Ms. Tripoli: In your opinion, what could be done by CMS or the executive branch to better ensure compliance with the hospital price transparency regulations?

Ms. TRIPOLI. I think, at the end of the day, this is about hospitals failing to comply. They have the requirements. We have been—it is a Federal rule. We have been in implementation for 2 years. At this point we would expect to see much higher compliance, and not just a—the—posting some prices, complete data files.

So I think, at the end of the day, this is about hospitals showing up and doing their part and complying with Federal rules.

Mr. JOHNSON. OK, all right.

Mr. Severn, you work to help patients obtain a good-faith estimate of what they will pay for services they need under the No Surprises Act, which mandated that providers furnish such estimates. It has been a challenge to implement this part of the law in cases where multiple providers or facilities are involved.

Do you have recommendations for Congress or CMS to improve data sharing to make good-faith estimates seamless and ensure patients have access to accurate cost information?

Mr. SEVERN. Thank you for the question. So to answer that question, I will give a couple of stats.

You know, we say there are 5,300 hospitals, it looks like as of today, that have prices posted; 4,600 over that have negotiated rates, 4,500 have cash prices. I think these numbers are important, because those stats are pretty high, and we are in this data every quarter. And so maybe a lot of things that you saw last year and the year before show you that there aren't as many prices. There are quite a few prices out there, what we call coverage in the market.

The next step, as you mentioned, is these prices turn into good-faith estimates, and these estimates need to be packaged. And the beautiful thing about No Surprises is that there is teeth to create an estimate that is accurate within $400. And so, to us, that is the next step. That is where this is going next is, great, your prices are out there. We need to get them to a patient before time of service, and then you need to be—it needs to be enforced that the estimate is accurate.

Mr. JOHNSON. Isn't it amazing how a free enterprise economy actually works to drive down costs when you tell people what they are going to pay for stuff?

Mr. Chairman, I yield back.

Mr. BUCSHON. The gentleman yields back, and I recognize Mrs.

Trahan from Massachusetts for her 5 minutes.

Mrs. TRAHAN. Thank you, Mr. Chair.

Healthcare in the United States operates on a free market system, where larger systems command higher rates of reimbursement with their market clout and smaller, often urban or rural systems have limited opportunity to negotiate higher prices. As many of my colleagues have said here today, this contributes to the strong getting stronger and the weak getting weaker, as providers with market clout can demand higher reimbursement from insurers.

During COVID we saw a number of rural hospitals closed because of this trend. And in the district I represent, we are seeing the same threat to access among urban community hospitals. We are told that hospital mergers and consolidation are supposed to increase efficiencies and lower costs, but community hospitals have not been part of market consolidation, and therefore they lack negotiating power. These hospitals don't have strong operating margins to begin with and provide care for some of the most under-served communities across the country, so they often aren't invited to join larger systems.

Mr. Ippolito, do larger hospitals and hospital systems charge more than smaller community hospitals for the same services because they cost more at larger facilities, or is it simply because these large hospital systems wield more negotiating power and can therefore fetch higher reimbursement rates for the services they provide?

Dr. IPPOLITO. It is to some degree both, but it is important to remember that the costs are endogenous. The hospital gets to choose how much things cost, and Partners has made different decisions about their underlying cost structure than, for example, a smaller community hospital.

But there is no getting around the second point. They have more negotiating leverage, and that is absolutely correct.

Mrs. TRAHAN. Thank you. In Massachusetts, outside of cities like Boston, we have lower-income communities that rely on stand- alone providers. These providers have the lowest prices and operate with the fewest resources. They cannot command prices, and many of them are limiting essential services and, in the worst cases, are on the brink of closing entirely.

Ms. Tripoli, where is access to care most threatened due to the limited market clout of smaller community hospitals?

Ms. TRIPOLI. I think, at the end of the day, what we know about the markets is that these large, dominant systems are able to buy up independent physician practices. And that is one of the greatest trends we are seeing right now in terms of vertical integration. And that has a direct impact not only on prices, but also access to care, and particularly primary care for many of the communities around our country.

And so one of the solutions we can do right now to end one of those incentives for big systems buying up smaller doctors' offices is to expand site-neutral payments, and—which will also result in significant savings for the system and also for the beneficiary.

Mrs. TRAHAN. So my followup question to that was that I am exploring policy solutions to address this access-to-care challenge that is disproportionately hurting low-income communities, especially in the district I represent.

So if you could share some of the challenges facing smaller community hospitals and some of the ways that we can improve reimbursement for these kinds of hospitals, that would be helpful.

Ms. TRIPOLI. That was directed for me?

Mrs. TRAHAN. Yes.

Ms. TRIPOLI. Again, I think one of the things we can do right off the bat, which is what is under discussion for this committee here today, is expanding site-neutral payments, which eliminates this perverse incentive for big systems to buy up independent doctors' offices, which has a direct impact on making sure that we have access to critical care in communities.

The other thing that I would just say is one of the other things we are seeing in terms of dominant market power is a lot of anti-competitive practices, including restricting providers from being able to go to competing systems, which has also a direct impact on access to care in communities. So I think taking a closer look at the different types of anticompetitive practices that are occurring between plans and providers, and prohibiting some of those practices that we know that lead to burnout, reduced access to care, drive up prices, and result in poorer quality care.

Mrs. TRAHAN. Great. Thanks so much. I yield back.

Mr. GUTHRIE. The gentlelady yields back. The Chair now recognizes Mr. Carter from Georgia for 5 minutes for the purpose of asking questions.

Mr. CARTER. Thank you, Mr. Chairman, and thank all of you for being here. I appreciate it very much.

This is my ninth year in Congress, and I have to tell you—I am just beginning my ninth year and, you know, when I first got here 8 years ago, the first thing I did was to go to the FTC and ask them to look at the vertical integration that exists with the insurance company owning the PBM, owning the pharmacy.

To me, it is a direct conflict of interest. All this could be resolved by just saying the insurance company can't own the PBM, and saying the PBM can't own the pharmacy. If we did away with that, we wouldn't have any problem. We would have what all of you have been calling for today, and that is competition, and that is what we need.

Obviously, transparency is a big part of it. I am not going to repeat everything that you have heard here. You know that 3 PBMs control 80 percent of the market—75, 80 percent of the market. That in itself is a big problem. When you have the insurance company that owns the PBM, you have steering going on because they are trying to get them to their pharmacy. All of that you understand.

I want to ask you, Ms. Bartlett, because I was intrigued. I haven't, unfortunately, been able to sit here the whole time to listen. But what was done in Montana with our good friend and former colleague, with—or who is now the Governor—I guess it may have been done before then, but nevertheless, thank you for what you did. But you mentioned that you all had changed PBMs, I think, at one point.

Did you know if the PBM before—were they engaging in spread pricing?

And all of you know what spread pricing is, I am assuming, and I am sure you do. So——

Mr. BARTLETT. Yes, thank you for the question. The PBM we had previously was engaged in spread pricing.

They also had contracted with CVS to be the rebate aggregator who would bring all the rebates in. And we were given $20 per drug rebate. And from my previous experience, I knew that that was way, way, way too low.

Mr. CARTER. Right.

Mr. BARTLETT. And then they also had contracted with a specialty pharmacy that was owned by an insurance company. And so——

Mr. CARTER. Go figure.

Mr. BARTLETT. Oh, yes. Going through that contract, you were able to see all the places that needed to be cleaned up. And so I terminated all those contracts and went for a transparent pass- through.

Mr. CARTER. You know, I mentioned earlier about the FTC. And finally, last summer, they are undertaking a study now, a 6B study looking at the impact that PBMs are having on independent retail pharmacies. Four percent of all independent retail pharmacies are going out of business every year, primarily because of the low reimbursement by the PBMs.

And of course, you know, it is such a problem, particularly when you think about the fact that the independent pharmacies adjudicate their claims through the insurance company. Therefore, the insurance company that owns the PBM that owns the pharmacy has all that information right there.

We had a case in middle Georgia just here in the last year where they were cut off by one of the PBMs and all of their patients were transferred to the mail order pharmacy that was owned by the PBM. That is—I mean, it is so obvious to me, and thank goodness my colleagues are getting it now and understanding what is going on. And thank goodness the FTC is undertaking this study.

I know you find it hard to believe—we get updates from them as to how the study is going, and they are having trouble getting the PBMs to cooperate. I can't imagine. But nevertheless, that is happening.

I want to mention—and I know it is self-serving, but I do have legislation, and it is bipartisan legislation. It is called the Drug Price Transparency in Medicaid Act of 2023. And it is to improve transparency and eliminate the use of spread pricing. You all know what is going on right now—it made news yesterday with the attorney general of Ohio and what he is doing—that is the kind of thing we need. That is the kind of action that needs to be taken.

Dr. Ippolito—I am sorry, I know you have been before us and before the Doctors Caucus, and thank you for your expertise in this field as well. But what about—you know, the thing that concerns me is employers don't get it, either. They don't understand. They don't know. What can we do to help employers understand and see just how rogue this is?

Dr. IPPOLITO. Well, I mean, I think what—you referenced your bill, and I think CBO will tell you—I am sure they have—that if you give the employers better information, their expectation is that they are going to change their behavior if they better understand, really, what the rebate levels are, what the gross spend and what the net spend really is.

Mr. CARTER. Right.

Dr. IPPOLITO. The only thing I will add—it has come up a couple times—you have got to make sure that those things actually incorporate more than just the PBM, but it has to include the rebate aggregator, the one level higher than the PBM, just to make sure that you get the full picture.

But I think their expectation is my expectation. If you know more, you are going to make a better decision and you are going to be—it is going to make it easier to compare the PBMs against each other if these fees and the costs are much clearer.

Mr. CARTER. You know, I will tell my age here, but I can remember practicing pharmacy and—when PBMs were nothing more than processors. That is all they did, was process claims. And then they evolved into this now that is causing—you know, all of us in Congress, and Democrats and Republicans alike, we want accessibility, affordability, and quality in healthcare. That is what we want.

Well, right now, pharmacists are the most accessible healthcare professionals in America. Ninety-five percent of all Americans live within 5 miles of a pharmacy. If you start doing away with independent retail pharmacies, that is going to end. Therefore, it will impact accessibility to healthcare in America.

I am sorry, Mr. Chairman, I know I am over, and I will yield back. Thank you.

Mr. GUTHRIE. The gentleman's time has expired, and he yields back. We will complete the members of the committee, and then go to people who are waiving on to the committee. So next would be Dr. Dunn from Florida.

You are recognized for 5 minutes.

Mr. DUNN. Thank you very much, Mr. Chairman.

You know, policies to promote transparency in healthcare pricing are a sure way to address the pressing issue of high healthcare costs. Empowering consumers with knowledge about the true cost of healthcare services and products will put more Americans in the driver's seat when it comes to their family's health and spending. President Trump executed a number of transparency policies across the healthcare continuum, from drugs to insurers to hospitals to doctors. And this committee must ensure that this compliance with these new rules continues or is enacted.

However, policies such as price caps and price setting actually pervert the market and limit access to consumer choices. That is not the path we should follow. Instead, I think we should be promoting the transparency that everybody has talked about so well tonight and thus competition to ensure healthcare markets operate in a way that serves the consumers.

Mr. Severn, we have seen greater compliance amongst insurers rather than hospitals when it comes to their respective transparency rules. But the size and complexity of the data files has made this information difficult for consumers to use in a meaningful way. I appreciate what Turquoise has been able to accomplish in the private sector when it comes to distilling these complex data sets to empower patients.

Will this data continue to improve the availability—the legibility, if you will—of the data and continue to improve with time, or should we consider tweaks to the regulation to assist with the processing of data?

Mr. SEVERN. Thank you for the question. You know, I will leave it up to others, not myself, to decide where best to tweak this.

But what I would recommend is there is a process right now for the insurance data to be modified through a technical back-and-forth that occurs on GitHub, which CMS runs. And over 9 months in the—since this data has come out, every month it has gotten more accessible, easier to work with. More companies and more third parties are making use of it, distributing it to patients and downstream.

So I would recommend continued tweaks, at least through the GitHub process with CMS, and then I will leave it to regulators to decide if more needs to happen in the text.

Mr. DUNN. How about enforcement?

Mr. SEVERN. Enforcement on the payer side is, you know, a little harder to address. I might not fully speak over that, because it kind of filters out to States and——

Mr. DUNN. OK, we haven't been doing it, for the most part. I think there's a couple of isolated instances, but we haven't been doing it.

Mr. Forge, the theme of this hearing is competition. It seems that you have, in fact, created competitive value for your patients in—by complying with the Hospital Price Transparency Rules as a community-based critical access hospital. How does price transparency enhance your ability to compete with larger competitors?

Mr. FORGE. Well, I think we have kind of addressed it a little bit earlier. I think the—what it focuses on for us, what we can really compete at is with quality. You know, when you are talking about competing on price, you know, volumes really takes the ticket right now. And so we are kind of, you know, where we are.

But if we can continue to provide a better product, and we can prove it, and a better service, maybe our volumes will continue to grow, we will gain more leverage. The cost has got to be a part of that equation.

Mr. DUNN. So I would say—I am a doctor in my real life. I would say that I have seen, you know, large hospital systems that simply did not compete on cost. They didn't use the benefit of their size to get low cost for themselves, which they would then—they didn't pass on to the consumer. So I think you have some potential to compete on cost, as well.

Dr. Ippolito, we have seen PBMs become vertically integrated with large health companies and pharmacies. I completely associate myself with the remarks of my colleague Mr. Carter. You have previously written, however, that the effects of that integration is somewhat unclear. I am fairly confident that such integration drives higher costs for consumers.

Do you have recommendations for transparency-oriented policies Congress could enact that would shed some light on the effects of that vertical integration?

Dr. IPPOLITO. Yes. So I will maybe clarify my prior writing.

The effects of vertical integration, as a general proposition, are a little bit less certain, just because conceptually there can be things like better adherence or better communication between various levels of the organization that could provide value.

That said, if you want to think about high level, what is important, you know, what do these contracts look like? Where are the incentives, right? Are there incentives to steer patients or steer volume to things that deliver, you know, revenues for you? If there is a choice between, for example, a pharmacy-dispensed product and a physician-administered one and you run a pharmacy, do you tend to steer people to the pharmacy?

Those are the kinds of questions I would be asking when it comes to vertically integrated firms like you are talking about.

Mr. DUNN. Thank—I want to thank the panel for their time today.

And, Mr. Chairman, I yield back.

Mr. GUTHRIE. The gentleman yields back. The Chair now recognizes Mr. Latta for 5 minutes for questions.

Mr. LATTA. Well, thank you, Mr. Chair, and thanks for today's hearing, and also thanks for our panelists.

I am sure the Chair has already said we have three different subcommittees that have been running today in the committee, so we appreciate your indulgence.

Mr. Forge, if I could start my questioning, what can or should the Federal Government do to make price transparency requirements and compliance criteria clearer—this has always been the tougher one—and more user-friendly for hospitals while also being useful for the—our patients out there?

Mr. FORGE. Well, I think, you know, basically, just simplification. You know, how do you simplify the regulations so that, you know, more hospitals can comply with them, you know, with less resources, less, you know, less effort, less work? We need simplification of these things.

The truth is we have to compete in rural America with big hospitals. We have to compete in that area. And so we need a little bit of help to make that easier for us to do so at that level.

Mr. LATTA. Well, you know, you bring up a question when you say "simplification" because, again, I know that when I go through my health facilities in the 5th district and around the region, you know, sometimes you look around and also we have had panels here before us of docs and other individuals, and I—you know, after a while you have to ask this question: How much time do you get to practice? How much time are you actually doing, really, the medical end of this job, instead of all of the paperwork?

And I know I have been in some doctors' offices that they have invited me in, and as I observed things for a little while, I say, "Who is actually practicing medicine here instead of filing forms?" So how do we—you know, how do we get the simplification in there? Because we all know it needs to be done. But how do we do it?

Mr. FORGE. Good question. I spend most of my days trying to solve that for our teams, as it is.

I think, you know, the volume of change in regulations is a big part of it. You know, we are adopting—adapting to new concepts, to new programs, to new deals every month, every year. And the volume of that becomes excessive. We need to kind of get back to why we are here.

An example would be simplifying the CPT codes. What do we have, 10,000 codes, you know, that we are working on? I know that is really important for value-based care, and I am all for that, but we have to figure out ways to make it easier for providers just to take care of patients and for us to get clear bills out to our patients.

Mr. LATTA. Well, thank you very much. Dr. Ippolito—I hope I pronounced that—is it "Eppolitto?"

Dr. IPPOLITO. Ippolito, but I have heard——

Mr. LATTA. Ippolito, I am sorry. We have heard much about transparency in the 340B program. And while I believe in the importance of transparency, I want to ensure that steps we take do not deny the resources from the hospitals that need them.

So do you believe we can increase transparency over the 340B program without serious consequences for our hospitals that use the program?

Dr. IPPOLITO. Yes, sure. When it comes to 340B, I think the first step is transparency on two elements. Number one, is it just functioning the way that we expect it to function? And then, number two, how are the hospitals actually using that money?

And I think the answers to those questions should inform any potential reform efforts that people have in mind. And they certainly would be relevant to your question about if you have a hospital that is genuinely delivering a lot of, say, uncompensated care and they are using their funds in that manner, then, you know, maybe we—even if you want to reform 340B, you want to make sure you protect that kind of institution. And so transparency seems like the first kind of step in that direction.

Mr. LATTA. Well, thank you. Let's see if—maybe I can do this real quickly in my last minute and 9 seconds for the panel: Would you each briefly opine on what you believe to be the most significant driver of high healthcare costs?

And maybe in 1 minute for all five of you. What is the driver in high healthcare costs?

Mr. SEVERN. Lack of competition and, particularly, the hospital spend, most likely.

Mr. FORGE. Complexity.

Mr. BARTLETT. The middlemen.

Ms. TRIPOLI. Consolidation, particularly in the hospital sector.

Dr. IPPOLITO. Yes, I would echo that: consolidation on the provider side.

Mr. LATTA. Well, Mr. Chairman, you know, I think if we can get it down in one word for an answer of what is driving the cost, I think we are doing pretty good.

But I want to thank our witnesses, and, Mr. Chairman, I thank you for holding today's hearing, and I yield back the balance of my time.

Mr. GUTHRIE. I thank the gentleman for yielding. Next will—I recognize Mr. Joyce for 5 minutes for questions.

Mr. JOYCE. Thank you for yielding, Mr. Chairman, and to the committee for having this hearing today on such an important topic.

As this committee looks to address healthcare costs, we need to make sure that we are addressing misguided incentives that are ballooning those costs. As has been mentioned here today, one of the biggest drivers in increasing spending over the last 10 years has been the 340B drug-pricing program. The 340B drug-pricing program was created in 1992 and aimed at enabling certain healthcare providers known as covered entities—and this is a quote— "to stretch scarce Federal resources to reach more eligible patients or provide more comprehensive services."

Between 2000 and 2020, the number of covered sites participating in the program grew from 8,100 to over 50,000. During this period, discounted purchases in the program grew from $4 billion to 38 billion from 2007 to 2020.

Mr. Chairman, I would like to ask unanimous consent to enter into the record an article from December in the Wall Street Journal to join the one entered by my friend and colleague Dr. Bucshon earlier today.

Mr. GUTHRIE. Any objection? Seeing none, so ordered.

[The information appears at the conclusion of the hearing.]

Mr. JOYCE. Thank you. Both of these detail a myriad of issues in a program which highlight the need for changes to be made.

I want to also be clear that we must ensure that any reform in this space cannot come at the expense of patient access to medications.

Dr. Ippolito, can you explain in detail how the 340B program is contributing to the overall trend of increased costs for patients that we are seeing in the healthcare marketplace right now?

Dr. IPPOLITO. Well, in terms of the patient effect, I think there's probably two things that would come to mind. The first is that, in theory, the money is supposed to be used to help fund care for patients, typically, that cannot afford to pay. So one of the big questions is, is that actually how the money is being used? And if it is not, that is something that is worth addressing.

And then I think the second point that I would emphasize is that this is another one of these policies that tends towards the direction of more consolidation, because it gives certain entities, hospitals, a big arbitrage opportunity over stand-alone physician practices. And so it pushes in the direction of more consolidation. That pushes in the direction of higher costs for patients.

Mr. JOYCE. So you brought up a very interesting point. So you addressed is this being utilized for the patients who need that care? Do you think it is? And do you think that that explains the $4 billion increase to $38 billion over 13 years, or is this being abused?

Dr. IPPOLITO. I think the perhaps most sort of damning answer is that I have no idea. I have no idea how the money is used, because I don't think there really is any effective oversight. I think it operates through HRSA, and I don't even know that there are standards for how the money is supposed to be spent, let alone how the oversight is supposed to work.

So that seems like an area that, for program integrity and just making sure it is doing what people want it to do, that seems like an area where transparency would be particularly useful.

Mr. JOYCE. So I addressed the district where I serve, Pennsylvania's 13th congressional district, which is rural and underserved, and I see great benefits from 340B programs for several of the rural hospitals. But I share your concerns if this process is being overutilized and abused.

Mr. Forge, to follow up on my colleague Dr. Bucshon's questions on reporting HRSA, do you think if Congress were to ask to compare current metrics on charity care with the total amount of savings that Pullman gets in a year from 340B or—from 340B programs, that the need for the program would outstrip any savings that the hospital will get?

Mr. FORGE. I am not sure that I can speak to that. But what I do know is that, in rural areas, hospitals that should benefit from 340B, in my experience, have had a tough time doing so. I think they are getting to the point where they are figuring it out, and we are starting to feel the benefits. But I don't think that all the places that should be feeling the benefits from 340B are feeling that.

Mr. JOYCE. Do you feel that there might be better metrics that we in Congress should use to fully grasp the value to patients that hospitals can provide with these programs, with these savings?

Mr. FORGE. Sure. I think maintaining viability and sustainability of these, you know, hospitals, these community-based hospitals in rural areas is the priority. So how do we, you know, look at 340B in these areas as an effective measure to keep these hospitals going, keep 24-hour emergency care services going, and make sure that these people have access to services where they live?

Mr. JOYCE. I thank you for your concise answer, because I don't think there is anything that hospitals should be afraid of when it comes to 340B transparency. If a hospital needs that support, it should be obvious, and it should be transparent. And for—the hospital that you run and in many districts are exactly who this program is meant to serve, but I do wonder whether this same story would be clear for every hospital. And I look forward to working with my colleagues in a bipartisan way to address this issue.

Thank you, Mr. Chair, and I yield back.

Mr. GUTHRIE. The gentleman yields back. The Chair now recognizes Mr. Pence from Indiana.

Oh, I am sorry, excuse me. The gentleman recognizes Mrs. Harshbarger for—yes, Harshbarger for 5 minutes for the purpose of questions.

Mrs. HARSHBARGER. Hey, thank you, Mr. Chairman, and thank you, witnesses, for being here today. This is informative for me.

I have been a pharmacist 37 years, and PBMs are just from the devil. OK?

And Ms. Bartlett, you are my kind of gal, OK? And I do want to ask you one question. You have already heard from Mr. Carter about the PBMs, but you said you used a transparent passthrough PBM. Can you tell me who that is?

Mr. BARTLETT. Yes, that was Navitus.

Mrs. HARSHBARGER. Navitus, OK. And there are some transparent PBMs out there.

Mr. BARTLETT. Yes, there are.

Mrs. HARSHBARGER. Integra, and——

Mr. BARTLETT. And you have to make sure it is in the contract.

Mrs. HARSHBARGER. Yes. I will be talking to you later.

Mr. BARTLETT. OK.

[Laughter.]

Mrs. HARSHBARGER. And I want to follow up on something that Mr. Griffith talked about, and I want to talk about that ProPublica report that was published last week.

And this is for Mr. Severn. You know, I am also concerned about the pricing, what they charge: a blood test, $1,000. And I have looked at these, because people bring them in to me. Remember, we are the most trusted healthcare professional. Everybody lives 5 minutes from a pharmacy. And by gosh, they utilize us. All right? I guess—are all laboratories that are not hospital-based required to post their prices?

Mr. SEVERN. Thanks for the question. The simple answer is yes. And that is what is so great. We had 18 months where we only had hospital prices, and now 9 months ago we are mixing nonhospital prices into the fray, which should create more competition.

Mrs. HARSHBARGER. So the labs have to report that, as well?

Mr. SEVERN. The——

Mrs. HARSHBARGER. If they are not hospital-based?

Mr. SEVERN. The insurance companies report the negotiated rates with labs on their behalf.

Mrs. HARSHBARGER. OK. Are they doing that?

Mr. SEVERN. Yes, we——

Mrs. HARSHBARGER. OK.

Mr. SEVERN. Billions of rates now just live on the Internet.

Mrs. HARSHBARGER. You know, we had the biggest—in the history of the country in my district, so there is no competition. We all know competition makes everything better, and it drives prices down. And there was a hospital—well, it really wasn't a hospital. They published their prices, their cash prices online on Facebook, compared it to the hospital, and people were angry, very angry. It is just getting the information out there.

And I guess this is for everyone: If suddenly the curtains were pulled back on all healthcare prices, and consumers could see prices systemwide in healthcare by the insurance payer and the plan as well as discounted cash prices, what would happen? What would happen?

And I will start with you, sir.

Mr. SEVERN. I think people would get in their cars and start driving to Pullman or somewhere more affordable.

[Laughter.]

Mr. FORGE. I think they would be confused.

Mrs. HARSHBARGER. They would.

Mr. FORGE. I think they would be confused.

Mrs. HARSHBARGER. They would be saying, "I have been paying too much for a long time."

Mr. FORGE. Yes, that is for sure.

Mrs. HARSHBARGER. Yes, ma'am.

Mr. BARTLETT. And I think employers would be very glad to see that, to see that their plan is paying much more than the cash price——

Mrs. HARSHBARGER. Those——

Mr. BARTLETT [continuing]. And compare it to their claims data and see that there is probably some medical spread pricing going on too.

Mrs. HARSHBARGER. Totally. Self-funded, they have no idea. They have no idea.

Mr. BARTLETT. You are right.

Mrs. HARSHBARGER. Yes, ma'am.

Ms. TRIPOLI. When we get to full transparency, I think it would give policymakers the tools to be able to intervene where prices have become completely irrational, so we can actually bring down the cost of care for the American people.

Mrs. HARSHBARGER. Yes.

Dr. IPPOLITO. Yes, like the last two, employers and policymakers might be the biggest users of that in the end.

Mrs. HARSHBARGER. Yes, where——

Dr. IPPOLITO. Where are the prices high, where are they low, and why?

Mrs. HARSHBARGER. We compare prices at Walmart versus Amazon, don't we? Well, why can't we do that with healthcare? We can. They call me for a price on a medication at the pharmacy, and I better be lower.

Though I could talk—I could ask you a whole lot of other questions, but I do have one for you, Dr. Ippolito, and it is about certificate of need. If you are talking about competition, you don't have competition in that arena, do you?

That is one glaring area where healthcare system lacks competition. And I hear about it from my constituents all the time. And these certificate-of-need regulations require hospitals and healthcare providers to obtain government approval before they can build new facilities, expand existing facilities, or purchase certain types of equipments, even beds.

Making matters worse, the laws allow existing providers to prevent competition by giving them the ability to object to new certificate-of-need application submitted by their would-be competitors. And many view these certificate-of-need laws as being the epitome of government interference, suppressing competition.

Do you agree that, as a whole, those certificate-of-need laws are misguided?

Dr. IPPOLITO. Yes. Well, I think at this point we have about 30, 40 years of evidence, and that evidence isn't particularly kind to certificate of need, however well-intentioned they were. At this point, I think we need as few impediments to competition as possible in the healthcare market.

Mrs. HARSHBARGER. Yes, I guess that is—my time is up. I will submit some more questions to you in writing, though. OK?

All right. With that, Mr. Chairman, I yield back.

Mr. GUTHRIE. Thank you. The gentlelady yields back, and the Chair now recognizes Ms. Kuster for 5 minutes for questions.

Ms. KUSTER. Thank you, Mr. Chairman, and thank you to our witnesses for being with us today.

As my colleagues on both sides of the aisle have stated, healthcare costs are unaffordable for literally millions of Americans. On top of high costs, patients are also navigating a confusing landscape where they can't realistically plan for how much life-saving treatment will cost them or if they will be able to afford it. This uncertainty often leads to decisions that only further harm a patient's health and burden the medical system, such as delaying care and rationing medication.

Patients rely on supports like the 340B program, which provides discounts on essential prescription drugs to vulnerable communities. Without programs like 340B, healthcare would simply be out of reach for too many. We can and must do better by our constituents.

One tool at our disposal are the efforts by this administration to increase transparency by enforcing existing compliance law that require hospitals and health plans to make the costs of services public, as we have been discussing today.

Another tool is increasing transparency about how hospital bills patients depending on where the care is provided. I am working to introduce bipartisan legislation to give patients the peace of mind that they will pay the same amount for care, regardless of where the care is provided.

Ms. Tripoli, Families USA has supported these site-neutral payment policies because they will save consumers money. How would changing hospital billing for clinically appropriate services help lower costs for patients?

Ms. TRIPOLI. Absolutely. It is really about just reducing—eliminating an incentive in the payment, the way we reimburse for care, that drives towards higher-cost outpatient care and allows hospitals, when they acquire physician practices, to rebrand them as outpatient facilities, they then tack on a facility fee, which consumers are paying directly, thousands of dollars.

I think we have seen from a variety of different projections, from MedPAC to CBO to the Committee for Responsible Budget, significant savings, not just for the system—estimates up to $153 billion over the next decade—also would include lowering premiums and cost sharing for Medicare beneficiaries by $94 billion. And for those in the commercial market up to $466 billion.

It is a no-brainer in terms of cost savings for the American people.

Ms. KUSTER. Thank you so much. Site-neutral policies are also a tool to help strengthen the Medicare program overall.

Mr. Ippolito, your recent report, "Procompetitive Health Care Reform Options for a Divided Congress," highlighted that site-neutral payments could reduce Medicare spending. How could expanding this policy save the Federal Government and taxpayers money?

Dr. IPPOLITO. Well, I mean, the savings to taxpayers are clear. Right now, Medicare pays substantially more for care if it is delivered in one of these settings that was just discussed, the ones that are owned by hospitals, as opposed to a physician-owned facility. And so I still want to emphasize, though, there's two pieces of this. There are direct savings to Medicare. There's direct savings to the government, the taxpayer. Those are very, very important. But there are also direct savings to beneficiaries in the form of out- of-pocket spending. Coinsurance can be a percentage of the price.

So if the price, the underlying price, is higher, the coinsurance is going to be higher.

And so that is an important thing to keep in mind here, and that is a near-term benefit of these policies.

Ms. KUSTER. Well, thank you. Another aspect of lowering costs for patients is ensuring they can choose less expensive generic drugs.

I am reintroducing my bipartisan bill, Increasing Transparency in Generic Drug Applications Act of 2022. This legislation would make it easier for lower-cost generic drugs to come to market, making lifesaving prescription drugs more affordable for patients across the country. By increasing transparency in the FDA's approval process, manufacturers will be able to bring more generic drug options to pharmacies faster.

We must continue to support a competitive drug market that encourages high-quality, lower-cost drug manufacturing. With that, I look forward to working with my Energy and Commerce colleagues on these important policies that can increase transparency and lower costs for patients and taxpayers.

And I yield back.

Mr. GUTHRIE. The gentlelady yields back. We are trying to figure out who is next in line.

And next is Mr. Obernolte.

Mr. Obernolte, you are recognized for 5 minutes for questions.

Mr. OBERNOLTE. Thank you very much, Mr. Chairman. Thank you to our witnesses.

Mr. Severn, I would like to start with you. You know, we have been having this robust discussion that is—we are talking about price transparency. But really, the consequence of our inability to have price transparency is that we don't have functional, free markets for healthcare in the United States. And we have seen the consequence of that not only in a lower standard of care here but in much, much higher pricing, which I think we are all kind of incentivized here, both there and here on the dais, to try and fix. Mr. Severn, I admire the work that you have been doing trying to enhance the visibility of price data. But, I mean, if we don't have a functional healthcare market where consumers are making decisions about where to go for their healthcare based on that data, then the data doesn't do us any good, because we need those consumers to be using the data to make decisions. And when we have got a market where most if not all the costs are borne by health insurance companies, then it is not the consumers making the choices.

So I know you have been talking about—I think your exact words were "getting more skin in the game from consumers," and I wanted to tunnel down on that a little bit. So you talked about high- deductible health plans, copays. What do you think is the optimal strategy?

I mean, realistically, given where we are with the Federal Government's regulation of healthcare markets, what are the realistic next steps to getting us to—more towards a functional healthcare market?

Mr. SEVERN. Thank you for the question. I think we are starting to see a ripple effect, where this data is making its way, you know, to smaller and smaller organizations and ultimately the consumer, you know, employers, care navigators, nurse care navigation companies, and then now we are starting to see many more tech companies like Turquoise pop up and put this data right in front of the consumer.

You know, our stats is that we have got—this time a year ago we had 12,000 people a month on our site, and now we have 50,000. So as you start to see more data filter in and more companies pop up, you see better consumer experiences.

And there is one piece of the transparency in coverage law that we haven't seen many payers use yet, which is issuing rebates back and writing off those rebates against the MLR. I think we are just going to keep seeing innovation, and we are only 9 months into this data being public.

Mr. OBERNOLTE. OK. Mr. Ippolito, kind of a similar line of questioning for you, and I am particularly interested, because I know you have done a lot of thinking about this. The other countries have done this a lot more thoroughly and with a lot more innovation than we have. We spend three times as much per capita as countries like Singapore, who have allowed consumers to take a much more active role in their choices about healthcare.

So what would you think about doing what Singapore has done, in pairing high-deductible health insurance plans with, essentially, a coinsurance program where the government sets aside 100 percent of the amount for the maximum deductible for a year, and gives it to the consumer in a health savings account and says, "Look, this is your money," you know, "This will meet 100 percent of your deductible, spend it on what you want to spend it on. But by the way, it rolls over if you don't use it at the end of the year. And if you don't use it after 5 years, it rolls over into a retirement account. So it is yours. It has got your name on it."

Would that kind of a system work here, do you think?

Dr. IPPOLITO. Yes, it is sort of like a prefunded HSA, kind of, it sounds like.

I think—whenever I think of those kinds of systems, I think there is a lot of promise. And I think one of the most important parameters that I focus on is it is not just that you have liability, it is that you have liability that you understand. And so, if you were to ask me to prioritize things, I would say making sure that people actually understand the incentives they face, not just that they know they are going to get a percentage of the bill, but making it clear.

So that means using things like reference pricing, using things like networks, which are very salient to people, using things like copayments, which are very salient to people. Those kinds of things, it is not just that you have the incentive, it is that the incentive is very clear to you. And then I think that kind of arrangement has a little bit more potential, and we are likely to see the benefits.

Mr. OBERNOLTE. Sure. Well, I mean—and I understand that we are talking about transparency and consumer pricing for healthcare here. And the panel—and I know everyone is pivoting back to that.

But, I mean, you said something, Dr. Ippolito, in your testimony that resonated so much I wrote it down. You said, "ample evidence that—there is ample evidence that healthcare spending in the United States reflects economic frictions rather than consumer choice." And my point is consumer choice doesn't matter when it is not consumers making the choices.

So when you hand them an account and you say, look, this is your money, here is a card, you can access it, do with it what you want, you are in charge of your healthcare," the health insurance system is there to backstop you if you have costs "that are greater than what this account can make, can bear, but this is your money. I mean, if you look at economic studies, it is very clear that kind of consumer buy-in is what is going to be required to make our healthcare markets in the United States function again.

And let me also point out in my remaining 14 seconds that Singapore, in addition to spending about a third what the U.S. does per capita for healthcare, has the highest quality healthcare in the world by any objective measurement. So there is a lot of room for improvement for us.

But thank you very much for your testimony today. I yield back, Mr. Chairman.

Mr. GUTHRIE. The gentleman yields back, and the Chair recognizes Mr. Pence for 5 minutes.

Mr. PENCE. Thank you, Mr. Chairman, and thank the witnesses for being here today.

Hoosiers and, as my congressman—as Congressman Crenshaw is very aware—and all Americans are facing higher medical costs and fewer options for care, particularly in rural communities. Complex medical fee structures, surprise billing, and confusing coverage plans have further eroded patient trust in our healthcare system. Improving healthcare price transparency, however, would inject needed competition for healthcare facilities and ultimately lower costs for patients. This is especially needed in the Hoosier State, which consistently ranks among having some of the highest hospital prices in the country.

Across southern Indiana, rural facilities are closing at an alarming rate, as they are all across the country, lowering access to care for vulnerable communities. Lack of competition has patients with fewer alternatives to access care, particularly in rural communities across Indiana's 6th district, my district. These issues are exasperated by unsustainable workforce shortages and skyrocketing labor costs.

There have been recent efforts to improve transparency, such as the Trump-Pence administration's 2019 HHS rule requiring hospitals to disclose standard charges, as well as transparency-in-coverage requirements for health insurers. However, it is clear there is still more that needs to be done so that Hoosiers and all Americans can make the best medical decisions for themselves and their families.

Dr. Ippolito, several years ago Congress took steps to harmonize Medicare payments between various sites of care for the same services provided through a site-neutral payment model. However, the services covered under the existing policy are relatively small—are a relatively small portion of outpatient services, since almost all existing facilities are grandfathered in by the legislation.

Do we know what portion of facilities are grandfathered in under this policy, and the scope of outpatient hospital spending the current policy impacts?

Dr. IPPOLITO. Well, you are certainly right that it is a very limited policy.

I don't know the number of facilities, but I can tell you that it represents less than a percentage of Medicare's total outpatient spending. I think it is 0.8 percent of Medicare's outpatient spending. So it affects a very small share.

Mr. PENCE. OK, thanks. How would patients be impacted if the policy were to apply to a greater universe of providers and services?

Dr. IPPOLITO. Well, Medicare and commercial market patients would benefit in the long run, because it reduces the incentive to keep consolidating the provider side in the market. In the immediate term, there is an obvious benefit to Medicare beneficiaries in the form of lower out-of-pocket spending. Their out-of-pocket is often a function of the price of the service. And if that price goes down, their out-of-pocket goes down.

Mr. PENCE. So it might be a good idea?

Dr. IPPOLITO. Well, I think so. But, you know, nobody voted for me, so——

Mr. PENCE. All right, thank you. And Mr. Chair, I yield back.

Mr. GUTHRIE. The gentleman yields back. The Chair now recognizes Mr. Crenshaw for 5 minutes for the purpose of asking questions.

Mr. CRENSHAW. Thank you to the Chair. Thank you to my friend from Indiana. I counted three mentions of Hoosiers.

[Laughter.]

Mr. CRENSHAW. It is a thing. All right.

So thank you all for being here. I appreciate your patience with us.

You know, I want to start out by saying, you know, let's frame this problem. So everybody needs healthcare. We can debate whether or not it is a right, per se, but everybody needs it, and we all agree that it is too expensive and that our payment system is largely to blame. It is not operating like a proper marketplace.

We have a couple of things that we want in our system. We want to increase quality. We want to maintain our innovative edge. We are one of the few countries that still maintains these promises of quality, but we want it to be cheaper and accessible. OK.

And now, I would articulate that the only forces that really drive down prices while also maintaining an innovative edge and quality are choice, competition, transparency. And that is what we are here to talk about today.

The complexity of healthcare makes transparency a really difficult problem. It is not like going to the grocery store. And so I would encourage this committee to focus on the entry point that everybody faces in healthcare, and that should be our legislative entry point, and that is primary care and what we can do to make primary care more accessible and easier for the patient, because that is your quarterback.

That is—that should be the person you use to navigate the rest of the immensely complex healthcare system. You can give me all the spreadsheets in the world on price transparency. I still can't figure it out. And I am a pretty experienced patient, OK? It is just—it is so complex.

And so I want to talk about primary care, and my favorite type of primary care, direct primary care, with you, Dr. Ippolito, if that is all right. A lot of the conversation today is about the traditional care model, where we have patients interacting with primary care providers, specialty care providers in different clinical settings, all of that. It is complex. It is overwhelming. Can you talk about how personalized care models like direct primary care can play in creating a wider, more competitive healthcare marketplace?

I guess I should define what I am talking about really quick, which is effectively a monthly fee for a primary care doctor, which is all inclusive. It doesn't matter how many visits you have, it is independent of insurance. It is essentially a subscription service for healthcare. And in the Houston area we are talking 60 to 70 bucks a month.

Dr. IPPOLITO. I mean, yes. So to echo a point I made earlier, given what we see in the healthcare market, we ought to be encouraging just about any kind of competition we can get. And so I think that is sort of the baseline.

When I think about direct primary care, you know, honestly, it fits pretty well within what you might think of as a sort of optimal insurance design if you were starting from scratch. That is, you really focus insurance on protecting people in the catastrophic situations, but then you try and have competition under a more normal pricing structure for more regular services. And I think that is— at least conceptually, that is what a lot of direct primary care seems to be trying to get at.

Mr. CRENSHAW. Do you think it could have a positive effect on overall healthcare spending?

Dr. IPPOLITO. You know, it is always tough with spending. I guess I will say two things.

The first is that, at least as I understand these models, they are often a capitated approach. Capitated payments do have really good incentives, right? So that is a good thing.

The second point, though, is that, when you think about primary care, it is often difficult to evaluate that on pure cost savings, because part of what you are doing is you are giving people access to care that they might need, right? And a lot of that care is really high value. Getting somebody on an antihypertensive or a statin is a really big ROI.

And so I don't know that I would emphasize pure cost savings. Instead, what I would do is say it is—there is a potential to really get more efficient spending, right?

Mr. CRENSHAW. Yes.

Dr. IPPOLITO. Especially——

Mr. CRENSHAW. Well, certainly because you are keeping people out of the emergency room, and what our goal should be, this continuity of care. Our goal should be every American knows who their primary care doctor is. That is definitely not the case right now. You think, like, do I call my—if you have a problem, do you— do I call my insurance? Do I just go to the ER? Nobody knows what to do. You need a quarterback.

All right, and I got 54 seconds. So Mr. Severn, could you talk to us about—you get all this data, you guys have all this experience gathering this data. Can you talk about what we should do to make it more transparent and readable to the consumer, so we can actually translate it?

Mr. SEVERN. We have talked about the hospital standard that, you know, is suggested right now, and I think we have pretty unanimously said we would love that standard to be enforced. And that does make these spreadsheets a little bit more apples-to-apples comparable.

It also—you know, I mentioned this a bit earlier—it has got a column that says "payment method." And there is a spectrum of complexity to these payment methods. And what you will find is not just price pressure, but you reward simpler payment methods. So I will go to the doctor that can say, hey, it is $50 up front versus some sliding fee or percent of charge.

Mr. CRENSHAW. OK. Thank you, and I yield back.

Mr. GUTHRIE. The gentleman yields back. The Chair now yields to Dr. Miller-Meeks for 5 minutes for the purpose of asking questions.

Mrs. MILLER-MEEKS. Thank you, Mr. Chair, and I thank all our witnesses who are here. It is a fascinating discussion. I could certainly ask questions for more than 5 minutes.

As an ophthalmologist, I moved our small three ophthalmology practices to have a cash-based payment and a discount for paying cash because it was simpler for patients than trying to navigate through their insurance company.

And I think it is interesting, as we talk about consolidation and competition and PBMs, that, you know, one of the biggest errors was in the establishment of Medicare, Medicare having different reimbursement for different States rather than a single reimbursement for a single procedure or a single visit, which would—then would have led to competition and medical tourism throughout the United States.

And in 2010, when the Affordable Care Act was being implemented, myself and many other individuals warned that prices would go up, that premiums would go up with the passage of the Affordable Care Act. We especially were concerned about consolidation, hospital-to-hospital consolidation, physician practices becoming larger physician practices or being purchased by hospitals, and that—we warned at that time that those procedures and things being done in doctor's offices would then move to hospital-based clinics, and the prices would go up.

And it is not just the price goes up. As Dr. Ippolito said, the patient's cost share is also much greater. So their out-of-pocket cost is also greater.

So consolidation increases healthcare prices and insurance premiums as well as worsens equal access for care to patients in rural communities and medically underserved communities. And why is that? Because consolidation threatens competition. It doesn't matter if you have price transparency if there is no competition. So as you drive out competition, the value of price transparency in certain areas decreases.

You know, we have seen an increasing number of physician groups get absorbed by health systems, such as the recent purchase of Oak Street Health by CVS and more physicians working in integrated groups and more Medicare beneficiaries being directly affected by the high cost of integration. For example, the numbers of diagnostic and imaging lab tests being performed in a hospital has increased dramatically. We are pushed as physicians within a hospital to do things within the hospital, and this has led to Medicare incurring tens of millions of dollars of unnecessary costs, as was pointed out.

And one of the things we talked about is the payment reform— or payment reform that we think Congress should consider, which is site neutrality. And what other things could we encourage providers to remain—other things to do to remain—providers to be independent, which could help with competition, Dr. Ippolito?

Dr. IPPOLITO. I am sorry. Could you repeat the last part of that?

Mrs. MILLER-MEEKS. What other things can we do, payment reforms can we do, to encourage both, you know, physicians——

Dr. IPPOLITO. Sure.

Mrs. MILLER-MEEKS [continuing]. To remain independent, site neutrality being one of those.

Dr. IPPOLITO. Sure. So, you know, think about any payment policy that pushes in the direction of consolidation. So site-neutral, making sure 340B doesn't push too far in that direction. That is one.

At the State—while there are State policies the Federal Government could, in principle, have effects on, things like certificate of need, which some States still do have—we have tons of evidence on that at this point—we can talk about things like scope of practice.

Especially when you talk about rural areas, the natural level of competition that is going to be supported is going to be lower. And so you have really got to push everywhere you can. You have got to think about where can we realistically harness telehealth, right? Certain areas, mental health, things like that, you have a lot of opportunity to use that.

But still, you know, at the end of the day, I think about the U.S. healthcare system in sort of three buckets. There's the really competitive markets, big cities; there's the plausibly competitive markets, a lot of midsized cities that may have one big, big provider; and then you have got rural areas. And you just do need to recognize that rural areas are a little bit different and be open to being a little bit more creative in those settings.

Mrs. MILLER-MEEKS. Thank you so much for that answer. And we have talked some about PBMs, and as a State senator in 2019 I put forward a bill in Iowa for transparency within the PBM and for the rebates, half of the rebate to go back to the person paying for the drugs. I got it through the Senate, but not the rebate part, the transparency part. We finally did not get it through the House that year, but we finally did. But 3 years later, we still don't have the transparency data coming forward, which we are finally getting to come forward.

And as you all know, the three largest PBMs—CVS Caremark, Express Scripts, and OptumRx—manage about 80 percent of all prescriptions in the United States, up from 48 percent a decade ago. And, you know, this is very pivotal in how we make decisions. We have—one of the PBM tactics—and I won't talk about all of them, but it is something that Representative Carter and I have worked on—is the growing practice of misappropriating patient assistance dollars for the benefit of the PBM's bottom line. A middle-man places increasing cost on patients by relying more on coinsurance and deductibles, copay assistance, an important bridge to ensure access to needed medications.

So Ms. Bartlett, what financial burdens do accumulators place on patients when copay assistance maximum is reached?

[No response.]

Mrs. MILLER-MEEKS. I may have to use—have you submit that in writing, because my time is——

Mr. BARTLETT. I definitely will.

Mrs. MILLER-MEEKS [continuing]. Expired, so——

Mr. BARTLETT. I definitely will. I got the question.

Mrs. MILLER-MEEKS. So if you would submit that in writing, I would thank you.

Thank you, Mr. Chair. I yield back.

Mr. GUTHRIE. Thank you. I thank the gentlelady for yielding back. We have now completed—the Members who are—of the committee—we have three that waived on, two that are present. So we—it looks like we have two more witnesses, so thank you all for your patience, and we will now go to our members of the full committee that are meeting here with us today, and the first will be Ms. Matsui from California.

You are recognized for 5 minutes.

Ms. MATSUI. Thank you very much, Mr. Chairman and Ranking Member Eshoo, for having this very important hearing today and allowing me to waive on. And thank you for the witnesses for being here today. I want to ask Mr. Forge a question.

I would like to briefly discuss the 340B program, which I know has been discussed here. But as many of my colleagues know, I have long been a champion of the 340B program, which is a critical part of the healthcare safety net that all our constituents depend on.

Unfortunately, there has been a lot of criticisms about this program lately, and I am concerned about some of the conversation around 340B happening today, which is why I felt compelled to waive on. 340B is, first and foremost, a program to provide discounted drugs to low-income patients. But some of the critics of this program seem to forget that 340B has another critical purpose: to help safety-net providers to provide critical services to under- served patients and to empower them to stay open, especially after the strains of the past few years.

Mr. Forge, can you share some of the programs or services Pullman Regional is able to offer because of your 340B discounts?

And what would happen if the hospital is no longer able to participate in the 340B program?

Mr. FORGE. Well, I want to answer you in a couple of different ways.

You know, first of all, it impacts more than just Pullman Regional Hospital. You know, there are local pharmacies who we contract with, which are really lifelines for small communities, you know, that they are serving. Colfax, Washington, is one that comes to mind.

You know, we are working in rural areas on 2 to 4 percent margins, you know, really tight margins. And so, you know, maintaining access to high-quality, board-certified physicians in our emergency room, for example, you know, making sure that, you know, we have 24-hour access to obstetric care, et cetera.

You know, 2 to 4 percent is not a lot, you know, it doesn't go a long ways. And so 340B, without that, you know, we would most likely have to cut some critical services to our service area as well as lose some lifeblood providers to our communities.

Ms. MATSUI. Oh, absolutely. Now, you mentioned pharmacies. One way that PhRMA and other 340B critics have attempted to chip away at the program is by restricting entities from using co tract pharmacies.

Mr. Forge, I know that Pullman Regional has relationships with several contract pharmacies to help you distribute your discounted drugs. Can you share why it is so important to your hospital and the patients you serve to use contract pharmacies?

Mr. FORGE. Well, you know, I have to say that we have had positive and negative experiences with contract pharmacies, and the most positive ones have been with the community-based, you know, pharmacies. So I kind of want to stick with that. You know, we haven't always had positive ones, but they are—and the reason why there is one better than the other, it really comes down to the service and—the customer service that goes back to the patient, goes back to the people that live in the community.

Ms. MATSUI. Certainly.

Mr. FORGE. You lose that a little bit with some of those bigger ones.

Ms. MATSUI. Certainly, yes. I have another question for you regarding transparency around 340B.

Some of the latest proposals on 340B reform have suggested a need for greater accountability. Mr. Forge, can you briefly describe the requirements your hospital already faces when it comes to submitting data to HRSA and maintaining records documenting compliance with 340B requirements?

Mr. FORGE. Sure. You know, I will talk, you know, back to my experiences. I have worked in multiple rural communities in critical access areas.

Some of the hospitals that I worked with were not able to meet the regulatory standards because of the high bar that they have, you know, within 340B. And therefore, those communities—in very rural Idaho, for example—weren't able to benefit from those.

You know, in other areas we had a little more expertise on our team. We were able to kind of pull that off in Wisconsin. And now, you know, back in Pullman, we are still figuring it out. We have to rely on outside resources to help us manage the 340B thing. That just tells you how complicated that it really is. We have multiple audits per year that really stress our team outside of normal operations—our finance teams, that is.

And so it is a standard that we are continuing to strive to do. We take it seriously. We want to be accountable to that. But that becomes more and more difficult as we go, and more complexity keeps being added.

Ms. MATSUI. Absolutely. You know, I understand, you know, but I am concerned about proposals that unnecessarily burden you. You have already gone through all of that.

I really appreciate the reminder of the importance of this program. I think we all agree that it is very important, and I don't want this program to be a scapegoat of high drug pricing and other problems that we know exist with our healthcare system. So I really do appreciate this committee bringing this up today, and I would really like to strengthen 340B and make sure it is there for the right reasons.

So thank you very much, and I yield back.

Mr. GUTHRIE. Thank you. The gentlelady yields back, and next will be Mr. Allen.

You are recognized for 5 minutes.

Mr. ALLEN. Thank you, Mr. Chairman, and thanks for waiving me on.

To give you a little background about why I am very interested in this is—and I want to thank the witnesses for staying with us and talking about this important issue. But back from 1991 to 2000—of course, I was running a construction business back then— and about 80 percent of our work was healthcare. And in fact, one of my clients asked me to serve as chairman of the hospital board, and I did that for—from 1991 to 2000.

And it was pretty interesting, how things evolved, because in the construction business you got to know what your costs are or you are not going to be in business very long. And what I learned about hospital accounting is—and one of the things we worked on—is we really didn't know what it cost us to do business. We knew that we charged a dollar, that at that time Medicare was paying about 60 cents on the dollar. And the insurance companies started—you know, they at one time were at $1. Of course, we had a functional free market healthcare system back then, and then they dropped below Medicare.

So I said we better figure out what our cost is here, or we are going to be out of business real quick. And unfortunately, that hospital is consolidated now, along with two other hospitals, and we have no locally owned or operated hospitals in my hometown of Augusta, Georgia.

And, you know, the—I was also asked to, as the ranking member on the Health, Employment, Labor, and Pensions Subcommittee over at Education and Workforce, which covers about 160 million lives all year, ERISA, healthcare, and I was—I was asked to serve on the Healthy Future Task Force Subcommittee.

And again, my question to all the experts—and we had some great testimony from folks talking to us about where healthcare is and what we got to do as far as affordability is concerned, but not one could tell me where our healthcare dollars are going. Not a single one. In fact, they said it was impossible. And I think it is because we don't have a functional free market system to compare anything to.

And so I said, "How do we peel the onion back here?" And—because we got tax dollars going into this, we got premium dollars going into this. And guess what? You know, we are—I was in Israel. Eight percent of their GDP, healthcare. Nobody complained about their healthcare system. And I have a hard time finding folks that are happy with the healthcare system, you know, with their healthcare or the providers happy with healthcare in this country. But, Ms. Tripoli, your organization advocates for patients. And so what is the most single important thing to make sure that patients know about how their healthcare dollars are being spent?

Ms. TRIPOLI. Well, I think you really nailed it, which is there has been an incredible shift over the last 60 years. Hospitals that used to be these community-based institutions have emerged into these megacost centers, and communities have watched their local hospitals disappear. It is a major problem. It is the number-one driver—it is one of the biggest drivers of unaffordable care in the form of higher prices.

So I think, for consumers, it is knowing that, it is knowing that their local hospital doesn't exist anymore. And so we need to think about the types of solutions that we can implement that are going to bring down the cost of care for the American people. It is the very solutions we are talking about today in terms of strengthening price transparency, codifying that rule——

Mr. ALLEN. Exactly, yes.

Ms. TRIPOLI [continuing]. Expanding site-neutral payments.

Mr. ALLEN. Yes, right. Well, good, thank you.

Mr. Severn, we—as part of the Healthy Future Task Force we had several companies—and Walmart is involved in what is called direct contracting for healthcare. Could you—and of course, obviously, they are doing it and our business community is going to figure this out, but we are going to have to have a functioning free market healthcare system to do it, because the government is driving everything right now.

But they have been able to use direct contracting to personalize care for their employees. Mr. Severn, can you comment on and tell us about your experience with direct contracting?

Mr. SEVERN. Prior to this transparency data being published in 2021, direct contracting was really only possible for large employers that could act as payers. They could pay the consultants, they could buy the data sets. With this new transparency data public, the barrier to direct contracting goes down, and so we will see more companies much smaller than Walmart have the ability to enter into direct contracts with providers, just based off the available——

Mr. ALLEN. Yes. And one of the things we wanted to do in our committee was to allow companies to form co-ops to do this, that they could then have the influence of a large contractor.

Listen, you all been great. Thank you so much for your testimony.

And thank you, Mr. Chairman, again.

Mr. GUTHRIE. Thank you.

Mr. ALLEN. I yield back.

Mr. GUTHRIE. I thank the gentleman for yielding, and we do have one more. We have Mr. Balderson from Ohio, who is waiving on for the hearing for 5 minutes.

You are recognized for 5 minutes for questions.

Mr. BALDERSON. Thank you, Mr. Chairman, I appreciate the waiver, and thank you all for hanging in there today. I will be brief.

Mr. Severn, from your experience with your patient-facing transparency tool, do you agree that, when provided accurate pricing data, patients make informed judgments on where they want to receive care?

Mr. SEVERN. The short answer is patients are just starting to learn that this data is there. And we are very early in seeing patients use this data. The best way to present the data is something simple, a consumer experience like we see elsewhere on Amazon or other e-commerce sites. Once that is possible on Turquoise and other sites, to say "this is the upfront cost, this is the only bill you are going to get," we will see a huge consumer uptake here. But we are just starting to see this at Turquoise.

Mr. BALDERSON. I agree. Unfortunately, CMS disagrees with you, since it denied an innovative health plan by claiming it is, and I quote, "not reasonable to expect prospective enrollees to understand" a new, unique plan.

Last year I wrote a letter, a bipartisan letter, to CMS in support of increasing access to innovative health plans that already are providing price transparency for patients. These plans are similar, somewhat similar, to the ones used in Montana by Ms. Bartlett, as they offer set reimbursement for anything you can do in the healthcare system. This allows consumers to shop for care and receive information about their cost obligations at any given provider—not just any given provider in their network, any given provider, period.

But what Mr. Severn is saying is that the consumers can and do have the ability to shop for value. As we increase the level of price transparency in our healthcare system, it is important to ensure that the entire system keeps up, and lessons learned in one place are applied to others to maximize their benefits for patients.

Mr. Forge, I myself come from rural Ohio, in Ohio's 12th congressional district, but I also have central Ohio, which has some of the big healthcare systems. Just like yours, though, the smaller one serves smaller communities. No one wants to be more punitive to the small community hospitals that are already stretched thin and trying to serve their patients, but we all agree that price transparency is important.

How do we work with these hospitals to make sure their price transparency experience is a positive one for the hospital and patients?

Mr. FORGE. Well, good question. I appreciate it.

Mr. BALDERSON. Thank you.

Mr. FORGE. I think, though, the first step is just recognizing that they need the help, right, recognizing that we need—you know, we need support, and making sure that it is a good experience.

But I think it comes back down to, you know, really thinking about those families and those individuals, and really helping those people with their medical literacy, helping them, you know, access programs like Mr. Severn here, and helping people access, you know, what people and the—that have bigger resources and bigger health systems have access to.

So it is recognizing it, you know, removing barriers, and continuing to focus on improving.

Mr. BALDERSON. OK. Thank you. My last question, Mr. Severn is for you again, I apologize.

Starting this year, insurers were required to provide personalized pricing information for 500 items and services to their enrollees. Have you tracked insurer compliance with this aspect of the rule?

Mr. SEVERN. We don't track insurer compliance with that aspect. We just look at the machine-readable file, the second piece of the requirement. That is what we track.

Mr. BALDERSON. How is it working?

Mr. SEVERN. You know, the stat we shared is 96 percent of covered lives are represented in the data across 181 payers as of today, which is much quicker than the hospital compliance—

Mr. BALDERSON. Yes, it is. Thank you.

Mr. Chairman, I yield back, and I thank you all again.

Mr. GUTHRIE. Thank you.

The gentleman yields back. Seeing no further witnesses, that concludes witness questions.

Thank you all so much for being here. I know it has been a long afternoon, but I know you are passionate about these issues as bipartisan. We are, as well, and look forward to making this the first of many efforts to get to the point where we are going to have transparency in the healthcare system, so that people can—we need healthcare systems to be—to exist, so they are going to need to do what they need to do—exist—but we also need information so people can make fair choices. So we are looking forward to that, moving forward.

I do have a list that I have shared with the ranking member of documents for the record from the majority and the minority. Any objection?

Without objection.

Ms. ESHOO. No objection, Mr. Chairman.

Mr. GUTHRIE. No objection, so it is so ordered.

[The documents appear at the conclusion of the hearing.[148]]

---

[148] The list of accepted documents has been retained in committee files and is included in the Documents for the Record at https://docs.house.gov/meetings/IF/IF14/20230328/115581/HHRG- 118-IF14-20230328-SD003.pdf.

Mr. GUTHRIE. And then I want to remind the Members they have 10 business days to submit questions for the record. And I ask the witnesses to respond to the questions promptly. Members should submit their questions by the close of business on April the 11th.

And without objection, the subcommittee is adjourned. [Whereupon, at 4:32 p.m., the subcommittee was adjourned.] [Material submitted for inclusion in the record follows:]

PATIENT RIGHTS ADVOCATE.ORG

1188 Centre Street
Newton, MA 02459

March 27, 2023

The Honorable Cathy McMorris Rodgers
Chair, Committee on Energy & Commerce
2125 Rayburn House Office Building
Washington, DC 20515

The Honorable Brett Guthrie
Chair, Health Subcommittee
2434 Rayburn House Office Building
Washington, D.C. 20515

The Honorable Frank Pallone, Jr.
The Honorable Frank Pallone, Jr.
2322 Rayburn House Office Building
Washington, DC 20515

The Honorable Anna Eshoo
Ranking Member, Health Subcommittee
272 Cannon House Office Building
Washington, DC 20515

Dear Chair McMorris Rodgers, Ranking Member Pallone, Chair Guthrie, and Ranking Member Eshoo:

In advance of tomorrow's hearing, Lowering Unaffordable Costs: Examining Transparency and Competition in Health Care, we wanted to share with you that the widespread noncompliance of hospitals with the federal Hospital Price Transparency Rule[149]1 (the "Rule") continues to be of great concern to both policy makers and American consumers.

[149] 45 CFR subtitle E, part 180, accessed February 13, 2023. https://www.federalregister.gov/documents/2019/11/27/2019-24931/medicare-and-medicaid-programs-cy-2020-hospital-outpatient-ppspolicy-changes-and-payment-ratesand#p-1010.

In light of the investigation of CMS enforcement practices announced in September 2022 by the HHS Office of Inspector General[150]2 and the call last November on behalf of the Committee on Energy and Commerce for the Government Accountability Office (GAO) to similarly investigate the Centers for Medicare and Medicaid Services (CMS), we are providing a timely update on recent research relating to compliance with the Rule.

PatientRightsAdvocate.org Independently Validated Report

- February 13, 2023: The PatientRightsAdvocate.org Fourth Semi-Annual Hospital Price Transparency Compliance Report[151] found that only 24.5% of 2,000 hospitals of the nations' largest hospital systems were fully compliant with the Rule, more than two years after the Rule took effect.

Independent, Peer-Reviewed Academic Research. Academic research published as recently as January 2023 sheds light on current poor compliance with the Rule and the urgent need for stronger enforcement actions:

- January 27, 2023: The Journal of General Internal Medicine reported that 35.9% of hospitals were in compliance[152] in the most recent time period examined in the study.
- January 17, 2023: The Journal of General Internal Medicine reported that only 19% of hospitals were in compliance.[153]
- January 5, 2023: JAMA Network Open noted the increase in penalties imposed by CMS one year after the Rule took effect, stated, "Despite the steeper penalties, the compliance rate remains low."[154]
- June 7, 2022: The Journal of the American Medical Association reported that only 5.7% of hospitals had both an adherent machine-readable file and an adherent shoppable display as required by the Rule, based on a review of 5,239 hospitals.[155]

Thank you again for your continued effort on this critical issue. We hope that any future updates on the status of compliance from a variety of independent sources will better inform the Committee's work.

---

150 https://oig.hhs.gov/reports-and-publications/workplan/summary/wp-summary-0000728.asp.

151 https://www.patientrightsadvocate.org/february-semi-annual-compliance-report-2023.

152 Henderson, M., Mouslim, M. Assessing Compliance with Hospital Price Transparency over Time. J GEN INTERN MED (2023). https://doi.org/10.1007/s11606-022-08020-3.

153 Loccoh EC, Khera R, van Meijgaard J, Marsh T, Warraich HJ. *Hospital Adherence to the Federal Price Transparency Mandate: Results from a Nationally Representative Sample*. J Gen Intern Med. 2023 Jan 17. doi: 10.1007/s11606-023- 08039-0. Epub ahead of print. PMID: 36650327.

154 Jiang JX, Krishnan R, Bai G. *Price Transparency in Hospitals—Current Research and Future Directions*. JAMA Netw Open. 2023;6(1):e2249588. doi:10.1001/jamanetworkopen.2022.49588.

155 Haque W, Ahmadzada M, Janumpally S, et al. *Adherence to a Federal Hospital Price Transparency Rule and Associated Financial and Marketplace Factors*. JAMA. 2022;327(21):2143–2145. doi:10.1001/jama.2022.5363.

Warmest Regards,

Cynthia A. Fisher Founder and Chairman
PatientRightsAdvocate.org

AAFP
AMERICAN ACADEMY OF FAMILY PHYSICIANS

March 28, 2023

The Honorable Brett Guthrie
Chairman
Health Subcommittee, House Committee on Energy & Commerce
U.S. House of Representatives 2125 Rayburn House Office Building
Washington, D.C. 20515

The Honorable Anna Eshoo Ranking Member
Health Subcommittee, House Committee on Energy & Commerce
U.S. House of Representatives 2125 Rayburn House Office Building
Washington, D.C. 20515

Dear Chairman Guthrie and Ranking Member Eshoo:

On behalf of the American Academy of Family Physicians (AAFP), representing more than 129,600 family physicians and medical students across the country, I write to express our appreciation for the Committee holding today's hearing on health care costs, titled "Lowering Unaffordable Costs: Examining Transparency and Competition in Health Care." The AAFP shares your commitment to making health care in the United States more accessible and affordable, and we write to offer our policy recommendations from the family medicine perspective.

The AAFP strongly believes that all individuals have a right to access timely, high quality, and affordable essential health care services, including comprehensive primary care. Family medicine and primary care are the only entities charged with longitudinal continuity of care for the whole patient.

The patient and primary care physician relationship and its comprehensiveness have the greatest effect on health care outcomes and costs over the long term, with evidence suggesting that improving affordable access to primary care improves health outcomes. Mortality rates are lower in regions with more primary care physicians – for every 10 additional primary doctors per 100,000 people, life expectancy increases by 51.5 days.[156] However, the current United States health care system fails to deliver comprehensive primary care because of the way primary care has been, and is currently, funded.

Every day, family physicians encounter patients who struggle to make ends meet, and the escalating costs of health care have led many patients to delay or forgo needed care. The Academy has long advocated to Congress in support of policies that will strengthen our nation's investment in primary care and improve patients' access to affordable health care. To meaningfully address health care costs through the lens of transparency and competition, *Congress must assess an array of policy areas including physician reimbursement, implementation of the No Surprises Act, and anti- competitive contracting practices.*

Physician Payment Reform

Independently practicing physicians need an environment that allows them to thrive, but the continuing consolidation of insurers and large health systems threatens their long-term viability. Consolidation increases health care prices and insurance premiums, as well as worsens equitable access to care for patients in rural and other medically underserved communities.[157,158] Congress should promote payment methods that boost competition in the marketplace and create greater choice for patients.

Despite evidence indicating that additional investments in primary care would improve population health and advance health equity, primary care has been historically underfunded in the U.S. Medicare and Medicaid have historically undervalued primary care. In the short-term, inadequate payment rates mean that primary care physicians lack the resources needed to provide comprehensive, continuous care for their patients and may be forced to accept fewer Medicare or Medicaid patients. In the long-run, payment distortions between primary and specialty care will continue to drive more physicians to go into higher paid specialties, worsening the maldistribution of the physician workforce. A recent Medicare Payment Advisory Commission (MedPAC) analysis highlighted that the median compensation remains much lower for primary care physicians than for physicians in certain other specialties, such as

[156] Basu S, Berkowitz SA, Phillips RL, Bitton A, Landon BE, Phillips RS. Association of Primary Care Physician Supply with Population Mortality in the United States, 2005-2015. JAMA Intern Med. 2019;179(4):506–514. doi:10.1001/jamainternmed.2018.7624.

[157] Yerramilli P, May FP, Kerry VB. Reducing Health Disparities Requires Financing People-Centered Primary Care. JAMA Health Forum. 2021;2(2):e201573. Available at: https://jamanetwork.com/journals/jama-health-forum/articleabstract/2776056.

[158] O'Hanlon CE, et al. Access, Quality, and Financial Performance of Rural Hospitals Following Health System Affiliation. December 2019. Health Affairs. Available at: https://www.healthaffairs.org/doi/full/10.1377/hlthaff.2019.00918.

radiology and surgical specialties – underscoring concerns about the mispricing of fee schedule services and its impact on the primary care pipeline.[159]

Medicare's current physician payment system is undermining physicians' ability to provide high quality, comprehensive care – particularly in primary care. Statutory budget-neutrality requirements and the lack of annual payment updates to account for inflation will, without intervention from Congress, continue to hurt physician practices and undermine patient care. In October, the Academy submitted robust recommendations to Congress on ways to reform the Medicare Access and CHIP Reauthorization Act (MACRA) to address challenges affecting our members and their patients. *We urge Congress to pass legislation to provide for an annual update to the Medicare Physician Fee based on the Medicare Economic Index (MEI) to ensure that payment rates keep pace with rising practice costs, enabling practices to keep their doors open.*

The AAFP also supports site neutral payment policies that would establish payment parity across care settings and has called for an expansion of site neutrality to all on-campus and off-campus hospital-based departments, as well as other facilities. We support reducing payment differences between sites of service since it enables patients to make more informed healthcare decisions by making costs more transparent. Payment parity also encourages patient choice based on quality rather than cost. It is the AAFP's policy that patients should have reasonable freedom to select their physicians, other providers, and healthcare settings. Importantly, whenever making a choice, patients and caregivers must be well-informed on the options available and possible effects of, and responsibilities involved with, each option. *Therefore, Congress should build upon past efforts to increase site neutrality and avoid any pressures to reverse these critical changes.*

Additionally, the Academy strongly supports the Centers for Medicare and Medicaid Services (CMS) proposal to implement a new add-on code for complex evaluation and management (E/M) visits: G2211. The G2211 code recognizes the inherent complexity of primary care office visits and provides commensurate Medicare reimbursement. We were disappointed that Congress elected to delay implementation of that code, and *we urge Congress to support full implementation of G2211 in the CY 2024 Medicare physician fee schedule.*

Congress must also act to bolster the primary care physician pipeline by enacting Medicaid payment parity. On average Medicaid, pays just 66 percent of the Medicare rate for primary care services and can be as low as 33 percent in some states.[160] This severely reduces the number of physicians who participate in Medicaid and limits access to health care for children and families. Increasing Medicaid payment rates will improve access to care for Medicaid patients, lead to better health outcomes, and reduce longstanding health disparities. *The AAFP urges Congress to pass the Kids' Access to Primary Care Act of 2023 (H.R. 952) to permanently raise Medicaid payment rates for primary care services to at least Medicare levels.*

---

[159] Medicare Payment Advisory Commission. (2021, March). Chapter 4 -Physician and other health professional services. Retrieved February 10, 2023, from https://www.medpac.gov/wpcontent/uploads/2021/10/ mar21_ medpac_report_ch4_sec.pdf.

[160] 7 Zuckerman, S., Skopec, L., & Aarons, J. (2021, February 01). Medicaid physician fees remained substantially Below fees paid by Medicare in 2019. Retrieved February 9, 2023, from https://www.healthaffairs. org/doi/abs/10.1377/hlthaff.2020.00611.

Price Transparency and Implementation of the No Surprises Act

As acknowledged above, the AAFP recognizes the value of transparency in health care, defined as reporting information that can be easily verified for accuracy. True transparency would provide accurate and meaningful information to patients, physicians and other stakeholders and improve quality at the point of care. To that end, the AAFP is supportive of ending surprise medical bills for patients and has long supported federal policies promoting price transparency and health care affordability. These policies improve data collection and enable patients and their health care teams to compare prices across facilities and insurers. As our members seek opportunities to enter into value-based care arrangements, it is critical they have access to information on provider's costs and quality performance to ensure they make informed decisions with their patients when making referrals.

However, the No Surprises Act (NSA) focuses on unanticipated medical bills from air ambulance providers, hospitals, emergency departments, and out of network clinicians and facilities. Congress did not intend for the NSA to impose burdensome regulatory requirements on primary care practices, who typically are in-network, provide high-value care to patients who have chosen to see them, and are already overburdened with administrative tasks. The AAFP has repeatedly shared *concerns* regarding regulatory implementation of the advanced explanation of benefits (AEOB) and good faith estimate (GFE) requirements of the NSA. The Department of Health and Human Services (HHS), Treasury, and Labor deferred enforcement of the AEOB requirement for patients with health insurance coverage, given several complex issues related to implementation and enforcement. The AAFP strongly *supported* this delay. The statute also requires that clinicians and facilities provide GFEs directly to uninsured or self-pay patients seeking to schedule a service. The GFE regulations are currently in effect and the AAFP has consistently shared concerns with the burden of implementing GFEs for uninsured and self-pay patients.

While we appreciate HHS guidance clarifying expectations for physicians, other clinicians, and facilities providing GFEs, family physicians continue to report that the GFE requirements are overly burdensome. Given that most primary care patients will opt to submit claims to their insurance provider for their care, the AAFP is deeply concerned that, once implemented, the AEOB requirements will add a much greater level of administrative burden and further diminish staff time devoted to caring for patients. Congress should urge the Departments to minimize new administrative requirements on primary care practices, given that they did not intend to target in-network, high-value primary care services with the passage of the NSA.

In addition to being inconsistent with the spirit of the NSA, AEOB requirements for primary care are likely to lead to confusion and frustration for patients. Primary care practices are typically patients' first point of contact within the health care system. Often, patients schedule appointments with their primary care physician due to the onset of new or worsening symptoms and the physician evaluates the patient to determine next steps. Before seeing the patient, it will be incredibly challenging for the practice to make a reasonable determination about the patients' condition or the resulting tests, treatments, referrals, or other services that may be needed. Requiring practices to generate the GFE will force them to guess, which will result in an inaccurate or irrelevant AEOB being sent to the patient, undermining the overall goal of the AEOB requirements.

Furthermore, the AAFP *supports* policies such the Medical Loss Ratio (MLR) requirements on health plans offering coverage in the individual market, which requires they submit data on the proportion of premium revenues spent on clinical services and quality improvement. This helps ensure health care resources are focused on patient care rather than insurer profits or administrative expense. These federal policies have helped advance affordability and improve equitable access to comprehensive health care coverage in the individual market.

Stop Anti-Competitive Contracting Practices that Harm Clinicians and Patients

The AAFP has long called for antitrust relief for physicians and advocates for legislation that would remove antiquated collective negotiation restrictions. Federal antitrust laws enforced by the Federal Trade Commission (FTC) prevent physicians from engaging in collective negotiation with insurers that are exempt from antitrust laws. Many of these statutes, originally intended to protect consumers from anticompetitive behavior, are increasingly ill-suited to today's rapidly changing health care workforce and marketplace.

The health insurance industry continues to be exempt from antitrust regulation — policy that stifles competition and blocks improvements to the nation's health care system. The AAFP calls on Congress to investigate the long-term consequences of health insurance market consolidation and supports legislation easing FTC restrictions on primary care physicians' contract negotiations. Family physicians should be able to work with third-party payers and negotiate contracts on a level playing field.

Congress should also prohibit the use of noncompete agreements in physician contracts. Noncompete agreements in health care impede patient access to physicians, deter advocacy for patient safety, limit physicians' ability to choose their employer, and stifle competition. Despite projected physician shortages, many health care employers still intentionally restrict physician mobility and workforce participation via noncompete agreements. Currently, noncompete agreements are enforced through a patchwork of state laws. Twelve states deem noncompete agreements unenforceable and against public policy; however public awareness of these laws remains low, and employers still intimidate employees with the threat of legal action. Thirty-eight states allow noncompete agreements in some form, judging enforceability on factors including job type, legitimacy of business interests, and reasonableness of duration, scope, and distance. Family physicians from across the country have expressed deep concerns about how noncompete agreements are forcing them to remain in undesirable employment situations which harm their financial and mental health or abandon their patients and travel long-distances or uproot their families to practice in a new geographic area. The AAFP urges Congress to pass legislation to ban noncompete clauses in physician employment contracts to ensure patients have access to their physicians and to allow physicians to freely practice medicine in their communities.

Thank you for the opportunity to offer these recommendations on ways to address health care costs and improve affordability. The AAFP looks forward to working with the Committee on policies that support primary care physicians and their patients through improved transparency and competition. Should you have any questions, please contact Erica Cischke, Director of Regulatory and Legislative Affairs at ecischke@aafp.org.

Sincerely,

Sterling N. Ransone, Jr., MD, FAAFP

Sterling N. Ransone, Jr., MD, FAAFP
Board Chair, American Academy of Family Physicians

American Hospital Association™
Advancing Health in America

Washington, D.C. Office
800 10th Street, N.W.
Two CityCenter, Suite 400
Washington, DC 20001-4956
(202) 638-1100

Statement of the American Hospital Association for theCommittee on Energy and Commerce Subcommittee on Health of the U.S. House of Representatives
"Lowering Unaffordable Costs: Examining Transparency and Competition in Health Care"
March 28, 2023

Chairman Guthrie, Ranking Member Eshoo, and members of the subcommittee, on behalf of our nearly 5,000 member hospitals, health systems and other health care organizations, our clinician partners — including more than 270,000 affiliated physicians, 2 million nurses and other caregivers — and the 43,000 health care leaders who belong to our professional membership groups, the American Hospital Association (AHA) appreciates the opportunity to provide the hospital perspective on transparency and competition in health care.

Given the hearing topics of transparency and competition could touch on a number of issues, we provided comments on the following areas: hospital compliance with the Hospital Price Transparency Rule and other transparency efforts; mergers and acquisitions; site neutral payment policies; the 340B program; and physician-owned hospital restrictions.

Hospital Price Transparency

Hospitals and health systems are committed to empowering patients with all the information they need to live their healthiest lives. This includes ensuring they have access to accurate price information when seeking care. Hospitals and health systems are working to comply with both state and federal price transparency policies, which are varied and sometimes conflicting. At the federal level, these include:

- Hospital Price Transparency Rule. As of Jan. 1, 2021, hospitals are required to publicly post via machine-readable files five different "standard charges": gross charges; payer-specific negotiated rates; de-identified minimum and maximum negotiated rates; and discounted cash prices. The rule also requires hospitals to provide patients with an out-of-pocket cost estimator tool or payer- specific negotiated rates for at least 300 shoppable services.

- Good Faith Estimates. The No Surprises Act requires hospitals and other providers to share Good Faith Estimates with uninsured/self-pay patients for most scheduled services. Future regulations will require unaffiliated providers to combine their estimates for an uninsured/self-pay patient into a single, comprehensive Good Faith Estimate for an episode of care.
- Advanced Explanation of Benefits. The No Surprises Act requires insurers to share advanced explanations of benefits with their enrollees, though implementation is currently on hold pending rulemaking. Hospitals will need to provide Good Faith Estimates to health insurers to operationalize this policy.

Hospital Price Transparency Rule

Over the past several years, the AHA has engaged hospitals and health systems in substantial education and engagement on the Hospital Price Transparency Rule. This includes:

- Establishing a CEO-level Price Transparency Task Force that helped guide the AHA in developing policies and sharing best practices with respect to price transparency and patient billing;
- Conducting education through multiple webinars, bi-weekly "office hours" with AHA and Healthcare Financial Management Association technical experts, issue briefs, case studies and podcasts;
- Providing an implementation guide, including implementation checklists and FAQs;
- Conducting a three-part webinar series on Health Care Consumer Expectations and Experiences with Kauffman Hall;
- Hosting a multi-stakeholder intensive design process, which included providers, payers, patient advocates, technology vendors and others, to develop solutions to improve the patient financial experience of care;
- Supporting CMS efforts to establish voluntary sample formats that hospitals may use to meet the federal requirement to make certain standard charges publiclyavailable through a machine-readable file by connecting the agency with experts from the hospital field; and
- Updating the AHA's Patient Billing Guidelines, which include a focus on helping patients access information on financial assistance.

CMS has a process in place to ensure hospital compliance with the Hospital Price Transparency Rule. This includes a review, usually involving direct discourse with the hospitals; if deficiencies are identified, a warning letter is sent from the agency; and if the deficiencies are not corrected, a corrective action plan is requested. Should a hospital continue to fail to come into compliance, CMS then applies a civil monetary penalty.

CMS found that in 2022, 70% of hospitals complied with both components of the Hospital Price Transparency Rule, including the consumer-friendly display of shoppable services information, as well as the machine-readable file requirements. This is an increase from 27%

in 2021. Moreover, when looking at each individual component of the rule, 82% of hospitals met the consumer-friendly display of shoppable services information requirement in 2022 (up from 66% in 2021) and 82% met the machine- readable file requirement (up from 30% in 2021).

These numbers show significant progress on the part of hospitals and health systems — while acknowledging the work that remains — in implementing these requirements. The lower compliance rate in 2021, however, should not be interpreted as a lack of hospital commitment to transparency. Instead, it reflects the incredible challenges hospitals were experiencing in 2020 and 2021 in addressing the most acute phases of the COVID-19 public health emergency, which strained hospitals' staff and required the diversion of personnel and financial resources. As the pandemic phase of COVID-19 winds down and hospitals have been able to resume more standard operations, they are able to dedicate the resources necessary to build the full suite of price transparency tools.

CMS also shared information regarding how it has interacted with hospitals to support compliance and the issuance of penalties:

> "As of January 2023, CMS had issued nearly 500 warning notices and over 230 requests for corrective action plans since the initial implementing regulation went into effect in 2021. Nearly 300 hospitals have addressed problems and have become compliant with the regulations, leading to closure of their cases. While it was necessary to issue penalties to two hospitals in 2022 for noncompliance (posted on the CMS website), every other hospital that was reviewed has corrected its deficiencies."

Unfortunately, some third parties continue to issue reports mischaracterizing whether hospitals are complying with the Hospital Price Transparency Rule, as was detailed in a letter AHA sent recently to House Energy and Commerce Chair Rodgers and Ranking Member Pallone. These reports fail to acknowledge CMS' requirements, such as how tofill in an individual negotiated rate when such a rate does not exist due to patient services being bundled and billed together. In this instance, CMS has said a blank cell would be appropriate since there is no negotiated rate to include. Despite this, some outside groups still count any file with blank cells as "noncompliant." This fundamental misrepresentation of the rules has only served to advance misinformation and confusion on the issue and distract from genuine productive discussions and efforts around what patients want in terms of transparency data and how best to provide that information.

In addition to the CMS report on compliance, we would draw your attention to a recent NBC Nightly News story, "Are hospitals complying with the federal price transparency law?" which highlights CMS' oversight work. We also would note that Turquoise Health, a health technology company that analyzes provider and payer data, has shown in its review similar uptake to the CMS results with respect to hospital compliance. In an October report, Turquoise found that through the third quarter of 2022, 76% of hospitals (4,909) have posted a machine-readable file.

Recommendations

Hospitals and health systems are eager to continue working towards providing the best possible price estimates for their patients. We ask Congress and the Administration to take the following steps to support these efforts, including:

- Review and streamline the existing transparency policies with a priority objective of reducing potential patient confusion and unnecessary regulatory burden on providers;
- Continue to convene patients, providers and payers to seek input on how to make federal price transparency policies as patient-centered as possible; and
- Refrain from advancing additional legislation or regulations that may further confuse or complicate providers' ability to provide meaningful price estimates while adding unnecessary costs to the health care system.

Hospital Mergers and Acquisitions

Mergers and acquisitions are one of the most important tools that some hospitals use to increase access, provide quality care and manage financial pressures and risk. These partnerships enable hospitals to expand service offerings, broaden networks and access to specialists, improve quality and better serve patients where they live. They also provide scale to help reduce costs associated with obtaining medical services, supplies and prescription drugs, and enable health systems to reduce other operational costs. Ultimately, hospital mergers and acquisitions expand and preserve access to care.

Emerging research has demonstrated a clear association between consolidation and quality improvement. For example, one study found that a full-integration approach is associated with improvements in mortality and readmission rates, among other qualityand outcome improvements.[161] Another study found significant reductions in mortality for a number of common conditions — including acute myocardial infarction, heart failure, acute stroke and pneumonia — among patients at rural hospitals that had merged or been acquired.[162]

Mergers and acquisitions help hospitals improve access to care by expanding the types of specialists and services available to patients. According to an analysis by Kaufman Hall, nearly 40% of affiliated hospitals added one or more services post-acquisition.

Mergers and acquisitions also are a vital tool that some health systems use to keep financially struggling hospitals open, thereby averting bankruptcy or even closure.[163] When hospitals become part of a health system, the continuum of care is strengthened for patients and the community, resulting in better care and decreased readmission rates.

Mergers and acquisitions have also played a critical role in preserving access to care in rural areas. An AHA analysis of the UNC Sheps Center data on rural hospital closures between 2010 and 2020 shows that slightly more than half of the hospitals that closed were independent. Health systems typically acquire rural hospitals when these hospitals are under financial

---

[161] https://jamanetwork.com/journals/jamanetworkopen/fullarticle/2787652.

[162] https://jamanetwork.com/journals/jamanetworkopen/fullarticle/2784342.

[163] https://www.aha.org/system/files/media/file/2021/10/KH-AHA-Benefits-of-Hospital-Mergers-Acquisitions- 2021-10-08.pdf.

distress. Research has shown that rural hospitals are less likely to close after acquisition compared to independent hospitals and that mergers have improved access and quality of care for rural hospitals.[164] Acquired hospitals typically form new collaborations or partnerships with larger health systems, which promotes access to specialists, telehealth and other care for rural patients.[165]

Medicare Outpatient Site Neutral Payment Reductions

The AHA strongly opposes additional site-neutral payment cuts, which threaten access to care, especially in rural and historically marginalized communities. Existing site- neutral payment policies have already negatively impacted the financial sustainability of hospitals and health systems, particularly as they continue to manage the aftermath of the COVID-19 pandemic as well as the challenges posed by workforce shortages, broken supply chains and historic levels of inflation that have increased the costs of caring for patients. In addition, underpayments from Medicare already put a strain on hospital finances by reimbursing hospitals significantly less than the cost of providing care for those beneficiaries. Further cuts would exacerbate that gap and may cause hospitals to significantly reduce services.

Site-neutral policies also fail to account for the fundamental differences between hospital outpatient departments (HOPDs) and other sites of care. The cost of caredelivered in hospitals and health systems takes into account the unique benefits that they provide to their communities. This includes the investments made to maintain standby capacity for natural and man-made disasters, public health emergencies, unexpected traumatic events as well as deliver 24/7 emergency care to all who come to the hospital, regardless of ability to pay or insurance status. Hospitals and health systems provide access to critical services and programs that may not be otherwise available, especially in low-income and rural communities.

Hospital facilities also treat patients who are sicker and have more chronic conditions than those treated in physician offices or ambulatory surgical centers, which requires a greater use of resources. In addition, hospital facilities must comply with a much more comprehensive scope of licensing, accreditation and other regulatory requirements compared to other sites of care.

Moreover, Medicare payments already fail to cover the costs of caring for Medicare beneficiaries — a fact that even the Medicare Payment Advisory Commission (MedPAC) has acknowledged. This underpayment is due in part to existing site-neutral payment policies that have substantially cut reimbursements; further site-neutral cuts would only exacerbate this gap. According to MedPAC, overall Medicare hospital margins were -6.3% in 2021 after accounting for temporary COVID-19 relief funds.

Without these temporary relief funds, the overall Medicare margin for 2021 remained depressed at -8.2% after hitting a staggering low of -12.3% in 2020. This marks nearly two decades in a row that Medicare payments have not covered patient costs. On average, Medicare only pays 84 cents for every dollar hospitals spend providing care to Medicare beneficiaries. Moreover, median hospital operating margins have stayed negative throughout 2022. Site-

164 https://www.ncbi.nlm.nih.gov/pmc/articles/PMC9250050/.

165 https://www.aha.org/system/files/media/file/2021/10/KH-AHA-Benefits-of-Hospital-Mergers-Acquisitions-2021 -10-08.pdf.

neutral cuts have already contributed to these shortfalls, and any further expansion of these policies will threaten patients' access to quality care.

Now more than ever, hospitals need stable and adequate reimbursements as they face challenging financial circumstances. Expanding site-neutral cuts to additional HOPDs would endanger the critical role that hospital-based outpatient departments play in their communities, including access to care for patients, especially the most medically complex.

340B Drug Pricing Program

The 340B Drug Pricing Program, for more than 30 years, has allowed hospitals to stretch limited federal resources to reduce the price of outpatient pharmaceuticals for patients as well as expand health services to the patients and communities they serve. 340B hospitals achieve savings by purchasing drugs at a discount. The amount of that discount depends on drug companies' pricing decisions, with the Health Resources and Services Administration (HRSA) estimating that the average discount is anywhere between 25% to 50%.

Hospitals use 340B savings to provide a range of vital programs and services, which include, but are not limited to, the provision of free or discounted drugs to low incomepatients, free care for uninsured patients and support for behavioral health clinics and community health programs. In fact, in the most recent year for which information is available, tax-exempt 340B hospitals provided nearly $68 billion in total benefits to their communities.[166] This drug pricing program is particularly important as drug prices continue to rise and hospitals face increased inflationary cost pressures across all their supplies and services. The AHA urges Congress to continue to protect this critical program and oppose efforts further restrict eligibility, which would result in reduced access to quality care for the patients and communities served by 340B hospitals.

The AHA is also alarmed by some drug companies' efforts to restrict access to 340B discounted drugs for 340B hospitals that have established community and specialty pharmacy arrangements. Since October 2022, over 20 drug companies have adopted these restrictive policies to the severe detriment of 340B hospitals and their patients. The financial impact on 340B hospitals is significant. For 340B critical access hospitals, AHA's survey reports average annual losses of over $500 thousand and 340B disproportionate share hospitals have average annual losses of nearly $3 million.[167] The AHA continues to actively support HRSA in its efforts to enforce the requirements for drug companies set forth in the 340B statute.

Restrictions on Physician-Owned Hospitals

America's community hospitals and health systems welcome fair competition, where health care entities can compete based in quality, price, safety and patient satisfaction. But physician-owned hospitals (POH) — where physicians cherry-pick the healthiest and best-insured patients and self-refer those patients to facilities in which they have an ownership interest —

166 Blog: 340B program helps advance health for patients, communities | AHA News.

167 Survey Brief: Drug Companies Reduce Patients' Access to Care by Limiting 340B Community Pharmacies | AHA.

represent the antithesis of competition. The AHA strongly opposes any changes that would either expand the number of POHs or ease restrictions on the growth of existing facilities.

Congress acted in 2010 to close the "whole hospital" loophole in the Stark law and placed restrictions on POHs. That provision represented a carefully crafted compromise to protect hospitals with a Medicare provider number as of Dec. 31, 2010 and allow those facilities to expand when increased hospital capacity is needed. Since 2010, eight POH hospitals have applied for the exceptions process and have been allowed to expand.

Several analyses, including by the Congressional Budget Office, MedPAC and independent researchers, have concluded that physician self-referral leads to greater per capita utilization of services and higher costs for the Medicare program. In fact, according to the Congressional Budget Office, closing the "whole hospital" exception loophole in the Stark law reduced the federal deficit by $500 million over ten years. Bills that would repeal the 2010 law would erase those savings and increase the federal deficit.

Furthermore, POHs tend to cherry-pick the most profitable patients and services, jeopardizing communities' access to full-service hospital care. The Government Accountability Office, CMS and MedPAC have found that patients in POHs tend to be healthier than patients with the same diagnoses who are taken care of by community hospitals. This practice of self-referring physicians carefully selecting their patients creates a destabilizing environment that leaves sicker and less-affluent patients to community hospitals, thereby placing these hospitals at a distinct financial disadvantage. This is because community hospitals rely on cross-subsidies from those services targeted by POHs to support essential, but under-reimbursed, services such as emergency, trauma and burn care. By siphoning off the most profitable services and patients, POHs threaten the ability of community hospitals to offer quality, comprehensive care and serve as the health care provider for all patients, regardless of income or insurance status, in their communities.

The Alliance to Fight for Health Care

Advancing employer-provided coverage

March 23, 2023

The Honorable Jason Smith
Chairman
Ways & Means Committee
United States House of Representatives
Washington, DC 20515

The Honorable Vern Buchanan
Chairman, Subcommittee on Health
Ways & Means Committee
United States House of Representatives
Washington, DC 20515

The Honorable Richard Neal
Ranking member
Ways & Means Committee
United States House of Representatives
Washington, DC 20515

The Honorable Lloyd Doggett
Ranking member, Subcommittee on Health
Ways & Means Committee
United States House of Representatives
Washington, DC 20515

Dear Chairman Smith, Chairman Buchanan, Ranking Member Neal, and Ranking Member Doggett:

Thank you for the opportunity to submit the following comments for the hearing record in connection with the March 23, 2023, Ways & Means Subcommittee on Health hearing on "Why Health Care is Unaffordable."

The Alliance to Fight for Health Care is a diverse coalition comprised of businesses, patient advocates, employer organizations, unions, health care companies, consumer groups and other stakeholders that support employer-provided health coverage. Together, we are working to ensure that employer-provided coverage remains an available and affordable option for working Americans and their families.

Employer-provided health care coverage is the backbone of the U.S. health care system—covering more than 178 million workers and their families. More people receive health insurance through an employer than all other sources of coverage combined—Medicare, Medicaid, Marketplace, Tricare and the Department of Veterans Affairs. Employer-provided coverage has always been efficient, effective, and stable, and through the COVID-19 pandemic, it has also proven to be resilient—with employers quickly stepping up to meet the health care needs of employees during the crisis.

Employer-provided coverage produces substantial return on the federal government's investment in it—both economically and when it comes to our health. Research finds that employer-provided coverage provides significant economic, social, and public health benefits. According to a National Bureau of Economic Research working paper, employer-provided coverage delivers significant value – at least $1.5 trillion in social value annually beyond the cost of insurance borne by businesses, workers, and government tax exemptions, at nearly $10,000 per person.

Despite economic uncertainty in 2022, more than 70% of large employers prioritized adding or expanding benefits or resources to meet employee needs. This included access to virtual care resources, expanded behavioral health, and alternative care arrangements, such as accountable care organizations and centers of excellence, that drive employees to high-value care.

Despite efforts, rising health care costs continue to be a top concern for both employers and employees. Health spending is increasing across all payers, and now exceeds 18% of U.S. Gross Domestic Product. From 2016 to 2020, the 9.3 % per person spending growth in the employer market was caused primarily by a 16% increase in average medical prices.

Health care costs continued to be a significant barrier to care for patients. A recent Morning Consult poll on health care issues conducted on behalf of the Alliance found health care costs are the No. 1 concern among insured Americans. What's more, 57% of insured adults said reducing health care costs should be Congress' top priority. But insured adults do not want to start over. Nearly 70% of insured adults, across the political spectrum, prefer to strengthen the existing system. Further, a majority of adults want Congress to work to lower the cost of health care for ALL Americans, not just those who receive coverage on the exchanges or in federal health care programs, like Medicare and Medicaid.

The Alliance to Fight for Health care agrees. We want to work with Congress this year to improve the U.S. health care system and reduce health care costs for ALL Americans by advancing policies to reduce health insurance premiums and increase affordability. And we come to the table with bipartisan ideas. For example, Congress could reduce cost and improve health outcomes for 178 million workers and their families enacting polices to:

- Remove restrictions preventing pro-patient competition in health care markets
- Protect patients from paying hospital prices for doctors' office visits
- Align value-based care incentives to benefit patients across all health care markets
- Give employers the flexibility to design programs to address chronic conditions and improve health outcomes

Policy Goal: Remove Restrictions Preventing Pro-Patient Competition in Health Care Markets

Employers want to create health plan designs that provide extra help to people with chronic or costly health conditions to improve health outcomes. Currently, "anti-tiering" and "anti-steering" clauses in contracts between providers and health plans restrict plans from creating innovative, high-value programs such as high-performance networks. Passing legislation, such as the Healthy Competition for Better Care Act, would enable more group health plans and health insurance issuers to enter into agreements with providers that guide enrollees to high-value providers and provide incentives to encourage enrollees to seek higher-quality, lower cost care. There is significant support for such proposals. Recent polling by the Alliance indicates that 85% of insured adults feel employers should be able to give employees who have enrolled in their company's health plan a discount for seeing a high-quality provider.

Policy Goal: Protect Patients from Paying Hospital Prices for Doctors' Office Visits

The Alliance supports lowering the cost of health care services through policy proposals such as site- neutral payment reform. Current Medicare and private health insurance payment policies pay more for services provided in hospital outpatient departments ("HOPD") – in other words, provider offices owned by but not located in the hospital. According to the Medicare Payment Advisory Commission (MedPAC), this disparity is incentivizing health care consolidation and higher-health care costs. As shown in an AMA survey, currently fewer than half of physicians now work in physician-owned practices, a trend that has sharply risen since 2012.

MedPAC discussed the payment disparity in their June 2022 report to Congress, "[I]n 2022, Medicare pays 141 percent more in a hospital outpatient department than in a freestanding office for the first hour of chemotherapy infusion." As noted by MedPAC, "partly in response to these incentives, in recent years hospitals have acquired more physician practices, and hospital employment of physicians has increased." MedPAC also notes that the resulting increased reimbursements are not linked to clear benefits, such as improved quality of care for beneficiaries, but they are linked to increased costs for patients.

Congress can build on site-neutral payment reform by requiring Medicare to align payment rates for certain services across the three main sites where patients receive outpatient care—HOPDs, ambulatory surgical centers (ASCs), and freestanding physician offices. MedPAC, in its June 2022 report, estimated expanding site-neutral payment policies in Medicare could generate $6.6 billion in annual savings for Medicare and taxpayers and lower cost-sharing for Medicare beneficiaries by $1.7 billion.

The savings if voluntarily adopted by the commercial market are likely even greater. New research by University of Minnesota economist Steve Parente conducted on behalf of the Alliance estimates that expanding site-neutral payment reform in Medicare and encouraging adoption in the commercial market could result in nearly $60 billion in savings annually in the commercial market.

Requiring transparency in reporting where care is provided (i.e., a hospital or a physician's office) is another commonsense step that can help improve clarity for all consumers. Congress should consider legislation such as The Transparency of Hospital Billing Act.

These policies can all be designed to protect vulnerable rural or safety net hospitals, while protecting patients from climbing costs and consolidation. There is significant support for site-neutral payment reform. The recent Morning Consult poll found 86% of insured adults, across political parties, believe health care costs should remain the same regardless of where the service is received.

Policy Goal: Align Value-Based Care Incentives to Benefit Patients Across All Health Care Markets

The Alliance believes that federal cost reduction and quality improvement efforts should seek to improve the health care market for all beneficiaries. Encouraging collaboration between public and private providers and payors could accelerate beneficial changes for all participants. Creating pathways to engage the group health market in CMS Innovation Center (CMMI) models more meaningfully will promote multi-payer collaboration and encourage public-private partnerships that improve quality, reduce costs, and advance the system as a whole.

All patients should have a seat at the table in advance of future model development and be part of an open dialogue to promote coordination and learning to help improve the system together.

Policy Goal: Give Employers the Flexibility to Design Programs to Address Chronic Conditions and Improve Health Outcomes

The Alliance also supports policies that reduce barriers to high value care, including enabling plans and employers to offer more high-value care pre-deductible. Laws and rules limiting pre-deductible coverage for chronic disease prevention, onsite medical clinics and telehealth inhibit employers' ability to offer high-value and potentially life-saving care to their employees on an equitable basis. Because of this, the Alliance supports legislation, including:

- The Chronic Disease Management Act (117th H.R. 3563/S. 1424), which allows greater flexibility to offer pre-deductible coverage for chronic disease prevention.
- The Telehealth Expansion Act (117th S. 1704), which makes permanent the flexibility for plans to offer telehealth pre-deductible.
- Legislation that allows employers to provide more robust services (like chronic disease management and primary care) at onsite medical clinics pre-deductible without charging cost- sharing.
- Legislation that permits plans below a specified actuarial value to make and plan participants to receive contributions to Health Savings Accounts (117th S. 2099).

You can find a longer list of our recommended policies – including the barriers they aim to address – on our website at www.fightforhealthcare.com.

We look forward to working together to advance public policy that makes health care more affordable, supports continued innovation, improves job-based coverage, and advances the health care system for all patients.

Respectfully,
The Alliance to Fight for Health Care

AMA
AMERICAN MEDICAL ASSOCIATION

Statement of the American Medical Association
U.S. House of Representatives Committee on Energy and Commerce, Subcommittee on Health
Re: Lowering Unaffordable Costs: Examining Transparency and Competition in Health Care
March 28, 2023

Division of Legislative Counsel 202-789-7426

Statement for the Record of the American Medical Association to the U.S. House of Representatives, Committee on Energy and Commerce, Subcommittee on Health Re: Lowering Unaffordable Costs: Examining Transparency and Competition in Health Care
March 28, 2023

The American Medical Association (AMA) appreciates the opportunity to submit the following Statement for the Record to the U.S. House of Representatives Committee on Energy and Commerce Subcommittee on Health as part of the hearing entitled, "Lowering Unaffordable Costs: Examining Transparency and Competition in Health Care." The AMA commends the

Subcommittee for focusing on the critically important issue of consolidation in health insurance, hospital, and pharmacy benefit manager (PBM) markets and the consequences for patients.

I. Health Insurance Competition Study

An important question of public policy is whether health insurance markets are competitive or whether health insurers possess market power. If insurers exercise market power, health plan premiums would be higher, and payments to providers and the quantity of health care would be lower, than if health insurance markets were competitive. High market concentration tends to lower competition and facilitate the exercise of market power. Unfortunately, the majority of U.S. health insurance markets are highly concentrated, as documented in a comprehensive study of U.S. markets.[168] The share of commercial markets in metropolitan statistical areas (MSA) that are highly concentrated rose from 71 percent to 75 percent between 2014 and 2021.

There is high concentration among health insurers in most Medicare Advantage (MA) markets as well. Seventy-nine percent of MA markets were highly concentrated in 2021. While MA markets have undergone a consistent though gradual decrease in average concentration since 2017, the decrease in average MA market concentration masks some merger activity that took place. By acquiring an insurer in another market where they do not already provide coverage, some MA insurers have been able to get bigger, such as Anthem did in commercial markets through its 2004 acquisition of WellPoint as well as each of those merging parties' acquisition of other Blue Cross Blue Shield insurers before that.

Most health insurance markets are ripe for the exercise of health insurer market power, which harms consumers and providers of care. These findings should prompt federal and state antitrustauthorities to vigorously examine the competitive effects of proposed horizontal and vertical mergers involving health insurers.

Given the uncertainty in predicting the competitive effects of consolidation, some mergers that are allowed cause competitive harm. For example, in 2008 a merger between UnitedHealthcare and Sierra was allowed under the condition that UnitedHealthcare divest most of its MA business in the Las Vegas area. Nonetheless, premiums in the commercial health insurance markets in Nevada increased in the wake of the merger.[169]

After years of largely unchallenged consolidation in the health insurance industry, a few subsequent attempts to consolidate have received closer scrutiny. Most notably, in 2015 two mergers involving four of the largest health insurers in the country were announced. Anthem attempted to acquire Cigna, and Aetna sought to acquire Humana. To help identify markets where mergers would cause competitive harm, the AMA used data from previous editions of the Competition in Health Insurance study (referenced above in footnote 1) to assess their competitive effects. Specifically, we calculated the changes in market concentration that would

---

[168] Guardado, J., Kane, C. *Competition in Health Insurance: A Comprehensive Study of U.S. Markets*. American Medical Association Division of Economic and Health Policy Research. 2022. Available at https://www.ama-assn.org/system/files/competition-health-insurance-us-markets.pdf. Accessed March 16, 2023.

[169] Guardado, J., Emmons, D., Kane, C. *The Price Effects of a Large Merger of Health Insurers: A Case Study of UnitedHealth-Sierra*. HMPI. 2013;1(3):16-35. Available at https://hmpi.org/wp-content/uploads/ 2017/02/ HMPI-Guardado-Emmons-Kane-Price-Effects-of-a-Larger-Merger-of-Health-Insurers.pdf. Accessed March 16, 2022.

result from the mergers and, according to the Department of Justice (DOJ)/Federal Trade Commission (FTC) Horizontal Merger Guidelines, classified markets based on how anti-competitive the mergers would be. We found that the mergers would be deemed anticompetitive in numerous markets across the United States.[170] Consistent with our findings and after close to a year of antitrust scrutiny, the DOJ and attorneys general from multiple states sued to block both acquisitions.[171] The DOJ and state attorneys general ultimately prevailed after an intense battle in the courts, which found that the mergers would cause harm to consumers and violate antitrust law. As a result, both mergers were abandoned by the merging parties. Our studies will continue to monitor competition in health insurance markets and be used to assess the competitive effects of proposed mergers among health insurers.

II. Pharmacy Benefit Managers

The lack of transparency surrounding pharmacy benefit managers and the impact it has on pharmaceutical costs to patients and the practice of medicine.

The AMA believes that the role of PBMs as "middlemen" among payers, pharmaceutical companies, and pharmacies goes beyond the negotiation of drug prices on behalf of their clients. The ability of patients and physicians to have the information they need to make key decisions regarding medication, and of policymakers to craft viable solutions to high and escalating pharmaceutical costs, has been hampered by these arrangements that are driving medications prices without a clear and justifiable reason. Patients today are facing insurmountable costs and administrative barriers to obtaining prescription drugs from a pharmacy, PBM, or through physician-administered treatments. The burden, however, is not solely caused by the escalating cost of pharmaceuticals, but the increase in medication utilization management policies due to those higher costs as well. As a result, patients may take greater clinical risks when treatments are cost prohibitive. If patients delay, forgo, or ration their pharmaceutical treatment, their health status may deteriorate, eventually requiring medical interventions in more costly care settings when their condition is at a more advanced stage of disease. In a health care delivery system in which racial and ethnic health care disparities are known to exist, market-driven barriers to care perpetuate disparitiesrather than promote equity for marginalized populations.

Issues and concerns surrounding the impact of unfair market forces on medication costs and access are not new; it is, however, of increasing concern that not only is patient affordability affected, but also the negative impacts felt by those affected by disparities have been exacerbated.[172] In a 2020 article published in the Journal of Managed Care + Specialty Pharmacy, the author notes that there has been a response to racial or ethnic disparities in medication use with more focus on social determinants of health. However, it is also acknowledged that "medication cost remains a formidable barrier to closing the disparities gap in medication use between Blacks and Whites, including both the uninsured and those having

[170] See https://www.ama-assn.org/about/competition-health-insurance-research. Accessed March 16, 2023.

[171] See lawsuits announcement at https://www.justice.gov/opa/pr/justice-department-and-state-attorneys-general-sue- block-anthem-s-acquisition-cigna-aetna-s. Accessed March 16, 2023.

[172] Kogut SJ., *Racial disparities in medication use: imperatives for managed care pharmacy*, J Manag Care Spec Pharm. 2020 Nov;26(11):1468-1474. doi: 10.18553/jmcp.2020.26.11.1468. PMID: 33119445; PMCID: PMC8060916.

a pharmacy benefit." The author points to the significant correlation between wealth and race in this equation, and furthermore notes that racial disparities have been documented in the utilization of essential evidence- based drug therapies, including but not limited to antidepressants, anticoagulants, diabetes medications, drugs for dementia, and statins. Statistics reported from the U.S. Bureau of Labor Statistics reflect that, in 2018, patients earning poverty-level wages were likely to prioritize rent payments or costs for food as a necessary trade-off to out-of-pocket prescription costs that consume a higher percentage of their weekly earnings. The author notes that, while patient cost sharing may be lower than it was comparably in the 1990s, the comparison of costs "does not take into account prices paid by those without health insurance, or the deviation in patient out-of-pocket spending that is associated with current pharmacy benefit designs."

These barriers also undoubtedly impact the physician's ability to provide uninterrupted optimal patient- centric care. In these scenarios, physicians are forced to navigate complex, and resource intensive requirements imposed by health insurers and PBMs.

The AMA has supported recently re-introduced legislation that promotes greater transparency of PBM operations and prohibits PBMs from engaging in unfair and deceptive reimbursement and payment practices.[173] The opaque nature of PBM negotiations and operations makes it exceedingly difficult for physicians to determine what treatments are preferred by a particular payer at the point-of-care, what level of cost-sharing their patients will face, and whether medications are subject to step therapy. We emphasize that this ultimately may lead to delays in necessary medication treatment, as well as being unaware of specific formulary and cost-sharing responsibilities, which can lead to an inability to afford and access necessary medications.

The AMA strongly supports efforts on the part of Congress, the FTC, and the U.S. Department of Health and Human Services to monitor and evaluate the utilization and impact of controlled distribution channels for prescription pharmaceuticals on patient access and market competition. The call for increased oversight and studies to prevent unfair or anticompetitive PBM practices is overwhelmingly welcomed.

In October 2022, the AMA released the findings from a new analysis[174] that reflects the widespread lack of competition in local PBM markets across the United States where PBMs provide services to commercial health insurers. This analysis is the first to shed light on variations in market shares and competition among PBMs and on the extent of vertical integration between health insurers and PBMs at the state andMSA-levels.

According to the analysis, commercial insurers largely use an external PBM for three services: rebate negotiation; retail network management; and claims adjudication (rather than conducting them in-house). The analysis assessed market competition for those three PBM services and concluded that, at the national level, a handful of PBMs have a large collective market share. The 10 largest PBMs had a collective share of 97 percent; the four largest PBMs had a collective share of roughly 66 percent.

At both the state and MSA-levels, the analysis found a high degree of market concentration for each of the three PBM services assessed by the study. Specifically, more than three of four

---

173 https://searchlf.ama-assn.org/letter/documentDownload?uri=%2Funstructured%2Fbinary%2Flet ter%2FLETTERS%2Flfrd.zip%2F2023-3-13-Letter-to-Senate-re-S-113-and-127-Acts-v3.pdf.

174 José R. Guardado, Competition in Commercial PBM Markeys and Vertical Integration of Health Insurers with PBMs, AMA Policy Research Perspectives (2022), https://www.ama-assn.org/system/files/prp-pbm-shares-hhi.pdf.

(about 78 percent) states had highly concentrated PBM markets; and more than four of five (85 percent) of MSA areas had highly concentrated PBM markets.

In terms of the extent of vertical integration between health insurers and PBMs, the study found that 69 percent of drug lives at the national level are covered by an insurer that is vertically integrated with a PBM. On average, 63 percent of state-level drug lives and 65 percent of MSA-level lives are vertically integrated. Six of the 10 largest PBMs are used exclusively by one insurer or a set of Blue Cross Blue Shield affiliates. Vertically integrated insurers may not allow non-vertically integrated insurer competitors to access their PBMs, or they could raise the cost of those PBM services. This could adversely affect non- vertically integrated insurers and ultimately patients through higher premiums.

Other research notes the increasing vertical integration of insurers, PBMs, specialty pharmacies, and providers, and provides an illustration of the major vertical business relationships among the largest companies in U.S. health care markets.

At this juncture, protecting patients and physicians from anticompetitive harm is another layer of complexity that warrants attention as Congress and the Administration continue to work through these issues to protect patients and ensure prescription drugs remain affordable and accessible. The AMA urges careful monitoring, and intervention when needed, of both horizontal and vertical integration to ensure competition in PBM and health insurance markets and patient access to care. Physicians experience and see first-hand the difficulty and burden high pharmaceutical costs have and continue to impose on their patients' care and remain concerned about the detrimental impact PBM business practices have on patients' access to and the cost of prescription drugs.

III. Physician-Owned Hospitals

The U.S. health care system is a market-based system that is not working as well as it could; it faces issues such as high and rising prices, suboptimal quality of care, and poor pricing practices.[175] This is partly the result of significant consolidation occurring in hospital markets around the country.[176] Many markets are now often dominated by one large, powerful health system, e.g., Boston (Partners), Pittsburgh (UPMC), and San Francisco (Sutter).[177] Consolidation has real-life consequences, as clearly laid out in a new book by Professors David Dranove and Lawton R. Burns about health care"megaproviders."[178] They found that in markets "where megaproviders dominate…, health care spending is higher, often much higher, and health care quality is no better, and sometimes lower."[179] Given that hospitals account for over 31 percent of total health spending, hospital market concentration is a leading cause of

---

175 Martin Gaynor, *Antitrust Applied: Hospital Consolidation Concerns and Solutions*, Statement before Subcommittee on Competition Policy, Antitrust, and Consumer Rights subcommittee of U.S. Senate, 117th Cong. 6, 2 (May 19, 2021) (Martin Gaynor, *Antitrust Applied*).

176 Martin Gaynor, *Antitrust Applied*, at 2; Emily Gee, *The High Price of Hospital Care*, Center for American Progress https://www.americanprogress.org/issues/healthcare/reports/2019/06/26/471464/high-price-hospital-care/. (Accessed March 16, 2023), Martin Gaynor and Robert Town, *The Impact of Hospital Consolidation-Update, the Synthesis Project*, Robert Wood Johnson Foundation (June 2012).

177 Martin Gaynor, *Antitrust Applied*, at 2.

178 David Dranove and Lawton R Burns, Big Med: Megaproviders and the High Cost of Health Care in America, 178 (2021). (Dranove).

179 Dranove, *supra,* at 178.

America's high health care cost.[180] Moreover, hospital market concentration is fast becoming a problem for which antitrust provides little prospect for relief.[181] The AMA is focused on this issue because this consolidation drives up health care costs and marginalizes physicians who want to remain independent.[182]

Consolidation is Driving Increased Health Care Costs

Increased levels of hospital market concentration are shown to lead to increased health costs.[18316] One study found that "prices at monopoly hospitals are 12 percent higher than those in markets with four or more rivals."[184] Another earlier study found that hospital mergers that occur within the same market led to, on average, a 2.6 percent increase in hospital prices; mergers also resulted in increased hospital spending and reductions in wages.[185] Other research has found that hospital mergers result in prices that are 10 to 40 percent higher than pre-merger.[186] These effects also endure; after a merger, hospital prices generally continue to rise for at least two years.[187] Advocates for mergers argue that these mergers will be able to provide better care or lower costs; however, larger health care systems generally have neither superior health outcomes nor lower costs.[188] Even if there are savings associated with hospital consolidation, they are typically not passed onto consumers.[189] Competition, not consolidation, has been proven an effective way to save lives without raising health care costs.[190]

Increased Hospital Concentration is Correlated with Worse Health Outcomes

Beyond increased costs, greater hospital market concentration has been shown to lead to worse health outcomes for patients. Antitrust policy in health care markets has a role to play in reducing the growth of disparities in health care access.[191] For example, in one study mortality rates after heart attacks were found to be higher, by a statistically significant measure, in more

---

180 Martin Gaynor, *Antitrust Applied*, at 5.

181 Dranove, *supra,* at 178.

182 Dranove, *supra,* at 178. The consolidation may also lead to enhanced hospital monopsony power in labor markets. Martin Gaynor, *Antitrust Applied* at 3.

183 Martin Gaynor and Robert Town, *supra*.

184 Zack Cooper, Stuart V Craig, Martin Gaynor, John Van Reenen, *The Price Ain't Right? Hospital Prices and Health Spending on the Privately Insured*, 134 The Quarterly Journal of Economics 1, 51 (February 2019). https:// academic.oup.com/qje/article-abstract/134/1/51/5090426?redirectedFrom=fulltext.

185 D. Arnold and C.M. Whaley, *Who Pays for Health Care Costs? The Effects of Health Care Prices on Wages,* RAND Corporation, 3 (2020).

186 Martin Gaynor, *Health Care Industry Consolidation*, Statement before the Committee on Ways and Means Health Subcommittee of the U.S. House of Representatives, 107th Cong. (September 9, 2011).

187 Martin Gaynor, *Antitrust Applied*, at 4.

188 Patrick S. Romano and David J. Balan, *A Retrospective Analysis of the Clinical Quality Effects of the Acquisition of Highland Park Hospital by Evanston Northwestern Healthcare*, 18 International Journal of the Economics of Business 1 (2011); Robert Lawton Burns, Jeffrey S. Mccullough, Douglas R. Wholey, Gregory Kruse, Peter Kralovec, and Ralph Muller. *Is the System Really the Solution? Operating Costs in Hospital Systems,* 72 Medical Care Research and Review 3, 247 (2015). doi:10.1177/1077558715583789.

189 Emily Gee, *Provider Consolidation Drives Up Health Care Costs*, Center for American Progress, (last accessed July 14th, 2021), https://www.americanprogress.org/article/provider-consolidation-drives-health-care-costs/.

190 Martin Gaynor, Rodrigo Moreno-Serra, and Carol Propper, *Death by Market Power: Reform, Competition, and Patient Outcomes in the National Health Service,* 5 American Economic Journal: Economic Policy 4, 134 (2013). doi:10.1257/pol.5.4.134.

191 Town, et al., *supra,* at page 10.

concentrated markets.[192] Another study found correlation between increased mortality rates for patients with heart diseases and higher hospital market concentration.[193] Preventing consolidation reduces costs; but more importantly, it leads to superior health outcomes for patients.

Antitrust Enforcement has Not Been Adequate to Reinvigorate Markets

Antitrust enforcement has not been able to sufficiently restore competition in hospital markets. In their new book, Professors David Dranove and Lawton R. Burns conclude that "antitrust agencies have taken a go-slow approach to enforcement, reflecting a combination of risk aversion, resource limits, and rules of the legal system."[194] The antitrust response has been inadequate notwithstanding the significant resources dedicated to restoring competition in health care. For example, between 2010 and 2018, over half of antitrust cases brough by the FTC were focused on the health care industry.[195] Yet, antitrust policy makes enforcement difficult. For example, many mergers are too small to require reporting to antitrust agencies. This allows hospitals to expand piecemeal and without supervision.[196] Similarly, the FTC cannot even enforce against anticompetitive conduct by not-for-profits; this presents a significant problem, considering how many hospitals are run as not-for-profits.[197] Consequently, the problem of concentrated hospital markets dominated by mega-providers driving up the high cost of health care in the United States requires new remedies.

Congress Should Lift the Ban It Placed on Physician-Owned Hospitals

Fortunately, there is something Congress can do. Low-hanging fruit would be removing barriers to health care market entry that Congress itself has erected. This includes the elimination of the restraint the Affordable Care Act (ACA) placed on Physician-Owned Hospitals (POHs). As explained by Joshua Perry, in An Obituary for Physician-Owned Specialty Hospitals, 23 Health Lawyer 2, 24 (2010), prior to the enactment of the ACA, physicians enjoyed a "whole hospital exception" to the Stark law— meaning that if they had an ownership interest in an entire hospital, and were authorized to perform services there, they could refer patients to that hospital. However, provisions within section 6001 of the ACA (42 U.S.C. 1395nn) essentially eliminate the Stark exception for physicians who do not have an ownership or investment interest and a provider agreement in effect as of December 31, 2010. Second, under current law the POH cannot expand its treatment capacity unless certain restrictive exceptions can be met. Thus, the ACA all but put an end to one source of new competition in hospital markets by banning new physician-owned hospitals that depend on Medicare reimbursement.

A 2020 report from Alexander Acosta, Alex M. Azar II, and Steven T. Mnuchin entitled, Reforming America's Healthcare System Through Choice and Competition, U.S. Department of Health and Human Services, U.S. Department of Treasury, U.S. Department of Labor

---

192 DP Kessler and MB McClellan, *Is Hospital Competition Socially Wasteful?* 115 Q J Econ. 2, 577 (2000).

193 T.B. Hayford, The Impact of Hospital Mergers on Treatment Intensity and Health Outcomes, 47 Health Services Research, 1008 (2012).

194 Dranove, supra, at 178.

195 Martin Gaynor, Antitrust Applied, at 17.

196 C. Capps, David Dranove, and C. Ody, Physician Practice Consolidation Driven By Small Acquisitions, So Antitrust Agencies Have Few Tools To Intervene, 36 Health Affairs 9, 1556 (2017).

197 Martin Gaynor, Antitrust Applied, at 18.

(2020), recommends that "Congress should consider repealing the ACA changes to physician self-referral law that limited physician-owned hospitals."[198] Congressional action would be especially welcome because physician-owned hospitals have developed an enviable track record for high quality and low-cost care.[199]

Reversing the ACA-imposed ban on new construction or expansion of existing physician-owned hospitals will both stimulate greater competition and provide patients with another option to receive high quality health care services. An April 12, 2021 Health Affairs article entitled, Reversing Hospital Consolidation: The Promise Of Physician-Owned Hospitals, explains how.

In sum, much of the U.S. hospital market lacks competition and restoring the whole hospital exception to the Stark law is the right prescription.

Conclusion

Competition is critical for well-functioning health care markets. When markets are not competitive and firms have market power, society is at a loss. Unfortunately, the majority of health insurance, hospital, and PBM care markets are not competitive. Mergers and acquisitions have contributed to these low levels of competition. Strong antitrust scrutiny of mergers in these markets is warranted. Also needed are policies that promote market entry, including lifting the statutory ban Congress imposed on physician-owned hospitals.

Federation of American Hospitals®

Charles N. Kahn III President and CEO
March 27, 2023

The Honorable Brett Guthrie Chair
House Energy and Commerce Health Subcommittee
2434 Rayburn House Office Building Washington, DC 20215

The Honorable Anna Eshoo Ranking Member
House Energy and Commerce Health Subcommittee
272 Cannon House Office Building Washington, DC 20215

198 Alexander Acosta, Alex M. Azar II, Steven T. Mnuchin, *Reforming America's Healthcare System Through Choice and Competition*, U.S. Department of Health and Human Services, U.S. Department of Treasury, U.S. Department of Labor (2020).

199 Id.

Dear Chairman Guthrie and Ranking Member Eshoo,

The Federation of American Hospitals (FAH) is pleased to provide this Statement for the Record regarding the House Energy and Commerce Health Subcommittee's hearing on "Lowering Unaffordable Costs: Examining Transparency and Competition in Health Care."

The FAH is the national representative of more than 1,000 leading tax-paying hospitals and health systems throughout the United States. FAH members provide patients and communities with access to high-quality, affordable care in both urban and rural areas across 46 states, plus Washington, DC and Puerto Rico. Our members include teaching, acute, inpatient rehabilitation, behavioral health, and long-term care hospitals and provide a wide range of inpatient, ambulatory, post-acute, emergency, children's, and cancer services.

The FAH and our member hospitals share the Subcommittee's goal of promoting a market-driven health care system that empowers patients with more choice and control over their health care decisions. We believe a more informed and engaged consumer will drive competition that accelerates progress towards higher quality and more affordable health care.

We look forward to working with the Energy and Commerce Health Subcommittee and appreciate the opportunity to provide input on several key policy platforms.

To help further the Subcommittee's goal of examining health care costs, this Statement for the Record addresses: hospital price transparency compliance; understanding the positive outcomes of hospital integration; the importance of maintaining the current ban on self-referral to physician-owned hospitals (POHs); opposing site-neutral payment cuts; and raising awareness of insurer and Medicare Advantage abuses.

Hospital Price Transparency Compliance

The FAH believes that all individuals deserve transparent, meaningful and easy to understand information, especially about their cost sharing responsibility, so they can make more informed decisions regarding their health care.

Our hospitals are committed to being compliant with the Centers for Medicare and Medicaid Services (CMS) Hospital Price Transparency Rule and are supportive of the Subcommittee's efforts to highlight the importance of patients knowing how much their care will cost before they receive it. It has been falsely reported that hospitals are intentionally avoiding complying with CMS's Hospital Price Transparency Rule. Just last month, CMS released a report that found that 70% of hospitals complied with both components of the regulation, including the consumer-friendly display of shoppable services information, as well as the machine-readable file requirements in 2022.[200] This is an increase from 27% in 2021. Moreover, when looking at each individual component of the rule, 82% of hospitals met the consumer- friendly display of shoppable services information requirement in 2022 (up from 66% in 2021) and 82% met the machine-readable file requirement (up from 30% in 2021). With this significant increase in compliance in just one year, significant progress has been, and will continue to be made, in complying with the important but cumbersome requirements. Thus,

[200] "Hospital Price Transparency: Progress and Commitment to Achieving Its Potential," Health Affairs Forefront, February 14, 2023.

hospitals and health systems remain committed to working with CMS to implement these policies and deliver reliable and usable pricing information to patients.

Understand Positive Effects of Hospital Integration

The nation's health care landscape is, by necessity, shifting towards integrated systems and coordinated care, and mergers do create sustainable market conditions for hospital care and services. This shift has naturally occurred within the health care industry and has been further fueled by health care policies that promote a more patient-centered, value-based health care delivery and payment system. Additionally, increasingly complex health care regulatory and administrative requirements such as those regarding electronic health records, cybersecurity, quality programs, and, increasingly, payer administrative hurdles, are extremely resource-intensive and difficult for an individual hospital or an individual physician or small group practice to navigate.

Hospital integration also is a response to inadequate, below the cost-of-care, public sector funding for hospitals, forcing hospitals to adapt to real-world economic and financial factors. The priority of any integration is to keep hospitals open, preserve or expand patients' access to care and continue to provide consistent, quality care around the clock to every patient treated in a hospital. By pursuing mergers and other integration efforts, hospitals are able to maintain their presence in the community, share and scale up best practices, and protect patients' access to essential and affordable quality care, especially in rural communities.

There have been multiple studies that point to the positive effect on quality as well as reduction in mortality associated with hospital mergers. For example, a study recently published in JAMA Network Open concluded that hospital mergers improve health outcomes in rural hospitals.[201] The researchers, who are affiliated with IBM Watson Health and the Agency for Healthcare Research and Quality, compared data from 172 merged rural hospitals and 266 comparison hospitals and found that in-hospital mortality rates were lower after the rural hospitals completed mergers. Researchers noted that "Mergers may enable rural hospitals to improve quality of care through access to needed financial, clinical, and technological resources, which is important to enhancing rural health and reducing urban-rural disparities in quality."

In addition, the American Hospital Association (AHA) has released numerous studies indicating that hospital integration benefits patients by providing higher quality care at a lower cost. A 2021 study reinforced the conclusions of previous reports: hospital acquisitions benefit patients by providing access to higher-quality care at a lower cost.[202] Specifically, a previous 2018 study found that mergers of hospitals within 30 miles of each other generated savings of more than $6.6 million in annual operating expenses at acquired hospitals.[203] The studies also determined that hospital acquisitions lead to improvements on key indicators of quality.

---

[201] Jiang HJ, Fingar KR, Liang L, Henke RM, Gibson TP. Quality of Care Before and After Mergers and Acquisitions of Rural Hospitals. JAMA Netw Open. 2021;4(9):e2124662. doi:10.1001/jamanetworkopen.2021.24662.

[202] Hospital Merger Benefits: An Econometric Analysis Revisited, conducted by economists at Charles River Associates, Sean May, Monica Noether and Ben Stearns, August 2021, and sponsored by the American Hospital Association.

[203] In Hospital Mergers: Foundation for a Modern, Efficient and High-Performing Health Care System of the Future, conducted by Charles River Associates, 2018, and sponsored by the American Hospital Association.

Empirical analysis continues to show a statistically significant reduction in inpatient readmission rates and a composite readmission/mortality outcome measure.[204]

Further, in 2013, the Center for Healthcare Economics and Policy released a comprehensive analysis of hospital integration studies, including 75 studies spanning the years 1996-2013, as well as 36 primary sources. The Center's analysis outlines improvements in health care for communities that result from mergers, including:

- Significant benefits to communities and patients in markets where hospitals remain open
- Preserved and expanded access to essential medical care.
- Improved service offerings and quality of care
- Sustained and necessary investment in technology, facilities and health IT
- Sensible reduction in excess capacity
- More competitive health care markets

As the health care landscape continues to evolve and providers accelerate efforts to improve patient outcomes and lower costs through coordinated care, the FAH will continue its efforts to inform the Subcommittee about health care competition and hospital integration. It is imperative that this issue is put in proper context, and focus is placed more holistically on the total landscape. The FAH is happy to discuss in further detail the positive effects of integration.

Maintain Current Ban on Self-Referral to Physician-Owned Hospitals (POH)

To help achieve the important goal of lowering health care costs, it is important that Congress continue to reject efforts by those who would seek to weaken the Stark Law ban on self-referral to POHs. Such arrangements are mired in conflicts of interest, and years of independent data show such arrangements result in over-utilization of Medicare services at significant cost to patients and the Medicare program. There is a substantial history of Congressional policy development and underlying research on the impact of self-referral to POHs. The empirical record is clear that these conflicts of interest arrangements of hospital ownership and self-referral by owner physicians promote unfair competition and result in cherry- picking of the healthiest and wealthiest patients, excessive utilization of care, and patient safety concerns. Today's policy includes 15 years of work by Congress, involving numerous hearings, as well as analyses by the HHS Office of inspector General (OIG), the Government Accountability Office (GAO), and the Medicare Payment Advisory Commission (MedPAC).

In 2010, Congress acted to protect the Medicare and Medicaid programs and the taxpayers that fund them by imposing a prospective ban on self-referral to new POHs. The FAH strongly believes that the foundation for the current law must not be weakened. It is noteworthy that Congressional Budget Office scoring of proposals to modify existing law consistently demonstrates that self-referral to POHs increases utilization, which increases Medicare costs and health care costs generally. The law helps ensure that full-service community hospitals can continue to meet their mission to provide quality care to all the patients in their communities.

---

[204] See Footnote 3.

Data from the health care consulting firm Dobson | Davanzo, released today by the FAH and AHA, shows that POHs, when compared to other hospitals, treat less medically complex and more financially lucrative patients, provide fewer emergency services, and treat fewer COVID- 19 cases.

Further, these arrangements have patient care margins more than 15 times those of non-POHs, they render less uncompensated care, and they treat fewer of dual-eligible (Medicaid and Medicare) patients. Even though POHs provide care to fewer patients with complex conditions, they are five times more likely to receive CMS's maximum penalty for readmissions. The new data reinforces many of the findings of earlier studies by the HHS OIG, GAO, and MedPAC, among others, documenting the conflicts of interest inherent with POHs that led to the Congressional ban in 2010. Those reports concluded that POHs:

- Cherry-pick patients by avoiding the less profitable Medicaid and uninsured patients;
- Treat fewer medically complex patients; and
- Provide fewer emergency services and often rely on publicly funded 911 services and acute care, community hospitals for these services for their own patients.

Thus, current law is key to ensuring that full-service community hospitals can continue to meet their mission to provide quality care to all patients in their communities. Weakening or unwinding the current ban opens the door to the very behaviors that Congress sought to prevent.

Oppose Site-Neutral Payment Cuts to Ensure Access to Care

The FAH strongly opposes site-neutral payment policies, as these types of policies would be detrimental for patient access to medically necessary care. Under a site-neutral payment policy, the payment for a service provided to a patient is similar regardless of the setting where the service is provided. The FAH agrees with the goal of ensuring patients receive the right care, at the right time, in the right setting. However, one-size-fits-all site-neutral payment policies ignore fundamental functional and cost structure differences between hospitals and physician offices, among other settings, and the unique, mission-critical services communities rely on hospitals to provide.

Site-neutral payments do not take into account one simple fact: hospitals and doctors' offices are not the same. Hospitals provide critical services to entire communities, including 24/7 access to emergency care and disaster relief. They need to maintain the ability to treat complex patients who require more intense care, and therefore require a different payment structure.

Hospital-affiliated sites offer patients more integrated care across health care settings, services for which hospitals need to be properly reimbursed to maintain coordinated, high-quality care for patients.

Increasingly, care is shifting from the inpatient to outpatient settings, meaning that patients now seen in hospital outpatient departments may require a higher level of care than traditionally offered in a physician's office. Reimbursement for outpatient services provided in a hospital outpatient department should reflect the higher overhead costs associated with providing care in that setting. Additionally, regulatory requirements such as the Emergency Medical

Treatment and Labor Act (EMTALA), hospital Conditions of Participation, hospital state licensure, and complex cost reports impose substantial resource and cost burdens that physician offices and ambulatory surgical centers do not have and therefore are not reflected in their payments.

On March 27, 2023, the AHA released a study that found that hospital outpatient departments treat underserved populations and sicker, more complex patients than other ambulatory care sites.[205] The study indicates that relative to patients seen in independent physician offices and ambulatory surgical centers, Medicare patients seen in hospital outpatient departments tend to be:

- Lower-income;
- Non-white;
- Eligible for Medicare based on disability and/or end-stage renal disease
- More severe comorbidities or complications;
- Dually-eligible for Medicare and Medicaid; and
- Previously seen in an emergency department or hospital setting.[206]

As seen in this recent study, site-neutral payment policies fail to distinguish between types of patients' hospitals serve when compared to other providers as well as the difference in level of care. Therefore, the one-size-fits-all site-neutral policies put the most vulnerable patients' access to care at risk.

Stop Insurer and Medicare Advantage Unfair Practices

The FAH is increasingly concerned by the alarming practices of Medicare Advantage (MA) and other insurance plans that harm patients by eroding access to and affordability of medically necessary care, and also require hospitals and caregivers to divert precious resources and time to respond to these tactics. These actions include excessive use of prior authorization, inadequate provider networks, extended observation care, retroactive reclassification of patient status (i.e., inpatient versus observation), and aggressive and arbitrary pre- and post-payment denial policies.

Some of these concerns were included in a recent HHS OIG Report[207] showing that MA organizations (MAOs) systemically apply problematic operating policies, procedures and protocols that limit care for MA enrollees. The OIG Report also identifies a pattern by which MAOs apply utilization controls to improperly withhold coverage or care from MA enrollees, as previously discussed. Specifically:

---

205 "Comparison of Medicare Beneficiary Characteristics Between Hospital Outpatient Departments and Other Ambulatory Care Settings"; prepared for the American Hospital Association, located at: https://www.aha.org/guidesreports/2023-03-27-comparison-medicare-beneficiary-characteristics-report.

206 See study results -https://www.aha.org/guidesreports/2023-03-27-comparison-medicare-beneficiary-characteristics-report.

207 Christi A. Grimm, U.S. Department of Health and Human Services Office of the Inspector General ("OIG"), OEI-09-18-00260, "Some Medicare Advantage Organization Denials of Prior Authorization Requests Raise Concerns About Beneficiary Access to Medically Necessary Care" (April 2022), https://oig.hhs.gov/oei/reports/OEI-09-18- 00260.pdf.

- Improper prior authorization denials. The OIG found that thirteen percent (13%) of prior authorization requests denied by MAOs would have been approved for beneficiaries under original Medicare.
- Improper denials for lack of documentation. The OIG found that in many cases beneficiary medical records were sufficient to support the medical necessity of the services provided.
- Improper payment request denials. The OIG found that eighteen percent (18%) of payment requests denied by MAOs actually met Medicare coverage rules and MAO billing rules.

These OIG findings reflect a broader pattern of MAO practices that inappropriately deny, limit, modify or delay the delivery of or access to services and care for MA beneficiaries. FAH members have regularly observed that MAOs abuse prior authorization requirements, maintain inadequate provider networks, use extended observation care, retroactively reclassify patient status (i.e., inpatient versus observation), improperly down code claims, and deploy inappropriate pre- and post-payment denial policies, and even deny claims for previously authorized services.

CMS recently acknowledged many of these concerns in two recently proposed regulations[208] that would constrain some of the bad behaviors MA plans employ related to prior authorization and non-coverage of items and services that would be covered for beneficiaries covered under the traditional Medicare fee-for-service program.

As the Subcommittee explores ways to improve health care costs and delivery, we urge you to investigate these practices and, at a minimum, exercise oversight authority to help ensure MA behaviors that protect patients through, for example, prior authorization reforms, comprehensive provider networks, and requiring MA plans to follow traditional Medicare's two- midnight rule for patient admissions.

****

The FAH appreciates the opportunity to offer these insights. We are committed to working with Congress and the Subcommittee to ensure the availability of affordable, accessible care to all Americans. Our goal is to build on what's working in America – starting with the strength of the employer-provided health coverage that millions of Americans rely on today, rather than government-run plans such as a public option or dismantling our current pluralistic system and replacing it with a one-size-fits-all government-controlled single payer system. We look forward to working with the Subcommittee to meet the significant challenges that hospitals face in treating patients and will be a resource as the Subcommittee examines access-promoting solutions. Our focus is providing access to quality care and we look forward to working with you to ensure this outcome.

If you have any questions or would like to discuss them further, please do not hesitate to contact me or a member of my staff at (202) 624-1534.

---

208 *See* https://www.cms.gov/newsroom/press-releases/cms-proposes-rule-expand-access-health-information-and-im prove-prior-authorization-process.

Sincerely,

The Alliance
Self-Funding Smart ®

House Committee on Energy and Commerce Subcommittee on Health
Hearing on Lowering Unaffordable Costs:
Examining Transparency and Competition in Health Care
March 28, 2023

The Alliance Employer Healthcare Purchasing Cooperative (The Alliance)
Statement for the Record

Chairs McMorris Rodgers and Guthrie and Ranking Members Pallone and Eshoo and members:

Thank you for holding a hearing on transparency and competition in healthcare – two issues that are critically important to employers across the nation that are committed to providing affordable health coverage to employees and their families despite the challenges of doing so.

The Alliance is a non-profit cooperative of 300+ self-funded employers who together purchase health care from over 34,000 doctors, medical professionals and facilities across the Midwest to provide health care to 110,000 employees and family members. Our cooperative was created by employers more than 30 years ago to pursue the triple aim on behalf of employers, employees and dependents, with transparency of cost and quality information as the foundation of the work we do.

The Alliance has been working for decades to provide reliable and actionable cost and quality information to our members and their employees and families. Our goal is to have a trustworthy source of valid and objective value measurement to (a) help our members steer employees and dependents toward the highest value health care available, (b) reward health care providers that are doing a great job with both cost and quality and (c) help member employees and their familes make informed decisions about their options for health care. While the complexity and opacity of the US health system has made this journey difficult, we believe transparency is foundational to achieving a health system that delivers the best outcomes and is affordable for U.S. workers.

The federal transparency efforts of the past several years hold great promise in helping us make rapid progress toward our goals of a truly free market health system informed by objective and reliable price and quality information, and we applaud Congress for its efforts to support this work. That said, we have a long way to go, and we provide these comments to help members of Congress move employers closer to their vision in the years ahead.

Hospital Transparency Rules

One day we hope to glean useable data from hospital transparency files to compare prices, but we are not there yet. That is because some facilities and systems see to do a good job complying with regulations while others are posting inaccurate prices that do not match contracted rates. Untilthe federal government requires uniformity among these files where prices are calculated exactly the same, the information will not be comparable. We believe CMS must develop a schema for hospital files and require hospitals to use it.

We also believe it is time for CMS to step up audit and enforcement activities. Last January marked the two-year anniversary of the implementation of hospital transparency requirements, and yet we cannot rely on machine-readable files (MRFs) for accurate information.

Health Plan (Issuer) Transparency Rules

The problem with issuer files is not uniformity of the data but the sheer volume of it.

Unlike hospital MRFs, there is schema in place for health plan MRFs, and issuers are required to include on MRFs all prices contracted. Because we use standard contracts with most providers, we legally have a "contracted rate" for thousands of CPT codes that will never be billed. In addition, issuers are allowed within the scheme to embed complex terms which can add rows of data to every MRF. We estimate that 98% of the data included in these files is meaningless, bloating them to a size that renders them undigestible for many organizations that do not have the capabilities to clean the data. We urge you to encourage CMS to reconsider decisions that have polluted the data available, and require instead accurate data for only the services that are commonly delivered by each provider.

In a similar vein, it is imperative that CMS require all prices to be expressed in a dollar amount instead of a percentage so that rates are comparable. A percentage is not helpful at all if the starting rates are missing, which is typically the case for providers who are not required to post chargemasters.

The Importance of Complete Good Faith Estimates

Even if hospital and issuer transparency files were perfect, there would still be critical pieces of information missing. Without these pieces, we are not able to help enrollees and family members understand costs or shop for care when they have the opportunity to do so.

The pieces of information we need, which good faith estimates may be able to deliver if designed correctly, is a complete estimate of all the charges a patient is likely to incur during an episode of care whether that be treatment, screening or a procedure, including related services from other providers, labs or imaging services. Without this information, the health plan's AEOB is unlikely to depict an accurate out of pocket cost, and we fear this will lead quickly to patients discounting good faith estimates and AEOBs as inaccurate and unhelpful.

We also believe Advanced EOBs should be provided to patients within days of scheduling, which would give plans more time to help enrollees shop for higher value care that may be available and beneficial to patients. If the goal is to help individuals shop for care, then they will need time to go through that process with the help of their employer or health plan.

Quality Data

We want to foster competition on both price and quality. While federal price transparency rules are still in their infancy, we see the potential, once mature, to provide consumers with the raw material needed to understand and compare prices and equip purchasers with analytics to negotiate with providers based upon more complete information. Meaningful ratings of quality are still elusive for the commercially insured market. Where CMS makes quality ratings publicly available, they are primarily based on the Medicare Fee for Service (FFS) population. A significant barrier to the acceptance of CMS' quality ratings is that providers are not being rated on their full population of patients.

To address this issue, we ask that:

- A national All Payer Claims Database be pursued which would provide the breadth of administrative data needed to compute a robust set of quality measures. And if the database includes allowed amounts, it would also enable payers to predict the total cost of care for any given episode – the holy grail of price transparency.
- CMS' quality measurement scope be expanded beyond Medicare and Medicaid. We need a federal agency to administer a quality measurement enterprise that operates in the public interest, not just the interests of the Medicare population. If CMS' scope cannot be expanded, there are other HHS agencies capable of leading HHS' measurement enterprise, such as the Agency for Healthcare Research and Quality.
- An HHS agency begin computing administrative-data derived measures that will optimally serve its programs as well as the transparency needs of the commercially insured population. For measures to realize their potential to effect health care costs for the public and private they need to use all payer claims data instead of or in addition to data from the Medicare FFS population. Taking this step of making these measure inclusive vs. restrictive is a tangible step toward the HHS goal of working in collaboration with private sector payers.
- A body comprised of public and private stakeholders be established to advise HHS on the identification and implementation of transparency strategies aimed at affecting the cost for the public and private sectors. CMS does commendable work listening to private sector priorities. However, given CMS' charge of serving the Medicare and Medicaid populations, the agency stops short of designing and acting in the interests of the public at large.
- The standardization of, and capability to, efficiently abstract electronic medical record (EMR) data for inclusion in administrative data sets be accelerated. Such EMR data is needed to measure quality in a number of complex, high cost clinical areas, such as

cancer care and various cardiac conditions. While HHS began work in this space nearly 20 years ago, the pace of making such EMR data available for measurement is insufficient. The Office of the National Coordinator for Health Information Technology (ONC) needs to play a stronger role in integrating EMRs in all aspects of the flow of information in support of measurement for transparency. Thus, HHS needs to restructure ONC in such a way to insulate it from the influences of any given stakeholder group thereby making it more accountable to the public good.

Anticompetitive Terms in Healthcare Contracts

The Alliance supports most of the provisions and aim of the Healthy Competition for Better Care Act introduced last session by Senator Mike Braun and Senator Tammy Baldwin. The bill tackles a number of anticompetitive contract terms that do not belong in any provider-payor contract.

However, we oppose exceptions for any health plan, including provider owned health plans. Exceptions that allow certain payors and providers to play by different rules is, in itself, anticompetitive in nature.

Consolidation

Horizontal and vertical provider consolidation is of great concern to our employer members and a threat to free market health care. How can a market work as intended if consumers have only one choice for the majority of the healthcare provided in their area? How can they find the highest value health care if all of the primary care physicians in their area are employed by hospital systems that require or financially incent them to refer care within the system?

In Wisconsin currently, three of our major provider systems are in some phase of a merger process. Others are on the horizon, with health system CEOs announcing publicly that they have to merge in order to keep up with competitors. We urge the committee to develop a commonsense and comprehensive anti-consolidation package that ensures that any healthcare consolidation allowed to move forward is in the best interests of the public.

Accountability

With transparency rules still in the early stages of adoption, we urge members of Congress to pursue the balance of the Shewart Cycle (Plan-Do-Check-Act) and begin to assess the impact of these rules. We need to examine what actions are taking place in response to transparency, particularly what the impact is on health care prices. We are already seeing evidence that awareness of price variation is leading some providers to demand higher rates, or “payor parity”, where dominant providers insist on raising prices to be equal to their most lucrative payor contracts. It’s incumbent upon Congress to monitor for these unintended consequences and hold provider and payors accountable for self-serving actions that work against the goal of making health care affordable for patients. At the very least, Congress should require an agency report that assesses year-over-year impact on prices.

Once again, we'd like to thank this administration, the former administration and the many members of Congress that support the ongoing march toward true healthcare cost and quality transparency. On behalf of our employer members, we are grateful for the opportunity to provide our comments on these important issues If we can be of further assistance to you, please do not hesitate to contact Melissa Duffy at mduffy@dcstrategies.org.

Sincerely,

Cheryl DeMars, CEO
Employers Health Care Alliance Cooperative (The Alliance)

PUTTING PATIENTS FIRST
NATIONAL HEALTH COUNCIL

National Health Council Statement for the Record
U.S. House of Representatives Committee on Energy and Commerce
Subcommittee on Health Hearing
"Lowering Unaffordable Costs: Examining Transparency and Competition in Health Care"
March 28, 2023

Chairs McMorris Rodgers and Guthrie and Ranking Members Pallone and Eshoo,

On behalf of the National Health Council (NHC), we thank you for holding this important and timely hearing on transparency and competition in health care. Patients are facing rising health insurance premiums, reduced access to care, and record levels of medical debt due to a health care system whose payment and delivery structures too often reward high-cost, low-quality care. Addressing transparency and competition is an important part of helping patients access and afford the care they need. It may be seen as only an incremental step, but it is paramount to ensuring patients can make better decision and helping patient advocates and policymakers craft policy that will improve the lives of people with chronic diseases and disabilities.

Created by and for patient organizations more than 100 years ago, the NHC brings diverse organizations together to forge consensus and drive patient-centered health policy. We promote increased access to affordable, high-value, sustainable health care. Made up of more than 150 national health- related organizations and businesses, the NHC's core membership includes the nation's leading patient organizations. Other members include health-related associations and nonprofit organizations including the provider, research, and family caregiver communities; and businesses representing biopharmaceutical, device, diagnostic, generic drug, and payer organizations.

Patients Need More Information

The current health care system is fragmented, opaque, and often driven by misaligned incentives. These factors combine to make care inaccessible and/or unaffordable, while making informed decision making difficult if not impossible. People with chronic diseases and disabilities each have unique challenges managing their conditions and different goals that they would like to achieve through their care. They want access to medicines and services that are going to best help them meet their needs, and they need information to help them and their providers decide what their best options are.

But unfortunately, this type of information is often unavailable, not understandable, or not actionable.

We have been pleased to see some steps in the right direction such as the creation of real-time benefit tools that can help providers let their patients know what cost-sharing requirements will be at the time or prescribing. Similarly, we are supportive of requirements for health care facilities to disclose the costs of routine services, though compliance and enforcement have lagged, and patients need better tools to comparison shop.

Finally, people with chronic conditions need better tools to pick a health care plan that best suits their needs. For a healthy individual, they may be best suited by plan with the lowest premium. However, if someone has a chronic condition that has intensive, consistent, and unique care needs, they need better information to pick the plan that best helps them manage their condition or conditions. They may need to know whether their specialists are in network, whether their medications are covered, dollar amounts for coinsurance for their medicines, and whether they are subject to utilization management such as prior authorization, step therapy, or copay accumulators. Much of this information is either absent from the Medicare Plan Finder or Healthcare.gov or difficult to find on these platforms. Patients need more information and better sorting and filtering options.

Patient Advocates and Policymakers Need More Information

Another benefit of transparency is its impact on public policy. As previously stated, the health care system is complex and opaque. This not only leads to difficulty in seeking appropriate and timely care, it also leads to difficulty in making needed policy changes. If patient advocacy organizations had better data about the incentives and decision- making in the health care system, we would be able to better analyze legislative and regulatory proposals and advocate for needed change. This would in turn help policymakers better understand the impact of changes on the lives of the American public.

For example, the hearing today will explore the role of Pharmacy Benefit Managers (PBMs), whose contracts with other firms in the drug supply chain are kept secret. The same can be said for other contracting arrangements throughout the health care system. Without understanding whether decisions account for patient perspectives, whether and how they are grounded in clinical evidence, and how incentives drive decisions, we far too often lack the data needed to educate our patient populations and analyze the impact of proposed legislation.

The NHC has long advocated for transparency across the health care system from every sector that impacts patients' lives. This includes health care providers, insurers, PBMs, and medical product manufacturers. It also includes government entities. For example, we would like to see the Centers for Medicare and Medicaid Services expand reporting on drug costs and spending, including price concessions and rebates, to help inform cost-containment strategies and drive informed action by health care stakeholders.

Conclusion

Once again, the NHC appreciates the opportunity to provide input into this important issue. Please do not hesitate to contact Eric Gascho, the National Health Council's Senior Vice President of Policy and Government Affairs, if you or your staff would like to discuss these issues in greater detail. He is reachable by phone at 202-973-0545 or via e-mail at egascho@nhcouncil.org.

NCPA
NATIONAL COMMUNITY PHARMACISTS ASSOCIATION
WWW.NCPA.ORG

Statement for the Record: The National Community Pharmacists Association (NCPA) United States House Health Subcommittee of the Committee on Energy and Commerce Hearing: "Lowering Unaffordable Costs: Examining Transparency and Competition in Health Care" March 28, 2023

Chairman Guthrie, Ranking Member Eshoo, and Members of the Subcommittee:

Thank you for conducting this hearing on lowering costs and increasing transparency and competition in healthcare. In this statement, NCPA will offer support and suggestions on several policy considerations that would lower out of pocket costs for patients' prescription drug costs, provide certainty for pharmacies, and protect taxpayers by bringing more transparency to Medicaid spending.

NCPA represents America's community pharmacists, including 19,400 independent community pharmacies. Almost half of all community pharmacies provide long-term care services and play a critical role in ensuring patients have immediate access to medications in both community and long-term care (LTC) settings. Together, our members represent a $78.5 billion healthcare marketplace, employ 240,000 individuals, and provide an expanding set of healthcare services to millions of patients every day. Our members are small business owners who are among America's most accessible healthcare providers.

Our pharmacies and the patients they serve have long had concerns about pharmacy benefit managers (PBMs), their anticompetitive practices, and the role they play in ever-increasing drug costs. These concerns have been further exacerbated because of the COVID-19 pandemic's impact on small businesses. Independently owned pharmacies have served as lifelines as essential businesses during the pandemic. However, PBM practices are causing these small businesses to struggle to remain viable and keep doors open to provide continued access and care. We appreciate the efforts of the Chair and Ranking Member to discuss PBM practices and their impact on drug prices for patients.

PBMs are not transparent about the rebate process and their profit margins. We often do not know how much the PBMs make on administrative service fees and spread pricing (the difference between how much they reimburse pharmacy and the higher price they charge the plan for administering that same prescription). More accurate reporting is needed to provide this transparency. To get a complete picture of PBM financials, we also need greater clarity on:

- Fees and claw backs charged to unaffiliated pharmacies;
- Methods to steer patients towards pharmacy benefit manager-owned pharmacies;
- Potentially unfair audits of independent pharmacies;
- Complicated and opaque methods to determine pharmacy reimbursement;
- The prevalence of prior authorizations and other administrative restrictions;
- The use of PBM-defined specialty drug lists and associated specialty drug policies; and
- The impact of rebates and fees from drug manufacturers on formulary design and the costs of prescription drugs to payers and patients.

Bring Transparency to the Medicaid Program and Prevent the Use of Spread Pricing by PBMs

H.R. 1613, the Drug Price Transparency in Medicaid Act was introduced by Reps. Buddy Carter (R-Ga.) Vincente Gonzalez (D-Tx.), Rick Allen (R-Ga.), Jake Auchincloss (D-Mass.), Elise Stefanik (R-NY), and Deborah Ross (D-NC). It would bring transparency to the Medicaid program by:

- Prohibiting spread pricing/requiring a full pass-through in all Medicaid managed care programs.
- Requiring pharmacy reimbursements in all state Medicaid managed care programs be at a rate of pharmacy's average acquisition costs and the state's Medicaid fee for service dispensing fee.
- Limiting payments to PBMs to solely administrative fees.
- Mandating National Average Drug Acquisition Costs (NADAC) reporting to CMS by all pharmacies participating in state Medicaid programs. This provision would provide much needed transparency in drug pricing and allow reimbursements to reflect the true acquisition costs of prescription drugs in Medicaid.

Bring Transparency for Employers and Consumers and Greater Enforcement Authorities

The Pharmacy Benefit Manager Transparency Act of 2023 (S. 127), introduced by Sens. Maria Cantwell (D- Wash.) and Chuck Grassley (R-Iowa), would increase drug pricing transparency for employers and plan sponsors and hold PBMs accountable for unfair and deceptive practices that drive up the costs of prescription drugs at the expense of consumers.

The bill:

- Prohibits deceptive, unfair pricing schemes, including spread pricing and arbitrary claw backs of payments made to pharmacies.
- Incentivizes transparent PBM practices by making clear that a PBM would not be in violation of the law if it:
  - Passes along 100 percent of rebates to health plan sponsor; AND
  - Provides full disclosure of cost, price, reimbursement and all charged fees, markups, and discounts to plan sponsor and pharmacy; OR
  - Provides the aggregate remuneration fees it receives from drug makers to health plans, payers, and any federal agency.
- Mandates transparency by requiring PBMs to file an annual report with the Federal Trade Commission (FTC), including the total amount they pocket through spread pricing and pharmacy fees.
- Clarifies the enforcement authority of the FTC and state attorneys general to prohibit unfair or deceptive business practices PBM-insurers use in commercial health insurance.

On March 22, 2023, the Commerce Committee marked up the legislation in an executive session. An amendment by Sens. Jon Tester (D-Mont.) and Shelley Moore Capito (R-W.Va.) was adopted that closes a loophole that could have allowed PBMs to continue to engage in the abusive practice of claw backs and protects the DIR final rule that limited post adjudication claw backs. S. 127, as amended, advanced out of the committee on a bipartisan 18-9 vote. NCPA hopes the full Senate will promptly take up this legislation to ensure PBM business practices that impact employers, patients and pharmacies are fair and transparent.

Ensure Patient Access to Pharmacies and Pharmacy Market Competition

Opaque and convoluted PBM and insurance plan pricing structures inhibit pharmacies from being able to plan their business operations without understanding what they will be reimbursed for a given drug or the services they provide for dispensing a given drug. Pharmacy performance/quality measures are being abused by plans/PBMs to secure fees from pharmacies rather than to fairly assess pharmacy performance.

Draft legislation in development by Reps. Morgan Griffith (R-Va.), Vicente Gonzalez (D-Tx.), Buddy Carter (R- Ga.), Lisa Blunt Rochester (D-Del.) and others would improve patient access to pharmacies and pharmacy market competition. This bill requires:

- The Secretary of HHS promulgate regulations to ensure PDP sponsors and MA-PD plans reasonably reimburse pharmacies.
  - This regulatory effort would help to ensure total reimbursement paid, net of all price concessions, fees, incentive payments, and any other form of remuneration

is reasonable for a pharmacy to acquire and dispense drugs and provide necessary pharmacy services.

- PDP sponsors and MA-PD plans beginning on January 1, 2024, to only use standardized measures established by the Secretary and relevant to the performance of a pharmacy based on the drugs a pharmacy dispenses.
- PDP sponsors and MA–PD plans to promptly furnish all pricing components to pharmacies, so that a pharmacy understands its final reimbursement and the purpose of any adjustments in reimbursement.

We are grateful that CMS has finalized its rulemaking that applies all pharmacy price concessions at the point of sale after years of Congressional efforts in support of DIR fee reform. However, while the final rule is a good start, additional statutory authority and clarity is needed that would allow CMS to move forward to address other issues, such as standardized quality metrics. We hope that Congress will work with us to standardize pharmacy quality metrics for pharmacy incentive payments this year, so that a more comprehensive pharmacy DIR fee reform can be implemented in 2024.

Conclusion

Prescription drug prices continue to grow at an alarming rate, while transparency and competition is decreasing. There are many factors in the pharmaceutical supply chain and delivery system that may contribute to these negative factors, including PBM "middlemen." NCPA stands ready to work with Congress and the administration to implement policies that will lower drug prices at the pharmacy counter for our patients.

PATIENT RIGHTS
ADVOCATE.ORG

March 20, 2023

The Honorable Cathy McMorris Rodgers
Chair,
Committee on Energy & Commerce
2125 Rayburn House Office Building
Washington, DC 20515

The Honorable Frank Pallone, Jr.
Ranking Member, Committee on Energy & Commerce
2322 Rayburn House Office Building
Washington, DC 20515

Dear Chair McMorris Rodgers and Ranking Member Pallone:

Thank you for your continued leadership on healthcare price transparency and for requesting the Government Accountability Office (GAO) to investigate hospitals' widespread noncompliance with the provisions of the Hospital Price Transparency Final Rule (the Rule).[209]

Unfortunately, more than two years since the Rule took effect, consumers still often cannot fully see in advance the prices they will be asked to pay so they can comparison shop before receiving care. Healthcare consumers – patients, employers, and unions – far too often cannot see the wide price variations they pay for hospital care, something they would not tolerate in any other industry. Hard-working Americans still face medical debt, garnished wages, and liens on their homes due to hospital overcharges, billing errors, and even fraud because they could not simply see fair market prices in advance.

Your letter to the GAO on November 4, 2022 cited numerous reports and articles from The Wall Street Journal,[210] Johns Hopkins,[211] Health Affairs,[212] and others indicating the widespread noncompliance of hospitals and pressing need for vigorous enforcement of the Rule. Additionally, your request provided a critical call to action for the GAO to help ensure the right of American consumers to benefit from this groundbreaking Rule that can empower them to lower their costs of care and coverage through a functional, competitive marketplace. Over 90% of Americans support healthcare price transparency,[213] which provides consumers access to fair, equitable prices, financial certainty, and the ability for remedy and recourse when they have been overcharged.

We were encouraged to learn that the Energy and Commerce Subcommittee on Health will be conducting a hearing on March 28, 2023 titled, *Lowering Unaffordable Costs: Examining Transparency and Competition in Health Care.* As you prepare for the upcoming hearing, we offer further clarification on the specific requirements of the Rule and our findings of widespread hospital noncompliance.

Last month, the American Hospital Association (AHA) dedicated a page on its website to our latest Semi-Annual Hospital Price Transparency Compliance Report[214] which found only 24.5% of the 2,000 of the nation's largest hospitals reviewed are fully complying with the Rule. The AHA suggests that our report "misconstrues, ignores and mischaracterizes" the level of compliance with the Rule. We are not surprised by its positions; the AHA is a special interest association representing the parties regulated under the rule. The organization alone spends nearly $30 million annually on lobbying efforts,[215] including unsuccessful litigation attempts to thwart the rule from being implemented. However, we are disappointed by the extent of misinformation on the AHA's webpage and in its recent letter transmitted to you as leaders of the House Energy and Commerce Committee, all while hiding behind its disingenuous assertion that the AHA is committed to delivering "reliable and useable pricing information to patients." We therefore offer the following responses and clarifications regarding our analysis:

---

209 84 Fed. Reg. 65524 (Nov. 27, 2019) (codified at 45 C.F.R. Part 180).

210 Melanie Evans, Anna Wilde Mathews, Tom McGinty, *Hospitals Still Not Fully Complying with Federal Price-Disclosure Rules,* Wall Street Journal (Dec. 30, 2021).

211 Johns Hopkins Bloomberg School of Public Health, Study Estimates That More than Half of U.S. Hospitals Not in Compliance with New Pricing Disclosure Rules in First Five Months (Dec. 9, 2021).

212 Health Affairs, Low Compliance from Big Hospitals On CMS's Hospital Price Transparency Rule (Mar. 16, 2021).

213 https://www.patientrightsadvocate.org/survey-2022.

214 Fourth Semi-Annual Hospital Price Transparency Report (Feb. 2023).

215 https://www.opensecrets.org/federal-lobbying/clients/summary?id=D000000116&cycle=2022.

1) The AHA cites a Centers for Medicare & Medicaid Services (CMS) statement referring to an "increase in hospitals meeting website assessment criteria from 27 percent to 70 percent between 2021 and 2022..."
   The phrase "meeting website assessment criteria" does not mean full compliance with the Rule. The quoted statement from CMS appeared in a February 14, 2023 blog post in Health Affairs[216] in which CMS described the website assessment it performed as merely an analysis of the consumer-friendly display of selected items or services: the easier of the two key components of hospital price transparency. In fact, in that blog post, CMS acknowledged the limitations of its website assessment, stating that, "the results cannot be used to determine compliance with respect to every regulatory requirement..."
   We stand by our report, the several reports cited in your letter to the GAO, and more recent peer reports indicating that very significant problems with compliance remain: The Journal of General Internal Medicine reported that only 19% of hospitals were in compliance in January of 2023,[217] the Journal of the American Medical Association (JAMA) Network Open noted that "compliance remained low" in January of 2023,[218] and JAMA reported only 5.7% compliance in June of 2022.[219]
   Even if 70% were an accurate reflection of overall compliance (which it is not), it would mean that more than 1,800 hospitals in the US are not compliant and that patients at nearly one-third of all U.S. hospitals do not have access to critical price information to make healthcare decisions. If CMS issued civil monetary penalties to those 1,800 hospitals, it would dramatically improve compliance, as we know because the two hospitals that were fined thus far immediately came into compliance with exemplary files.
   Stating that the problem is not as bad as last year, even with AHA's misleading representation of compliance figures, is not something of which the AHA nor its constituent hospitals should be proud.
2) The next section of the AHA webpage ('On using formulas instead of dollar amounts') uses quotes that come from a CMS Frequently Asked Questions (FAQ) document in which CMS provides its opinion on various aspects of the Rule and suggests that when hospital prices are determined by algorithms, it should be acceptable for hospitals to provide the algorithms rather than reducing them to dollars-and-cents prices.[220]
   We believe CMS instead should be guided by the Rule which states: "The term 'rate' is defined in the Oxford dictionary as 'a fixed price paid or charged for something, especially goods or services.' We therefore use the terms 'rate' and 'charge'

---

[216] Meena Seshamani & Douglas Jacobs, *Hospital Price Transparency: Progress and Commitment to Achieving Its Potential*, Health Affairs Forefront (Feb. 14, 2023).

[217] Loccoh EC, Khera R, van Meijgaard J, Marsh T, Warraich HJ. *Hospital Adherence to the Federal Price Transparency Mandate: Results from a Nationally Representative Sample.* J Gen Intern Med. 2023 Jan 17. doi: 10.1007/s11606-023-08039-0. Epub ahead of print. PMID: 36650327.

[218] Jiang JX, Krishnan R, Bai G. *Price Transparency in Hospitals—Current Research and Future Directions*. JAMA Netw Open. 2023;6(1):e2249588. doi:10.1001/jamanetworkopen.2022.49588.

[219] Haque W, Ahmadzada M, Janumpally S, et al. *Adherence to a Federal Hospital Price Transparency Rule and Associated Financial and Marketplace Factors*. JAMA. 2022;327(21):2143–2145. doi:10.1001/jama.2022.5363.

[220] Hospital Price Transparency Frequently Asked Questions (updated Nov. 29, 2022).

interchangeably throughout this final rule."[221] Thus, under the plain text of CMS's own Rule, "standard charges" means all of the prices, even if an algorithm produces multiple potential prices.

The referenced FAQ guidance was not promulgated through notice and comment rulemaking as required by the Administrative Procedure Act, so it is not binding, especially in light of clear and specific language in the final rule. Even if the guidance were binding, the CMS guidance only allows the use of a formula where it is impossible to provide a rate. Unfortunately, this section of the guidance provides an escape hatch that is being abused by hospitals; instead of converting the formulas into dollars-and-cents prices, many continue to posting formulas that are uninterpretable by both consumers and software tools.

3) AHA next quotes the CMS FAQ which seeks to explain the phrase "as applicable" as permitting use of the notation, "N/A."

   Although CMS provided an exception in its FAQs for the limited circumstances under which a hospital may enter an "N/A" rather than a price for a cell in its file, the AHA goes too far by defending hospitals' egregious use of this exception.[222] This specific issue was addressed in a recent (February 25, 2023) NBC Nightly News Story about CMS's failure to robustly enforce the Rule. We strongly urge you to view it. Specifically, please note the comment made by CMS Administrator Chiquita Brooks-LaSure that "N/A, according to our rules, means 'we [the hospital] don't do the procedure.'"

   If CMS had conducted its compliance reviews with any diligence, it would have discovered that many hospitals' machine-readable files provide an "N/A" value instead of a price for items and services that those hospitals do, in fact, provide. Our analysis found that hospitals failed to include payer-negotiated prices that the payers disclosed in their Transparency in Coverage files, which also are required by law and are available to CMS. CMS needed only to perform a basic crosscheck to confirm that the content in one file reflects corresponding content in another; if it had done so, CMS would have discovered much more noncompliance.

   We also found that some hospitals' files contained "N/A" in more than 90% of the fields in their machine-readable files—a patently implausible number of items or services to assume that a hospital simply does not offer those items or services to its patients. The Administrator's comment flatly contradicts the easily ascertainable facts about the use of "N/A" entries, and the AHA's bluster in support of this widespread practice is misplaced.

4) AHA proceeds to tackle the issue of price files placed in obscure locations on hospital websites by citing a CMS statement that "many publicly available web pages . . . are discoverable using simple internet searches . . . ." Consistently with this statement about many pages, our report stated that "a significant number of hospitals posted their files in obscure locations on their websites"

   AHA neglects to acknowledge the Rule's express requirement that "[a] hospital must select a publicly available website for purposes of making public the standard charge

221 84 Fed. Reg. at 65539.

222 In fact, we believe CMS should not have granted this exception to the Rule's requirements, especially not by subregulatory guidance without inviting and considering comments from patients and other stakeholders.

information . . . [and] information must be displayed in a prominent manner and clearly identified with the hospital location . . . ." (emphasis added).[223] Failing to provide a link that an average patient could find or requiring an individual to know to do a web search for the right search terms to find the prices that are provided for transparency to consumers is not displaying the price file in a "prominent manner."

5) AHA's next bone of contention is our observation about hospitals posting price files in JSON computer file format.
   Here again, the AHA misrepresents our statements and positions. We did not say that this format is not permitted. We only pointed out that we have not yet seen a JSON file accompanied by appropriate documentation or schema information—practices that multiple third-party software engineers with whom we have consulted have confirmed is customary in the industry.
6) The AHA then attacks our comment that some hospital price files are needlessly large and many hospitals provide full data disclosures in considerably smaller files.
   Here again, we merely comment on practices that some hospitals have adopted that strike us as suspicious because they are out of sync with common practices for the posting and sharing of substantial bodies of data. We are happy to provide statements from academic researchers and/or other sophisticated users as to the issues they face resulting from these unnecessary large file size increases.

The AHA's reaction does, of course, reveal one important truth: The power of true healthcare price transparency presents a profound challenge to health systems that for decades have enjoyed little to no accountability for their high prices. It comes as no surprise they have sought to influence CMS's implementation of the Rule and have been able to achieve a very lenient interpretation and scant enforcement of these critical requirements. It also comes as no surprise that the AHA is representing "effort" by hospitals—rather than *compliance*—as progress and defending practices by hospitals that have the effect of hiding price data rather than being transparent. It is surprising and problematic that CMS is supporting this approach.

Some reporters covering healthcare price transparency have referenced a review performed by a for-profit entity, Turquoise Health, which found that 76% of hospitals have posted a machine- readable file.[224] We do acknowledge that a majority of hospitals have posted a machine-readable file. However, merely posting a machine-readable file is not compliance; the file itself must meet several criteria to satisfy the Rule: It must be in a digital, machine-readable format and prominently displayed on a publicly available website, must have standard charge information that is "easily accessible, without barriers," and must include a description, the gross charge, the payer- specific negotiated charge by payer and plan, the de-identified minimum and maximum negotiated charge, the discounted cash price, and billing code.

The difference between Turquoise's report and ours is simple: Turquoise rates hospitals with varying levels of compliance; we consider hospitals missing any data as noncompliant. We note that Turquoise is primarily providing pricing information to hospitals and health insurers in order to compare prices among themselves. Yet, the primary purchasers of healthcare and coverage – patients, unions, and employers – are still largely unable to do comparative analysis across hospitals and plans due to continued widespread obfuscation.

---

[223] 45 C.F.R. § 180.50(b), (d).

[224] https://turquoise.health/mrf_transparency_score.

Our small team reviews 4,000 hospitals per year alongside an independent validator; semi-annually, 2,000 hospitals are comprehensively reviewed in two months. It is totally feasible for CMS to comprehensively review all 6,000 hospitals each year. In its blog, CMS revealed only a cursory website review of 600 hospitals so far, over the course of two years. It is absolutely necessary for CMS to hold hospitals accountable to enable a functional, competitive marketplace to lower costs and empower consumers to protect from overcharges and save. We also believe it is critical for CMS to clearly articulate its methodology for evaluating compliance against binding regulations. Our team has been fully transparent about our methodology and has disclosed all the hospitals we have reviewed; it is imperative that CMS be transparent as well.

Again, we commend your bipartisan leadership in requesting that the GAO investigate hospital non-compliance, along with your upcoming hearing on March 28th. Thank you for empowering American healthcare consumers – workers, employers, and unions – to obtain functional markets with fair, equitable prices and lower their costs of care and coverage.

Warmest Regards,

Cynthia A. Fisher

Cynthia A. Fisher Founder and Chairman
PatientRightsAdvocate.org

New York Times
Profits Over Patients
How a Hospital Chain Used a Poor Neighborhood to Turn Huge Profits
Bon Secours Mercy Health, A Major Nonprofit Health System, Used the Poverty of Richmond Community Hospital's Patients to Tap into a Lucrative Federal Drug Program

By Kae Thomas and Jessica Silver-Greenberg
Published Sept. 24, 2022, Updated Sept. 27, 2022

Link to Artile

RICHMOND, Va. — In late July, Norman Otey was rushed by ambulance to Richmond Community Hospital. The 63-year-old was doubled over in pain and babbling incoherently. Blood tests suggested septic shock, a grave emergency that required the resources and expertise of an intensive care unit.

But Richmond Community, a struggling hospital in a predominantly Black neighborhood, had closed its I.C.U. in 2017.

It took several hours for Mr. Otey to be transported to another hospital, according to his sister, Linda Jones-Smith. He deteriorated on the way there, and later died of sepsis. Two people who cared for Mr. Otey said the delay had most likely contributed to his death.

"He should have been able to go to the hospital and get the treatment he needed," Ms. Jones-Smith said. "He should have been saved."

Ringed by public housing projects, Richmond Community consists of litle more than a strapped emergency room and a psychiatric ward. It does not have kidney or lung specialists, or a maternity ward. Its magnetic resonance imaging machine frequently breaks, and was out of service for seven weeks this summer, said two medical workers at the hospital, who requested anonymity because they still work there. Standard tools like an otoscope, a device used to inspect the ear canal, are often hard to come by.

Yet the hollowed-out hospital — owned by Bon Secours Mercy Health, one of the largest nonprofit health care chains in the country — has the highest profit margins of any hospital in Virginia, generating as much as $100 million a year, according to the hospital's financial data.

The secret to its success lies with a federal program that allows clinics in impoverished neighborhoods to buy prescription drugs at steep discounts, charge insurers full price and pocket the difference. The vast majority of Richmond Community's profits come from the program, said two former executives who were familiar with the hospital's finances and requested anonymity because they still work in the health care industry.

The drug program was created with the intention that hospitals would reinvest the windfalls into their facilities, improving care for poor patients. But Bon Secours, founded by Roman Catholic nuns more than a century ago, has been slashing services at Richmond Community while investing in the city's wealthier, white neighborhoods, according to more than 20 former executes, doctors and nurses.

"Bon Secours was basically laundering money through this poor hospital to its wealthy outposts," said Dr. Lucas English, who worked in Richmond Community's emergency department until 2018. "It was all about profits."

More than half of all hospitals in the United States are set up as nonprofits, a designation that allows them to make money but avoid paying taxes. Although Bon Secours has taken a financial hit this year like many other hospital systems, the chain made nearly $1 billion in profit last year at its 50 hospitals in the United States and Ireland and was sitting on more than $9 billion in cash reserves. It avoids at least $440 million in federal, state and local taxes every year that it would otherwise have to pay, according to an analysis by the Lown Institute, a nonpartisan think tank.

In exchange for the tax breaks, the Internal Revenue Service requires nonprofit hospitals to provide a benefit to their communities. But an investigation by The New York Times found that many of the country's largest nonprofit hospital systems have drifted far from their charitable roots. The hospitals operate like for-profit companies, fixating on revenue targets and expansions into affluent suburbs.

Many of these hospitals have for years slashed staffing levels, leaving them unprepared for a flood of severely ill Covid-19 patients. Others, borrowing tricks from business consultants, have trained staff to squeeze payments from poor patients who should be eligible for free care.

In a statement, a spokeswoman for Bon Secours Mercy Health said the hospital system had spent nearly $10 million on improvements to Richmond Community Hospital since 2013, including opening a pharmacy and renovating the cafeteria, emergency department and other areas. The chain also invested nearly $9 million since 2018 in the neighborhood surrounding the hospital, she said.

Bon Secours's chief executive, John M. Starcher Jr., made about $6 million in 2020, according to the most recent tax filings.

"Our mission is clear — to extend the compassionate ministry of Jesus by improving the health and well- being of our communities and bring good help to those in need, especially people who are poor, dying and underserved," the spokeswoman, Maureen Richmond, said. Bon Secours did not comment on Mr. Otey's case.

In interviews, doctors, nurses and former executives said the hospital had been given short shrift, and pointed to a decade-old development deal with the city of Richmond as another example.

In 2012, the city agreed to lease land to Bon Secours at far below market value on the condition that the chain expand Richmond Community's facilities. Instead, Bon Secours focused on building a luxury apartment and office complex. The hospital system waited a decade to build the promised medical offices next to Richmond Community, breaking ground only this year.

'Glorified Emergency Room'

For Dr. Richard Jackson, 69, an internal medicine specialist whose family has been caring for patents in this city for more than a century, walking the mostly empty halls of Richmond Community Hospital is a painful reminder of what has been lost.

The hospital was founded in 1907 by Black doctors who were not allowed to work at the white hospitals across town. In the 1930s, Dr. Jackson's grandfather, Dr. Isaiah Jackson, mortgaged his house to help pay for an expansion of the hospital. His father, also a doctor, would take his children to the hospital's fundraising telethons.

In 1980, Richmond Community moved to its current site in the East End neighborhood, where there was no other hospital. The modest building did not have an emergency room or a maternity ward. But in addition to the intensive care unit, it had specialists in cancer as well as heart and lung disease. Dr.

Jackson recruited many of them from Howard University, where he had atended medical school.

But in the 1990s, the changing health care industry threatened the hospital's survival. Large insurance companies began requiring customers to use specific networks of hospitals and doctors, in a bid to pressure providers to lower their rates. Independent institutions like Community — as it is known in the neighborhood — could not compete with larger chains, and the hospital struggled to atract patents.

The doctors, who owned the hospital as part of a for-profit partnership, sold it to Bon Secours in 1995.

Bon Secours was one of the dominant players in Richmond, with major medical centers throughout the city. It initially invested in the hospital, opening the emergency department, according to a history of Richmond Community by Cassandra Newby-Alexander at Norfolk State University.

But as the years passed, Bon Secours began stripping the hospital's services, including the I.C.U. The unit had only five beds, but doctors regarded it as the heart of the hospital, the place to provide critical care for the sickest patents and those recovering from major surgery.

Removing the I.C.U. "really takes the meat and potatoes out of being a hospital," Dr. Jackson said. "It's a glorified emergency room."

With the I.C.U. closed, the hospital's two lung specialists had nowhere to treat critically ill patents. They retired, and Bon Secours did not replace them. A team of cardiologists let a few years later. Other specialists, including gastrointestinal doctors and neurologists who were part of Bon Secours's broader network, rarely treated patients at Richmond Community.

Doctors and nurses said that when they had protested the closure of the I.C.U. and other cuts, Bon Secours argued that patients could still receive care at the chain's other hospitals.

But that promise was undermined by the arrival of the coronavirus, which disproportionately affected Black and low-income residents in the East End. In the census tract that includes Richmond Community Hospital, the Covid death rate has been 81 percent higher than the city's overall rate, according to data provided by the Virginia Department of Health.

In the summer of 2021, as the Delta variant surged through the city, a woman in the emergency room with Covid declined and needed an I.C.U. with a ventilator, according to three people involved in her case.

For hours, the staff couldn't get her to another hospital. Eventually, she was transferred to Memorial Regional Medical Center, also owned by Bon Secours, but died after arriving. Her death let some who had cared for her at Community wondering if she would have survived had she shown up at a different hospital.

Bon Secours declined to comment on whether the hospital's lack of an I.C.U. contributed to the Covid death toll.

The pandemic exacerbated a problem that doctors and nurses said they had long faced — getting patients access to other hospitals in the Bon Secours system.

The East End is home to Richmond's largest Black population and, despite recent interest from real estate investors, lacks some basic services. In 2019, it got its first supermarket.

In some of the neighborhoods surrounding the hospital, more than half the households do not have a car, according to research done by Virginia Commonwealth University. The public bus route to St. Mary's, a large Bon Secours facility in the northwest part of the city, takes more than an hour. There is no public transportation from the East End to Memorial Regional, nine miles away.

"It became impossible for me to send people to the advanced heart valve clinic at St. Mary's," said Dr. Michael Kelly, a cardiologist who worked at Richmond Community until Bon Secours scaled back the specialty service in 2019. He said he had driven some patents to the clinic in his own car.

Richmond Community has the feel of an urgent-care clinic, with a small waiting room and a tan brick facade. The contrast with Bon Secours's nearby hospitals is striking.

At the chain's St. Francis Medical Center, an Italianate-style compound in a suburb 18 miles from Community, golf carts shutle patients from the lobby entrance, past a marble fountain, to their cars.

In December, Bon Secours kicked off a $108 million construction project at St. Francis to expand its I.C.U. and maternity ward. Not long before that, Bon Secours broke ground on a free-standing emergency room that would be an extension of St. Francis in suburban Chesterfield County. The news release boasted that it would offer CT, M.R.I. and ultrasound imaging.

Dr. Samuel Hunter, 81, who worked for more than four decades as a pathologist at Richmond Community until he left in May, said the disparity reminded him of his childhood in segregated Florida, where Black children like him learned from textbooks that white students had already used.

"I know what it feels like to have secondhand things," he said.

A Lucrative Drug Program

When Bon Secours bought Richmond Community, the hospital served predominantly poor patients who were either uninsured or covered through Medicaid, which reimburses hospitals at lower rates than private insurance does. But Bon Secours turned the hospital's poverty into an asset.

The organization seized on a federal program created in the 1990s to give a financial boost to nonprofit hospitals and clinics that serve low-income communities. The program, called 340B afer the section of the federal law that authorized it, allows hospitals to buy drugs from manufacturers at a discount — roughly half the average sales price. The hospitals are then allowed to charge patients' insurers a much higher price for the same drugs.

The theory behind the law was that nonprofit hospitals would invest the savings in their communities. But the 340B program came with few rules. Hospitals did not have to disclose how much money they made from sales of the discounted drugs. And they were not required to use the revenues to help the underserved patients who qualified them for the program in the first place.

In 2019, more than 2,500 nonprofit and government-owned hospitals participated in the program, or more than half of all hospitals in the country, according to the independent Medicare Payment Advisory Commission.

Starting in the mid-2000s, big hospital chains figured out how to supercharge the program. The basic idea: Build clinics in wealthier neighborhoods, where patients with generous private insurance could receive expensive drugs, but on paper make the clinics extensions of poor hospitals to take advantage of 340B.

Since 2013, Bon Secours has opened nine such satellite clinics in wealthier parts of the Richmond area, according to federal records. Even though the outposts are miles from Richmond Community, they are legally structured as subsidiaries of the hospital, which entitles them to buy drugs at the discounted rate.

The Bon Secours Cancer Institute at St. Mary's, for example, administers cancer drugs to patients in an office suite on the tree-lined campus of St. Mary's Hospital.

Thanks to 340B, Richmond Community Hospital can buy a vial of Keytruda, a cancer drug, at the discounted price of $3,444, according to an estimate by Sara Tabatabai, a former researcher at Memorial Sloan Ketering Cancer Center.

But the hospital charges the private insurer Blue Cross Blue Shield more than seven times that price — $25,425, according to a price list that hospitals are required to publish. That is nearly $22,000 profit on a single vial. Adults need two vials per treatment course.

The way hospitals use the 340B program is "nakedly capitalizing on programs that are intended to help poor people," said Dr. Peter B. Bach, a biotechnology executive and researcher whose work has shown that hospitals participating in the 340B program have increasingly opened clinics in wealthier areas since the mid-2000s.

Bon Secours did not disclose how much money it earned through the program, but said the funds "help us address health disparities while providing community support and outreach." It said it had provided nearly $18 million in free care to poor parents at Richmond Community

Hospital since 2018. In 2020, the hospital provided $3.8 million in free care to low-income parents, or about 2.6 percent of its total expenses, slightly above the national average.

The federal agency that oversees the 340B program, the Health Resources and Services Administration, said that hospitals and clinics were regularly audited, and that the Biden administration had proposed requiring them to report how they spent profits generated through the program. Such a change would require congressional approval.

In 2020, the most recent year for which data is available, Richmond Community Hospital — including its satellite offices — had a profit margin of nearly 44 percent, the highest in the state, according to an analysis by Virginia Health Information, a nonprofit group that collects financial data from hospitals.

That year, the hospital brought in more than $110 million in revenue, after expenses and losses were deducted, according to Virginia Health Information. According to two former Bon Secours executives familiar with the hospital's financial operations, the vast majority of Richmond Community's profit since 2013 has come from the 340B program.

Bon Secours's other hospitals have not done as well. St. Mary's, considered the most prestigious Bon Secours facility in Richmond, brought in $83 million in 2020.

'Unabashedly Profit-Oriented'

On a sunny October day in Richmond in 2012, two cheerleaders for Washington's National Football League team smiled for cameras as they gripped a large sign between them.

"Bon Secours Training Center," read the sign, which combined the Bon Secours fleur-de-lis logo with a bust of a Native American, the football team's logo at the time.

The team, Bon Secours and the State of Virginia were unveiling a major economic deal that would bring $40 million to Richmond, add 200 jobs and keep the Washington team — now known as the Commanders — in the state for summer training.

The deal had three main parts. Bon Secours would get naming rights and help the team build a training camp and medical offices on a lot next to Richmond's science museum.

The city would lease Bon Secours a prime piece of real estate that the chain had long coveted for $5,000 a year. The parcel was on the city's west side, next to St. Mary's, where Bon Secours wanted to build medical offices and a nursing school.

Finally, the nonprofit's executives promised city leaders that they would build a 25,000-square-foot medical office building next to Richmond Community Hospital. Bon Secours also said it would hire 75 local workers and build a fitness center.

"It's going to be a quick timetable, but I think we can accomplish it," the mayor at the time, Dwight C. Jones, said at the news conference.

Today, physical therapy and doctors' offices overlook the football field at the training center.

On the west side of Richmond, Bon Secours dropped its plans to build a nursing school. Instead, it worked with a real estate developer to build luxury apartments on the site, and delayed its plans to build medical offices. Residents at The Crest at Westhampton Commons, part of the $73 million project, can swim in a saltwater pool and work out on communal Peloton bicycles. On the ground floor, an upscale Mexican restaurant serves cucumber jalapeño margaritas and a Drybar offers salon blowouts.

The land next to Richmond Community Hospital, by contrast, remained inactive until February of this year, when Bon Secours broke ground on the complex.

Former executives at the chain said a series of management changes in Bon Secours's Richmond region, coupled with a change in mayoral administrations, had distracted attention from the project. And a merger with an Ohio hospital chain in 2018 accelerated the push for higher revenues, according to former administrators and doctors.

"There was a major shift from being mission-oriented to being unashamedly, unabashedly profit- oriented," said Dr. Jones, the former mayor who helped broker the original deal.

Bon Secours said that since 2018, it had spent more than $19 million supporting organizations and initiatves throughout metropolitan Richmond, including more than $8 million on local businesses and charities in the East End. The work near Richmond Community Hospital is projected to be finished by the end of this year. Hospital executives have said they plan to house mental health, hospice and other services there.

Disaster Medicine

For years, doctors and nurses at Richmond Community have often felt as if they were working on a batlefield, doing their best with severely limited supplies and facilities.

Kristen Schnurman, who began her career as a physician assistant at Bon Secours in 2014 and left in 2019, said she had once confided in a doctor that she was not learning proper medical care.

"He said to me — and this will always stick with me — 'You're not learning medicine, you're learning disaster medicine,'" she said.

In the summer of 2016, with temperatures soaring past 90 degrees, the hospital's air-conditioning went out for several weeks, making it hoter inside than out on the street.

When asked about the air-conditioning and lack of basic supplies at Richmond Community, Bon Secours declined to comment. Ms. Richmond, the Bon Secours spokeswoman, said it would replace the M.R.I. machine as part of a $5.3 million capital improvement plan.

Dr. Kelly, the cardiologist, stopped treating patients at the hospital in 2019. But there is one man's story that haunts him.

The man, who was in his 50s, arrived at the emergency room showing signs of a heart atack. To prevent permanent damage, the man needed to be swifly catheterized, a procedure that would insert a balloon into his blocked artery and force it open.

Bon Secours did not have the tools for the catheterization, so Dr. Kelly arranged for the patient to be transferred quickly to Memorial Regional.

But Memorial could not guarantee a bed would be ready, Dr. Kelly said. So the patient waited for several hours in the Community emergency room. "All we could do was watch it happen," Dr. Kelly recalled.

The patient survived, he said, but the delay damaged his heart. For the rest of his life, the man will be at risk for extreme fatigue and dangerously low blood pressure, Dr. Kelly said.

Every time that Bon Secours took away a service from Community, executives gave doctors the same justification: Patients were just an ambulance ride away from hospitals in the broader system.

But Dr. Kelly and other doctors said many patients had wound up like the man with the heart atack. “We very, very often were stuck for many hours with patients who absolutely needed advanced care,” Dr. Kelly said.

Other patients faced a different problem: Specialists who saw patients at other Bon Secours locations would not travel to the hospital.

This spring, Doris Scarborough, 79, went to Richmond Community to have her toe partly amputated. Poor circulation had turned the toe black and gangrenous. She said her podiatrist had told her that she would lose some of her toe, but was likely to keep her leg if she had a standard procedure known as revascularization.

Richmond Community did not offer this procedure. Ms. Scarborough had to have it done at the specialist’s office, and it took more than two weeks to get an appointment. Weeks after the procedure, Ms. Scarborough lost her entire toe.

Dr. Foluso Fakorede, a cardiologist and an expert on racial disparities in amputation, said many people in poor, nonwhite communities faced similar delays in getting the procedure. “I am not surprised by what’s transpired with this patient at all,” he said.

Because Ms. Scarborough does not drive, her nephew must take time off work every time she visits the vascular surgeon, whose office is 10 miles from her home. Richmond Community would have been a five-minute walk. Bon Secours did not comment on her case.

“They have good doctors over there,” Ms. Scarborough said of the neighborhood hospital. “But there does need to be more facilities and services over there for our community, for us.”

Susan C. Beachy contributed research.

AMERICAN BENEFITS COUNCIL

Written Statement for the Record For the Hearing of the U.S. House of Representatives Committee on Energy and Commerce, Subcommittee on Health Entitled Lowering Unaffordable Costs: Examining Transparency and Competition in Health Care
April 15, 2021

Chairs McMorris Rodgers and Guthrie and Ranking Members Pallone and Eshoo:

The American Benefits Council (“the Council”) thanks you for holding this important hearing, “Lowering Unaffordable Costs: Examining Transparency and Competition in Health Care.” We applaud your focus on examining ideas to drive down the cost of health care through transparency and competition.

The Council is dedicated to strengthening employer-sponsored benefit plans. The Council represents more major employers – over 220 of the world's largest corporations – than any other association that exclusively advocates on the full range of employee benefit issues. Members also include organizations supporting employers of all sizes.

Collectively, Council members directly sponsor or serve benefit plans covering virtually all Americans participating in employer-sponsored programs.

Providing health coverage to more than 178 million Americans,[225] employers play a critical role in the health care system and drive innovations from which the entire health system benefits. With a vested interest in securing the health and well-being of their employees, employers deliver high-value, innovative coverage. But they are deeply concerned about rising health care costs and other impediments to innovation. The only way to effectively address the cost of health care is to understand the root causes of rising costs and take action that targets those underlying drivers – including a lack a transparency and competition.

Transparency and competition are the foundation of an affordable, high-quality and value-driven health care market. Accordingly, legislation that increases transparency and competition are among the top health policy priorities outlined in the Council's February 27 letter to Congress[226] and restated below. We call on Congress to enact reforms that support employers' efforts to lower health care costs for workers and their families through greater transparency and competition by taking action to:

- Expand site neutral payment reforms
- Restrict hospital billing practices that fuel consolidation and mask appropriate payment amounts
- Restrict anti-competitive contracting provisions
- Ensure federal antitrust laws are fully applied to horizontal and vertical integration
- Support implementation of the No Surprises Act
- Reject legislation that would exacerbate consolidation and market failures
- Support greater price transparency
- Support quality transparency and meaningful, harmonized metrics
- Support drug pricing transparency, competition and value and increased PBM accountability

There is a health care affordability crisis in this country. We commend you for shining a light on the critical role that a lack a transparency and competition play in fueling this crisis. The time is now for Congress to act on implementing these reforms that will make the health care market more transparent and competitive and, therefore, make health care more affordable and accessible in communities across the country, including underserved communities.

---

[225] U.S. Census Bureau, Health Insurance Coverage in the United States: 2021 (September 2022), Table 1.

[226] American Benefits Council, Health Priorities for the 118th Congress, American Benefits Council (February 27, 2023).

Market Consolidation, a Lack of Transparency and Fundamental Market Failures Stifle Competition and Patient Choice and Increase Health Care Costs

The pandemic served to spur a number of transformational innovations in health care delivery – such as the increased use of telehealth – that can enhance access to affordable, value-driven care. However, impediments remain. Misaligned incentives reward providers for quantity rather than quality. Market consolidation and lack of transparency and fundamental market failures stifle competition and patient choice and increase costs.

The national health expenditure grew to $4.3 trillion in 2021, representing almost one-fifth (18.3%) of the U.S. gross domestic product.[227] The annual growth in national health spending is expected to average 5.1% over 2021-2030 and reach nearly $6.8 trillion by 2030.[228] During this same period, private health insurance spending growth is projected to average 5.7%. According to a study by the Kaiser Family Foundation, annual premiums for employer-sponsored family health coverage reached $22,463 for family coverage in 2022, with workers on average paying $6,106 toward the cost of their coverage.[229] The average premium for family coverage has increased 20% over the last five years and 43% over the last ten years. This trajectory is unsustainable.

Compounding the problem is that employer health plans already pay much higher prices for health care goods and services than public plans. According to an analysis by the Congressional Budget Office (CBO).[230]

The main reason for the growth of per-person spending by commercial insurers—and for the difference from the growth of per-person spending by Medicare [fee-for-service (FFS)]—has been rapid increases in the prices that commercial insurers pay for hospitals' and physicians' services.

According to a RAND Corporation report, in 2020, across all hospital inpatient and outpatient services, employers and private insurers paid hospitals 224% of what Medicare would have paid for the same services.[231]

Employers have grown increasingly frustrated with rising health care costs. Top executives at nearly 87% of large employers surveyed in a 2021 poll believed the cost of providing health benefits to employees will become unsustainable in the next five-to-10 years.[232]

The cost of health care is a top concern for voters as well. According to the recent Morning Consult poll for the Alliance to Fight for Health Care, 83% of insured adults say they are concerned about costs (with 44% very concerned.) Reducing health care costs was cited as the top health care reform priority for a majority (57%) of insured adults, topping covering more people (19%) and covering more health care services (24%). In polling conducted for the

---

[227] U.S. Centers for Medicare and Medicaid Services (CMS), *NHE Fact Sheet* (Updated December 14, 2022).

[228] CMS news release, "CMS Office of the Actuary Releases 2021-2030 Projections of National Health Expenditures" (March 28, 2022).

[229] Kaiser Family Foundation, *2022 Employer Health Benefits Survey* (October 27, 2022).

[230] Congressional Budget Office, *The Prices That Commercial Health Insurers and Medicare Pay for Hospitals' and Physicians' Services* (January 20, 2022).

[231] Rand Corporation, Prices Paid to Hospitals by Private Health Plans: Findings from Round 4 of an Employer-Led Transparency Initiative (2022).

[232] Kaiser Family Foundation news release, "Vast Majority of Large Employers Surveyed Say Broader Government Role Will Be Necessary to Control Health Costs and Provide Coverage, Survey Finds" (April 29, 2021).

Alliance to Fight for Health Care, almost 80% of voters want Congress to work to lower health care costs for all Americans, no matter how or where they get their health coverage.[233]

Hospital spending is the largest health spending category in the United States, accounting for almost one-third of all expenditures. In 2021, hospital spending totaled $1.3 trillion (Centers for Medicare & Medicaid Services (CMS)).[234] Spending on hospital services accounts for 44% of total personal health care spending for the privately insured and hospital price increases are key drivers of recent growth in per capita spending among the privately insured.[235] Also, a recent literature review by CBO found that providers' market power was a key reason for variation in the prices that commercial insurers pay for hospitals' and physicians' services across the United States.[236]

As one 2020 report on price transparency highlighted:

> One of the greatest challenges to affordable health care is the high cost of American hospitals. The most important driver of higher prices for hospital care, in turn, is the rise of regional hospital monopolies. Hospitals are merging into large hospital systems, and using their market power to demand higher and higher prices from the privately insured and the uninsured.[237]

Consolidation corrodes the competitive market forces needed to align health care cost with value, resulting in higher costs for plans and patients alike. An estimated 117 million people live in a concentrated hospital market whereas 160 million reside in a competitive hospital market, according to an Urban Institute analysis.[238] Prices at monopoly hospitals are 12% higher than those in markets with four or more rivals.[239]

Moreover, consolidation has not come with demonstrated improvement in the quality of care.[240] Substantial economic literature has demonstrated that provider consolidation leads (on average) to "less bang for the buck"— higher prices without higher quality or access.[241] Substantial evidence links hospital mergers to increases in prices. At the same time, many private hospital systems are becoming vertically integrated with physician organizations. Such integration can direct patient referrals to higher-priced hospitals within the system and away

---

233 Alliance to Fight for Health Care & Morning Consult, Coverage and Reforming the System (February 21, 2023).

234 CMS Office of the Actuary Press Release, "National Health Spending Grew Slightly in 2021" (December 14, 2022).

235 Rand Corporation, *Nationwide Evaluation of Health Care Prices Paid by Private Health Plans* (2020).

236 Congressional Budget Office (CBO), *Policy Approaches to Reduce What Commercial Insurers Pay for Hospitals' and Physicians' Services* (September 29, 2022).

237 The Foundation for Research on Equal Opportunity, *Affordable Hospital Care Through Competition and Price Transparency* (January 31, 2020).

238 Urban Institute, *Introducing a Public Option or Capped Provider Payment Rates into Concentrated Insurer and Hospital Markets* (March 2021).

239 Zack Cooper, Stuart V Craig, Martin Gaynor and John Van Reenen, "The Price Ain't Right? Hospital Prices and Health Spending on the Privately Insured," *Quarterly Journal of Economics, vol. 134, no. 1* (February 2019), pp. 51–107.

240 As noted in Rand Corporation, *Impact of Policy Options for Reducing Hospital Prices Paid by Private Health Plans* (2021), pp. 2, "A review of all hospital mergers between 2009 and 2013 found that hospital mergers do not lead to improvements in quality (Beaulieu et al., 2020). Likewise, research has found that vertical integration does not lead to increases in the quality of care (Short and Ho, 2019; Post, Buchmueller and Ryan, 2018; Machta et al., 2019). See also Kaiser Family Foundation, *What We Know About Provider Consolidation* (September 2, 2020).

241 The Hamilton Project, *A Proposal to Cap Provider Prices and Price Growth in the Commercial Health-Care Market* (March 2020), pp 7.

from lower-priced community providers.[242] Addressing consolidation, restoring competition and better aligning incentives with value are essential to lowering health care costs.

Policy Priority **Expand site-neutral payment reforms.**

A way to decrease incentives for consolidation is for Congress and the U.S. Department of Health and Human Services (HHS) to expand implementation of site- neutral payment reform which aligns payment rates for certain services across the three main sites where patients receive outpatient care. Policies that reduce providers' incentive to consolidate would "deter some hospitals and physicians from merging with or acquiring rival firms, which would slow the consolidation of markets."[243]

One such incentive results from differences in payment rates for the same or similar services at different sites of outpatient care - hospital outpatient departments (HOPDs), ambulatory surgical centers (ASCs) and freestanding physician offices. Medicare (and private health insurance) generally pay the highest rates for services provided in HOPDs and lowest rates for services performed in freestanding physician offices. For services provided in freestanding clinician offices, Medicare makes a single payment to the practitioner under the physician fee schedule. For services provided in HOPDs or ASCs, Medicare makes two payments: one for the clinician's professional fee and one for the HOPD or ASC facility fee under the relevant payment system. For example, in 2022, Medicare paid 141 percent more in an HOPD than in a freestanding office for the first hour of chemotherapy infusion (counting both the professional fee and facility fee).

According to the Medicare Payment Advisory Commission (MedPAC), which advises Congress on Medicare payment policy, this disparity is incentivizes consolidation of physician practices with hospitals—that result in care being provided in settings with the highest payment rates. This increases costs without significant improvements in patient outcomes.[244] MedPAC's recommendations to align payment rates across the different ambulatory settings for a greater number of services would have resulted in an estimated $6.6 billion savings to Medicare in 2019 and $1.7 billion reduction in beneficiary cost-sharing. Effects for the commercial market are likely even greater. New research by University of Minnesota economist Steve Parente estimates that expanding site-neutral payment reform could result in nearly $60 billion in savings annually if adopted in the commercial market.[245]2

We urge Congress and HHS to expand site-neutral payment reforms while protecting access to care in underserved rural and urban communities. This would discourage provider consolidation and hospital acquisitions of physician practices.

---

[242] Ibid.

[243] Id (Footnote 12) at pp 16.

[244] Medicare Payment Advisory Commission report to Congress, *Medicare and the Health Care Delivery System* (June 2022).

[245] Alliance to Fight for Health Care briefing presentation, *The Untapped Potential of Site-Neutral Payment Reform* (February 1, 2023), pp 27.

Policy Priority **Restrict hospital billing practices that fuel consolidation and mask what should be the appropriate payment amounts.**

A troubling trend arises from provider consolidation as large hospital systems purchase physician practices and shift billing practices to portray services delivered at these sites as 'hospital services' as opposed to 'professional services' in order to receive the higher facility reimbursement fee. Congress should pass legislation to promote "honest billing" practices by allowing payors to distinguish between sites of service in order to apply the appropriate payment amount.

Policy Priority **Remove barriers to employer innovation by restricting anti-competitive contracting provisions that impede value-driven care.**

In concentrated markets, prices do not flow from competitive negotiations, but from the outsized leverage that market concentration affords. Large hospital systems attempt to leverage their significant market share by forcing plans to contract with all affiliated facilities and prevent educating patients about lower-cost, higher-quality care. These anti-competitive contract terms in the form of "all-or-nothing," "anti-steering," "anti- tiering" and "most-favored-nation" contract provisions foster inflated costs and limit plan sponsor's flexibility in plan design to promote access to high-value care.

The Council urges Congress to address the anti-competitive contract terms that disrupt market dynamics and raise the cost of health care services across the system. Legislation, such as the bipartisan Healthy Competition for Better Care Act from the last Congress would, in the aggregate, increase competition and promote lower costs by restricting such contract terms. Congress should enact such legislation.

Policy Priority **Support the Federal Trade Commission (FTC) and U.S. Department of Justice (DOJ) in ensuring that federal antitrust laws are fully applied to horizontal and vertical integration in the health care system.**

The FTC should establish stricter review and enforcement of hospital and physician practice consolidation, including mergers and hospital acquisitions of physician practices, upon completion of its study under the Merger Retrospective Program. Based on the results of the study, the FTC should make recommendations to Congress to prevent consolidation and increase market competition.

Policy Priority **Support implementation of the No Surprises Act to protect patients *and* lower health care costs.**

We have seen the corrosive effect of private-equity backed consolidation on the health care market in the context of surprise medical bills from out-of-network providers, resulting in higher patient costs. Out-of-network providers of emergency and ancillary services in which patients had no meaningful choice in their selection exploited their leverage to remain out-of-network and charge exorbitant prices or extract much higher prices to join a network. In the No Surprises Act (NSA), Congress acted to address this market failure. Despite the efforts of some providers to undermine the NSA through continual litigation and flooding the dispute resolution process with specious claims, implementation of the legislation should not veer from the twin goals the law sought to achieve – protecting patients from surprise medical bills and lowering costs for all consumers.

Policy Priority **Reject legislation that would exacerbate market failures and raise costs for employers and employees.**

The dialysis market is a stark example of the detrimental impact of consolidation.

The nation's two largest dialysis providers control more than 80% of the market, giving them significant leverage to raise prices for private payers. A research letter published in the Journal of the American Medical Association, Internal Medicine found that commercial insurers paid one of the largest dialysis providers, on average, over $1,000 per treatment, roughly four times Medicare's fixed costs.[246] Legislation such as the inappropriately named Restore Protections for Dialysis Patients Act will give the duopoly even more leverage to raise prices for private payers and widen the gap between Medicare and the commercial market and should be rejected.

Policy Priority **Support greater price transparency in the health care system.**

A competitive and value-driven health care market is predicated on transparency. Increased access to pricing data will enable market forces to work more effectively and efficiently, ultimately leading to better cost and quality outcomes. Many employers that have had success decreasing the rate of health care spending have done so by analyzing their plan data to better understand how much is being spent on specific services and then using plan design features to encourage lower utilization overall or engagement of higher-value, relatively lower-cost providers. Programs focused on value-based benefit design and value-based payment reform can potentially transform our system by realigning incentives to keep participants healthier – while at the same time lowering costs. These changes are not feasible without transparency and plan sponsor access to pricing and quality data.

We strongly support the U.S. Department of Health and Human Services (HHS) regulations requiring hospitals to provide increased price transparency. We have urged HHS to undertake vigorous enforcement and to further increase the penalties for noncompliance.

Our plan sponsor members are doing their part to support increased transparency.

They recognize that access to pricing data is critical to unleashing the power of employers to drive lower cost and higher value health care. As such, we support the regulations

246 JAMA Network/JAMA Internal Medicine, *A Comparison of Payments to a For-profit Dialysis Firm From Government and Commercial Insurers* (May 13, 2019).

implementing the transparency provisions under Section 2715A of the Public Health Service Act, as well as the transparency provisions for group health plans contained in the Consolidated Appropriations Act, 2021 (CAA). Employers have made great efforts to comply with the full range of requirements. We want to ensure the optimal utility of these requirements to support those employer efforts.

We are hopeful that the emphasis by policymakers on the need for transparency continues to gain momentum, allowing employers not only access to their data, but the freedom to use market intelligence to truly analyze how their health care dollars are spent and take action to direct those resources to high-quality, cost-effective providers.

Policy Priority **Support quality transparency and meaningful, harmonized metrics.**

We recognize that price is just one side of the value equation – quality is the other.

However, the efforts by employers to pursue innovative strategies that improve the value of health care are hampered by inconsistent and incomplete quality metrics. Some employers are already providing quality reporting, or others are working toward that goal, but challenges remain.

Federal programs can spur these efforts by adopting uniform measures across federal programs. Congress can promote consensus measures of value to incentivize value-based payments.

Yet, the most significant issue in systematic, universal quality measurement is access to data. It is often difficult for employers to get robust clinical quality and patient experience data at the practice or individual doctor level to validate high performing networks. Having carriers report with complete transparency to employers at the individual provider level the aggregate performance of those providers for the entire patient mix on leading, validated clinical quality indicators is essential. Congress and federal regulators should facilitate cost-effective access to quality data to allow employers, other innovators and academics to define and evolve the quality metrics.

Harmonized quality measures coupled with price metrics are the foundation for employer's innovative payment reforms. We note, however, that while increased price transparency will be most effective when coupled with quality information, price transparency efforts should proceed apace even if quality transparency will take additional time to realize.

Policy Priority **Support meaningful drug pricing transparency, competition and value and increased Pharmacy Benefit Manager (PBM) accountability.**

The Council strongly supports legislation to require greater transparency and accountability with respect to PBMs. Employers appreciate that pharmaceutical drug therapies have played a significant role in treating and curing injury, illness and disease. They allow millions of Americans to overcome debilitating conditions, return to work and live longer, healthier, more productive lives. Moreover, money spent wisely on drugs can reduce hospital, physician and other medical expenditures.

Nonetheless, prescription drug costs continue to represent a considerable portion of overall plan costs. In an effort to manage drug costs, employers have implemented innovative strategies while ensuring that employees and families have access to needed drugs and services. Many of these strategies have been developed by, or in concert with, PBMs. However, employers remain deeply concerned about prescription drug costs, particularly the cost of specialty drugs, and the absence of appropriate price – and cost – transparency across the entire drug pricing system.

The current rebate structure is complex and opaque for many employers, making it hard for them and plan participants and beneficiaries to understand the true prices and value of drugs. One of our main goals has been to support initiatives that increase transparency throughout the pharmaceutical distribution system to ensure that public and private payers spend resources more wisely. This includes increased transparency with respect to rebates paid by manufacturers to PBMs. Increased transparency and accountability could help employers and employees make better informed purchasing decisions and lead to higher value pharmacy expenditures. Reforms are needed to enable value-based pricing that ensures the price we pay for prescription drugs reflects the benefits they provide and protects meaningful innovation.

* * * * *

We urge you to advance bipartisan solutions to lower costs and enhance the value of health care. The hearing today is an important step in addressing this challenge for both employers and working families. The Council stands ready to assist you in any way possible. Please contact Ilyse Schuman, Senior Vice President, Health Policy, ischuman@abcstaff.org with any questions.

CONSUMERS F1RST

The Alliance to Make the Health Care System Work for Everyone

Statement for the Record
House Committee on Energy and Commerce Subcommittee on Health
Hearing on "Lowering Unaffordable Costs: Examining Transparency and Competition in Health Care"
Prepared by Consumers First: *The Alliance to Make the Health Care System Work for Everyone*
March 28, 2023

Chairs McMorris Rodgers and Guthrie and Ranking Members Pallone and Eshoo, on behalf of Consumers First and our undersigned allies we want to thank you for holding this important and timely hearing on transparency and competition in health care, and to offer our sincere appreciation to all of the witnesses and committee Members who are lifting up the impact that unaffordable health care costs have on people all across this country. As an alliance that brings together the interests of consumers, employers, labor unions, and primary care clinicians working to realign and improve the fundamental economic incentives and design of the health care system, Consumers First thanks you for being responsive to our call to action[247] and stands ready to support you as you embark on this critical work.

Our country is in the midst of a health care affordability crisis where consumers, employers, workers, and clinicians are struggling in a health care system whose payment and delivery structure incentivizes high cost, low quality care. Families are experiencing rising health insurance premiums, reduced access to care, and record levels of medical debt.[248]

This crisis is overwhelmingly being driven by health care industry consolidation - particularly among hospitals - that has eliminated healthy competition and led to irrational health care prices and anticompetitive behavior.[249]iii Hospital prices have become highly problematic as the role of hospitals in our economy has shifted over the last 60 years from charitable institutions to corporate entities, resulting in a fundamental misalignment between the business interests of the hospital sector and the interests of our nation's families, workers and employers. The impact is stark:

- Since 2010, more than 1,600 hospitals have merged, and the number of doctor's offices being bought by health care monopolies has increased dramatically, with more than half of all physicians now being employed by hospital-owned practices.[250,251,252]

---

[247] https://familiesusa.org/wp-content/uploads/2023/01/Consumers-First-letter-to-118th-Congress-final-1.23.23.pdf.

[248] Gaynor, M. "*Examining the Impact of Health Care Consolidation" Statement Before the Committee on Energy and Commerce, Oversight and Investigations Subcommittee, U.S. House of Representatives.* 2018. https://www.researchgate.net/publication/323228757_Examining_the_Impact_of_Health_Care_Consolidation_Statement_before_the_Committee_on_Energy_and_Commerce_Oversight_and_Investigations_Subcommittee_US_House_of_Representatives .

[249] Jaime S. King et al., Preventing Anticompetitive Healthcare Consolidation: Lessons From Five States (Source on Healthcare Price and Competition and Nicholas C. Petris Center on Health Care Markets and Consumer Welfare, University of California Berkeley School of Public Health, June 2020), https://sourceonhealthcare.org/profile/preventing- anticompetitive-healthcare-consolidation-lessons-from-five-states/; Martin Gaynor, Kate Ho, and Robert J. Town, "The Industrial Organization of Health-Care Markets," Journal of Economic Literature 53, no. 2 (June 2015): 235–284.

[250] Chart 2.9: Announced Hospital Mergers and Acquisitions, 2005–2017," TrendWatch Chartbook 2018: Trends Affecting Hospitals and Health Systems (Washington, DC: American Hospital Association, 2018), https://www.aha.org/system/files/2018- 07/2018-aha-chartbook.pdf.

[251] Gaynor, M. "Examining the Impact of Health Care Consolidation" Statement Before the Committee on Energy and Commerce, Oversight and Investigations Subcommittee, U.S. House of Representatives. 2018. https://www.researchgate.net/publication/323228757_Examining_the_Impact_of_Health_Care_Consolidation_Statement_before_the_Committee_on_Energy_and_Commerce_Oversight_and_Investigations_Subcommittee_US_House_of_Representatives.

[252] Updated Physician Practice Acquisition Study: National and Regional Changes in Physician Employment, 2012-2018," Physicians Advocacy Institute (PAI), February 2019, http://www.physiciansadvocacy institute.org/Portals/0/assets/docs/021919-Avalere-PAI-Physician-Employment-Trends-Study-2018-Update.pdf?ver=2019-02-19-162735-1.

- Since 2015, hospital prices increased by more than 30 percent, accounting for one-third of U.S. health care spending, and growing *four times* faster than workers' paychecks.[253,254,255]
- High hospital prices result in one-quarter of a trillion dollars in waste each year, which accounts for a quarter of *all* waste annually generated by the US health system.[256]
- And importantly, hospital prices are not only high, but have become essentially irrational. In 2020, across all hospital inpatient and outpatient services, employers and private insurers paid on average 224 percent of what Medicare pays for the same services.[257]
- Prices at hospitals in concentrated markets are 12 percent higher than those in markets with four or more rivals without any demonstrated improvement in the quality or access to care.[258,259,260] All the while, the workforce in these concentrated markets suffers - wages for nurses and other health care workers decrease significantly after mergers and acquisitions.[261]
- Prices for the exact same service vary widely: A colonoscopy at a single medical center in Mississippi can range from $782 to $2,144 depending on insurance.[262] At one health system in Wisconsin, an MRI costs between $1,093 and $4,029 depending on level of insurance.[263] Across the country, the average price for a knee replacement ranges from $21,976 in Tucson, Arizona to $60,000 in Sacramento California.[264]

---

253 Kurani, N. et al. *How Has U.S. Spending on Healthcare Changed Over Time?*. Health System Tracker, Peterson-KFF. 2022. https://www.healthsystemtracker.org/chart-collection/u-s-spending-healthcare-changed- time/#Contribution%20to%20change%20in%20total%20national%20health%20expenditures,%20from%202019-2020,%20by%20spending%20category.

254 *Policy Approaches to Reduce What Commercial Insurers Pay for Hospitals' and Physicians' Services.* Congressional Budget Office. 2022. https://www.cbo.gov/publication/58222.

255 Desilver, D. *For Most U.S. Workers, Real Wages Have Barely Budged in Decades.* Pew Research Center. 2018. https://www.pewresearch.org/fact-tank/2018/08/07/for-most-us-workers-real-wages-have-barely-budged-for-decades/.

256 Shrank, W. et al. Waste in the US Health Care System: Estimated Costs and Potential for Savings. JAMA. 2019. https://jamanetwork.com/journals/jama/article-abstract/2752664.

257 Whaley, C. et al. Prices Paid to Hospitals by Private Health Plans. RAND. 2022. https://www.rand.org/pubs/research_reports/RRA1144-1.html.

258 Cooper, Z. et al. The Price Ain't Right? Hospital Prices and Health Spending on the Privately Insured. The Quarterly Journal of Economics. 2019. https://academic.oup.com/qje/article-abstract/134/1/51/5090426?redirectedFrom=fulltext&login=false.

259 Gaynor, M. Diagnosing the Problem: Exploring the Effects of Consolidation and Anticompetitive Conduct in Health Care Markets. Statement before the Committee on the Judiciary Subcommittee on Antitrust, Commercial, and Administration Law.
U.S. House of Representatives. 2019. https://www.congress.gov/116/meeting/house/109024/witnesses/HHRG-116-JU05-Bio-GaynorM-20190307.pdf.

260 *The Impact of Hospital Consolidation on Medical Costs.* NCCI Insights. 2018. https://www.ncci.com/Articles/Pages/II_Insights_QEB_Impact-of-Hospital-Consolidation-on-Medical-Costs.aspx.

261 Prager, E. Schmitt, M. *Employer Consolidation and Wages: Evidence from Hospitals.* American Economic Association. 2021. https://www.aeaweb.org/articles?id=10.1257/aer.20190690.

262 Kliff, S. Katz, J. *Hospitals and Insurers Didn't Want You to See These Prices. Here's Why.* The Upshot. The New York Times. 2021. https://www.nytimes.com/interactive/2021/08/22/upshot/hospital-prices.html.

263 Kliff, S. Katz, J. *Hospitals and Insurers Didn't Want You to See These Prices. Here's Why.* The Upshot. The New York Times. 2021. https://www.nytimes.com/interactive/2021/08/22/upshot/hospital-prices.html.

264 *National Chartbook of Health Care Prices.* The Health Care Cost Institute. 2016. https:// healthcostinstitute.org/national- chartbook-health-care-prices-2015.

It is time to implement policy changes that will make the health care sector more competitive, make health care more affordable, and allow our nation's families to access the health and health care they deserve.

The Energy and Commerce Committee has a key role to play in both uncovering concerning health industry behavior through bipartisan oversight and hearings such as this one, and addressing those behaviors through legislation. We urge the Committee to consider well-vetted, bipartisan, and commonsense legislation that would remedy some of the most obvious health system failings, and to take on rising health industry consolidation among hospitals, insurers, and other health care organizations that enables anticompetitive behaviors, prevents healthy competition in markets and results in monopolies that have the ability to set outrageous and unjustifiable prices.

Price transparency. One crucial way this Committee can address provider consolidation and encourage competition in the health care system is through price transparency. Unveiling prices is a critical step towards achieving truly affordable health care, improved health, and more competitive health care markets across the U.S. health care system. Price transparency pulls back the curtain on prices so that policymakers, researchers, employers, and consumers can see how irrational health care prices have become and take action to rein in pricing abuses. Further, unveiling prices can inform where the highest and most irrational prices are occurring in the health care system, so policymakers can implement more targeted policy solutions to bring down the cost of health care. We strongly support the administration's efforts to increase hospital price transparency and urge Congress to strengthen and codify the Hospital Price Transparency Rule.

Site-neutral payments. Another area we encourage the Committee to pursue is addressing payment differentials across sites of service that financially incentivize further consolidation. The continuation of this perverse payment incentive drives up costs and incentivizes consolidation with no corresponding improvement in quality or access. We urge the Committee to consider implementing site-neutral payment policies across the board as recommended by MedPAC,[265] and to eliminate site-dependent reimbursement distortions that indirectly incentivize acquisition of non-hospital patient access points.

Anti-competitive contracting. We also urge the Committee to take a closer look at anticompetitive practices and clauses in health care contracting agreements, which occur in a variety of places including between providers and insurers and in clinician and health care worker employment arrangements. In contracts between provider entities and insurers, large entities in highly consolidated markets have the upper hand in contract negotiations to build networks and set prices. As a result, many of these contracts include terms that limit access to higher-quality, lower-cost care. When anticompetitive terms are present in health care clinician and worker employment contracts, they can further stifle competition, lead to burnout

---

265 "Aligning fee-for-service payment rates across ambulatory settings," *Report to the Congress: Medicare and the Health Care Delivery System*, MedPAC, June 2022, https://www.medpac.gov/wp- content/uploads/2022/06/Jun22_Ch6_MedPAC_Report_to_Congress_SEC.pdf.

exacerbating workforce shortages,[266] impede patient access to preferred providers and care, and in some cases lead to higher prices for health care services[267].

We also encourage you to work with colleagues on the House and Senate Judiciary Committees to ensure that the Federal Trade Commission and U.S. Department of Justice Antitrust Division are appropriately resourced and have the legal tools needed to exert meaningful oversight of health care merger and acquisitions, including examining the impact on patient access to quality care.

Enacting these policies would set critical groundwork to reduce inflated spending throughout the system and make health care more affordable and value-driven for consumers.[268]

Consumers First and our undersigned allies look forward the discussion today and to working with you to enact bipartisan and commonsense improvements to our nation's health care payment and delivery system. Please contact Jane Sheehan, Director of Federal Relations at Families USA, JSheehan@familiesusa.org, for further information and to let us know how we can best be of service to you.

Sincerely,

Consumers First Steering Committee

American Academy of Family Physicians American Benefits Council

American Federation of State, County & Municipal Employees American Federation of Teachers Families USA

Purchaser Business Group on Health Supporting Organizations

Allergy & Asthma Network

American Medical Student Association APIAHF

Center for Independence of the Disabled, NY Colorado Consumer Health Initiative Connecticut Oral Health Initiative, Inc.

Consumers for Affordable Health Care Consumers for Quality Care Democratic Disability Caucus of Florida Florida Voices for Health

Health Access California Health Care Voices MomsRising

National Alliance of Healthcare Purchaser Coalitions National Partnership for Women & Families

New Jersey Citizen Action

Northwest Health Law Advocates (WA State) Pennsylvania Health Access Network

Small Business Majority

Tennessee Health Care Campaign, Inc The Arc

The ERISA Industry Committee Third Way

U.S. PIRG (Public Interest Research Group) Universal Healthcare Foundation of CT Utah Health Policy Project

---

266 Smith EB, "Ending Physician Noncompete Agreements—Time for a National Solution," *JAMA Health Forum.* 2021;2(12):e214018. doi:10.1001/jamahealthforum.2021.4018 https://jamanetwork.com/journals/jama-health-forum/fullarticle/2786894.

267 Hausman, Naomi, and Kurt Lavetti. 2021. "Physician Practice Organization and Negotiated Prices: Evidence from State Law Changes." *American Economic Journal: Applied Economics*, 13 (2): 258-96.DOI: 10.1257/app.20180078 https://www.aeaweb.org/articles?id=10.1257/app.20180078.

268 *Policy Approaches to Reduce What Commercial Insurers Pay for Hospitals' and Physicians' Services.* Congressional Budget Office. 2022. https://www.cbo.gov/publication/58222.

Virginia Organizing

LUGPA
Integrated Practices
Comprehensive Care

Large Urology Group Practice Association Testimony for the Energy and Commerce Health Subcommittee Hearing: "Lowering Unaffordable Costs: Examining Transparency and Competition in Health Care"

March 28, 2023

Chairman Guthrie and Ranking Member Eshoo, the Large Urology Group Practice Association (LUGPA) is honored to submit this testimony to the Energy & Commerce Committee on how to strengthen the health care system. LUGPA represents 150 urology group practices in the United States, with more than 2,100 physicians who, collectively, provide more than one-third of the nation's urology services. But our focus on public policy is on assisting all independent physician practices and the patients we care for.

The U.S. health care system is becoming increasingly consolidated by large hospital systems, which are buying up their competition, driving up prices and shrouding the cost of care from patients who are paying an increasing share of the bill. Congress and the Biden Administration can help reverse these troubling trends by pursuing several fundamental policies:

1) Enforce the hospital transparency rule, which will empower patients to make prudent decisions on where to get their health care;
2) Support independent physician practices by equalizing payments for similar services across different sites-of-service;
3) Require a minimum level of charity care (e.g. 3.8% -- the average amount provided by for-profit hospitals) for a hospital to earn a non-profit designation to be exempt from taxation and eligible for the 340B drug program;
4) Repeal the inpatient only list;
5) Reform the Stark law to eliminate the prohibition of physician ownership of hospitals and codify and simplify the reforms to value-based entities implemented through regulation in 2020.

American Patients Are Bearing the Brunt of Increasing Hospital Power

An increasing share of healthcare expenditures is being transferred to patients. Individual healthcare expenditures in 2023 are double what they were in 2016. Individual healthcare spend is estimated to increase at 9.9% per annum. The US ranks 19th of the G20 nations in share of healthcare costs borne by patients; only the Czech Republic is higher, with patients paying approximately 50% higher than average—in addition, the rate of increase in the US is amongst the highest in the world.[269]

These healthcare costs are severely economically burdensome to patients. A report from the Kaiser Family Foundation found that nearly 1 in 4 patients diagnosed with cancer will declare bankruptcy or lose their home within 5 years of their diagnosis. In 2022, 38% of Americans report delaying important healthcare decisions due to cost concerns. Even more concerning is that these burdens are disproportionately borne by socioeconomically disadvantaged groups.[270]

---

[269] OECD Out-of-pocket Health Spending, 1990-2021, accessed at: https://data.oecd.org/healthres/health-spending.html.

[270] Health Care Debt In The U.S.: The Broad Consequences Of Medical And Dental Bills. Accessed at: https://www.kff.org/report-section/kff-health-care-debt-survey-main-findings/.

Hospital mergers and acquisitions are contributing to rising costs of care[271] Once acquired, physicians have been shown to alter referral patterns to use more expensive hospital services.[272,273] Hospitals have focused on acquiring physician practices because that strategy simultaneously quashes competition in the local market for services such as outpatient surgery and radiation therapy and creates downstream revenue through referrals for surgery and ancillary services. This downstream revenue a physician generates for a hospital employer far surpasses the cost of the employed physician's salary.5 A few examples, as presented in the Merritt Hawkins 2019 Physician Inpatient/Outpatient Revenue Survey, include urologists generating $2,161,458 while receiving an average salary of $386,000, gastroenterologists generating $2,695,277 while receiving an average salary of $487,000, and ophthalmologists generating $1,440,217 while receiving an average salary of $300,000.[274]

Sadly, patients are not aware that hospitals can mandate that their employed doctors use hospital- owned services that are vastly more expensive and yet may be less convenient and offer no better care.

Site of service payment differentials are an artefact of historical realities that did not anticipate the tremendous technological and clinical innovations which have advanced the complexity and types of care available in outpatient settings and, concomitantly, reduced costs associated with the delivery of that care. Yet, the policy of paying hospitals substantially more (often more than twice as much) for the identical services provided in a physician office, infusion center or ambulatory surgery center (ASC), paradoxically, acts as a disincentive to pursuing innovations that shift care out of the higher cost hospital setting, thereby perpetuating inflationary cost trends and inhibiting patient access.

These payment differentials waste taxpayer and beneficiary dollars and provides mega-hospital systems with additional resources and incentives to acquire physician practices, promote consolidation, limit competition and restrict treatment options for patients. A recent study by Avalere for the Physician Advocacy Institute found that the percentage of hospital-employed physicians increased by more than 70% from July 2012 through January 2018. During that timeframe, hospital acquisitions of physician practices more than doubled. In 2017 and 2018 alone, an additional 8,000 physician practices were acquired by hospitals. The trend is disturbing—with the proportion of independent physicians steadily dropping from 48.5% in 2012 to 31.4 percent in 2018.

This trend should be of great concern to policymakers. The hospitals site of service is vastly more expensive than physician practices, even when furnishing the identical health care services.[275] As an example, Medicare pays hospitals more than twice the amount as physician offices for the infusion of the identical drug that requires the same nurse staff time and technical training; i.e. for the CPT code 96413 "Chemo admin; intravenous infusion; up to 1 hr." the HOPD rate is $325.64 vs. the in-office rate of $140.16.

---

[271] Rabbani M. Non-profit hospital mergers: the effect on healthcare costs and utilization. Int J Health Econ Manag. 2021 Dec;21(4):427-455.

[272] Whaley CM, Zhao X, Richards M, et al. Higher Medicare Spending on Imaging and Lab Services After Primary Care Physician Group Vertical Integration. Health Aff (Millwood). 2021 May;40(5):702-709.

[273] Carlin CS, Feldman R, Dowd B. The impact of hospital acquisition of physician practices on referral patterns. Health economics. 2016 Apr;25(4):439-54.

[274] 5 Merritt Hawkins 2019 Physician Inpatient/Outpatient Revenue Survey.

[275] Hayes J, Hoverman JR, Brow ME, et. al. Cost differential by site of service for cancer patients receiving chemotherapy. Am J Manag Care. 2015 Mar 1;21(3):e189-96.

Nonprofit Hospitals Are Abusing Their Tax-Exempt Status

Nonprofit hospitals enjoy sizable federal, state and local tax exemptions in exchange for meeting requirements to provide services such as free care for the poor.[276] These hospitals also have access to special federal programs, like the 340B drug discount program, in exchange for the expectation that they adhere to their non-profit obligations and use these programs to support vulnerable patients in underserved communitis. Today, about 50 percent of the hospitals in the United States are nongovernment not-for-profit community hospitals.[277] In exchange for their substantial tax savings and goodwill, these hospitals are expected to provide services in the public interest, including free or discounted care and financial assistance to patients who are unable to pay.

Recent public reporting by investigative journalists in the New York Times,[278] the Wall Street Journal,[279] and other prominent outlets demonstrate that many not-for-profit hospitals are not fulfilling their mission to serve America's neediest patients.[280] To the contrary, these public reports clearly show that some hospitals are going after the most vulnerable patients through financial duress during hospital intake process and abusive collections practices for unpaid medical bills.[281,282] These stories are even more remarkable when you consider that compliance with recent transparency rules are abysmal, nearly two years after implementation began.[283] A majority of hospitals aren't complying with a CMS rule on price transparency, according to a study published in JAMA. Under the rule, which was finalized in 2019 and took effect in January 2021, hospitals have to publicize their negotiated rates with payers for common services. But early data shows that's often not the case. The study, conducted by researchers at Harvard Medical School, randomly sampled 100 hospitals, as well as the 100

---

276 Kaiser Family Foundation, "Hospital Charity Care: How It Works and Why It Matters," Zachary Levinson, Scott Hulver, and Tricia Neuman, https://www.kff.org/health-costs/issue-brief/hospital-charity-care-how-it-works-and why-it-matters/.

277 American Hospital Association, "Fast Facts on U.S. Hospitals, 2022," https://www.aha.org/statistics/fast-facts-us-hospitals.

278 How a Hospital Chain Used a Poor Neighborhood to Turn Huge Profits, Sep. 27, 2022, at https://www.nytimes.com/2022/09/24/health/bon-secours-mercy-health-profit-poor-neighborhood.html?smid=tw-share.

279 Many Hospitals Get Big Drug Discounts. That Doesn't Mean Markdowns for Patients. *The Wall Street Journal.* Available at https://www.wsj.com/articles/340b-drug-discounts-hospitals-low-income-federal-program-11671553899.

280 They Were Entitled to Free Care. Hospitals Hounded Them to Pay. The New York Times. Available at https://www.nytimes.com/2022/09/24/business/nonprofit-hospitals-poor-patients.html.

281 See Senator Baldwin's letter to Ascension, citing its 10-year partnership with a debt collection company that had to cease operations in Minnesota following a state investigation that found it embedded debt collectors among hospital staff and assigned patient scores based on their ability to pay, according to the letter. Senator Baldwin also noted that the partnership is still ongoing and particularly unusual given that nonprofit health systems are held to strict standards that bar aggressive billing and debt collection practices. A STAT news article analyzing Ascension's private equity operations, suggests many investments did not align the nonprofit's mission of providing charitable benefits to the community. Available at https://www.baldwin.senate.gov/download/ascension-financial-letter_final.

282 See Letter from Senators Warren and Wyden to McKinsey. A recent investigation by the *New York Times* uncovered a deal between Providence and McKinsey that resulted in a plan to use predatory tactics to pressure patients into paying for their care, no matter their income or ability to pay. As a result, more than 55,000 patients were pursued by debt collectors when they should have been offered discounts due to their socioeconomic status. Available at https://www.warren.senate.gov/download/20230220-letter-to-mckinsey-re-nonprofit-hospitals.

283 Patients Rights Advocates. Fourth Semi-Annual Hospital Price Transparency Report, Feb. 2023, available at https://www.patientrightsadvocate.org/february-semi-annual-compliance-report-2023.

highest-earning hospitals of 2017. Of the randomly selected facilities, 83% were noncompliant with at least one of the rule's requirements. The top-earning hospitals were more compliant but not by much, with 75% noncompliant with at least one requirement.[284]

Even as they do not comply with their obligations borne from their not-for-profit status, these hospitals are increasingly taking advantage of mergers and other business decisions that can actually reduce access and drive up costs for all consumers, without verifiable increase in quality of care.[285] These types of mergers can deprive communities of critical care and result in workforce wages reductions,[286] even as many hospital executives are seeing massive growth in their income.[287]

Recommendations to Congress and the Biden Administration

1) Enforce the hospital transparency law

The hospital transparency rule had two laudable requirements. First, hospitals have to publish discounted cash prices applicable to all uninsured patients and payer-specific negotiated rates for all services. Additionally, hospitals have to publish price data, including expected out-of-pocket costs, for "shoppable services" such as an X-ray that can be scheduled in advance, in an easily understandable format to facilitate shopping across different sites of care, such as a price estimator tool. Hospitals who fail to comply are theoretically liable for $100 per day per patient. But the law has been rarely enforced. CMS should raise the penalty to $500 per infraction and actually enforce the law for the vast majority of hospitals that remain out-of-compliance.

As patients bear an increasing burden of their healthcare costs, hospital price transparency is crucial to restore patient agency in managing their physical, emotional, and financial well-being.

2) Establish a threshold of charity care in the tax code for non-profit hospital status.

Currently, hospitals do not have to provide a specified level of charity care in order to be categorized "non-profit" and thus exempt from state, local and federal taxation and to be eligible for the 340B drug discount program. A recent study in Health Affairs documented that for-profit hospitals actually provide about 50 percent more charity care than non-profit

284 *JAMA Health Forum*. 2021;2(3):e210316. doi:10.1001/jamahealthforum.2021.0316.

285 Associate Secretary for Planning & Evaluation, HHS, available at https://aspe.hhs.gov/sites/default/files/documents/0d2c04fec395bc8c573c5b20c189cdd0/enviromental-scan-consolidation-hcm.pdf. *See also* https://www.vox.com/policy-and-politics/2023/1/20/23560762/hospital-mergers-uk-study-deaths-read missions. (According to VOX, in 2005, about half of US hospitals were part of a larger system. By 2017, two-thirds were. Most places in the US have what is considered a highly concentrated hospital market, which means one company operates most of the hospital facilities in the area.).

286 *See ASPE* report.

287 https://www.medpagetoday.com/special-reports/features/103127 (Focused on NC hospitals, this report noted that CEOs and top executives at North Carolina's nonprofit hospitals made over $1.75B between 2010 and 2020, as worker wages were stymied, medical debt mounted, and a lack of transparency persisted.

hospitals (3.8 percent vs 2.3 percent).[288] Congress should establish a minimum threshold of bona fide charity care for hospitals to reap the many benefits of their non-profit status, including not paying taxes and being made eligible for hugely profitable 340B drugs which they dispense at substantial markups. What metric for a hospital's non-profit status can be more important than providing indigent patients, needed free care? We suggest a threshold equal to the amount for-profit hospitals provide: 3.8 percent.

3) Close the site-of-service payment disparities

Medicare pays substantially more for services performed on an outpatient basis at hospitals than it does for the same services performed in physician offices and ambulatory surgery centers. This fuels consolidation where these sites can be acquired by hospitals and designated as part of a hospital and paid as such. Congress could eliminate these payment disparities and save $141 billion over 10 years in Medicare. But Congress need not entirely equalize payments to make progress in this area. For example, it could raise physician payments for identical treatments by 25% and lower hospital payments by 50%. This would still provide substantial net savings to the program, but importantly provide much needed resources to physician practices which have received cuts in recent years and confront a decade of payment freezes while hospitals receive compounding market basket payment updates.

4) Repeal the Inpatient Only (IPO) List.

CMS recently reversed the reform the Trump Administration had initiated and that was only in the first year of a three-year phase-in by reinstating the inpatient only list of 298 procedures. CMS simultaneously removed 256 procedures that had been added to the ASC-payable list. This reversal occurred despite the acknowledged blistering pace of technological innovation and the sustained trend of increased volume and complexity of cases safely moving into the outpatient setting such that the healthcare intelligence firm Sg2 projects that 85 percent of all healthcare procedures will be performed on an outpatient basis by 2028. Arbitrarily defining an IPO list creates an unnecessary barrier and presumes that the government knows better than practicing physicians when it comes to determining the appropriate site of service in which to perform a procedure.

Not only does the elimination of the IPO list and expansion of the ASC Covered Procedures List (CPL) promote beneficiary access to safe and convenient sites of care while expanding access to innovation, but it also contributes to significant savings in Medicare spending as surgical procedures in the ASC are paid half the amount as the hospital. ASCs have already saved Medicare $28 billion from 2011 to 20188 and could save much more if physicians had the ability to move appropriate procedures to that setting. This can occur in a more robust way by eliminating the inpatient only list and restoring those procedures to the ASC-payable list.

---

[288] Bai, et al. "Analysis Suggests Government and Nonprofit Hospitals' Charity Care is Not Aligned with Their Favorable Tax Treatment". Health Affairs, April 2021.

5) Simplify and Modernize the Stark Self-Referral Law

It has been shown that competition in the healthcare market improves outcomes and reduces costs.[289] Regrettably, acquisition of physician practices by hospitals and the increasing trend of hospitals to form monolithic health systems serves only to stifle that competition. An additional example of this is that physicians are barred from owning hospitals and are subject to antiquated laws enacted 35 years ago. The Affordable Care Act permanently barred new physician-owned hospitals and barred growth of current physician-owned hospitals – as a payoff to the hospital industry, which was asked to accept market basket payment reductions to help fund the insurance expansion.

Brian Miller noted as a result of ACA's statutory ban, "more than $275 million of planned economic activity spread across 45 hospital expansion projects ceased. More than 75 new hospitals either planned or under development were prematurely terminated, representing more than $2.2 billion in economic losses. Intangible losses include the loss of the "physician entrepreneur" and user-driven innovation in the face of increasing corporatization of medical practice, both likely contributing to the increase in physician professional dissatisfaction… Premature foreclosure of the POH marketplace inhibited the development of the US version of the "focused factory" model of specialized hospitals or integrated Reversing Hospital Consolidation: model of specialized hospitals or integrated practice units, a feature seen in other markets."[290]

LUGPA worked closely with aligned stakeholders to encourage updating existing regulations governing the Stark statute and strongly supports the administrative reforms made by both CMS and the HHS Office of the Inspector General (OIG) in December of 2020. The OIG administrative changes created three new safe harbors to encourage value-based care models: (1) care coordination arrangements without requiring the parties to assume risk; (2) value-based arrangements with substantial downside financial risk; and (3) value-based arrangements with full financial risk. Essentially simultaneously, CMS adopted revisions to the Medicare self-referral statute also designed to support value-based payment arrangements in the Medicare program. Although these regulatory changes were helpful in advancing the adoption of payment arrangements that reward value over volume, they remain constrained by the underlying statutes and furthermore, these regulations are complex and hard to understand by providers. As a result, practitioners have been reluctant to enter new or innovative payment arrangements for fear of triggering inadvertent violations of the underlying statutes or investigations by overzealous prosecutors. In addition, adoption of these programs is hampered by logistical challenges for practices remain as compliance is carried out while dealing with real-time patient pressures and practice resource constraints.

LUGPA looks forward to working with the committee to help improve access, enhance quality and reduce costs for our patients. please feel free to contact Dr. Kapoor (dkapoor@solarishp.com) at (516)-342-8170 if LUGPA can provide additional information to assist the committee as it considers these issues.

---

289 Gaynor M, Moreno-Serra R, Propper C. Death by market power: reform, competition, and patient outcomes in the National Health Service. American Economic Journal: Economic Policy. 2013 Nov 1;5(4):134-66.

290 Brian Miller et al. "Reversing Hospital Consolidation: the Promise of Physician-Owned Hospitals" Health Affairs Blog April 2021.

Respectfully submitted,

Evan R. Goldfischer, MD
President

Deepak A. Kapoor, M.D.
Chairman, Health Policy

Executive Order on Promoting Competition in the American Economy

July 09, 2021

By the authority vested in me as President by the Constitution and the laws of the United States of America, and in order to promote the interests of American workers, businesses, and consumers, it is hereby ordered as follows:

Section 1. Policy

A fair, open, and competitive marketplace has long been a cornerstone of the American economy, while excessive market concentration threatens basic economic liberties, democratic accountability, and the welfare of workers, farmers, small businesses, startups, and consumers.

The American promise of a broad and sustained prosperity depends on an open and competitive economy. For workers, a competitive marketplace creates more high-quality jobs and the economic freedom to switch jobs or negotiate a higher wage. For small businesses and farmers, it creates more choices among suppliers and major buyers, leading to more take-home income, which they can reinvest in their enterprises. For entrepreneurs, it provides space to experiment, innovate, and pursue the new ideas that have for centuries powered the American economy and improved our quality of life. And for consumers, it means more choices, better service, and lower prices.

Robust competition is critical to preserving America's role as the world's leading economy.

Yet over the last several decades, as industries have consolidated, competition has weakened in too many markets, denying Americans the benefits of an open economy and widening racial, income, and wealth inequality. Federal Government inaction has contributed to these problems, with workers, farmers, small businesses, and consumers paying the price.

Consolidation has increased the power of corporate employers, making it harder for workers to bargain for higher wages and better work conditions. Powerful companies require workers to sign non-compete agreements that restrict their ability to change jobs. And, while many occupational licenses are critical to increasing wages for workers and especially workers of color, some overly restrictive occupational licensing requirements can impede workers' ability to find jobs and to move between States.

Consolidation in the agricultural industry is making it too hard for small family farms to survive. Farmers are squeezed between concentrated market power in the agricultural input industries — seed, fertilizer, feed, and equipment suppliers — and concentrated market power in the channels for selling agricultural products. As a result, farmers' share of the value of their agricultural products has decreased, and poultry farmers, hog farmers, cattle ranchers, and other agricultural workers struggle to retain autonomy and to make sustainable returns.

The American information technology sector has long been an engine of innovation and growth, but today a small number of dominant Internet platforms use their power to exclude market entrants, to extract monopoly profits, and to gather intimate personal information that they can exploit for their own advantage. Too many small businesses across the economy depend on those platforms and a few online marketplaces for their survival. And too many local newspapers have shuttered or downsized, in part due to the Internet platforms' dominance in advertising markets.

Americans are paying too much for prescription drugs and healthcare services — far more than the prices paid in other countries. Hospital consolidation has left many areas, particularly rural communities, with inadequate or more expensive healthcare options. And too often, patent and other laws have been misused to inhibit or delay — for years and even decades — competition from generic drugs and biosimilars, denying Americans access to lower-cost drugs.

In the telecommunications sector, Americans likewise pay too much for broadband, cable television, and other communications services, in part because of a lack of adequate competition. In the financial-services sector, consumers pay steep and often hidden fees because of industry consolidation. Similarly, the global container shipping industry has consolidated intoa small number of dominant foreign-owned lines and alliances, which can disadvantage American exporters.

The problem of economic consolidation now spans these sectors and many others, endangering our ability to rebuild and emerge from the coronavirus disease 2019 (COVID-19) pandemic with a vibrant, innovative, and growing economy. Meanwhile, the United States faces new challenges to its economic standing in the world, including unfair competitive pressures from foreign monopolies and firms that are state-owned or state-sponsored, or whose market power is directly supported by foreign governments.

We must act now to reverse these dangerous trends, which constrain the growth and dynamism of our economy, impair the creation of high-quality jobs, and threaten America's economic standing in the world.

This order affirms that it is the policy of my Administration to enforce the antitrust laws to combat the excessive concentration of industry, the abuses of market power, and the harmful effects of monopoly and monopsony — especially as these issues arise in labor markets, agricultural markets, Internet platform industries, healthcare markets (including insurance, hospital, and prescription drug markets), repair markets, and United States markets directly affected by foreign cartel activity.

It is also the policy of my Administration to enforce the antitrust laws to meet the challenges posed by new industries and technologies, including the rise of the dominant Internet platforms, especially as they stem from serial mergers, the acquisition of nascent competitors, the aggregation of data, unfair competition in attention markets, the surveillance of users, and the presence of network effects.

Whereas decades of industry consolidation have often led to excessive market concentration, this order reaffirms that the United States retains the authority to challenge transactions whose previous consummation was in violation of the Sherman Antitrust Act (26 Stat. 209, 15 U.S.C. 1 et seq.) (Sherman Act), the Clayton Antitrust Act (Public Law 63-212, 38 Stat. 730, 15 U.S.C. 12 et seq.) (Clayton Act), or other laws. See 15 U.S.C. 18; Standard Oil Co. v. United States, 221 U.S. 1 (1911).

This order reasserts as United States policy that the answer to the rising power of foreign monopolies and cartels is not the tolerance of domestic monopolization, but rather the promotionof competition and innovation by firms small and large, at home and worldwide.

It is also the policy of my Administration to support aggressive legislative reforms that would lower prescription drug prices, including by allowing Medicare to negotiate drug prices, by imposing inflation caps, and through other related reforms. It is further the policy of my Administration to support the enactment of a public health insurance option.

My Administration further reaffirms the policy stated in Executive Order 13725 of April 15, 2016 (Steps to Increase Competition and Better Inform Consumers and Workers to Support Continued Growth of the American Economy), and the Federal Government's commitment to the principles that led to the passage of the Sherman Act, the Clayton Act, the Packers and Stockyards Act, 1921 (Public Law 67-51, 42 Stat. 159, 7 U.S.C. 181 et seq.) (Packers and Stockyards Act), the Celler-Kefauver Antimerger Act (Public Law 81-899, 64 Stat. 1125), the Bank Merger Act (Public Law 86-463, 74 Stat. 129, 12 U.S.C. 1828), and the Telecommunications Act of 1996 (Public Law 104-104, 110 Stat. 56), among others.

Sec. 2. The Statutory Basis of a Whole-of-Government Competition Policy

a) The antitrust laws, including the Sherman Act, the Clayton Act, and the Federal Trade Commission Act (Public Law 63-203, 38 Stat. 717, 15 U.S.C. 41 et seq.), are a first line of defense against the monopolization of the American economy.
b) The antitrust laws reflect an underlying policy favoring competition that transcends those particular enactments. As the Supreme Court has stated, for instance, the Sherman Act "rests on the premise that the unrestrained interaction of competitive forces will yield the best allocation of our economic resources, the lowest prices, the highest quality and the greatest material progress, while at the same time providing an environment conducive to the preservation of our democratic political and social institutions." Northern Pac. Ry. Co. v. United States, 356 U.S. 1, 4 (1958).
c) Consistent with these broader policies, and in addition to the traditional antitrust laws, the Congress has also enacted industry-specific fair competition and anti-monopolization laws that often provide additional protections. Such enactments include the Packers and Stockyards Act, the Federal Alcohol Administration Act (Public Law 74-401, 49 Stat. 977, 27 U.S.C. 201 et seq.), the Bank Merger Act, the Drug Price Competition and Patent Term Restoration Act of1984 (Public Law 98-417,

98 Stat. 1585), the Shipping Act of 1984 (Public Law 98-237, 98 Stat. 67, 46 U.S.C. 40101 et seq.) (Shipping Act), the ICC Termination Act of 1995 (Public Law 104- 88, 109 Stat. 803), the Telecommunications Act of 1996, the Fairness to Contact Lens Consumers Act (Public Law 108-164, 117 Stat. 2024, 15 U.S.C. 7601 et seq.), and the Dodd- Frank Wall Street Reform and Consumer Protection Act (Public Law 111-203, 124 Stat. 1376) (Dodd-Frank Act).

d) These statutes independently charge a number of executive departments and agencies (agencies) to protect conditions of fair competition in one or more ways, including by:
   (i) policing unfair, deceptive, and abusive business practices;
   (ii) resisting consolidation and promoting competition within industries through the independent oversight of mergers, acquisitions, and joint ventures;
   (iii) promulgating rules that promote competition, including the market entry of new competitors; and
   (iv) promoting market transparency through compelled disclosure of information.
e) The agencies that administer such or similar authorities include the Department of the Treasury, the Department of Agriculture, the Department of Health and Human Services, the Department of Transportation, the Federal Reserve System, the Federal Trade Commission (FTC), the Securities and Exchange Commission, the Federal Deposit Insurance Corporation, the Federal Communications Commission, the Federal Maritime Commission, the Commodity Futures Trading Commission, the Federal Energy Regulatory Commission, the Consumer Financial Protection Bureau, and the Surface Transportation Board.
f) Agencies can influence the conditions of competition through their exercise of regulatory authority or through the procurement process. See 41 U.S.C. 1705.
g) This order recognizes that a whole-of-government approach is necessary to address overconcentration, monopolization, and unfair competition in the American economy. Such an approach is supported by existing statutory mandates. Agencies can and should further the polices set forth in section 1 of this order by, among other things, adopting pro-competitive regulations and approaches to procurement and spending, and by rescinding regulations that create unnecessary barriers to entry that stifle competition.

Sec. 3. Agency Cooperation in Oversight, Investigation, and Remedies

a) The Congress frequently has created overlapping agency jurisdiction in the policing of anticompetitive conduct and the oversight of mergers. It is the policy of my Administration that, when agencies have overlapping jurisdiction, they should endeavor to cooperate fully in the exercise of their oversight authority, to benefit from the respective expertise of the agencies and to improve Government efficiency.
b) Where there is overlapping jurisdiction over particular cases, conduct, transactions, or industries, agencies are encouraged to coordinate their efforts, as appropriate and consistent with applicable law, with respect to:
   (v) the investigation of conduct potentially harmful to competition;
   (vi) the oversight of proposed mergers, acquisitions, and joint ventures; and
   (vii) the design, execution, and oversight of remedies.

c) The means of cooperation in cases of overlapping jurisdiction should include, as appropriate and consistent with applicable law:
   (i) sharing relevant information and industry data;
   (ii) in the case of major transactions, soliciting and giving significant consideration to the views of the Attorney General or the Chair of the FTC, as applicable; and
   (iii) cooperating with any concurrent Department of Justice or FTC oversight activities under the Sherman Act or Clayton Act.

d) Nothing in subsections (a) through (c) of this section shall be construed to suggest that the statutory standard applied by an agency, or its independent assessment under that standard, should be displaced or substituted by the judgment of the Attorney General or the Chair of the FTC. When their views are solicited, the Attorney General and the Chair of the FTC are encouraged to provide a response to the agency in time for the agency to consider it in advance of any statutory deadline for agency action.

Sec. 4. The White House Competition Council

a) There is established a White House Competition Council (Council) within the Executive Office of the President.

b) The Council shall coordinate, promote, and advance Federal Government efforts toaddress overconcentration, monopolization, and unfair competition in or directly affecting the American economy, including efforts to:
   (i) implement the administrative actions identified in this order;
   (ii) develop procedures and best practices for agency cooperation and coordination on matters of overlapping jurisdiction, as described in section 3 of this order;
   (iii) identify and advance any additional administrative actions necessary to further the policies set forth in section 1 of this order; and
   (iv) identify any potential legislative changes necessary to further the policies set forth in section 1 of this order.

c) The Council shall work across agencies to provide a coordinated response to overconcentration, monopolization, and unfair competition in or directly affecting the American economy. The Council shall also work with each agency to ensure that agency operations are conducted in a manner that promotes fair competition, as appropriate and consistent with applicable law.

d) The Council shall not discuss any current or anticipated enforcement actions.

e) The Council shall be led by the Assistant to the President for Economic Policy and Director of the National Economic Council, who shall serve as Chair of the Council.

f) In addition to the Chair, the Council shall consist of the following members:
   (i) the Secretary of the Treasury;
   (ii) the Secretary of Defense;
   (iii) the Attorney General;
   (iv) the Secretary of Agriculture;
   (v) the Secretary of Commerce;
   (vi) the Secretary of Labor;
   (vii) the Secretary of Health and Human Services;
   (viii) the Secretary of Transportation;

(ix) the Administrator of the Office of Information and Regulatory Affairs; and
(x) the heads of such other agencies and offices as the Chair may from time to time invite to participate.

g) The Chair shall invite the participation of the Chair of the FTC, the Chair of the FederalCommunications Commission, the Chair of the Federal Maritime Commission, the Director of the Consumer Financial Protection Bureau, and the Chair of the Surface Transportation Board, to the extent consistent with their respective statutory authorities and obligations.
h) Members of the Council shall designate, not later than 30 days after the date of this order, a senior official within their respective agency or office who shall coordinate with the Council and who shall be responsible for overseeing the agency's or office's efforts to address overconcentration, monopolization, and unfair competition. The Chair may coordinate subgroups consisting exclusively of Council members or their designees, as appropriate.
i) The Council shall meet on a semi-annual basis unless the Chair determines that a meeting is unnecessary.
j) Each agency shall bear its own expenses for participating in the Council.

Sec. 5. Further Agency Responsibilities

a) The heads of all agencies shall consider using their authorities to further the policies set forth in section 1 of this order, with particular attention to:
   (i) the influence of any of their respective regulations, particularly any licensing regulations, on concentration and competition in the industries under their jurisdiction; and
   (ii) the potential for their procurement or other spending to improve the competitiveness of small businesses and businesses with fair labor practices.
b) The Attorney General, the Chair of the FTC, and the heads of other agencies with authority to enforce the Clayton Act are encouraged to enforce the antitrust laws fairly and vigorously.
c) To address the consolidation of industry in many markets across the economy, as described in section 1 of this order, the Attorney General and the Chair of the FTC are encouraged to review the horizontal and vertical merger guidelines and consider whether to revise those guidelines.
d) To avoid the potential for anticompetitive extension of market power beyond the scope of granted patents, and to protect standard-setting processes from abuse, the Attorney General and the Secretary of Commerce are encouraged to consider whether to revise their position on the intersection of the intellectual property and antitrust laws, including by considering whether torevise the Policy Statement on Remedies for Standards-Essential Patents Subject to Voluntary F/RAND Commitments issued jointly by the Department of Justice, the United States Patent and Trademark Office, and the National Institute of Standards and Technology on December 19, 2019.
e) To ensure Americans have choices among financial institutions and to guard against excessive market power, the Attorney General, in consultation with the Chairman of the Board of Governors of the Federal Reserve System, the Chairperson of the Board

of Directors of the Federal Deposit Insurance Corporation, and the Comptroller of the Currency, is encouraged to review current practices and adopt a plan, not later than 180 days after the date of this order, for the revitalization of merger oversight under the Bank Merger Act and the Bank Holding Company Act of 1956 (Public Law 84-511, 70 Stat. 133, 12 U.S.C. 1841 et seq.) that is in accordance with the factors enumerated in 12 U.S.C. 1828(c) and 1842(c).

f) To better protect workers from wage collusion, the Attorney General and the Chair of the FTC are encouraged to consider whether to revise the Antitrust Guidance for Human Resource Professionals of October 2016.

g) To address agreements that may unduly limit workers' ability to change jobs, the Chair of the FTC is encouraged to consider working with the rest of the Commission to exercise the FTC's statutory rulemaking authority under the Federal Trade Commission Act to curtail the unfair use of non-compete clauses and other clauses or agreements that may unfairly limit worker mobility.

h) To address persistent and recurrent practices that inhibit competition, the Chair of the FTC, in the Chair's discretion, is also encouraged to consider working with the rest of the Commission to exercise the FTC's statutory rulemaking authority, as appropriate and consistent with applicable law, in areas such as:

   (i) unfair data collection and surveillance practices that may damage competition, consumer autonomy, and consumer privacy;

   (ii) unfair anticompetitive restrictions on third-party repair or self-repair of items, such as the restrictions imposed by powerful manufacturers that prevent farmers from repairing their own equipment;

   (iii) unfair anticompetitive conduct or agreements in the prescription drug industries, suchas agreements to delay the market entry of generic drugs or biosimilars;

   (iv) unfair competition in major Internet marketplaces;

   (v) unfair occupational licensing restrictions;

   (vi) unfair tying practices or exclusionary practices in the brokerage or listing of real estate; and

   (vii) any other unfair industry-specific practices that substantially inhibit competition.

(i) The Secretary of Agriculture shall:

   (i) to address the unfair treatment of farmers and improve conditions of competition in the markets for their products, consider initiating a rulemaking or rulemakings under the Packers and Stockyards Act to strengthen the Department of Agriculture's regulations concerning unfair, unjustly discriminatory, or deceptive practices and undue or unreasonable preferences, advantages, prejudices, or disadvantages, with the purpose of furthering the vigorous implementation of the law established by the Congress in 1921 and fortified by amendments. In such rulemaking or rulemakings, the Secretary of Agriculture shall consider, among other things:

      A. providing clear rules that identify recurrent practices in the livestock, meat, and poultry industries that are unfair, unjustly discriminatory, or deceptive and therefore violate the Packers and Stockyards Act;

      B. reinforcing the long-standing Department of Agriculture interpretation that it is unnecessary under the Packers and Stockyards Act to demonstrate industry-wide harm to establish a violation of the Act and that the "unfair, unjustly discriminatory, or deceptive" treatment of one farmer, the giving to one farmer of an "undue or unreasonable preference or advantage," or the subjection of one farmer to an "undue or unreasonable prejudice or

C. disadvantage in any respect" violates the Act;
D. prohibiting unfair practices related to grower ranking systems — systems in which the poultry companies, contractors, or dealers exercise extraordinary control over numerous inputs that determine the amount farmers are paid and require farmers to assume the risk of factors outside their control, leaving them more economically vulnerable;
E. updating the appropriate definitions or set of criteria, or application thereof, for undue or unreasonable preferences, advantages, prejudices, or disadvantages under the Packers and Stockyards Act; and adopting, to the greatest extent possible and as appropriate and consistent with applicable law, appropriate anti-retaliation protections, so that farmers may assert their rights without fear of retribution;

(ii) to ensure consumers have accurate, transparent labels that enable them to choose products made in the United States, consider initiating a rulemaking to define the conditions under which the labeling of meat products can bear voluntary statements indicating that the product is of United States origin, such as "Product of USA";

(iii) to ensure that farmers have greater opportunities to access markets and receive a fair return for their products, not later than 180 days after the date of this order, submit a report to the Chair of the White House Competition Council, with a plan to promote competition in the agricultural industries and to support value-added agriculture and alternative food distribution systems through such means as:

A. the creation or expansion of useful information for farmers, such as model contracts, to lower transaction costs and help farmers negotiate fair deals;
B. measures to encourage improvements in transparency and standards so that consumers may choose to purchase products that support fair treatment of farmers and agricultural workers and sustainable agricultural practices;
C. measures to enhance price discovery, increase transparency, and improve the functioning of the cattle and other livestock markets;
D. enhanced tools, including any new legislative authorities needed, to protect whistleblowers, monitor agricultural markets, and enforce relevant laws;
E. any investments or other support that could bolster competition within highly concentrated agricultural markets; and
F. any other means that the Secretary of Agriculture deems appropriate;

(i) to improve farmers' and smaller food processors' access to retail markets, not later than 300 days after the date of this order, in consultation with the Chair of the FTC, submit a report to the Chair of the White House Competition Council, on the effect of retail concentration and retailers' practices on the conditions of competition in the food industries, including any practices that may violate the Federal Trade Commission Act, the Robinson-Patman Act (Public Law 74-692, 49 Stat. 1526, 15 U.S.C. 13 et seq.), or other relevant laws, and on grants, loans, and other support that may enhance access to retail markets by local and regional food enterprises; and

(ii) to help ensure that the intellectual property system, while incentivizing innovation, does not also unnecessarily reduce competition in seed and other input markets beyond that reasonably contemplated by the Patent Act (see 35 U.S.C. 100 et seq. and 7 U.S.C. 2321 et seq.), in consultation with the Under Secretary of Commerce for Intellectual Property and Director of the United States Patent and Trademark Office, submit a report to the Chair of the White House Competition Council, enumerating and describing any relevant concerns of the Department of Agriculture and strategies for addressing those concerns across intellectual property, antitrust, and other relevant laws.

j) To protect the vibrancy of the American markets for beer, wine, and spirits, and to improve market access for smaller, independent, and new operations, the Secretary of the Treasury, in consultation with the Attorney General and the Chair of the FTC, not later than 120 days after the date of this order, shall submit a report to the Chair of the White House Competition Council, assessing the current market structure and conditions of competition, including an assessment of any threats to competition and barriers to new entrants, including:

(iii) any unlawful trade practices in the beer, wine, and spirits markets, such as certain exclusionary, discriminatory, or anticompetitive distribution practices, that hinder smaller and independent businesses or new entrants from distributing their products;

(iv) patterns of consolidation in production, distribution, or retail beer, wine, and spirits markets; and

(v) any unnecessary trade practice regulations of matters such as bottle sizes, permitting, or labeling that may unnecessarily inhibit competition by increasing costs without serving any public health, informational, or tax purpose.

k) To follow up on the foregoing assessment, the Secretary of the Treasury, through the Administrator of the Alcohol and Tobacco Tax and Trade Bureau, shall, not later than 240 days after the date of this order, consider:

(vi) initiating a rulemaking to update the Alcohol and Tobacco Tax and Trade Bureau's trade practice regulations;

(vii) rescinding or revising any regulations of the beer, wine, and spirits industries thatmay unnecessarily inhibit competition; and

(viii) reducing any barriers that impede market access for smaller and independent brewers, winemakers, and distilleries.

l) To promote competition, lower prices, and a vibrant and innovative telecommunications ecosystem, the Chair of the Federal Communications Commission is encouraged to work with the rest of the Commission, as appropriate and consistent with applicable law, to consider:

(i) adopting through appropriate rulemaking "Net Neutrality" rules similar to those previously adopted under title II of the Communications Act of 1934 (Public Law 73-416, 48 Stat. 1064, 47 U.S.C. 151 et seq.), as amended by the Telecommunications Act of 1996, in "Protecting and Promoting the Open Internet," 80 Fed. Reg. 19738 (Apr. 13, 2015);

(ii) conducting future spectrum auctions under rules that are designed to help avoid excessive concentration of spectrum license holdings in the United States, so as to prevent spectrum stockpiling, warehousing of spectrum by licensees, or the creation of barriers to entry, and to improve the conditions of competition in industries that depend upon radio spectrum, including mobile communications and radio-based broadband services;

(iii) providing support for the continued development and adoption of 5G Open Radio Access Network (O-RAN) protocols and software, continuing to attend meetings of voluntary and consensus-based standards development organizations, so as to promote or encourage a fair and representative standard-setting process, and undertaking any other measures that might promote increased openness, innovation, and competition in the markets for 5G equipment;

(iv) prohibiting unjust or unreasonable early termination fees for end-user communications contracts, enabling consumers to more easily switch providers;

(v) initiating a rulemaking that requires broadband service providers to display a broadband consumer label, such as that as described in the Public Notice of the Commission issued on April 4, 2016 (DA 16–357), so as to give consumers clear, concise, and accurate information regarding provider prices and fees, performance, and network practices;

(vi) initiating a rulemaking to require broadband service providers to regularly report broadband price and subscription rates to the Federal Communications Commission for the purpose of disseminating that information to the public in a useful manner, to improve price transparency and market functioning; and Communications Commission for the purpose of disseminating that information to the public in a useful manner, to improve price transparency and market functioning; and

(vii) initiating a rulemaking to prevent landlords and cable and Internet service providers from inhibiting tenants' choices among providers.

m) The Secretary of Transportation shall:

(i) to better protect consumers and improve competition, and as appropriate and consistent with applicable law:

A. not later than 30 days after the date of this order, appoint or reappoint members of the Advisory Committee for Aviation Consumer Protection to ensure fair representation of consumers, State and local interests, airlines, and airports with respect to the evaluation of aviation consumer protection programs and convene a meeting of the Committee as soon as practicable;

B. promote enhanced transparency and consumer safeguards, as appropriate and consistent with applicable law, including through potential rulemaking, enforcement actions, or guidance documents, with the aims of:

1. enhancing consumer access to airline flight information so that consumers can more easily find a broader set of available flights, including by new or lesser known airlines; and

2. ensuring that consumers are not exposed or subject to advertising, marketing, pricing, and charging of ancillary fees that may constitute an unfair or deceptive practice or an unfair method of competition;

C. not later than 45 days after the date of this order, submit a report to the Chair of the White House Competition Council, on the progress of the Department of Transportation's investigatory and enforcement activities to address the failure of airlines to provide timely refunds for flights cancelled as a result of the COVID-19 pandemic;

D. not later than 45 days after the date of this order, publish for notice and comment a proposed rule requiring airlines to refund baggage fees when a passenger's luggage is substantially delayed and other ancillary fees when passengers pay for a service that is not provided;

E. not later than 60 days after the date of this order, start development of proposed amendments to the Department of Transportation's definitions of "unfair" and "deceptive" in 49 U.S.C. 41712; and

F. not later than 90 days after the date of this order, consider initiating a rulemaking to ensure that consumers have ancillary fee information, including "baggage fees," "change fees," and "cancellation fees," at the time of ticket purchase;

(ii) to provide consumers with more flight options at better prices and with improved service, and to extend opportunities for competition and market entry as the industry evolves:

A. not later than 30 days after the date of this order, convene a working group within the Department of Transportation to evaluate the effectiveness of existing commercial aviation programs, consumer protections, and rules of the Federal Aviation Administration;

B. consult with the Attorney General regarding means of enhancing effective coordination between the Department of Justice and the Department of Transportation to ensure competition in air transportation and the ability of new entrants to gain access; and

C. consider measures to support airport development and increased capacity and improve airport congestion management, gate access, implementation of airport competition plans pursuant to 49 U.S.C. 47106(f), and "slot" administration;

(iii) given the emergence of new aerospace-based transportation technologies, such as low-altitude unmanned aircraft system deliveries, advanced air mobility, and high-altitude long endurance operations, that have great potential for American travelers and consumers, yet also the danger of early monopolization or new air traffic control problems, ensure that the Department of Transportation takes action with respect to these technologies to:

A. facilitate innovation that fosters United States market leadership and market entry to promote competition and economic opportunity and to resist monopolization, while also ensuring safety, providing security and privacy, protecting the environment, and promoting equity; and

B. provide vigilant oversight over market participants.

n) To further competition in the rail industry and to provide accessible remedies for shippers, the Chair of the Surface Transportation Board (Chair) is encouraged to work with the rest of the Board to:

(i) consider commencing or continuing a rulemaking to strengthen regulations pertaining to reciprocal switching agreements pursuant to 49 U.S.C. 11102(c), if the Chair determines such rulemaking to be in the public interest or necessary to provide competitive rail service;

(ii) consider rulemakings pertaining to any other relevant matter of competitive access, including bottleneck rates, interchange commitments, or other matters, consistent with the policies set forth in section 1 of this order;

(iii) to ensure that passenger rail service is not subject to unwarranted delays and interruptions in service due to host railroads' failure to comply with the required preference for passenger rail, vigorously enforce new on-time performance requirements adopted pursuant to the Passenger Rail Investment and Improvement Act of 2008 (Public Law 110-423, 122 Stat. 4907) that will take effect on July 1, 2021, and further the work of the passenger rail working group formed to ensure that the Surface Transportation Board will fully meet its obligations; and

(iv) in the process of determining whether a merger, acquisition, or other transaction involving rail carriers is consistent with the public interest under 49 U.S.C. 11323-25, consider a carrier's fulfillment of its responsibilities under 49 U.S.C. 24308 (relating to Amtrak's statutory rights).

o) The Chair of the Federal Maritime Commission is encouraged to work with the rest of the Commission to:

(i) vigorously enforce the prohibition of unjust and unreasonable practices in the context of detention and demurrage pursuant to the Shipping Act, as clarified in "Interpretive Rule on Demurrage and Detention Under the Shipping Act," 85 Fed. Reg. 29638 (May 18, 2020);

(ii) request from the National Shipper Advisory Committee recommendations for improving detention and demurrage practices and enforcement of related Shipping Act prohibitions; and

(iii) consider further rulemaking to improve detention and demurrage practices and enforcement of related Shipping Act prohibitions.

p) The Secretary of Health and Human Services shall:

(i) to promote the wide availability of low-cost hearing aids, not later than 120 days after the date of this order, publish for notice and comment a proposed rule on over-the-counter hearing-aids, as called for by section 709 of the FDA Reauthorization Act of 2017 (Public Law 115-52, 131 Stat. 1005);

(ii) support existing price transparency initiatives for hospitals, other providers, and insurers along with any new price transparency initiatives or changes made necessary by the No Surprises Act (Public Law 116-260, 134 Stat. 2758) or any other statutes;

(iii) to ensure that Americans can choose health insurance plans that meet their needs and compare plan offerings, implement standardized options in the national Health Insurance Marketplace and any other appropriate mechanisms to improve competition and consumer choice;

(iv) not later than 45 days after the date of this order, submit a report to the Assistant to the President for Domestic Policy and Director of the Domestic Policy Council and to the Chair of the White House Competition Council, with a plan to continue the effort to combat excessive pricing of prescription drugs and enhance domestic pharmaceutical supply chains, to reduce the prices paid by the Federal Government for such drugs, and to address the recurrent problem of price gouging;

(v) to lower the prices of and improve access to prescription drugs and biologics, continue to promote generic drug and biosimilar competition, as contemplated by the Drug Competition Action Plan of 2017 and Biosimilar Action Plan of 2018 of the Food and Drug Administration (FDA), including by:

A. continuing to clarify and improve the approval framework for generic drugs and biosimilars to make generic drug and biosimilar approval more transparent, efficient, and predictable, including improving and clarifying the standards for interchangeability of biological products;
B. as authorized by the Advancing Education on Biosimilars Act of 2021 (Public Law 117-8, 135 Stat. 254, 42 U.S.C. 263-1), supporting biosimilar product adoption by providing effective educational materials and communications to improve understanding of biosimilar and interchangeable products among healthcare providers, patients, and caregivers;
C. to facilitate the development and approval of biosimilar and interchangeable products, continuing to update the FDA's biologics regulations to clarify existing requirements and procedures related to the review and submission of Biologics License Applications by advancing the "Biologics Regulation Modernization" rulemaking (RIN 0910-AI14); and
D. with the Chair of the FTC, identifying and addressing any efforts to impede generic drug and biosimilar competition, including but not limited to false, misleading, or otherwise deceptive statements about generic drug and biosimilar products and their safety or effectiveness;

(vi) to help ensure that the patent system, while incentivizing innovation, does not also unjustifiably delay generic drug and biosimilar competition beyond that reasonably contemplated by applicable law, not later than 45 days after the date of this order, through the Commissioner of Food and Drugs, write a letter to the Under Secretary of Commerce for Intellectual Property and Director of the United States Patent and Trademark Office enumerating and describing any relevant concerns of the FDA;

(vii) to support the market entry of lower-cost generic drugs and biosimilars, continue the implementation of the law widely known as the CREATES Act of 2019 (Public Law 116-94, 133 Stat. 3130), by:

A. promptly issuing Covered Product Authorizations (CPAs) to assist product developers with obtaining brand-drug samples; and
B. issuing guidance to provide additional information for industry about CPAs; and

(viii) through the Administrator of the Centers for Medicare and Medicaid Services, prepare for Medicare and Medicaid coverage of interchangeable biological products, and for payment models to support increased utilization of generic drugs and biosimilars.

q) To reduce the cost of covered products to the American consumer without imposing additional risk to public health and safety, the Commissioner of Food and Drugs shall work with States and Indian Tribes that propose to develop section 804 Importation Programs in accordance with the Medicare Prescription Drug, Improvement, and Modernization Act of 2003 (Public Law 108-173, 117 Stat. 2066), and the FDA's implementing regulations.

r) The Secretary of Commerce shall:
   (i) acting through the Director of the National Institute of Standards and Technology (NIST), consider initiating a rulemaking to require agencies to report to NIST, on an annual basis, their contractors' utilization activities, as reported to the agencies under 35 U.S.C. 202(c)(5);
   (ii) acting through the Director of NIST, consistent with the policies set forth in section 1 of this order, consider not finalizing any provisions on march-in rights and product pricing in the proposed rule "Rights to Federally Funded Inventions and Licensing of Government Owned Inventions," 86 Fed. Reg. 35 (Jan. 4, 2021); and
   (iii) not later than 1 year after the date of this order, in consultation with the Attorney General and the Chair of the Federal Trade Commission, conduct a study, including by conducting an open and transparent stakeholder consultation process, of the mobile application ecosystem, and submit a report to the Chair of the White House Competition Council, regarding findings and recommendations for improving competition, reducing barriers to entry, and maximizing user benefit with respect to the ecosystem.

s) The Secretary of Defense shall:
   (i) ensure that the Department of Defense's assessment of the economic forces and structures shaping the capacity of the national security innovation base pursuant to section 889(a) and (b) of the William M. (Mac) Thornberry National Defense Authorization Act for Fiscal Year 2021 (Public Law 116-283, 134 Stat. 3388) is consistent with the policy set forth in section 1 of this order;
   (ii) not later than 180 days after the date of this order, submit to the Chair of the White House Competition Council, a review of the state of competition within the defense industrial base, including areas where a lack of competition may be of concern and any recommendations for improving the solicitation process, consistent with the goal of the Competition in Contracting Act of 1984 (Public Law 98-369, 98 Stat. 1175); and
   (iii) not later than 180 days after the date of this order, submit a report to the Chair of the White House Competition Council, on a plan for avoiding contract terms in procurement agreements that make it challenging or impossible for the Department of Defense or service members to repair their own equipment, particularly in the field.

t) The Director of the Consumer Financial Protection Bureau, consistent with the pro-competition objectives stated in section 1021 of the Dodd-Frank Act, is encouraged to consider:
   (i) commencing or continuing a rulemaking under section 1033 of the Dodd-Frank Act to facilitate the portability of consumer financial transaction data so consumers can more easily switch financial institutions and use new, innovative financial products; and
   (ii) enforcing the prohibition on unfair, deceptive, or abusive acts or practices in consumer financial products or services pursuant to section 1031 of the Dodd-Frank Act so as to ensure that actors engaged in unlawful activities do not distort the proper functioning of the competitive process or obtain an unfair advantage over competitors who follow the law.

u) The Director of the Office of Management and Budget, through the Administrator of the Office of Information and Regulatory Affairs, shall incorporate into its recommendations for modernizing and improving regulatory review required by my Memorandum of January 20, 2021 (Modernizing Regulatory Review), the policies set forth in section 1 of this order, including consideration of whether the effects on competition and the potential for creation of barriers to entry should be included in regulatory impact analyses.

v) The Secretary of the Treasury shall:
   (i) direct the Office of Economic Policy, in consultation with the Attorney General, the Secretary of Labor, and the Chair of the FTC, to submit a report to the Chair of the White House Competition Council, not later than 180 days after the date of this order, on the effects of lack of competition on labor markets; and
   (ii) submit a report to the Chair of the White House Competition Council, not later than 270 days after the date of this order, assessing the effects on competition of large technology firms' and other non-bank companies' entry into consumer finance markets.

Sec. 6. General Provisions

a) This order shall be implemented consistent with applicable law and subject to the availability of appropriations.

b) Where not already specified, independent agencies are encouraged to comply with the requirements of this order.

c) Nothing in this order shall be construed to impair or otherwise affect:
   (i) the authority granted by law to an executive department or agency, or the head thereof;

   or

   (ii) the functions of the Director of the Office of Management and Budget relating to budgetary, administrative, or legislative proposals.

d) This order is not intended to, and does not, create any right or benefit, substantive or procedural, enforceable at law or in equity by any party against the United States, its departments, agencies, or entities, its officers, employees, or agents, or any other person.

JOSEPH R. BIDEN JR.
THE WHITE HOUSE,
July 9, 2021.

Policy Solutions for Hospital Consolidation

By Brian J. Miller and Jesse M. Ehrenfeld

November 2022

Key Points

Addressing consolidation in the health care services market is an imperative, as health care services now represent over 51 percent of national health care expenditures, 90 percent of metropolitan statistical areas are considered consolidated for hospital services, and 65 percent of metropolitan statistical areas are considered consolidated for outpatient specialty care.

Robust research has documented the harms of hospital consolidation, including higher prices for services, higher insurance premiums and consumer cost sharing, lack of quality gains, and decrements in the patient experience.

Policymakers have multiple tools to improve antitrust enforcement, modify existing payment policies that drive consolidation, and promote entry in the market for hospital care and other health care services.

With over $178 billion in the Coronavirus Aid, Relief, and Economic Security (CARES) Act funds distributed to health care providers over the past two years, recent concern has focused on how incumbent and often well-resourced health systems deployed government funding. Examples are numerous, with the financially stable Cleveland Clinic[1] receiving CARES Act funds while reporting record 2021 operating income during the pandemic. With over $12 billion in long-term investments[2] and easy access to debt financing even during the height of the pandemic, with a $650 million credit line and $447 million in investment income, the Cleveland Clinic was well positioned to weather a multiyear financial storm. Despite pandemic financial pressures, the organization turned a net profit due to receiving over $352 million in CARES Act funds.[3] The Cleveland Clinic purchased a financially distressed hospital from the Sisters of Mercy Health System in the clinic's home Ohio market in December 2020[4] and opened a private hospital in London in 2022.[5]

In this context, policymakers have appropriately begun to question the market power of health care systems in consolidated markets. While many recent policy efforts have focused on prescription drug prices, health care services represent a significant portion of the nation's health care expenditures, with hospital care representing 30.8 percent or $1.1 trillion annually, while spending on physician services has reached 19.6 percent of national expenditures or over $800 billion annually.[6] Ninety percent of metropolitan statistical areas (MSAs) represent highly concentrated hospital markets as defined by the Federal Trade Commission (FTC) and Department of Justice (DOJ) Antitrust Division guidelines. Thus, hospital consolidation is a recent subject of policy interest, with the US Senate Committee on the Judiciary's Subcommittee on Competition Policy, Antitrust, and Consumer Rights holding a 2021 hearing on hospital consolidation.[7] Yet hospital markets are not the only component of care delivery that is consolidated. Ambulatory markets are also consolidated, with an estimated 39 percent of MSAs similarly considered consolidated for primary care physicians and 65 percent for specialty care.[8]

The exercise of hospital market power is not just a scholarly question; it directly affects consumers. During 2022 rate negotiations, MaineHealth, a health system operating in a highly concentrated market,[9] gave notice to the major health insurer Elevance (formerly Anthem) that it would withdraw Maine Medical Center in Portland from its health plan network,[10] and the CEO penned an op-ed about it in the local paper.[11] With thousands of consumers potentially facing out-of-network charges despite the hospital exhibiting a pre-pandemic operating margin of nearly 10 percent[12] or four times the industry median,[13] the contracting dispute was eventually resolved, albeit with the terms of the contract remaining sealed.[14]

Because of increasing local and national focus on hospital consolidation, in this report we review the harms of hospital consolidation, government policies promoting consolidation, and policy options to combat consolidation.

The Harms of Consolidation: An Illness Infecting American Health Care

The harms of hospital consolidation are well-documented, including higher prices for clinical services,[15] with prices in monopoly hospitals 12 percent higher than those in markets with four or more rivals and prices increasing 6 percent after mergers of geographically close hospitals. Higher prices ultimately drive higher insurance premiums across plan markets including employer-sponsored insurance[16] and Affordable Care Act (ACA) exchange marketplaces.[17] Unfortunately, rising insurance premiums correspond with higher consumer cost-sharing payments,[18] as health plans shift costs to employees through rising deductibles, co-pays, and coinsurance rates. The pocketbook is not the only area where consumers are hurt: Early evidence suggests that higher health care costs can indirectly suppress wage growth,[19] compounding the effects of rising costs.

As part of a natural market response, health plans titrate and narrow managed care networks to lower cost and preserve or improve quality.[20] This reduces patient choice in already consolidated care delivery markets. While quality gains and systems engineering are often used to justify hospital mergers,[21] health services research suggests otherwise. A retrospective study of hospital mergers using multiple databases crossing health system ownership and quality performance data denoted no improvements in outcomes-measured quality after mergers. These were denoted by common measures such as 30-day readmission rates or 30-day mortality. In fact, there was a modest decline in patient experience metrics.[22]

While traditional measures of cost and quality trend in the wrong direction for consumers, there are additional meaningful market harms. New bipartisan interest in labor market competition is an emerging lens through which to examine hospital consolidation, with many health professionals including physicians, nurses, and pharmacists facing monopsony power when they enter labor markets in consolidated regions. Health systems with market power in labor markets can prevent the free movement of labor through the use of noncompete agreements,[23] with labor market harms being a recent competition policy interest to the DOJ Antitrust Division[24] and the FTC.[25] For clinical staff, noncompete restrictions serve as a barrier and are further compounded by the need to update licensure or certification if relocating across state lines. Hospital consolidation and the subsequent loss and externalization of control over the clinical practice environment drive physician burnout,[26] with over two-thirds of physicians exhibiting signs of burnout.[27]

Finally, innovation losses—while challenging to measure—are another harm of hospital consolidation. What does this mean? Healthy competition results in improvements in systems, clinical operations, and administrative processes, resulting in lower cost and higher quality. A lack of competition produces the opposite: ossification and stagnation.

While innovation losses over time are generally not measurable, other economic indicators shed light on the magnitude of this problem. Labor productivity, a measure typically improving over time, has remained flat for over two decades, with the Bureau of Labor Statistics noting flat labor productivity growth (i.e., no growth) for over two decades in private community hospitals.[28] Anecdotally, our clinical knowledge supports this theme. Innovation in medical devices and pharmaceutical products has driven much of the past 30 years of the revolution in cardiac care after a myocardial infarction (i.e., heart attack) or development of heart failure with coronary stents, catheters, pacemakers, implantable cardioverter-defibrillators, and new pharmaceuticals such as angiotensin receptor blockers, angiotensin receptor-neprilysin inhibitors, and antiplatelet agents.

Combating Consolidation: Improving Antitrust Enforcement

Effective antitrust enforcement promotes a robust competitive marketplace through review and challenge of anticompetitive mergers coupled with policing of anticompetitive corporate behavior. With over 1,412 mergers from 1998 to 2015[29] and an estimated 50–70 hospital and clinic mergers occurring annually,[30] providing the FTC adequate staff and funding for hospital merger enforcement is crucial.

Enforcement is predicated on adequate agency situational awareness. Policymakers initially addressed this problem through the 1976 Hart-Scott-Rodino (HSR) Antitrust Improvements Act, which requires that parties in transactions meeting certain financial requirements[31] file a premerger notification[32] with the FTC and DOJ Antitrust Division and observe a waiting period before consummating the transaction—or risk civil penalties. The HSR Act purposely exempts small transactions from premerger notification to not increase the regulatory burden on small enterprises in addition to avoiding generating unnecessary transactions for FTC staff to review.

At the same time, health policy experts have noted that small physician practice acquisitions have driven a sizable portion of care delivery consolidation,[33] motivated by hospital acquisition and private equity funding.[34] While the HSR Act does not preclude antitrust enforcement against small transactions, enforcement in the absence of information presents a unique challenge. To provide competition authorities with better information regarding small transactions, some competition policy experts have proposed lowering the HSR reporting threshold to capture small transactions.[35] Even if narrowed to a specific industry or sector, creating such a reporting requirement would slow the growth of many small businesses, the lifeblood of American innovation and productivity.

Alternative policy interventions include providing targeted information to antitrust agencies, state attorneys general, and policy researchers through creating a state competition index, currently a topic of legislative interest.[36] The Department of Health and Human Services Office of the Assistant Secretary for Planning and Evaluation (ASPE) could undertake an annual, state-level study characterizing publicly reported horizontal and vertical mergers in the market for health care services (e.g., hospitals, ambulatory practices, etc.) and health plans. To improve market transparency, ASPE could describe and enumerate the number of specific types of health care facilities in operation annually and compute the Herfindahl-Hirschman Index for the markets for general acute care hospital services, ambulatory medical services by specialty, and other services as relevant. This would provide transparency to antitrust agencies' and researchers' changes in market structure, promoting targeted enforcement instead of increasing regulatory reporting burdens for small businesses.

At the same time, to facilitate targeted and effective competition policy advocacy[37] by the FTC[38] and the DOJ Antitrust Division,[39] ASPE could characterize the number and type of anticompetitive state laws preventing hospital and health care service market entry—namely, certificate of need (CON)[40] and certificate of public advantage (COPA) laws. CON laws present in 35 states require providers to seek state regulatory approval before offering new services or technology (e.g., new computer tomography scanner) or opening new clinical facilities. A regulatory process manipulated by current market incumbents,

CON frequently prevents expanded access. COPA laws serve a similar function, albeit for hospital mergers, replacing competition with regulation.[41]

Other enforcement areas are worth further policy attention. By historical precedent, the FTC reviews hospital and physician practice mergers, including nonprofit hospitals (which represent approximately half of all domestic hospitals).[42] Merger enforcement can be undertaken through Section 5 of the FTC Act and/or Section 7 of the Clayton Act,[43] the latter of which includes nonprofit and for-profit enterprises. However, FTC enforcement against anticompetitive practices occurs through Section 5 of the FTC Act, which is limited to "persons, partnerships, or corporations,"[44] thus excluding nonprofit hospitals and health systems. Consequently, the DOJ Antitrust Division assumes responsibility for and brings such cases under the Sherman Antitrust Act, rather than directing cases to the staff at the agency with preexisting industry expertise. Policymakers have recognized this inefficiency in antitrust enforcement, having introduced legislation to attempt to correct it.[45]

A final area of concern for antitrust enforcers is anti-steering and anti-tiering provisions in managed care contracts. Health plans use network design to direct consumers to high-quality, low-cost physicians and facilities. Tiering providers (i.e., preferred, non-preferred, and out of network) and tying favorable cost sharing to physicians steer consumers.[46] At times, this may fractionate hospitals and health systems, with some facilities and physicians being "preferred" with favorable cost sharing to drive patient volume and others being non-preferred or even out of network.

Health systems have responded in kind by inserting anti-steering and anti-tiering clauses into managed care contracts. While recent enforcement efforts have targeted this contracting behavior as anticompetitive, with the DOJ Antitrust Division winning a recent case against Atrium Health for the use of anti-steering provisions,[47] this represents an evolving area of health care antitrust enforcement with unclear market penetration. The National Academy for State Health Policy has introduced model legislative language to address anticompetitive contracts,[48] with pending legislation directing a first step in having the Government Accountability Office (GAO) study anticompetitive contracting terms.[49] Supporting antitrust authorities through empowering the GAO or ASPE to study the prevalence and effects of such practices across payer markets would provide both the FTC and DOJ Antitrust Division a guidebook for targeted enforcement.

Removing the Government's Foot from the Consolidation Accelerator

Antitrust enforcement alone is not sufficient: Policymakers must remove the government's foot from the accelerator of consolidation. Historical attempts to control cost created consolidation as an unintended consequence. Policymakers have historically deployed centralized administrative pricing (i.e., price regulation) within the Medicare fee-for-service (FFS) program in an attempt to control costs.

In an FFS system, cost is a function of price, volume, and the intensity of service (i.e., the degree of resources applied to an individual clinical problem). Clinicians and beneficiaries jointly determine the volume and intensity, while market regulators set the price. As price decreases, clinicians can modulate the volume and intensity of care, undermining price regulation.[50] Within the Medicare administrative pricing model, FFS Medicare operates as a static system subject to annual payment updates through annual Centers for Medicare & Medicaid Services (CMS) rulemaking. Unlike a dynamic market system, policy arbitrage is a key strategy for providers in a static system.

A classic example of payment policy arbitrage in a static system is the lack of site-neutral payment. What is site-neutral payment? It is paying the same amount for a service regardless of where it is performed. Consider the following example.

If a physician sees a new patient for a 30-minute visit, the physician can bill Medicare under the physician fee schedule for an evaluation and management service. If a hospital purchases that same practice and designates the practice a provider-based facility (either on campus or off campus, with the boundary at 250 yards and less than 35 miles, respectively),[51] the facility bills as a hospital outpatient department. Functionally, the hospital submits a claim, billing Medicare under the outpatient prospective payment system (OPPS),[52] and it bills separately for the professional service component and receives reduced reimbursement as a facility fee.

For a 30-minute office visit, the physician fee schedule payment rate for calendar year 2017 was $109.46 for a new patient, while if delivered in a hospital outpatient setting, the total would be 68.5 percent higher or $184.44, with $106.56 for the ambulatory payment classification collected under the OPPS and $77.88 for the facility fee.[53] This higher total reimbursement is beneficial for hospitals that collect higher revenue for the same service but harmful to patients, who experience higher Part B coinsurance amounts due to bigger bills for the same clinical service.

Payment policy arbitrage through a lack of site-neutral payment drove hospital acquisition of physician practices, benefiting health systems through increased revenue. Recognized as a problem by both the Medicare Payment Advisory Commission[54] and the Office of Inspector General,[55] a partial fix was included as part of the Bipartisan Budget Act (BBA) of 2015.[56] The BBA prohibited new off-campus provider-based hospital clinics from qualifying for higher payment; however, it left existing arrangements untouched. The Trump administration attempted to correct the problem, implementing a cut to previously grandfathered off-campus facilities,[57] triggering a merry-go-round of hospital industry lawsuits,[58] subsequent CMS attempts at rulemaking,[59] and appeals[60] that ultimately resulted in the preservation of site-neutral payment policy.[61] The Biden administration has continued to support this site-neutral payment for hospital outpatient departments, with a new proposed exemption for rural sole community hospitals.[62]

Other examples abound, including differential payment for services provided at subacute rehabilitation facilities compared with those at inpatient rehabilitation facilities or differences in payment for the same surgical procedure completed at an ambulatory surgical center (e.g., in a hospital operating room). The Committee for a Responsible Federal Budget projected that implementation of site-neutral payment would save Medicare $217–$279 billion over a decade,[63] an estimate inclusive only of direct effects.

In other cases, CMS has directly perpetuated the problem. Consider the case of the "inpatient-only list," a list of procedures for Medicare beneficiaries that can only be performed in a hospital setting.[64] The market regulator set the price for such procedures to $0 in the ambulatory setting, foreclosing competition and perpetuating a static marketplace. This ignores innovation and freezes the market for medical services at a single point in time.

For example, 30 years ago, outpatient elective total hip and knee replacements were considered unsafe and rarely performed. Today, over one in four elective total hip and knee joint replacements are performed in the outpatient setting.[65] Regulators should not preferentially designate the site of care, an action that policymakers can correct by banning the use of an inpatient-only list, currently a topic of legislative interest.[66]

Promoting Market Entry

Physician-owned hospitals (POHs) represent a pragmatic lever through which policymakers can promote hospital market entry,[67] directly combating hospital consolidation. The history behind this issue is a story of competitors banning competition, as new POHs are statutorily excluded from participation in the Medicare program, with recently introduced companion bills in the Senate and House of Representatives[68] targeting this concern.

In the 1980s, to improve clinical operations, a small number of physicians across the US independently pooled their capital and opened hospitals. Hospital industry concerns unsurprisingly rapidly emerged, including accusations of POHs cherry-picking healthy patients and so leaving community hospitals with sicker patients, engaging in adverse selection against Medicare and Medicaid patients, and skimping on charity or uncompensated care.

Academic and government-sponsored reports revealed complexity in this marketplace: A 2003 GAO study found that surgical-specialty POHs served fewer Medicaid patients, while cardiac hospitals served—unsurprisingly, given the natural history of cardiac disease—more Medicare patients than did general community hospitals.[69]

Claims regarding charity care were similarly suspect: CMS staff research found that a small sample of cardiac and orthopedic surgical-specialty hospitals provided less uncompensated care than their nonprofit competitors did. When tax payments were considered, the total aggregate community benefit was an order of magnitude larger.[70] One important point lost in the policy discussion: POHs are a market split equally between community or general acute care hospitals and surgical-specialty hospitals, the latter type being comprised of three primary submarkets (cardiac, orthopedic, and general surgical hospitals).[71]

While POHs were permitted through an exception in self-referral law (called "Stark Law," which is discussed below) known as the "whole hospital exception," the hospital industry achieved an 18-month moratorium in 2003 on new and expanded POHs participating in Medicare, eventually reenacted and expanded to a full-fledged ban as part of the negotiations surrounding passage of the ACA.[72] Economic consequences were real, with market foreclosure estimated at $1.8 billion in economic losses for construction projects alone, as at least 100 new hospitals or significant expansions that were either planned or under development were prematurely terminated.[73]

Recent research has also demonstrated relative benefits of physician owners: Physician-owned orthopedic hospitals have lower cost and higher quality, with physician-owned cardiac hospitals demonstrating higher quality and equivalent cost. Finally, physician-owned community hospitals have equivalent cost and quality compared to their nonprofit and for-profit competitors,[74] yet consumers still benefit from lower costs and higher quality associated with increased competition.

Policymakers have attempted to address hospital industry concerns. Patient acuity—or cherry-picking healthier patients—is a problem best addressed by payment policy, wherein payers can adjust payment for differential acuity and complexity. CMS did just that in response to hospital industry concerns regarding overpayment of physician-owned specialty hospitals. In 2007, CMS updated the inpatient prospective payment system to better account for complicating conditions and case mix index.[75] Section 6001 of the ACA is now a statutory solution for a regulatory problem, as it bans market entry for a single market participant. Policymakers can right this wrong and promote hospital competition by repealing Section 6001.

Stark Law proffers another opportunity for policy intervention to promote market entry. Rising Medicare program expenditures in the 1980s and a series of academic studies demonstrating increased use of physician-owned services[76] prompted oversight and eventual statutory regulation and prohibition of many clinical operational practices. Weighed against rigidity and concerns regarding a loss of physician agency[77] and acknowledging valid concerns regarding budgetary sustainability of Medicare, induced demand, and ethical questions, a series of reforms (i.e., Stark Law) were passed in both statute[78] and rulemaking.[79]

In accordance with Stark Law, physicians are prohibited from making self-referrals for designated health services (DHS) to an entity in which they or a family member have a direct financial relationship and are subsequently billing the Medicare program. The definition of a DHS is broad, including imaging services, home health services, and durable medical equipment. While recent policy efforts have aimed to create exceptions to Stark Law regulations to promote value-based care,[80] implementation remains challenging for the average physician: The most recent value-based care rulemakings on Stark Law and Anti-Kickback Statute registered at 191[81] and 212 pages, respectively.[82] Thus, regulatory understanding and compliance costs remain well outside the operating purview of all but the largest health systems.

The health care ecosystem when Stark Law was originally passed compared to today is noticeably different. The 1980s marked the peak of FFS medicine, soon followed by the rise of managed care. Today, 48 percent of the Medicare program enrollment is in Medicare Advantage, a risk-adjusted capitated public-private program,[83] while almost half of Medicaid spending is channeled through risk-adjusted capitation paid to a Medicaid managed care organization.[84] Incentives within a capitated payment model are different, as the health plan loses money from fraud, waste, and abuse including inappropriate use or facility or provider-induced demand.

Even outside of capitated payment, FFS medicine today is different, as payers have new technological tools to survey for and prevent inappropriate use, including utilization review, prior authorization, and automated prepayment claims editing. Furthermore, benefit design can deploy market forces to control for inappropriate utilization or induced demand through bundling and other tools of health finance.

Stark Law persists as an aging relic in a changed world. Patients, many of whom experience challenges with both health[85] and health insurance literacy,[86] depend on their families and physicians to make decisions about their health, goals, and efficient and effective use of health care products and services. Limiting shared decision-making transfers these burdens onto patients at a time when they are least equipped to handle them. For example, a morbidly obese heart failure patient who has a bad back and knees, can barely walk, and depends on Social Security Disability Income, Medicare, and Medicaid would be forced to cobble together coordinated, integrated orthopedic care from their primary care physician, orthopedic surgeon, and physical therapist, even though that's not their role.

Stark Law presupposes that nonprofit and for-profit corporations are less self-interested parties than physicians are. In many cases, corporations mandate or otherwise enforce corporate self-referral on physicians, scoring providers based on "within system" versus external referrals. Yet this very activity can be part of the key to offering integrated care delivery, as organizations can coordinate and systematize care for complex patients.

When physician-owned and -operated organizations attempt to construct integrated care delivery, they face statutory prohibitions imposed through Stark Law, while corporations instead face regulatory oversight. Regulation, not prohibition, is the appropriate mechanism for combating waste, fraud, and abuse. Policymakers should consider reforms to Stark Law, including the potential of a general waiver under a managed care setting—that is, for beneficiaries enrolled in Medicare Advantage plans and Medicaid managed care organizations,[87] where utilization review practices, prepayment claims edits, and other technological tools can combat the harms of self-referral.

Conclusions

With health care services representing over 51 percent of national health care expenditures, over 90 percent of MSAs considered consolidated for hospital services, and 65 percent of MSAs considered consolidated for outpatient specialty care, addressing consolidation in the market for health care services is a policy imperative. Robust research has documented the many harms of hospital and care delivery consolidation, including higher prices for services and associated increased consumer cost sharing, higher insurance premiums, lack of quality gains, and decrements in measures of patient experience. Policymakers have multiple tools available to improve and target antitrust enforcement, modify existing payment policies that currently drive consolidation, and repeal statutory bans on market entry to promote entry in the market for hospital care and other health care services.

About the Authors

Brian J. Miller is a nonresident fellow at the American Enterprise Institute and an assistant professor of medicine and business (courtesy) at the Johns Hopkins University. He previously served as a special adviser at the Federal Trade Commission (FTC) and is currently an expert witness on health insurance for the FTC.

Jesse M. Ehrenfeld is a professor of anesthesiology and senior associate dean at the Medical College of Wisconsin. He is the director of the Advancing a Healthier Wisconsin Endowment and a member of the American Medical Association Board of Trustees.

Notes

1. Marissa Plescia, "Cleveland Clinic's Operating Income More Than Triples in 2021," *Becker's Hospital Review*, March 2, 2022, https://www.beckershospitalreview.com/finance/cleveland-clinic-s-operating-income-more-than-triples-in-2021.html.

2. Ernst & Young, "Consolidated Financial Statements and Supplementary Information: The Cleveland Clinic Foundation d.b.a. Cleveland Clinic Health System Years Ended December 31, 2021 and 2020 with Reports of Independent Auditors," 2021, https://my.clevelandclinic.org/-/scassets/files/org/about/financial-statements/cchs-2021-w-ob-nonob.pdf?la=en.

3. Robert King, "Cleveland Clinic Posts Increased Q3 Income, but Profits Still Down for First 9 Months of 2020," Fierce Healthcare, November 30, 2020, https://www.fiercehealthcare.com/hospitals/cleveland-clinic-posts-49m-profit-for-first-nine-months-2020-as-covid-19-hampers-finances.

4. Robert King, "Cleveland Clinic Makes Deal with Sisters of Charity to Acquire Mercy Medical Center," Fierce Healthcare, December 8, 2020, https://www.fiercehealthcare.com/hospitals/cleveland-clinic-makes-deal-sisters-charity-to-acquire-mercy-medical-center.

5. Heather Landi, "Cleveland Clinic Expands into Europe with Opening of Private London Hospital near Buckingham Palace," Fierce Healthcare, March 29, 2022, https://www.fiercehealthcare.com/providers/cleveland-clinic-opens-private-london-hospital-near-buckingham-palace.

6. Micah Hartman et al., "National Health Care Spending in 2020: Growth Driven by Federal Spending in Response to the COVID-19 Pandemic," *Health Affairs* 41, no. 1 (2022): 13–25, https://www.healthaffairs.org/doi/abs/10.1377/hlthaff.2021.01763.

7. Committee on the Judiciary, Subcommittee on Competition Policy, Antitrust, and Consumer Rights, "Antitrust Applied: Hospital Consolidation Concerns and Solutions," May 19, 2021, https://www.judiciary.senate.gov/meetings/antitrust-applied-hospital-consolidation-concerns-and-solutions.

8. Brent D. Fulton, "Health Care Market Concentration Trends in the United States: Evidence and Policy Response," *Health Affairs* 36, no. 9 (2017): 1530–38, https://www.healthaffairs.org/doi/10.1377/hlthaff.2017.0556.

9. The Herfindahl-Hirschman Index (HHI) for hospital services in Portland, Maine, increased from 3,203 in 2016 to 4,058 in 2020. An HHI of zero represents perfect competition, while 10,000 represents a perfect monopoly. The antitrust agencies generally consider a market above 2,500 to be highly concentrated. See Health Care Cost Institute, "Hospital Concentration Index: An Analysis of U.S. Hospital Market Concentration," June 2022, https://healthcostinstitute.org/hcci-originals/hmi-interactive#HMI-Concentration-Index; and US Department of Justice, "Herfindahl-Hirschman Index," July 31, 2018, https://www.justice.gov/atr/herfindahl-hirschman-index.

10. MaineHealth, "MaineHealth Gives Notice to Remove Maine Medical Center from Anthem's Health Insurance Network Beginning in 2023," April 7, 2022, https://www.mainehealth.org/News/2022/04/MaineHealth-gives-notice-to-remove-Maine-Medical-Center-from-Anthem-health-insurance-network.

11. Andy Mueller, "Commentary: Time Is Running Out for Deal Between Anthem, MaineHealth, CEO Says," *Portland Press Herald*, June 23, 2022, https://www.pressherald.com/2022/06/23/commentary-time-is-running-out-for-deal-between-anthem-mainehealth-ceo-says.

12. See Maine Health Data Organization, "Hospital Financial Information Report II," 2020, 9, https://mhdo.maine.gov/_pdf/Report%202_2020.pdf.

13. Ron Shinkman, "Hospital Margins Hit Hard by Pandemic, but CARES Act Provided Huge Relief, Moody's Finds," Healthcare Dive, March 26, 2021, https://www.healthcaredive.com/news/hospital-margins-hit-hard-by-pandemic-but-cares-act-provided-huge-relief/597391.

14. MaineHealth, "MaineHealth and Anthem Blue Cross and Blue Shield in Maine Reach Agreement," August 17, 2022, https://www.mainehealth.org/News/2022/08/MaineHealth-and-Anthem-Blue-Cross-and-Blue-Shield-in-Maine-Reach-Agreement.

15. Zack Cooper et al., "The Price Ain't Right? Hospital Prices and Health Spending on the Privately Insured," *Quarterly Journal of Economics* 134, no. 1 (2019): 51–107, https://academic.oup.com/qje/article-abstract/134/1/51/5090426?redirectedFrom=fulltext.

16. Erin E. Trish and Bradley J. Herring, "How Do Health Insurer Market Concentration and Bargaining Power with Hospitals Affect Health Insurance Premiums?," *Journal of Health Economics* 42 (2015): 104–11, https://www.ncbi.nlm.nih.gov/pmc/articles/PMC5667641.

17. Andrew S. Boozary et al., "The Association Between Hospital Concentration and Insurance Premiums in the ACA Marketplaces," *Health Affairs* 4 (2019): 668–74, https://www.healthaffairs.org/doi/pdf/10.1377/hlthaff.2018.05491.

18. "The average single coverage annual deductible among covered workers with a deductible has increased 25% over the last five years and 79% over the last ten years." See Kaiser Family Foundation, "2020 Employer Health Benefits Survey," October 8, 2020, https://www.kff.org/report-section/ehbs-2020-summary-of-findings.

19. Katherine Baicker and Amitabh Chandra, "The Labor Market Effects of Rising Health Insurance Premiums," *Journal of Labor Economics* 24, no. 3 (2006), https://www.journals.uchicago.edu/doi/abs/10.1086/505049?mobileUi=0&; and Daniel Arnold and

Christopher M. Whaley, "Who Pays for Health Care Costs? The Effects of Health Care Prices on Wages," RAND Corporation, 2020, https://www.rand.org/pubs/working_papers/WRA621-2.html.

20. Daniel Polsky, Zuleyha Cidav, and Ashley Swanson, "Marketplace Plans with Narrow Physician Networks Feature Lower Monthly Premiums Than Plans with Larger Networks," *Health Affairs* 35, no. 10 (2016): 1842–48, https://www.healthaffairs.org/doi/full/10.1377/hlthaff.2016.0693.

21. Complaint, Advocate Health Care Network, Advocate Health and Hospitals Corporation, and NorthShore University Healthsystem, FTC Docket No. 9369 (December 17, 2015), https://www.ftc.gov/system/files/documents/cases/151218ahcpt3cmpt.pdf; Melanie Blackman, "CHI Franciscan, Virginia Mason Announce Final Merger Agreement," HealthLeaders, January 5, 2021, https://www.healthleadersmedia.com/strategy/chi-franciscan-virginia-mason-announce-final-merger-agreement; Tom Kruse et al., "New IDS Merger Aims to Improve Value and Access for Its Communities," Healthcare Financial Management Association, September 23, 2022, https://www.hfma.org/topics/cost-effectiveness-of-health/article/new-ids-merger-aims-to-improve-value-and-access-for-its-communit.html; and CHI Health at Home, "Dignity Health and Catholic Health Initiatives to Combine to Form New Catholic Health System Focused on Creating Healthier Communities," https://www.chihealthathome.com/content/health-at-home/en/news/dignity-health-catholic-health-initiatives-combine.html.

22. Nancy D. Beaulieu et al., "Changes in Quality of Care After Hospital Mergers and Acquisitions," *New England Journal of Medicine* 382, no. 1 (2020): 51–59, https://www.nejm.org/doi/full/10.1056/NEJMsa1901383.

23. John O'Shea and David Balat, "Noncompete Agreements for Physicians: Clear and Consistent Policy Is Needed," Texas Public Policy Foundation, April 2022, https://www.texaspolicy.com/wp-content/uploads/2022/04/2022-04-RR-RoH-BalatOshea-NoncompeteAgreementsforPhysicians.pdf.

24. US Department of Justice, "Public Workshop on Competition in Labor Markets," November 25, 2020, https://www.justice.gov/atr/events/public-workshop-competition-labor-markets.

25. Federal Trade Commission, "Non-Competes in the Workplace: Examining Antitrust and Consumer Protection Issues," January 9, 2020, https://www.ftc.gov/news-events/events/2020/01/non-competes-workplace-examining-antitrust-consumer-protection-issues.

26. National Academy of Medicine, "The Influence of the External Environment on Clinician Burnout and Professional Well-Being," in *Taking Action Against Clinician Burnout: A Systems Approach to Professional Well-Being* (Washington, DC: National Academies Press, 2019), 101, https://www.nap.edu/catalog/25521/taking-action-against-clinician-burnout-a-systems-approach-to-professional.

27. Tait D. Shanafelt et al., "Changes in Burnout and Satisfaction with Work-Life Integration in Physicians over the First 2 Years of the COVID-19 Pandemic," *Mayo Clinic Proceedings* (2022): 1–11, https://www.mayoclinicproceedings.org/article/S0025-6196(22)00515-8/fulltext#articleInformation.

28. US Bureau of Labor Statistics, "Private Community Hospitals Labor Productivity," https://www.bls.gov/productivity/highlights/hospitals-labor-productivity.htm.

29. Martin Gaynor, "Examining the Impact of Health Care Consolidation," testimony before the Oversight and Investigations Subcommittee, Committee on Energy and Commerce, US House of Representatives, February 14, 2018, https://energycommerce.house.gov/sites/democrats.energycommerce.house.gov/files/documents/Testimony-Gaynor-OI-Hrg-on-Examining-the-Impact-of-Health-Care-Consolidation-2018-02-14.pdf.

30. See Lina M. Khan and Richard A. Powers, *Hart-Scott-Rodino Annual Report: Fiscal Year 2020*, Federal Trade Commission and US Department of Justice, Table X, https://www.ftc.gov/system/files/documents/reports/hart-scott-rodino-annual-report-fiscal-year-2020/fy2020_-_hsr_annual_report_-_final.pdf.

31. Federal Trade Commission, "Revised Jurisdictional Thresholds for Section 7A of the Clayton Act," *Federal Register* 87, no. 15 (January 24, 2022): 3541, https://www.federalregister.gov/documents/2022/01/24/2022-01214/revised-jurisdictional-thresholds-for-section-7a-of-the-clayton-act.

32. Hart-Scott-Rodino Premerger Notification Program, "What Is the Premerger Notification Program? An Overview," Federal Trade Commission, March 2009, https://www.ftc.gov/sites/default/files/attachments/premerger-introductory-guides/guide1.pdf.

33. Cory Capps, David Dranove, and Christopher Ody, "Physician Practice Consolidation Driven by Small Acquisitions, So Antitrust Agencies Have Few Tools to Intervene," *Health Affairs* 36, no. 9 (2017): 1556–63, https://www.healthaffairs.org/doi/10.1377/hlthaff.2017.0054.

34. Sally Tan et al., "Trends in Private Equity Acquisition of Dermatology Practices in the United States," *JAMA Dermatology* 155, no. 9 (2019): 1013–21, https://jamanetwork.com/journals/jamadermatology/fullarticle/2738309.

35. Fiona M. Scott Morton, "Diagnosing the Problem: Exploring the Effects of Consolidation and Anticompetitive Conduct in Health Care Markets," testimony before the Subcommittee on Regulatory Reform, Commercial and Antitrust Law, Judiciary Committee, US House of Representatives, https://www.congress.gov/116/meeting/house/109024/witnesses/HHRG-116-JU05-Wstate-MortonF-20190307.pdf.

36. Competition in State Health Markets Act., H.R. 8130, 117th Cong., 2nd sess. (2022), https://www.congress.gov/bill/117th-congress/house-bill/8130?s=1&r=6.

37. James C. Cooper, Paul A. Pautler, and Todd J. Zywicki, "Theory and Practice of Competition Advocacy at the FTC," Federal Trade Commission, https://www.ftc.gov/sites/default/files/documents/public_events/FTC%2090th%20Anniversary%20Symposium/040910zywicki.pdf; and Federal Trade Commission, "Stats & Data 2020," 2020, https://www.ftc.gov/system/files/attachments/stats-data-2020/annual_highlights_2020_stats_and_data_infographic.pdf.

38. Federal Trade Commission, "Legal Library: Advocacy Filings," https://www.ftc.gov/legal-library/browse/advocacy-filings.

39. US Department of Justice, "Competition Policy and Advocacy Section," August 25, 2022, https://www.justice.gov/atr/about-division/cpa-section.

40. Matthew D. Mitchell, "Certificate-of-Need Laws: How They Affect Healthcare Access, Quality, and Cost," George Mason University, Mercatus Center, May 21, 2021, https://www.mercatus.org/Certificate-of-Need-Laws-How-They-Affect-Healthcare-Access-Quality-and-Cost.

41. Lina M. Khan et al., "FTC Policy Perspectives on Certificate of Public Advantage," Federal Trade Commission, August 15, 2022, https://www.ftc.gov/system/files/ftc_gov/pdf/COPA_Policy_Paper.pdf.

42. American Hospital Association, "Fast Facts on U.S. Hospitals, 2022," https://www.aha.org/statistics/fast-facts-us-hospitals.

43. 15 U.S.C. § 18.

44. 15 U.S.C. § 45.

45. Oversight of Anti-Competitive Behavior of Non-Profit Hospitals Act, H.R. 8129, 117th Cong., 2nd sess. (2022), https://www.congress.gov/bill/117th-congress/house-bill/8129?s=1&r=7.

46. Anna D. Sinaiko, "Variations in Patient Response to Tiered Physician Networks," *American Journal of Managed Care* 22, no. 6 (2016): 420–25, https://www.ajmc.com/view/variations-in-patient-response-to-tiered-physician-networks.

47. US Department of Justice, "Atrium Health Agrees to Settle Antitrust Lawsuit and Eliminate Anticompetitive Steering Restrictions," press release, November 15, 2018, https://www.justice.gov/opa/pr/atrium-health-agrees-settle-antitrust-lawsuit-and-eliminate-anticompetitive-steering; and *United States of America and the State of North Carolina v. Carolinas Healthcare System*, 3:16-cv-00311-RJC-DCK (W.D.N.C. April 24, 2019), https://www.justice.gov/atr/case-document/file/1157461/download.

48. National Academy for State Health Policy, "NASHP Model Act to Address Anticompetitive Terms in Health Insurance Contracts," April 12, 2021, https://www.nashp.org/nashp-model-act-to-address-anticompetitive-terms-in-health-insurance-contracts.

49. Addressing Anti-Competitive Contracting Clauses Act, H.R. 8135, 117th Cong., 2nd sess. (2022), https://www.congress.gov/bill/117th-congress/house-bill/8135?s=1&r=1.

50. Centers for Medicare & Medicaid Services, "Estimated Volume-and-Intensity Response to a Price Change for Physicians' Services," August 13, 1998, https://www.cms.gov/Research-Statistics-Data-and-Systems/Research/ActuarialStudies/downloads/physicianresponse.pdf.

51. 42 CFR § 413.65.

52. Medicare Payment Advisory Commission, "Outpatient Hospital Services Payment System," November 2021, https://www.medpac.gov/wp-content/uploads/2021/11/medpac_payment_basics_21_opd_final_sec.pdf.

53. See example in Centers for Medicare & Medicaid Services, "Medicare Program: Changes to Hospital Outpatient Prospective Payment and Ambulatory Surgical Center Payment Systems and Quality Reporting Programs," *Federal Register* 83, no. 225 (November 21, 2018): 58818, https://www.federalregister.gov/documents/2018/11/21/2018-24243/medicare-program-changes-to-hospital-outpatient-prospective-payment-and-ambulatory-surgical-center#p-1580.

54. Medicare Payment Advisory Commission, "March 2020 Report to Congress: Medicare Payment Policy," March 13, 2020, https://www.medpac.gov/document/http-www-medpac-gov-docs-default-source-reports-mar20_entirereport_sec-pdf.

55. Department of Health and Human Services, Office of Inspector General, "Hospital Ownership of Physician Practices," September 1999, https://oig.hhs.gov/oei/reports/oei-05-98-00110.pdf; and Department of Health and Human Services, Office of Inspector General, "CMS Is Taking Steps to Improve Oversight of Provider-Based Facilities, but Vulnerabilities Remain," June 2016, https://oig.hhs.gov/oei/reports/oei-04-12-00380.pdf.

56. Bipartisan Budget Act of 2015, Pub L. No. 117-74 § 603, https://www.congress.gov/bill/114th-congress/house-bill/1314.

57. Centers for Medicare & Medicaid Services, "CMS Finalizes Rule That Encourages More Choices and Lower Costs for Seniors," press release, November 2, 2018, https://www.cms.gov/newsroom/press-releases/cms-finalizes-rule-encourages-more-choices-and-lower-costs-seniors; and Centers for Medicare & Medicaid Services, "Medicare Program: Changes to Hospital Outpatient Prospective Payment and Ambulatory Surgical Center Payment Systems and Quality Reporting Programs," 2018, https://s3.amazonaws.com/public-inspection.federalregister.gov/2018-24243.pdf.

58. Paige Minemyer, "Judge Strikes Down Trump Administration's Site-Neutral Payments," Fierce Healthcare, September 17, 2019, https://www.fiercehealthcare.com/hospitals-health-systems/judge-strikes-down-trump-administration-s-site-neutral-payments-rule.

59. Victoria Bailey, "CMS to Start Reprocessing Site-Neutral Outpatient Claims," Revcycle Intelligence, September 13, 2021, https://revcycleintelligence.com/news/cms-to-start-reprocessing-site-neutral-outpatient-claims.

60. Robert King, "Appeals Court Rules HHS Has Authority to Implement Site-Neutral Payments, Dealing Blow to Hospitals," Fierce Healthcare, July 17, 2020, https://www.fiercehealthcare.com/hospitals/appeals-court-rules-hhs-has-authority-to-implement-site-neutral-payments-dealing-blow-to; and Dave Muoio, "Supreme Court Review of Appellate Decision on Site-Neutral Payments Is Unnecessary, HHS Says in New Filing," Fierce Healthcare, May 17, 2021, https://www.fiercehealthcare.com/hospitals/supreme-court-review-appellate-decision-site-neutral-payments-unnecessary-hhs-says-new.

61. Dave Muoio, "Supreme Court Declines to Hear AHA's Appeal of Site-Neutral Payments Decision," Fierce Healthcare, June 28, 2021, https://www.fiercehealthcare.com/hospitals/supreme-court-declines-to-hear-aha-s-appeal-site-neutral-payments-decision.

62. Centers for Medicare & Medicaid Services, "CY 2023 Medicare Hospital Outpatient Prospective Payment System and Ambulatory Surgical Center Payment System Proposed Rule (CMS 1772-P)," July 15, 2022, https://www.cms.gov/newsroom/fact-sheets/cy-2023-medicare-hospital-outpatient-prospective-payment-system-and-ambulatory-surgical-center.

63. Committee for a Responsible Federal Budget, "Equalizing Medicare Payments Regardless of Site-of-Care," February 23, 2021, https://www.crfb.org/papers/equalizing-medicare-payments-regardless-site-care.

64. Centers for Medicare & Medicaid Services, "Medicare Program: Hospital Outpatient Prospective Payment and Ambulatory Surgical Center Payment Systems and Quality Reporting Programs; Price Transparency of Hospital Standard Charges; Radiation Oncology Model," *Federal Register* 86, no. 218 (November 16, 2021), https://www.federalregister.gov/d/2021-24011/p-1897.

65. Jack M. Bert, Jessica Hooper, and Sam Moen, "Outpatient Total Joint Arthroplasty," *Current Reviews in Musculoskeletal Medicine* 10 (2017): 567–74, https://www.ncbi.nlm.nih.gov/pmc/articles/PMC5685972/pdf/12178_2017_Article_9451.pdf.

66. Consumer Choice of Care Act, H.R. 8134, 117th Cong., 2nd sess. (2022), https://www.congress.gov/bill/117th-congress/house-bill/8134?s=1&r=2.

67. Brian J. Miller, "Reversing Hospital Consolidation: The Promise of Physician-Owned Hospitals," Health Affairs Forefront, April 12, 2021, https://www.healthaffairs.org/do/10.1377/forefront.20210408.980640.

68. Patient Access to Higher Quality Health Care Act, S. 4130, 117th Cong., 2nd sess. (2022), https://www.congress.gov/bill/117th-congress/senate-bill/4130; and Patient Access to Higher Quality Health Care Act, H.R. 1330, 117th Cong., 1st sess. (2021), https://www.congress.gov/bill/117th-congress/house-bill/1330/titles?r=2&s=1.

69. Government Accountability Office, "Specialty Hospitals: Information on National Market Share, Physician Ownership, and Patients Served," April 18, 2003, https://www.gao.gov/assets/gao-03-683r.pdf.

70. Community benefit represented 3.74 percent of revenue for cardiac physician-owned hospitals (POHs), 7.23 percent of revenue for orthopedic POHs, and 0.87 percent of revenue for nonprofit community hospitals. See Centers for Medicare & Medicaid Services, "Study of Physician-Owned Specialty Hospitals Required in Section 507(c)(2) of the Medicare Prescription Drug, Improvement, and Modernization Act of 2003," 2005, Table 6.1, https://www.cms.gov/Medicare/Fraud-and-Abuse/PhysicianSelfReferral/Downloads/RTC-StudyofPhysOwnedSpecHosp.pdf.

71. Dan Blumenthal et al., "Access, Quality, and Costs of Care at Physician Owned Hospitals in the United States: Observational Study," *BMJ* (2015): 351, https://www.bmj.com/content/351/bmj.h4466.

72. Patient Protection and Affordable Care Act, Pub. L. No. 111-148 § 6001, https://www.cms.gov/Medicare/Fraud-and-Abuse/PhysicianSelfReferral/Downloads/Section_6001_of_the_ACA.pdf.

73. CCO Healthcare Partners, "Legislation Limiting Physician Owned Hospitals Has Immense Impact on Local Economies," January 17, 2011, https://news.cision.com/cco-healthcare-partners/r/legislation-limiting-physician-owned-hospitals-has--immense-impact-on-local-economies,g537478; CCO Healthcare Partners, "Physician Hospitals of America Survey: Affordable Care Act Blocks 6300 Jobs & $1.8 Billion in Construction Spending," November 29, 2011, https://news.cision.com/cco-healthcare-partners/r/physician-hospitals-of-america-survey--affordable-care-act-blocks-6300-jobs----1-8-billion-in-constr,c9193669; and Physician-Led Healthcare for America, "Impact of Implementation of Section 6001," February 21, 2011, https://physiciansled.com/wp-content/uploads/2022/10/Economic-Impact-of-Section-6001-2.21.2011-For-WEB.pdf.

74. Brian J. Miller et al., "Cost and Quality of Care in Physician-Owned Hospitals: A Systematic Review," George Mason University, Mercatus Center, September 7, 2021, https://www.mercatus.org/publications/healthcare/cost-and-quality-care-physician-owned-hospitals-systematic-review.

75. Centers for Medicare & Medicaid Services, "Improving Medicare's Hospital Inpatient Prospective Payment System to Better Recognize the Costs of Care," April 13, 2007, https://www.cms.gov/newsroom/fact-sheets/improving-medicares-hospital-inpatient-prospective-payment-system-better-recognize-costs-care.

76. J. M. Mitchell and E. Scott, "Physician Ownership of Physical Therapy Services: Effects on Charges, Utilization, Profits, and Service Characteristics," *JAMA* 268, no. 15 (1992): 2055–59, https://pubmed.ncbi.nlm.nih.gov/1404742; and B. J. Hillman et al., "Frequency and Costs of Diagnostic Imaging in Office Practice—a Comparison of Self-Referring and Radiologist-Referring Physicians," *New England Journal of Medicine* 323, no. 23 (1990): 1604–8, https://pubmed.ncbi.nlm.nih.gov/2233949.

77. E. Haavi Morreim, "Conflicts of Interest: Profits and Problems in Physician Referrals," *JAMA* 262, no. 3 (1989): 390–94, https://jamanetwork.com/journals/jama/article-abstract/378029.
78. Omnibus Budget Reconciliation Act of 1989, Pub. L. No. 101-239 (1989); and Omnibus Budget Reconciliation Act of 1993, Pub. L. No. 103-66 (1993).
79. Health Care Financing Administration, "Medicare Program: Physicians' Referrals to Health Care Entities with Which They Have Financial Relationships," *Federal Register* 66, no. 3 (January 4, 2001): 856–965, https://www.govinfo.gov/content/pkg/FR-2001-01-04/pdf/01-4.pdf; Centers for Medicare & Medicaid Services, "Medicare Program: Physicians' Referrals to Health Care Entities with Which They Have Financial Relationships (Phase II)," *Federal Register* 69, no. 59 (March 26, 2004): 16054–146, https://www.govinfo.gov/content/pkg/FR-2004-03-26/pdf/04-6668.pdf; and Centers for Medicare & Medicaid Services, "Medicare Program: Physicians' Referrals to Health Care Entities with Which They Have Financial Relationships (Phase III)," *Federal Register* 72, no. 171 (2007): 51012–99, https://www.govinfo.gov/content/pkg/FR-2007-09-05/pdf/07-4252.pdf.
80. Centers for Medicare & Medicaid Services, "Modernizing and Clarifying the Physician Self-Referral Regulations Final Rule (CMS-1720-F)," November 20, 2020, https://www.cms.gov/newsroom/fact-sheets/modernizing-and-clarifying-physician-self-referral-regulations-final-rule-cms-1720-f.
81. Centers for Medicare & Medicaid Services, "Medicare Program: Modernizing and Clarifying the Physician Self-Referral Regulations," *Federal Register* 85, no. 232 (December 2, 2020): 77492–682, https://www.govinfo.gov/content/pkg/FR-2020-12-02/pdf/2020-26140.pdf.
82. Centers for Medicare & Medicaid Services, "Medicare and State Health Care Programs: Fraud and Abuse; Revisions to Safe Harbors Under the Anti-Kickback Statute, and Civil Monetary Penalty Rules Regarding Beneficiary Inducements," *Federal Register* 85, no. 232 (December 2, 2020): 77684–895, https://www.govinfo.gov/content/pkg/FR-2020-12-02/pdf/2020-26072.pdf.
83. Meredith Freed, "Medicare Advantage in 2022: Enrollment Update and Key Trends," Kaiser Family Foundation, August 25, 2022, https://www.kff.org/medicare/issue-brief/medicare-advantage-in-2022-enrollment-update-and-key-trends.
84. Kaiser Family Foundation, "Total Medicaid MCO Spending," 2019, https://www.kff.org/other/state-indicator/total-medicaid-mco-spending.
85. Mark Kutner et al., "The Health Literacy of America's Adults: Results from the 2003 National Assessment of Adult Literacy," US Department of Education, National Center for Education Statistics, September 2006, https://nces.ed.gov/pubs2006/2006483.pdf.
86. Mira Norton, Liz Hamel, and Mollyann Brodie, "Assessing Americans' Familiarity with Health Insurance Terms and Concepts," Kaiser Family Foundation, November 11, 2014, https://www.kff.org/health-reform/poll-finding/assessing-americans-familiarity-with-health-insurance-terms-and-concepts.
87. Brian J. Miller, Jesse M. Ehrenfeld, and Albert W. Wu, "Competition or Conflict of Interest—Stark Choices," *JAMA Health Forum* 2, no. 2 (2021): e210150, https://jamanetwork.com/journals/jama-health-forum/fullarticle/2776935.

Bill of the Month
The $18,000 Breast Biopsy: When Having Insurance Costs You a Bundle

By Lauren Sausser
August 23, 2022

Dani Yuengling of Conway, South Carolina, researched how much a needle biopsy of a lump in her breast might cost. The hospital website showed it would be about $1,400 for someone without insurance. She reasoned her bill with insurance would be less. Instead, the sticker price was close to $18,000, and she was on the hook for more than $5,000 — the balance of her deductible. (GAVIN MCINTYRE FOR KHN)

When Dani Yuengling felt a lump in her right breast last summer, she tried to ignore it.

She was 35, the same age her mother had been when she received a breast cancer diagnosis in 1997. The disease eventually killed Yuengling's mom in 2017.

npr

This story also ran on NPR. It can be republished for free.

Send Us Your Medical Bills

Do you have an exorbitant or baffling medical bill? Join the KHN and NPR ‘Bill of the Month’ Club and tell us about your experience. We’ll feature a new one each month.

SUBMIT YOUR BILL

“It was the hardest experience, seeing her suffer,” said Yuengling, who lives in Conway, South Carolina.

After a mammogram confirmed the lump needed further investigation, Yuengling scheduled a breast biopsy for Valentine’s Day this year at Grand Strand Medical Center in Myrtle Beach.

Among many concerns she had ahead of that appointment — the first being a potential cancer diagnosis — Yuengling needed to know how much the biopsy would cost. She has a $6,000 annual deductible — the amount her health plan requires she pay before its contribution kicks in — and she wasn’t close to hitting that. Whatever the procedure cost, Yuengling knew she’d be on the hook for most of it.

But the hospital wouldn’t give her a price. She was told her providers wouldn’t know what type of biopsy needle they needed until the procedure was underway and that would impact the price.

The hospital’s online “Patient Payment Estimator” showed Yuengling an uninsured patient would owe about $1,400 for the procedure.

“That’s fine. No big deal,” she thought to herself, confident it would be cheaper for her because she did have insurance. A Google search indicated it could be closer to $3,000, but Yuengling thought that price seemed reasonable, too.

She wasn’t fretting too much about money as she underwent the procedure. It soon brought the good news that she didn’t have cancer.

Then the bill came.

The Patient: Dani Yuengling, now 36, who is covered by Cigna through her employer, a human resources contractor for the Mayo Clinic.

Medical Service: An ultrasound-guided breast biopsy.

Service Provider: Grand Strand Medical Center, a 403-bed, for-profit hospital in Myrtle Beach, South Carolina. It is one of 182 hospitals owned by Nashville- based HCA Healthcare, which generated $58.7 billion in revenue last year.

Total Bill: $17,979 for the procedure, including lab work, pharmacy charges, and sterile supplies. Cigna's in-network negotiated rate was $8,424.14, of which the insurance company paid the hospital $3,254.47. Yuengling was billed $5,169.67, the balance of her deductible.

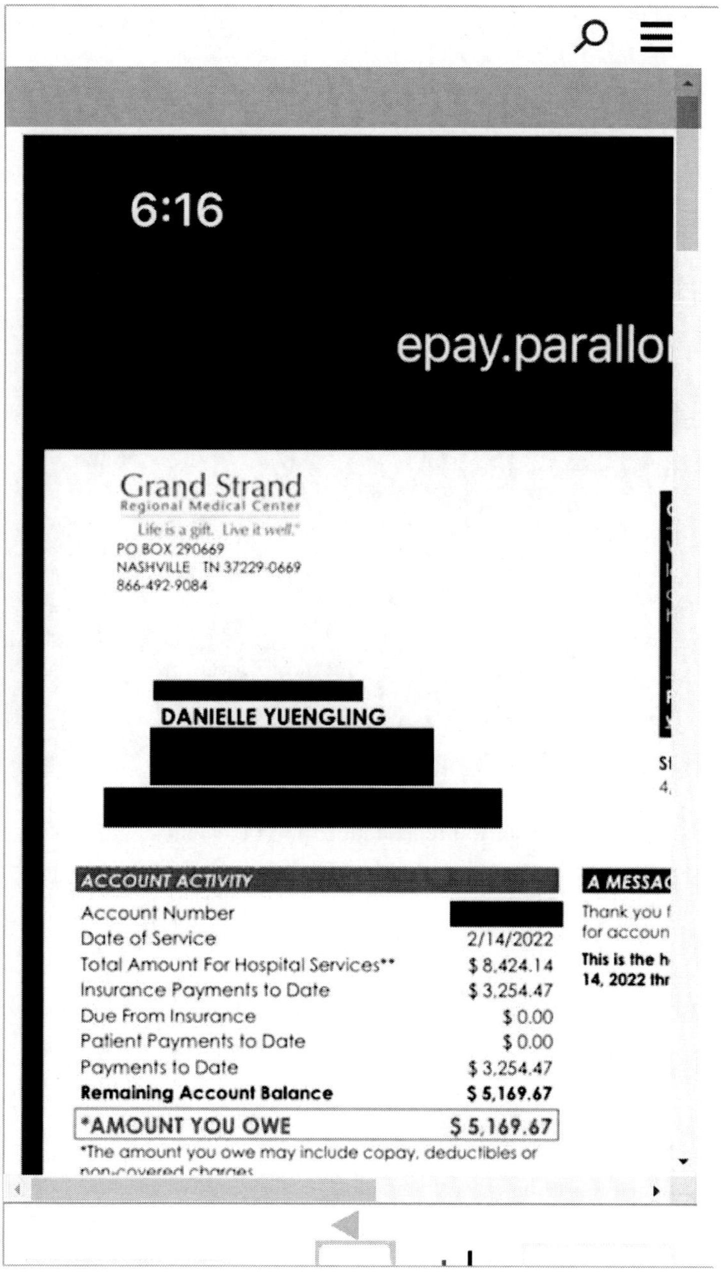
6:16

epay.parallo

Grand Strand
Regional Medical Center
Life is a gift. Live it well.
PO BOX 290669
NASHVILLE TN 37229-0669
866-492-9084

[redacted]
DANIELLE YUENGLING
[redacted]

ACCOUNT ACTIVITY

Account Number	[redacted]
Date of Service	2/14/2022
Total Amount For Hospital Services**	$ 8,424.14
Insurance Payments to Date	$ 3,254.47
Due From Insurance	$ 0.00
Patient Payments to Date	$ 0.00
Payments to Date	$ 3,254.47
Remaining Account Balance	**$ 5,169.67**
***AMOUNT YOU OWE**	**$ 5,169.67**

*The amount you owe may include copay, deductibles or non-covered charges

A MESSAG
Thank you f
for accoun
This is the h
14, 2022 thr

What Gives: It's not uncommon for uninsured patients — or any patient willing to pay a cash price — to be charged far less for a procedure than patients with health insurance. For the nearly 30% of American workers with high-deductible plans, like Yuengling, that means using insurance can lead to a far bigger expense than if they had been uninsured or just pulled out a credit card to pay in advance.

Ge Bai, an associate professor at Johns Hopkins Bloomberg School of Public Health, recently published *research on this topic* and said hospitals in the U.S. often set their cash prices lower than the prices they charge to treat commercially insured patients.

"We can very confidently say this is very common," said Bai, who advised that all patients, regardless of their insurance status, inquire about the cash price before undergoing a procedure. "It should be a norm."

Dani Yuengling lost her mother to breast cancer and takes her health seriously. But after a frustrating experience with a very high bill for a biopsy, she's reluctant to get follow-up care. (GAVIN MCINTYRE FOR KHN)

Grand Strand charged Yuengling's insurance an extraordinarily high price for her procedure. By comparison, according to the federal government's website, Medicare patients who need an ultrasound-guided biopsy similar to the one Yuengling received would pay only about $300 — their required 20% coinsurance for outpatient care. Medicare would pay the hospital the remainder of the bill, about $1,200. The hospital expected more than five times the Medicare price from Yuengling and her insurer.

Patients in Conway with private health insurance who are treated at other hospitals also typically are charged less than what Yuengling paid for the same procedure — on average about $3,500, according to Fair Health Consumer, an organization that analyzes health insurance claims.

And uninsured patients who pay cash prices and need an ultrasound-guided breast biopsy at the nearby Conway Medical Center are likely to owe even less — about $2,100, according to Allyson Floyd, a spokesperson for the hospital.

Meanwhile, Grand Strand Medical Center spokesperson Caroline Preusser blamed "a glitch" involving the hospital's online calculator for the inaccurate information Yuengling received and said the correct estimate for the cash price for a breast biopsy at the hospital is between $8,000 and $11,500 "depending on the exact procedure and equipment used."

The hospital removed certain procedures from the payment estimator until they can be corrected, Preusser wrote. She did not say how long that would take.

share

shots - health news

An $18,000 biopsy? Paying cash might have been cheaper than using her insurance KAISER HEALTH NEWS

listen 6:50

© 2022 npr

Resolution: Yuengling tried disputing the charges with the hospital. She called the billing department and was offered a 36% discount, lowering the amount she needed to pay to $3,306.29. Grand Strand Medical Center allows patients to set up payment plans, but Yuengling decided to charge the full amount to a credit card because she wanted the whole thing to go away.

> "I could not sleep. It was driving me crazy. I was having migraines. I was sick to my stomach," she said. "I hate having debt. I didn't want to think about it. Obviously, that didn't work because I'm still thinking about it."

She said she requested on multiple occasions to speak to the hospital's patient advocate and was eventually connected with an outside company, Parallon, which conducted an audit of her bill. She eventually received a letter dated May 26 from the hospital's Revenue Integrity Department. It stated: "After a review of the charges in question and your medical record, the following was identified; The charges on your account were appropriate."

"I don't know why I actually expected a different outcome," she said.

The hospital has requested that Yuengling return for a follow-up appointment related to the biopsy. She has refused.

Harlow Sumerford, a spokesperson for HCA Healthcare, told KHN in an email that the hospital system apologizes for any confusion caused by the payment estimator "and we are working to fix the issue."

(GAVIN MCINTYRE FOR KHN).

The Takeaway: With a family history of breast cancer, Yuengling was right to follow up with her doctor after feeling a lump. After failing to get a clear answer on her costs from Grand Strand Medical Center, she could have taken an additional step to explore what other hospitals in the area charge. Although her physician referred her to Grand Strand, she was not obligated to use that hospital. She could have saved a significant amount of money by opting to undergo the procedure elsewhere.

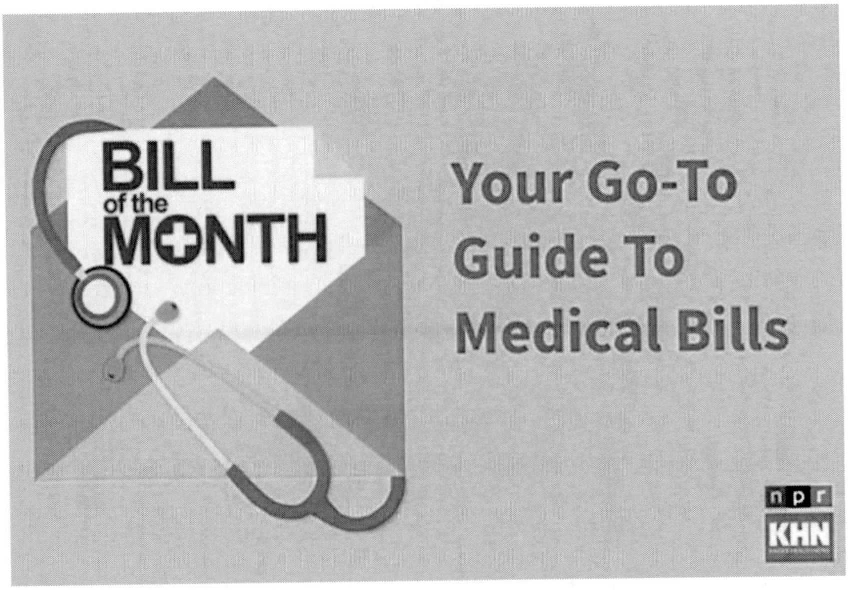

Bill of the Month Resources

Related Links

The Ambulance Chased One Patient Into Collections
His-and-Hers Cataract Surgeries, But His Bill Was 20 Times as Much Her First Colonoscopy Cost Her $0. Her Second Cost $2,185. Why?
After Medical Bills Broke the Bank, This Family Headed to Mexico for Care

Furthermore, patients like Yuengling who have a high-deductible insurance plan should consider paying cash prices for certain procedures and not involving their insurance company at all.

Jacqueline Fox, a health care attorney and a professor at the University of South Carolina School of Law, said she isn't aware of any law that would prohibit a patient from doing that. After all, she pointed out, patients with health insurance pay cash prices for prescription medications all the time. It stands to reason they could do the same for medical procedures.

But some facilities make this difficult. Grand Strand Medical Center, for example, offers "self-pay" patients an "uninsured discount," but that discount is limited to people who have "no third party payer source of payment or do not qualify for Medicaid, Charity or any other discount program the facility offers," according to the hospital's website. Only patients confirmed to have no health insurance are offered information about the discount.

In some cases, paying a cash price for a procedure might not make financial sense in the long run because none of it would be applied toward the deductible. Patients might save money on one procedure but end up paying their full deductible if unexpected medical expenses mount later during the calendar year.

Insured patients should reach out to their health plan for a good-faith estimate before a procedure. Under the No Surprises Act, health plans are supposed to give members an idea of their total out-of-pocket costs upon request. Ask for an "Advanced Explanation of Benefits," said Sabrina Corlette, a research professor at the Georgetown University McCourt School of Public Policy, though she points out this part of the law isn't being enforced yet.

The No Surprises Act also allows patients to file complaints with the federal government regarding their medical bills — whether or not they carry health insurance.

Yuengling filed her complaint in June.

Stephanie O'Neill contributed the audio portrait with this article.

Bill of the Month is a crowdsourced investigation by KHN and NPR that dissects and explains medical bills. Do you have an interesting medical bill you want to share with us? Tell us about it!

Lauren Sausser: lsausser@kff.org, @laurenmsausser

(GAVIN MCINTYRE FOR KHN).

NFIB

555 12th Street NW, Suite 1001
Washington, D.C. 20004

1-800-552-5342
NFIB.com

The Honorable Brett Guthrie
Chairman
Subcommittee on Health
House Energy & Commerce Committee
U.S. House of Representatives
Washington, D.C. 20515

The Honorable Anna Eshoo
Ranking Member
Subcommittee on Health
House Energy & Commerce Committee
U.S. House of Representatives
Washington, D.C. 20515

Dear Chairman Guthrie, Ranking Member Eshoo, and Members of the House Energy & Commerce Subcommittee on Health,

On behalf of the National Federation of Independent Business (NFIB), the nation's leading small business advocacy organization, thank you for convening a hearing focused on lowering unaffordable healthcare costs and examining transparency and competition in healthcare.

Small businesses are the backbone of our economy and play a critical role in creating jobs and driving economic growth. For over 40 years, NFIB members have identified the rising cost of health insurance as their top concern.[291] However, Congress has failed to address the causes of rapidly rising health insurance costs.

A recent NFIB survey found that 56% of small employers currently offer health insurance to employees while 44% do not.[292] The data clearly shows that the most significant reason small employers do not offer health insurance is cost, with 65% of respondents reporting cost as the primary reason.[293] Furthermore, 98% of small employers are concerned that the cost of providing health insurance to their employees will become unsustainable in the next 5-10 years.[294]

Small business owners are forced to make difficult decisions in response to this unaffordability crisis. The percentage of small businesses offering health insurance has dropped dramatically in the last decade. Meanwhile, the businesses that do offer coverage have to pass the costs along to their customers. Nearly half of small employers (46%) report raising their prices to keep up with rising health insurance costs. Moreover, almost half of small employers now earn less due to health insurance premium increases over the last five years.[295] Since 2014, some counties nationwide have witnessed small business premiums skyrocketing to 130%.[296]

Healthcare unaffordability is not just a problem for small businesses but for the entire economy. Sixty-three percent of all employers believe offering health insurance to recruit and retain employees is a very or moderately important factor in their business.[297] As small businesses struggle to rebound from crippling inflation, worker shortages, and looming supply chain disruptions, it is critical that they can compete with larger firms in attracting and retaining talent. Health costs make remaining competitive an impossible task for small employers as they do not enjoy the same regulatory flexibilities and economies of scale.

NFIB recommends that Congress implement policies that lower healthcare costs for small employers and their employees while expanding choice and flexibility in benefit offerings and reducing regulatory burdens.

Small businesses support price transparency. In a recent NFIB member ballot, more than three- quarters (77%) of small business owners support requiring insurers to provide price information for healthcare services. And small businesses can benefit greatly from greater price transparency.

---

291 Holly Wade & Andrew Heritage, NFIB Research Center, Small Business Problems and Priorities, 2020, https://assets.nfib.com/nfibcom/NFIB-Problems-and-Priorities-2020.pdf.

292 Holly Wade & Madeleine Oldstone, Small Business Health Insurance Survey, NFIB Research Center, March 2023 https://strgnfibcom.blob.core.windows.net/nfibcom/Health-Insurance-Survey-2023.pdf.

293 Ibid.

294 Ibid.

295 Ibid.

296 Internal Revenue Service. (2022) Instructions for Form 8941, *Credit for Small Employer Health Insurance Premiums*. pp. 10-30 https://www.irs.gov/pub/irs-pdf/i8941.pdf.

297 Holly Wade & Madeleine Oldstone, Small Business Health Insurance Survey, NFIB Research Center, March 2023 https://strgnfibcom.blob.core.windows.net/nfibcom/Health-Insurance-Survey-2023.pdf.

When healthcare providers and insurers are required to disclose the costs of their services and treatments, small businesses can make more informed decisions about which plans and providers to choose. This enables them to negotiate better rates with their insurers and avoid overpaying for healthcare services. According to a study by the RAND Corporation, improving price transparency could decrease hospital spending by as much as $26.6 billion a year.[298]

Small businesses can also benefit from greater competition in the healthcare industry. Consolidation in local healthcare markets can be particularly harmful to small employers, which may already have limited options for providers in their area. According to the Congressional Budget Office (CBO), hospital markets have become more highly concentrated in recent years, with the share of concentrated systems increasing from 63% to 70%.[299] Consolidation undoubtedly has resulted in higher prices in the commercial market: A 2020 review of published research by the Medicare Payment Advisory Commission (MedPAC) concluded that the "preponderance of evidence suggests that hospital consolidation leads to higher prices."[300]

The same is true of Pharmacy Benefit Managers (PBMs), which continue to further consolidate and negatively impact employers and their employees through higher costs. The three largest PBMs control at least 80% of the health plan pharmacy benefit market,[301] and control, through PBM- affiliated pharmacies, more than 65% of total prescription revenues ($122.2 billion in 2021) from pharmacy-dispensed specialty drugs. In contrast to other claims that consolidation would help consumers with greater efficiencies and lower prices, it has only resulted in less transparency and made the system more opaque. PBM reform is necessary to lower prescription drug costs. By increasing transparency, ending spread pricing, allowing patient choice, and encouraging competition, PBMs can be incentivized to offer higher quality and more affordable services to small businesses and their employees.

Small business owners support increased competition and oppose increased consolidation in healthcare. In a recent NFIB member ballot, more than 80% of small business owners support legislation to rein in healthcare consolidation and anti-competitive business practices.

NFIB remains committed to partnering with you to ensure that small businesses and their employees can access affordable health insurance coverage: When small businesses thrive, our communities thrive.

We greatly appreciate your consideration of these vital policy issues and look forward to working with you to protect and defend the small business community.

Sincerely,

Kevin Kuhlman

Kevin Kuhlman,

---

298 Liu, Jodi L., Zachary M. Levinson, Nabeel Qureshi, and Christopher M. Whaley, *Impact of Policy Options for Reducing Hospital Prices Paid by Private Health Plans*. Santa Monica, CA: RAND Corporation, 2021. https://www.rand.org/pubs/research_reports/RRA805-1.html.

299 Congressional Budget Office. *S.1895, Lower Health Care Costs Act Cost Estimate.* July 16, 2019 https://www.cbo.gov/system/files/2019-07/s1895_0.pdf.

300 MedPAC, "March 2020 Report to the Congress: Medicare Payment Policy," March 13, 2020.

301 1 Fein, A. (2022). DCI's Top 15 Specialty Pharmacies of 2021—And Three Factors That Will Reshape 2022. Drugchannels.net.

Vice President,
Federal Government Relations NFIB

PCMA

Statement for the Record
Pharmaceutical Care Management Association 325 7th Street, NW Suite 900, Washington, DC 20004
Submitted to the United States House of Representatives Energy & Commerce Committee Subcommittee on Health
"Lowering Unaffordable Costs: Examining Transparency and Competition in Health Care"
March 28, 2023

Introduction

The Pharmaceutical Care Management Association (PCMA) appreciates the opportunity to provide this statement about the role of the pharmacy benefit manager (PBM) industry in the market for prescription drugs, focusing on how PBMs benefit patients and taxpayers. PCMA is the national association representing America's pharmacy benefit companies, which administer prescription drug plans and operate home delivery and specialty pharmacies for more than 275 million Americans with health coverage through public and private employers, labor unions, Medicare, Medicaid, the Federal Employees Health Benefits (FEHB) program, and the exchanges established by the Affordable Care Act (ACA). Our members work closely with health plans and health insurance issuers to secure lower costs for prescription drugs and achieve better health outcomes.

PBMs have always focused on lowering drug costs for patients and a wide range of health plan sponsors. Our comments to the Committee review the policies that PCMA members support to encourage competition as the most effective way to lower prescription drug costs for patients and the private sector and government entities that provide or arrange for prescription drug coverage. We then highlight some of the ways pharmacy benefit companies currently work to improve care and lower costs for patients and reduce health benefit costs for employers. We end with an explanation of how our industry supports meaningful, actionable transparency to further enhance market competition, while detailing the numerous disclosure requirements with which PBMs already comply.

Any attempt at understanding the factors driving drug costs must include a look at the entire supply chain including drug companies, Pharmacy Services Administrative Organizations (PSAOs), pharmacy wholesalers, manufacturer wholesalers, employer benefit consultants, pharmacies, and others with impact on the cost of prescription drugs. We encourage the

Committee to review all these entities as it assesses how to improve the prescription drug market.

Pharmacy Benefit Companies Support Policies to Encourage Competition as the Best Way to Lower Prescription Drug Costs

PBMs work to improve prescription drug affordability by providing prescribers with information about less expensive generic alternatives, setting performance standards for pharmacies to encourage generic fills, and ensuring patients are aware of lower cost alternatives. Due in large part to these efforts by PBMs, 90 percent of prescription drug fills are generics.[302] Pharmacy benefit companies also support increased uptake of biosimilars through business decisions, such as preferring both the brand and a biosimilar to ensure patients and providers have the proper incentives to choose lower cost options and the choice to continue with a drug they may be reluctant to move away from, and policy proposals, including eliminating the interchangeability designation to reduce costs and confusion, stopping patent abuses, and making it easier for Medicare Part D plans to update formularies as new biosimilars come to market.

Toward that end, PCMA recently proposed the following three keys in a policy platform supportive of a more sustainable health care future:

Key #1: Ensure System Sustainability by Promoting Competition. Enabling a robust private prescription drug marketplace that promotes competition is the best way to drive down prescription drug costs and make more affordable alternatives available for patients.

Key #2: Support and Equip Clinicians with Tools and Data to Serve Patients Optimally. Pharmacy benefit experts support efforts to help clinicians, including pharmacists and other health care practitioners, "practice at the top of their license" to optimize use of their clinical expertise and counseling abilities. Pharmacy benefit companies also work to increase clinicians' administrative efficiency by offering information and tools to help serve patients.

Key #3: Enhance Patient Outcomes and Improve the Patient Experience. Pharmacy benefit companies use their prescription drug expertise to support better health outcomes and provide recommendations to meet each patient's needs.

Our Affordable Future policy platform proposes numerous solutions to build on the private market system and facilitate collaboration among patients, regulators, PBMs, clinicians, health plans, and pharmacies to work toward a more functional, equitable, and affordable market for prescription drugs.

PCMA supports numerous pieces of legislation that have been introduced and advanced by this Committee in previous Congresses that would address tactics that undermine competition in the pharmaceutical market. The Bringing Low-cost Options and Competition while Keeping Incentives for New Generics (BLOCKING) Act would discourage parking of 180-day exclusivity by a first generic applicant while allowing the FDA to approve a subsequent generic application under certain conditions prior to the first applicant's date of commercial marketing. The Protecting Consumer Access to Generic Drugs Act would make it illegal for brand-name and generic drug manufacturers to enter into agreements in which the generic manufacturer is

---

[302] AAM. 2021. https://accessiblemeds.org/sites/default/files/2021-10/AAM-2021-US-Generic-Biosimilar-Medicines-Savings-Report-web.pdf.

paid to keep a generic equivalent off the market. We encourage the Committee to again consider these and other proposals to improve competition in the prescription drug market.

Earlier this year, the Senate Judiciary Committee approved a package of bills on a bipartisan basis that align with the solutions proposed by our organization, and PCMA continues to support the Interagency Patent Coordination and Improvement Act of 2023, the Prescription Pricing for the People Act of 2023, the Stop STALLING Act, the Preserve Access to Affordable Generics and Biosimilars Act, and the Affordable Prescriptions for Patients Act. PCMA also supported Senator Rosen's Expanding Access to Affordable Prescription Drugs and Medical Devices Act to improve the competitive landscape for prescription drugs.

Pharmacy Benefit Companies Improve Care for Patients

PBMs Simplify the Patient Experience

People with insurance filled more than 6.4 billion prescriptions in retail pharmacies in 2021.[303] Every day, that amounts to nearly 15 million prescriptions, so it is critical that patients can pick up their prescriptions as quickly as possible at the pharmacy counter (or at home via mail delivery) to establish and maintain medication adherence. PBMs perform many essential functions that combine disparate information and expertise, as well as advanced technology to facilitate and streamline getting a prescription filled as seamlessly as possible.[304]

To optimize the patient experience when a pharmacy initiates the process of filling a prescription drug, once the pharmacy enters the prescription into its system, the prescribing information is sent electronically to the patient's PBM, which checks the pharmacy benefit information to confirm the patient's insurance status and cost-sharing amount, as well as the patient's medication history for any errors or possible harmful drug interactions. While pharmacies have records of the prescriptions they fill as well as those filled by other pharmacies in the same chain, they do not have records of prescriptions filled by other pharmacies using a different system – for example, those outside their chain. However, if a patient uses insurance, their PBM will have the ability to see all their prescriptions. Technology allows real-time, almost instantaneous access to this information which the PBM uses to determine if there is any reason that a prescribed drug should not be taken by a patient and can alert the pharmacist to any dangerous interactions before the patient receives any medication and pays any associated cost sharing. All of this happens rapidly, seamlessly, and behind the scenes to improve patient safety and care.

Part D plans and the PBMs that administer them are also required to provide real-time benefit tools to give patients and prescribers cost sharing and benefits information at the point of prescribing.

---

303 IQVIA. The Use of Medicines in the U.S. 2022. April 2022. Available at https://www.iqvia.com/insights/the-iqvia- institute/reports/the-use-of-medicines-in-the-us-2022.

304 Pharmaceutical Care Management Association (PCMA). PBM Technology and Expertise Improves Patient Health Outcomes. June 2016. March 8, 2022. Available at https://www.pcmanet.org/pbm-technology-and-expertise-improves-patient-health-outcomes/.

PBMs Lower Drug Costs for Patients

PBMs, working with those providing insurance, encourage patients through formulary design and cost-sharing incentives to use the most affordable drugs, which are usually generics. For many brand drugs, PBMs negotiate directly with drug manufacturers who compete for formulary placement by offering a type of discount called rebates.[305] For drugs on the preferred tier of a plan's formulary, patients typically have lower cost sharing.[306] As competing products enter the market, PBMs gain the flexibility to leverage competitor products to negotiate deeper drug discounts for patients and employers.[307]

PBMs have also led the industry in creating contracts that account for the value of specialty and high-cost medications.[308] Value-based arrangements are at the forefront of new drug payment designs and will be critical to managing the costs of next-generation therapies like cell and gene therapies, orphan drugs, and ultra-expensive specialty drugs. Value-based contracts will betterallow plans to manage these high costs, and plan sponsors will need broad flexibility to craft and employ value-based contracts.

The Medicare Part D program, where older Americans and those living with disabilities can choose among private plans to get their drug benefits, is a great example of PBM value. PBMs support Part D plans by negotiating rebates and discounts and promoting better pharmacy quality, passing 99.6 percent of those savings from those negotiations to the Part D plans, which in turn use them to enhance drug benefits and keep premium costs reliably low for beneficiaries.[309]

Savings from PBMs benefit health plans, employers, retirees, and patients directly. Prescriptions cost health plans and employers an average of $1,315 per person per year, with patients paying an average of $180 for their prescriptions, or 14 percent.[310] Without PBMs and the savings they generate, drug costs could be $2,000 per person per year.[311]

---

[305] Foley Hoag. The History of Rebates in the Drug Supply Chain and HHS' Proposed Rule to Change Safe Harbor Protection for Manufacturer Rebates. April 2, 2019. Available at https://foleyhoag.com/publications/ebooks-and-white-papers/2019/march/the-history-of-rebates-in-the-drug-supply-chain.

[306] Congressional Budget Office (CBO). Prescription Drugs: Spending, Use, and Prices. January 17, 2020. Available at https://www.cbo.gov/system/files/2022-01/57050-Rx-Spending.pdf.

[307] Congressional Budget Office (CBO). Prescription Drugs: Spending, Use, and Prices. January 17, 2020. Available at https://www.cbo.gov/system/files/2022-01/57050-Rx-Spending.pdf.

[308] Pharmacy Benefit Management Institute. Solving America's High Drug Cost Problem: Prevent Drug Company Tactics that Increase Costs and Undermine Clinical Quality. January 2021. Available https://www.pcmanet.org/wp-content/uploads/2021/01/Solving-America%E2%80%99s-High-Drug-Cost-Problem_whitepaper_FINAL2.pdf.

[309] Government Accountability Office (GAO). Medicare Part D: Use of Pharmacy Benefit Managers and Efforts to Manage Drug Expenditures and Utilization. August 13, 2019. Available at https://www.gao.gov/products/gao-19-498.

[310] Visante. The Return on Investment (ROI) on PBM Services. February 2020. An analysis prepared by Visante on behalf of PCMA Available at https://www.pcmanet.org/wp-content/uploads/2020/02/ROI-on-PBM-Services-FINAL_.pdf.

[311] Visante. The Return on Investment (ROI) on PBM Services. February 2020. An analysis prepared by Visante on behalf of PCMA Available at https://www.pcmanet.org/wp-content/uploads/2020/02/ROI-on-PBM-Services-FINAL_.pdf.

Pharmacy Benefit Companies Reduce Costs for Employers

Employers need choice and flexibility when it comes to designing prescription drug benefits that meet the health and affordability needs of unique employee populations. Employers and other health plan sponsors vary dramatically in size, resources, and function and serve diverse populations. Employer health plan sponsors know more about their financial resources and plan participants than any other entity, and they use that information to make choices about how to best serve their unique populations.

PBMs have an established record of negotiating with drug manufacturers and pharmacies to reduce drug costs. PBMs work to bring drug prices down for employers, both large and small, and others who provide health insurance. No employer, union, retiree health plan, pension fund, or other health plan has to hire or use a PBM. But virtually all do choose to hire a PBM to lower the cost of providing health care coverage and to better serve the patients they represent.

PBM clients choose their PBMs through a transparent and highly competitive bidding process. With more than 70 full-service PBMs in the market, including regular new entrants, unions, employers, and health plans have a tremendous diversity of opportunities to contract with the PBM that best meets their unique needs.[312]

Employers and health plans serving federal programs rely on PBM expertise to secure savings through price concessions from pharmaceutical companies (through formularies and other tools), administer medication adherence and health coaching programs, and provide overall guidance and expertise on pharmacy benefit design and coverage. Employers report about 80 percent satisfaction with the cost-saving, health-improving services provided by their PBM.

For all those sponsoring health insurance, it is important that there is choice among PBMs and the ability to decide how to set up their drug benefits to best serve their unique populations.

Some may choose a PBM based on its scale, ability to negotiate deep discounts or manage the risk of price changes. Others choose to hire PBMs based on their innovative care management programs or different levels of service. For small employers, many of whom may struggle to provide health insurance to employees, PBMs both lower drug costs and provide cost predictability, enabling them to stretch their benefit dollars even further.

One method that PBMs use to lower drug costs is incentivizing the use of lower-cost generic alternatives to name-brand drugs. Indeed, generic dispensing has grown over the past decade as more generics have entered the market and patients have responded to health plan designs encouraging their use, so that now roughly 90 percent of prescriptions filled in the United States are for generic drugs, at a fraction of the cost of their brand-name equivalents.[313] PBMs also employ other tools designed to deliver high-quality drug benefits while bringing down costs.[314]

---

[312] Pharmaceutical Care Management Association (PCMA). The PBM Marketplace Is Highly Competitive. April 2021. Available at https://www.pcmanet.org/wp-content/uploads/2021/04/PBM-Landscape-2021.pdf.

[313] US Food and Drug Administration (FDA). Generic Drugs. February 5, 2021. Available at https://www.fda.gov/drugs/buying-using- medicine-safely/generic-drugs.

[314] Pharmacy Benefit Management Institute (PBMI). Solving America's High Drug Cost Problem: Prevent Drug Company Tactics that Increase Costs and Undermine Clinical Quality. 2020. Available at https://www.pcmanet.org/wp-content/uploads/2021/01/Solving-America%E2%80%99s-High-Drug-Cost-Problem_whitepaper_FINAL2.pdf. Pharmacy Benefit Management Institute (PBMI). 2017 Trends in Specialty Drug Benefits. 2017. Available at www.pbmi.com/research. Pharmacy Benefit Management Institute (PBMI). 2016 Trends in Drug Benefit Design. 2016. Available at www.pbmi.com/research.

Plan sponsors should have the option of determining how they would like to pay the pharmacy benefit company they select for their services. "Spread pricing" is a risk-based contracting model in which employers choose to let the pharmacy benefit company hold the risk that plan participants may use more expensive pharmacies to acquire drugs in exchange for the option to keep the savings when a patient uses a less expensive pharmacy, as well as to take a loss when they use costlier pharmacies. Today, employers can choose spread pricing or "pass-through" contracting, in which the plan sponsor pays whatever the pharmacy charges. While larger employers typically select pass-through contracts, as they have the scale to deal with the variability of pharmacy charges, smaller employers often choose spread contracts because of the pricing predictability and savings they derive.

As a result, PBMs have a pro-competitive influence on the prescription drug marketplace, and PBM services provide a significant and measurable benefit for businesses and others providing health insurance. Without PBMs in the marketplace, those organizations would be left to negotiate drug costs on their own or pay the full costs of these drugs.

PBMs Support Meaningful, Actionable Transparency to Enhance Market Competition

Transparency that helps patients and payers is necessary across the entire prescription drug chain. PBMs support and practice actionable transparency that empowers patients, their physicians, those sponsoring health coverage, and policymakers, so that they can make informed decisions that can lead to lower prescription drug costs. Actionable transparency encourages consumers to shop for coverage that best fits their health needs and budgets, and once covered, use the most cost-effective, highest-value healthcare goods and services. It enables prescribers and patients to avoid pharmacy-counter surprises and helps ensure that physicians can prescribe drugs that are affordable for patients. To that end, PBMs provide patients and prescribers with real-time benefit tools (RTBTs), which provide real-time information on exactly where the patient is with respect to progressing through a deductible or another benefit phase, what drugs are on the patient's formulary, and exactly what cost sharing to expect for a given drug at the pharmacy. PBMs also provide patients with information on in-network pharmacies, premiums, general cost- sharing, and benefits for their prescription drug coverage.

PBMs provide health plans, employer plan sponsors, and consumers with a broad array of accurate, actionable information on price and quality to make efficient purchasing decisions. PBMs' customers are able to set the terms of the transparency and information they want to receive, as well as their audit rights, as part of their contracts.

In recent years, Congress has added more requirements for PBMs to report to federal agencies, as well as public reporting in more aggregated form, in both cases with appropriate protections for confidential data to avoid encouraging tacit collusion, efforts that we support.

Exposing Proprietary Pricing Information Can Raise Drug Prices

The FTC has historically spoken out against over-exposing information about private business dealings because such an approach is deeply damaging to a competitive marketplace, stating, "If pharmaceutical manufacturers learn the exact amount of the rebates offered by their competitors (either because the safeguards on subsequent disclosure by purchasers and prospective purchasers are insufficient or because the mandated disclosure to prescribers provides sufficient information for pharmaceutical manufacturers to calculate these amounts) then tacit collusion among manufacturers is more feasible. Consequently, the required disclosures may lead to higher prices for PBM services and Pharmaceuticals."[315]

Likewise, the Federal Trade Commission has noted that there are limits to the benefits of transparency and unintended consequences that can result.[316]

The FTC is not alone in this assertion. Recently, in speaking about concerns related to anticompetitive information exchanges, Principal Deputy Assistant Attorney General Doha Mekki noted on behalf of the Department of Justice (DOJ) that, "Courts have long recognized that the exchange of competitively sensitive information can subvert the competitive process and harm competition." Attorney General Mekki also spoke of the United States Supreme Court's concern that sharing current pricing information risks greater harm than sharing old, stale information, and specifically stated that, "transparency in the health care arena may lead to tacit collusion and higher prices."[317] She went on to say:

> Courts also have looked at the degree to which the exchanged data has been aggregated. These decisions considered how, in light of the facts and market realities at the time, the information could facilitate and result in the type of behavior that the antitrust laws condemn. The Second Circuit explained in Todd that "[p]rice exchanges that identify particular parties, transactions, and prices are seen as potentially anticompetitive because they may be used to police a secret or tacit conspiracy to stabilize prices Courts prefer
>
> that information be aggregated in the form of industry averages, thus avoiding transactional specificity." But facial aggregation of data alone has been held to be insufficient to save otherwise problematic information exchanges. In Todd, the Second Circuit looked beyond data that appeared to be somewhat aggregated to conclude that the defendants had the ability to effectively disaggregate it, raising serious antitrust concerns.[318]

For these reasons, it is important to carefully protect data that helps to maintain a competitive market and ensure it is never released publicly. As Mekki warns, such information sharing would likely damage the private market, "A softening of competition through tacit

---

315 FTC. 2004. https://www.ftc.gov/sites/default/files/documents/advocacy_documents/ftc-comment-hon.greg-aghazarian-concerning-ca.b.1960-requiring-pharmacy-benefit-managers-make-disclosures-purchasers-and-prospective-purchasers/v040027.pdf.

316 See FTC Staff Comment to the Honorable James L. Seward Concerning New York Senate Bill 58 on Pharmacy Benefit Managers (PBMs), FED. TRADE COMM'N. March 2009. Available at https://www.ftc.gov/sites/default/files/documents/advocacy_documents/ftc-staff-comment-honorable-james-l.seward-concerning- new-york-senate-bill-58-pharmacy-benefit-managers-pbms/v090006newyorkpbm.pdf.

317 DOJ. *Principal Deputy Assistant Attorney General Doha Mekki of the Antitrust Division Delivers Remarks at GCR Live: Law Leaders Global 2023*. 2022. https://www.justice.gov/opa/speech/principal-deputy-assistant-attorney-general-doha-mekki-antitrust- division-delivers-0.

318 Ibid. Includes information sourced from *Todd*, 275 F.3d at 212-2013.

coordination, facilitated by information sharing, distorts free market competition in the process."

Additionally, the Congressional Budget Office has framed the transparency and disclosure considerations clearly in this often-quoted statement:

> The disclosure of drug rebates could affect Medicare spending through two principal mechanisms. First, disclosure would probably make rebates less varied among purchasers, with large rebates and small rebates tending to converge toward some average rebate. Such compression, for reasons discussed below, would tend to reduce the rebates that PDPs received and thus would raise Medicare costs. Second, for a range of medical conditions, drugs appropriate for treatment are available from only a few manufacturers; disclosure of drug-by drug rebate data in those cases would facilitate tacit collusion among those manufacturers, which would tend to raise drug prices. (CBO March 12, 2007)

PCMA encourages the Committee, as it reviews how to improve the prescription drug market to help lower costs for patients and businesses, to focus its efforts on actionable transparency that reduces drug costs versus transparency that raises them.

PBMs Already Comply with Numerous Disclosure Requirements

Pharmacy benefit companies already operate under federal transparency requirements and adhere to myriad contractually required transparency provisions imposed by their own business and government partners.

PBMs are subject to regulations promulgated by the Department of Health and Human Services (HHS), the Department of Labor, the Department of Treasury, the Food and Drug Administration, and states. PBM practices are overseen by state Medicaid agencies, state-based consumer protection agencies, private accreditation organizations, and their own clients – health plan sponsors and PBMs are directly regulated by state departments of insurance or other state agencies.

Exchange plans must report data on numerous administrative processes like coverage determinations and prior authorization in a way that potential enrollees can access and understand them. Exchange plans must also report data confidentially to CMS regarding generic dispensing rates for retail and mail order pharmacies; aggregate amounts and types of rebates, discounts, price concessions, and service fees; total prescriptions covered; and the difference between the amount the health plan pays the PBM and the amount that the PBM pays retail and mail order pharmacies.

Part D plans must make available to enrollees and potential enrollees all relevant aspects of their benefit design, and report confidentially to CMS the same information as exchange plans, through annual reporting. Part D plans also submit Prescription Drug Event (PDE) data, which is a summary of Part D claims activity with additional data elements including pharmacy dispensing fees. As part of the bid and reconciliation processes, PBMs (via the Part D plans) must report estimated pharmacy and manufacturer Direct and Indirect Remuneration (DIR), including rebates and other price concessions.

It is important to note that government reporting by PBMs is not static but an ongoing, evolving construct. Indeed, CMS routinely updates required Medicare Part D filings to encompass more information, including with respect to PDE and DIR filings. For example, new pharmacy DIR rules take effect on January 1, 2024. Under these new rules, the negotiated price for a Part D covered drug must reflect the lowest possible reimbursement a network pharmacy will receive for a drug and must include all pharmacy price concessions. CMS has already issued detailed guidance on how these changes are to be included in PDE and DIR filings, including changes related to calculating beneficiary cost sharing taking into account the application of pharmacy price concessions at point of sale.[319] Also, CMS has several other major expansions underway to the PDE submissions for 2025 related to Inflation Reduction Act implementation, and we expect to see more for 2026.

Moreover, reporting is not limited to federal health care programs and the exchanges. For commercial plans, Departments of Treasury, HHS, and Labor as well as the Office of Personnel Management (OPM) require PBMs to report:

- The 50 most frequently dispensed brand prescription drugs.
- The 50 costliest prescription drugs by total annual spending.
- The 50 prescription drugs with the greatest increase in expenditures from the previous year.
- Prescription drug rebates, fees, and payments by drug manufacturers in each therapeutic class of drugs, as well as for each of the 25 drugs that yielded the highest amount of rebates.
- The premium and out-of-pocket cost impact of prescription drug rebates, fees, and other payments. PBMs may report these data directly to the government or to their clients. The clients (plan sponsors, issuers, and the FEHB program carriers generally) are required to submit this information, along with some of their own data regarding premiums, aggregated at the state/market level, rather than separately for each plan.

The Departments must biannually issue a report based on the data, but otherwise must keep the data confidential and may not release proprietary information.

PBMs may report these data directly to the government or to their clients. These business partners (including plan sponsors, issuers, and the FEHB program carriers generally) are required to submit this information aggregated at the state/market level, rather than separately for each plan.

Beyond government reporting requirements, much of the PBMs' operational specifics are available to plan enrollees through other provisions of the ACA and Social Security Act including the Summary of Benefits and Coverage, Medicare Plan Finder, and real-time benefit tools that provide current information on prescription drug benefits.

Finally, the Securities and Exchange Commission (SEC) also requires publicly traded health plans and PBMs to report quarterly and annual financial information to the SEC.

---

[319] CMS HPMS memo. October 14, 2022. Available at https://www.cms.gov/httpseditcmsgovresearch-statistics-data-and- systemscomputer-data-and-systemshpmshpms-memos-archive/hpms-memos-wk-2-october-10-14.

Conclusion

The PBM industry is the only stakeholder in the prescription drug supply chain dedicated to seeking lower costs. PBMs do that work for the employer, union, retiree plan, health plan, and government entities who hire them, and, most importantly, for the patients for whom those health plan sponsors provide coverage. As pharmacy benefit experts, PBMs generate tremendous value, estimated at $145 billion annually for society,[320] and save payers and patients an average of $1,040 per person per year.[321] For many years, evidence has also shown a return of 10:1 on investments in PBM services for their private sector and government partners.[322] As a result, PBMs will lower the cost of health care by $1 trillion this year alone.[323]

PBMs are able to negotiate for lower drug costs when they can bring competition between pharmaceutical manufacturers and between pharmacies to bear. PBMs lower prescription drug costs by using these negotiations to deliver discounts and rebates, promoting the use of generic medications, encouraging better pharmacy quality, and offering things like home delivery for those on chronic medications.

Through their work, PBMs are contributing to lower costs for health coverage, lower costs for medications, and better and more affordable access for patients, which means more people getting the medications they need to lead healthier lives.

PCMA would be happy to provide additional information to the Committee on the value pharmacy benefit companies bring to patients, health plan sponsors, and society, and looks forward to working collaboratively with Congress and other stakeholders to build on the existing private market framework to make medications more affordable and accessible for patients.

Arnold Ventures

New Poll: Majority of Voters Support Aggressive Congressional Action to Lower Hospital Prices

Survey findings Reflect Voter Frustration with a Dysfunctional Market

Health care has become increasingly unaffordable for everyday Americans, including individuals and families with private insurance. As health care costs continue to climb, a new survey finds a majority of voters from across the political spectrum think it is very important for Congress to lower hospital prices, the main driver of rising costs for the privately insured.

---

320 National Bureau of Economic Research. 2022. https://www.nber.org/papers/w30231.

321 Visante. 2023. https://www.pcmanet.org/wp-content/uploads/2023/01/Pharmacy-Benefit-Managers-PBMs-Generating-Savings-for-Plan-Sponsors- and-Consumers-January-2023.pdf.

322 Visante. 2023. https://www.pcmanet.org/wp-content/uploads/2023/01/The-Return-on-Investment-ROI-on-PBM-Services-January-2023.pdf.

323 Visante. The Return on Investment (ROI) on PBM Services. An analysis prepared by Visante on behalf of PCMA. February 2020. Available at https://www.pcmanet.org/wp-content/uploads/2020/02/ROI-on-PBM-Services-FINAL_.pdf.

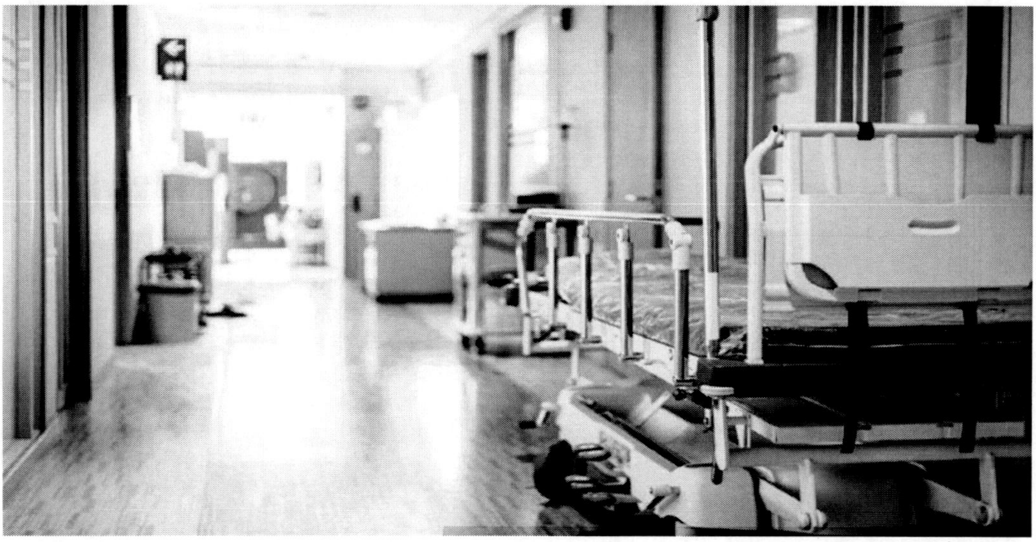

Getty Images

By the:

Commercial Sector Prices Team

TOPIC	Commercial Sector Prices
PUBLISHED	**Mar 23, 2023**
SHARE	

Have an evidence-based week

Get The Abstract from Arnold Ventures delivered to your inbox.

This site is protected by reCAPTCHA and the Google Privacy Policy and Terms of Service apply.

This new survey — from the bipartisan polling team of Guy Molyneux and Geoff Garin from Hart Research Associates and Bob Ward from Fabrizio Ward, and supported by Arnold Ventures — finds that voters overwhelmingly view hospital prices as not only high, but unreasonable given the care that patients receive. The survey findings also demonstrate that voters from across the political spectrum support a range of policies to lower high hospital prices for the privately insured, including policies to address hospital consolidation, ban anticompetitive practices, expand site-neutral payments, and directly limit the prices hospitals can charge.

Voters' main worry: that Congress won't do enough to limit health care prices, not that they will go too far. Building on a 2021 survey on high hospital prices from the same bipartisan polling team, these survey results underscore the strong voter demand for congressional action on unaffordable hospital prices.

These survey findings reflect voter frustration with a dysfunctional market.

The prices that hospitals charge the privately insured far exceed the prices that Medicare pays, with some hospitals charging as much as three to five times Medicare rates. Prices vary wildly for the same service even within the same city, and more and more markets
monopolies that engage in anticompetitive behavi

As a result, health care prices continue to climb, cr
employers, and taxpayers. About 40% of U.S. adult
to cost. More than 100 million Americans have me
as wage garnishment. Unaffordable health care pri
slow wage growth for consumers. Increased emplo
grow, shape their hiring and compensation choice:

Public, policymaker, and media attention o federal action.

Policymakers are stepping up to address out-of-co
Indiana, and other states pursued policies to addre
monopolies. This year, states spanning the politica
ban facility fees, and address anticompetitive cont
and California.

At the same time, bipartisan policymakers at the federal level are exploring ways to strengthen price transparency, expand site-neutral payments, and limit health care consolidation. The House Ways and Means and Energy and Commerce Committees are holding hearings on health care affordability and transparency and competition, respectively. Legislation to strengthen price transparency has been introduced recently. In the previous Congress, legislation to expand site-neutral payments and take on anticompetitive contracting practices was also introduced.

Polling results

Voters demand Congress take action on hospital prices.

— Nine in 10 voters (89%) say it is important for this Congress to take action to reduce hospital prices, including 95% of Biden voters and 85% of Trump voters; 60% say it is very important.

— By a wide majority, more voters (74%) are concerned that Congress won't do enough to limit prices than are worried Congress will get too involved in setting prices (26%).

There is broad consensus that hospital prices are out of control.

— 80% of voters say hospital prices are unreasonable, including more than 3 in 4 Biden voters (78%) and more than 4 in 5 Trump voters (83%).

— 75% of voters think the prices that hospitals and doctors charge privately insured patients for medical services are too high relative to Medicare.

— When asked about limiting hospital prices to
(51%) said a rate of twice what Medicare pays

Large majorities of voters support a range of p

— Voters from both sides of the aisle broadly su

— Requiring hospitals to publicly disclos

— Limiting outpatient fees to the same p

— Preventing hospitals from engaging in

— Limiting mergers and acquisitions (74

— Limiting the prices that hospitals can c

More than 7 in 10 voters support aggressive action to lower prices, including limiting the prices that hospitals can charge to privately insured patients to 2X what Medicare pays.

— There is broad bipartisan support for directly limiting prices, with 76% of Biden voters and 70% of Trump voters supporting it.

— 59% of voters believe that limiting the prices hospitals can charge to no more than twice the price Medicare pays would lower health care costs for them. A solid majority of voters in both parties still support limiting the prices hospitals can charge even after hearing both sides' arguments.

Resources

2023 Hospital Prices Polling Executive Summary
DOCUMENT

2023 Health Care Prices Survey
DOCUMENT

Chartbook: 2023 Health Care Prices Survey
DOCUMENT

Coverage and Reforming the System: Polling Presentation

February 2023

The Alliance to Fight for Health Care

Advancing employer-provided coverage

Key Findings

1) The cost of health care is a serious concern. Eight in ten insured adults are concerned about the cost of care, with seven in ten concerned about the ability to pay, and/or the cost of prescription drugs.
2) More than four in five insured adults feel employers should be able to give employees who have enrolled in their company's health plan a discount for seeing a high-quality doctor.
3) Three in four insured Americans believe that when the identical health service is provided in two different sites – such as a doctor's office and outpatient clinic – the price should be the same.
4) Nearly 90% of insured adults believe their health coverage should not be taxed.

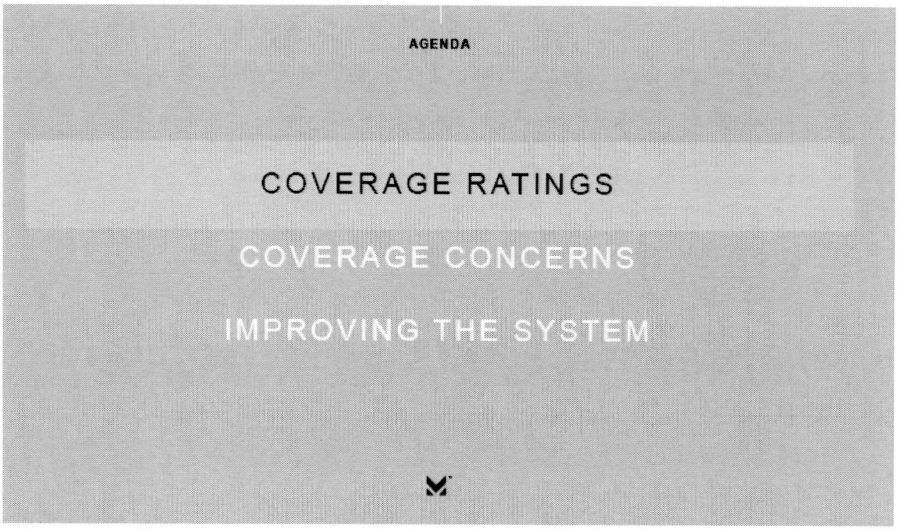

MORNING CONSULT

COVERAGE RATINGS

Three-quarters of insured adults who receive employer-sponsored care, including a bipartisan majority, rate the care they receive positively.

How would you rate your current employer-sponsored health care?

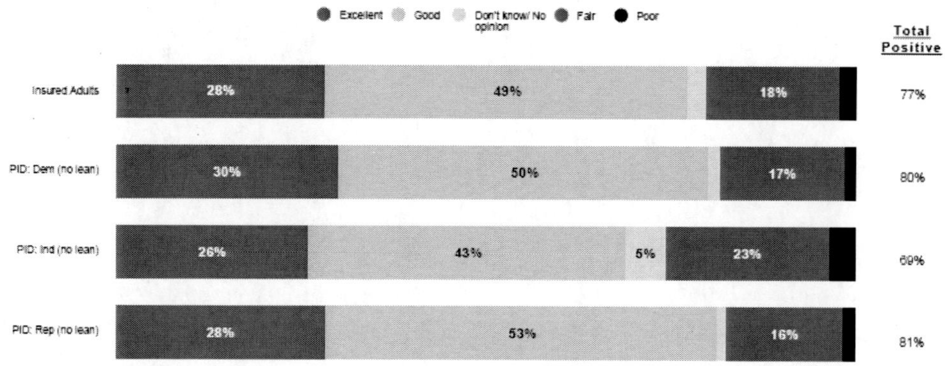

MORNING CONSULT

COVERAGE RATINGS

Those who are insured through an employer-sponsored plan are much less likely to want to switch their plan to Medicare or Medicaid while those who are insured through the marketplace/ exchange are more likely to want to switch to employer-sponsored care.

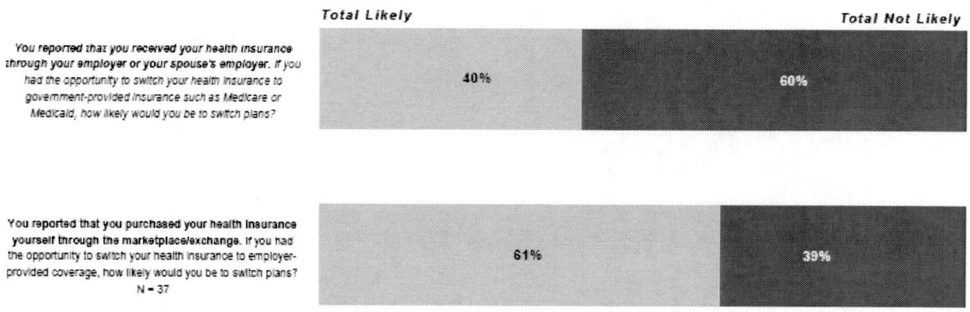

MORNING CONSULT

COVERAGE RATINGS

Insured adults, including most adults across the political spectrum, prefer to select a private plan from their employer where their employer covers most of the cost.

Regardless of what type of health insurance you have right now, which kind of coverage would you prefer to have?

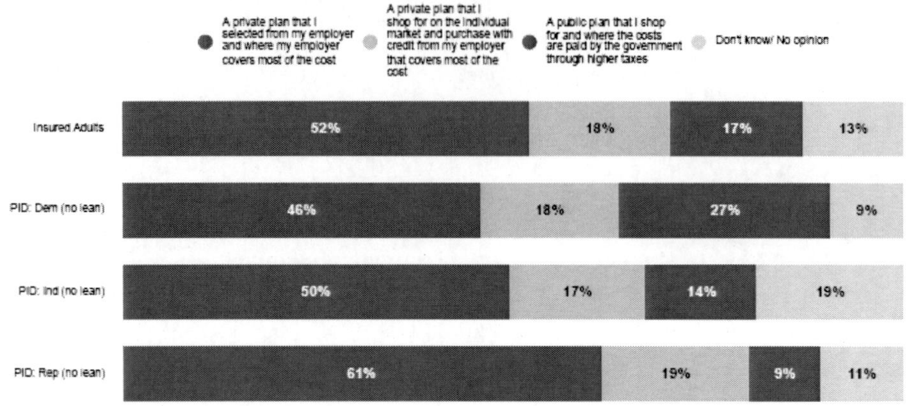

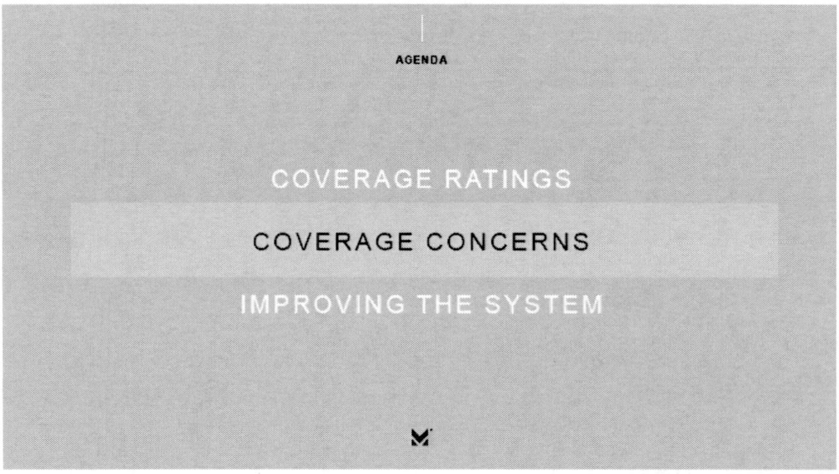

MORNING CONSULT

COVERAGE CONCERNS

Eight in ten insured adults are concerned about the cost of care, with seven in ten concerned about the ability to pay, and/or the cost of prescription drugs.

How concerned are you, if at all, about each of the following?

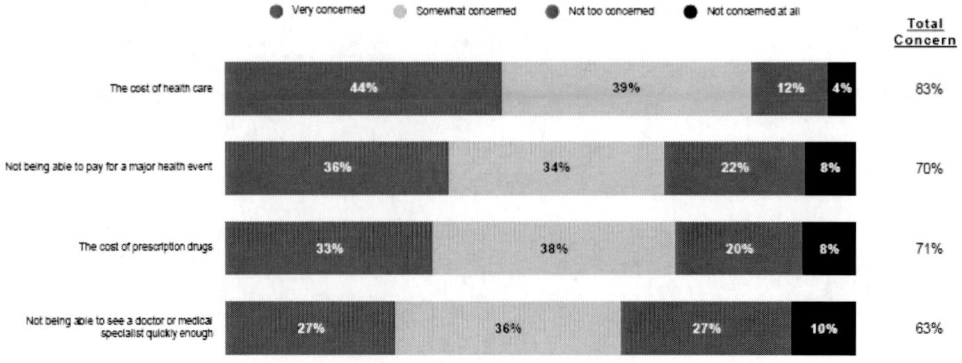

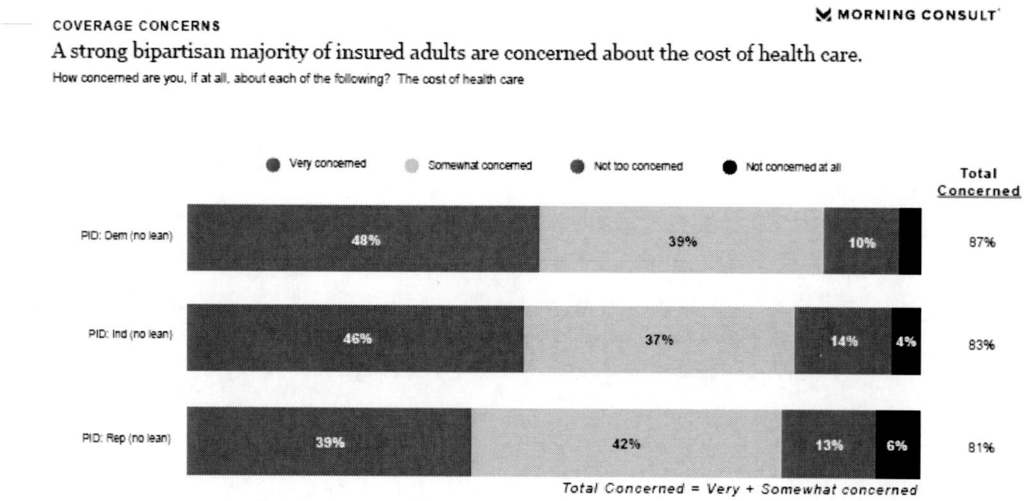
MORNING CONSULT
COVERAGE CONCERNS
A strong bipartisan majority of insured adults are concerned about the cost of health care.
How concerned are you, if at all, about each of the following? The cost of health care
Very concerned
Somewhat concerned
Not too concerned
Not concerned at all
Total Concerned
PID: Dem (no lean)
48%
39%
10%
87%
PID: Ind (no lean)
46%
37%
14%
4%
83%
PID: Rep (no lean)
39%
42%
13%
6%
81%
Total Concerned = Very + Somewhat concerned

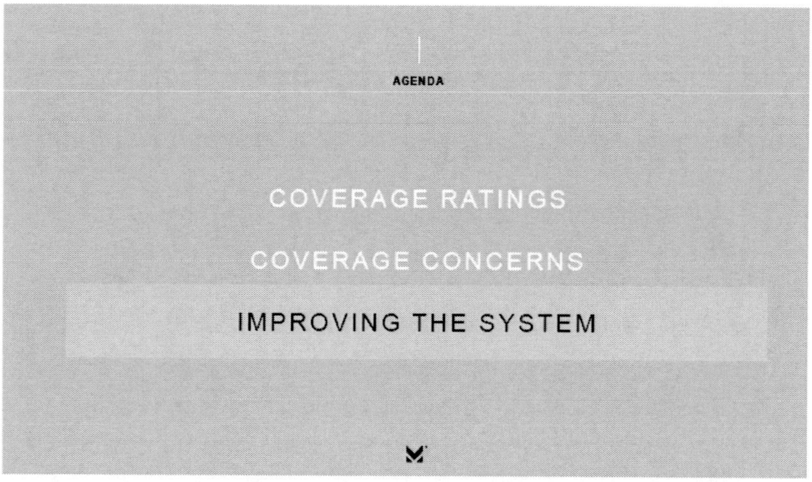
AGENDA
COVERAGE RATINGS
COVERAGE CONCERNS
IMPROVING THE SYSTEM

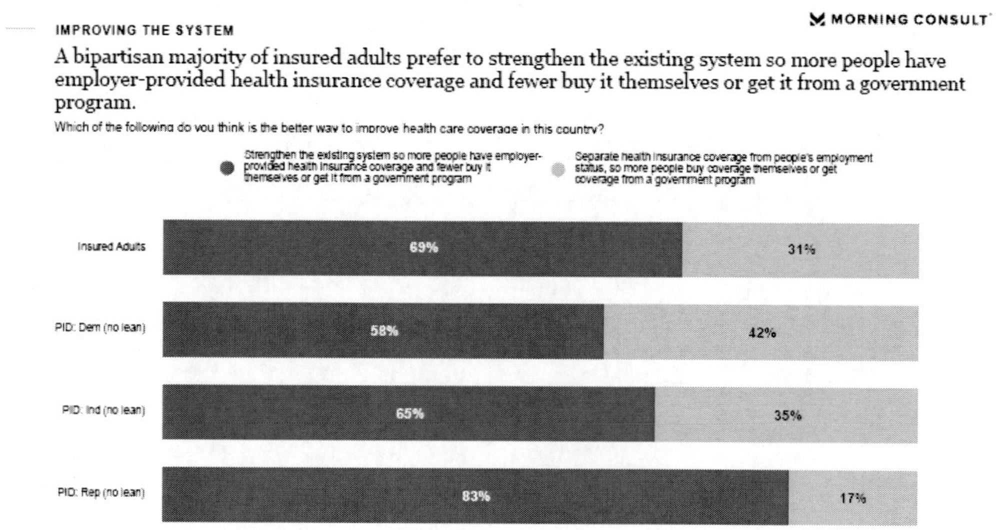
MORNING CONSULT
IMPROVING THE SYSTEM
A bipartisan majority of insured adults prefer to strengthen the existing system so more people have employer-provided health insurance coverage and fewer buy it themselves or get it from a government program.
Which of the following do you think is the better way to improve health care coverage in this country?
Strengthen the existing system so more people have employer-provided health insurance coverage and fewer buy it themselves or get it from a government program
Separate health insurance coverage from people's employment status, so more people buy coverage themselves or get coverage from a government program
Insured Adults
69%
31%
PID: Dem (no lean)
58%
42%
PID: Ind (no lean)
65%
35%
PID: Rep (no lean)
83%
17%

MORNING CONSULT

IMPROVING THE SYSTEM

Four in five insured adults, including across political party, feel lawmakers should work to lower health care costs for *all* Americans, no matter where they get their coverage.

Which of the following statements comes closest to your opinion, even if neither is exactly right?

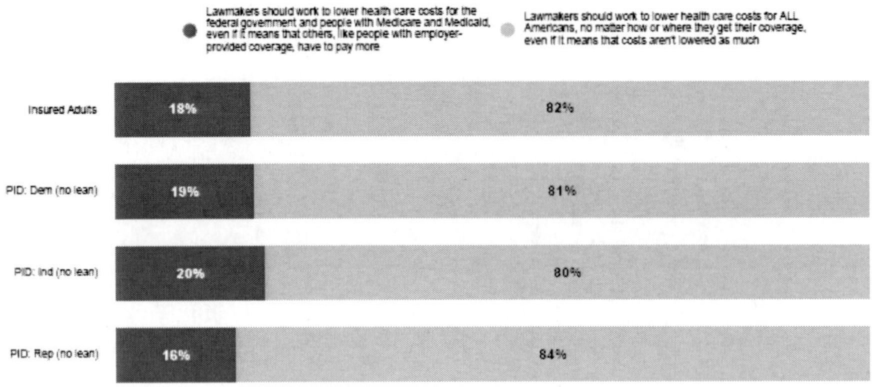

MORNING CONSULT

IMPROVING THE SYSTEM

More than four in five insured adults feel employers should be able to give employees who have enrolled in their company's health plan a discount for seeing a high-quality doctor.

Which of the following statements comes closest to your opinion, even if neither is exactly right?

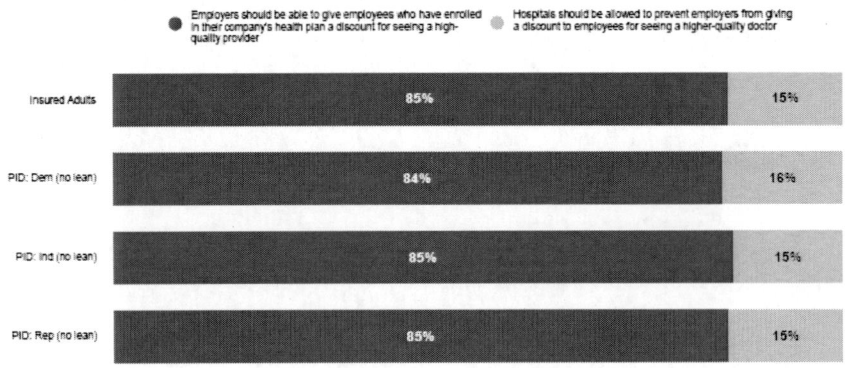

MORNING CONSULT

IMPROVING THE SYSTEM

Across the political spectrum, insured adults believe health care costs should remain the same regardless of where the service is received.

Sometimes the cost of an identical health treatment or procedure can differ depending on where the service is received. Which statement do you agree with more, even if neither state exactly how you feel?

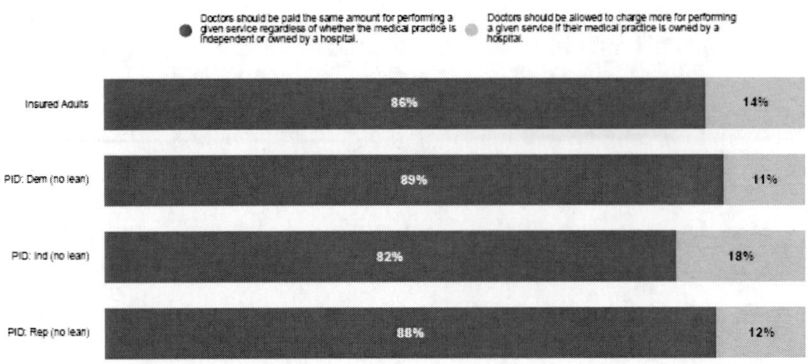

MORNING CONSULT

IMPROVING THE SYSTEM

Reducing health care costs emerges as the top priority for health care reform.

Of the following, which should be made the single most important priority when it comes to health care reform?

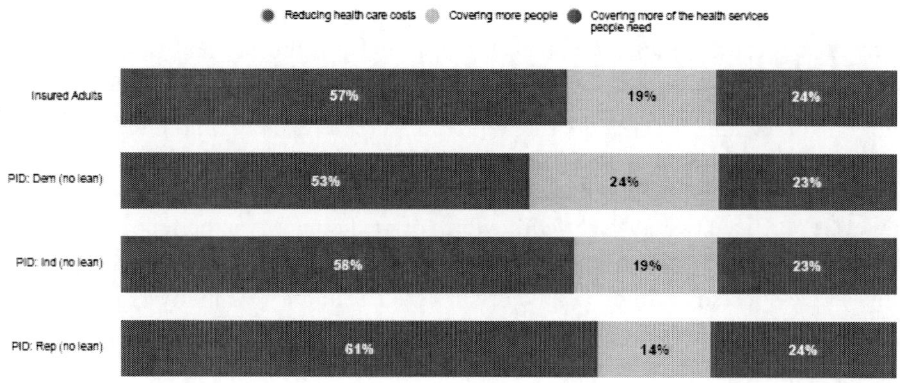

MORNING CONSULT

IMPROVING THE SYSTEM

Nearly nine in ten insured adults feel employer – sponsored care should continue to be tax free.

Which of the following statements comes closest to your opinion, even if neither is exactly right?

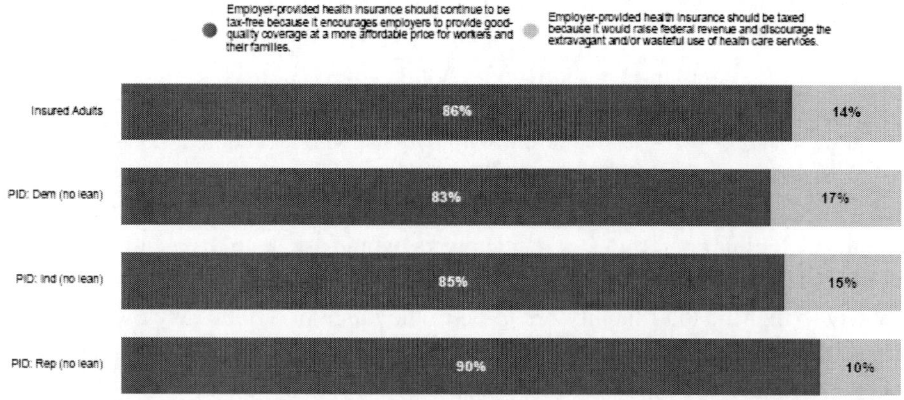

Building Something Worth Building for All Patients

Michael Burgess

March 24, 200810.1377/FOREFRONT.20080324.000367

To paraphrase the great American architect, Frank Lloyd Wright: no man should write about building who has not himself built something worth building. As a physician who helped build an ambulatory surgery center (ASC), I conform to Mr. Wright's formula and am glad to pen some thoughts about my personal experiences with the facility.

Let me begin by stipulating that I am neither a statistician, an economist, nor an academic. I have, however, practiced twenty-five years' worth of medicine. My experience is far-ranging: from a multispecialty practice, to a solo practice, and then in a single-specialty group. It was as a part of this single-specialty group I helped organize and start an ASC in my Texas hometown. And now, by virtue of the fact that I have been elected to Congress, one could argue that I've become an expert in almost anything.

Therefore, I am grateful to have the opportunity to provide some alternative insights into the conclusions outlined in the piece by Jon Gabel and colleagues titled "Where Do I Send Thee? Does Physician-Ownership Affect Referral Patterns to Ambulatory Surgery Centers?"

While the overall piece is thoughtful, I take issue with some of the conclusions. First and foremost, it is unfair to assume that self-pay patients fall into one of two categories: those seeking cosmetic surgery or those who are wealthy. There are also those who lack health insurance.

Like other patients, the uninsured require and request surgery as well. In my own practice of obstetrics and gynecology, it was in dealing with patients who lacked health insurance where the payment disparity among different facilities became most apparent. Many times I encountered patients who desired operations, such as tubal ligation, but lacked health insurance. If they chose to pay for this operation, our local hospital would ask them to pay up front between $8,000 and $12,000. If, however, they were to make the same inquiry at an outpatient surgical center, they would find the total facility fee to be in the range of $1,000. My own modest fee for this procedure was in the neighborhood of $400, which would be unchanged whether the surgery was performed in a hospital facility or an ASC.

In response to these facts, I would simply ask the rhetorical question: in which scenario was I more likely to be paid my fee? That in which the patient had paid $1,000 for the facility or a figure about ten times as high? Invariably the patient's finances would be depleted by the hospital charge, and the physician's fee would often go unpaid.

Thus, if a patient with no insurance presented to my practice for an elective procedure, my likelihood of receiving compensation might, in fact, be increased if the patient were referred to an ASC, regardless of ownership.

Ownership encourages quality. Payment disparities are certainly a challenge. But, there are many other health care concerns today, including the issues of quality of care and payment for performance. One of the most controversial and complex subjects is physician-ownership of medical facilities, as evidenced by Gabel and colleagues' discussion. There is an old axiom that says no one ever checks the water in the battery of a rental car. There is a lot to be said for pride of ownership in any facility, including one's own office or one's ASC.

The relative efficiency of ASCs. Paperwork and policy are also problems when it comes to modern-day health care. In my own twenty-five years of clinical practice, I had multiple struggles with hospital administration. Indeed, sometimes the conventional wisdom was that my local hospital behaved like an absentee landlord. I recall very vividly a five-year effort to get filtered drinking water for my hospitalized patients. It is not a battle I would like to relive at any point in the future.

Additionally, timing and schedules are critical parts of any medical practice. I was fortunate to have a robust roster of patients. So I began scheduling minor procedures on a day that I typically took out of the office. If I were to do four procedures at my local hospital, turnover time after each case would approach one hour. As a consequence, I could complete those four extra cases each week, but it would consume a large amount of time.

If, however, those four cases were performed in an ASC, turnover time was much shorter. It allowed me to place the patient safely in the recovery room, speak with her family, and dictate a procedure note before it was time to start the next case. This meant that those four cases could be accomplished by mid-morning and I could be off about other pursuits. Turnover time was reduced because the correct incentives were in place to make the facility run smoothly and safely.

The need for better data on physician owners of ASCs. While I disagree with several of Gabel and colleagues' assertions, I do concur with their statements about the difficulty in interpretation of data because of the lack of public information about physician owners of ambulatory surgery centers. In fact, without this relevant data, any conclusion drawn becomes suspect – relying on broad generalities, or merely reinforcing preconceived notions. It is frequently hard to correct for observer bias.

Additionally, the statements on the difference between Medicaid and Blue Cross Blue Shield – in other words, those ranging from the lowest to the highest payer – were somewhat confusing. As a clinician, why would I want to invest more of my most valuable commodity (time) to treat a patient for which my reimbursement is lowest? In the interest of precious time, it seems that the incentive for treating the Medicaid patient would be tilted toward the ASCs, so that it could be done more efficiently.

Whenever I am confronted with a set of medical choices, my first default question is always, "Is it safe?" Secondly, I might consider, "What is the least complicated option for me and my patient?" And third, "What are the clinical as well as the business outcomes?" Thus, if I found myself recommending a procedure for a patient, and it could be safely performed in a surgery center, regardless of the amount of available compensation, the ease of scheduling and the rapidity of performance would tend to influence me toward the outpatient facility.

There also might be a case to be made in terms of differentiation by specialties. Generalists such as gynecologists or general surgeons will typically have a broad mix of patients. Their diagnoses might reveal a different pattern than those among physicians who were more narrowly focused within a more well-defined specialty.

Differing attitudes toward the provision of health care. Finally, within the discussion section for this piece, perhaps the focus should not be on why the lowest reimbursement patients (Medicaid) were referred least often to an ASC. Instead, we should determine why Medicaid is the lowest payer. We should also explore what this says about those who want to expand the government's role in paying for health care.

The paper talks about 11 a.m. on a Sunday morning. The statement is made that this might be the most segregated hour of the week. I am not certain about the source of that data, but I do wonder if there is a mindset of a segment of the population who believe that they should pay nothing for medical care versus those who search for an affordable option when hospital costs have increased to a level would preclude their use.

The fact remains that both hospitals and ASCs are necessary for providing good, efficient, and cost-effective care in modern medicine. Physicians are more inherently aware of this fact than any other profession. Therefore, it is not surprising that they would want to provide these types of facilities or partner with their hospitals to provide these types of facilities, to provide the best possible care for their patients in an efficient and cost-effective manner. After all, it is patient care that really matters at the end of the day, and this begins and ends with doctors.

Right to Shop for Public Employees: How Health Care Incentives Are Saving Money in Kentucky

March 8, 2019

Jared Rhoads
The Dartmouth Institute for
Health Policy and Clinical Practice
FGA

Key Findings

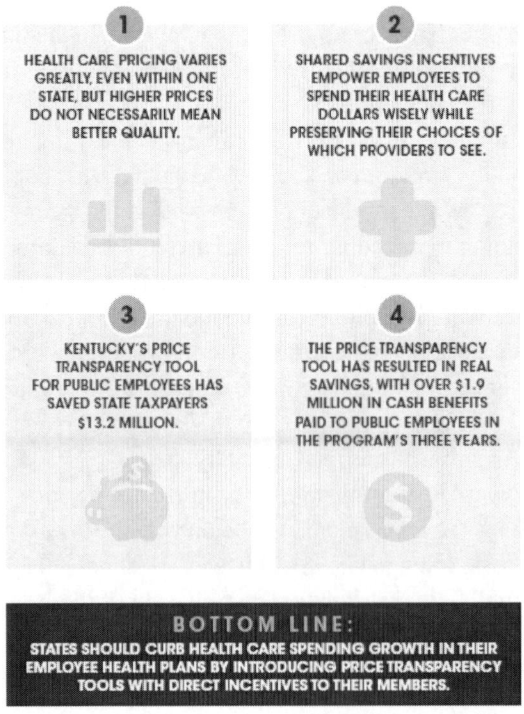

The Problem: The Rising Cost Of Coverage for State Employees

Across the country, states spend in excess of $30 billion to insure roughly 2.7 million public employee households.[324,325] The coverage offered by state employee health plans is often generous, and uptake is high. Among state and local governments, for instance, roughly 89 percent of workers are offered health benefits, and 79 percent of these workers enroll.[326] Premiums also tend to be expensive— indeed, higher than private sector premiums due to the characteristics of state employees (e.g., age, marital status, and educational attainment).[327] These factors converge to make health benefits for public employees a costly budget item for states.

Many states have looked for ways to control costs. Various approaches have included increasing the employee contribution, rolling out wellness programs, and offering high-deductible options. Some of these approaches have helped to slow the rise in costs, but all have substantial tradeoffs, and few are actually popular among public employees.[328,329,330]

For the state of Kentucky, the challenges are much the same. State officials must manage the health care costs of the roughly 150,000 public employees and their family members (260,000 beneficiaries in total, including retirees) in the state employee health plan, called the Kentucky Employee Health Plan (KEHP).[331]

---

324 Governing,"State government employment: Totals by job type: 1960-2016," Governing (2017), http:// www.governing.com/ gov-data/public-workforce-salaries/state-government-employment-by-agency-job-type-current-historical-data.html.

325 Pew Charitable Trusts and MacArthur Foundation, "State employee health plan spending," Pew Charitable Trusts and MacArthur Foundation (2014), http://www.pewtrusts.org/~/media/Assets/2014/08/ StateEmployeeHealth CareReportSeptemberUpdate.pdf.

326 Bureau of Labor Statistics,"Employee benefits in the United States," U.S. Department of Labor (2018), https://www.bls.gov/ news.release/pdf/ebs2.pdf.

327 Bureau of Labor Statistics,"Why are employer-sponsored health insurance premiums higher in the public sector than in the private sector?," U.S. Department of Labor (2018), https://www.bls.gov/opub/mlr/2018/article/ pdf/employer- sponsored-health-insurance-premiums.pdf.

328 Mark Japinga, et al,"State employee health plans can be leaders and drivers of value-based initiatives," Duke Margolis Center for Health Policy (2017), https://healthpolicy.duke.edu/sites/default/files/atoms/files/ duke_seph_12.8.17-final.pdf.

329 Pew Charitable Trusts and MacArthur Foundation,"State health care spending," Pew Charitable Trusts and MacArthur Foundation (2016), https://www.pewtrusts.org/-/media/assets/2016/05/state-health-care-spen ding.pdf.

330 Katherine Barrett and Richard Greene,"States' answer to rising health-care costs for employees? You pay for it," Governing (2017), http://www.governing.com/topics/mgmt/gov-rising-health-premiums-state-employees.html.

331 Commonwealth of Kentucky,"Kentucky employees' health plan: Seventeenth annual report," Commonwealth of Kentucky (2017), https://personnel.ky.gov/KGHIB/Annual%202017%20Report.pdf.

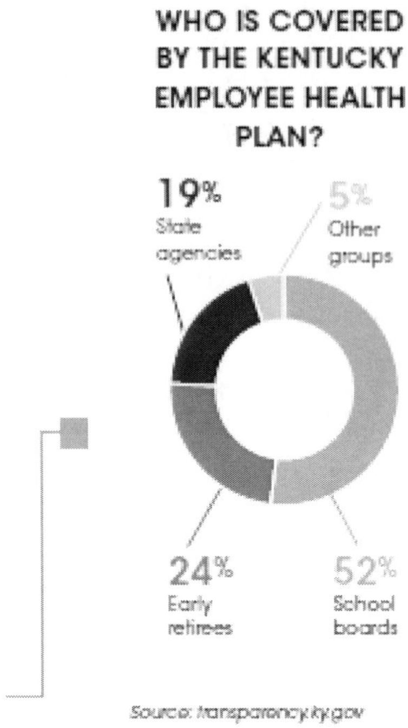

Kentucky Grapples with Rising Health Care Costs

> Over 70 percent of consumers use a higher- cost option for things like scans and tests when a lower-cost option is available.

Between 2008 and 2011, Kentucky increased the amount that state employees could contribute to their health insurance by 55 percent.[332] However, by 2012, the average total premium for an employee and dependents was still over $1,200 per month. To control costs, Kentucky then increased deductibles in two of their more popular plans—achieving some cost control but also increasing employee out-of-pocket costs, an unpopular move.[333]

Kentucky state officials searched for new approaches to keep health care costs under control while lessening the burden on state employees, a win-win for both the state and its employees.

Two factors seemed to be contributing to the problem: a lack of employee awareness about the prices of health care goods and services and a lack of employee interest and motivation to make prudent choices.

At the time, employees had neither the ability nor the incentive to shop around for the most affordable services when they needed care. Prices were not readily available for routine diagnostic imaging services such as abdominal CT scans and digital mammograms or for

---

[332] Ibid.

[333] Jason Bailey,"Shifting health costs to employees has become way state plugs budget," Kentucky Center for Economic Policy (2016), https://kypolicy.org/shifting-health-costs-employees-become-way-state-plugs-budget/.

relatively minor procedures such as cataract surgery and corrective nasal/ sinus surgery. Prices were even harder to obtain for major surgeries and procedures, such as arthroscopic knee surgery and total hip replacement.

Even within a small geographic area,the price of a procedure like an MRI can vary greatly. Without knowledge about these price variations, Kentucky health care consumers were at risk of selecting a needlessly expensive provider, hospital, or diagnostic center. According to transparency company data, it is estimated that over 70 percent of consumers use a higher-cost option for things like scans and tests when a lower-cost option is available.[334]

Prices for the Same Service Can Vary Greatly in Kentucky

Price variation for in-network negotiated rates for MRI services in various Kentucky markets

Numberof MRI Providers	Region	Low	High	Cost Difference
13	Frankfort	$261	$1,073	311%
19	Lexington	$261	$1,135	335%
29	Louisville	$253	$1,503	494%
5	Paducah	$289	$1,439	398%
58	Erlanger	$401	$3,811	850%
6	Pikeville	$685	$1,735	153%

Source: Vitals.

One idea One idea best value by offering price transparency tools and shared-savings incentives

Similarly, without any incentive to shop around for the best value, Kentucky health care consumers did not have a strong reason to care whether they were using a high-cost option. From the consumer perspective, they had paid their insurance premium, some had paid their deductible, and they faced similar co-pays no matter which provider they saw. The fact that one provider might charge twice that of an equivalent provider across the street was more of a concern for the state—which was responsible for paying the claim—than the patient.

Recognizing these factors, one idea emerged as a mutually- beneficial, commonsense solution: encouraging employees to shop for the best value by offering price transparency tools and shared-savings incentives.

Bringing Shopping Options to Kentucky Public Employees

In 2013 and 2014, as Kentucky prepared to launch their new incentive program, state officials formed a cost reduction strategy around the idea of educating members about health care costs. The state ultimately selected Vitals SmartShopper, a technology-enabled third-party service, to empower KEHP members with the ability to shop for health care and keep part of the savings.

The implementation of the Vitals SmartShopper program began as a pilot for state employees in 2013 and was expanded to the full population after proving successful. With no

[334] Information provided by Rob Graybill, Vice President of Product and Sales Strategy, on July 17, 2018.

new complicated back-end information technology for the state to adopt, implementation of the program went smoothly.

After the program was implemented on January 1, 2015, the focus for KEHP turned from program setup to program promotion, enrollment, and optimization.

Information about the program was disseminated via announcements and printed materials, as well as by state officials and KEHP staff who visited work sites. Kentucky Department of Employee Insurance Commissioner Jenny Goins, for example, visited road crews and other groups of public employees to encourage them to sign up for the program.[335] KEHP also worked with the state wellness vendor and other administrative departments to encourage participation—in 2018, KEHP offered a $15 registration reward in the form of a Visa gift card to the first 1,000 people to sign up. Within 24 hours of the program going live, every gift card had been claimed.

Three years in, participation in the program is growing. Employees across all age groups have enrolled, with individuals in the 56 to 65 year old age category comprising the largest user group, demonstrating that the program is not just an offering for younger, tech-savvy employees.

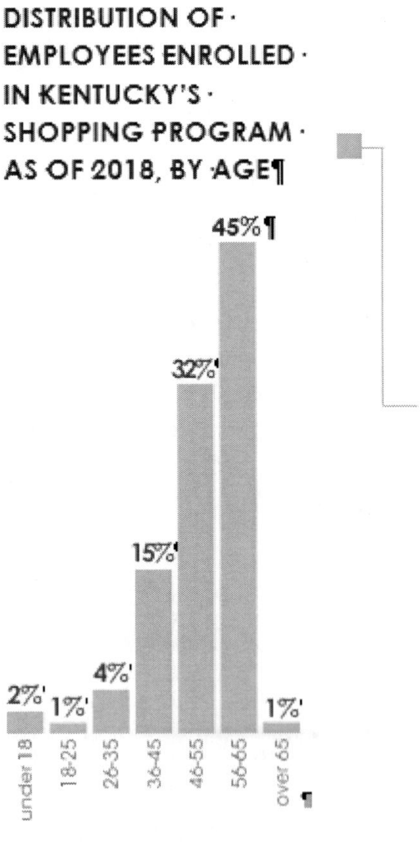

Source: Kentucky Department of Employee Insurance, 2018

335 Information provided by Jenny Goins, Commissioner, Kentucky Department of Employee Insurance on September 10, 2018.

What It Takes to Set up a Shared-Savings Program

States need to be innovative. Price trans- parency and shopping tools might sound like they are too good to be true, but they aren't. Trans- parency works because this program uses incentives, and Kentucky members like incentives. It's money in their pocket.

Jenny Goins,
Commissioner, Department of Employee Insurance

Transparency Vendor

- Implement and administer website and technology
- Run call center
- Partner in education and engagement
- Administer shopping
- Issue reward checks
- Issue tax forms
- Get users registered

Insurer

- Provide eligibility data
- Provide claims data

Public Department/Agency

- Procure service
- Partner in education and communication
- Get users activated

Five Lessons Learned from Kentucky's Incentive Program

Kentucky's experience has shown that empowering patients with a price transparency tool results in taxpayer savings and direct and incentives to members without sacrificing quality

The Vitals SmartShopper program empowers Kentucky public employees to shop for health care services by sharing price information and rewarding them with cash payments when they choose a low-cost provider. All public employees and retirees who are eligible for insurance coverage are eligible to use SmartShopper.

Under the shopper program, incentive rewards differ across services. Incentives generally range from $25 to $500 based on the cost and the savings potential of the service. Employees can go to the lowest cost provider and receive the maximum incentive for a given service, or in many cases they can also go to the second or third most cost-effective provider and still receive a (slightly lower) incentive. For instance, the predetermined incentive for choosing the most cost-effective MRI provider for an abdominal MRI is $150, $75 for the second most cost-effective provider, and $50 for the third most cost-effective provider. Kentucky's experience has shown that empowering patients with a price transparency tool results in taxpayer savings and direct savings and incentives to members without sacrificing quality.

More Than $13 Million In Savings and Nearly $2 Million In Incentives, and Counting

According to data from the state through mid-2018, Vitals Smartshopper has saved state taxpayers a total of $13.2 million in health care costs.[336] Over 19,000 incentives have been paid to members for a total of $1,919,460 back into the pockets of public employees.[337] The average savings to the state per claim that was "shopped" is $546.[338] Kentucky's program is experiencing a return on investment of 2.7:1 overall, with a target for 2018 of 3:1.[339] According to Vitals, as additional services are added such as lab, physical therapy, and infusion, ROI will continue to grow.

336 Jenny Goins,"Healthcare transparency success story," Kentucky Department of Employee Insurance (2018).

337 Ibid.

338 Ibid.

339 Ibid.

Kentucky Public Employees Are Shopping

The shopper program has been popular among public employees. Through mid-2018, about 42 percent of eligible households used the program to look up information about prices and rewards, and 57 percent of those employees actively chose a more cost-effective provider. So far, the program has spread more rapidly among female employees, with 81 percent of shoppers being female. These overall levels of interest are consistent with public polling that has shown that more than eight out of 10 voters want the right to know the cost of non-emergency procedures ahead of time, and that about seven out of 10 support the idea of rewarding patients directly when they shop to save money.[340]

There are several reasons member engagement has been so strong. Program implementers devoted adequate attention and energy to three key areas: 1) spreading the word about the program so that awareness was high, 2) getting people to register for the program so that there were not any barriers or delays later on when they needed to shop for care, and 3) reminding people to use the program when they need to shop for care (for instance, by automatically mailing postcards to members when members miss an opportunity to earn an incentive).

Kentucky Public Employees Are Shopping for Different Services and Procedures

KEHP has found that of all the procedures and services currently eligible for shared savings, routine screenings and diagnostic imaging are the most commonly shopped services. The top

[340] Foundation for Government Accountability, "Poll: Voters want the right to shop for health care," Foundation for Government Accountability (2018), https://thefga.org/poll/poll-voters-want-right-shop-health-care/.

five most frequently shopped services are: 1) Mammogram, 2) MRI, 3) Colonoscopy, 4) CT Scan, and 5) Ultrasound. As the list of services expands over time, the shopping program will also potentially help lower out-of- pocket costs for employees with chronic health conditions.

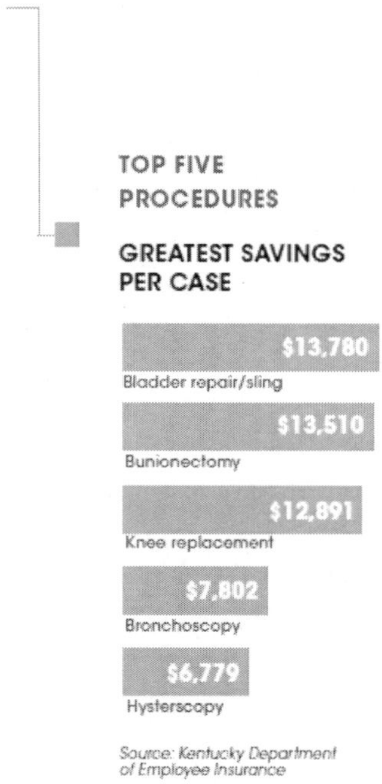

Shoppable Procedures and Rewards for Kentucky State Employees

SHOPPABLE PROCEDURES	PATIENT REWARD
Bronchoscopy	$200
Colonoscopy	$150
CT Scan Chest	$150
Eye Surgery – Cataract Removal	$150
Hip Replacement	$500
Mammogram	$25
MRI Lower Limb	$150
Shoulder Rotator Cuff Repair	$250
Ultrasound of Head and Neck	$50

Source: Vitals, incentive based on using the most cost-effective provider.

As expected, the services that generate the largest savings per case are not necessarily the same services that account for the greatest overall savings. According to data through May 2018, the top procedure in terms of savings per case was bladder repair surgery, and the top procedure in terms of cumulative savings were MRIs.

Most KEHP employees have an opportunity to pick a more cost-effective choice and receive an incentive. According to Vitals, 85 percent of KEHP members do not already go to low-cost providers. Moreover, the lower-cost options that the program helps to identify do not require a great amount of travel. The average distance that enrollees drive to save money is only eight miles.

Kentuckians Are Not Overusing Services or Sacrificing Quality

Skeptics expressed concerns that shopping incentives will lead to lower-quality care. However, the Kentucky experience reveals no evidence to suggest that consumers are sacrificing quality of care in order to save money. In fact, the opposite is true as patients are now making decisions based on location, cost, and quality for the first time.

Patients who shop around do not always choose the lowest cost option—many still choose a costlier procedure and forgo the cash incentive. In these cases, shoppers are freely expressing their preference, which could be based on an opinion they have about quality or other factors such as convenience and location.

Some have also speculated that shared savings will lead to overutilization. The experience at KEHP and at other cli- ents of Vitals SmartShopper show that this fear is unfounded. According to Vitals, KEHP has not experienced any unwarranted utilization spikes from people seeking care just to receive a cash reward. The one area in which Vitals has seen a slight increase in utilization is in recommended preventive services such as mammograms and colonoscopies, which most clinicians and observers would agree is a good thing and could eventually lower health care costs over the long run. In fact, outreach and education programs have specifically encouraged this change in patient behavior.

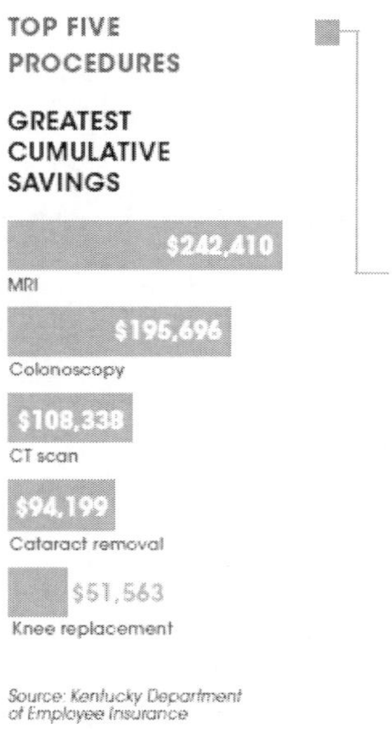

Kentucky's Shopper Program Could Reduce the Cost of Care in the Long Term

Not only does the Vitals SmartShopper program yield short-term benefits, it might also lead to long-term benefits for Kentuckians in the form of lower health care prices. In response to the price transparency initiative, some hospitals and imaging centers have become aware that their prices are high and have lowered their prices to rank higher on the lists provided to shoppers. For example, one high-cost regional hospital inquired how much they would need to lower their imaging rates to be listed competitively in the shopper program. Working with the provider and the health plan, the hospital lowered their imaging rates for MRIs and CTs by roughly 30 percent to rank higher in the shopper program.[341] Similarly, some providers that are already low- cost have reached out to Vitals to provide more information about additional services that they also offer at their locations at competitive prices, which can help expand the set of services eligible for incentives.

Lessons for Other States

At a time when most states have shifted at least some of their health care costs back to public employees, new approaches need to be explored that empower patients to help drive costs down long-term. States should consider offering shared savings incentives for smarter health care shopping in order to control health care costs and empower patients with choices.

> States should consider offering shared savings incentives for smarter health care shopping in order to control health care costs and empower patients with choices.

Appendix 1

NOTICE USED BY THE KENTUCKY EMPLOYEE HEALTH PLAN IN THE 2014 BENEFIT SELECTION GUIDE TO COMMUNICATE TO MEMBERS ABOUT THE TRANSPARENCY SHOPPING PROGRAM.

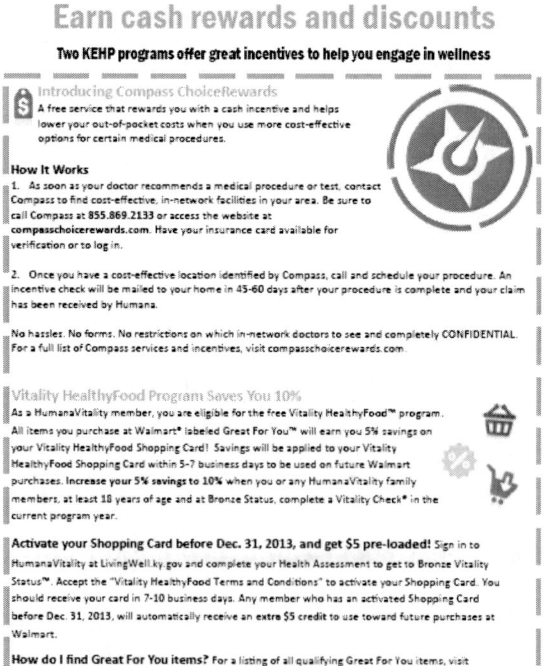

Earn cash rewards and discounts

Two KEHP programs offer great incentives to help you engage in wellness

Introducing Compass ChoiceRewards

A free service that rewards you with a cash incentive and helps lower your out-of-pocket costs when you use more cost-effective options for certain medical procedures.

How It Works

1. As soon as your doctor recommends a medical procedure or test, contact Compass to find cost-effective, in-network facilities in your area. Be sure to call Compass at 855.869.2133 or access the website at **compasschoicerewards.com**. Have your insurance card available for verification or to log in.

2. Once you have a cost-effective location identified by Compass, call and schedule your procedure. An incentive check will be mailed to your home in 45-60 days after your procedure is complete and your claim has been received by Humana.

No hassles. No forms. No restrictions on which in-network doctors to see and completely CONFIDENTIAL. For a full list of Compass services and incentives, visit compasschoicerewards.com.

Vitality HealthyFood Program Saves You 10%

As a HumanaVitality member, you are eligible for the free Vitality HealthyFood™ program. All items you purchase at Walmart* labeled Great For You™ will earn you 5% savings on your Vitality HealthyFood Shopping Card! Savings will be applied to your Vitality HealthyFood Shopping Card within 5-7 business days to be used on future Walmart purchases. **Increase your 5% savings to 10%** when you or any HumanaVitality family members, at least 18 years of age and at Bronze Status, complete a Vitality Check* in the current program year.

Activate your Shopping Card before Dec. 31, 2013, and get $5 pre-loaded! Sign in to HumanaVitality at LivingWell.ky.gov and complete your Health Assessment to get to Bronze Vitality Status™. Accept the "Vitality HealthyFood Terms and Conditions" to activate your Shopping Card. You should receive your card in 7-10 business days. Any member who has an activated Shopping Card before Dec. 31, 2013, will automatically receive an **extra $5 credit** to use toward future purchases at Walmart.

How do I find Great For You items? For a listing of all qualifying Great For You items, visit LivingWell.ky.gov and select "On Healthy Foods" in the Get Discounts box or call the number on the back of your member ID card. NOTE: Sam's Club stores and Walmart.com are excluded.

Compass SmartShopper was purchased and is now operated by Vitals SmartShopper.

[341] Information provided by Rob Graybill, Vice President of Product and Sales Strategy, Vitals, on July 17, 2018.

Appendix 2

NOTICE USED BY THE KENTUCKY EMPLOYEE HEALTH PLAN IN THE 2016 BENEFIT SELECTION GUIDE TO COMMUNICATE TO MEMBERS ABOUT THE TRANSPARENCY SHOPPING PROGRAM.

Vitals SmartShopper — Transparency Vendor

How fast can you earn up to $500?

How about 5 minutes?

STEP 1: Create a secure account

STEP 2: Shop online or by phone

STEP 3: Earn cash rewards

vitalssmartshopper

With the fully mobile Vitals SmartShopper™, you can shop common medical services from anywhere, including your doctor's office. When you choose a cost-effective location, you earn a cash reward!

Recent program enhancements include quality information and a helpful out-of-pocket cost calculator tool.

It only takes a minute to create a new account:

1. Visit www.vitalssmartshopper.com and click on the "First Time Users" tab.
2. In the Card I.D. # prompt, enter your Anthem I.D. number exactly as it appears on your insurance card.
3. Follow the prompts to fill in the remaining requested information and click "Login."

Congratulations! Your new account is created. Now you're ready to shop health care services and start earning cash rewards. Or register by phone at

Procedure	Your Reward
Colonoscopy	up to $150
CT Scans	up to $150
Ear, Nose & Throat	up to $150
Gall Bladder Removal	up to $250
Hip Replacement Surgery	up to $500
Knee Surgery	up to $250
Mammograms	up to $25
MRIs	up to $150
PET Scans	up to $150
Ultrasounds (non-maternity)	up to $50

This is a partial list of procedures covered. For a complete list, visit www.vitalssmartshopper.com. Dollar amounts vary depending on medical service and location.

[redacted]

HEALTHCARE
LEADERSHIP
COUNCIL

March 28, 2023

The Honorable Brett Guthrie
Chairman
Energy and Commerce Committee
Subcommittee on Health
Washington, D.C. 20515

The Honorable Anna Eshoo
Ranking Member
Energy and Commerce Committee
Subcommittee on Health
Washington, D.C. 20515

Dear Chairman Guthrie and Ranking Member Eshoo:

The Healthcare Leadership Council (HLC) appreciates the opportunity to provide comments in advance of your hearing, "Lowering Unaffordable Costs: Examining Transparency and Competition in Health Care."

HLC is a coalition of chief executives from all disciplines within American healthcare. It is the exclusive forum for the nation's healthcare leaders to jointly develop policies, plans, and programs to achieve their vision of a 21st century health system that makes affordable, high-quality care accessible to all Americans. Members of HLC – hospitals, academic health centers, health plans, pharmaceutical companies, medical device manufacturers, laboratories, biotech firms, health product distributors, post-acute care providers, home care providers, and information technology companies – advocate for policies that increase the quality and efficiency of healthcare by ensuring the development of new and improved lifesaving, life-enhancing medical innovations.

The Centers for Medicare and Medicaid Services (CMS) has issued transparency rules for hospitals and health plans. HLC supports bipartisan efforts to further deliver healthcare price and quality information to consumers, but we believe price transparency is a complex issue and we encourage much deliberation and further discussion to ensure consumers are receiving relevant information. HLC continues to work toward a future in which public and private sector healthcare organizations securely share information in an efficient, effective manner that utilizes standard formats and is useful and understandable to healthcare consumers.

HLC members have proven they can harness data to improve care and value in healthcare. There continue to be opportunities to work collectively toward a future of better healthcare and health by improving the accessibility and quality of health data to accelerate progress in medicines, technologies, and healthcare delivery. HLC members would like to highlight important key concepts that should be taken into consideration for any legislation addressing healthcare pricing transparency.

More specifically, HLC recommends eliminating unnecessary regulatory barriers that create a burdensome environment in our healthcare system.

1) Transparency of healthcare costs and payments must continue to provide information that is of practical use to consumers to allow them to make the right healthcare decisions. It is critically important that consumers be able to understand any pricing information that is made available.
2) Any sharing of cost or payment data with consumers should be released alongside information on quality to drive value in healthcare. There is a significant risk that consumers, when given pricing information without accompanying quality ratings, could make erroneous assumptions about quality based on cost – defeating our efforts to drive toward better value. We urge Congress to take a thoughtful approach to the release of any cost data to ensure that it is presented in a way that allows consumers to make a judgment based on value rather than cost.
3) Lastly, HLC supports further efforts to modernize the current fraud-and-abuse legal framework in the context of new care delivery and payment models.

While CMS took an important first step to modernize the Stark laws and Anti-Kickback statute to allow for patient-centered collaborations, more work needs to be done. The regulations still leave barriers standing in the way for important healthcare sectors, including drug and device manufacturers and clinical laboratories, who are ready to work with physicians, hospitals, health plans and other stakeholders in innovative partnerships to improve value and protect and strengthen patient health. Congress can act to remove the barriers that continue to exist and open the door to these collaborations.

HLC and its members stand ready to work on healthcare price transparency policy with you and your colleagues. Please feel free to reach out to Tina Grande, Executive Vice President for Policy at the Healthcare Leadership Council at (202) 449-3433 or tgrande@hlc.org with any questions or for additional details.

Sincerely,

Mary R. Grealy President

FGA

Lowering Unaffordable Costs: Examining Transparency and Competition in Health Care

Jonathan Ingram, Vice President of Policy and Research
Hayden Dublois, Data and Analytics Director

America's health care system is built upon a lack of transparency. In most states, it is nearly impossible for individuals and families to compare the cost of health care services and procedures like they would when shopping for gas, groceries, or housing. This intentional lack of transparency confuses consumers, hides true costs, and drives up prices.[342]

In the past several years, the U.S. Department of Health and Human Services has updated several federal regulations that require hospitals and insurers to provide more transparency, introducing accountability into America's health care system.

Unfortunately, the Biden administration has done little to monitor compliance with these transparency requirements and has even unlawfully stopped enforcement.

State-Level Transparency Reforms Led to Federal Action

The Foundation for Government Accountability (FGA) has worked in more than a dozen states on health care transparency efforts for many years.[343,344] These states' experiences paved the way for— and helped inform—eventual federal action on transparency.[345,346] Indeed, FGA research on those experiences was relied upon in evaluating and proposing transparency rules.[347,348]

---

342 Hayden Dublois and Jonathan Ingram, "How America's hospitals are hiding the cost of health care," Foundation for Government Accountability (2022), https://thefga.org/research/americas- hospitals-are-hiding-the-cost-of-health-care.

343 Josh Archambault, "Right to shop: The next big thing in health care," Forbes (2016), https://www.forbes.com/sites/theapothecary/2016/08/05/right-to-shop-the-next-big-thing-in- health-care.

344 Josh Archambault et al., "Comments for CMS-1694-P," Foundation for Government Accountability (2018), https://www.regulations.gov/comment/CMS-2018-0046-0702.

345 Ibid.

346 Foundation for Government Accountability, "FGA applauds CMS's price transparency final rule," Foundation for Government Accountability (2019), https://thefga.org/press/fga-applauds-cms- price-transparency-final-rule.

347 Centers for Medicare and Medicaid Services, "Medicare and Medicaid programs: CY 2020 hospital outpatient PPS policy changes and payment rates and ambulatory surgical center payment system policy changes and payment rates – Price transparency requirements for hospitals to make standard charges public," U.S. Department of Health and Human Services (2023), https://www.govinfo.gov/content/pkg/FR-2019-11-27/pdf/2019-24931.pdf.

348 Josh Archambault et al., "Comments for CMS-1694-P," Foundation for Government Accountability (2018), https://www.regulations.gov/comment/CMS-2018-0046-0702.

The Biden Administration Is Not Enforcing Transparency Requirements

In 2022, FGA conducted an independent review of more than 6,400 hospitals, revealing widespread non-compliance with those transparency requirements.[349] Altogether, more than 63 percent of hospitals were not complying with the transparency rule.[350] Some of these hospitals refused to disclose cash prices, negotiated rates with private insurance plans, prices for some services, or even any prices at all.[351] In some states, non-compliance is even more pronounced. In Maryland, for example, just five percent of hospitals were complying with federal transparency requirements.[352]

Unfortunately, the Biden administration has done little to enforce these requirements. It took nearly a year and a half after the rule became effective for Centers for Medicare & Medicaid Services (CMS) to issue the first fines.[353] But even these actions were little more than a minor slap on the wrist. The only fines issued so far have gone to two hospitals in Georgia's Northside Hospital System.[354] However, the fine amounts levied after nearly 18 months of non-compliance totaled less than 0.1 percent of the hospital system's annual gross revenue.[355] Put another way, these fines represented just 40 minutes of the hospital system's annual revenue.[356]

Worse yet, the Biden administration is stonewalling efforts to shine light on its lack of enforcement. In March 2022, FGA filed a Freedom of Information Act (FOIA) request with CMS seeking information on warnings, corrective action plans, fines, and other penalties issued in relation to the hospital price transparency rule.[357] Although federal law gives agencies just 20 business days to respond to FOIA requests, the Biden administration refused to produce any records associated with the rule more than five months later, despite repeated follow up attempts.[358] This stonewalling led FGA to file a lawsuit against the Biden administration in federal court, forcing them to produce the relevant public records.[359,360,361] The federal court

349 Hayden Dublois and Jonathan Ingram, "How America's hospitals are hiding the cost of health care," Foundation for Government Accountability (2022), https://thefga.org/research/americas-hospitals-are-hiding-the-cost-of-health-care.

350 Ibid.

351 Ibid.

352 Ibid.

353 Ibid.

354 Ibid.

355 Ibid.

356 Ibid.

357 Ibid.

358 Ibid.

359 Ibid.

360 Foundation for Government Accountability, "FGA files lawsuit against the Biden administration's Centers for Medicare and Medicaid Services (CMS) for stonewalling requests regarding hospital price transparency," Foundation for Government Accountability (2022), https://thefga.org/press/fga-lawsuit-biden-cms-hospital-price-transparency.

361 Jonathan Ingram and Hayden Dublois, "Hospitals move to hike prices by 15% and Team Biden does nothing to stop it," New York Post (2022), https://nypost.com/2022/08/29/hospitals-move- to-hike-prices-by-15-and-team-biden-does-nothing-to-stop-it.

ordered the Biden administration to stop evading FGA's records request, though the litigation and related document production remains ongoing.[362]

Further, the Biden administration has issued unlawful guidance to actually block the enforcement of health care transparency rules, including transparency requirements for drug prices.[363] In March 2023, FGA filed suit in federal court to challenge these unlawful actions.[364,365]

FGA thanks the Subcommittee on Health for its commitment to making the health care system more transparent and accountable to the American people.

Presidential Documents

Federal Register
Vol. 84, No. 124
Thursday, June 27, 2019

Title 3-
The President

Executive Order 13877 of June 24, 2019

Improving Price and Quality Transparency in American Healthcare to Put Patients First

By the authority vested in me as President by the Constitution and the laws of the United States of America, it is hereby ordered as follows:

Section 1. Purpose. My Administration seeks to enhance the ability of patients to choose the healthcare that is best for them. To make fully informed decisions about their healthcare, patients must know the price and quality of a good or service in advance. With the predominant role that third- party payers and Government programs play in the American healthcare system, however, patients often lack both access to useful price and quality information and the incentives to find low-cost, high-quality care. Opaque pricing structures may benefit powerful special interest groups, such as large hospital systems and insurance companies, but they generally leave patients and taxpayers worse off than would a more transparent system.

---

[362] Foundation for Government Accountability, "Judge orders Biden's CMS to stop evading lawful requests for hospital price transparency records," Foundation for Government Accountability (2022), https://thefga.org/press/judge-biden-cms-stop-evading-requests-hospital-price- transparency.

[363] Foundation for Government Accountability, "FGA lawsuit filed in federal court against Biden officials to enforce drug price transparency rule," Foundation for Government Accountability (2023), https://thefga.org/additional-research/fga-lawsuit-filed-in-federal-court-against-biden- officials-to-enforce-drug-price-transparency-rule.

[364] Ibid.

[365] Brianna Herlihy, "Biden admin hit with lawsuit for ignoring Trump-era drug price transparency rule," Fox News (2023), https://www.foxnews.com/politics/biden-admin-hit-lawsuit-ignoring-trump-era-drug-price-transparency-rule.

Pursuant to Executive Order 13813 of October 12, 2017 (Promoting Healthcare Choice and Competition Across the United States), my Administration issued a report entitled "Reforming America's Healthcare System Through Choice and Competition." The report recommends developing price and quality transparency initiatives to ensure that healthcare patients can make well- informed decisions about their care. In particular, the report describes the characteristics of the most effective price transparency efforts: they distinguish between the charges that providers bill and the rates negotiated between payers and providers; they give patients proper incentives to seek information about the price of healthcare services; and they provide useful price compari- sons for "shoppable" services (common services offered by multiple providers through the market, which patients can research and compare before making informed choices based on price and quality).

Shoppable services make up a significant share of the healthcare market, which means that increasing transparency among these services will have a broad effect on increasing competition in the healthcare system as a whole. One study, cited by the Council of Economic Advisers in its 2019 Annual Report, examined a sample of the highest-spending categories of medical cases requiring inpatient and outpatient care. Of the categories of medical cases requiring inpatient care, 73 percent of the 100 highest- spending categories were shoppable. Among the categories of medical cases requiring outpatient care, 90 percent of the 300 highest-spending categories were shoppable. Another study demonstrated that the ability of patients to price-shop imaging services, a particularly fungible and shoppable set of healthcare services, was associated with a per-service savings of up to approximately 19 percent.

Improving transparency in healthcare will also further protect patients from harmful practices such as surprise billing, which occurs when patients re- ceive unexpected bills at highly inflated prices from out-of-network providers they had no opportunity to select in advance. On May 9, 2019, I announced principles to guide efforts to address surprise billing. The principles outline how patients scheduling appointments to receive facility-based care should have access to pricing information related to the providers and services they may need, and the out-of-pocket costs they may incur. Having access to this type of information in advance of care can help patients avoid excessive charges.

Making meaningful price and quality information more broadly available to more Americans will protect patients and increase competition, innovation, and value in the healthcare system.

Sec. 2. Policy. It is the policy of the Federal Government to ensure that patients are engaged with their healthcare decisions and have the information requisite for choosing the healthcare they want and need. The Federal Gov- ernment aims to eliminate unnecessary barriers to price and quality transparency; to increase the availability of meaningful price and quality information for patients; to enhance patients' control over their own healthcare resources, including through tax-preferred medical accounts; and to protect patients from surprise medical bills.

Sec. 3. Informing Patients About Actual Prices. (a) Within 60 days of the date of this order, the Secretary of Health and Human Services shall propose a regulation, consistent with applicable law, to require hospitals to publicly post standard charge information, including charges and information based on negotiated rates and for common or shoppable items and services, in an easy-to-understand, consumer-friendly, and machine-readable format using consensus-based data standards that will meaningfully inform patients' deci- sion making and allow patients to compare prices across hospitals. The regulation should require the posting of standard charge information for services, supplies, or fees billed by the hospital or provided by employees of the hospital. The regulation should also require hospitals to regularly update the posted information and establish a monitoring mechanism for the Secretary to ensure compliance with the posting requirement, as needed. (b) Within 90 days of the date of this order, the Secretaries of Health and Human Services, the Treasury, and Labor shall issue an advance notice of proposed rulemaking, consistent with applicable law, soliciting comment on a proposal to require healthcare providers, health insurance issuers, and self-insured group health plans to provide or facilitate access to informa- tion about expected out-of-pocket costs for items or services to patients before they receive care.

(c) Within 180 days of the date of this order, the Secretary of Health and Human Services, in consultation with the Attorney General and the Federal Trade Commission, shall issue a report describing the manners in which the Federal Government or the private sector are impeding healthcare price and quality transparency for patients, and providing rec- ommendations for eliminating these impediments in a way that promotes competition. The report should describe why, under current conditions, lower-cost providers generally avoid healthcare advertising.

Sec. 4. Establishing a Health Quality Roadmap. Within 180 days of the date of this order, the Secretaries of Health and Human Services, Defense, and Veterans Affairs shall develop a Health Quality Roadmap (Roadmap) that aims to align and improve reporting on data and quality measures across Medicare, Medicaid, the Children's Health Insurance Program, the Health Insurance Marketplace, the Military Health System, and the Veterans Affairs Health System. The Roadmap shall include a strategy for establishing, adopting, and publishing common quality measurements; aligning inpatient and outpatient measures; and eliminating low-value or counterproductive measures.

Sec. 5. Increasing Access to Data to Make Healthcare Information More Transparent and Useful to Patients. Within 180 days of the date of this order, the Secretary of Health and Human Services, in consultation with the Secretaries of the Treasury, Defense, Labor, and Veterans Affairs, and the Director of the Office of Personnel Management, shall increase access to de-identified claims data from taxpayer-funded healthcare programs and group health plans for researchers, innovators, providers, and entrepreneurs, in a manner that is consistent with applicable law and that ensures patient privacy and security. Providing access to this data will facilitate the develop- ment of tools that empower patients to be better informed as they make decisions related to healthcare goods and services. Access to this data will also enable researchers and entrepreneurs to locate inefficiencies and oppor- tunities for improvement, such as patterns of performance of medical proce- dures that are outside the recommended standards of care. Such data may be derived from the Transformed Medicaid Statistical Information System (T-MSIS) and other sources. As part of this process, the Secretary of Health and Human Services shall make a list of priority datasets that, if de-identified, could advance the policies set forth by this order, and shall report to the President on proposed plans for future release of these priority datasets and on any barriers to their release.

Sec. 6. Empowering Patients by Enhancing Control Over Their Healthcare Resources. (a) Within 120 days of the date of this order, the Secretary of the Treasury, to the extent consistent with law, shall issue guidance to expand the ability of patients to select high-deductible health plans that can be used alongside a health savings account, and that cover low-cost preventive care, before the deductible, for medical care that helps maintain health status for individuals with chronic conditions. (b) Within 180 days of the date of this order, the Secretary of the

Treasury, to the extent consistent with law, shall propose regulations to treat expenses related to certain types of arrangements, potentially including direct primary care arrangements and healthcare sharing ministries, as eligible medical expenses under section 213(d) of title 26, United States Code. (c) Within 180 days of the date of this order, the Secretary of the Treasury, to the extent consistent with law, shall issue guidance to increase the amount of funds that can carry over without penalty at the end of the year for flexible spending arrangements.

Sec. 7. Addressing Surprise Medical Billing. Within 180 days of the date of this order, the Secretary of Health and Human Services shall submit a report to the President on additional steps my Administration may take to implement the principles on surprise medical billing announced on May 9, 2019.

Sec. 8. General Provisions. (a) Nothing in this order shall be construed to impair or otherwise affect:

(i) the authority granted by law to an executive department or agency, or the head thereof; or

(ii) the functions of the Director of the Office of Management and Budget relating to budgetary, administrative, or legislative proposals.

b) This order shall be implemented consistent with applicable law and subject to the availability of appropriations.

c) This order is not intended to, and does not, create any right or benefit, substantive or procedural, enforceable at law or in equity by any party against the United States, its departments, agencies, or entities, its officers, employees, or agents, or any other person.

THE WHITE HOUSE,
June 24, 2019.

[FR Doc. 2019-13945
Filed 6-26-19; 11:15 am]
Billing code 3295-F9-P

Chris Severn QFR Responses

Lowering Unaffordable Costs: Examining Transparency and Competition in Health Care

Attachment 1—Additional Questions for the Record the Honorable Dan Crenshaw

Mr. Severn, I often think of the patient provider relationship. Services are ordered with the patient's best interest in mind, but in a large marketplace, there are often different treatment options available with varying cost.

1) What opportunities exist to make existing health pricing data meaningful to patients and providers, particularly before a service is actually provided in the exam room or at the point-of-service, so that we can lower costs?

First and foremost, the existing health pricing data must be adapted into consumer-friendly service packages. Healthcare prices are currently represented by over 10,000 hyper-granular medical billing codes that were not designed for a consumer audience. As a result, there is no common language for providers to communicate cost information to patients, and technology innovators working to improve the patient financial experience similarly lack the same standard.

To address this need, former CMS Administrator Seema Verma and Niyum Gandhi, CFO and Treasurer at Mass General Brigham, formed Project Clarity[366], a multi-stakeholder collaborative with an ultimate goal to empower adopters of existing price transparency regulations (payers, providers, technical implementers, etc.) to produce pricing information that is consumer-friendly. This work is supported technically by Turquoise Health, CareJourney, the Healthcare Cost Institute and others.

In 2022, this group published its first draft set of 10 open-source, consumer friendly service packages. It is committed to publishing another 100 service package definitions in 2023 for public use. The group aims for these service packages to become the lingua franca of Good Faith Estimates required by the No Surprises Act in 2023 and beyond.

Secondly, as you note, patients should not solely shoulder the burden to shop for affordable care. These healthcare prices must make their way into the primary care physician's workflow at the point of care. Technology innovators are working to embed healthcare pricing data into electronic health record software. However, for this technology to reach full impact on lowering costs, it is up to providers, health insurers and the government to properly incentivize referring providers to route patients towards more affordable care.

2) Which health services or procedures provide the greatest immediate opportunity for price transparency?

Outpatient services are particularly fit for immediate price transparency disruption if they meet the following criteria:

- High volume
- Low clinical variation in quality (commodity services provided in multiple locations)
- Moderately expensive (a few hundred to single digit thousands): These services fall below an insured patient's deductible but are high priced enough to incentivize shopping

These services are typically ordered by primary care physicians or specialty care physicians during a patient consult. The following service categories meet these criteria:

---

366 https://projectclarity.health/.

- High cost imaging (MRI, CT, PET)
- Routine outpatient surgical (Colonoscopy and diagnostic gastrointestinal services, certain biopsies, low-complexity orthopedic and cardiac services)
- Physician-administered injectable drugs (Part B drugs)
- High cost labs and diagnostic studies (e.g., Holter monitors or sleep studies)

While lower priced services such as office visits and therapy consults do not pose an immediate opportunity for significant price savings, as there is less rate variability and more weight placed on provider quality, patient outcomes may improve as these prices become public. Kaiser Family Foundation polling shows that 24% of adults have delayed doctor's office visits due to cost.[367]

Often, these cost concerns come from lack of education that preventive visits and consults are frequently covered or have low cost share for the patient. Preventive care can catch serious illness sooner, reducing overall costs of care for severe episodes.

As pricing innovation evolves alongside consumer education, more complex and high-priced hospital services will also be impacted by price transparency data. First, the industry must innovate to package complex care into more predictable, consumer-friendly episodes.

FAMILIESUSA
THE VOICE FOR HEALTH CARE CONSUMERS

May 2, 2023

The Honorable Brett Guthrie, Chair
Health Subcommittee
Committee on Energy and Commerce
U.S. House of Representatives
Washington, DC 20515

The Honorable Anna Eshoo, Ranking Member
Health Subcommittee
Committee on Energy and Commerce
U.S. House of Representatives
Washington, DC 20515

Dear Chairman Guthrie and Ranking Member Eshoo:

Thank you again for the opportunity to testify before the House Energy and Commerce Health Subcommittee at the March 28 hearing "Lowering Unaffordable Costs: Examining Transparency and Competition in Health Care." After the hearing, members of the Committee submitted questions for the record, which I've answered below.

If any committee members or staff would like to discuss these issues further, please contact Jane Sheehan, Director of Federal Relations at Families USA (JSheehan@familiesusa.org). It's an honor to support the committee's critical work to expand and improve access to high quality, affordable health care. Please don't hesitate to be in touch if there is anything more we can do to be of service to that shared mission.

---

[367] https://www.kff.org/health-costs/poll-finding/kff-health-tracking-poll-march-2022/.

Sincerely,

Sophia Tripoli, MPH
Senior Director of Health Policy Families USA

Sophia Tripoli, Senior Director of Health Policy, Families USA Answers to Questions for the Record
House Energy and Commerce Health Subcommittee
Lowering Unaffordable Costs: Examining Transparency and Competition in Health Care

March 28, 2023

Questions for the Record from the Honorable Cathy McMorris Rodgers

1) I was encouraged to read in the 2023 Medicare Trustees Report that CMS actions, including the removal of hip and knee procedures off the "inpatient only list" and allowing patients to receive and doctors to perform additional services in the more efficient and less expensive outpatient seFng, have reduced total Medicare expenditures and contributed to extending the program's solvency a little longer through 2031. How should Congress think about additional actions to enhance patient and provider choices by encouraging more services to be safely administered in the outpatient seFng?

Ensuring the solvency of the Medicare Trust Fund is vital to our efforts to make high-quality, affordable care accessible to all consumers. Inpatient settings are the most expensive settings in which health care services are delivered, and they should be reserved for the treatment of patients that need more intensive levels of care, whether due to severity of the health condition or clinical determination of need for extended observation and/or treatment necessitating a longer hospital stay.[368] Moving additional medical services to less expensive outpatient settings, when clinically safe and appropriate, is an important step to reducing high health care costs and ensuring health care resources are used effectively.

Importantly, Congress should continue to focus their legislative efforts on policy solutions that address the underlying drivers of unaffordable health care such as unchecked provider consolidation, particularly among hospitals, that allows large health care corporations to

---

[368] For instance, according to Medicare's Two-Midnight Rule, inpatient care is generally covered if the patient requires a hospital stay that is longer than two midnights, with certain exceptions. Otherwise, the expectation is for patients whose stays are shorter than two midnight to be treated with outpatient care. For more information, see *Fact Sheet: Two Midnight Rule,* CMS, October 13th, 2015, https://www.cms.gov/newsroom/fact-sheets/fact-sheet-two-midnight-rule-0.

leverage market power to drive up prices.[369] This includes addressing underlying distortions in payment systems such as site of service payment differentials that incentivize hospitals to buy independent physicians' offices and rebrand them as outpatient facilities in order to generate higher reimbursements and increase prices.[370] Policy solutions that address these broken financial incentives such as site neutral payment are critical to increase competition and lower health care costs for the American people.

We also encourage Congress to consider additional reforms to Medicare that would shore up the Medicare Trust Fund, such as strengthening oversight of improper billing and upcoding in Medicare Advantage plans.[371]

a) Would allowing more procedures to be done in outpatient seFngs, like Ambulatory Surgery Centers, enhance competition among providers and encourage hospitals to compete with ASCs and other hospitals who offer outpatient services?

The U.S. health care system should be designed to ensure medical services are delivered in the safest, most effective, and least expensive care setting possible. This is a fundamental principle in the efficient allocation of health care dollars and resources.[372]

Under the current Medicare payment system, hospitals and other health care facilities are reimbursed at a higher rate for medical services performed in hospital outpatient departments (HOPDs) and other "provider-based" outpatient facilities than for the same services performed in a physician's office or ambulatory surgical center (ASC), even when the services can be delivered safely in either setting.[373,374,375,376]

These misaligned payment incentives entice large hospital corporations and health systems to drive care delivery into higher-cost settings, often resulting in hospitals buying up doctors' offices in order to rebrand them as HOPDs to get higher reimbursements. This practice leads to increasingly anticompetitive markets where large hospital corporations have outsized market power and can demand higher prices for all consumers.[377]

---

369 Emily Gee, Ethan Gurwitz, *Provider Consolidation Drives up Health Care Costs,* Center for American Progress, December 5, 2018, , https://www.americanprogress.org/article/provider-consolidation-drives-health-care-costs/

370 Karyn Shwartz, et al., *What We Know About Provider Consolidation,* KFF, September 2nd, 2020 What We Know About Provider Consolidation | KFF. See also, *Hospital Acquisition of Physician Practices Drives up Cost,* AHIP, August 20th, 2021https://www.ahip.org/news/articles/hospital-acquisition-of-physician-practices-drives-up-cost

371 *Ten Options to Secure the Medicare Trust Fund,* CRFB, June 16th, 2022. Ten Options to Secure the Medicare Trust Fund | Committee for a Responsible Federal Budget (crfb.org)

372 "Medicare and the Health Care Delivery System Chapter 6, Aligning fee-for-service payment rates across ambulatory settings", MedPAC, June 2022 https://www.medpac.gov/wpcontent/uploads/2022/06/Jun22_MedPAC_Report_to_Congress_SEC.pdf.

373 84 Fed. Reg. 39616.

374 Amanda Cassidy, "Site-Neutral Payments", Health Affairs, July 24th, 2014, https://www.healthaffairs.org/do/10.1377/hpb20140724.283836.

375 Eric Lopez, "How Much More Than Medicare Do Private Insurers Pay? A Review of the Literature", April 15th, 2020 https://www.kff.org/medicare/issue-brief/how-much-more-than-medicare-do-private-insurers-pay-a-review-of-the-literature/.

376 Jeffrey Clemens, Joshua Gottlieb, "In the Shadow of a Giant: Medicare's Influence on Private Physician Payments", December 16th, 2016https://www.ncbi.nlm.nih.gov/pmc/articles/PMC5509075/.

377 Michael E. Chernew, "Disparities in Payment Across Sites Encourages Consolidation", January 27th, 2021 https://www.ncbi.nlm.nih.gov/pmc/articles/PMC7839635/.

The broken payment incentives driving care towards higher-cost HOPDs not only contribute to anticompetitive markets and higher health care costs overall, but also have direct negative financial impacts on individual patients.[378] For example, Medicare beneficiaries pay higher copays at hospital outpatient departments than they do in physician offices. Ultimately this means patients are getting hit financially in multiple ways – in the form of higher copays for specific services, and again in the form of higher premiums and expenses resulting from excess costs to Medicare that occur when HOPDs are paid more than twice as much as physicians for the same service.[379]

b) Does research and existing data suggest patients would still be able to receive quality and safe care for certain additional services in outpatient settings?

Research points to a number of medical services that can be safely and effectively delivered in lower cost settings such as a physician's office instead of a more expensive hospital-based setting.[380] In fact, a variety of medical services that were once exclusively delivered on an inpatient basis are routinely being delivered safely and effectively in outpatient and ambulatory settings, including endoscopies, colonoscopies, and cataract surgeries.[381] Based on MedPAC analysis and recommendations, we urge Congress to enact site neutral payment policies for select medical services that can be safely delivered in multiple care settings, ending the longstanding distortion in the Medicare payment system that incentives big hospital corporations to buy physician practices and shift health care services to higher cost settings.[382]

Questions for the Record from the Honorable Frank Pallone, Jr.

Hospital mergers and acquisitions have been increasing. 90 percent of metropolitan hospital markets in the U.S. are highly concentrated, and many regions are dominated by a single system.

Studies suggest health care in industry consolidation is driving up the prices of health care services for families.

1) Can you describe some of the trends you are seeing and explain the incentives for growing industry consolidation?

At its core, our nation's affordability crisis is driven by a fundamental misalignment between the business interests of the health care sector and the health and financial security of our nation's families – a business model that allows industry to set prices that have little to do with the quality of the care they offer. These high and irrational prices are largely due to trends

[378] Department of Health and Human Services Office of Inspector General, June 2022 https://oig.hhs.gov/oas/reports/region7/71802815.pdf.

[379] 84 FR 39616, August 9, 2019.

[380] "Report to Congress: Medicare Payment Policy", MedPAC, March 2023 https://www.medpac.gov/wp-content/uploads/2023/03/Mar23_MedPAC_Report_To_Congress_SEC.pdf.

[381] Ibid. See also, Michael Abrams, "Accelerating the Shift of Care to Lower Cost Settings", March 11th, 2019 Accelerating the Shift of Care to Lower Cost Settings (ajmc.com).

[382] Ibid.

in health care industry consolidation that have eliminated competition and allowed monopolistic pricing to push our nation's families to the brink of financial ruin.[383]

America's health care affordability crisis stems from high, rising, and variable prices across a wide range of health care goods and services, including prescription drugs and diagnostic tools such as MRIs and CT scans. For example, the price of Humira — a drug used to treat arthritis — is more than four times as expensive in our country as in the United Kingdom and almost twice as expensive as in Germany.[384] The average price of a hospital-based MRI in the United States is $1,475.[385] That same scan costs $503 in Switzerland and $215 in Australia.[386] These higher prices for an identical service are the main driver of the dramatic increase in per capita health care spending in our country, where health care accounted for nearly 20% of the nation's GDP in 2020, far exceeding health care spending by any other industrialized country.[387]

These irrational and unjustifiable prices are largely due to trends in health care industry consolidation that have eliminated competition and allowed monopolistic pricing to flourish.[388] This consolidation has taken place without meaningful regulatory oversight or intervention, and is becoming more acute.[389] In fact, there are few truly competitive health care markets left, with 95% of metropolitan statistical areas (MSAs) having highly concentrated hospital markets, nearly 80% of MSAs having highly concentrated specialist physician markets, and 58% of MSAs having highly concentrated insurer markets.[390]

---

383 Robert A. Berenson et al., "Addressing Health Care Market Consolidation and High Prices", The Urban Institute https://www.urban.org/sites/default/files/publication/101508/addressing_health_care_market_consolidation_and_high_prices_1.pdf. See also, Naomi N. Levey, "100 Million People in America are Saddled with Health Care Debt," Kaiser Health News, June 16, 2022, Health https://khn.org/news/article/diagnosis-debt-investigation-100-million- americans-hidden-medical-debt/.

384 Nisha Kurani, Dustin Cotliar, and Cynthia Cox, "How Do Prescription Drug Costs in the United States Compare to Other Countries?" Peterson-KFF Health System Tracker, February 8, 2022, https://www.healthsystemtracker.org/.

385 18 Michael Chernew et al., "Are Health Care Services Shoppable? Evidence from the Consumption of Lower-Limb MRI Scans", Working Paper 24869 Cambridge, MA: National Bureau of Economic Research, July 2018, revised January 2019https://www.nber.org/system/files/working_papers/w24869/w24869.pdf.

386 Sarah Kliff, "The Problem Is the Prices: Opaque and Sky High Bills Are Breaking Americans — and Our Health Care System," Vox, October 16, 2017, https://www.vox.com/policy-and-politics/2017/10/16/16357790/health-care- pricesproblem.

387 Emma Wager, Jared Ortaliza, and Cynthia Cox, "How Does Health Spending in the U.S. Compare to Other Countries?" Peterson-KFF Health System Tracker, January 21, 2022, https://www.healthsystemtracker.org/chart-collection/healthspending-u-s-compare-countries-2/#GDP%20per%20capita%20and%20health%20consumption%20spending%20 per%20capita,%202020%20(U.S.%20dollars,%20PPP%20adjusted).

388 Robert A. Berenson et al., Addressing Health Care Market Consolidation and High Prices, The Urban Institute https://www.urban.org/sites/default/files/publication/101508/addressing_health_care_market_consolidation_and_high_prices_1.pdf. See also, Congressional Budget Office, "Policy Approaches to Reduce What Commercial Insurers Pay for Hospitals' and Physicians' Services", September 2022. https://www.cbo.gov/system/files/2022-09/58222-medical-prices.pdf.

389 Gerard Anderson and Peter Hussey, and Varduhi Petrosyan, "It's Still the Prices, Stupid: Why the US Spends So Much on Health Care, and a Tribute to Uwe Reinhardt," Health Affairs 38, 2019, https://www.healthaffairs.org/doi/10.1377/.

390 Jaime S. King et al., "Preventing Anticompetitive Healthcare Consolidation: Lessons from Five States" Center on Health Care Markets and Consumer Welfare of the University of California Berkeley School of Public Health, June 2020, https://sourceonhealthcare.org/profile/preventing-anticompetitive-healthcare-consolidation-lessons-from- five-states/.

- Hospital consolidation: Hospital mergers are occurring more frequently both within and across health care markets, leading to higher prices in both cases. According to the American Hospital Association, there were 1,577 hospital mergers from 1998 to 2017.[391],[392] An estimated 40% of those mergers took place from 2010 to 2015.[393]
- *Insurance consolidation:* Insurance markets are not as highly concentrated as providers, but there is evidence of markets with little competition between insurers. Between 2006 and 2014, the four-firm concentration ratio —the extent of market control held by the four largest firms, Aetna, Blue Cross Blue Shield, United and Anthem — for the sale of private insurance increased from 74% to 83%.[394]
- *Vertical Integration:* The number of hospital-acquired physician practices grew from 35,700 in 2012 to more than 80,000 in 2018.[395] Over this same time period, the percentage of physicians employed by a hospital or health system nearly doubled, from 25% to 44%.[396] Recent research found that over 55% of physicians are now employed in hospital-owned practices.[397] This trend was accelerated by the COVID-19 pandemic, which exacerbated the financial vulnerabilities of independent and smaller physician practices and threatened the near collapse of entire sectors of the health care system — particularly primary care.[398] Nearly 23,000 physicians left independent practice to work for a hospital or other corporate entity after the onset of the COVID-19 pandemic, while hospitals and other corporate entities acquired nearly 21,000 additional physician practices from 2019 to 2020, representing a 25% increase in corporate-owned practices.[399]

Nowhere is the negative impact of consolidation more evident than the rising cost of hospital stays and services, which have increased dramatically in the last decade and make up

---

391 "Chart 2.9: Announced Hospital Mergers and Acquisitions, 1998–2015," TrendWatch Chartbook 2016, American Hospital Association, 2016.

392 Chart 2.9: Announced Hospital Mergers and Acquisitions, 2005–2017," TrendWatch Chartbook 2018: Trends Affecting Hospitals and Health Systems, American Hospital Association, 2018.

393 Martin Gaynor, "Examining the Impact of Health Care Consolidation," statement before the U.S. House Committee on Energy and Commerce Oversight and Investigations Subcommittee, February 14, 2018.

394 Leemore S. Dafny, "Evaluating the Impact of Health Insurance Industry Consolidation: Learning from Experience," The Commonwealth Fund, November 2015, https://www.commonwealthfund.org/publications/issue-briefs/2015/nov/evaluatingimpact-health-insurance-industry-consolidation.

395 "Updated Physician Practice Acquisition Study: National and Regional Changes in Physician Employment, 2012-2018," Physicians Advocacy Institute (PAI), February 2019, http://www.physiciansadvocacyinstitute.org/Portals/0/assets/docs/021919-Avalere-PAI-Physician-Employment-Trends-Study-2018-Update.pdf?ver=2019-02-19-162735-117.

396 PAI, "Physician Practice Acquisition Study."

397 Shruthi Venkatesh, "The Impact of Hospital Acquisition on Physician Referrals." Carnegie Mellon University, Pittsburgh, 2019.

398 Avalere Health, "COVID-19's Impact on Acquisitions of Physician Practices and Physician Employment 2019-2020," Physicians Advocacy Institute, June 2021, http://www.physiciansadvocacyinstitute.org/Portals/0/assets/docs/Revised-6-8-21_PAI-PhysicianEmployment-Study-2021-FINAL.pdf?ver=K6dyoekRSC_c59U8QD1V-A%3D%3D.

399 Ibid.

a large portion of increasing health care costs overall.[400,401,402] These cost increases have occurred despite lower hospital utilization and are largely due to escalating prices, which are the result of hospitals buying other hospitals and community doctors to eliminate competition and form big health care corporations and medical monopolies.[403,404]

Americans in many communities have watched as their local hospitals became health systems, and those health systems were bought by large health care corporations. What most in the public and policymaking community have not realized is how much this has destroyed any real competition in our health care sector; allowing hospitals to dramatically increase their prices every year.[405],[406] Between 1990 and 2023, hospital prices have increased 600% - and just since 2015, hospital prices have increased as much as 31% nationally, now accounting for nearly one-third of U.S. health care spending, and growing more than four times faster than workers' paychecks.[407,408,409,410]

High and Irrational Prices Fueled by a Lack of Transparency

Importantly, hospital prices are not only high, but have become essentially irrational:

- In 2020, across all hospital inpatient and outpatient services, employers and private insurers paid on average 224% of what Medicare pays for the same services.[411]
- Prices at hospitals in concentrated markets are 12% higher than those in markets with four or more rivals without any demonstrated improvement in the quality or access to

---

400 "2020 Health Care Cost and Utilization Report", Health Care Cost Institute, May 2022. https://healthcostinstitute.org/images//pdfs/HCCI_2020_Health_Care_Cost_and_Utilization_Report.pdf.

401 Emily Gee, *The High Price of Hospital Care*, Center for American Progress, June 26, 2019 https://www.americanprogress.org/article/high-price-hospital-care/.

402 Nisha Kurani and Cynthia Cox, "What drives health spending in the U.S. compared to other countries" Peterson-KFF Health System Tracker, September 25, 2020, https://www.healthsystemtracker.org/. See also, Zack Cooper, et al., *Hospital Prices Grew Substantially Faster Than Physician Prices for Hospital Based Care in 2007-14*. Health Affairs, February 2019. https://doi.org/10.1377/hlthaff.2018.05424.

403 "2020 Health Care Cost and Utilization Report", Health Care Cost Institute, May 2022. https://healthcostinstitute.org/images//pdfs/HCCI_2020_Health_Care_Cost_and_Utilization_Report.pdf.

404 Robert A. Berenson et al., *Addressing Health Care Market Consolidation and High Prices*, The Urban Institute https://www.urban.org/sites/default/files/publication/101508/addressing_health_care_market_consolidation_and_high_prices_1.pdf.

405 Martin Gaynor, "What to Do About Health-Care Markets? Policies to Make Health-Care Markets Work", March 2020 https://www.brookings.edu/wp-content/uploads/2020/03/Gaynor_PP_FINAL.pdf.

406 Robert A. Berenson et al., *Addressing Health Care Market Consolidation and High Prices*, The Urban Institute https://www.urban.org/sites/default/files/publication/101508/addressing_health_care_market_consolidation_and_high_prices_1.pdf.

407 Nisha Kurani and Cynthia Cox, "What drives health spending in the U.S. compared to other countries" Peterson-KFF Health System Tracker, September 25, 2020, https://www.healthsystemtracker.org/.

408 Drew DeSilver, "For Most U.S. Workers, Real Wages Have Barely Budged in Decades," Pew Research Center, August 7, 2018, https://www.pewresearch.org/fact-tank/2018/08/07/for-most-us-workers-real-wages-have-barely-budged-fordecade.

409 "2020 Health Care Cost and Utilization Report", Health Care Cost Institute, May 2022. https://healthcostinstitute.org/images//pdfs/HCCI_2020_Health_Care_Cost_and_Utilization_Report.pdf.

410 "The Healthcare Cost Crisis: An American Epidemic" West Health https://healthcostcrisis.org/.

411 Whaley, C. et al, "Prices Paid to Hospitals by Private Health Plans", RAND, 2022 https://www.rand.org/pubs/research_reports/RRA1144-1.html.

care.[412],[413],[414] All the while, the workforce in these concentrated markets suffers - wages for nurses and other health care workers decrease significantly after mergers and acquisitions.[415]

- Prices for the exact same service vary widely, sometimes even within a single hospital system:
  - A colonoscopy at a single medical center in Mississippi can range from $782 to $2,144 depending on insurance.[416]
  - At one health system in Wisconsin, an MRI costs between $1,093 and $4,029 depending on level of insurance.[417]
  - Across the country, the average price for a knee replacement ranges from $21,976 in Tucson, Arizona to $60,000 in Sacramento California.[418]
  - The price of an MRI at Mass General Hospital in Boston Massachusetts ranged from $830 to $4,200 depending on the insurance carrier.[419]

What's more, consumers and employers, who are the ultimate purchasers of health care, have limited insight into what the prices of health care services are, until after they've received a bill. For the majority of Americans – 66% – who receive health care through private insurance,[420] health care prices are established in closed-door negotiations between large hospital corporations and health plans based on who has more market power.[421] These health care prices, often referred to as the negotiated rate, are buried in proprietary contracts without insight into or oversight over the price of health care services by the public and policymakers.[422] Health care is one of the only markets in the U.S. economy in which consumers are blinded to

---

412 Cooper, Z. et al, "The Price Ain't Right? Hospital Prices and Health Spending on the Privately Insured", The Quarterly Journal of Economics, 2019. https://academic.oup.com/qje/article-abstract/134/1/51/5090426?redirectedFrom=fulltext&login=false.

413 Martin Gaynor, "Diagnosing the Problem: Exploring the Effects of Consolidation and Anticompetitive Conduct in Health Care Markets. Statement before the Committee on the Judiciary Subcommittee on Antitrust, Commercial, and Administration Law", U.S. House of Representatives, March 7th, 2019. https://www.congress.gov/116/meeting/house/109024/witnesses/HHRG-116-JU05-Bio-GaynorM-20190307.pdf.

414 "The Impact of Hospital Consolidation on Medical Costs" NCCI Insights, July 11th, 2018. https://www.ncci.com/Articles/Pages/II_Insights_QEB_Impact-of-Hospital-Consolidation-on-Medical-Costs.aspx.

415 Prager, E. Schmitt, M, "Employer Consolidation and Wages: Evidence from Hospitals". American Economic Association, February 2021 https://www.aeaweb.org/articles?id=10.1257/aer.20190690.

416 Sara Kliff, Josh Katz, " Hospitals and Insurers Didn't Want You to See These Prices. Here's Why" The New York Times, August 22nd, 2021 https://www.nytimes.com/interactive/2021/08/22/upshot/hospital-prices.html.

417 Ibid.

418 National Chartbook of Health Care Prices, The Health Care Cost Institute, 2016. https://healthcostinstitute.org/national-chartbook-health-care-prices-2015.

419 Sara Kliff, Josh Katz, "Hospitals and Insurers Didn't Want You to See These Prices. Here's Why" The New York Times, August 22nd, 2021 https://www.nytimes.com/interactive/2021/08/22/upshot/hospital-prices.html.

420 US Census, Health Insurance Coverage in the United States, 2020, https://www.census.gov/library/publications/2021/demo/p60-274.html.

421 Sara Kliff, Josh Katz, "Hospitals and Insurers Didn't Want You to See These Prices. Here's Why" The New York Times, August 22nd, 2021 https://www.nytimes.com/interactive/2021/08/22/upshot/hospital-prices.html.

422 Jaime King, Testimony before the House Committee on Energy and Commerce and Subcommittee on Oversight and Investigations, July 17, 2018, https://democrats-energycommerce.house.gov/sites/democrats.energycommerce.house.gov/files/documents/Testimony-King-OI-Hrg-on-Examining-State-Efforts-to-Improve-Transparency-of-Health-Care-Cost-2018-07-17.pdf.

the price of a service until they receive a bill after the services is delivered.[423] It is the epitome of a broken market that threatens the financial security of American families and fails to serve their needs.

2) Can you briefly describe how consolidation impacts affordability and quality of care for consumers?

Unchecked industry consolidation, particularly among large hospital corporations, has allowed hospitals to dramatically increase their prices every year.[424] Between 1990 and 2023, hospital prices have increased 600% - and just since 2015, hospital prices have increased as much as 31% nationally, now accounting for nearly one-third of U.S. health care spending, and growing more than four times faster than workers' paychecks.[425,426,427,428]

Commercial health care prices are not only high but also vary widely across the United States because of this unchecked industry consolidation. Two individuals living in two different cities, even those in close proximity and with a similar cost of living, can be paying significantly different prices for health care with no connection to input costs or care quality. For example, the average price for a knee replacement for a patient in Tucson, Arizona, is $21,976, while the same procedure costs about $38,000 more in Sacramento, California.[429] Patients in New Mexico pay about 25% above the national average of health care prices, while those in Arizona pay 15% below the national average.[430] Prices also can vary significantly within a U.S. health care market — even within a single hospital system. For example, the price of an MRI at Mass General Hospital in Boston, Massachusetts, ranged from $830 to $4,200, depending on the insurance carrier.[431]

These irrational and unjustifiable prices, largely due to trends in health care industry consolidation that have eliminated competition and allowed monopolistic pricing to flourish, are directly harming the financial security and health and well-being of Americans across the country.[432] Almost half of all Americans have reported having to forgo medical care due to the

---

423 Danielle Scheurer, "Lack of Transparency Plagues U.S. Health Care System", The Hospitalist, May 1, 2013. https://www.the-hospitalist.org/hospitalist/article/125866/health-policy/lack-transparency-plagues-us-health- care-system.

424 Michael Chernew et al., "Are Health Care Services Shoppable? Evidence from the Consumption of Lower-Limb MRI Scans, Working Paper 24869" (Cambridge, MA: National Bureau of Economic Research, July 2018, revised January 2019), https://www.nber.org/system/files/working_papers/w24869/w24869.pdf.

425 Nisha Kurani and Cynthia Cox, "What drives health spending in the U.S. compared to other countries" Peterson-KFF Health System Tracker, September 25, 2020, https://www.healthsystemtracker.org/.

426 Drew DeSilver, "For Most U.S. Workers, Real Wages Have Barely Budged in Decades," Pew Research Center, August 7, 2018, https://www.pewresearch.org/fact-tank/2018/08/07/for-most-us-workers-real-wages-have-barely-budged-fordecade.

427 "2020 Health Care Cost and Utilization Report", Health Care Cost Institute, May 2022. https://healthcostinstitute.org/images//pdfs/HCCI_2020_Health_Care_Cost_and_Utilization_Report.pdf.

428 "The Healthcare Cost Crisis: An American Epidemic" West Health https://healthcostcrisis.org/.

429 Alison Kodjak, "That Surgery Might Cost You a Lot Less in Another Town, "National Public Radio, April 27, 2016, https://www.npr.org/sections/health-shots/2016/04/27/475880565/that-surgery-might-cost-you-a-lot-less-in-another-town.

430 Ibid.

431 Sara Kliff, Josh Katz, "Hospitals and Insurers Didn't Want You to See These Prices. Here's Why" The New York Times, August 22nd, 2021 https://www.nytimes.com/interactive/2021/08/22/upshot/hospital-prices.html.

432 Robert A. Berenson et al., Addressing Health Care Market Consolidation and High Prices, The Urban Institute https://www.urban.org/sites/default/files/publication/101508/addressing_health_care_market_consolidation_and

cost, and almost a third have indicated that the high cost of medical care is interfering with their ability to secure basic needs like food and housing,[433] and over 40 percent of American adults – 100 million people – face medical debt.[434] High and rising health care costs are a critical problem for national and state governments, and affect the economic vitality of middle-class and working families, crippling the ability of working people to earn a living wage. Today's real wages — wages after accounting for inflation — are roughly the same as four decades ago, while employer health insurance premiums have risen dramatically.[435] At the same time, nearly 90% of large employers say that rising health care costs will threaten their ability to provide health care benefits to employees over the next five to 10 years if costs are not lowered.[436]

3) Recent investigations into hospital closures have raised concerns about the role of private equity in health care. Can you describe how private equity arrangements may impact affordability and patient access to care?

The role of private equity in driving unaffordable health care and impacting patient access to care is most evident around the abusive practice of surprise medical billing, where many private equity firms built an entire business model around keeping certain providers out of network in order to balance bill America's families.[437] There is also evidence that private equity ownership of hospitals is creating conditions that lead to poorer quality of care and worse patient outcomes.[438] One study found that private equity owned hospitals have lower patient satisfaction scores and fewer full time equivalent employees per occupied bed, the latter of which is consistently associated with lower quality care and poorer patient health outcomes.[439],[440],

There are numerous examples of private equity firms buying up hospitals, diverting resources away from medical care and into administrative spending, often in the form of fees to the private equity firms themselves, and then closing critical hospital services or entire

_high_prices_1. pdf. See also, Congressional Budget Office, Policy Approaches to Reduce What Commercial Insurers Pay for Hospitals' and Physicians' Services, September 2022. https://www.cbo.gov/system/files/2022-09/58222- medical-prices.pdf.

433 "Americans' Views on Healthcare Costs, Coverage and Policy", NORC at the University of Chicago and West Health, March 2018 https://www.norc.org/NewsEventsPublications/PressReleases/Pages/survey-finds-large-number-of-people-skipping-necessarymedical-care-because-cost.aspx.

434 Naomi N. Levey, "100 Million People in America are Saddled with Health Care Debt", Kaiser Health News, June 16, 2022, https://khn.org/news/article/diagnosis-debt-investigation-100-million-americans-hidden-medical-debt/.

435 Drew DeSilver, "For Most U.S. Workers, Real Wages Have Barely Budged in Decades," Pew Research Center, August 7, 2018, https://www.pewresearch.org/fact-tank/2018/08/07/for-most-us-workers-real-wages-have-barely-budged-fordecade. See also, Gary Claxton et al., Health Benefits in 2022: Premiums Remain Steady, Many Employers Report Limited Provider Networks for Behavioral Health. Health Affairs, October 27, 2022. https://www.healthaffairs.org/stoken/tollfree/2022_11_CLAXTON/full.

436 "Vast Majority of Large Employers Surveyed Say Broader Government Role Will Be Necessary to Control Health Costs and Provide Coverage, Survey Finds," Kaiser Family Foundation, April 29, 2021, Vast Majority of Large Employers Surveyed Say Broader Government Role Will Be Necessary to Control Health Costs and Provide Coverage, Survey Finds | KFF.

437 https://www.arnoldventures.org/stories/part-3-as-purveyors-of-surprise-medical-billing-private-equity-has-fought-lawmakers-attempts-to-protect-patients.

438 https://bfi.uchicago.edu/insight/research-summary/does-private-equity-investment-in-healthcare-benefit-patients-evi dence-from-nursing-homes/.

439 https://www.ncbi.nlm.nih.gov/pmc/articles/PMC9125965/.

440 How Inadequate Hospital Staffing Continues to Burn Out Nurses and Threaten Patients - Penn LDI (upenn.edu).

facilities.[441,442] The result is reduced access and availability of key health care services for marginalized and medically underserved communities such as those based in rural areas.[443,444,445]

Questions for the Record from the Honorable Robin Kelly

1) Can you discuss how the final rule can help policymakers better understand the drivers of healthcare costs and implement policies to improve affordability?

The Hospital Price Transparency Rule is a critical step towards meaningful health care price transparency, for the first-time requiring hospitals to release negotiated rates with insurers. In order to be useful for consumers, all hospitals must comply with the rule and CMS must standardize how hospitals report this information to maximize its effectiveness.

Unveiling the prices of health care goods and services allows consumers and employers to become better informed, empowered purchasers of health care. It also enables researchers and policymakers to analyze prices in U.S. health markets in order to make targeted policy decisions that drive high-value care across the health care system.[446] The most critical pricing information to support that work is the negotiated rate for a service, which is widely recognized as the underlying price of health care goods and services.[447] But revealing prices alone is not enough. To provide a comprehensive view into U.S. health care markets and truly drive healthy competition, price must be paired together with data on quality so that consumers, employers, policymakers, and researchers can assess the actual value of health care services and goods.[448]

Unveiling health care prices and quality data has the power to disrupt the status quo by shifting market dynamics. It would force the health care sector to compete based on rational prices and quality of care rather than predicating success on the ability to buy up competition, price gouge, and generate a high volume of high-priced services that do not improve patient

---

441 Buy and Bust: When Private Equity Comes for Rural Hospitals | KFF Health News; "Less about people and more about profits": Investors' role in next week's closure of San Antonio hospital under scrutiny - CBS News; Hospital shutdown in Pennsylvania spurs questions about private equity in health care - CBS News.

442 Sajith Matthews, Renato Roxas, "Private equity and its effect on patients: a window into the future", May 23rd, 2022https://www.ncbi.nlm.nih.gov/pmc/articles/PMC9125965/.

443 Jonathan Lapook, et al, April 2^{5th,} 2023 "Less about people and more about profits": Investors' role in next week's closure of San Antonio hospital under scrutiny - CBS News.

444 Sajith Matthews, Renato Roxas, "Private equity and its effect on patients: a window into the future", May 23rd, 2022. https://www.ncbi.nlm.nih.gov/pmc/articles/PMC9125965/.

445 Jonathan Lapook, Michael Kaplan, December 6, 2022 https://www.cbsnews.com/news/pennsylvania-delaware-county-memorial-hospital-shutdown-private-equity-health-care/.

446 Robert A. Berenson et al., Addressing Health Care Market Consolidation and High Prices: The Role of the States (Washington, DC: Urban Institute, January 2020), https://www. urban.org/sites/default/files/publication/ 101508/addressing_health_care_market_consolidation_and_high_prices_3. Pdf.; Jaime S. King, "Examining State Efforts to Improve Transparency in Healthcare Costs for Consumers," testimony before the U.S. House Committee on Energy and Commerce and Subcommittee on Oversight and Investigations, July 17, 2018, https://democrats-energycommerce.house.gov/sites/democrats.energycommerce.house.gov/files/documents/ Testimony-King.

447 Kng, "Examining State Efforts."

448 Berenson et al., *Market Consolidation and High Prices;* King, "Examining State Efforts.

health. This shift is essential to align the business interests of the health care sector with the financial security and health outcomes of our nation's families.

2) What are some examples of industry gaming that is clouding the pricing data?

Hospitals are deploying various tactics to either buck price transparency requirements outright or make the information they disclose very hard to understand.[449] Many hospitals have posted no information on negotiated rates at all.[450] Some hospitals post incomplete required information (that is, using "NA" or blanks).[451] And other hospitals post prices in the form of a percentage of Medicare payment (for example, "120% of Medicare") or as a percentage of gross charges, even though the Hospital Price Transparency rule explicitly requires hospitals to list the standard charges, including negotiated rates for each individual item or service, rather than listing those prices as a percentage of a second value such as a Medicare payment rate wherever possible.[452]

Please see a recent Families USA report on price transparency for additional discussion of industry gaming of price transparency reporting.

Questions for the Record from the Honorable Angie Craig

According to a recent analysis published in the Minneapolis Star Tribune entitled "A Minnesota family's desperate search for care reveals state's mental health crisis", reimbursement for mental health generally is lower than for other diagnoses.

1) Can you explain this trend?

Unfortunately, Minnesota's experience is echoed in many other states that are experiencing acute shortages of behavioral health providers and behavioral health inpatient beds. Underpayment of behavioral health care relative to physical health care, by both commercial insurers and Medicaid, results in many providers staying out-of-network.[453,454] This effectively makes behavioral health care inaccessible to millions of people. There are many facets to

---

449. Sophia Tripoli and Adam Axler, The Power of Price Transparency: Unveiling Health Care Prices to Promote Accountability and Lower Costs, Families USA (April 19, 2023), https://familiesusa.org/resources/the-power-of-price-transparency-unveiling-health-care-prices-to-promote-accountability-and-lower-costs/; The Fourth Semi-Annual Hospital Price Transparency Compliance Report, PatientsRightsAdvocate.org, February 2023, https://www.patientrightsadvocate.org/february-semi-annual-compliance-report-2023; Justin Lo et al., "Ongoing Challenges with Hospital Price Transparency," Peterson-KFF Health System Tracker, February 10, 2023, https://www. healthsystemtracker.org/brief/ongoing-challenges-with-hospital-price-transparency/.

450 PatientRightsAdvocate.org, Price Transparency Report

451 PatientRightsAdvocate.org, Price Transparency Report.

452 45 C.F.R. Part 180.50(b) – Requirements for making public hospital standard charges for all items and services, Required data elements; U.S. Centers for Medicare and Medicaid Services (CMS), "Hospital Price Transparency Frequently Asked Questions," CMS.gov, last modified November 29, 2022, https://www.cms.gov/files/document/hospital-price-transparency-frequently-asked-questions.pdf.

453 Sarah Kliff, "The Problem Is the Prices: Opaque and Sky High Bills Are Breaking Americans — and Our Health Care System," Vox, October 16, 2017, https://www.vox.com/policy-and-politics/2017/10/16/16357790/health-care-pricesproblem.

454 https://www.americanprogress.org/article/the-behavioral-health-care-affordability-problem/

addressing this critical problem in the health care system including strengthening the behavioral health workforce, building sustainable and adequate reimbursement, and improving access to mental health and behavioral health care services. One critical dimension of solving this problem is putting in place stronger network adequacy standards, and enforcement of both mental health parity and network adequacy requirements. With 163 million people living in mental health professional shortage areas, there is also an urgent need to invest in the development of the mental health workforce.[455]

2) That same analysis suggests that health plans for people in Medicaid paid significantly less than commercial health insurers for mental health diagnoses. Can you explain that?

In general, Medicaid reimburses providers for health care services at a lower payment rate compared to commercial insurance. And across both types of payors, payment rates for mental health services in particular are often lower than payment rates for equivalent non-mental health services. For example, in Medicaid, psychiatrists in many states are paid less than primary care providers for delivering similar services.[456] Although states directly set reimbursement rates for providers in fee-for-service Medicaid, most people who receive Medicaid are in managed care plans, and these plans are the ones setting rates for behavioral health providers.

States and the federal government have an important role to play in ensuring people who rely on Medicaid for health care have access to the behavioral health services that they need. For example, they can set standards for network adequacy and strengthen oversight and enforcement. California is an example of a state that recently has stepped up its standards to ensure that networks have enough mental health professionals that are accepting new patients.[457]

3) How can we increase competition across the health care sector to bring down costs for patients?

There are a number of promising reforms that Congress should institute to promote healthy competition across the U.S. health care system and bring down costs for patients. One crucial way Congress can address provider consolidation and encourage health care competition is through passing legislation that strengthens the Hospital Price Transparency rule, including by sharpening data requirements and establishing standard formats, eliminating loopholes for hospitals, and further increasing penalties to encourage greater hospital compliance. Price transparency regulations are an important tool to pull back the curtain on prices so that policymakers, researchers, employers, and consumers can see how irrational health care prices have become and take action to rein in hospital pricing abuses.

---

[455] https://data.hrsa.gov/topics/health-workforce/shortage-areas.

[456] Tami Mark, et al, "Comparison of Medicaid Reimbursements for Psychiatrists and Primary Care Physicians," *Psychiatric Services,* July 24, 2020, https://doi.org/10.1176/appi.ps.202000062.

[457] National Health Law Program, "NHeLP welcomes new mental health network adequacy reporting for California plans," February 1, 2023, https://healthlaw.org/nhelp-welcomes-new-mental-health-network-adequacy-reporting-for-california-plans/.

Congress should also address payment differentials across sites of service that incentivize further consolidation and are a major driver of unaffordable care for America's families. Market inefficiencies that come from site-specific payment rates are a significant problem, which if addressed, could save American families and payers billions of dollars.[458] These site payment differentials drive care delivery from physician offices to higher-cost hospital outpatient departments.[459] This shift is a major driver of higher spending on health care services which require lower resources such as office visits and minor procedures.[460] And importantly, these payment differentials create a financial incentive for hospitals to consolidate by buying physician offices and rebranding them as off-campus outpatient hospital departments (HOPDs) and facilities in order to receive higher payments.[461]

Lastly, Congress should take a closer look at anticompetitive practices and clauses in health care contracting agreements, which occur in a variety of places including between providers and insurers and in clinician and health care worker employment arrangements.[462] In contracts between provider entities and insurers, large entities in highly consolidated markets have the upper hand in contract negotiations to build networks and set prices. As a result, many of these contracts include terms that limit access to higher-quality, lower-cost care. When anticompetitive terms are present in health care clinician and worker employment contracts, they can further stifle competition, lead to burnout exacerbating workforce shortages,[463] impede patient access to preferred providers and care, and lead to higher prices for health care services.[464]

4) As I am sure you are well aware, medical debt can be crushing, and Minnesotans are feeling the weight just as many other Americans are. How can comprehensive health care price transparency give my constituents financial certainty and peace of mind that they won't be bankrupted by their care?

Every person should have the right to know what a health care procedure costs at a hospital or health care facility, whether it is an X-ray, an MRI, or a surgery. Health care is one of the only sectors in the U.S. economy where consumers and purchasers are blinded to the price of a service until after that service has been delivered and they receive a bill.[465] For the two thirds

---

458 Committee for a Responsible Federal Budget, Moving to Site Neutrality in Commercial Insurance Payments, February 14, 2023. https://www.crfb.org/papers/moving-site-neutrality-commercial-insurance.

459 Ibid.

460 Ibid.

461 Ibid.

462 A notable example of a hospital system allegedly employing anticompetitive contracting practices was in the case of Sutter Health, based in California. Health care prices in northern California, where Sutter Health operated, grew four times faster than prices across the rest of the state between 2004 and 2013. Glenn A. Melnick and Katya Fonkych, "Hospital Prices Increase in California, Especially Among Hospitals in the Largest Multi-Hospital Systems," Inquiry 53 (June 2016), https://www.researchgate.net/publication/303891826_Hospital_Prices_Increase_in_California_Especially_Among_Hospitals_in_the_Largest_Multi-hospital_Systems. See also, Jenny Gold, Surprise Settlement in Sutter Health Antitrust Case, October 16, 2019, Kaiser Health News. https://khn.org/news/surprise-settlement-insutter-health-antitrust-case/.

463 Erik B. Smith, Ending Physician Noncompete Agreements—Time for a National Solution, Journal of American Medical Association (JAMA), December 3, 2021. https://jamanetwork.com/journals/jama-health-forum/fullarticle/2786894.

464 Prager, E. Schmitt, M. Employer Consolidation and Wages: Evidence from Hospitals. American Economic Association. 2021. https://www.aeaweb.org/articles?id=10.1257/aer.20190690.

465 King, "Examining State Efforts."

of Americans who receive health care through private insurance, health care prices are established in closed-door negotiations between large hospital corporations and health plans, and based on which organization has more market power.[466]

These health care prices — often referred to as negotiated rates — are buried in proprietary contracts without insight into or oversight over the price of health care services by the public and policymakers.[467] This lack of transparency is alarming, particularly given that high and rising health care prices are the primary driver of our nation's health care affordability crisis.[468]

Price transparency holds the promise of unveiling underlying prices of health care services and goods so that consumers and employers can be better informed and empowered purchasers of health care, and so that researchers and policymakers can analyze prices in U.S. health markets to make targeted policy decisions that drive high-value care into the health care system. The most critical pricing information is the negotiated rate, which is widely recognized as the underlying price of health care services and goods.[469] Unveiling price data will force the health care sector to compete based on rational prices rather than by buying up doctors' offices to price gouge and generate a high volume of high-priced services that do not improve patient health. Unveiling health care prices has the power to disrupt the status quo market dynamics – a shift that is essential to align the business interests of the health care sector with the financial security and health outcomes of our nation's families.

Benedic Ippolito, PhD, Senior Fellow, American Enterprise Institute Answers to Questions for the Record Subcommittee on Health House Committee on Energy and Commerce Lowering Unaffordable Costs: Examining Transparency and Competition in Health Care

March, 28.2023

The Honorable Cathy McMorris Rodgers

I was encouraged to read in the 2023 Medicare Trustees Report that CMS actions, most notably removing hip and knee procedures off the "inpatient only list" and allowing patients to receive

---

466 Berenson et al., *Market Consolidation and High Prices;* King, "Examining State Efforts."

467 John Della Volpe, "Executive Summary of National Healthcare Survey," SocialSphere, February 24, 2022, https://www.patientrightsadvocate.org/feb2022surveyresults.

468 Noam N. Levey, "100 Million People in America Are Saddled with Health Care Debt," Kaiser Health News, June 16, 2022, https://khn.org/news/article/diagnosis-debt-investigation-100-million-americans-hidden-medical-debt/; Institute of Medicine, *Best Care at Lower Cost: The Path to Continuously Learning Health Care in Ame*rica, Mark. Smith et al., eds. (Washington, DC: National Academies Press, 2013), https://www.nap.edu/ catalog/13444/best-care-at-lower-cost-the-path-to-continuously-learning; Gerard F. Anderson, Peter Hussey, and Varduhi Petrosyan, "It's Still the Prices, Stupid: Why the US Spends So Much on Health Care, and a Tribute to Uwe Reinhardt," *Health Affairs* 38, no. 1 (January 2019): 87–95, https://www.healthaffairs. org/doi/10.1377/hlthaff.2018.05144.

469 Danielle Scheurer, "Lack of Transparency Plagues U.S. Health Care System," *The Hospitalist*, May 1, 2013, https://www.the-hospitalist.org/hospitalist/article/125866/health-policy/lack-transparency-plagues-us-health-care-system; Ann Boynton and James C. Robinson, "Appropriate Use of Reference Pricing Can Increase Value," *Health Affairs Forefront*, July 7, 2015, https://www.healthaffairs.org/do/10.1377/forefront. 20150707. 049155/full/; Sarah Kliff and Josh Katz, "Hospitals and Insurers Didn't Want You to See These Prices. Here's Why," *The New York Times*, August 22, 2021, https://www.nytimes. com/interactive/ 2021/08/22/upshot/ hospital-prices.html.

and doctors to perform additional services in the more efficient and less expensive outpatient setting have reduced total Medicare expenditures and contributed to extending the program's solvency a little longer through 2031. How should Congress think about additional actions to enhance patient and provider choices by encouraging more services to be safely administered in the outpatient setting?

1) Would allowing more procedures to be done in outpatient settings, like Ambulatory Surgery Centers, enhance competition among providers and encourage hospitals to compete with ASCs and other hospitals who offer outpatient services?

Recent empirical analysis has emphasized the importance of provider competition in moderating the growth of health costs.[470] In many areas, competitive concerns are especially pronounced within the inpatient hospital market, placing particular emphasis on procompetitive policies that affect this market. Allowing a greater number of procedures to be done outside of the inpatient setting would generally help improve competition for these types of services. Indeed, one would expect this kind of dynamic to emerge in a well-functioning health care market. As services become less likely to make use of inpatient services, payers would have a strong incentive to encourage enrollees to make use of more competitive, lower-cost settings. It is worth noting that under its current criteria for removing procedures from the IPO list, CMS considers whether most outpatient departments or ASCs are equipped to provide it.[471] Thus, one would expect relatively immediate competition from such a change.

2) Does research and existing data suggest patients would still be able to receive quality and safe care for certain additional services in outpatient settings?

The continued advance of technology and improvements to clinical practice all but ensure that the answer to this question is "yes." This is particularly true since health care providers can still make clinical judgements about site of service on a case-by-case basis. Moreover, this consideration is reflected in CMS' approach to removing items from this list. As they note,[472] "...over time, given advances in technology and surgical technique, we would continue to evaluate services to determine whether they should be removed from the IPO list. Our goal is to ensure that inpatient only designations are consistent with the current standards of practice. We have asserted in prior rulemaking that, insofar as advances in medical practice mitigate concerns about these procedures being performed on an outpatient basis, we would be prepared to remove procedures from the IPO list and provide for payment for them under the OPPS (65 FR 18443)."

---

470 For a discussion, see Loren Adler and Benedic Ippolito "Procompetitive Health Care Reform Options for a Divided Congress," *American Enterprise Institute and The Brookings Institution* (March 16, 2023).

471 See https://public-inspection.federalregister.gov/2022-23918.pdf.

472 https://public-inspection.federalregister.gov/2022-23918.pdf.

The Honorable Earl L. "Buddy" Carter

As a pharmacist, I've seen firsthand the obstacles patients face in filling their prescriptions. Manufacturer copay assistance is one of the ways many patients today are able to better afford their prescription medicines. According to a recent study, manufacturer copay assistance was found to close important affordability gaps, increasing utilization by 4.8 to 16.7 percent which in turn raised health outcomes by 1.0 to 3.3 percent. Unfortunately, "copay accumulator" schemes that PBMs have developed pocket a patient's copay assistance; my bill, the HELP Copays Act, would ban this practice. Dr. Ippolito, you have written about the need for more transparency in the role of PBMs for plan sponsors or insurers. However, pharmacists like me see patients struggle with PBM transparency too, including understanding their coverage and benefits which often hide details on tactics like copay accumulators with hard to understand language.

1) Dr. Ippolito - Do you think there is a role for increased PBM transparency for patients so that they can actually understand their pharmacy benefit and accurately predict their out- of-pocket costs for their plan year so they don't experience copay surprise from accumulator programs?

Well-functioning markets require that consumers understand the costs and benefits of products which they buy. Within health insurance markets, it is critical that consumers understand the premiums, coverage, and cost sharing obligations of different insurance plans. Copay accumulators can play an important role in patients' cost sharing, so efforts to make them more transparent are sensible and can help consumers make more informed decisions that better reflect their preferences. In particular, one could imagine consumers weighing a tradeoff between greater protection against large out-of-pocket shocks you describe and other plan features, like premiums.

The Honorable Dan Crenshaw

One of the most under-discussed supply-side barriers to competition are state certificate- of-need laws. My state of Texas recognizes the burden and does not have them, but in the more than 30 states that maintain these laws (Certificate of Need State Laws (ncsl.org)), new health care providers are typically prohibited from entering the market without a government-ordained "certificate-of-need." Nearly 20 years ago, the FTC said these laws were not successful in containing costs, and that they can actually increase prices by fostering anticompetitive barriers to entry (Improving Health Care: A Dose of Competition (ftc.gov)). Dr. Ippolito, unsurprisingly these well-intentioned but misguided laws are a result of poor federal policy, specifically incentives created in 1970s for states to adopt these laws.

1) Do you believe that they are contributing to increased federal spending on health care? Should Congress engage in a conversation about the merits of these state laws today?

Certificate of Need (CON) laws were originally motivated by the concern that if health care investments were unchecked, they might lead to excessive use of unneeded services or a wasteful "arms race" over costly services with dubious value. Moreover, they were advertised as a mechanism to direct investments where they were most needed, potentially increasing access to care in certain areas. However, as you note, they also represent a barrier to entry that can raise serious concerns. CON laws directly increase the costs of market entry by requiring a potential entrant to spend time and resources navigating the process. In addition, it allows states to block potential entrants. This latter feature can be particularly concerning if CON laws provide an opportunity for regulatory capture by dominant, incumbent providers who seek to limit their own competition. This concern has grown more pronounced over time as consolidation in many parts of the health care market—but particularly hospital markets—has increased. Given the long history of CON laws, including the elimination of these laws in many states, one would expect ample evidence of their purported benefits. Instead, the evidence tends to support concerns that CON laws have an overall negative effect on health care markets.[473] As you note, available evidence has prompted federal antitrust agencies to express significant concerns with CON laws. Given this, it strikes me as reasonable to consider whether Congress has a role in encouraging the remaining states to move away from these policies.

The Honorable Frank Pallone, Jr.

1) There is little insight into how PBMs negotiate arrangements and rebates with drug manufacturers and what impact this has on health plans and patients. Increasing transparency with respect to contracting arrangements between PBMs and drug manufacturers has been proposed as a mechanism for lowering drug prices. Can you describe what benefit more transparency would have here?

Across markets it is very difficult for purchasers to compare products when their costs and benefits are unclear. This is a potentially significant issue in the market for PBM services. In particular, the relatively complex and opaque fee structure (including, but not limited to, rebates) can make it difficult to assess the true cost of a PBM contract. This also makes it more challenging to compare one PBM against another, potentially muting competition between them. Greater transparency in this area can help plan sponsors better evaluate contracts and generate more competition between PBMs.

2) As you mentioned in your testimony, there have been bipartisan proposals in Congress that would require PBMs to disclose certain information to plan sponsors and employers. Do you believe this is a proposal that would effectively lower costs while also providing plan sponsors with additional information to leverage better arrangements?

Prior legislative efforts, like the Lower Health Care Costs Act of 2019, have included provisions that would require PBMs to disclose more information about rebates, costs, and fees.[474] Providing clearer information about these contract features to plan sponsors and

---

[473] For a discussion, see Mitchell, Matthew "Certificate-of-Need Laws: How They Affect Healthcare Access, Quality, and Cost." Mercatus Center. May 21, 2021.

[474] For the complete text, see https://www.congress.gov/bill/116th-congress/senate-bill/1895.

employers should help them better assess the costs and benefits of different contracts and generate more cost competition between PBMs. All else equal, this should reduce costs. This expectation is shared by the Congressional Budget Office, which estimated that prior proposals along these lines would lower federal deficits.[475]

3) What role has market consolidation played with respect to PBMs? Do you believe consolidation has increased anti-competitive contracting arrangements?

The PBM market is relatively consolidated, with three firms controlling roughly 80 percent of the market.[476] Fewer, larger PBMs has the potential to increase their leverage when negotiating with drug makers, but also allow PBMs to potentially retain a larger share of spending than would occur in a more competitive market. These countervailing forces are worth policy attention. Beyond horizontal consolidation, the major PBMs are also vertically integrated with other entities in the health care market, including insurers, specialty pharmacies, and providers. Vertical integration has the potential to influence the way that PBMs behave with regards to other parts of the health care market. For example, it is possible that they may engage in behavior that benefits other parts of the vertically integrated company (e.g., by preferencing their own specialty pharmacy or otherwise driving volume and spending towards firms that are part of the same vertically integrated entity). These types of behaviors can potentially increase coordination or avoid double marginalization, but also raise competitive concerns. Whether these types of vertical relationships result in anticompetitive behavior is worth attention and is likely a case where greater transparency would help policymakers better assess the validity of these concerns.

4) You discussed in your testimony how consolidation is leading to increased costs for consumers and employers. Can you describe some of the consolidation that is occurring and how this is impacting our health system at large?

The very high level of U.S. health care spending would not represent a major problem if that spending accurately reflected the preferences of consumers. However, there is significant evidence that much of that spending instead reflects market imperfections, like highly consolidated markets.

For example, the following figure from Fulton (2017) illustrates the fraction of Metropolitan Statistical Areas that are considered highly consolidated (defined as an HHI over 2,500) from 2010-2016. Consolidation is very high in many areas (e.g., hospital sector) and rising in others (e.g., many physician markets). Given additional mergers and acquisitions since the publication of this paper, these data likely understate the level of consolidation in the current market.

---

[475] Congressional Budget Office, "S. 1895, Lower Health Care Costs Act,' July 26, 2019.

[476] Drug Channels. "The Top Pharmacy Benefit Managers of 2021: The Big Get Even Bigger." April 5, 2022.

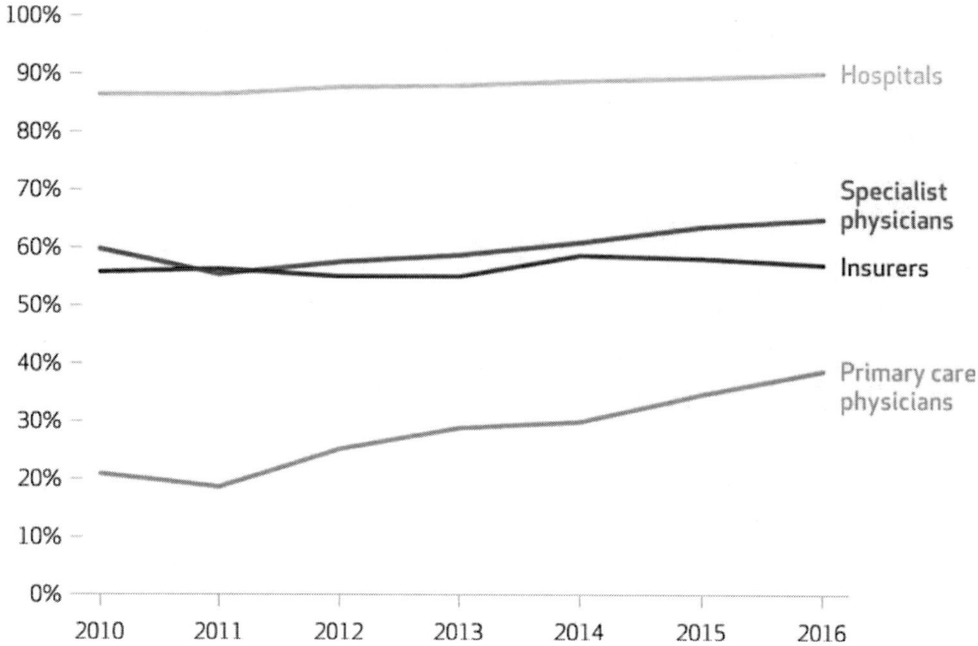

Note: Figure from Fulton (2017).

Figure. Percentages of MSAs with HHI over 2,500 for hospitals, physicians, and insurers.

Markets with limited competition allow dominant firms—whether providers, insurers, PBMs, or any market actor—to charge high prices while facing less pressure to improve quality. These costs are ultimately borne by consumers in multiple ways. Particularly in the private market, consolidated entities increase the cost of insurance, which now stands over $22,000 per year for a family plan in the employer market.[477] Employees bear the burden of these costs in two ways. First, this can increase the premiums directly paid by employees and increase their out-of-pocket spending. Second, this reduces wage growth of employees. Even if employers nominally shoulder a large share of these costs, doing so increases the cost of employing a worker and reduces the amount they can pay in cash. Economic evidence has shown this link across multiple settings.[478] In short, by increasing health costs, consolidation has first-order implications for consumers.

5) Can you describe ways Congress can address market consolidation and help lower costs?

Congress can consider a number of policies to attenuate market concentration and increase cost pressures throughout the health care market. (Many of the following policy options are discussed in greater detail in Adler and Ippolito, 2023).[479] First, it can change payment policies that currently incentive consolidation. This includes adopting site- neutral payments within the

---

[477] KFF, "2022 Employer Health Benefits Survey." October 27, 2022.

[478] For example, see Gruber, Jonathan. "The incidence of mandated maternity benefits." The American economic review (1994): 622-641.

[479] Adler, Loren and Benedic Ippolito. "Procompetitive Health Care Reform Options for a Divided Congress." AEI and Brookings. March 16, 2023.

Medicare program where appropriate, reforming incentives created by drug payments in the Medicare Part B program, and altering the 340B program. Second, the federal government could in principle incentivize states to change a host of policies that can reduce competition. This includes Certificate of Need policies, Scope of Practice restrictions, and Certificates of Public Advantage. Third, Congress can consider changes to antitrust enforcement in these markets. Regulators could be given more insight into possible anticompetitive consolidation by lowering thresholds for required reporting of transactions and by requiring reporting in cases where a single owner engages in a large number of small transactions (in conjunction, they could work to improve transparency about ownership structures more generally). They could also consider strengthening antitrust statutes by reducing the bar for regulators to challenge a merger in these markets (e.g., some have proposed requiring only that a merger "meaningfully" or "materially" lessens competition rather than "substantially" so).[480]

[480] For a discussion, see Testimony of Leemore S. Dafny before the U.S. House Committee on the Judiciary Subcommittee on Antitrust, Commercial and Administrative Law on "How Health Care Consolidation Is Contributing to Higher Prices and Spending, and Reforms That Could Bolster Antitrust Enforcement and Preserve and Promote Competition in Health Care Markets."

Chapter 2

Lowering Unaffordable Costs: Legislative Solutions to Increase Transparency and Competition in Healthcare*

Committee on Energy and Commerce

Wednesday, April 26, 2023
House of Representatives, Subcommittee on Health,
Committee on Energy and Commerce,
Washington, DC.

The subcommittee met, pursuant to call, at 10:00 a.m. in the John D. Dingell Room 2123 of the Rayburn House Office Building, Hon. Brett Guthrie (chairman of the subcommittee) presiding.

Members present: Representatives Guthrie, Burgess, Latta, Griffith, Bilirakis, Johnson, Bucshon, Hudson, Carter, Pence, Crenshaw, Joyce, Harshbarger, Miller-Meeks, Obernolte, Rodgers (ex officio), Eshoo (subcommittee ranking member), Sarbanes, Ca´rdenas, Ruiz, Dingell, Kuster, Kelly, Barraga´ n, Blunt Rochester, Craig, Schrier, Trahan, and Pallone (ex officio).

Also present: Representatives Allen, Matsui, and Schakowsky. Staff present: Alec Aramanda, Professional Staff Member, Health; Kate Arey, Digital Director; Jolie Brochin, Clerk, Health; Sarah Burke, Deputy Staff Director; Corey Ensslin, Senior Policy Advisor, Health; Seth Gold, Professional Staff Member, Health; Grace Graham, Chief Counsel, Health; Nate Hodson, Staff Director; Tara Hupman, Chief Counsel; Peter Kielty, General Counsel; Chris Krepich, Press Secretary; Carla Rafael, Senior Staff Assistant; Emma Schultheis, Staff Assistant; Michael Taggart, Policy Director; Dray Thorne, Director of Information Technology; Lydia Abma, Minority Policy Analyst; Jacquelyn Bolen, Minority Health Counsel; Waverly Gordon, Minority Deputy Staff Director and General Counsel; Tiffany Guarascio, Minority Staff Director; Stephen Holland, Minority Senior Health Counsel; Saha Khaterzai, Minority Professional Staff Member; Una Lee, Minority Chief Health Counsel; Rick Van Buren, Minority Senior Health Counsel; and C.J. Young, Minority Deputy Communications Director.

Mr. GUTHRIE. The subcommittee will come to order.

So the Chair recognizes himself for 5 minutes for an opening statement.

---

* This is an edited, reformatted and augmented version of Hearing Before the Subcommittee on Health of the Committee on Energy and Commerce House of Representatives Serial No. 118–27, dated APRIL 26, 2023.

In: Healthcare: Costs, Competition and Transparency
Editor: Liam Moore
ISBN: 979-8-89530-633-8

Opening Statement of Hon. Brett Guthrie, A Representative in Congress from the Commonwealth of Kentucky

We are here today because the healthcare costs continue to rise, further limiting America's budgets that have already been stretched by the inflation driven by the spending in the last couple of years. We are considering 17 bills and discussion drafts to advance price transparency and improve competition within the healthcare system to ultimately lower costs.

This legislation hearing builds on our bipartisan work last month. In our educational hearing we heard from experts and witnesses from across the political and policy spectrum who share our goal to lower costs for patients. Republicans and Democrats on this committee are reaching across the aisle to advance solutions, and these bipartisan efforts can be seen in many of the proposals before us today.

Transparency can reveal the true value of each step in the healthcare supply chain and empower patients and employers to get the best deal on high-quality care. Many of our proposals before the subcommittee today will shine a light on prescription drug middlemen and further policies to make the healthcare system more competitive to lower costs. The Transparent Price Act, introduced by the leaders of the full committee, will help build upon the Trump administration's hospital and insurers' transparency rules to ensure patients and employers are getting the best deal possible. While transparency is necessary for a functioning market, there must also be competition to lower prices and increase quality. As such, we are reviewing a number of policies designed to reduce incentives to consolidate and require providers to compete with one another on both price and quality, all with the goal of benefiting patients. For example, today we will examine a number of proposals that will ensure patients aren't paying more for the same service in one care setting versus another. I look forward to hearing what the impacts of these policies could be for patients, both in the quality of care they would receive and how these would impact their out-of-pocket spending.

One proposal recommended by MedPAC would save $1.7 billion annually. Similarly, another policy would simply require CMS to assess the impact that regulatory decisions may have on consolidation in healthcare to see if Federal regulations may be unintentionally driving consolidation. Improving competition will help ensure seniors maintain access to the highest quality healthcare services at the best possible prices.

Another theme repeatedly heard during last month's bipartisan educational hearing is the need to address pricing practices by pharmacy middlemen. Patients are facing rising costs at the drug counter resulting from the growing influence of a small number of pharmacy benefit managers. Due consolidation within the PBM industry, 80 percent of all drug claims are adjudicated by three PBMs.

It is the subcommittee's duty to ensure this consolidation is driving value and improving outcomes. That is why I strongly support the bipartisan PBM Accountability Act to provide key information to employers about the drug costs and their coverage for their employees. With that information, employers can truly know what benefit their PBM may be providing.

There is also bipartisan legislation from the—from Representative Carter that would finally ban spread pricing in Medicaid. In 2019 it was reported that PBMs earned $123 billion in Kentucky alone through spread pricing. Medicaid programs should find a more transparent way to pay PBMs for their services.

Finally, I want to thank Representative Eshoo for working with me on the MVP Act. The innovation coming the next few years is game changing, including potential one-time cures for rare diseases, sickle cell anemia, and hemophilia. However, the Medicaid system is not set up to pay for high-cost treatments. Medicaid programs operate on an annual budget and need more flexibility to help ensure patients gain access to these therapies. This bipartisan legislation builds on a Trump administration regulation that would give Medicaid programs the flexibility needed over time and enter into contracts that provide patients with access to novel cell and gene therapies. This payment model also ensures States aren't on the hook to pay for treatments that fail patients.

In closing, I look forward to today's hearing to discuss these bipartisan ideas to lower healthcare costs, and look forward to working with my subcommittee colleagues to advance these policies.

[The prepared statement of Mr. Guthrie follows:]

Congressman Brett Guthrie Opening Statement as Prepared for Delivery

We are here today because health care costs continue to rise, further limiting Americana's budgets which have already been stretched thin by inflation driven by Democrats spending spree.

We are considering 17 bills and discussion drafts to advance price transparency and improve competition within the health care system. This legislative hearing builds on our bipartisan work last month. In our educational hearing, we came together to hear from experts and witnesses from across the political and policy spectrum who share our goal to lower costs for patients. Now, on the vast majority of these proposals, Republicans and Democrats on this committee are reaching across the aisle to advance solutions.

Transparency can reveal the true value of each step in the health care supply chain and empower patients and employers to get the best deal on high quality care. Many of the proposals before the subcommittee today will shine a light on prescription drug middlemen and further polices to make the health care system more competitive to lower costs. The Transparent PRICE Act, introduced by the leaders of the full committee, will improve upon the Trump Administration's hospital and insurer price transparency rules to ensure patients and employers are getting the best possible deal.

While transparency is necessary to a functioning market, there must also be competition to lower prices and increase quality. As such, we are reviewing a number of policies designed to reduce incentives to consolidate and require providers to compete with one another on both price and quality, all with the goal of benefitting patients. For example, by ending the practice of requiring Medicare and patients to pay more for certain services at hospitals – when those same services can be performed safely in doctor's offices or Ambulatory Surgical Centers – seniors can save billions. One proposal put forth by MedPAC, which we are discussing today, is estimated to have saved seniors $1.7 billion if it had been in place in 2019.

Similarly, another policy would simply require CMS to assess the impact regulatory decisions may have on consolidation in health care, so that we can better understand how federal regulations may be unintentionally driving consolidation. Improving competition will help ensure seniors maintain access to the highest quality health care services at the best possible prices.

Another theme heard repeatedly last month's bipartisan educational hearing is the need to address opaque pricing practices by pharmacy middlemen. Patients are facing rising costs at the drug counter, resulting from the growing influence of a small number of pharmacy benefit managers caused by the consolidation within the PBM industry. 80% of all drug claims are adjudicated by three PBMs.

I strongly support the bipartisan PBM Accountability Act to provide key information to employers about the drug costs of their employees. With that information, employers can hold PBMs accountable and understand what benefit their PBM may be providing. There's also bipartisan legislation from Representative Carter that would finally ban spread pricing in Medicaid. In 2019, it was reported that PBMs earned $123 million in Kentucky alone through spread pricing. Medicaid programs should find a more transparent way to pay PBMs for their services.

Finally, I want to thank Ms. Eshoo for working with me on the MVP Act. The innovation coming the next few years is game changing – potential one time cures for rare diseases, sickle cell, hemophilia - but our system is not set up for that. Medicaid programs operate on annual budget, and while a multi million dollar drug is cost effective in a lot of these cases, states need more flexibility. This bipartisan legislation builds on a Trump Administration regulation that would give Medicaid programs the flexibility needed to pay over time and enter into contracts that provide patients with access to novel cell and gene therapies while ensuring states aren't on the hook to pay for treatments that fail patients.

In closing, I look forward to today's hearing to discuss these bipartisan ideas to lower health care costs and look forward to working with my subcommittee colleagues to advance these policies. I yield back.

Mr. GUTHRIE. I yield back, and I now recognize the gentlelady from California, Representative Eshoo, for 5 minutes for an opening statement.

Opening Statement of Hon. Anna G. Eshoo, A Representative in Congress from the State of California

Ms. ESHOO. Thank you, Mr. Chairman, and good morning, colleagues.

Today we are considering 17 legislative proposals to lower costs and increase transparency in our healthcare system.

Administrator Brooks-LaSure, welcome to the subcommittee. This is your first time, and we are very glad to have you with us. Our last hearing on this topic showed that the United States spends more on healthcare than our peer countries, but we have significantly worse health outcomes. Simply put, we are not getting the best value for our healthcare dollar.

Hospital care is the largest health spending category in the United States, accounting for 31 percent of all healthcare spending in 2021. Since 2000, hospital prices have increased over 200 percent, and are predicted to continue rising in the coming years. When hospital prices increase, out-of-pocket costs for Medicare beneficiaries, who are often on fixed incomes, increase as well.

The proposals before us today raise very interesting and important questions on how to lower costs and improve health outcomes, including how to implement targeted site-neutral policies, while protecting patient access and rural hospitals.

Aligning payment rates across outpatient settings could save Medicare more than 141 billion—with a B—dollars over 10 years. But we should heed MedPAC's recommendation to ensure that we prioritize safety and access when advancing our policies: how to bring more transparency to the 340B program without creating unnecessary barriers, how to further competition in the healthcare industry to better serve patients and to decrease costs.

I am also pleased that we are discussing two bills that I am co-leading. The PBM Accountability Act will finally shed a light on the opaque drug pricing system that PBMs use during their dealings with manufacturers and insurance plans to make enormous profits. It would also save the Government, the Federal Government, over $2 billion in the next 10 years.

The Medicaid Value-Based Payments for Patients Act will codify a CMS rule to help ensure Medicaid enrollees have access to breakthrough gene therapies for dreaded diseases, as the chairman said, for sickle cell anemia and certain cancers. And I am pleased to partner with the chairman on this legislation, and continue—and I look forward to continuing to carefully craft and tailor it.

Finally, we are considering bipartisan legislation to codify existing price transparency rules for hospitals and insurers and prevent payment reductions to disproportionate share hospitals under the Medicaid program. I fully support these bills.

So thank you, Madam Administrator, for being with us today. We look forward to the—your answers to our questions. And I know we have a second panel, and I see some of the panelists in the hearing room—and thank you for being with us.

[The prepared statement of Ms. Eshoo follows:]

Committee on Energy and Commerce

Opening Statement as Prepared for Delivery of Subcommittee on Health Ranking Member Anna Eshoo

Hearing on "Lowering Unaffordable Costs: Legislative Solutions to Increase Transparency and Competition in Health Care"
April 26, 2023

Today, we consider 17 legislative proposals to lower costs and increase transparency in our healthcare system.

Welcome CMS Administrator Brooks-LaSure to the Subcommittee for the first time. We are very glad to have you with us.

Our last hearing on this topic showed that the U.S. spends more on healthcare than our peer countries but we have significantly worse health outcomes. Simply put, we aren't getting the best value for our healthcare dollar.

Hospital care is the largest health spending category in the U.S., accounting for 31% of all health care spending in 2021.

Since 2000, hospital prices have increased over 200 percent and are predicted to continue rising in the coming years.

When hospital prices increase, out-of-pocket costs for Medicare beneficiaries who are often on fixed incomes increase as well.

The proposals before us today raise interesting and important questions on how to lower costs and improve health outcomes, including:

- How to implement targeted site-neutral policies while protecting patient access and rural hospitals. Aligning payment rates across outpatient settings could save Medicare more than $141 billion over 10 years, but we should heed MedPAC's recommendation to ensure we prioritize safety and access when advancing policies.
- How to bring more transparency to the 340B program without creating unnecessary barriers; and
- How to further competition in the healthcare industry to better serve patients and decrease costs.

I'm also pleased that we're discussing two bills that I co-led.

The PBM Accountability Act will finally shed a light on the opaque drug pricing system that pharmacy benefit managers (PBMs) use during their dealings with manufacturers and insurance plans to make enormous profits. It will also save the federal government over $2 billion in the next ten years.

The Medicaid Value-Based Payments for Patients Act will codify a CMS rule to help ensure Medicaid enrollees have access to breakthrough gene therapies for dreaded diseases such as sickle cell anemia and certain cancers. I'm pleased to have partnered with Chairman Guthrie on this legislation, and I look forward to continuing to carefully craft and tailor it.

Finally, we're considering bipartisan legislation to codify existing price transparency rules for hospitals and insurers and prevent payment reductions to disproportionate share hospitals under the Medicaid program. I fully support these bills.

So, thank you Madame Administrator for being with us today. We look forward to your answers to our questions.

Ms. ESHOO. And with that, Mr. Chairman, I yield back the balance of my time.

Mr. GUTHRIE. Thank you. The gentlelady yields back. The Chair will now recognize the Chair of the full committee, Chair Rodgers, for 5 minutes for an opening statement.

Opening Statement of Hon. Cathy Mcmorris Rodgers, a Representative in Congress from the State of Washington

Mrs. RODGERS. Good morning, and welcome to Administrator Brooks-LaSure of the Centers for Medicare and Medicaid Services, and a range of stakeholders on proposals to lower the cost of healthcare for Americans through increased transparency and competition.

This committee has a rich history of plowing the hard ground necessary to legislate and address issues from data privacy to mental health. And I am proud that we are coming together on another top priority for the American people.

Each day it seems we hear a new and more unbelievable story of patients struggling to afford their care and navigate the system: a 4-year-old getting bills his parents can't protest; entire books dedicated to helping people challenge hospital bills and overcome denials of care issued by insurance companies that receive billions in premiums and subsidies each year. Addressing these challenges won't be easy, but I know this committee is up to the task.

Transparency is essential for patients and employers to know and plan for their healthcare costs. It is foundational to rebuilding the doctor-patient relationship. Seven proposals before us improve transparency in the system, and I am thankful for Ranking Member Pallone for leading H.R. 2691, the Transparent Price Act, with me.

Our bill has been years in the making, and it is a culmination of a lot of bipartisan work and discussions to bring price transparency to the forefront. Our bill builds on regulations released by the Trump administration and enforced by the Biden administration, which just had to levy two more fines against hospitals to comply.

Thank you, Ranking Member Pallone, for working with me for years now on this important issue, starting with ensuring implementation of the rule and now building on it with legislation.

More proposals also help people understand what happens when their insurer owns their doctor, pharmacy, a PBM, and if that is driving value and unaffordable costs for the system. Five bills and proposals look to reduce what patients and employers pay for medicines through transparency and competition.

And lastly, a number address incentives for consolidation in Federal healthcare programs. At our bipartisan hearing last month we heard a story about a senior from Ohio with painful arthritis. The cost of her annual steroid injection increased from $30 to $1,400 because her office clinic reclassified as a hospital department, even though it was the exact same service with the—from the exact same provider and the exact same building.

Today patients in Medicare pay more at hospitals than out-patient centers or physician offices for the same services. Several proposals would advance site-neutral payments for certain services that can be routinely done safely in a doctor's office, such as drug administration, diagnostic tests, imaging procedures, to name a few. For these services Medicare and patients would pay the same amount, regardless of where they are performed.

Ideas for site-neutral payments are bipartisan. Presidents Obama and Trump proposed them in their budgets. Before this committee, Secretary Becerra committed to working on these policies. This is the right thing to do for patients. The Committee for a Responsible Federal Budget estimated site-neutral payments would save Medicare patients $94 billion over 10 years.

Let's be clear. Hospitals are integral. They are integral parts of our communities. And we recognize the effects of high labor cost, inflation, and ever-increasing government regulation. But the question before us is this: Should we support hospitals through a complex and opaque network of cross-subsidies with unintended consequences like consolidation that increase costs for patients, or do we separately work on a transparent, accountable way to support hospitals that need it?

I am glad that the American Hospital Association is here today, and I hope we can come together to address these issues for patients to get the care they need at the cost that they can afford. And as I close, I want to again thank Ranking Member Pallone and all my colleagues on this committee, the subcommittee Chair, the Ranking Member Eshoo, for leading—all the Members that are coming together—to lead on solutions in a bipartisan way. This is bigger than any one person or political party. It is about people, especially the most vulnerable, who, for way too long, have struggled in a healthcare system that is too expensive and too complex.

Many are discussion drafts before us today, and we are having this hearing to understand what work needs to be done to move these policies forward. And I invite all the stakeholders to provide constructive feedback to inform our bipartisan work. Patients all over the country are hopeful that this Congress may finally work together to address healthcare costs and complexity, and I am proud that Energy and Commerce is leading the way.

[The prepared statement of Mrs. Rodgers follows:]

Congresswoman Cathy McMorris Rodgers Health Subcommittee Hearing 4.26.23
Opening Statement
As Prepared for Delivery

Welcome

Good morning.

Today, we will hear from Administrator Brooks-LaSure and a range of stakeholders on proposals to lower the costs of health care for Americans through increased transparency and competition.

This committee has a rich history of plowing the hard ground on issues from data privacy to mental health ... and I'm proud we're coming together on another top priority for the American people.

Each day it seems we see a new and more unbelievable story of patients struggling to afford their care and navigate the system:A 4-year-old getting bills his parents can't protest.

Entire books dedicated to helping people challenge hospital bills and overcome denials of care issued by insurance companies that receive billions in premiums and subsidies each year. Addressing these challenges won't be easy, but I know this committee is up to the task.

Today's Bills

Transparency is essential for patients and employers, to know and plan for their health care costs. It's foundational to rebuilding the doctor-patient relationship.

Seven proposals before us improve transparency in the system, and I'm thankful for Ranking Member Pallone for leading H.R. 2691, the Transparent PRICE Act, with me.

Our bill has been years in the making, and it is a culmination of a lot of bipartisan work and discussions to bring price transparency to the forefront.

Our bill builds on regulations released by the Trump Administration and enforced by the Biden Administration, which just had to levy two more fines against hospitals to comply.

Thank you, Ranking Member Pallone, for working with me for years now on this important issue, starting with ensuring implementation of the rule and now building on it with this legislation.

More proposals also help people understand what happens when their insurer owns their doctor, pharmacy, a PBM, and if that is driving value or unaffordable costs for the system.

Five bills and proposals look to reduce what patients and employers pay for medicines through transparency and competition...

And lastly, a number address incentives for consolidation in federal health care programs.

At our bipartisan hearing last month, we heard a story about a senior from Ohio with painful arthritis.

The cost of her annual steroid injection increased from $30 to $1,400 because her office clinic reclassified as a hospital department, even though it was the exact same service, from the exact same provider, in the exact same building.

Today, patients and Medicare pay more at hospitals than outpatient centers or physician offices for the same services.

Several proposals would advance "site-neutral payments" for certain services that can be routinely done safely in a doctor's office, such as Drug administration... diagnostic tests... imaging procedures... to name a few.

For these services, Medicare and patients would pay the same amount, regardless of where they are performed.

Ideas for site neutral payments are bipartisan.

Presidents Obama and Trump proposed them in their budgets.

Before this Committee, Secretary Becerra committed to working on these policies.

This is the right thing to do for patients.

The Committee for a Responsible Federal Budget estimated site neutral policies would save Medicare patients $94 billion over ten years.

Let's be clear:

Hospitals are integral parts of our communities and we recognize the effects of high labor costs, inflation, and ever-increasing government regulation.

But the question before us is:

Should we support hospitals through a complex and opaque network of cross-subsidies with unintended consequences, like consolidation, that increase costs for patients? or do we separately work on a transparent, accountable way to support hospitals that need it?

I am glad the American Hospital Association is here today. I hope we can come together to address these issues for patients to get the care they need at a cost they can afford.

Conclusion

As I close, I again want to thank Ranking Member Pallone and all my colleagues for leading on solutions in a bipartisan way.

This is bigger than any one person or political party.

It's about people, especially the most vulnerable, who for too long have struggled in a health care system that is too expensive and too complex.

Many are discussion drafts… We are having this hearing to understand what work needs to be done to move these policies forward.

I invite all stakeholders to provide constructive feedback to inform our bipartisan work.

Patients all over the country are hopeful that Congress may finally work together to address the health care cost and complexity, and I'm proud E&C continues to lead the way.

Mrs. RODGERS. I yield back.

Mr. GUTHRIE. Thank you. The gentlelady yields back. The Chair now recognizes the ranking member of the full committee, the gentleman from New Jersey, Rep. Pallone, for 5 minutes for opening statement.

Opening Statement of Hon. Frank Pallone, Jr., A Representative in Congress from the State of New Jersey

Mr. PALLONE. Thank you, Mr. Chairman. And I want to start out by saying I appreciate Ranking Member Rodgers' comments about working with us on various legislation, but I am concerned that we are holding a hearing on legislative efforts to lower healthcare costs at the same time that the Republican leadership prepares to bring Speaker McCarthy's what I consider irresponsible and e treme Default on America Act to the House floor.

The Speaker's bill will raise costs for American families, kick millions of people off their health insurance, and cut $100 billion from the Medicaid program so they can provide huge new giveaways to billionaires and big corporations. Republicans are manufacturing a debt crisis to justify these cruel cuts. They are holding the American economy hostage, and this brinkmanship will be catastrophic to our economy and make it harder for American families to make ends meet.

Republicans are also rushing the bill to the floor without holding any hearings or a markup. So much for regular order. Last Congress, when Democrats were in charge, we held several days of markups that included robust debates for both the American Rescue Plan and the Inflation Reduction Act. But now they are in charge, and Republicans are moving to the Default on America Act without an open or transparent process, or any process at all, really. And we haven't had the opportunity to hear from experts about the bill's implications, probably because Republicans know how deeply unpopular these ideas are.

So if Republicans succeed in cutting $100 billion from Medicaid, the consequences will be devastating and will be felt by every beneficiary, provider, and plan that relies on Medicaid. Republicans claim their bill would encourage Medicaid beneficiaries to work, but it is clear that this is just a pretext to cut Medicaid.

As a reminder, the Congressional Budget Office found that Medicaid work requirements do not increase employment. They merely result in individuals losing coverage as a result of bureaucratic red tape. Two-thirds of adults on Medicaid are already working, and those who are not generally have caregiver responsibilities, are dealing with physical or mental health issues that make work difficult, or are experiencing other barriers to unemployment like lack of education or training. If Republicans actually cared about increasing employment among Medicaid beneficiaries, they would have included policies to address those barriers.

Now, turning to the topic of today's hearing, I do believe we should be working together to bring greater transparency and competition to our healthcare system. But I have some concerns about the process leading up to today's hearing.

My Republican colleagues shared a vast majority of the discussion drafts we will be discussing a week before the hearing was noticed. Given the broad array of topics and bills, I am disappointed that we did not have adequate time to fully vet some of these policies and provide the minority's input from the beginning.

So I hope my Republican colleagues will commit to work in a bipartisan manner as we consider these policies moving forward. And I know that the Ranking Member Rodgers has already said that she is committed to that. After all, we have been working together on H.R. 2691, the Transparent Price Act, which I introduced with Chair Rodgers.

Patients deserve greater transparency in the prices they pay for healthcare. Today consumers are not able to easily obtain price information on healthcare services. Sometimes the price information that is provided is inaccurate and misleading, making it difficult to compare across providers or determine the true value of the care. And I know that we are going to work on that together. I just heard the chairwoman, Chairwoman Rodgers, say that.

I am also concerned by reports that many hospitals are either acting slowly or not yet complying with the hospital price transparency final rule, making it even more difficult for consumers to access price information. H.R. 2691 codifies the existing requirements for both hospitals and insurers, and it will also improve the accessibility and usability of the price information for consumers. I am also pleased we are considering two bills that will increase transparency into pharmacy benefit manager practices by helping employers, consumers, and State Medicaid agencies better understand drug price information which can help lower healthcare costs.

We will also discuss legislation that I support to cancel the $8 billion in cuts currently scheduled for Federal payments to Medicaid disproportionate share hospitals, and a bill to require hospitals to disclose ownership data. Studies show that health consolidation is leading to higher care prices for consumers, and I am particularly concerned about the role of private equity in hospital consolidation. I look forward to hearing from the witnesses on how these trends may be impacting healthcare affordability and access to coverage.

So I look forward to the witnesses' testimony. [The prepared statement of Mr. Pallone follows:]

Committee on Energy and Commerce

Opening Statement as Prepared for Delivery of Ranking Member Frank Pallone, Jr.

Health Subcommittee Hearing on "Lowering Unaffordable Costs: Legislative Solutions to Increase Transparency and Competition in Health Care"
April 26, 2023

Today, Committee Republicans are holding a hearing on legislative efforts to lower health care costs at the same time their leadership prepares to bring Speaker McCarthy's irresponsible and extreme Default on America Act to the House floor. The Speaker's bill will raise costs for American families, kick millions of people off their health insurance, and cut $100 billion from the Medicaid program so they can provide huge new giveaways to billionaires and big corporations.

Republicans are manufacturing a debt crisis to justify these cruel cuts. They are holding the American economy hostage. This brinkmanship will be catastrophic to our economy and make it harder for American families to make ends meet.

Republicans are also rushing the bill to the floor without holding any hearings or a markup. So much for regular order. Last Congress, when Democrats were in charge, we held several days of markups that included robust debates for both the American Rescue Plan and the Inflation Reduction Act. But now that they are in charge, Republicans are moving the Default on America Act without an open or transparent process, or any process at all. We haven't had the opportunity to hear from experts about the bill's implications, probably because Republicans know how deeply unpopular these ideas are.

If Republicans succeed in cutting $100 billion from Medicaid, the consequences will be devastating and will be felt by every beneficiary, provider, and plan that relies on Medicaid. Republicans claim their bill would encourage Medicaid beneficiaries to work, but it's clear that this is just a pretext for them to cut Medicaid. As a reminder, the Congressional Budget Office found that Medicaid work requirements do not increase employment—they merely result in individuals losing coverage as a result of bureaucratic red tape.

Two-thirds of adults on Medicaid are already working and those who are not, generally have caregiver responsibilities, are dealing with physical or mental health issues that make work difficult, or are experiencing other barriers to employment like lack of education or training. If Republicans actually cared about increasing employment among Medicaid beneficiaries, they would have included policies to address those barriers.

Turning to the topic of today's hearing, I do believe we should be working together to bring greater transparency and competition to our health care system, but I have significant concerns about the process leading up to today's hearing.

My Republican colleagues shared a vast majority of the discussion drafts we will be discussing a week before the hearing was noticed. Given the broad array of topics and bills, I am disappointed that we did not have adequate time to fully vet some of these policies and provide the minority's input from the beginning. I hope my Republican colleagues will commit to work in a bipartisan manner as we consider these policies moving forward.

After all, we have been working together on H.R. 2691, the Transparent PRICE Act, which I introduced with Chair Rodgers. Patients deserve greater transparency in the prices they pay for health care. Today, consumers are not able to easily obtain price information on health care services. Sometimes, the price information that is provided is inaccurate and misleading, making it difficult to compare across providers or determine the true value of the care.

I am concerned by reports that many hospitals are either acting slowly or not yet complying with the Hospital Price Transparency final rule, making it even more difficult for consumers to access price information. H.R. 2691 codifies the existing requirements for both hospitals and insurers. It will also improve the accessibility and usability of the price information for consumers.

I am also pleased we are considering two bills that will increase transparency into pharmacy benefit manager practices by helping employers, consumers, and state Medicaid agencies better understand drug price information which can help lower health care costs.

We will also discuss legislation that I support to cancel the $8 billion in cuts currently scheduled for federal payments to Medicaid disproportionate share hospitals, and a bill to require hospitals to disclose ownership data. Studies show that health consolidation is leading to higher care prices for consumers. I am particularly concerned about the role of private equity in hospital consolidation, and I look forward to hearing from the witnesses on how these trends may be impacting health care affordability and access to coverage.

I look forward to the witnesses' testimony, and I yield back.

Mr. PALLONE. And with that, Mr. Chairman, I yield back.

Mr. GUTHRIE. Thank you. The gentleman yields back. And I will just say that this is a bipartisan hearing, and we want to work together as we move forward to see if we can get the bipartisan solutions on the bills that you referenced, as the chairman committed to. So thanks.

So this morning we have with us today the Administrator for Centers for Medicare and Medicaid Services.

We appreciate you being here. And as you know, you have 5 minutes for an opening statement, and the yellow light will give you kind of an update. And I know you have a tight timeframe, so we are going to try to keep our questions to the 5 minutes as well. So we need to move forward so everybody gets a chance to answer their questions.

So I would like to welcome the Administrator here today, Ms. Chiquita Brooks-LaSure, and we appreciate you being here, and you are now recognized for 5 minutes for your opening statement.

Statement of the Hon. Chiquita Brooks–Lasure, Administrator, Centers for Medicare and Medicaid Services

Ms. BROOKS-LASURE. Thank you so much, Chairs McMorris Rodgers and Guthrie, Ranking Members Pallone and Eshoo, and members of the subcommittee. I just really want to thank you for the opportunity to discuss the Centers for Medicare and Medicaid Services' work to lower costs and increase transparency across the healthcare system.

As the Nation's largest payer for healthcare, CMS plays a key role in incentivizing high-quality care and smarter spending across the healthcare system. And I would like to highlight some of the work we have been doing.

Drug costs account for a growing portion of overall healthcare costs, and too often people are forced to choose between paying for their prescriptions or meeting other basic needs. CMS is hard at work implementing the Inflation Reduction Act. And thanks to this law, people with Medicare prescription drug coverage are already beginning to see lower out-of-pocket costs. This includes Medicare beneficiaries that need insulin, which now will no longer pay—will pay $35 for a month's supply.

CMS has also taken action to discourage drug companies from increasing their prices faster than the rate of inflation. And we continue to work on the IRA provisions that cap total out-of-pocket drug costs and allow Medicare to negotiate with drug manufacturers for the first time in the history of the program. Our efforts are lowering costs for people with Medicare and the program overall while improving access to innovative, lifesaving treatments.

In addition to lowering costs, CMS's efforts to increase transparency across the healthcare system will incentivize competition, improve consumer experience, and result in additional savings for our healthcare system and for patients. People should know the cost of their healthcare services and what they will be required to pay before they seek care. CMS is working hard to get this information into their hands, the CMS hospital price transparency rules providing public access to standard hospital charges, and we will continue to work to ensure that available information is meaningful and useful.

It is important that this information is available to all Americans, which is why we took action last year to increase the penalty for noncompliance to over $2 million annually. And I am pleased to announce today that we are updating our enforcement process to shorten the time by which hospitals must come into compliance after a deficiency is identified. Further, for hospitals that have not made any good-faith attempt to satisfy the requirements, we will no longer be sending a warning notice, and we will move straight to the corrective action plan phase.

In addition to improving the transparency of hospital prices, we are working to improve transparency from private health plans so that people know the cost of a covered item or service before receiving care. These data will help people to make informed decisions, and allows third-party developers to create price transparency tools that will help people shop for health plans and for doctors. It is critical to provide Americans with cost information before they receive care.

Additionally, CMS is also working to implement the No Surprises Act to protect patients from surprise medical bills after care has been received.

We are also committed to expanding transparency efforts across healthcare consolidation and its impacts on prices. In particular, consolidation in healthcare can leave rural and underserved areas with inadequate or more expensive healthcare options.

CMS is working to make public information on mergers, acquisitions, consolidations, and changes of ownership for hospitals and nursing homes enrolled in Medicare. Making facility ownership information available supports efforts to identify poor performers, better understand the impacts of consolidation, and help patients and caregivers make more informed decisions about their care.

Thank you for allowing me to highlight some of CMS's efforts to lower costs and increase transparency while continuing to expand access to high-quality, affordable care. We are committed to building on the work that we have done to address rising healthcare costs in a way that helps us advance health equity, expand access, improve health outcomes, and increase transparency. Thank you.

[The prepared statement of Ms. Brooks-LaSure follows:]

Statement of Chiquita Brooks-Lasure, Administrator Centers for Medicare & Medicaid Services on "Lowering Unaffordable Costs: Legislative Solutions to Increase Transparency and Competition in Health Care" Before the U.S. House Committee on Energy and Commerce, Subcommittee on Health April 26, 2023

Chairs McMorris Rodgers and Guthrie, Ranking Members Pallone and Eshoo, and Members of the Subcommittee, thank you for the opportunity to discuss the Centers for Medicare & Medicaid Services' (CMS's) work to lower health care costs and increase price transparency across the health care system.

As the nation's largest payer for health care, CMS plays a key role in incentivizing high-quality care and smarter spending across the industry. CMS programs cover over 170 million people across the United States, including more than 92 million people enrolled in Medicaid, the Children's Health Insurance Program (CHIP), and the Basic Health Program, over 64 million people enrolled in Medicare, and over 16 million Americans who selected or were automatically re-enrolled in health insurance coverage through HealthCare.gov Marketplaces and State-based Marketplaces (SBMs) during the 2023 open enrollment.[1,2] Efforts across the Agency are based on a foundation of goals that aim to advance health equity, eliminate avoidable differences in health outcomes experienced by people who are disadvantaged or underserved, and provide the care and support that our enrollees need to thrive.

We greatly appreciate the additional tools and resources provided by Congress through historic legislation such as the Patient Protection and Affordable Care Act (P.L. 111-148), and more recently, the American Rescue Plan Act (P.L. 117-2), the Inflation Reduction Act (P.L. 117- 169), the Bipartisan Safer Communities Act (P.L. 117-159) and the Consolidated Appropriations Acts, 2021 (P.L. 116-260), 2022 (P.L. 117-103), and 2023 (P.L. 117-328). Thanks to provisions in these important laws, the Administration has made tremendous progress toward increasing access to affordable treatments, strengthening the Medicare program, lowering prescription drug costs, and expanding access to health coverage in Medicaid and through the Marketplace.

CMS is committed to building on the work we have done to date, and is continuing to find ways to address rising health care costs—including both costs to the health care system overall and out-of-pocket costs borne by patients—in a way that allows us to advance health equity, expand access, improve health outcomes, and increase transparency.

Implementing the Inflation Reduction Act and Lowering Drug Costs

Drug costs account for a growing portion of overall health care costs, and Americans are often forced to make difficult decisions between paying for their prescriptions or other basic needs, like paying their rent or putting food on the table. On average, one in four Americans who take prescription drugs struggle to afford their medications. Nearly 3 in 10 American adults who take prescription drugs say that they have skipped doses, cut pills in half, or not filled prescriptions due to cost.[3] In 2021, prescription drug spending increased by 7.8% to $378 billion, compared to 3.7% in 2020.[4] CMS is responding to this growing problem by taking proactive steps to reduce what Americans pay at the pharmacy counter and to reduce overall drug spending within our programs.

Among other efforts, CMS is hard at work implementing provisions of the Inflation Reduction Act (IRA), which lowers prescription drug spending for millions of people with Medicare, redesigns the Part D program, keeps prescription drug premiums stable, and strengthens the Medicare program both now and in the long run. Thanks to this work, people with Medicare prescription drug coverage are already beginning to see lower out-of-pocket costs. For example, beginning in January of this year, people with Medicare prescription drug

---

[1] CMS FY 2022 Financial Report: https://www.cms.gov/files/document/cms-financial-report-fiscal-year-2022.pdf.

[2] CMS Press Release, "Biden-Harris Administration Celebrates the Affordable Care Act's 13th Anniversary and Highlights Record-Breaking Coverage" https://www.cms.gov/newsroom/press-releases/biden-harris-administration-celebrates-affordable-care-acts-13th-anniversary-and-highlights-record.

[3] Executive Order on Lowering Prescription Drug Costs for Americans, https://www.whitehouse.gov/briefing-room/presidential-actions/2022/10/14/executive-order-on-lowering-prescription-drug-costs-for-americans/.

[4] National Health Expenditure Data Fact Sheet, https://www.cms.gov/research-statistics-data-and-systems/statistics-trends-and-reports/nationalhealthexpenddata/nhe-fact-sheet.

coverage now have coverage of vaccines recommended by the Advisory Committee on Immunization Practices (ACIP), such as the shingles vaccine, at no cost. Starting October 1, 2023, most adults enrolled in Medicaid or CHIP will also have access to ACIP-recommended adult vaccines with no cost-sharing. And, as of January this year, people with Medicare prescription drug coverage who use insulin now pay no more than $35 per one-month supply of covered insulin. The President's Fiscal Year (FY) 2024 Budget builds on this progress by proposing to extend this $35 cap on insulin products for a monthly prescription to group and individual market plans.

Moving forward, CMS will continue our efforts to lower drug costs for the American people. In 2024, CMS will implement provisions of the IRA to remove burdensome coinsurance costs for people with Medicare prescription drug coverage whose out-of-pocket spending places them in the catastrophic coverage phase, and extend full cost-sharing assistance to all enrollees in the Low-Income Subsidy (LIS) program, lowering premiums and cost-sharing for an estimated 300,000 beneficiaries. And in 2025, for the first time, a cap on out-of-pocket drug costs for people with Medicare prescription drug coverage means millions of Americans won't pay more than $2,000 a year for their prescriptions, and they will have the option to pay their prescription costs in monthly amounts spread over the year rather than all at once.

Medicare Drug Price Negotiation Program

CMS is also focused on taking steps to lower drug costs leveraging new authority under the IRA for Medicare to negotiate directly with drug manufacturers for the price of certain high-expenditure brand-name drugs that don't have competition. Medicare's new ability to negotiate drug prices will mean lower drug costs for people with Medicare and the Medicare program, improving access to innovative, life-saving treatments for people that need them. Earlier this year, CMS took our first steps toward implementing the Medicare Drug Price Negotiation Program. The initial program guidance,[5] published on March 15, 2023, specifies the requirements and procedures for implementing the Negotiation Program for the first round of negotiations, which will occur during 2023 and 2024 and result in prices effective in 2026.

Among other things, the initial guidance details how CMS intends to identify selected drugs, consider factors in negotiation, conduct the negotiation process, and establish the requirements for manufacturers of selected drugs. CMS sought public comment on key elements of the initial guidance, and we will continue to provide multiple comment opportunities for members of the public, people with Medicare and their families, beneficiary and consumer advocates, pharmaceutical manufacturers, health care providers, and other stakeholders to provide input as we move forward with implementing the law.

Medicare Prescription Drug Inflation Rebate Program

CMS is also implementing the provisions of the IRA that discourage drug companies from increasing their prices faster than the rate of inflation. The Medicare Prescription Drug Inflation Rebate Program will require manufacturers to pay rebates to the Medicare Trust Fund in cases of price increases for certain drugs that exceed inflation, particularly brand name drugs, which make up 80 percent of all prescription drug spending. Since one of the primary drivers of

---

[5] Medicare Drug Price Negotiation Program: Initial Memorandum, Implementation of Sections 1191 – 1198 of the Social Security Act for Initial Price Applicability Year 2026, and Solicitation of Comments, https://www.cms.gov/files/document/medicare-drug-price-negotiation-program-initial-guidance.pdf.

increased prescription drug spending has been increases in spending per prescription, requiring rebates for price increases above inflation for drugs already on the market may help reduce future growth in Medicare prescription drug spending. Thanks to these policies, CMS is already reducing coinsurance for some people with Medicare Part B coverage.

Ensuring Sustainability Across CMS Programs

We are committed to fulfilling our obligation under the law to be a good steward of CMS programs, ensuring that taxpayer dollars are spent appropriately and improving the long-term sustainability of these programs.

Strengthening Medicare

The Administration is working to strengthen the Medicare program for current and future generations, and our efforts are getting results. This year's Medicare Board of Trustees Report estimates that the solvency of the Medicare Hospital Insurance Trust Fund has been extended by three years since last year's report.[6] Adopting the proposals in the President's FY 2024 Budget would further extend the solvency of the Medicare Hospital Insurance Trust Fund by at least 25 years by making the wealthy pay their fair share in taxes and by furthering efforts to lower prescription drug costs. Proposals in the budget would build on efforts in the Inflation Reduction Act (IRA) to lower prescription drug costs and would invest $8 billion to enhance Medicare benefits, such as expanding access to diabetes prevention services, behavioral health services including addiction services, nutrition and obesity counseling, and community health workers. Additionally, the budget proposes to align income and asset determination processes for people with Medicare, easing administrative burdens for states and removing enrollment barriers for individuals who seek help affording premiums and cost-sharing.

Strengthening the Medicare Advantage (MA) Program

All parts of Medicare should provide equitable, high-quality care that people can afford and that will be available for our children and grandchildren. This includes Medicare Advantage (MA), which now serves roughly 50% of all Medicare beneficiaries. To strengthen and improve the MA program, we released a series of regulations that take significant steps to protect beneficiaries, improve transparency and enrollee access to correct information, and protect the sustainability of MA by improving payment accuracy and recovering overpayments.

Most recently, on April 5, 2023, CMS finalized a rule focused on key consumer protections. As examples, the final rule includes changes to protect people exploring MA and Part D coverage from confusing and potentially misleading marketing practices. It also provides important protections regarding utilization management policies and coverage criteria that ensure that MA enrollees receive the same access to medically necessary care that they would receive in Traditional Medicare, while also streamlining prior authorization requirements and minimizing disruptions in access to care for enrollees.

On March 31, 2023, CMS finalized payment policies in the Calendar Year 2024 Medicare Advantage and Part D Rate Announcement[7] that improve payment accuracy, support continued

---

[6] 2023 Annual Report of the Boards of Trustees of the Federal Hospital Insurance and Federal Supplementary Medical Insurance Trust Funds, https://www.cms.gov/oact/tr/2023.

[7] Calendar Year 2024 Medicare Advantage and Part D Rate Announcement, https://www.cms.gov/Medicare/Health-Plans/MedicareAdvtgSpecRateStats/Announcements-and-Documents.

substantial value and choice in MA, and continue our efforts to improve and stabilize Medicare. Payment to MA plans is projected to be 3.32% higher, on average, in 2024 than 2023 based on the final 2024 Rate Announcement.

As required by law, CMS adjusts payments to health plans offering MA to reflect the expected health care costs of enrollees based on disease factors and demographic characteristics through a process known as "risk adjustment." This ensures CMS pays more for enrollees with greater health care needs and reduces incentives for plans to favor healthier beneficiaries. CMS routinely makes updates to the MA risk adjustment model to reflect more recent utilization and cost patterns and to ensure MA payments accurately reflect the costs of care for MA enrollees. Consistent with updates made in the past, in the 2024 Rate Announcement, CMS finalized a three-year phase-in approach to make updates to the risk adjustment model.

The updated risk adjustment model will more accurately pay for greater health care needs. As a result, the final policies will help ensure MA plan payments better reflect the costs of care for people enrolled in MA, with higher payments going to plans serving people with more health care needs, such as people with diabetes, depression, and other complex conditions like substance use disorder. The updated risk adjustment model includes more than 350 depression diagnosis codes and more than 300 diabetes diagnosis codes. Additionally, CMS will continue to make higher MA payments for an enrollee who is dually-eligible compared to someone who is not, for each diagnosis. The final policies help ensure people in MA can continue to access the care they need, including people who are dually-eligible for Medicare and Medicaid and people with chronic and complex medical conditions.

In January 2023, CMS also finalized policies to improve federal oversight of improper payments in MA through the Risk Adjustment Data Validation (RADV) Program. RADV audits—our primary tool to address improper payments in the MA program—involve the review of medical records submitted by MA plans to verify that the medical diagnoses reported by MA organizations for risk adjusted payments are accurate and documented in the medical record.

These changes will allow CMS to recover overpayments and support the fiscal sustainability of Medicare going forward.

These regulations work together with other efforts to improve access to care through MA, advance health equity, and strengthen Medicare's ability to serve seniors and people with disabilities today and in the future. In addition to protecting beneficiaries and the stability and sustainability of MA, CMS is also advancing health equity and driving quality in MA health coverage by establishing a health equity index in the Star Ratings program that will reward MA and Medicare Part D plans that provide excellent care for underserved populations.

Improving Price Transparency and Consumer Experience

In addition to lowering costs and increasing access to care, CMS's ongoing efforts to increase transparency across the health care system will help to incentivize competition, improve consumer experience, and realize additional savings across the health care system, including for patients. Lack of accessible information on prices makes it challenging for consumers to shop for services and limits competition. Over the past several years, CMS has implemented—and is continuing to implement—numerous complementary policies to promote transparency across the health care system.

Hospital Price Transparency Rule

In November 2019, CMS finalized a rule[8] establishing requirements for hospitals operating in the U.S. to establish, update, and make public a list of their standard charges for the items and services they provide, effective January 2021. While federally owned or operated hospital facilities, such as facilities operated by the U.S. Department of Veterans Affairs, military treatment facilities operated by the U.S. Department of Defense, and hospitals operated by an Indian Health Program, are deemed by CMS to have already met the requirements, the remainder are required to make their standard charges public in two ways: 1) a comprehensive, machine- readable file that includes all standard charges for all items and services provided by the hospital; and 2) a consumer-friendly display comprising at least 300 shoppable services, which can be satisfied through the release of a shoppable services file or by offering an online price estimator tool.

In 2021, CMS undertook rulemaking[9] to increase the penalty for noncompliance with the requirements. As a result, the maximum potential penalty amount was increased beginning in 2022 to $10 per bed per day, for hospitals with a bed count over 30, up to a maximum daily civil monetary penalty amount of $5,500. Therefore, the annual penalty amount increased from just over $100,000 annually per hospital to over $2 million annually per hospital in 2022. Between January and February 2021, and again between September and November 2022, CMS proactively conducted assessments of the websites of hundreds of randomly sampled hospitals to evaluate their compliance with the new requirements. A comparison of the results[10] shows progress in hospitals' implementation efforts since the Hospital Price Transparency regulation first went into effect, with 82 percent of hospitals in the sample meeting consumer-friendly display criteria, up from 66 percent; 82 percent posting a machine-readable file that met the website assessment criteria, up from 30 percent; and 70 percent doing both, up from 27 percent. While these results are encouraging, CMS takes seriously the concerns it has heard from consumers and stakeholders that hospitals are not making their standard charge information available online.

When a hospital is identified as potentially noncompliant (for example, through complaints made by individuals or entities to CMS, analyses related to compliance, or an audit), CMS begins a comprehensive review and works to bring hospitals into compliance. When deficiencies are found, a warning notice is sent to the hospital; if those deficiencies are not remedied, CMS requests a corrective action plan. If a hospital fails to respond to CMS's request for corrective action or comply with the requirements of the corrective action, CMS then issues a notice of imposition of a civil monetary penalty.

As of April 2023, CMS has issued over 730 warning notices and 269 requests for corrective action plans. CMS has issued civil monetary penalties to four hospitals for noncompliance

---

[8] "Medicare and Medicaid Programs: CY 2020 Hospital Outpatient PPS Policy Changes and Payment Rates and Ambulatory Surgical Center Payment System Policy Changes and Payment Rates. Price Transparency Requirements for Hospitals To Make Standard Charges Public" https://www.govinfo.gov/content/pkg/FR-2019-11-27/pdf/2019- 24931.pdf.

[9] "Medicare Program: Hospital Outpatient Prospective Payment and Ambulatory Surgical Center Payment Systems and Quality Reporting Programs; Price Transparency of Hospital Standard Charges; Radiation Oncology Model" https://www.govinfo.gov/content/pkg/FR-2021-11-16/pdf/2021-24011.pdf.

[10] HealthAffairs "Hospital Price Transparency: Progress And Commitment To Achieving Its Potential" https://www.healthaffairs.org/content/forefront/hospital-price-transparency-progress-and-commitment-achieving-its- potential.

(posted on the CMS website);[11] every other hospital that was reviewed through a comprehensive compliance review has corrected its deficiencies or is in the process of doing so, and CMS helps hospitals come into compliance by conducting extensive technical assistance with hospitals throughout the compliance process.

CMS continues to collaborate and work with hospitals and stakeholders to increase and improve compliance with the hospital price transparency requirements. Importantly, we have been engaging interested parties, including consumer groups, hospitals, researchers, and other industry experts, to obtain their feedback on the most useful and meaningful ways to display hospital standard charge information. For example, in response to stakeholder feedback that the price transparency machine-readable files can be difficult to use and understand, in November 2022, CMS released several sample formats with a standardized set of data elements for machine- readable files that hospitals could elect to adopt. When developing the data elements and sample formats, CMS sought public input on best practices through a Request for Information[12] as well as a technical experts panel comprised of industry experts from hospitals, technology, and academia. Further increasing standardization could help hospitals better comply with the regulations, aid CMS enforcement, and facilitate third parties' abilities to develop innovative products that make prices more accessible and meaningful for consumers.

CMS is also taking action to streamline its enforcement efforts, including by expediting the timeframes by which hospitals must come into full compliance upon submitting a corrective action plan. Moving forward, CMS plans to take additional aggressive steps to identify and prioritize action against hospitals that have failed entirely to post files. By taking these additional steps, we believe that, together with stakeholders and members of the public, we can further unlock the potential of hospital price transparency and achieve greater competition in the health care system and lower costs for patients.

Price Transparency in Private Health Coverage

In addition to improving the transparency of prices for services provided by hospitals, CMS now requires additional price transparency from private health coverage. Health plan price transparency helps consumers know the cost of a covered item or service before receiving care, allowing them to make more informed decisions.

In November 2019, CMS, along with the Departments of Labor and the Treasury (the Departments), finalized the Transparency in Coverage Final Rules[13] implementing requirements in the ACA for most group health plans and issuers of group or individual health insurance to publicly post pricing information for covered items and services. These rules have several components. First, as of July 1, 2022, most group health plans and issuers of group or individual health insurance coverage are required to publicly post pricing information for certain covered items and services. This pricing information can be used by third parties, such

[11] https://www.cms.gov/hospital-price-transparency/enforcement-actions.

[12] Included as part of the proposed rule "Medicare Program: Hospital Outpatient Prospective Payment and Ambulatory Surgical Center Payment Systems and Quality Reporting Programs; Organ Acquisition; Rural Emergency Hospitals: Payment Policies, Conditions of Participation, Provider Enrollment, Physician Self-Referral; New Service Category for Hospital Outpatient Department Prior Authorization Process; Overall Hospital Quality Star Rating" https://www.federalregister.gov/documents/2022/07/26/2022-15372/medicare-program-hospital- outpatient-prospective-payment-and-ambulatory-surgical-center-payment.

[13] "Transparency in Coverage" https://www.federalregister.gov/documents/2020/11/12/2020-24591/transparency-in-coverage#h-11.

as researchers and app developers to help consumers better understand the costs associated with their health care.

The Departments envision that third-party developers and other entities will download, process, and compile this data, creating more advanced price transparency tools that will help consumers shop among plans and providers, as well as giving the broader public information on patterns in health care costs and generate opportunities for innovation. For example, with pricing information, researchers can better assess the cost-effectiveness of various treatments; state regulators can better review issuers' proposed rate increases; patient advocates can better help guide patients through care plans; employers can adopt incentives for consumers to choose more cost-effective care; and entrepreneurs can develop tools that help doctors better engage with patients.

Next, by plan or policy years beginning on or after January 1, 2023, most group health plans and issuers of group or individual health insurance coverage are required to establish an internet- based price comparison tool that discloses personalized pricing information for 500 covered items and services[14] to their participants, beneficiaries, and enrollees through an online consumer tool, or in paper form, upon request. Cost estimates must be provided in real-time based on cost- sharing information that is accurate at the time of the request. By plan or policy years beginning on or after January 1, 2024, the internet-based comparison tool must include this information for all items and services.

Surprise Billing

In addition to implementing transparency provisions under the ACA, in September 2021, CMS implemented critical rights and protections for consumers under the No Surprises Act (NSA).[15] The NSA was enacted in December 2020 as part of the Consolidated Appropriations Act, 2021 (CAA), and CMS, together with our colleagues at the Departments of Labor and the Treasury, and the Office of Personnel Management, has been working to implement the law and ensure that consumers receive the benefits of the protections they are entitled to. In addition to expanding and improving the quality of information about costs available to consumers before they receive services, the NSA protects consumers enrolled in private coverage from receiving surprise medical bills when they receive most emergency services, non-emergency services from out-of-network providers at in-network facilities, and services from out-of-network air ambulance service providers. On September 16, 2022, the Departments issued a Request for Information (RFI) on implementing NSA requirements that plans and issuers provide enrollees an Advanced Explanation of Benefits. The RFI seeks information and recommendations on transferring data from providers and facilities to plans, issuers, and carriers; other policy approaches; and the economic impacts of implementing these requirements. Implementing the Advanced Explanation of Benefits requirement is a key priority for CMS. We want to ensure that, when consumers receive these documents, it provides meaningful, actionable information for them.

The NSA also requires all providers to provide 'good faith estimates' of expected charges to uninsured and self-pay consumers prior to receiving a healthcare service. Starting January 1, 2022, uninsured and self-pay consumers can access the patient-provider dispute resolution

[14] "Transparency in Coverage," 85 Fed. Reg. 72158, 72182-72190 (November 12, 2020).

[15] "Requirements Related to Surprise Billing; Part II" https://www.federalregister.gov/documents/2021/10/07/2021-21441/requirements-related-to-surprise-billing-part-ii.

process if they are billed an amount substantially in excess of the good faith estimate they received before the item or service was furnished. Uninsured or self-pay consumers who receive a final bill that exceeds the initial estimate by $400 or more can dispute the final charges using this newly-established process.

In order to ensure that consumers, group health plans, health insurance issuers, providers, facilities, and providers of air ambulance services have the tools and information necessary to understand and comply with these new requirements, in January 2022, the Departments launched the No Surprises Help Desk, which allows consumers, providers, and payers to ask questions concerning the NSA and submit complaints about potential violations of the law. The Help Desk refers complaints to the appropriate federal agency for follow up action. In some cases, states are the appropriate enforcement agencies. To assist stakeholders with the resolution of payment disputes and ensure fair payment, the Departments also set up an online portal for disputing parties and certified independent dispute resolution entities to resolve these disputes through the Federal Independent Dispute Resolution (IDR) process.

Between April 15, 2022, the date the Departments launched the Federal IDR portal, and December 5, 2022, disputing parties initiated over 164,000 cases through the Federal IDR portal—almost ten times the number initially estimated by the Departments for the full calendar year.

A significant portion of backlogged disputes are pending eligibility determinations. The process of determining whether a dispute is eligible for the Federal IDR process has been a more significant burden for certified IDR entities than either the Departments or the certified IDR entities initially expected. To address this issue, the Departments have engaged a contractor and government staff to conduct pre-eligibility reviews, which include outreach and technical assistance in support of the certified IDR entities' eligibility determinations. The Departments anticipate that continuing these efforts in 2023, in addition to pursuing other major reforms to accelerate throughput, will allow certified IDR entities to focus on making payment determinations and expedite the resolution of initiated disputes.

To implement the NSA and the transparency provisions of Title II of Division BB of the CAA, 2021, the Departments were provided a one-time appropriation of $500 million, which expires at the end of 2024. However, most of the added statutory requirements are permanent, and the Departments will have ongoing responsibilities such as enforcement of plan, issuer, and provider compliance; complaints collection and investigation; as well as auditing comparative analyses of nonquantitative treatment limits for mental health and substance-use disorder plan benefits. That is why the President's FY 2024 Budget includes a request for $500 million to replenish and extend the No Surprises Act Implementation Fund, ensuring the Departments will have sufficient funding to enforce this law in the future.

Hospital and Nursing Home Ownership Data

Hospital and nursing facility consolidation can leave underserved areas with inadequate or more expensive health care options. Making facility ownership information transparent supports efforts to identify common owners that have had histories of poor performance, to analyze data and trends on how market consolidation increases consumer costs, without necessarily improving quality of care, and to evaluate the relationships between ownership and changes in health care costs and outcomes.[16]

In April 2022, as part of the President's efforts to increase competition and transparency, CMS publicly released for the first time data on mergers, acquisitions, consolidations, and changes of ownership from 2016-2022 for hospitals and nursing homes enrolled in Medicare. This data, now available on data.cms.gov, is a powerful new tool for researchers, state and federal enforcement agencies, and the public to better understand the impacts of consolidation on health care prices and quality of care. In September 2022, CMS released additional data publicly on the ownership of approximately 15,000 nursing homes certified as a Medicare Skilled Nursing Facility, regardless of any change in ownership, including providing more information about organizational owners of nursing homes. In December 2022, CMS released detailed information on the ownership data of more than 7,000 Medicare-certified hospitals. And just last week the agency released ownership data for all Medicare-certified hospice and home health agencies. For the first time, anyone can now review detailed information on the ownership of more than 6,000 hospices and 11,000 home health agencies certified to participate in the Medicare program on the CMS website.[17]

In February 2023, CMS issued a proposed rule to require nursing homes to disclose additional ownership and management information, including information regarding individuals or entities that provide administrative services or clinical consulting services to the nursing homes. The proposed rule would also require additional information about entities that lease or sublease property to nursing homes and defines "private equity company" and "real estate investment trust ownership" for the purposes of provider enrollment and disclosure. Building on the proposals in the rule, CMS has taken steps to require Medicare skilled nursing facilities and other providers to disclose private equity company and real estate investment trust ownership interests via a revision to the Medicare enrollment application used by these providers.

In addition to fostering competition that drives high-quality care, transparent ownership data benefits the public by assisting patients, and their loved ones, in making more informed decisions about care. Analyzing this data will support CMS efforts to develop policy approaches that can improve competition in health care, a key priority for the Administration's strategy to reduce health care costs.

Moving Forward

The Administration has made expanding access to high-quality, affordable health care a top priority. We are working to not only lower prescription drug and health care costs but to make sure consumers fully understand the costs they will be expected to pay before they receive care.

CMS appreciates the work of Congress in passing groundbreaking legislation to help us achieve these goals, and we look forward to continuing to work together as we move forward

[16] ASPE, Ownership of Skilled Nursing Facilities: An Analysis of Newly-Released Federal Data, https://aspe.hhs.gov/sites/default/files/documents/fd593ae970848e30aa5496c00ba43d5c/aspe-data-brief-ownership- snfs.pdf.

[17] "For the First Time, HHS Is Making Ownership Data for All Medicare-Certified Hospice and Home Health Agencies Publicly Available" https://www.cms.gov/newsroom/press-releases/first-time-hhs-making-ownership- data-all-medicare-certified-hospice-and-home-health-agencies.

with implementation and continue finding ways to advance health equity, lower health care costs, and improve transparency across our nation's health care system.

Mr. GUTHRIE. Thank you, I appreciate that. And I will say that you have a hard stop. We want everybody to have the opportunity to ask questions, so I am going to be enforcing the 5-minute rule on questions.

So don't ask a question with 10 seconds left to go. So I will get started. I will—the Chair will now recognize myself for 5 minutes for questions.

And Administrator Brooks-LaSure, we will start with Alzheimer's disease. It has touched every family. And there has been a lot of attention to a decision to severely—by CMS—to severely restrict access to an entire class of FDA-approved Alzheimer's drug treatments. And the Veterans Administration announced it will cover one of these therapies, Lecanemab, which CMS will only cover in limited circumstances.

And in the case of Lecanemab, what is unnecessary and unreasonable about this FDA-approved drug with the Medicare-age patients?

And would you talk broader, or more of FDA and the Alzheimer treatments that have come forward that are only very limited cover by CMS?

Ms. BROOKS-LASURE. Thank you so much for the question about coverage of Alzheimer's drugs.

As you know, and we all know, Alzheimer's disease is incredibly devastating. And I want to thank all the advocates who are caring for the millions of Americans who suffer from a devastating illness. And it touches so many families, including my own.

I will start by saying it is CMS's responsibility to make sure, when we approach the coverage process, that we evaluate all the evidence and, of course, take in the work of the FDA. When FDA fully approves drugs—and in this case, for the treatment of Alzheimer's disease—that means that the FDA has made a determination that it will affect the disease itself. And when FDA fully approves drugs for Alzheimer's disease, CMS will cover it more broadly.

What—our requirements are that, once the drug is fully approved by the FDA, we encourage doctors and ask doctors who are prescribing the medication to make sure that information is available through our registry. And we are doing that because we need to continue to develop evidence of and understand the impact on the drug. But we will——

Mr. GUTHRIE. Do you believe CMS would benefit from Congress providing greater clarity into the phrase "reasonable and necessary" in the Medicare program?

Ms. BROOKS-LASURE. I would say that we have very clear guidelines, and we have outlined in our national coverage determinations how we approach our responsibility that we have from Congress, which is to evaluate coverage in Medicare populations. And we absolutely take the work that we get from the FDA as we consider our coverage.

Mr. GUTHRIE. OK. I know there are—other Members are going to address that as well, so I want to get to one question on the bill before us before we move forward. But that is concerning to all of us. It is bipartisan. I have heard both sides of the aisle talk about the access to this drug for Alzheimer's patients, and we are all concerned about it.

But before leaving office, President Trump finalized a Medicaid rule in place to permit manufacturers to submit multiple best prices, including a bundle sell option as well as value-based best price, to submit to a non-VBP best price opinion—option as well. We will have legislation, bipartisan legislation with myself and Chair—or Ranking Member Eshoo. H.R.

266, the MVP Act, would codify the rule. Will you commit to working with Ranking Member Eshoo and me to codify this rule?

Ms. BROOKS-LASURE. I will absolutely commit to working with you on outcomes-based options for Medicaid. This is something that we are very interested in in the administration, and have started to put together a proposal from the Innovation Center and would love to work with you on that.

Mr. GUTHRIE. So could you go further, and just discuss how this rule—because we have talked about the expensive treatments for sickle cell, for hemophilia that could—people who suffer from these diseases could greatly benefit from these programs. Could you just go and discuss more how these therapies will help patients by providing flexibility for Medicaid programs to structure them?

Ms. BROOKS-LASURE. Certainly. And while I won't talk about specific proposals, I will say that what we have seen across States is them needing to have more strategies as innovative therapies come to market that affect a limited number of people but where these illnesses are incredibly devastating.

And you talked about sickle cell disease. There are others, but sickle cell in particular, where it is so important that people know—that the doctors know how to treat that disease, and that they—people get those therapies. It is critical that States are able to cover those in a way that is affordable to them so that we can ensure access, and I would love to work with you on additional strategies.

Mr. GUTHRIE. Yes, I remember talking with Dr. Francis Collins, the previous NIH director, and he said that—he said, "I never used the word 'cure' for a lot of diseases, but sickle cell can be cured with some of these treatments, and we need to make sure people have access to them."

Ms. BROOKS-LASURE. Absolutely.

Mr. GUTHRIE. And so we look forward to—all of us—working together with the administration and from our side of the Capitol, or the—of DC to make sure we work together to move this forward.

My time has expired, and the Chair now recognizes the ranking member for 5 minutes for questions.

Ms. ESHOO. Thank you, Mr. Chairman.

I am very glad that the chairman raised the issue of Alzheimer's, the drug. We did not have a conversation with each other coming into this hearing, but I want to take up the same issue. And it is a demonstration that there is a really deep concern on both sides of the aisle on this.

I see, as I expressed to you when we spoke, a disconnect between CMS, the FDA, and the VA on new treatments for mild Alzheimer's. By July 6th, as you know, the FDA will determine whether Lecanemab is—it is a new treatment for mild Alzheimer's— whether it—that it will qualify for full approval. This will be the traditional FDA approval that is the gold standard, not an accelerated approval. That is already in place.

The VA has already said it will cover this drug as long as patients meet the criteria for use. Currently—and I am sure you are well aware—tens of thousands of veterans with mild Alzheimer's can go to their VA neurologist, be assessed, and receive a prescription. But it is unclear whether the estimated 1 million Medicare patients who could benefit from the treatment would be able to access the FDA-approved drug in July. And in order to access the drug, they may need to enroll in what you described to me as a CMS-approved prospective comparative study like a registry.

So I have just a few quick questions. They are not long answers, they are really yes-or-no.

Has Medicare ever required participation in a registry for a fully FDA-approved drug before?

Ms. BROOKS-LASURE. Let me start by saying that registries are not a study. So—just to be clear.

Ms. ESHOO. But have you ever done this before?

Ms. BROOKS-LASURE. We have. Registries are something that we have done, but I can get back to you on details about that.

Ms. ESHOO. Has CMS published any details about the required registry for fully approved Alzheimer's treatments, besides the general description that is in the April 22 memo?

Ms. BROOKS-LASURE. Not beyond that, but we——

Ms. ESHOO. OK.

Ms. BROOKS-LASURE [continuing]. Intend——

Ms. ESHOO. Do you know of any doctors' offices or health systems who are prepared to enroll Medicare Alzheimer's patients in the registry beginning in July?

Ms. BROOKS-LASURE. We welcome doctors to do so.

Ms. ESHOO. No, but have you—do you know of any that are prepared to enroll, any doctors——

Ms. BROOKS-LASURE. We wouldn't know that until——

Ms. ESHOO [continuing]. Or health systems?

Ms. BROOKS-LASURE. We wouldn't know that until FDA fully——

Ms. ESHOO. Have you published any information to Alzheimer's patients and their families explaining how to get the drug under Medicare?

Ms. BROOKS-LASURE. We will do so.

Ms. ESHOO. But it is not done.

Ms. BROOKS-LASURE. That is correct.

Ms. ESHOO. OK. So here is the thing. If doctors don't know, if patients don't know, and Medicare doesn't really seem to know what this registry entails, how are Medicare patients going to get the drug potentially beginning in July? That is really the $64,000 question in my mind.

Let me describe to you two constituents. One is a grandfather and a veteran. He has coverage. He has been diagnosed. His wife was also diagnosed. She is not a veteran. How do I, or any of us, explain that to our constituents?

This is, as you said and have said many times, this is a devastating disease, and I don't think this can be treated as 17 months of a little additional hope.

Any—this drug comes out, families across the country are going to be clamoring for it. Medicare is not prepared, from your answers. You are adding layers to this. The VA is doing something very different. And there is, as I said, there is a huge concern here.

This is a progressive disease. We know that early intervention with progressive diseases is really essential.

So I hope that you will leave this hearing with a new commitment and a new view of how to do this, because you are not prepared. And the beginning of July is, like, 2 months away—8, 9 weeks away.

So I will give you the opportunity to——

Mr. GUTHRIE. We are out of——

Ms. ESHOO. Well, all right, yes.

Mr. GUTHRIE. I am sorry, we are out of time. Hopefully, you will have a chance during the hearing to answer that——

Ms. ESHOO. I really, really——

Mr. GUTHRIE [continuing]. Because I want to hear your answer, as well.

Ms. ESHOO. Well, OK.

Mr. GUTHRIE. Absolutely.

Ms. ESHOO. Thank you, Mr. Chairman.

Mr. GUTHRIE. The Chair now recognizes Dr. Burgess for 5 minutes for questions.

Mr. BURGESS. I thank the chairman and the ranking member for bringing this up. I will just stay in the same vein for a moment. The AMA puts out a—what is called a Morning Rounds every morning. Yesterday the AMA Morning Rounds was—talked about how scientists are targeting mild cognitive impairment, the early Alzheimer's stages, with aggressive treatment. And if we don't have these things in our armamentarium because—not because of the FDA, which is a perennial problem, but it is you, with a coverage determination that removes a tool from what doctors are able to use.

It actually wasn't what I wanted to talk about. There's a lot of things. I am going to submit some stuff to you in—for questions for the record.

I do have to say, you know, Texas has had an issue with expanding Medicaid coverage to 6 months, which they did in the last legislative session. It actually was blocked by CMS for reasons that I don't understand. You—I wrote you a letter, the Texas delegation wrote you a letter. You responded and said you received it last November, but it really wasn't a satisfactory response.

I know the State legislature is working on something now. Yes, time marches on. Things are likely to change, but CMS needs to provide us an answer why they blocked this action by the Texas legislature, which I feel would have helped patients who were falling out of coverage after 3 months, as used to be standard practice. Granted, 6 months is not as good as 12 months, but it was a start, and Texas should have been allowed to have that State flexibility.

Now, what I really want to talk about is the bill that does away with the prohibition in Medicare physician-owned hospitals. And we have talked about this a lot in this committee. It is just fundamentally wrong that, because of an academic degree that I have, I am not able to engage in a lawful practice in this country. And yet you brought up in your testimony that consolidation in healthcare allows hospitals to own doctors. This is nuts. Hospitals can own doctors, but doctors can't own hospitals. Why is that OK?

So I do have a number of statements for the record. I have got a study that I want to submit for the record, Mr. Chairman.

Mr. GUTHRIE. Without objection, so ordered.

Mr. BURGESS. So let me just ask you, are you doing an analysis on—with this consolidation rulemaking that you are working on or anything in the CMMI model development, are you looking at removal of this prohibition on physician-owned hospitals?

Ms. BROOKS-LASURE. Thank you for the question. We need to follow the statute, which sets out what the requirements are and when—and in terms of physician-owned hospitals, which we are doing so.

And in terms of consolidation, our focus and our authority is around transparency. And that is why we have been working very hard to make it clear where we have ownership in nursing homes, hospitals, hospice, home health. That is where our authority lies.

Mr. BURGESS. Well, look. It was a physician-owned hospital in the Rio Grande Valley that saved a lot of people during the pandemic. Had they not stepped up—and they had to get a special waiver from the agency in order to just take care of the patient population they had to take care of, all because they were a physician-owned hospital.

So I am just simply going to ask, will you commit to work with me on this bipartisan issue to ensure CMS examines the considerations in the rulemaking process?

Ms. BROOKS-LASURE. I would be happy to work with you.

Mr. BURGESS. And let me further ask—CMS, in its recent inpatient prospective payment system proposed rule—you narrowed the opportunity for physician-owned hospitals to expand, raising barriers to entry and increasing costs. Will you work with me on that?

Ms. BROOKS-LASURE. I would absolutely work with you where—notice and comment, and happy to work with you on it.

Mr. BURGESS. Are you aware of a working paper coauthored by the Department of Justice and Federal Trade Commission staff addressing hospital competition and restrictions on physician-owned hospitals?

Ms. BROOKS-LASURE. I am definitely aware that DoJ is working on hospital consolidation.

Mr. BURGESS. So the Biden Executive order notes the need for improved labor market competition. This working paper notes that repealing the ban on physician-owned hospitals will increase labor market competition. Do you agree with that?

Ms. BROOKS-LASURE. I would have to review the document, thank you.

Mr. BURGESS. And we will make sure you have it available.

Look, we talk about access and particularly rural access. Physician-owned hospitals is a way to rapidly provide that access. And again, it is just fundamentally wrong that a hospital can own a doctor, but a doctor can't own a hospital.

Thank you, Mr. Chairman. I will yield back.

Mr. GUTHRIE. Thank you. I thank the gentleman for yielding back. The Chair now recognizes my friend from New Hampshire, Ms. Kuster, for 5 minutes.

Ms. KUSTER. Thank you, Mr. Chairman, and thank you for holding this hearing.

I want to thank all of the guests in the audience and my colleagues for addressing Alzheimer's. This was something that we lived with in our family, and I appreciate your advocacy.

I am going to turn to a different topic. I am glad to see that my bill, the PBM Accountability Act, was included for discussion. I want to thank the Chair. It is great to work with you, Chairman Guthrie and Ranking Member Eshoo and Congressman Buddy Carter, to introduce this legislation that brings transparency to pharmacy benefit manager operations and lowers costs for patients.

Administrator Brooks-LaSure, thanks so much for your testimony. I would like to focus on the challenges facing the Medicaid program, particularly the unwinding process and the threat from our colleagues on the other side of the aisle of work requirements.

In the past 3 years, Medicaid enrollment has grown substantially and the number of uninsured Americans, fortunately, has dropped. Nearly 95 million people had health insurance through Medicaid as of March of 2023. As we move to a new phase of the pandemic with the end of the public health emergency and States beginning the process of redetermining who is eligible for Medicaid coverage, we must recognize the risk to individuals and their families and the public health risks that we all became so aware of during the pandemic.

Estimates find that as many as 15 million Americans could lose health insurance coverage because of these redeterminations, including 6.8 million who would still be eligible for coverage and incorrectly lose their Medicaid. These numbers are staggering, but they can hide the true challenge that people in every single district across this country will experience.

Picture a family who loses coverage and is unable to access care, preventative services, behavioral healthcare, necessary medications because of factors completely outside their control: 6.8 million people will have an experience where logistics lead to them getting kicked off the Medicaid rolls, whether it be agency staffing shortages, low electronic renewal rates, or outreach barriers.

I want to ask you, Administrator, can you detail the efforts that CMS has made in coordination with States to prevent people from unnecessarily losing their Medicaid coverage?

Ms. BROOKS-LASURE. Thank you so much for highlighting how important of an issue it is for us to make sure we hold on to the millions of people who have coverage in the Medicaid program.

If we have learned anything over the last couple of years, it is how important it is that everyone has access to affordable healthcare in this country. It is important for the individuals themselves, their families, and for all of us to be safe and secure. We are at record-low levels of uninsured across this country, with over 92 million people who are enrolled in Medicaid and CHIP, many of them caregivers, hard-working individuals who have multiple jobs, who are in school, who are taking care of family and friends.

And so, for—when we think about the unwinding, what we are doing here at CMS is working very closely with States both on the Medicaid side as well as the marketplace side, and thinking about healthcare.gov to make sure that people are aware of the need to update their contact information and update their information if they get unwinding letters from States. And we are encouraging States to automatically enroll as much as they can, to automatically rely on data that they have in house.

We are also wanting to work with partners, community organizations, health plans, providers, everyone who touches a Medicare— Medicaid beneficiary. And I have been thrilled with some of the work that the private sector has been interested in doing and already beginning to make sure that people are aware of the importance of staying on their healthcare coverage.

Ms. KUSTER. Thank you. Medicaid, as we know, is the single largest payer for mental health services in the U.S. and is increasingly playing a larger role in the reimbursement for substance use disorder services.

My time is very short, but I am very concerned that recent analysis shows that the work requirement in a Medicaid program would jeopardize access to care for 21 million people, leaving millions without critical coverage when seeking mental health and recovery. Would you—would instituting Medicaid work requirements affect how patients and communities respond?

Ms. BROOKS-LASURE. What we have found over time is that whenever we put up red tape barriers to people being able to enroll in coverage——

Mr. GUTHRIE. Your time is expired.

Ms. BROOKS-LASURE [continuing]. It affects——

Mr. GUTHRIE [continuing]. The 5 minutes. I apologize. Hopefully, you will have an opportunity to answer as we move forward.

Ms. KUSTER. Thank you very much, and I will——

Mr. GUTHRIE. Thank you.

Ms. KUSTER [continuing]. Yield back.

Mr. GUTHRIE. The gentlelady yields back. The Chair recognizes Mr. Latta from Ohio for 5 minutes for questions.

Mr. LATTA. Well, thanks, Mr. Chairman, and thanks for holding this very important hearing today.

And, you know, there is broad bipartisan consensus that the price of healthcare is unaffordable and that government spending is out of control. As has been pointed out a little bit earlier, the United States spent about 4.3 trillion on healthcare in 2021, which represents about one-fifth of the U.S. gross domestic product. Unfortunately, without congressional action, healthcare spending is expected to increase to nearly 6.8 trillion by 2030. We all know this is unmanageable, and we need to find some solutions so we can put the patients first.

And, you know, I—in reading your testimony, when you were talking about the income—or the Inflation Reduction Act, under the IRA you state that lowers prescription drug spending for millions of people with Medicare, redesigns Part D, and keeps drug premiums stable, and strengthens the Medicare program both now and in the long term.

But let me ask this. You know, we know one thing: The United States leads the world out there in finding drug and new cures. And I know the gentlelady from California was talking about on the Alzheimer's side. But, you know, when we just went through COVID, I remember sitting in those early meetings around the table when COVID was just at its—we were just starting to deal with it. And sitting around with individuals from companies—and within a year, you know, we had three different types of medications out there. Nowhere else in the world could—did that occur but here in the United States. But it is because of—you know, we have here in this country.

Is there a concern at CMS that with what has been placed in the law right now could inhibit the creation of these new drugs and cures?

Because, again, it is just not one type of a cure out there that we need. In Alzheimer's, a cure that we have got to have—and I know on both sides of our families that we have seen the devastating effect of that horrible, horrible disease. But I am really concerned about what is going to happen into the future for companies being able to go out there and find these drugs, and make— get these drugs to the market.

Ms. BROOKS-LASURE. We share the goal that—of making sure that drug companies still absolutely have the incentive to be as innovative as they have been. And you are so right, that the drug companies were incredible in making sure that we were safe from COVID–19 with coming—bringing vaccines to market. And it is our every intention at CMS to make sure that we run the drug negotiation process in a way that continues to foster innovation but also makes sure that we can provide it to Medicare beneficiaries.

Mr. LATTA. OK, let me follow up, though. Because when you say that you are going to have that innovation out there, how are you going to provide that?

Because, again, this is something that everybody is talking about right now. But how is CMS going to make sure that you are going to be able to have—that the United States leads the world, and everybody sees is the envy of the world, in getting, you know, lifesaving cures to the market that we have to have?

Ms. BROOKS-LASURE. I would answer your question in two ways. First of all, we are working very closely with drug companies as we work on our guidance, and that is something I have personally done, as well as our staff have met with many, many companies and talked to them through what our process is going to be.

Second of all, the drug negotiation is something drug companies do every day. They do it with companies all across America, as well as, of course, the world. But they do it in our drug benefit right now. And we are building on that work, and taking all of that into account.

The drugs that we will be negotiating are drugs that have been on the market for many, many years. There are drugs that, by law, are going to be drugs that are top spenders where they have been on market for many years. But we will continue to work with policymakers and stakeholders to listen to concerns, listen to issues that they raise with their guidance, just like we are right this minute.

Mr. LATTA. Well, in my last 50 seconds—I know the chairman is being very good on keeping the time—because, you know, the United States—and we have had the hearings in here, we have seen the facts that around the—not only around the—you know, this hemisphere, but around the globe, when a lot of countries out there say what their costs are, really it is not apples to apples out there. It is really—because what is happening out there, we are seeing that the United States has a lot more drugs that could be provided, but other countries that are out there, they only have a certain number of drugs, and then those individuals might need a certain type of cancer drug, and the Government says, “You can’t have it, you are going to have to have this,” but it might not be the drug that they are going to have to have for—to get them cured.

So I just want to make sure that CMS always remembers that the United States is going to lead out there, because it is absolutely essential that we do to make sure that we have the best healthcare and the cures here, in the United States.

Mr. Chairman, I yield back.

Mr. GUTHRIE. Thank you. The gentleman yields back. The Chair now recognizes Mr. Ca′ rdenas from California for 5 minutes.

Mr. CA′RDENAS. Thank you very much, Chairman Guthrie, and also Ranking Member Eshoo, for holding this hearing.

And to Administrator Brooks-LaSure, thank you so much for weighing in on these transparency-related issues.

Before discussing proposals we are considering today, I feel like I must mention the threats we are seeing to Medicaid. There is a bill before us this very week that will institute what amounts to a significant cut to Medicaid access under the guise of work requirements. In fact, just yesterday HHS released new analysis showing that around 21 million Americans’ coverage and access to care would be threatened under the Medicaid work requirement proposal put forth by my Republican colleagues.

We have seen this before. And not only does it force people out of their insurance, it does nothing to boost employment. We can look at Arkansas as a case study. The State implemented these work and reporting requirements, and, as a result, thousands of people were disenrolled for failure to comply. For many of these people, they were kicked off not just because they were—not because they were ineligible, but because it was so difficult to navigate the reporting process. And that is really the point. The proposal is cruel, and a thinly veiled attempt to restrict access to coverage to American citizens, which brings me to my question.

Administrator Brooks-LaSure, why is access to Medicaid so critical, and how do work requirements and the reporting around them further disadvantage already vulnerable populations?

Ms. BROOKS-LASURE. Thank you so much for your question about how important coverage is.

I think we have gotten a lesson, as a country, of how important it is, not only with the COVID–19 pandemic, where it was critical that people could have access to vaccines and treatments, but also when we think about tackling our other crises in this country like maternal health, where we need to make sure that women are getting healthcare before they are pregnant, while they are pregnant, and afterwards to address health outcomes and so on down the list in terms of mental health.

You mentioned the experience that we saw in Arkansas, where people who would have met the requirements where they were working or where they would have been exempted lost coverage. That is what often happens in these situations. I spoke to a family during my time pre-CMS Administrator, when work requirements were in discussions. And I remember talking to a woman whose brother was disabled who absolutely would have qualified for an exemption, but she was very overwhelmed by the paperwork that she needed to fill out and the—and how confusing it was.

That is what happens when we put up barriers to people getting care, and it is critical that we make sure that people in this country are covered, not just for them, but for all of us.

Mr. CA´RDENAS. Is depression a medical condition?

Ms. BROOKS-LASURE. Depression is a medical condition.

Mr. CA´RDENAS. Could somebody find themselves diagnosed with clinical depression and want to work but for a period of time is having a difficulty being employed?

If that is the case, and the person isn't employed, and they are not able to navigate the system of paperwork, would that be denying somebody access to healthcare that they obviously critically need?

Ms. BROOKS-LASURE. It is so important that people are healthy so that they are able to work, so that they are able to live their lives. And absolutely, what we have seen is that people have gotten illnesses when they are uninsured, and that has prohibited their ability to be in the workforce. And that is what we don't want as a country. To make sure our economy continues to grow, to make sure that people are able to achieve the American dream, it is critical that we have that basic protection.

Mr. CA´RDENAS. Thank you. And I am very concerned about these requirements, and I am grateful for your defense of Medicaid on the record.

Now I also want to be sure to discuss the role of safety net hospitals in providing critical care to medically underserved and lowincome communities. I am glad to see policy proposals that would delay Medicaid DSH cuts, as this funding has been critical to upholding services in safety net settings.

Administrator Brooks-LaSure, if we do not step in, what type of impact would you expect for safety net hospitals, many of which are still struggling in the wake of COVID–19 pandemic, which is still with us?

Ms. BROOKS-LASURE. Yes, hospitals have been on the forefront of the pandemic and have been keeping so many of us safe and healthy through the last couple of years.

We know that the safety net has—disproportionately serves the underserved, and DSH payments do go to help support the payments for particularly them supporting the uninsured.

Mr. CA´RDENAS. Thank you so much. My time having been expired——

Mr. GUTHRIE. OK, the——

Mr. CA´RDENAS [continuing]. I yield back.

Mr. GUTHRIE. The gentleman yields back. I appreciate that. The Chair now recognizes the Chair of the full committee, Chair McMorris Rodgers, for 5 minutes.

Mrs. RODGERS. Thank you, Mr. Chairman.

Just to clarify regarding the proposal that the Republicans have on the floor for work requirements for Medicaid, the Democrats keep talking about millions. CBO just yesterday suggested that it estimated 600,000 may lose their Medicaid if these able-bodied adults with no children choose not to work, volunteer, or get training 20 hours a week. So if you are pregnant, you are not included. If you are a parent with children, not included. If you are mentally or physically unfit, the bill text is very clear, not included.

And I just want to get that on the record, because I don't want people to be concerned, people that—we all believe it is very important that Medicaid is a very important safety net. What we are trying to do is protect that safety net and encourage the able-bodied adults without children to work, volunteer, or get some training, come alongside them, and it is their decision.

Administrator, if—I wanted to ask some questions here. If you could ask Congress—you know, back to transparency now—if you could ask Congress for one specific improvement to price transparency rules, what would they be?

Ms. BROOKS-LASURE. What a question. I think that we have been given authority on price transparency, as we have talked about, with health plans and hospitals.

I will say that some of our transparency—our guidance on hospitals is probably very limited; there is one sentence in the statute. But I really would love to work with you to increase our authority on price transparency.

Mrs. RODGERS. OK, thank you for that. Ranking Member Pallone and I have proposed improvements to these rules, and I am glad that in your testimony you mentioned the importance of needing to standardize hospital price transparency data.

I believe that you are still not doing enough with the authority that you have, and there hasn't been enough enforcement across the board. I am specifically disappointed that you did not mention enforcing the existing requirement that PBMs disclose their drug prices. That is something that is included in the bill. So I just would like to ask, what has kept you from doing more to enforce these requirements?

Ms. BROOKS-LASURE. Certainly, and thank you for your leadership on price transparency and the push to encourage all of the entities to submit data.

On PBMs in particular, and price transparency on prescription drugs, because our rules interacted with new legislation that passed in No Surprises Act, we took a step and wanted to make sure it was coordinated, but we are committed to continuing to make sure——

Mrs. RODGERS. So the——

Ms. BROOKS-LASURE [continuing]. That information——

Mrs. RODGERS. Thank you. I will just take my—reclaiming my time. There is a lot more to be done. And this hearing is about competition, transparency. Healthcare businesses like PBMs continue to rapidly consolidate, finding new and innovative ways to add complexity, hide where the money is going. And we are fighting to pass strong transparency laws.

I bring up these key transparency provisions because, from the last bipartisan effort to address cost, they are not being implemented. Congress banned gag clauses, but I routinely hear from employers who cannot access their own health claims data. Patients are supposed to get good-faith estimates on cost when they schedule an appointment, but CMS is not enforcing this for patients with employer-sponsored insurance.

And I do not want this committee's efforts—we are going through a lot of work, hearings, bills to hopefully get a bill—you know, many bills—signed into law. I don't want it to languish for years while CMS prioritizes their other agenda. So failure to do the implementation harms the very patients that we are coming together to help in a bipartisan way. So will you commit to work with this committee to get properly implemented and enforced the bipartisan legislation?

Ms. BROOKS-LASURE. We continue to work to enforce the law, and absolutely will work with you on that.

Mrs. RODGERS. Thank you. We are seeing a dramatic growth in a newer kind of consolidation under payers. In other words, insurance companies purchasing healthcare providers. And to a patient it means your insurance company might own the doctor you see, the pharmacy where you get your medicine, and the PBM that decides how much you pay for that medicine. And I think we all have questions about what that means for patients and the costs that they pay and the quality of care that they receive.

Administrator, one of the proposals before us contemplates collecting numerous data points to tell us about the health of and the spending on patients who see doctors or pharmacies owned by insurance companies and PBMs, compared to patients that see independent doctors and pharmacies. Have you attempted to collect this data to better understand the effects of vertical integration?

Ms. BROOKS-LASURE. I do not believe we have authority to do so, but I am happy to look in at the issue.

Mrs. RODGERS. OK.

Ms. BROOKS-LASURE. But we very much support transparency around ownership and increased transparency.

Mrs. RODGERS. OK, lots more to come. Thanks for being here. I yield back.

Mr. GUTHRIE. Thank you. The gentlelady yields back. The Chair recognizes the Ranking Member Pallone for 5 minutes.

Mr. PALLONE. Thank you, Mr. Chairman.

Administrator Brooks-LaSure, thank you for coming here today. And as I am sure you have seen, last week the Republicans released their bill, what I call Default on America Act. And of course, it includes a provision that would threaten access to care for millions of low-income Americans and cut over $100 billion from Medicaid.

So last Congress, when Democrats were moving through reconciliation, Republicans repeatedly complained about the lack of regular order. And of course, we put those bills through multiple days of markups, considered probably dozens of Republican amendments, and debated for hours. And Republicans are skipping all of that and trying to rush a bill to the floor without so much as a hearing today. So I am going to take this opportunity to ask some of the questions I would have asked if Republicans had been willing to hold themselves to the same standards they held Democrats to last Congress.

And I know you have already been asked about the work requirements, but I want a little more information. Would you expect people to lose access to health insurance if Medicaid were to adopt a work requirement?

Ms. BROOKS-LASURE. I would expect that. And I would say again that it is not just people who are subject to the requirements that often get caught up in red tape. It is—can often be people who are exempted.

So, for example, in Arkansas what we found is that there was an individual who had health insurance, who was working, didn't realize that he needed to fill out the paperwork, lost his job, lost his insurance, had a health condition that made him unable to work. That—those stories replicate across barriers so often.

Mr. PALLONE. Now, this—thank you. The Centers for Medicare and Medicaid Services have previously said that the administrative burden can make it difficult for beneficiaries to comply with Med- icaid work requirements. Is it fair to say that many beneficiaries lose coverage because they get tangled up in red tape? And that is, I guess, your example, but if you want to——

Ms. BROOKS-LASURE. That is an example. I think we have seen it.

It is also—States are in the process of working on unwinding.

If—we want them focused on making sure they are meeting all the requirements that were established by the Congress at the end of the year and making sure, again, that we are holding on to coverage so that we are addressing health outcomes like maternal health, like mental health, and making sure we have a strong and healthy workforce.

Mr. PALLONE. So, Administrator, CMS has said that research shows that most Medicaid beneficiaries are either already working or subject to an exemption, and that this—and I quote— "this makes it challenging for such a work requirement to produce any meaningful impact on employment outcomes."

In other words, work requirements and Medicaid don't actually increase work. Is that correct?

Ms. BROOKS-LASURE. There has been no link when we have seen work requirements in States to an increase in employment.

Mr. PALLONE. All right. And to summarize, I mean, again, I know you have talked about this quite a bit with some of the previous Members asking questions, but to summarize, work requirements, in my opinion, won't increase employment. They will cause people to lose health insurance, and many of these people will still be eligible and just get caught up in the red tape, and is that correct?

And if you wanted to talk about——

Ms. BROOKS-LASURE. That is certainly our expectation, and based on our experience over the last many, many decades. When we establish new requirements for people, they form barriers to the people who are subject to them as well as to others.

Mr. PALLONE. Well, thank you. It is clear from your answers that—you know, why Republicans wanted to skip regular order on this bill. And that is because the Republicans' so-called work requirements is nothing more than another attempt by Republicans to take health insurance away from people and cut over $100 billion from Medicaid. And I am disappointed that my colleagues are choosing to ram this cruel and harmful policy through the House of Representatives without so much as a hearing. And I hope my colleagues will join me in recognizing this bill for what it is: another transparent attempt to take healthcare away from millions of Americans, unfortunately.

And with that, Mr. Chair, I yield back.

Mr. GUTHRIE. The gentleman yields back. The Chair now recognizes Mr. Griffith of Virginia for 5 minutes for questions.

Mr. GRIFFITH. Good morning. In CMS's recent notice of benefit and payment parameters rule, CMS finalized a policy that your agency has originally estimated would render more than 60,000 plans illegal to be on the ACA exchange. As many as 2.7 million people may lose their plan or have to scramble to try to find a new plan.

You just finished a whole discussion of people getting caught up in the red tape. Madam Administrator, aren't you the red tape? Aren't you all the ones who are saying you can't do this, you can't do that, particularly when it comes to these ACA exchange programs?

Ms. BROOKS-LASURE. I would say that we are working very hard to make sure that people can enroll in coverage, and that they have good options.

Mr. GRIFFITH. But you have taken 60,000 options, plans off the table.

Ms. BROOKS-LASURE. So the provision that I think you are referring to is our requirement around making sure that people understand the difference between their plans. People will have many dozens of choices. What we found in research and what we found from this experience of States——

Mr. GRIFFITH. And that may be true in some areas, but there have been times in my district, a rural district that is economically stressed, where there has only been one plan available, and now that has changed. There's a couple of plans available, but we are not going to have dozens. And then you have taken 60,000 plans nationwide across the board off the table.

And on top of that, we have seen price increases in the ACA plans. It stands to reason, does it not, that when you limit the number of plans, you create an incentive for price increases. Isn't that true?

Ms. BROOKS-LASURE. I would disagree.

Mr. GRIFFITH. OK, you disagree. I want to come back to that in a minute.

Where I had originally planned on starting before you talked about getting caught up in red tape, and I am back here going, "But you are the red tape," I wanted to talk about Alzheimer's. We have got a bunch of folks here from the Alzheimer's Association, including a former aide of mine in the Virginia legislature, Josh Myers, who is with us today. If you look around, you will see a lot of purple behind you.

This committee worked hard to change the way the FDA did its work so that we could get things that—medicines that take a long time to show benefit or to have an impact out there on the marketplace, because Alzheimer's is not something that you cure in a day or a week or 2 weeks. You have got to have years of using these medicines, particularly the—if I am saying it right—the amyloid plaque medications. And we changed those rules. We worked hard in this committee, this subcommittee, so that the FDA could approve it.

My question to you is then, the FDA has approved it; when did CMS decide or get authority to operate like a scientific regulatory body, when that is the FDA's job? And isn't that what you are doing? You have turned yourself into a regulating body, a scientific regulatory body, by denying paying for the Alzheimer's medication that this subcommittee, and this committee on a bipartisan basis, worked hard to make sure was available to the patients of Alzheimer's.

Ms. BROOKS-LASURE. Thank you for your question. And as we have all been talking about, Alzheimer's disease is incredibly devastating, both to the individuals who have it, and the families.

What we—our requirement by law is to do a determination of whether a drug is covered—whether it is reasonable and necessary for the Medicare population.

For the drugs that have been a—that have received accelerated approval——

Mr. GRIFFITH. And the FDA says it is reasonable and necessary. When the physician says it is reasonable and necessary—isn't it true you are just trying to cost shift?

Ms. BROOKS-LASURE. Our decisions are based on our requirements, the ones that we need to follow.

Mr. GRIFFITH. So you say we need to change your laws.

Ms. BROOKS-LASURE. Of course, Congress has the authority——

Mr. GRIFFITH. Has that authority.

Ms. BROOKS-LASURE [continuing]. To change our rules.

Mr. GRIFFITH. I just don't understand why you are going against what our clear wishes were from this committee, this subcommittee, and this—and the Congress of the United States.

I have time maybe to go into one other direction. On those plans that you ruled illegal for the ACA, one of those is a company that has—is a disrupter. It is trying to try a new model where they get rid of a lot of the middlemen and therefore don't have a network. They approve all drugs approved by the FDA. They will pay for them. It is a novel approach coming out of Ohio. You all ruled if you don't have a network, you can't be on an ACA plan. How does that make any sense?

Ms. BROOKS-LASURE. I would say what CMS focuses on is making sure that we know that if someone is enrolled in a health plan, they will have access to their doctors. And so that is our——

Mr. GRIFFITH. Well, this plan allows them access to any doctor they want, unlike the other ACA plans. It sounds like to me this is exactly what you ought to be moving forward to approving.

I appreciate your time, and I yield back.

Mr. GUTHRIE. The time has expired, the gentleman yields back.

The Chair now recognizes Dr. Ruiz for 5 minutes for questions.

Mr. RUIZ. Thank you. Thank you for holding this important hearing.

Lowering the cost of healthcare along with increasing access to care are two of my top priorities. So I am especially glad the Supporting Safety Net Hospitals Act, which will eliminate the pending cuts to disproportionate share hospital payments for the next 2 years, is included in this hearing for consideration.

You see, I grew up, practiced medicine, and now represent a district that is woefully medically underserved and in dire need of better, more equitable access to healthcare. In my district alone, I have four DSH hospitals: Pioneer, El Centro, Palo Verde, and San Gorgonio hospitals, all of which will be significantly impacted by these cuts. These hospitals that care for our most underserved populations are already operating on razor-thin margins, and any cuts could mean hospital closures, and we certainly cannot risk that. Many of my constituents are already forced to travel a significant distance to get to a hospital, so any hospital closure will lead to even worse access.

In addition to helping keep the doors open to DSH hospitals—or the DSH hospitals' doors open, such as El Centro, Pioneer, Palo Verde, San Gorgonio hospitals, we also need to address the healthcare provider shortage that is plaguing our country. One of the ways that we can do that is by increasing the utilization of community health workers and promotoras.

Administrator Brooks-LaSure, you say in your testimony that proposals in the President's budget to invest $8 billion to enhance Medicare benefits, such as expanding access to diabetes prevention services, behavioral health services, including addiction services, nutrition and obesity counseling, and community health workers. Can you expand on what the administration wants to do to increase access to community health workers?

And what is your understanding between the difference of community health workers and promotoras, and will those changes also help promotoras?

Ms. BROOKS-LASURE. Thank you so much for your focus on making sure that people, particularly the underserved, deliver care. And what we know is that there are so many types of organizations that are providing critical needs. And you mentioned safety net hospitals, which are on the forefront in many respects; Community Health Centers, where so many people get their private primary care——

Mr. RUIZ. Let me just kind of refocus, because I only have a certain amount of time, and my specific question is can you expand on what the administration wants to do to increase access to community health workers, or promotoras?

Ms. BROOKS-LASURE. So we are very committed to making sure that people who are helping to make sure that folks are connected to healthcare coverage and healthcare services, we are using our authority where we can, and welcome the opportunity to continue.

Mr. RUIZ. OK, thank you. I am working on legislation on—to increase access to community health workers and promotoras, and would love to partner with you on those efforts moving forward.

Ms. BROOKS-LASURE. Thanks.

Mr. RUIZ. Good?

Ms. BROOKS-LASURE. Mm-hmm.

Mr. RUIZ. OK. So switching topics to the No Surprises Act, this landmark policy was a huge win for patients who are now left out in the middle of paying—payment disputes between providers and insurance companies and are no longer receiving these balance bills, surprise medical bills.

But as you mentioned in your testimony, there is a significant portion of backlog disputes that are pending eligibility determinations. And I am sure you can imagine that I am hearing from a lot of folks about this backlog and the significant amount of time it is taking to get a resolution on their cases. And I think that the unanticipated backlog is indicative of just how important it was that we addressed the issue of surprise billing.

So I am pleased to hear you say that the departments are working to increase staff in order to address the backlog in eligibility determination, so that cases can be decided more quickly by the certified independent dispute resolution entities. So can you give us a status update on staffing, as well as how long you estimate it will take to clear the current backlog?

Ms. BROOKS-LASURE. I think you are very right in saying that the volume that we have gotten shows just how important of an issue No Surprises has been.

Mr. RUIZ. So can you give us——

Ms. BROOKS-LASURE. But yes, we will——

Mr. RUIZ [continuing]. A status update on staffing, as well as how long you estimate it will take to clear the current backlog?

Ms. BROOKS-LASURE. We are working very hard on that, and will continue to, and happy to follow up.

Mr. RUIZ. OK. So I will follow up with you on that one for a status update. Staffing is going to be very important. I do think that there are a lot of rural hospitals who serve in underserved areas who rely on us making sure that this backlog is cleared as soon as possible.

So with that, I thank you, and I yield back my time.

Mr. GUTHRIE. Thank you. The gentleman yields back. The Chair now recognizes Mr. Carter from Georgia for 5 minutes.

Mr. CARTER. Thank you, Mr. Chairman, and thank you very much for this hearing. This is something you know that I am very passionate about, and I can't tell you how much I appreciate it.

Administrator, thank you for being here. Just for the record, I am a pharmacist. I have practiced pharmacy over 40 years before I became a Member of Congress. I started when I was 10, by the way.

[Laughter.]

Mr. CARTER. But nevertheless, one of the issues that is most important to me is transparency and drug pricing. I was the one behind the counter who had to go and watch the senior citizen make a decision between buying groceries and buying her medicine. I was the one behind the counter who watched the mother in tears as she tried to find the money to pay for her child's antibiotic. And I set as my goal when I got here 8 years ago to do something about that.

The first thing I did was to go to the FTC and to ask them to look at the vertical integration that exists within the drug pricing chain, where the insurance company owns the PBM that owns the pharmacy that, in many cases, employs the provider. I asked them to look at that. Finally, after 71⁄2 years, they undertook a study last summer to look at the impact that the practices of the PBMs are having on independent retail pharmacies.

You know, this is a bipartisan issue. This is a nonpartisan issue. I never went to the counter and asked, "Are you a Republican or a Democrat?" The price was always the same. High drug prices impact everyone here in America, all Americans. That is why we have to do something about it.

Chair Rodgers asked you a question a little while ago, and I want to get clarification and be fair here. I believe she asked you if you had—I don't know whether she was talking about transparency or about the vertical integration, and you said you had no authority in that area. Was it about the transparency?

Ms. BROOKS-LASURE. It was about vertical integration.

Mr. CARTER. About the—OK, fair enough. I do believe that is the responsibility of the FTC, and I think the FTC has failed, has failed Americans in not undertaking that responsibility. And that is why I applaud them for this study that they are doing right now. And it is not just pharmacy, and it is not just drug pricing. It is consolidation within healthcare, period. You know, we had in this committee—we had the CBO, the Congressional Budget Office, before us in a meeting. We had the Director and we had 20 staff members. I asked them directly to give me one—just one—example of where consolidation in healthcare has saved money. They could not give me one. One example of where consolidation in healthcare has saved money, and they could not give me one.

You know, we all want the same things. Republicans and Democrats want the same thing. We want affordability, accessibility. We want quality in healthcare. That is what we want. And when we talk about accessibility, we have to talk about independent retail pharmacies, because 95 percent of all Americans live within 5 miles of a pharmacy, yet 4 percent of all independent retail pharmacies are going out of business every year as a result of the practices primarily of PBMs.

Now, I have got a bill here. You know what spread pricing is, and you understand it. We have got a bill, Drug Pricing Transparency in Medicaid Act. You understand that the State of Ohio, the attorney general, has just recently undertaken a lawsuit against the PBMs, referring to them as gangsters. And that is exactly what they are.

I just want to ask you, do you agree that more transparency is needed when PBMs are now vertically integrated, and own the insurance company that owns the PBMs that owns the pharmacy that in many cases employs the provider?

Ms. BROOKS-LASURE. I agree that transparency is important.

Mr. CARTER. Well——

Ms. BROOKS-LASURE. I did want to mention one thing that we have done—and it really did come from talking with pharmacists— was trying to increase the transparency with fees that are paid and to make sure that pharmacists would understand what the rules were. And it is something that we will continue to work on.

Mr. CARTER. What do you think you can do in helping us with transparency?

Ms. BROOKS-LASURE. I am happy to—our staff is happy to work with you on ideas around transparency.

Mr. CARTER. Well, we got plenty of them.

If we eliminated spread pricing, do you think that we could save money here in America?

Ms. BROOKS-LASURE. I think it is—as with——

Mr. CARTER. If I could, there was a study done—and it is a little aged now, it was done a little bit over a year ago—by the Berkeley Research Group that showed—and listen, and if you remember one thing, then remember this: It showed that only 37 percent of the price of a drug goes to the pharmaceutical manufacturer, which begs the question, where does the 63 percent go? It goes to the PBM, it goes to the middlemen. That is where the problem is. That is where we can control drug prices at.

I want to ask you to please commit that you will work with us to bring forth more drug transparency. We have got bipartisan legislation that we are working on now.

Ms. BROOKS-LASURE. I commit that we will work with you on——

Mr. CARTER. Thank you, and thank you for being here today, and I yield back.

Mr. GUTHRIE. Thank you. The gentleman's time has expired. The Chair now recognizes Representative Barraga´ n from California for 5 minutes for questions.

Ms. BARRAGA´N. Thank you, Mr. Chairman, for holding this hearing.

Thank you, Administrator Brooks-LaSure, for being here, for all the work that you do at CMS.

Before I want to start, I want to recognize advocates out here in our purple-colored shirts that are advocating for Alzheimer's. As you know, as many people have heard, my mother has Alzheimer's. She is 82 years old. And the issue of Alzheimer's and access to care, access to drugs, and making sure it is equitable is an issue that is not only near and dear to me, but requires advocacy.

Your testimony highlights that part of the goal that you have is to have equity. And it says "efforts across the Agency are based on a foundation of goals that aim to advance health equity, eliminate avoidable differences in health outcomes experienced by people who are disadvantaged or underserved."

We know that Alzheimer's impacts all Americans. We know that Latino communities are growing, and they are at huge risk of being those that are going to be impacted by Alzheimer's. And I have seen firsthand—and a lot of our families have seen firsthand—the devastation.

You and I have had conversation before, both through letters that I have sent to CMS asking them to reconsider its national coverage determination. We have had a meeting. You were very generous with your time. I appreciate your willingness to do that. I have held a press conference. I am going to continue to hold press conferences, and I have introduced legislation to try to fix—and what I see as a fix—to CMS's unprecedented decision to tightly restrict coverage for a whole class of Alzheimer's drugs.

And this is a bipartisan issue. This is something that we have heard from colleagues on both sides of the aisle and something that is, I think, meaningful and a failure, really, of CMS to provide meaningful coverage for the class of therapies targeting Alzheimer's disease. CMS's decision continues to concern me. And so I want to follow up to a letter I had sent to you and a response that you provided on March 27th, just a couple of weeks ago.

Administrator, you stated in your response letter to me on March 27th, when I urged you to reconsider the coverage policy—you said that—and I am quoting from the letter— "If the FDA approves a drug within this class based on a direct measure of clinical benefit, CMS will provide enhanced access and coverage for people with Medicare participating in CMS-approved studies, such as nationwide, registry-based study." And I am ending the quote there.

From my understanding, this means that CMS will continue its policy of only providing coverage for those enrolled in a CMS-approved study, which is concerning to me. Is that—is that accurate?

Ms. BROOKS-LASURE. No, in the sense of—I—and we will work to clarify what we mean by "registry," because it is clear that there is a misunderstanding.

When we say "registry," all that we are indicating is that individuals who are taking the drug, their doctors will put that information in a privately owned registry so that some of the other factors that are prescribed by the drug can be included. But it in no way limits people from getting access to the drug.

Ms. BARRAGA´N. But don't they have to be——

Ms. BROOKS-LASURE. Whatever is on the FDA label——

Ms. BARRAGA´N. Don't they have to be part of a study?

Ms. BROOKS-LASURE. It is not a study in the sense of it will just be included. The people who will be eligible will be based on the FDA label. So whatever—when FDA approves the drug, they say it—whichever populations they say it is appropriate for, that will be the basis of which people will get the drug.

Ms. BARRAGA´N. So you are basically saying that all patients indicated for—for example, the drug lecanemab—and any future therapies in the class will have coverage for the drug upon full approval?

Ms. BROOKS-LASURE. That is right.

Ms. BARRAGA´N. Do you know when such registries will be ready for patients to enroll and begin receiving treatment?

Ms. BROOKS-LASURE. We encourage——

Ms. BARRAGA´N. And will the registry be available the day of the FDA's approval, or will there be a delay?

Ms. BROOKS-LASURE. That is certainly our goal. Private-sector entities right now can start setting them up.

Ms. BARRAGA´N. OK. Administrator, can you tell us what other FDA-approved drug has been denied coverage by CMS?

Ms. BROOKS-LASURE. We have never denied a drug for an FDA- approved drug. We have done coverage with evidence development, which we are doing here.

Ms. BARRAGA´N. Well, except for this, right, except for this drug?

Ms. BROOKS-LASURE. We are not denying coverage. We have said that for an accelerated approval drug, it needs to be covered in the—under a clinical trial. And when it reaches Federal full approval by FDA, we will cover it more broadly.

Ms. BARRAGA´N. I think that is a little inaccurate, and that is my

concern, is it has been FDA approved, say, on an accelerated basis, and this is the first time that the CMS has not covered a drug, is my understanding——

Mr. GUTHRIE. I believe we have extended our time.

Ms. BARRAGA´N [continuing]. That was FDA-approved.

Mr. GUTHRIE. I agree——

Ms. BARRAGA´N. I am sorry.

Mr. GUTHRIE [continuing]. That accelerated approval is full approval, my understanding.

Ms. BARRAGA´N. I yield back.

Mr. GUTHRIE. Thank you for that. But I agree with you, 100 percent.

The Chair recognizes Dr. Bucshon for 5 minutes for questions.

Mr. BUCSHON. Thank you, Chairman Guthrie, and thank you, Administrator, for appearing today.

So following up on that, has the FDA told you that accelerated approval is not full approval and should be treated differently?

Ms. BROOKS-LASURE. We have many conversations with the FDA. We consider accelerated approval in a different category than full.

Mr. BUCSHON. OK, you do, but the FDA does not. So I want to just make that clear.

I am sure, like all of us here today, that you support lowering drug costs for all Americans, particularly seniors on Medicare who live on a fixed income. So I am curious why CMS chose to increase the taxpayer cost of cancer drugs and other expensive medications for serious diseases by 37 percent recently.

What I am referring to is that CMS traditionally paid 340B hospitals, which acquire drugs at a discount in order to reach more patients and expand care, which—I support the program—and provide more comprehensive services to those folks at around 80 percent of the average sales price. But as of September 2022, CMS reimburses for these drugs at 6 percent above average sales price. Why?

Ms. BROOKS-LASURE. We—and as you probably are aware, under the previous administration the policy was changed, and we have gone back to the original policy, as dictated by Congress.

Mr. BUCSHON. OK. Actually, it was a Supreme Court ruling, probably, that has really—

Ms. BROOKS-LASURE. That is right.

Mr. BUCSHON [continuing]. Caused that. But for the record, Justice Kavanaugh, in the ruling, ruled that CMS's first option is to pay for 340B drugs based on hospital survey data. And I understand that CMS has that survey data, which indicates that it should be paying for 340B drugs, that average sales price, minus 28.7 percent. Just saying.

So it is a little disingenuous to say you are—you know, and try to blame it on the Trump administration, and say you are going back to previous policy. It is based on a Supreme Court ruling. However, your interpretation of the ruling, I would argue, is inaccurate.

I have one additional question as it relates to this 340B court case. It is my understanding that CMS has not yet announced how it will handle payments for 340B drugs made prior to last September 28th. What is the plan?

Ms. BROOKS-LASURE. We plan—intend to issue it very soon.

Mr. BUCSHON. So you don't have a plan that you have publicly issued yet?

Ms. BROOKS-LASURE. That is correct. We will publicly do so in the next couple——

Mr. BUCSHON. OK. Do you have an estimate about what the expense will be, what the cost will be?

Ms. BROOKS-LASURE. We will issue that as part of the rule.

Mr. BUCSHON. OK. It is going to be in the billions and billions of dollars. I understand that. I mean, I believe in our system, you know, and the court made a ruling, and there we go.

Mr. Chairman, I don't really have any further questions. I just have a comment on the hearing in general. This is a great hearing for the American people. This is about lowering healthcare costs for all Americans regardless of your ZIP Code. It is about making sure Americans have access to FDA-approved drugs. It is about maintaining innovation and—in the healthcare marketplace. And at the end of the day, again, it is about access to quality, affordable healthcare services for the people that we all represent.

So I just want to commend the committee and the chairman of the subcommittee and the staff on the Republican side and both sides of the aisle on Energy and Commerce for this hearing. I have been in Congress for 13 years. I am a healthcare provider. And I am not using hyperbole here, but I think this is potentially one of the most important healthcare hearings that I have participated in since I have been on the committee.

Ms. ESHOO. Would the gentleman yield?

Mr. BUCSHON. I will yield.

Ms. ESHOO. I thank the gentleman.

I just would like to add something to the record in the exchange between Congresswoman Barraga´ n on it takes over a year, Madam Administrator, up to 17 months for approval on medical devices in terms of what you are referencing, the system you want to use for this drug. That is not acceptable. It really isn't. And so I just wanted to get that down for the record. And I appreciate——

Mr. BUCSHON. Yes, and I would yield——

Ms. ESHOO [continuing]. It, and I yield back.

Mr. BUCSHON. I reclaim my time. I want to make a comment on what Ms. Eshoo just said. I had—I am aware of a device in the past that I was involved in—many of us were—that took 5 years to get a national coverage decision of an FDA-approved medical device, limiting access. So the discussion around Alzheimer's drugs and other medications where CMS is not making quick decisions on drugs that have been through the FDA process needs to be looked at. I yield.

Mr. GUTHRIE. The gentleman yields back. The Chair now recognizes Ms. Representative Lisa Blunt Rochester from Delaware for 5 minutes.

Ms. BLUNT ROCHESTER. Thank you, Mr. Chairman, and thank you, Administrator Brooks-LaSure, for your testimony.

I am grateful that we are considering policies to lower unaffordable healthcare costs, and I would like to focus on a few programs that protect the health and economic security of low-income seniors.

I believe one of the most underdiscussed provisions of the Inflation Reduction Act is the expansion of the Medicare Part D low-income subsidy program, also called Extra Help. The low-income subsidy program pays Medicare Part D prescription drug premiums and cost-sharing for over 13 million individuals with low incomes who meet certain resource criteria. An estimated 40 percent of low- income Medicare beneficiaries spend 20 percent or more of their very modest income on premiums and other healthcare costs, which makes programs like the low-income subsidy program a lifeline for some seniors.

The Inflation Reduction Act expanded cost-sharing assistance to enrollees in the low-income subsidy program beginning in 2024. Can you tell us how this provision will lower drug costs for vulnerable Americans and what CMS will do to ensure that all people who qualify can take advantage of this new benefit?

Ms. BROOKS-LASURE. Thank you, Congresswoman, for highlighting what is one of the most exciting provisions of the Inflation Reduction Act.

Every year there are new provisions that take effect, and in 2024 we are very excited to expand coverage. We encourage seniors right now to look and see if they are eligible for what we call our Medicare savings programs and our low-income subsidy, because if you are already enrolled, you will automatically have access when next year starts to these additional protections around cost sharing.

It also expands the number of people who are going to be eligible. And so, as part of our annual open enrollment period, we are very focused on trying to get the word out to everyone to make sure that they enroll in this coverage if they are eligible.

Ms. BLUNT ROCHESTER. And you mentioned Medicare savings programs, and MSPs are also programs that help those with limited income and resources pay for Medicare Part A and B cost sharing. However, MedPAC has noted that many Medicare beneficiaries and providers do not know about the MSPs, and many beneficiaries who are eligible may be particularly—may be really difficult to reach them because they live in rural areas or they are homebound or have limited English proficiency or have vision, hearing, or cognitive difficulties.

Furthermore, conflicting enrollment and eligibility requirements between the MSPs and related Federal programs serving similar low-income individuals like the LIS program have resulted in low-income individuals having—there are being just inefficiencies in the—and creating underenrollment.

The President has proposed several reforms to ease the administrative burdens for States and remove enrollment barriers. Can you describe these proposals and how they would help low-income seniors afford their healthcare costs?

Ms. BROOKS-LASURE. We are incredibly focused on Medicare savings programs because so many people who are eligible for them are not enrolled, and that is something that we are very focused on. States administer them, and so we are really trying to make the connections even closer between the Medicare program—so when someone calls our call center, that they get connected to the State to get enrolled, and trying to limit the paperwork as—in terms of what people need to fill out.

Ms. BLUNT ROCHESTER. I would also like to associate myself with the comments of many of my colleagues about how important this hearing is.

Also, to the advocates who are here today, the Alzheimer's advocates wearing your purple, I always say, you know, as we said, this has touched so many of us, whether it is my grandmother, my mother, one of my good neighbors, that the reason why you wear purple is because this is not a red issue or a blue issue, it is an American issue. So thank you so much for your advocacy.

And I yield back.

Mr. BUCSHON [presiding]. The gentlewoman yields back. I now recognize Mr. Johnson from Ohio for 5 minutes for his questioning. Mr. JOHNSON. Well, good morning and thank you, Administrator Brooks, for making time in your busy schedule to speak with our committee. As I understand it, this is the first time that you have been in front of Congress, despite being in your role for nearly 2 years.

I take Congress' oversight role very seriously. And while we are on the topic of transparency in the healthcare space, I think it is reasonable to question the Biden administration's commitment to transparency, given that we haven't heard directly from you before our committee previously. So I appreciate having the opportunity to do that today.

You know, in late 2019 the Trump administration proposed and later finalized rulemaking to increase price transparency for patients, giving the American people all of the information about their healthcare as vital to ensuring they receive the care and treatment they deem necessary for their own lives and the lives of their loved ones. Since that rule went into effect, there have been varying reports of price transparency compliance among hospitals. To date, CMS has issued only four penalties for noncompliance. Yet a number of academic and nongovernmental studies have concluded that the number is much, much higher.

So my first question: Ms. Brooks, could you explain why there is such disagreement with concern to transparency compliance?

I mean, what metrics is CMS using that would cause such confusion about who is following the rules and who isn't?

Ms. BROOKS-LASURE. Thank you for your questions about transparency and the work of the committee, and we are very committed to implementing the rule.

Mr. JOHNSON. No, I want to—but I need you—Ms. Brooks, I need you to answer my question.

Ms. BROOKS-LASURE. Certainly.

Mr. JOHNSON. What metrics are you using that would cause the confusion about who is and who isn't following the rules?

Ms. BROOKS-LASURE. Some of the differences that people have where—in the different studies, in terms of whether people are complying, is because people have been looking at different metrics.

So we are looking at what our rules require. And I will give you an example, if that is helpful.

So there have been some questions where hospitals, for example, might have "N/A." The reason why they may do that is because they don't offer that service. And according to our rules, they don't need to do so.

Mr. JOHNSON. Well, when cross-referencing hospital pricing data with insurance company data under transparency in coverage, patient advocate groups are finding real dollars-

and-cents amounts in insurance company price data fields, whereas hospitals have posted N/As, blanks, dashes, and hyphens. So it is not that they are not offering those services, because the insurance companies are saying they are.

How can CMS consider hospitals that enter such data as compliant in good faith, as you did in an interview with NBC Nightly News, without first verifying the accuracy of the data?

Ms. BROOKS-LASURE. So as we have been talking about, we are working to implement the legislation. And when anyone lets us know that they think a hospital is in violation, we undertake a review, and we look to——

Mr. JOHNSON. And you have only found that four times out of all of the hospitals?

Ms. BROOKS-LASURE. No, that is not right. What we have done is we send first a warning notice if they have met certain standards, if they—if—we send a warning notice, we ask them to do a corrective action plan.

And what we have found is, by—the vast majority of hospitals, when they find out that they have not been in compliance, come into compliance, because that is our goal. Our goal is not to impose penalties, although we will absolutely do so, and we have increased our penalties. We are focused on getting hospitals into compliance, and that is why today we are shortening our timeframes.

Mr. JOHNSON. Well, then why is CMS blindly accepting hospital files, some of which have been flagged by various outside groups as compliant, without first verifying that the rates are legitimate?

Ms. BROOKS-LASURE. We review when we get a complaint, and happy to follow up on specifics.

Mr. JOHNSON. Well, I submit, Mr. Chairman, we are not going to get to transparency—and we all know what transparent does. Transparency improves competition, it ends up improving quality, and it lowers cost. That is across any industry. Price transparency is essential to lowering healthcare costs. And when you consider that healthcare costs are the most—are the largest part driving America's national debt, it is the most expensive part of what the Federal Government spends. This is a really important topic, Mr. Chairman. I yield back.

Mr. BUCSHON. The gentleman yields back. I now recognize Dr. Schrier from Washington for her 5 minutes for questions.

Ms. SCHRIER. Thank you, Dr. Bucshon, Mr. Chairman, and thank you, Administrator Brooks-LaSure, for coming to speak with us today. It is great to see you, and welcome.

You know, the last couple of years have been really hard for the medical community. Doctors and nurses and respiratory therapists were overwhelmed by the demands of the pandemic. Many put their health and their family's health at risk in order to care for patients. Some physicians had to pause elective procedures. Many shifted to telemedicine, as you know. And because of some of these financial strains, many small offices needed to close their doors.

At the same time, every year we scramble and panic by the end of the year to prevent cuts to Medicare reimbursement rates. And this is happening at a time of inflation and high wages. And it is hard for small and large practices to keep their doors open. In fact, according to the AMA, the failure of Medicare reimbursement to keep pace with inflation has had such a big impact on physician payment, it translates to a 26 percent drop in inflation-adjusted Medicare pay for doctors. And that is not a way to keep a system functioning.

Add to that early resignations and retirements, and there is a lot of strain on the system. What happens, then, to these small practices is that the big ones eat them up, and you end up with consolidation and a lack of competition and higher prices. And if those large systems can't stay afloat, what they will do is number—limit the number of Medicaid and Medicare patients that they will see in order to get by, and then patient access is impacted.

And so I am wondering, Administrator Brooks-LaSure, what do you see as the best way to bring down costs, increase transparency, have fair reimbursement, keep competition, and how can we help in Congress?

Ms. BROOKS-LASURE. Well, thank you so much for highlighting what we are hearing across the country, just how much doctors and other clinicians are struggling during—that is something that has been happening for many years, and certainly over the last couple of years, when the healthcare system has been incredibly strained. We are happy to work with you to continue to think about how we can support our workforce, how we can really try to make sure that all offices can continue to be able to thrive in different types of environments.

Ms. SCHRIER. Let's work together on physician reimbursement. I know the community, and all of us at some point will really appreciate that.

A quick question about transparency and pricing. I know we have talked a lot today about listing—list prices for procedures at hospitals, which seems really, really helpful on the surface, but it mostly applies to people who either have high deductibles or who are uninsured. And when I look at my explanation of benefits, there is a negotiated price that is far lower than that list price.

And so I am just wondering, given that many—most Americans are not paying the sticker price or a percentage of that sticker price, how much impact are these listed prices really going to have on the cost of healthcare in this country?

Ms. BROOKS-LASURE. It is a really important point. So we do have rules and requirements around health plans providing information about the—about procedures. And I think, for people who are insured, that can be a more helpful understanding of what their costs are going to be. But yes, if you have health insurance, you are going to likely choose the doctors that—and who are in your network.

The list prices, I would say, are a first step in transparency. They certainly are helpful for the uninsured, but also for third-party developers to use that information, and I know this committee heard from one such entity that can help with making the information more accessible.

Ms. SCHRIER. Thank you. I have one other issue, and I don't expect an answer, I just look forward to working with you to ease this problem.

I hear about this issue regularly from my patients, my constituents who are also patients, and it strikes a nerve with me because I have Type 1 diabetes, and have been using a pump for, like, almost 40 years. Patients on insulin pump therapy who have Medicare—even those who, like me, have been on a pump for decades and are stable and their doctor only thinks they need to come in once a year—they need to go see their physician every 3 months to get authorization to use an insulin pump. This puts them at risk for running out, it is a use of medical dollars that we shouldn't be spending. And I would just say that on these and other inefficiencies in the system, I would love to continue to work with you.

I am out of time, and I yield back.

Ms. BROOKS-LASURE. I am happy to talk.

Mr. BUCSHON. The gentlelady yields back—I agree with you on the insulin pump issue—and at this point I yield to Mrs. Harshbarger from Tennessee for her line of questioning.

Mrs. HARSHBARGER. Thank you, Mr. Chairman, and thank you for being here today, Madam Administrator.

I was concerned by the about-face that your agency took in the last 2 weeks reversing decades of policy that has otherwise precluded Federal healthcare coverage for undocumented immigrants. In that rule your agency wrote, "However, given the broad aim of the ACA to increase access to health coverage, we now assess that this rationale for excluding certain noncitizen groups from such coverage was not only statutorily mandated, it failed to best effectuate congressional intent in the ACA."

And I find it hard to believe that suddenly this administration, unlike the prior two administrations, now knows what congressional intent was and, all of a sudden, somehow you are aware of a statutory mandate that none of us knew about, including the Obama administration who passed the law.

Now, there's two documents, Mr. Chairman. In fact, I have these documents from the Obama administration that made it clear that DACA recipients were not eligible for Medicare or Medicaid or ACA coverage. And I would like to submit these for the record, Mr. Chairman.

So I guess my question——

Mr. BUCSHON. Without objection.

[The information appears at the conclusion of the hearing.]

Mrs. HARSHBARGER. My question to you, Madam Administrator, is how can you legally justify this sudden departure from the law?

Ms. BROOKS-LASURE. The Biden-Harris administration is focused on making sure that everyone has access to affordable coverage consistent with the law. We have made a determination that people who are brought to this country when they were children, known as DACA recipients, a closed cohort, so everyone who is a DACA——

Mrs. HARSHBARGER. Was that——

Ms. BROOKS-LASURE [continuing]. Under——

Mrs. HARSHBARGER [continuing]. By Executive order, or——

Ms. BROOKS-LASURE. It is under——

Mrs. HARSHBARGER. It is not congressional intent.

Ms. BROOKS-LASURE [continuing]. Administrative authority.

Mrs. HARSHBARGER. All right. I want to change subjects right quick.

In late 2021 CMS published a 9-page FAQ with the last Q&A stating, "It is a Stark violation if medical practices simply mail or otherwise deliver an oral drug to a patient." And I have practices in my district and in my State like Tennessee Oncology, and they are alarmed because they routinely send these oral drugs to patients in rural areas like my area as a convenience, or as a medical necessity when the patient is too sick to pick the drug up.

And as a pharmacist for over 35 years, I cannot understand, when an oral drug has been prescribed by a physician and dispensed for a patient, how in the world that constitutes a Stark violation when it actually costs that practice money to send it and mail it to a patient?

And I am saying that because a number of my House colleagues and I will be sending a letter urging you to retract that FAQ. And very recently, even HHS Secretary Becerra said at one of our committee hearings he would absolutely work with me and our colleagues on this issue.

So I just need a yes or no. Do you really intend that Medicare seniors who are too sick or without transportation to possibly go without their cancer drugs or any of these critical therapies?

Ms. BROOKS-LASURE. I am happy to work with you on this.

Mrs. HARSHBARGER. Fantastic. And as my colleague, Buddy Carter, mentioned, we have heard a lot about PBMs today, and how they operate in the shadows. There's many, many things we could talk about that, and even Secretary Becerra recently told the Senate Appropriations Committee that, with regard to PBMs, transparency would be helpful to see how they are operating, and the moment we try to do something, we likely find ourselves in court. We are trying to move the dial. That came from the Secretary.

And I have two questions, but I do want to tell you about a bill that I just put out this week. It is bipartisan legislation. It is called the PBM Sunshine Accountability Act. And what this would do would require public reporting of PBM information that the HHS Secretary already gets under current law. And it enhances the reporting to include the rebates and fees that PBMs and its financial affiliates receive from drug manufacturers and health insurers so we better understand the rebates and fees that companies are receiving when they are—where they are coming from, and what is not passed on to the clients and the patients. Would you be in support of something like that?

Ms. BROOKS-LASURE. I would be happy to work with you on that. Mrs. HARSHBARGER. Absolutely. And I have got a couple other questions, but I know my time is about up, and it concerns the No Surprises Act. And in 2020, when it was passed into law, it required to make publicly available by June 27th, 2023, a report on drug rebates, drug reimbursements, and pricing trends in commercial health insurance. And are you on track to meet this deadline?

Ms. BROOKS-LASURE. We are working to do this provision, yes.

Mrs. HARSHBARGER. OK. I know my time is up, so I yield back.

Thank you.

Mr. BUCSHON. The gentlelady yields back. Is Ms. Kelly ready for her line of questioning?

I yield now to Ms. Kelly for 5 minutes.

Ms. KELLY. Hello, Administrator. Good to see you.

Ms. BROOKS-LASURE. Nice to see you.

Ms. KELLY. Thank you, Chair Guthrie and Ranking Member Eshoo, for holding today's hearing.

Administrator Brooks-LaSure, thank you for being here today.

When we passed the American Rescue Plan, my legislation was included to extend Medicaid postpartum coverage from 60 days to 1 full year. This extension has been a crucial lifeline for mothers and their infants, and I am proud to say that this is no longer a temporary measure. Currently, 32 States and Washington, DC, have already made this extension permanent. Even other States like Alabama, Tennessee, Kansas, Oklahoma, and Nebraska have enacted postpartum Medicaid extension legislation.

The expansion of Medicaid postpartum coverage is a critical part of our efforts to address, as you know, the maternal health crisis in this country, as the Medicaid program finances about 4 in 10 births in the U.S.

Sadly, mothers aren't the only victims of our maternity care system: 1 out of every 1,000 babies born in the U.S., approximately 6 babies die.

Extending postpartum—Medicaid postpartum coverage to 1 year is part of our ongoing efforts to break down barriers to accessing care. I am deeply concerned that work requirements—I know someone mentioned it before—in Medicaid will undo our progress.

Administrator, are Medicaid work requirements a benefit or a hindrance to Congress' effort to make Medicaid more accessible to low- income individuals as well as new moms?

Ms. BROOKS-LASURE. Thank you so much for your work on maternal health, and it is very exciting that every time I talk we have more States that have come in to extend coverage postpartum.

And I think it is really important, when we think about the maternal health crisis, to remember that part of it is making sure that women have coverage before they are pregnant. That is one of the key pieces, that people have coverage so they can live healthy lives, they can work. And the vast majority of people on the Medicaid program are working. They are caregivers. They are students.

But what we have seen over time is that, when there are additional barriers to enrollment, that it creates people getting lost in the red tape. And that can mean people who are subject to the requirements, but very often it also means people who are exempt but need to make sure that they produce the right documents and produce the right forms and that they go through it. And let's remember who these people are. They are people working multiple jobs, who are juggling a lot of life.

And so I think it is—as we have seen, it is critical for people to have health insurance coverage, both for themselves, for their families, and for us, as a country, to make sure that we are safe when a pandemic hits.

Ms. KELLY. Thank you so much for your response.

On August 1st, 2022, CMS finalized the proposed rule, and will award a birthing-friendly hospital designation in the fall of 2023 to hospitals that have participated in a national or statewide quality collaborative and carried out the recommended intervention. This is the first-ever hospital quality designation by HHS that specifically focuses on maternal health.

How will these hospital programs be evaluated to ensure that the awarded organizations' outcomes are higher than the organizations without the designation?

Ms. BROOKS-LASURE. I am so excited about the work that we have been able to do on the birthing-friendly designation, particularly because the private sector has really partnered with us and is using it even more broadly. So more than half of the country will be able to look to see these designations for hospitals.

These are hospitals that will have agreed to have taken the recommendations from their maternal health experts and included those, and we intend to continue to get information from the public commenters about quality measures that we will hold these hospitals accountable for.

Ms. KELLY. I just want to thank you for all of your hard work, and your staff, and for being accessible and helping our office so much.

Thank you, and I yield back.

Mr. BUCSHON. The gentlelady yields back. I now recognize Dr. Joyce for his 5 minutes for his line of questioning.

Mr. JOYCE. Thank you for yielding, Mr. Chairman, and for holding this hearing today.

First, I would like to add my voice to the list of those concerned of what CMS has decided on restricting coverage for antiamyloid treatment for Alzheimer's disease. The CMS standard is defined in statute as "reasonable and necessary for the diagnosis or treatment of illness or injury, or to improve functioning of a malformed body member."

I would like to thank my colleague, Rep. Barraga′ n, for working on legislation with me to mitigate this misguided decision and would urge that this panel take lifesaving measures to address this issue.

Administrator Brooks-LaSure, I was encouraged to see the President's Executive order on competition take on hospital consolidation by noting that this consolidation has left many areas, particularly rural communities, with inadequate or more expensive healthcare options. Can you please elaborate on actions—and please be specific—your agency has taken to address hospital consolidation?

Ms. BROOKS-LASURE. Thanks. Thank you so much, Congressman, for your mentioning of the administration's real focus on consolidation.

Our authority at CMS on consolidation is really around transparency, and that is what we are focused on, making sure that there is ownership information available to people as they are choosing plans. There are other agencies across the administration with additional authority, of course. That is our focus.

Mr. JOYCE. Thank you. Building on this work, I am hopeful that you will be encouraged to see these bipartisan bills—draft as a way to address the President's Executive order by removing incentives for greater hospital and provider consolidation. Importantly, they are built on a foundation of work from the presidential administrations from both parties, nonpartisan groups like MedPAC, and academics and think tanks across the ideological spectrum.

Will you commit to work with us on these policies to mitigate consolidation and promote competition?

Ms. BROOKS-LASURE. I will absolutely do so.

Mr. JOYCE. This year over eight Humira biosimilars will launch in the U.S., with expectations of producing significant cost savings for patients and the healthcare systems. Medicare alone, it is estimated, could save over $2 billion if it had access to these biosimilars.

In order for patients and the Medicare program to realize these savings, biosimilars must have immediate access to Part D formularies. What policy actions is CMS taking to ensure that these Humira biosimilars are available to beneficiaries?

Ms. BROOKS-LASURE. We are certainly excited about innovative drugs that come to market in particularly biologics and other generics. I am happy to talk in more depth about what we do to encourage Part D formularies—Part D plans to cover——

Mr. JOYCE. I personally welcome that discussion. I think it is so important for patients across America.

Earlier this year I sent a bipartisan letter asking CMS to take action about biosimilars and formulary access. One point that I raised was having CMS update guidance to ensure maintenance charge—maintenance change policies were updated to include a broad array of biosimilars. What is the status of this request?

And will you commit to doing a thorough review to ensure that biosimilar formulary access is not only permitted but is also done in a way that ensures patients can utilize them?

Ms. BROOKS-LASURE. We will follow up with your request, and——

Mr. JOYCE. Thank you.

Ms. BROOKS-LASURE [continuing]. I will get you a status update.

Mr. JOYCE. I appreciate that commitment.

Finally, I would like to thank you, Mr. Chairman and Ranking Member Eshoo, for the work that you have done on the MVP Act and echo my support for this important legislation.

One of the things that is so important about the MVP Act is it adequately is flexible for many different disease states. As a physician, I understand how different some outcomes could be across different disease states. For example, the outcomes that you might measure and the length of time you would measure them might look different for a gene therapy for muscular atrophy than outcomes for hemophilia. The multiple best price approach would allow payers and States to establish VBAs that could encompass multiple outcomes, including one for diseases where a pay-over- time arrangement is truly the most appropriate way.

Can you discuss how important it is that the best price approach capture different types of VBAs in order for them to work across all disease states?

Ms. BROOKS-LASURE. I certainly agree, and am excited that the committee is going to focus on outcome-based proposals to make sure that we can—make sure that States can afford to cover drugs, that people have access to them, and ones that really support these innovative—

Mr. JOYCE. Thank you for——

Ms. BROOKS-LASURE [continuing]. Therapies.

Mr. JOYCE [continuing]. Your commitment to access. My time has expired, and I yield.

Mr. BUCSHON. The gentleman yields. I now recognize Mr. Sarbanes for 5 minutes.

Mr. SARBANES. Thank you very much, Mr. Chairman. I appreciate it.

Administrator, thank you for being with us today and for your testimony about the many efforts that CMS is undertaking to create a more transparent, accessible, and affordable healthcare system. We certainly appreciate it.

Last year, as you know, Congress finally—finally, after many, many decades, really—took the historic step of standing up to Big Pharma and enacting policies that are already—we are seeing it— lowering healthcare costs for millions of seniors in the Medicare program.

As the Inflation Reduction Act reforms continue to be implemented over the coming years, we must continue to build on this success, and I am glad the subcommittee today is undertaking what is a bipartisan discussion of some of the issues that contribute to rising healthcare costs today.

Too often, when asked to identify the driver of the high cost of prescription drugs, the various actors in the supply chain point the finger at others, and the veil of secrecy surrounding so many healthcare pricing and contracting practices makes it virtually impossible for anyone to fully and accurately—and certainly, not easily—follow the money trail. This is, in fact, an intentional design feature that allows Big Pharma to continue to increase its prices and, along with pharmacy benefit managers, its profits.

So, Administrator, how can the administration's current work to increase transparency help policymakers better understand these pricing practices, get behind this design, and help patients make more informed decisions about their healthcare?

Ms. BROOKS-LASURE. Thank you for noting just how monumental the Inflation Reduction Act is.

I get asked a lot of questions as CMS Administrator, but I don't know one that I get asked about the most more than prescription drug coverage and the ability of people to pay for their prescriptions in this country. And we are really moving forward and tremendously excited about the opportunity to bring additional benefits to negotiate, and we are committed to transparency as far as our authority allows and want to continue to work with you on all of the proposals that you are considering.

Mr. SARBANES. Let me turn to increasing transparency and better understanding of some of the drivers of healthcare costs. If we have a better understanding of these factors, we can address them more effectively, which will, in turn, improve patient access and care overall.

In Maryland, as you know, we have been working to improve patient care while lowering systemwide healthcare costs for decades. Since the 1970s, we have had a hospital all-payer system. It is unique now. And our current total-cost-of-care model uses global hospital budgets to incentivize value-based care, eliminate the need for charity hospitals, and strengthen the quality and comprehensiveness of care provided to all individuals regardless of their geographic location in the State or their insurance status. It is really a visionary approach.

And Maryland's total-cost-of-care model also allows our State to invest in other health system goals, like lowering the maternal mortality rate and the opioid overdose mortality rate, decreasing the number of children who visit emergency rooms for asthma, reducing adult Marylanders' risk of diabetes, and so on.

So, Administrator, what benefits do patients and providers do value-based approaches like the one that we have done in Maryland offer, and how can we work to incentivize and expand similar approaches across the country in this effort to lower costs and improve access to care for all Americans?

Ms. BROOKS-LASURE. Thank you for raising Maryland's innovative approach to paying for care, and it is one of the models that, through our CMS Innovation Center, we are really focused on trying to create other opportunities for States for other types of programs to really be able to operate and move to much more of a value-based, outcomes-based program.

We have a number of demonstrations that are underway and ones that we are intending to pursue, and really encourage all stakeholders to reach out to us about ideas.

Mr. SARBANES. Thanks very much. I look forward to continuing to engage with CMS and others to further strengthen Maryland's total-cost-of-care model and apply lessons learned from that success to drive future healthcare initiatives.

I yield back, Mr. Chairman.

Mr. BUCSHON. The gentleman yields back. I now recognize Mrs. Miller-Meeks for her 5 minutes.

Mrs. MILLER-MEEKS. Thank you, Mr. Chair, and thank you, Ms. LaSure, for being here.

There were those of us who spoke very eloquently during the Affordable Care Act that provisions within the Affordable Care Act would lead to increased consolidation, both hospital ownership of physician practices, larger physician practices, and that consolidation would lead to procedures being done at hospitals at higher cost and ultimately would lead to increased healthcare costs.

And in 2019 and in 2020, almost 50,000 physicians left private practice to work for hospitals or other corporate entities. Roughly 70 percent of physicians are now employed by larger systems, meaning just 3 out of 10 doctors practice independently. Hospitals are motivated to gobble up physician practices because they are able to bill Medicare roughly double the amount that private practices are.

Not only do payment differences in Medicare cost the Government and taxpayers more money, but it costs seniors more because they are paying inflated coinsurance amounts for services that would cost significantly less if provided by a nonhospital-owned practice.

For example, a level 2 nerve injection in 2023 done in a physician's office would result in a $226 payment from Medicare. That same injection provided by a hospital outpatient department would result in a $741 payment. Same service, but a $515 payment increase due to it being provided in a different location, putting the patient and the Government on the hook to cover the delta.

And I am in a district that has numerous both critical access hospitals, community hospitals, and in-between hospitals. And so I am very sensitive to, you know, the concerns of my rural hospitals, but when we are talking about the entire healthcare system and the cost of the healthcare system and trying to provide increased access and increased quality care, I think this is concerning.

A 2020 estimate from the Congressional Budget Office projected $141 billion in savings, and I think that has now been increased to 158 by some more recent studies, $158 billion over the next 10 years, if site-neutral payment reforms were implemented.

And let me also say that I was a physician in academic medicine and in private practice, and a hospital-employed physician.

MedPAC has also supported site-neutral payment reform, not only because it would reduce cost to beneficiaries but because it would reduce incentives for vertical integration or consolidation in our healthcare system, which, as we all know, drives up costs.

Can you detail CMS's plans to implement site-neutral payment reform, and how can Congress help?

Ms. BROOKS-LASURE. Well, thank you so much for talking about how important rural hospitals are, which is something that I have been spending a lot of my time and travels just hearing from rural hospitals, their issues, as well as the issues around consolidation, which I think we all are very much concerned about.

I would say that, as you know, for the most part, Medicare payment policy is determined by statute. And so we are following the way that we pay according to what Congress has passed. In some limited circumstances we have implemented site-neutral payments where we feel that we have authority, but happy to work with you in ways that we can continue to make sure that people can get care in the most appropriate setting.

Mrs. MILLER-MEEKS. And we are also seeing a concerning trend of physicians being purchased by payers, with one health insurance company now owning 7 percent of all physicians in the United States. So another vertical integration that is extraordinarily worrisome.

And do you believe it is better or worse for patient care when physicians leave private practice?

Ms. BROOKS-LASURE. We certainly want to make sure that people have access to care and access to choices, and consolidation can be an issue with that.

Mrs. MILLER-MEEKS. Thank you so much for your testimony and for being here.

I want to also echo the sentiments—my mother had Alzheimer's, so I appreciate all of you here in purple supporting Alzheimer's and our support for getting drugs that have been approved through the FDA on to the marketplace and covered. So I echo the sentiments of my colleague.

Thank you, Mr. Chair. I yield back.

Mr. BUCSHON. The gentlelady yields back. I now recognize Mrs. Trahan for 5 minutes.

Mrs. TRAHAN. Thank you to the chairman and to ranking member for holding this important hearing today. Thank you to our witness, Administrator Brooks-LaSure.

I first want to start my remarks by voicing my strong appreciation for our hospitals and their workers, for the unbelievable job that they do in our communities. Whether it is a global pandemic, a natural disaster, a marathon bombing, a mass shooting, our Nation's hospitals are always there, and American patients expect them to be there, capable of meeting their needs in times of crisis.

You know, many of my colleagues on this committee know that, when appropriate, I will take opportunity to talk about a critical safety net hospital in my district: Lawrence General Hospital. Law- rence General serves a majority of Medicaid patients in a city that is 80 percent Hispanic or Latino. Under extremely challenging circumstances, the nurses, doctors, and administrators at Lawrence General have continued to deliver high-quality, affordable care to the underserved.

Like many safety net hospitals coming out of COVID, Lawrence is struggling financially. Administrator Brooks-LaSure, how important is it to maintain access to care for underserved areas like Lawrence, Massachusetts?

And what is the agency doing to protect the Nation's safety net providers?

Ms. BROOKS-LASURE. Thank you so much for mentioning how important our Nation's hospitals are in all sorts of situations, but certainly over the last couple of years, as we have been going through the COVID–19 pandemic.

We are absolutely committed to doing everything we can within our own authority and have been looking at ways that we can support a host of hospitals, certainly including safety net hospitals which care for the most underserved, and would love to continue to work with you all on that.

Mrs. TRAHAN. So I fully believe this committee has the responsibility to legislate in a way that allows our hospitals to deliver care while also lowering costs for American patients. Many of the bills in this hearing today are in the discussion draft phase. So I do look forward to working with my Republican colleagues to finalize them in a bipartisan manner.

Administrator Brooks-LaSure, it is my understanding—and as my colleague from Iowa just mentioned—that in recent years there have been efforts by CMS to implement site-neutral payment policies for certain services. However, there are exemptions to the statutory requirement for rural sole community hospitals, cancer hospitals, and children's hospital to maintain access to appropriate care. Has CMS measured how some exemptions to site-neutral payment policies have maintained access to care in underserved areas?

And how would extending similar exemptions to the Nation's safety nets help them financially?

Ms. BROOKS-LASURE. I am happy to follow up with you on that question.

Mrs. TRAHAN. Thank you. Safety net hospitals often rely heavily on Medicaid and Medicare reimbursements to provide care to underserved populations. And any reduction in reimbursement rates could potentially impact their financial sustainability and their ability to provide essential services in their communities.

We know that CMS supports the Nation's hospitals. Can you share how CMS is thinking about lowering Medicare costs for patients while balancing the need to protect and defend these critical providers?

Ms. BROOKS-LASURE. We certainly, within our authority, are very focused on pulling all of the levers that we can, and happy to continue our discussions around that.

Mrs. TRAHAN. Well, I look forward to following up. I mean, it is worth noting that site-neutral payments can be a complex issue. While I am here to lower healthcare costs for patients, promote price transparency, and encourage competition among healthcare providers, I do want to make sure we are keeping in mind any unintended consequences that may limit access to care because of the discussion drafts in the hearings today.

So I look forward to working closely with you, with my Republican colleagues to continue to work on the policies before us today.

And thank you, Mr. Chair. I yield back.

Mr. GUTHRIE [presiding]. The gentlelady yields back. The Chair now recognizes Mr. Crenshaw from Texas for 5 minutes for questions.

Mr. CRENSHAW. Thank you, Mr. Chair.

Thank you, Administrator, for being here. I think we all share the common ground of lowering healthcare costs and, especially, shoring up hospital safety nets. And without appropriate protections that stem from costs from charity care, access is impaired and everyone's healthcare costs go up.

I want to talk about the Medicaid Disproportionate Share Hospital program, the DSH program. It is an example where we provide very transparent payment to hospitals that do provide that charity care. Our healthcare system is complex. It is highly regulated. But the DSH program goes around this by directly giving straightforward payments to hospitals that are doing the good work of serving patients without coverage.

Unfortunately, this is often—this program has been cut in favor of other priorities like the Affordable Care Act, and it has been cut as a budget gimmick. Now, we have kicked the can down the road by delaying those cuts for years and years and years. I am proud to partner with Congresswoman Clarke on bipartisan legislation to create a fully paid-for, 2-year solution to Medicaid DSH funding, which covers the costs of safety net hospitals that treat these at- need, uninsured populations, avoiding these cuts also in a way that is more fiscally responsible.

I just want you to comment on that and underscore how important the DSH program is. I mean, you know, which hospitals bear the brunt of potential DSH cuts?

Ms. BROOKS-LASURE. As you were mentioning, so many of our safety net hospitals are the ones who would lose payments, according to DSH, because DSH really focuses on people—on hospitals that serve a disproportionate share of uninsured or Medicaid beneficiaries.

Mr. CRENSHAW. So I am going to assume that you would agree that we should probably——

Ms. BROOKS-LASURE. Yes.

Mr. CRENSHAW [continuing]. Not cut those in the future.

Ms. BROOKS-LASURE. I would say that it is very important that we maintain coverage for safety net hospitals.

Mr. CRENSHAW. And do you agree with the assessment?

I mean, the Affordable Care Act's cuts were problematic for these healthcare safety net programs.

Ms. BROOKS-LASURE. I would say that it is important that, particularly as we still have uninsured in the country, to make sure that hospitals are paid for caring for them.

Mr. CRENSHAW. Yes, I mean, I would point out for the record, I mean, one of the problems here was that the DSH cuts did come from the ACA. There was a miscalculation of how many Medicaid enrollees would be in the program. It doesn't matter if it was an expansion State or a nonexpansion State. I mean, I am—Ms. Clarke is helping me lead this, obviously, and that is New York. So the last question I have: Do you agree DSH payments are an accountable and direct mechanism with which to subsidize hospitals?

And as we rethink incentives in the system, could DSH be a good model for transparency when we do need to support hospitals in need?

Ms. BROOKS-LASURE. I do think that DSH is an incredibly important program, and a way of really understanding who is serving the——

Mr. CRENSHAW. Well, it is an important program. But, I mean, the framework, the way it is actually——

Ms. BROOKS-LASURE. Yes, I would agree with you——

Mr. CRENSHAW [continuing]. Administered, do you think——

Ms. BROOKS-LASURE [continuing]. That there is——

Mr. CRENSHAW [continuing]. It is a good model?

Ms. BROOKS-LASURE. I think that there is a lot of wisdom to having some understanding of what the mixed-payer mix looks like in terms of payment.

Mr. CRENSHAW. I want to talk about primary care access in the Medicaid program. You know, a simple question: Do you think there is a physician shortage, and where do you see that most pronounced?

Ms. BROOKS-LASURE. I would agree with you that we are seeing workforce challenges, and it is not everywhere, but it is in so many of our rural areas. And you mentioned primary care. We absolutely have a lack of primary care in many parts of the country.

Mr. CRENSHAW. Yes. I am introducing bipartisan legislation that would seek to—open access to independent primary care physicians in State Medicaid programs, particularly through recurring preset payments. We call that direct primary care. And I am doing this because in too many parts of my State—and throughout the coun try, actually—there is a shortage of primary care physicians to serve this critical population. The patient-to-physician ratio in rural areas is 39 to 100,000 people, compared to 53 to 100,000 in urban areas. And we are looking to have a shortage in the United States of as many as 55,000 primary care doctors.

So I think this is very important legislation. I urge my colleagues to support it for obvious reasons. You know, access to primary care reduces emergency room utilization, improves outcomes, probably reduces overall healthcare spending. You know, we often talk about getting people access to coverage, but that isn't care. I think this legislation would go far in allowing States to experiment with their own Medicaid programs.

There is no question in there, but if you have any last remarks or positive things to say about that, go ahead.

[Laughter.]

Ms. BROOKS-LASURE. Just to agree with you that it is crucial that we do more to support primary care in this country.

Mr. CRENSHAW. Great. Thank you. And I yield back.

Mr. GUTHRIE. Thank you. The gentleman yields back. The Chair, seeing none on the minority side, will recognize Mr. Bilirakis from Florida for 5 minutes for questions.

Mr. BILIRAKIS. Thank you. I appreciate it, Mr. Chairman.

Administrator Brooks-LaSure, I have expressed concerns about the practice of large health systems purchasing independent, free- standing physician offices and then subsequently billing for the same services by the same providers at a significantly higher hospital rate. The Office of Inspector General and others have explained that this dynamic has created adverse incentives for consolidation and inappropriate billing practices that ultimately cost the Medicare program and cost patients who have to pay 20 percent copay for hospital outpatient services.

So I wanted to ask you about the process CMS undertakes after a hospital purchases a physician office practice to subsequently bill at the hospital rate as a hospital outpatient department. Can you please tell us what CMS does and what the process involves to ensure that hospital-acquired freestanding physician offices are compliant with the relevant conditions of participation and other provider-based facility requirements in Medicare in order to bill as a hospital?

And then I have a followup, as well.

Ms. BROOKS-LASURE. Certainly. And as I thank the committee for really focusing on hospital consolidation and our concerns around what that is meaning for physician offices, our role is to certainly put out, based on Congress, payment policies. And when hospitals agree to get payment from us, they agree to follow the rules around all of our guidances. And we certainly will investigate if a hospital is billing incorrectly.

Mr. BILIRAKIS. Yes, that is my followup: Will you commit to work with members of this committee to ensure this process is efficient and effective and ensuring these facilities meet the necessary requirements to bill as hospitals?

Ms. BROOKS-LASURE. Yes.

Mr. BILIRAKIS. OK. Very important for our patients too.

Next, I also wanted to ask you about CMS's transitional coverage of emerging technologies rule. We are almost 2 years after the agency's repeal of the original MSET rule, which we had expressed was incredibly disappointing at the time. CMS promised to replace it with a new TSET rule to provide Medicare coverage for new medical breakthrough device technologies but has yet to do so despite the target date supposedly set for this month. That is why I led bipartisan legislation in this space to provide this pathway into law, since it is clear CMS has little interest in advancing innovation for patients.

Again, Administrator, can you tell us when will CMS release and implement your final TSET rule?

And what is CMS planning to do to ensure this simply isn't another CED process but instead a meaningful separate pathway for new devices with existing, sound data that does not require additional evidence generation?

If you could answer that, I would appreciate that very much.

Ms. BROOKS-LASURE. Yes. We are committed to releasing updated guidance this spring, and I will just say that we have been working and talking with stakeholders, device companies to make sure that they have an understanding of our roles, and will—we will absolutely put that out very soon.

Mr. BILIRAKIS. OK, very good. We are going to stay on you with that.

One of the themes on our agenda today is about discouraging additional consolidation in the marketplace. In one of our draft bills, the Provider and Payers Compete Act would require HHS, during its annual rulemaking on Medicare provider payments, to consider the effects these regulatory changes have on further consolidation in the marketplace. I have been concerned about how the physician fee schedule, for example, is contributing to these trends.

How will you ensure your agency is doing what it can, from a regulatory standpoint, to prevent additional consolidation, whether it is through the physician fee schedule or other rules that affect provider reimbursement?

Ms. BROOKS-LASURE. I would be happy to work with you on any and all ideas that you have for us in terms of our authority.

Mr. BILIRAKIS. All right, very good. Thank you. I guess my time has run out.

Thank you, Mr. Chairman. I yield back.

Mr. GUTHRIE. The gentleman yields back, and that concludes all Members present who have asked questions or—questions. Thank you for being here today.

I think just the one thing I can say both sides have absolutely agreed on, that we need to work on the Alzheimer drug and make sure that people have access as we move forward.

I appreciate the opportunity for you—I appreciate you being here, but I did have three letters for the record I forgot to submit for the record. I showed the ranking member. It is for our bill, so it is supporting our bill together. And then Dr. Burgess offered one I am not sure I correctly submitted for the record.

So without objection, so ordered.

[The information appears at the conclusion of the hearing.]

Mr. GUTHRIE. Thank you for being here, and we appreciate your time, and we got you—our agreed-upon time, so we appreciate that. And now we will get ready for panel 2.

[Pause.]

Mr. GUTHRIE. The second—the hearing will come back to order, and we will be prepared for the second panel. I will introduce our witnesses, and then we will recognize each other for 5 minutes for questions.

I think most of you have testified or seen this, that you all have a light. When—you have a green light. When the light gets yellow, it means to start summarizing, and to be ready to finish. And when it is red, it means time has expired. So you have 5 minutes for moving forward.

So I am going to introduce the witnesses, and we will begin the questions—the opening statements.

So first, Ms. Ashley Thompson, senior vice president of public policy analysis and development for the American Hospital Association.

Next we have Karen [sic] Bass, chief policy and external affairs officer for the Pharmaceutical Care Management Association.

Our next witness will be Brian Connell, executive director of Federal affairs for Leukemia & Lymphoma Society.

The next witness is Sean Cavanaugh, chief policy officer for Aledade—sounded like a Kentucky Derby horse name, so —that is coming up in a couple of weeks, so watch Kentucky.

Our next witness will be Ilyse Schuman, a senior vice president of health policy for American Benefits Council.

And then Mr. Loren Adler, associate director of the USC–Brook- ings Schaeffer Initiative for Health Policy.

We appreciate you all being here, taking the time. I know you have—most of you were able to listen to the first panel, and know what some of us are thinking and what our thoughts are, so we appreciate that. We appreciate you being here. All of us are going to be working together to work on these pieces, specific pieces of legislation before you today.

And so with that I will begin with—our first witness will be Ashley Thompson, senior vice president of public affairs.

Statement of Ashley Thompson, Senior Vice President, Public Policy Analysis and Development, American Hospital Association; Kristin Bass, Chief Policy and External Affairs Officer, Pharmaceutical Care Management Association; Brian Connell, Executive Director, Federal Affairs, The Leukemia & Lymphoma Society; Sean Cavanaugh, Chief Policy Officer, Aledade; Ilyse Schuman, Senior Vice President, Health Policy, American Benefits Council; and Loren Adler, Fellow And Associate Director, USC-Brookings Schaeffer Initiative for Health Policy, Economic Studies, Brookings Institution

Statement of Ashley Thompson

Ms. THOMPSON. Chair Rodgers, Ranking Member Pallone, Chair Guthrie, and Ranking Member Eshoo, and members of the committee and subcommittee, I appreciate the opportunity to testify on behalf of the American Hospital Association's 5,000 member hospitals and health systems.

Hospitals and health systems are cornerstone of communities across our Nation. The more than 6 million people who work there provide care, compassion, and comfort for the sick and injured 24/ 7, 365 days a year. Last year they delivered 3.5 million babies and provided emergency care for 123 million people. They are at the forefront of developing new techniques and technologies to prevent, diagnose, and treat disease and are responsible for training the next generation of doctors and other clinicians.

While hospitals' commitments to caring never wavers, the reality is right now they are facing many significant challenges. These include historic workforce shortages resulting in a national crisis, soaring costs of providing care, cracks in the supply chain, overwhelming regulatory and administrative burdens, and severe underpayment by Medicare and Medicaid.

These challenges are jeopardizing access to care and services for patients and communities. Some hospitals are being forced to cancel or close critical services, particularly in rural areas. Patients are experiencing longer wait times to receive care. As all of you are hearing, hospitals are boarding patients ready for discharge with- out any additional reimbursement because post-acute care facilities and nursing homes do not have space. Several hospitals are struggling to remain open.

The AHA appreciates the subcommittee's dedication to healthcare affordability, a goal that all of our members fundamentally share. Thus, I appreciate the opportunity to comment on five of the issues addressed by the subcommittee's legislative proposals. Moreover, the AHA looks forward to discussing them further with committee members and staff over the next several weeks.

First, as you know, the hospital price transparency rule went into effect 2 years ago during one of the most difficult periods of the pandemic. Since then, hospitals have made significant progress complying with these regulations. According to CMS, 70 percent of hospitals have adhered to both components of the rule, despite its complexity and lack of clarity. Hospitals are eager to continue their compliance efforts, and the Transparent Price Act affords an opportunity to continue to work together towards this goal.

Secondly, the AHA strongly opposes legislation that would lead to additional site-neutral payment cuts and threaten access to patient care. There is nothing neutral about site-neutral policies. Compared to other healthcare settings, hospital outpatient departments treat patients who are often older, poorer, sicker, and with more complex medical conditions. Hospital outpatient departments also must comply with more comprehensive licensing, accreditation, and regulatory requirements. Additionally, hospitals are required to maintain standby capacity for disasters, public health emergencies, and unexpected traumatic events, as well as deliver emergency care regardless of insurance status.

Third, the AHA strongly supports the 340B drug discount program, which is crucial to helping hospitals stretch limited Federal resources and expand health services to patients and communities. We appreciate the subcommittee's interest in making sure all stakeholders meet 340B program integrity requirements. Already, 340B hospitals must attest to meeting all program requirements, recertify their eligibility annually, participate in audits conducted by HRSA and drug manufacturers, and maintain records and inventories of all 340B and non-340B prescription drugs. The AHA would oppose efforts to create significant new reporting requirements for 340B hospitals. In addition, any measures that increase transparency for 340B providers also should include greater transparency for drug companies.

Fourth, the AHA opposes changes that would either expand the number of physician-owned hospitals or ease restrictions on the growth of existing facilities. Studies show that physician-owned hospitals cherry-pick patients who are less medically complex and more financially lucrative, as well as provide limited or no emergency services.

Finally, I would like to express strong support for the Medicaid DSH legislation. We appreciate that Congress has, on a bipartisan basis, kept the Medicaid DSH cuts from going into effect. Hospitals care for a significant number of low-income, uninsured, and Medicaid patients, and the Medicaid DSH program is critical to maintaining access to essential services for these individuals.

Thank you for the opportunity to testify. I look forward to taking your questions.

[The prepared statement of Ms. Thompson follows:]

Testimony of the American Hospital Association for the Committee on Energy and Commerce Subcommittee on Health of the U.S. House of Representatives
"Lowering Unaffordable Costs: Legislative Solutions to Increase Transparency and Competition in Health Care"
April 26, 2023

Chairman Guthrie, Ranking Member Eshoo, and members of the Subcommittee, I am Ashley Thompson, senior vice president of public policy analysis and development, at the American Hospital Association (AHA). On behalf of our nearly 5,000 member hospitals and health systems, along with our clinician partners, I appreciate the opportunity to testify today.

We appreciate the Subcommittee's ongoing interest in addressing transparency and competition in health care. Advancing the health of our patients is a priority for the AHA and its members, whether it is providing for their health care needs or sharing the information they require to make informed care decisions.

We welcome the opportunity to discuss the legislation the Subcommittee is considering as it applies to the Hospital Price Transparency Rule; site-neutral payment policies; mergers and acquisitions; the 340B Drug Pricing Program; physician-owned hospital restrictions; and the Medicaid Disproportionate Share Hospital (DSH) Program.

Understanding the Current Environment

Our nation is facing significant health care challenges. These include an increased prevalence of chronic disease, skyrocketing demand for behavioral health care, especially among children and adolescents, sicker patients and a workforce that is struggling to continue caring for others while simultaneously addressing their own health care needs. Hospitals and health systems exist to care for our communities as well as provide a safe, meaningful place to work. Many of the underlying drivers of poor health are caused by larger societal factors that go far beyond hospitals' walls. Yet, patients arrive at hospitals expecting for their needs to be addressed, and the nurses, doctors, technicians and other staff we rely upon are struggling to keep up with demand.

Hospitals' and health systems' ability to continue to serve their patients and communities is challenged by substantial resource constraints. A report released last week by the AHA details the extraordinary financial pressures continuing to affect hospitals and health systems, as well as access to patient care. The report found expenses across the board saw double digit increases in 2022 compared to prepandemic levels, including for workforce, drugs, medical supplies and equipment, as well as other essential operational services such as IT, sanitation, facilities management, and food and nutrition services.

Among other findings, the report showed:

- Overall hospital expenses have increased by *17.5% between 2019 and 2022.* This far outpaced Medicare reimbursement, which *only increased 7.5%* during this same time.
- Labor costs, which on average account for about half of hospitals' total budget, have increased 20.8% between 2019 and 2022. This is in large part due to a greater reliance on contract staffing agencies to fill workforce gaps and to meet patient demand. The outcome of this has been a staggering *258% increase in total contract labor expenses for hospitals in 2022 compared to 2019.*
- For the first time in history, *the median price of a new drug exceeded $200,000* — more than triple the median annual household income in the U.S. At the same time, price increases for existing drugs continue to outpace inflation, which helped drive a *19.7% increase in drug expenses per patient between 2019 and 2022.*
- Hospital supply expenses per patient increased 18.5% between 2019 and 2022, outpacing increases in inflation by nearly 30%. Specifically, *hospital expenses for emergency services supplies — which include ventilators, respirators and other critical equipment — experienced a nearly 33% increase* during the same time period.

These factors led to the most financially challenging year for hospitals and health systems since the beginning of the COVID-19 pandemic, leaving over half of hospitals operating at a financial loss at the end of 2022, and with negative operating margins continuing into 2023.

In addition, the fiscal year (FY) 2024 Hospital Inpatient Prospective Payment System proposed rule by the Centers for Medicare & Medicaid Services (CMS) puts forward an inadequate proposed inpatient hospital payment update of 2.8%, despite hospitals incurring near decades-high inflation and increased costs for labor, equipment, drugs and supplies. The AHA has repeatedly requested that CMS and the Administration address shortcomings in its previous market basket forecasts for all hospitals. For example, CMS" inpatient payment update was a full three percentage points less than what actual market basket inflation was in 2022. These inadequate inflationary adjustments – in addition to Medicare's existing underpayments to hospitals – do not reflect the economic reality in which our hospitals are providing care to our communities.

Workforce challenges also are taking a significant toll on hospitals and health systems. Long building structural changes in the health care workforce, combined with the profound impact of the COVID-19 pandemic, have left hospitals and health systems facing a national staffing emergency that is jeopardizing patient access to care. Patients requiring additional care after a hospitalization – such as skilled nursing, behavioral health or therapy-at-home — face growing delays in accessing those services due to personnel shortages. These delays also put incredible strain on hospitals and health systems, as they must bear the costs of caring for patients during these excess days without appropriate reimbursement, and they add burden on an already stretched workforce.

The shortages have been challenging for acute care hospitals as well as post-acute care and other providers receiving patient transfers from acute care hospitals, such as psychiatric hospitals. As a result, post-acute care and other providers have been unable to accept new patients, creating patient bottlenecks at acute care hospitals.

Rehabilitation and long-term care hospitals also report similar patient bottlenecks, with difficulties discharging their patients to other post-acute care providers, such as skilled nursing facilities.

Hospital Price Transparency Rule

Hospitals and health systems are committed to empowering patients with all the information they need to live their healthiest lives. This includes ensuring they have access to accurate price information when seeking care. Hospitals and health systems are working to comply with both state and federal price transparency policies, which are varied and sometimes conflicting. At the federal level, these include the Hospital Price Transparency Rule. As of Jan. 1, 2021, hospitals are required to publicly post via machine-readable files five different "standard charges": gross charges; payer-specific negotiated rates; de-identified minimum and maximum negotiated rates; and discounted cash prices. The rule also requires hospitals to provide patients with an out-of-pocket cost estimator tool or payer-specific negotiated rates for at least 300 shoppable services.

CMS has a process in place to ensure hospital compliance with the Hospital Price Transparency Rule. This includes a review, usually involving direct discourse with the hospitals; if deficiencies are identified, a warning letter is sent from the agency; and if the deficiencies are not corrected, a corrective action plan is requested. Should a hospital continue to fail to come into compliance, CMS then applies a civil monetary penalty.

CMS found that in 2022, 70% of hospitals complied with both components of the Hospital Price Transparency Rule, including the consumer-friendly display of shoppable services information, as well as the machine-readable file requirements. This is an increase from 27% in 2021. Moreover, when looking at each individual component of the rule, 82% of hospitals met the consumer-friendly display of shoppable services information requirement in 2022 (up from 66% in 2021) and 82% met the machine- readable file requirement (up from 30% in 2021).

These numbers show significant progress on the part of hospitals and health systems — while acknowledging the work that remains — in implementing these requirements. The lower compliance rate in 2021, however, should not be interpreted as a lack of hospital commitment to transparency. Instead, it reflects the incredible challenges hospitals were experiencing in 2020 and 2021 in addressing the most acute phases of the COVID-19 public health emergency, which strained hospitals' staff and required the diversion of personnel and financial resources. As the pandemic phase of COVID-19 winds down and hospitals have been able to resume more standard operations, they are able to dedicate the resources necessary to build the full suite of price transparency tools.

CMS also shared information regarding how it has interacted with hospitals to support compliance and the issuance of penalties:

> "As of January 2023, CMS had issued nearly 500 warning notices and over 230 requests for corrective action plans since the initial implementing regulation went into effect in 2021. Nearly 300 hospitals have addressed problems and have become compliant with the regulations, leading to closure of their cases. While it was necessary to issue penalties to two hospitals in 2022 for noncompliance (posted on the CMS website), every other hospital that was reviewed has corrected its deficiencies."

Unfortunately, some third parties continue to issue reports mischaracterizing whether hospitals are complying with the Hospital Price Transparency Rule, as was detailed in a letter AHA sent recently to House Energy and Commerce Chair Rodgers and Ranking Member Pallone. These reports fail to acknowledge CMS' requirements, such as how to fill in an individual negotiated rate when such a rate does not exist due to patient services being bundled and billed together. In this instance, CMS has said a blank cell would be appropriate since there is no negotiated rate to include. Despite this, some outside groups still count any file with blank cells as "noncompliant." This fundamental misrepresentation of the rules has only served to advance misinformation and confusion on the issue and distract from genuine productive discussions and efforts around what patients want in terms of transparency data and how best to provide that information.

In addition to the CMS report on compliance, we would draw your attention to a recent report from Turquoise Health that found about 84% of hospitals had posted a machine- readable file containing rate information by the end of first-quarter 2023, up from 65% the previous quarter.

Recommendations

Hospitals and health systems are eager to continue working toward providing the best possible price estimates for their patients. We ask Congress and the Administration to take the following steps to support these efforts, including:

- Review and streamline the existing transparency policies with a priority objective of reducing potential patient confusion and unnecessary regulatory burden on providers;
- Continue to convene patients, providers and payers to seek input on how to make federal price transparency policies as patient-centered as possible; and
- Refrain from advancing additional legislation or regulations that may further confuse or complicate providers' ability to provide meaningful price estimates while adding unnecessary costs to the health care system.

Medicare Outpatient Site-Neutral Payment Reductions

The AHA strongly opposes additional site-neutral payment cuts, which threaten access to care, especially in rural and historically marginalized communities.

Existing site-neutral payment policies have already had a significantly negative impact on the financial sustainability of hospitals and health systems, particularly as they continue to manage the aftermath of the COVID-19 pandemic as well as the challenges posed by workforce shortages, broken supply chains and historic levels of inflation that have increased the costs of caring for patients. Such policies have contributed to Medicare's chronic failure to cover the cost of caring for its beneficiaries, putting a strain on hospitals' ability to continue to care for their communities. Further cuts would only exacerbate this shortfall and may cause hospitals to significantly reduce services or close altogether.

Site-neutral policies also fail to account for the fundamental differences between hospital outpatient departments (HOPDs) and other sites of care. The cost of care delivered in hospitals and health systems takes into account the unique benefits that they provide to their communities. This includes the investments made to maintain standby capacity for natural and man-made disasters, public health emergencies and unexpected traumatic events, as well as deliver 24/7 emergency care to all who come to the hospital, regardless of ability to pay or insurance status. Hospitals and health systems provide access to critical services and programs that may not be otherwise available, especially in low-income and rural communities.

Hospital facilities also treat patients who are sicker and have more chronic conditions than those treated in physician offices or ambulatory surgical centers, which requires a greater use of resources. In addition, hospital facilities must comply with a much more comprehensive scope of licensing, accreditation and other regulatory requirements compared to other sites of care, such as ambulatory surgery centers (ASCs) and physician offices (see chart below).

Specifically, physicians often refer sicker patients with higher-risk conditions to hospital-based settings for safety reasons, as hospitals are better equipped to handle complications and emergencies, which often require the use of additional resources that other settings do not typically provide. Indeed, nearly half of all Medicare beneficiaries live with four or more chronic conditions and one-third have one or more limitations in activities of daily living

(ADL). Compared to independent physician offices and ASCs, data[18] show that, on average, HOPDs treat Medicare patients who are suffering from more severe chronic conditions and have higher prior utilization of hospitals and emergency departments. Such co-morbid conditions may include morbidly obese patients, patients with mental health issues, such as dementia, and disabled patients. Because some co-morbid conditions can make even simple procedures more dangerous and increase the likelihood of complications, it is prudent to utilize the greater capacities and capabilities of HOPDs to assist patients if something goes wrong during a procedure. In fact, patients experiencing unexpected life or limb-threatening complications in physician offices and ASCs are usually emergently transferred to the closest hospital via an ambulance.

Regulatory Requirements/Roles	Hospital Outpatient Department	Ambulatory Surgery Center	Physician Office
24/7 Standby Capacity for ED Services	✓		
Backup for Complications Occurring in Other Settings	✓		
EMTALA	✓		
Uncompensated Care/Safety Net	✓		
Teaching/Graduate Medical Education	✓		
Special Capabilities (burn, trauma, neonatal, psychiatric services, etc.)	✓		
Required Government Cost Reports	✓		
Equipment Redundancy Requirements	✓		
Disaster Preparedness and Response	✓	✓	
Annual Hazard Vulnerability Analysis	✓	✓	
Stringent Ventilation Requirements and Infection Control Codes	✓	✓	
Fire and Life Safety Codes (NFPA 101)	✓	✓	
Essential Electrical System (NFPA 99)	✓	✓	
Evacuation and Relocation and Quarterly Fire Drills	✓	✓	
Infection Control Program	✓	✓	
Quality Assurance Program	✓	✓	
Joint Commission Accreditation	✓	✓	

[18] https://www.aha.org/system/files/media/file/2023/03/Comparison-of-Medicare-Beneficiary-Characteristics- Between-Hospital-Outpatient-Departments-and-Other-Ambulatory-Care-Settings.pdf.

Many such examples exist in which less healthy patients are, for clinical and safety reasons, referred to HOPDs rather than other settings. This includes diagnostic cardiac catheterization procedures, which sometimes reveal blockages in the coronary arteries and require immediate interventions that cannot be safely provided in an ASC or physician office. Another example is total knee arthroplasty (TKA) procedures. While these services often can be successfully performed for healthier Medicare patients in an ASC setting, it is not appropriate for others in the Medicare population who have co-morbid conditions and ADL limitations. For instance, patients undergoing TKA are at increased risk of myocardial infarction (with patients 80 years or older at highest risk) and deep vein thrombosis with the potential to propagate a potentially lethal pulmonary embolus.

Moreover, according to the Medicare Payment Advisory Commission (MedPAC), for the past 20 years, Medicare payments have failed to cover the costs of caring for Medicare beneficiaries. This underpayment is due in part to existing site-neutral payment policies that have substantially cut reimbursements; further site-neutral cuts would only exacerbate this gap. According to MedPAC, overall Medicare hospital margins were - 6.3% in 2021 after accounting for temporary COVID-19 relief funds. Without these temporary relief funds, the overall Medicare margin for 2021 remained depressed at - 8.2% after hitting a staggering low of -12.3% in 2020. Indeed, on average, Medicare only pays 84 cents for every dollar hospitals spend providing care to Medicare beneficiaries. Moreover, overall median hospital operating margins were negative throughout 2022 and into the beginning of 2023. Site-neutral cuts have already contributed to these shortfalls, and any further expansion of these policies will threaten patients' access to quality care.

It is important to understand that site-neutral policies generally rely upon an assumption that Medicare's physician fee schedule rates are fair and accurate. They are not. The physician fee schedule "conversion factor" in 2023 is almost $3 less than it was 25 years ago, in 1998. This is even without considering inflation. In addition to inadequate reimbursement, physicians, and the entire health care workforce writ large, are grappling with physical and emotional strain, burnout and shortages. They are facing enormous challenges, including skyrocketing administrative and regulatory burden in the form of, for example, electronic health record requirements, and increasing violence in their workplace, not to mention the once-in-a-lifetime pandemic that brought the entire health care system to the brink of collapse. As a result, our members report that physicians in their community regularly express the sentiment that their freestanding practices are no longer viable. And, rather than allow their communities to go without this critical care, hospitals acquire the practice in order to maintain patient access.

Now more than ever, hospitals need stable and adequate reimbursements as they face challenging financial circumstances. Expanding site-neutral cuts to additional HOPDs would endanger the critical role that HOPDs play in their communities, including access to care for patients, especially the most medically complex.

Hospital Mergers and Acquisitions

Mergers and acquisitions are one of the most important tools that some hospitals use to increase access, provide quality care and manage financial pressures and risk. These partnerships enable hospitals to expand service offerings, broaden networks and access to specialists, improve quality and better serve patients where they live. They also provide scale to help reduce costs associated with obtaining medical services, supplies and prescription drugs, and enable health systems to reduce other operational costs. Ultimately, hospital mergers and acquisitions expand and preserve access to care.

Emerging research has demonstrated a clear association between consolidation and quality improvement. For example, one study found that a full-integration approach is associated with improvements in mortality and readmission rates, among other quality and outcome improvements.[19]2 Another study found significant reductions in mortality for a number of common conditions — including acute myocardial infarction, heart failure, acute stroke and pneumonia — among patients at rural hospitals that had merged or been acquired.[20]3 Being part of a system also can help hospitals comply with new, resource-intensive regulatory requirements. For example, hospitals affiliated with systems are more likely to have a price transparency score of 5 out of 5 stars, according to a recent report by Turquoise Heath.

Mergers and acquisitions help hospitals improve access to care by expanding the types of specialists and services available to patients. According to an analysis by Kaufman Hall, nearly 40% of affiliated hospitals added one or more services post-acquisition. Mergers and acquisitions also are a vital tool that some health systems use to keep financially struggling hospitals open, thereby averting bankruptcy or even closure.[21] When hospitals become part of a health system, the continuum of care is strengthened for patients and the community, resulting in better care and decreased readmission rates.

Mergers and acquisitions also have played a critical role in preserving access to care in rural areas. An AHA analysis of the UNC Sheps Center data on rural hospital closures between 2010 and 2020 shows that slightly more than half of the hospitals that closed were independent. Health systems typically acquire rural hospitals when these hospitals are under financial distress. Research has shown that rural hospitals are less likely to close after acquisition compared to independent hospitals and that mergers have improved access and quality of care for rural hospitals.[22] Acquired hospitals typically form new collaborations or partnerships with larger health systems, which promotes access to specialists, telehealth and other care for rural patients.[23]

340B Drug Pricing Program

The 340B Drug Pricing Program allows hospitals to stretch limited federal resources to reduce the price of outpatient pharmaceuticals for patients as well as expand health services to the patients and communities they serve. 340B hospitals achieve savings by purchasing drugs at a discount. The amount of that discount depends on drug companies' pricing decisions, with the discount increasing the more the drug companies decide to raise the price of their drugs. The Health Resources and Services Administration (HRSA) estimates that the average discount is anywhere between 25% to 50%.

---

[19] https://jamanetwork.com/journals/jamanetworkopen/fullarticle/2787652.

[20] https://jamanetwork.com/journals/jamanetworkopen/fullarticle/2784342.

[21] https://www.aha.org/system/files/media/file/2021/10/KH-AHA-Benefits-of-Hospital-Mergers-Acquisitions-2021-10-08.pdf.

[22] https://www.ncbi.nlm.nih.gov/pmc/articles/PMC9250050/.

[23] https://www.aha.org/system/files/media/file/2021/10/KH-AHA-Benefits-of-Hospital-Mergers-Acquisitions-2021-10-08.pdf.

Hospitals use 340B savings to provide a range of vital programs and services, which include, but are not limited to, the provision of free or discounted drugs to low-income patients, free care for uninsured patients and support for behavioral health clinics and community health programs. In fact, in the most recent year for which information is available, tax-exempt 340B hospitals provided nearly $68 billion in total benefits to their communities. This program is particularly important as drug prices continue to rise and hospitals face increased inflationary cost pressures across all their supplies and services. The AHA urges Congress to continue to protect this critical program and oppose efforts to further restrict eligibility, which would result in reduced access to quality care for the patients and communities served by 340B hospitals.

We appreciate the Subcommittee's support for the 340B program and interest in making certain all stakeholders meet the 340BB program integrity requirements. 340B hospitals must annually recertify their eligibility to participate and attest to meeting all the program requirements; participate in audits conducted by HRSA and drug manufacturers; and maintain auditable records and inventories of all 340B and non-340B prescription drugs. The AHA is working with its 340B member hospitals, through the AHA Good Stewardship Principles, on efforts to strengthen the 340B program by helping 340B hospitals support greater transparency in communicating publicly the immense value the program brings to patients and communities.

However, the AHA would oppose efforts to create significant new reporting requirements for 340B hospitals that do not reflect the true value or intent of the 340B program. Reporting on a drug's reimbursement amount would not provide relevant information because the reimbursement amount is the same for 340B hospitals and non-340B hospitals alike. 340B savings for a hospital are based on the difference between what the hospital paid to acquire the drug under 340B versus what the hospital would have paid to acquire the drug outside of the 340B program. Focusing on these measures and hospitals' charity care numbers alone would not provide policy makers with an accurate picture of the myriad benefits the patients and communities receive due to a hospitals' participation in the 340B program. 340B hospitals are committed to transparency, but believe transparency should involve mutual concessions. Any measures that increase transparency for 340B providers also should include greater transparency for drug companies, including how they set their prices and how much they decide to increase their prices.

As part of any effort to make changes to the 340B program, the AHA encourages Congress to address the alarming efforts by some drug companies' to restrict access to 340B discounted drugs for 340B hospitals that have established community and specialty pharmacy arrangements. Since October 2022, over 20 drug companies have adopted these restrictive policies to the severe detriment of 340B hospitals and their patients. The financial impact on 340B hospitals is significant. For 340B critical access hospitals, AHA's survey reports average annual losses of over $500,000 and 340B disproportionate share hospitals have average annual losses of nearly $3 million. The AHA continues to actively support HRSA in its efforts to enforce the requirements for drug companies set forth in the 340B statute.

Restrictions on Physician-Owned Hospitals

America's community hospitals and health systems welcome fair competition, where health care entities can compete based on quality, price, safety and patient satisfaction. But physician-owned hospitals (POH) — where physicians cherry-pick the healthiest and best-insured patients and self-refer those patients to facilities in which they have an ownership interest — represent the antithesis of competition. The AHA strongly opposes any changes that would either expand the number of POHs or ease restrictions on the growth of existing facilities.

Congress acted in 2010 to close the "whole hospital" loophole in the Stark law and placed restrictions on POHs. That provision represented a carefully crafted compromise to protect hospitals with a Medicare provider number as of Dec. 31, 2010 and allow those facilities to expand when increased hospital capacity is needed. Since 2010, eight POHs have applied for the exceptions process and have been allowed to expand.

Several analyses, including by the Congressional Budget Office, MedPAC and independent researchers, have concluded that physician self-referral leads to greater per capita utilization of services and higher costs for the Medicare program. In fact, according to the Congressional Budget Office, closing the "whole hospital" exception loophole in the Stark law reduced the federal deficit by $500 million over 10 years. Bills that would repeal the 2010 law would erase those savings and increase the federal deficit.

Furthermore, POHs tend to cherry-pick the most profitable patients and services, jeopardizing communities' access to full-service hospital care. The Government Accountability Office, CMS and MedPAC have found that patients in POHs tend to be healthier than patients with the same diagnoses who are taken care of by community hospitals. This practice of self-referring physicians carefully selecting their patients creates a destabilizing environment that leaves sicker and less-affluent patients to community hospitals, thereby placing these hospitals at a distinct financial disadvantage. This is because community hospitals rely on cross-subsidies from those services targeted by POHs to support essential, but under-reimbursed, services such as emergency, trauma and burn care. By siphoning off the most profitable services and patients, POHs threaten the ability of community hospitals to offer quality, comprehensive care and serve as the health care provider for all patients, regardless of income or insurance status, in their communities.

Medicaid DSH Program

Congress established the Medicaid DSH program to provide financial assistance to hospitals serving a disproportionate number of low-income patients to ensure Medicaid and uninsured patients have access to health care services. These hospitals also provide critical community services, such as trauma and burn care, maternal and child health care, high-risk neonatal care and disaster preparedness resources. The patients they serve are among those that need care the most and often experience challenges accessing it, including children, the poor, the disabled and the elderly.

Reductions to the Medicaid DSH program were enacted as part of the Affordable Care Act, with the reasoning that hospitals would have less uncompensated care as health insurance coverage increased. Under current statute, the Medicaid DSH cut is $8 billion for each of the next four fiscal years (2024-2027, for a total of $32 billion for all four years).

Unfortunately, the projected coverage levels have not been realized and hospitals continue to care for patients for whom they are not receiving payment. The redetermination process that began on April 1 also may lead to additional individuals becoming uninsured as states decide who remains eligible for the Medicaid program. In addition, hospitals are dealing with financial instability due to the long-lasting impact of the COVID-19 pandemic as well as the increased inflationary costs they have incurred for the staffing, supplies, drugs and equipment necessary to be able to serve their communities.

Consequently, the need for the Medicaid DSH payments is still vital for the hospitals that rely on the program. Congress has, with bipartisan support, prevented the cuts from going into effect previously. *The AHA supports efforts to once again address the Medicaid DSH reductions.*

Conclusion

We thank you for the opportunity to share the hospital and health system field's perspective and appreciate that these topics are priority areas for the Subcommittee, as they are for our field and our patients. We look forward to continuing to work with you to address these important issues.

Mr. GUTHRIE. Thank you. Thank you for your statement. The Chair now recognizes Ms. Bass.

You are recognized for 5 minutes for an opening statement.

Statement of Kristin Bass

Ms. BASS. Good afternoon, Chairman Guthrie, Ranking Member Eshoo, and members of the subcommittee. My name is Kristin Bass, and I am the chief policy and external affairs officer for PCMA, the national association representing America's pharmacy benefit companies. I appreciate the invitation to share our industry's views on the legislation under consideration. We are grateful for the opportunity to work with both majority and minority staff, and your willingness to hear a variety of views.

It is important to understand what pharmacy benefit companies do to best evaluate how legislative change may impact their ability to help secure drug savings and drive affordability for patients. We are proud that pharmacy benefit companies are hired to administer prescription drug plans for more than 275 million Americans who have health coverage through public and private employers, labor unions, Medicare, other Federal programs, and the exchanges, and we are proud of the physicians, pharmacists, and other health professionals who help design the prescription drug coverage options PBMs offer, and administer the medication quality and safety programs they provide.

To be clear, no employer or plan sponsor has to hire or use a pharmacy benefit company, but virtually all choose to do so to secure savings on drugs and to better serve the patients in their plans. Employers select a PBM through a transparent and highly competitive bidding process. With over 70 full-service pharmacy benefit companies in the market and regular new entrants, plan sponsors can choose to contract with the company that best meets their unique needs. Some may choose based on scale and ability to negotiate deep discounts. Others prioritize innovative care management programs and different levels of service.

As part of their bid request, plan sponsors define and appropriately demand what information, transparency, and audit rights they need, and those are memorialized in their contracts. Our companies provide their clients with a broad array of actionable, accurate information on price and quality to make efficient purchasing and plan design decisions. And in recent years, Congress and Federal regulators have added numerous additional requirements for PBMs to report to Federal agencies and to provide aggregated public reporting.

So why do plan sponsors choose to use a pharmacy benefit company? They rely on our companies' expertise to secure savings through price concessions from drug companies, to partner with lower-cost, higher-quality pharmacies, and to prove medication adherence. For small employers who may struggle even to provide health benefits, pharmacy benefit companies offer options for cost predictability, enabling them to stretch their benefit dollars further.

Plan sponsors also choose how best to use the savings that PBMs deliver, whether to lower premiums, lower costs at the pharmacy counter, or make benefits more robust. The pharmacy benefit company delivers the savings, and the employer plan sponsor decides how to use them.

As we evaluate the legislation before the subcommittee today, we have two major concerns that carry through many of the bills proposed to address prescription drug costs.

First, the legislation would limit choice by dictating terms to the market, taking away flexibility that is needed for managing drug costs, keeping health coverage affordable, and helping patients stay on their meds. We should avoid government mandates that could increase costs and decrease innovation.

Second, none of the legislation being considered today would address the price of prescription drugs, but may instead increase costs not only by limiting choice but by stacking the deck in favor of drug companies when it comes to negotiations for rebates. We have to be cognizant of what happens when one side in a negotiation gets confidential information about their competitors' negotiated rates. It only leads to higher costs.

Instead, we encourage the subcommittee to address the actual cause of the affordability challenge: the price set by the drug company and the rampant patent abuses that have blocked competition. To that end, we greatly appreciate the leadership of many members of this subcommittee who have supported policies to ensure more competition and choice by getting generics and biosimilars to market without delay.

Thank you for inviting me to appear before the subcommittee today. Our companies exist to secure savings and improve health outcomes for plan sponsor employers, unions, and government programs, and, most importantly, the patients we serve. I hope that you will keep this important and valued role front of mind as you consider these bills as well as my written testimony, which details unintended consequences about the specific bills before you.

We look forward to continuing our work with you and the patients and payers we serve to secure affordability, access, and adherence to the medications Americans need. I am happy to answer any questions.

[The prepared statement of Ms. Bass follows:]

Testimony of Kristin Bass
Chief Policy and External Affairs Officer
Pharmaceutical Care Management Association
Submitted to the United States House of Representatives Energy & Commerce Committee, Subcommittee on Health
"Lowering Unaffordable Costs: Legislative Solutions to Increase Transparency and Competition in Health Care"
April 26, 2023

Introduction

Good morning, Chairman Guthrie, Ranking Member Eshoo, and other members of the Subcommittee. My name is Kristin Bass, and I am the Chief Policy and External Affairs Officer for the Pharmaceutical Care Management Association (PCMA). PCMA is the national association representing America's pharmacy benefit companies, which administer prescription drug plans and operate home delivery and specialty pharmacies for more than 275 million Americans with health coverage through public and private employers, labor unions, retiree plans, Medicare, Medicaid, the Federal Employees Health Benefits (FEHB) program, and the exchanges established by the Affordable Care Act (ACA). Our members work closely with health plans and health insurance issuers to secure lower costs for prescription drugs and achieve better health outcomes.

I appreciate the opportunity to testify before you to share the thoughts and concerns of the pharmacy benefit industry regarding the legislative proposals under consideration. Pharmacy benefit managers (PBMs) have always focused on lowering prescription drug costs for patients and a wide range of health plan sponsors – specifically by:

- Negotiating rebates from brand drug companies and discounts from drugstores to reduce costs for patients, their families, and health plans – saving payers and patients an average of $1,040 per patient per year.[24]
- Encouraging the use of more affordable alternative brand drugs, such as generics and biosimilars.
- Offering services that benefit patients, such as home delivery, which saves patients time and money while increasing access and care coordination.
- Managing and helping patients access high-cost specialty medications.
- Reducing waste, preventing potentially harmful drug interactions, and improving adherence.

Today, in addition to discussing the legislative proposals that have been introduced, I will review the policies that PCMA members support to encourage a competitive market for prescription drugs, highlight some of the ways pharmacy benefit companies currently work to lower costs for patients and reduce health benefit costs for employers and other plan sponsors,

---

[24] Visante. The Return on Investment (ROI) on PBM Services. An analysis prepared by Visante on behalf of PCMA. January 2023. Available athttps://www.pcmanet.org/wp-content/uploads/2023/01/The-Return-on-Investment-ROI-on- PBM-Services-January-2023.pdf.

and explain how PBMs support meaningful, actionable transparency to further enhance market competition. Just like PCMA's members, the PBM market is dynamic, diverse, and continues to grow. As of March 2023, there are 73 full-service PBMs in the U.S., with six new PBMs entering the market since 2021.[25]

As an industry, we welcome any opportunity to discuss and advance ways to improve the prescription drug marketplace so Americans can better afford their prescription drugs. There are many bills before the Committee today, all intended to lower health care costs and improve consumers' ability to make informed choices; however, some of these well-intended proposals will have unintended consequences that would do the exact opposite, increasing costs and reducing choice.

PCMA's testimony today considers mainly the bills and discussion drafts addressing prescription drug costs filed for this committee's consideration, which are limited in scope and focus almost exclusively on the role of PBMs, rather than the companies responsible for setting the prices of the drugs they make and sell. We believe any attempt at understanding the factors driving drug costs must include a look at the entire supply chain, including drug companies, large pharmacy collectives known as Pharmacy Services Administrative Organizations (PSAOs), wholesale distributors, employer benefit consultants, pharmacies, and all others with impact on the cost of prescription drugs. For instance, there is irrefutable evidence of certain drug companies repeatedly abusing the patent system to keep more affordable alternatives from entering the marketplace, which allows those companies to arbitrarily set and increase prescription drug prices.

As it assesses how best to improve the prescription drug market, we encourage the Committee to review all these entities, their business models, profit incentives and underlying motives for pushing or attempting to block certain pieces of legislation as it assesses how to improve the prescription drug market.

Pharmacy Benefit Companies Support Policies to Encourage Competition as the Best Way to Lower Prescription Drug Costs

PBMs work to improve prescription drug affordability by providing prescribers with information about less expensive generic alternatives, setting performance standards for pharmacies to encourage generic fills and adherence, and ensuring patients are aware of lower cost alternatives. Due in large part to these efforts by PBMs, 90 percent of prescriptions are filled with generics.[26] Pharmacy benefit companies also support increased uptake of biosimilars by preferring both the brand and a biosimilar to ensure patients and providers have the incentive to choose lower-cost options and the choice to continue with a drug from which they may be reluctant to switch. Our industry supports policy proposals to increase biosimilar uptake, including eliminating the interchangeability designation to reduce costs and confusion, stopping abuse of the patent system, and making it easier for Medicare Part D plans to update formularies as new biosimilars come to market.

---

[25] PCMA. The PBM Marketplace Continues to Evolve. April 2023.

[26] AAM. 2021. https://accessiblemeds.org/sites/default/files/2021-10/AAM-2021-US-Generic-Biosimilar-Medicines-Savings- Report-web.pdf.

PCMA supports numerous pieces of legislation that have been introduced and advanced by this committee in previous Congresses that would address tactics that undermine competition in the pharmaceutical market. We also support policies to address drug companies' abuses of the patent system that allow them to extend monopoly pricing well beyond their products' original patent expirations. Drug companies too often block competition and are responsible for setting and increasing prices. Improving competition in the marketplace by cracking down on this abuse will help lower costs for patients and families.

We encourage the Committee to consider these and other proposals to improve competition in the prescription drug market.

PBMs Support Meaningful, Actionable Transparency to Enhance Market Competition

Transparency that helps patients and payers is necessary across the entire prescription drug supply and payment chain. PBMs support and practice actionable transparency that empowers patients, their physicians and pharmacists, those sponsoring health coverage, and policymakers to make informed decisions that can lead to lower prescription drug costs. Actionable transparency encourages consumers to shop for coverage that best fits their health needs and budgets, and through their health coverage, use the most cost-effective, highest-value health care goods and services. It enables prescribers and patients to avoid pharmacy-counter surprises and helps ensure that physicians can prescribe drugs that are affordable for patients. To that end, PBMs provide patients and prescribers with real-time benefit tools, which provide information about a patient's progress through a deductible or another benefit phase, what drugs are on the patient's formulary, and exactly what cost sharing to expect for a given drug at the pharmacy. PBMs also provide patients with information on in-network pharmacies, premiums, general cost- sharing, and benefits for their prescription drug coverage.

PBMs provide health plans, employer plan sponsors, and consumers with a broad array of accurate, actionable information on price and quality to make efficient purchasing decisions. As part of their requests for proposals (RFPs) when putting their pharmacy benefits out to bid, PBMs' customers lay out the terms of the transparency and information they want to receive, as well as their audit rights, and those are memorialized in their contracts.

In recent years, Congress has added more requirements for PBMs to report to federal agencies, as well as public reporting in more aggregated form. In both cases, these bills included appropriate protections for confidential data to avoid encouraging tacit collusion, and PCMA supported these efforts. We have also supported legislation that is now law, which provides Congressional support agencies, including Congressional Budget Office (CBO), Government Accountability Office (GAO), Medicare Payment Advisory Commission (MedPAC), and Medicaid and CHIP Payment and Access Commission (MACPAC), with access to Medicare and Medicaid claims-level data to ensure you are able to perform appropriate oversight.

We have very significant objections, however, to *H.R. 2691, the Transparent PRICE Act,* which requires public disclosure of drug-specific information, including the average amount paid by a plan (net of rebates, discounts, and price concessions) for each specific drug dispensed or administered by each participating provider. With this information, each pharmacy and drug manufacturer will know its competitors' price concessions and will be able to determine whether it could have gotten the same business with a lesser price concession. Thus, we believe public disclosure of this too granular, too recent information creates a very high risk for tacit collusion and that patients and plan sponsors will pay more for prescription drugs as a result.

While we support the aim of *H.R. 2679, the PBM Accountability Act,* to provide detailed utilization and cost information to plan sponsors, we strongly believe that it is unnecessary to legislate provision of this information as employers can request these data as part of their RFPs.

We appreciate that the bill's sponsors have included a provision that would avoid giving drug- specific confidential information on discounts and rebates to manufacturers, wholesalers, pharmacies, and others in the supply chain who could use it in an anti-competitive manner.

However, the bill still includes a requirement for PBMs to provide information to which they are typically not privy, namely detailed information about drug copay coupons and other forms of manufacturer direct financial assistance to patients. To comply with this requirement, we ask that the bill include a requirement for manufacturers to provide the required drug copay coupon and patient assistance program information to PBMs.

As the Committee considers these proposals, we want to caution against another unintended consequence that could arise from the enactment of either or both bills. Extensive, unharmonized but duplicative reporting requirements create administrative burdens to which larger PBMs may be able to adapt, but smaller PBMs may find overly burdensome or wholly unworkable, forcing them to either close their doors or consolidate, reducing the competitive market for PBMs. It is also important to note that while larger PBMs may be able to adapt, these added reporting burdens on top of the existing requirements outlined below could lead to higher costs for consumers.

PBMs Already Comply with Numerous Disclosure Requirements

As noted in PCMA's written statement in response to the Committee's hearing on this subject last month, "Examining Transparency and Competition in Health Care," pharmacy benefit companies already operate under federal transparency requirements and adhere to myriad contractually required transparency provisions imposed by their own business and government partners.

PBMs are subject to transparency regulations promulgated by the Departments of Health and Human Services (HHS), Labor, and Treasury, the Office of Personnel Management, and states. PBM practices are overseen by state Medicaid agencies, state-based consumer protection agencies, private accreditation organizations, and their own customers – health plan sponsors. PBMs are also directly regulated by state departments of insurance or other state agencies.

Exchange plans must report data to CMS on numerous administrative processes such as coverage determinations and prior authorization in a way that both enrollees and potential enrollees can access and understand them. Exchange plans must also report data confidentially to CMS regarding generic dispensing rates for retail and mail order pharmacies; aggregate amounts and types of rebates, discounts, price concessions, and service fees; total prescriptions covered; and the difference between the amount the health plan pays the PBM and the amount that the PBM pays retail and mail order pharmacies.

Medicare Part D plans must make available to enrollees and potential enrollees all relevant aspects of their benefit design, and report confidentially to CMS the same information as exchange plans, through annual reporting. Part D plans also submit to CMS Prescription Drug Event (PDE) data, which is a summary of Part D claims activity with additional data elements including pharmacy dispensing fees. As part of the annual bid and reconciliation processes, PBMs (via the Part D plans) must report to CMS estimated pharmacy and manufacturer Direct and Indirect Remuneration (DIR), including rebates and other price concessions.

It is important to note that government reporting by PBMs is not static but an ongoing, evolving construct. Indeed, CMS routinely updates required Medicare Part D filings to encompass more information, including with respect to PDE and DIR filings. For example, new pharmacy DIR rules take effect on January 1, 2024. Under these new rules, the negotiated price for a Part D covered drug must reflect the lowest possible reimbursement a network pharmacy will receive for a drug and must include all pharmacy price concessions. CMS has already issued detailed guidance on how these changes are to be included in PDE and DIR filings, including changes related to calculating beneficiary cost sharing taking into account the application of pharmacy price concessions at point of sale.[27] Also, CMS has several other major expansions underway to the PDE submissions for 2025 related to Inflation Reduction Act implementation, and we expect to see more for 2026.

Moreover, reporting is not limited to federal health care programs and exchanges. For commercial plans, the Departments of Treasury, HHS, and Labor as well as the Office of Personnel Management (OPM) require PBMs to report:

- The 50 most frequently dispensed brand prescription drugs.
- The 50 costliest prescription drugs by total annual spending.
- The 50 prescription drugs with the greatest increase in expenditures from the previous year.
- Prescription drug rebates, fees, and payments by drug manufacturers in each therapeutic class of drugs, as well as for each of the 25 drugs that yielded the highest amount of rebates.
- The premium and out-of-pocket cost impact of prescription drug rebates, fees, and other payments.

PBMs may report these data directly to the government or to their customers. The customers (plan sponsors, issuers, and the FEHB program carriers generally) are required to submit this information, along with some of their own data regarding premiums, aggregated at the state/market level, rather than separately for each plan. The Departments must biannually issue a report based on the data, but otherwise must keep the data confidential and may not release proprietary information. The first such report will be issued in June 2024.

PBMs may report these data directly to the government or to their customers. These customers (including plan sponsors, issuers, and the FEHB program carriers generally) are required to submit this information aggregated at the state/market level, rather than separately for each plan.

Beyond government reporting requirements, much of the PBMs' operational specifics are available to plan enrollees through other provisions of the Affordable Care Act and Social Security Act, including the Summary of Benefits and Coverage, Medicare Plan Finder, and real- time benefit tools that provide current information on prescription drug benefits.

---

[27] CMS HPMS memo. October 14, 2022. Available at https://www.cms.gov/httpseditcmsgovresearch-statistics-data-and-systemscomputer-data-and-systemshpmshpms-memos-archive/hpms-memos-wk-2-october-10-14.

Finally, the Securities and Exchange Commission (SEC) also requires publicly traded health plans and PBMs to report quarterly and annual financial information to the SEC.

Exposing Proprietary Pricing Information Can Raise Drug Prices

PCMA continues to be concerned about potential unintended consequences of bills that expose proprietary pricing and contract information. The Federal Trade Commission (FTC) has historically spoken out against over-exposing information about private business dealings because such an approach is deeply damaging to a competitive marketplace, stating, "If pharmaceutical manufacturers learn the exact amount of the rebates offered by their competitors (either because the safeguards on subsequent disclosure by purchasers and prospective purchasers are insufficient or because the mandated disclosure to prescribers provides sufficient information for pharmaceutical manufacturers to calculate these amounts) then tacit collusion among manufacturers is more feasible. Consequently, the required disclosures may lead to higher prices for PBM services and Pharmaceuticals."[28]

Likewise, the FTC has noted that there are limits to the benefits of transparency and unintended consequences can result.[29]

The FTC is not alone in this assertion. Recently, in speaking about concerns related to anticompetitive information exchanges, Principal Deputy Assistant Attorney General Doha Mekki noted on behalf of the Department of Justice (DOJ) that, "Courts have long recognized that the exchange of competitively sensitive information can subvert the competitive process and harm competition." Attorney General Mekki also spoke of the United States Supreme Court's concern that sharing current pricing information risks greater harm than sharing old, stale information, and specifically stated that, "transparency in the health care arena may lead to tacit collusion and higher prices."[30] She went on to say:

> Courts also have looked at the degree to which the exchanged data has been aggregated. These decisions considered how, in light of the facts and market realities at the time, the information could facilitate and result in the type of behavior that the antitrust laws condemn. The Second Circuit explained in Todd that "[p]rice exchanges that identify particular parties, transactions, and prices are seen as potentially anticompetitive because they may be used to police a secret or tacit conspiracy to stabilize prices. Courts prefer that information be aggregated in the form of industry averages, thus avoiding transactional specificity." But facial aggregation of data alone has been held to be insufficient to save otherwise problematic information exchanges. In Todd, the Second Circuit looked beyond data that appeared to be somewhat aggregated to

---

28 FTC. 2004. https://www.ftc.gov/sites/default/files/documents/advocacy_documents/ftc-comment-hon.greg- aghazarian-concerning-ca.b.1960-requiring-pharmacy-benefit-managers-make-disclosures-purchasers-and-prospective-purchasers/v040027.pdf.

29 See FTC Staff Comment to the Honorable James L. Seward Concerning New York Senate Bill 58 on Pharmacy Benefit Managers (PBMs), FED. TRADE COMM'N. March 2009. Available at https://www.ftc.gov/sites/default/files/documents/advocacy_documents/ftc-staff-comment-honorable-james-l.seward-concerning-new-york-senate-bill-58-pharmacy-benefit-managers-pbms/v090006newyorkpbm.pdf.

30 DOJ. *Principal Deputy Assistant Attorney General Doha Mekki of the Antitrust Division Delivers Remarks at GCR Live: Law Leaders Global 2023*. 2022. https://www.justice.gov/opa/speech/principal-deputy-assistant-attorney-general-doha-mekki-antitrust-division-delivers-0.

conclude that the defendants had the ability to effectively disaggregate it, raising serious antitrust concerns.[31]

For these reasons, it is important to carefully protect data that helps to maintain a competitive market and ensure it is never released publicly. As Mekki warns, such information sharing would likely damage the private market, "A softening of competition through tacit coordination, facilitated by information sharing, distorts free market competition in the process."

Additionally, the Congressional Budget Office has framed the transparency and disclosure considerations clearly in this often-quoted statement:

> The disclosure of drug rebates could affect Medicare spending through two principal mechanisms. First, disclosure would probably make rebates less varied among purchasers, with large rebates and small rebates tending to converge toward some average rebate. Such compression, for reasons discussed below, would tend to reduce the rebates that PDPs received and thus would raise Medicare costs. Second, for a range of medical conditions, drugs appropriate for treatment are available from only a few manufacturers; disclosure of drug-by drug rebate data in those cases would facilitate tacit collusion among those manufacturers, which would tend to raise drug prices.[32]

PCMA encourages the Committee, as it reviews how to improve the prescription drug market to help lower costs for patients and businesses, to focus its efforts on actionable transparency that reduces drug costs versus transparency that raises them.

Pharmacy Benefit Companies Support Plan Sponsors' Ability to Choose What Works for Them

Public and private health plan sponsors vary dramatically in size, resources, and function, serving diverse populations. Employers, union and retiree plans, states, and others who provide health care coverage know more about their financial resources and plan participants than any other entity, and they need the ability to design plans tailored to the unique needs of their participants. No public or private employer, union, retiree health plan, pension fund, or other health plan is required to hire or use a PBM, but virtually all do, and the vast majority are happy with the services their PBMs provide, with employers reporting about 80 percent satisfaction with the cost-saving, health-improving services provided by their PBM. As health plan sponsors strive to create accessible, affordable benefits that meet the needs of the populations they cover, policymakers should avoid mandates that could increase costs and decrease quality.

Health plans, including those serving federal programs, rely on PBM expertise to secure savings through price concessions from pharmaceutical companies, administer medication adherence and health coaching programs, and provide overall guidance and expertise on pharmacy benefit design and coverage. PBM clients choose their PBMs through a transparent

---

[31] Ibid. Includes information sourced from *Todd*, 275 F.3d at 212-2013.

[32] Congressional Budget Office. Letter from Congressional Budget Office to Honorable Joe Barton and The Honorable Jim McCrery, p. 2. Available at: https://www.cbo.gov/sites/default/files/110th-congress-2007-2008/reports/03-12-drug%20rebates.pdf.

and highly competitive bidding process. With more than 70 full-service PBMs in the market – including new entrants – health plan sponsors have an opportunity to evaluate the differentiated value propositions of multiple PBMs and select the one that best meets their needs.[33] Some may base selection criteria on PBMs' scale, ability to negotiate deep discounts, or effectiveness managing the risk of price changes. Others may base selection criteria on PBMs' innovative care management programs or different levels of service. For small employers, many of whom may struggle to provide health insurance to employees, PBMs both lower their overall drug costs and provide cost predictability, enabling them to stretch their benefit dollars even further.

PBMs also manage pharmacy benefits for state Medicaid programs with both Medicaid managed care organizations (MCOs) and fee-for-service (FFS) coverage. Nationally, PBMs saved Medicaid $22 billion from 2013 to 2018 combined; however, the potential for additional savings remains untapped.[34] In the commercial market, PBMs have the flexibility to:

- drive use of the highest therapeutic quality, lowest-cost drugs and shift utilization from brands to generics as clinically appropriate;
- develop preferred pharmacy networks;
- advance evidence-based, clinically effective utilization; and
- leverage data analytics to detect and prevent fraud, waste, and abuse.

As drug prices continue to increase and expensive gene and cell therapies come to market, state Medicaid programs will face increasing budgetary pressures. Optimal use of PBMs tools in state Medicaid programs would save a total of $112 billion over 10 years, $43 billion for states, and $69 billion for the federal government.[35]

Plan sponsors, including state Medicaid programs, should continue to have the option of determining how they would like to pay the pharmacy benefit company they select for their services. "Spread pricing" is a risk-based contracting model in which the client (in this case, a state Medicaid program) may choose to contract for predictability. Under a spread pricing model, a state would let the pharmacy benefit company hold the risk that Medicaid recipients may use more expensive pharmacies to acquire drugs. In exchange for that risk, the state lets the PBM keep the savings when a patient uses a less expensive pharmacy, but the PBM takes a loss when patients use costlier pharmacies. Today, states and other plan sponsors can choose spread pricing or, alternatively, "pass-through" contracting, in which the plan sponsor pays whatever the pharmacy charges. While some may select pass-through contracts because they have the scale or budget to deal with the variability of pharmacy charges, others, including a number of state Medicaid programs, choose spread contracts because of the pricing predictability and savings they derive. It is important to note that while this type of risk-based contracting has been portrayed as drug-by-drug difference between what a plan pays for an individual drug and what is paid by the PBM to the pharmacy, spread contracts are based on a plan sponsor's overall drug spend. In contrast, under administrative, or pass-through, contracts, plan sponsors bear financial risk for their total drug spend. Many employers, including small businesses, prefer the price predictability of spread contracting.

---

[33] Pharmaceutical Care Management Association (PCMA). The PBM Marketplace Is Highly Competitive. April 2021. Available at https://www.pcmanet.org/wp-content/uploads/2021/04/PBM-Landscape-2021.pdf.

[34] Unitedhealth Group. 2019. Available at https://www.unitedhealthgroup.com/content/dam/UHG/PDF/2019/UHG-PBM-Medicaid-Savings.pdf.

[35] Ibid.

Among the bills offered for consideration today is H.R.1613, the Drug Price Transparency in Medicaid Act of 2023, which prohibits the use of spread pricing in Medicaid, limiting state choice. State Medicaid programs are never required to select risk-based contracting models. State Medicaid programs that do not wish to use spread pricing can – and do – select other payment arrangements. We believe states should have that flexibility.

We are further concerned that the proposed legislation's application of the Medicaid equal access protection at section 1902(a)(30) of the Social Security Act to PBMs appears to give the Centers for Medicare & Medicaid Services (CMS) direct rate setting authority with respect to pharmacy reimbursement. The equal access protection, a federal directive imposed on states as the primary administrators of the Medicaid program to ensure sufficient payments providers, should not be repurposed and imposed on PBMs who generally have no contractual privity with the state Medicaid agency. We are unclear whether the intent of the Committee is to broaden Medicaid's rate setting authority, or otherwise bypass MCOs in contracting with PBMs. We oppose making this change and urge the subcommittee to appropriately consider this potential consequence.

CMS' May 15, 2019 guidance on Medicaid's Medical Loss Ratio (MLR) already ensures that PBMs are not excessively profiting from state Medicaid programs by requiring that pharmacy spread is included in the plan's 15 percent non-claims administrative expense, in addition to eligibility and coverage verification, claims processing, utilization review, or network development, expenditures, and profits. As explained in the guidance:

> The PBM is required to classify and report revenues and expenditures associated with the administration of the Medicaid covered outpatient drug benefit to the managed care plan in the same manner that the managed care plan would be required itself to classify and report this information if the managed care plan had administered the covered outpatient drug benefit directly. Even if the managed care plan pays the PBM a capitated amount in a risk-based arrangement, the managed care plan and PBM must classify and report revenues and expenditures associated with the administration of the Medicaid covered outpatient drug benefit consistent with 42 CFR 438.8. That is, the managed care plan may not use the entire capitated payment to the PBM as incurred claims. Rather, the PBM must calculate incurred claims as the amounts paid to the retail or mail-order pharmacy.[36]

As part of this reporting process, states are able to make informed decisions about their Medicaid drug benefits. They should continue to have that choice.

Medicare Part D Pharmacy Network Requirements Support Robust Beneficiary Access to Prescription Drugs

Maintaining a competitive market for prescription drugs requires participation from all participants in the supply chain. Where a patient acquires a drug can impact its cost significantly. Policies that restrict pharmacy benefit companies' ability to develop pharmacy networks drive costs up, while well-managed pharmacy networks offer savings to both plan sponsors and enrollees. Health plan sponsors may select – or in the case of Medicare Part D, prefer – specific networks of pharmacies to provide drugs to their enrollees at competitive

[36] CMS. 2019. https://www.medicaid.gov/federal-policy-guidance/downloads/cib051519.pdf.

prices. Nationally, 76% of employers report using a tailored pharmacy network, and employees typically save about 38% out-of-pocket using in-network vs. out-of-network pharmacies.[37] To preserve the benefits of pharmacy networks, it is important to understand the critical role of pharmacy services administrative organizations (PSAOs) in supporting pharmacies.

Pharmacies large and small are important partners in delivering care to patients. Most pharmacy networks are designed to provide patients with a variety of options allowing them to get the drugs they need where they need them. Approximately 83% of independent pharmacies use large PSAOs to negotiate favorable contracts with pharmacy benefit companies. Data shows the independent pharmacy market is stable, growing 0.4% over the last year,[38] and it is the only sector of retail pharmacy that has experienced growth over the last 10 years. By leveraging the power of large PSAOs to negotiate with pharmacy benefit companies on their behalf, independent pharmacies can secure favorable contract terms and, on average, higher reimbursements than chain drugstores.[39] PSAOs and PBMs also provide pharmacies with software, such as Pharmacy Quality Solutions' Electronic Quality Improvement Platform for Plans and Pharmacies (EQuIPP), which allow pharmacies to access their contracted pharmacy measures and compare benchmark measures of their contracts across plans and against other pharmacies.

There are many types of pharmacies – retail, specialty, hospital, clinic, home care, mail order pharmacy, compounding, and assisted living or long-term care – to name a few. These pharmacies vary and not all pharmacies can or should do all things because they offer differing levels of expertise and services to ensure patients are getting what they need to secure the best health outcomes. In fact, there are more than 60,000 retail pharmacies in the United States, including large chains, mass merchants, grocery stores, and 23,000 independent community pharmacies.

Health plans with a variety of sites of care in their networks are able to promote access, affordability, and value. For example, the right mix of brick-and-mortar, mail, and specialty pharmacies improves adherence to therapy and patient safety.

The discussion draft legislation to amend title XVIII of the Social Security Act to promote transparency of common ownership interests under Parts C and D of the Medicare Program may disincentivize business model efficiencies and be a disservice to beneficiaries and the broader PBM market by increasing administrative burdens. The excessive reporting requirements imposed by this proposal on vertically integrated plans could also impair the ability of Part D plans to meet the program's standards for network adequacy. Further, other members of the prescription drug supply chain may be impacted as they are vertically integrated as well. For example, wholesalers often own PSAOs and or pharmacies, as well as operating the equivalent of pharmacy franchises.

---

37 PBMI. 2020. "2019 Trends in Drug Benefit Design."

38 MCPA. 2022. https://ncpa.org/newsroom/news-releases/2022/10/02/ncpa-releases-2022-digest-report.

39 Health Evaluations. 2021. https://www.pcmanet.org/wp-content/uploads/2021/01/PSAO-Report_Health- Evaluations.pdf. See also: Milliman. 2020. https://cdn.ymaws.com/www.floridapharmacy.org/resource/ resmgr/docs_2021_legislative_session/milliman_report.pdf; Ohio Medicaid. 2018. https://www.gongwer-oh.com/public/130/pbmredacted.pdf.; Ohio Department of Medicaid. 2019.https://medicaid.ohio.gov/wps/wcm/connect/gov/2ef5a8b4-0f15-4ef4-8883-11fd6238e101/ODM-HDS-Summary.pdf?MOD=AJPERES&CONVERT_TO=url&CACHEID=ROOTWORKSPACE.Z18_K9I401S01H7F40QBNJU3SO1F56-2ef5a8b4-0f15-4ef4-8883-11fd6238e101-nAkMJJ4.

PBMs Help Patients Afford Their Drugs

As we understand it, the legislative proposal before the Committee *to establish patient protections with respect to highly rebated drugs* attempts to prevent patients from paying out-of-pocket cost sharing that exceeds the net cost of their drug. This is a scenario outside the norm because the market already offers solutions to prevent it from happening. PBMs support efforts to address high out-of-pocket costs for patients and offer health plans' myriad programs in the commercial market, including benefit design options that allow up to full rebate pass-through at the point of sale. The bill also proposes a complicated requirement to base cost sharing on the net price of a drug from the previous calendar year, which is impractical because rebate contracts change every year. For example, a rebate could drop precipitously from one year to the next, as is likely to happen with respect to the insulins for which manufacturers just dropped prices. To minimize operational complexity, cost sharing should be based on a good faith estimate of net price for the current year, as rebates are not known until well after a year's end.

We are also concerned about the likely significant market distortion that would result from the provisions of the bill prohibiting health plans from receiving from drug manufacturers a rebate, reduction in price, or other remuneration for a highly rebated drug that was not covered in a previous year, unless the reduction in price is reflected at the point of sale to the enrollee; and any such other remuneration is a flat-fee-based service fee not contingent on the total volume of sales. For example, this provision essentially requires a point-of-sale rebate if a PBM negotiates to a lower overall cost of a competitor's drug and puts it on the formulary. This would lead to premium increases. In addition, manufacturers would know that PBMs would want to avoid premium increases, and it would strengthen manufacturers' hands in negotiations for drugs that already have patent protections and monopoly pricing. We urge the subcommittee to eliminate this provision from the legislation to avoid this unintended market distortion.

In addition to offering programs to keep out-of-pocket costs low, PBMs work with those providing insurance to encourage patients through formulary design and cost-sharing incentives to use the most affordable drugs, which are usually generics. Generic dispensing has grown over the past decade as more generics have entered the market and patients have responded to health plan designs encouraging their use.[40] PBMs also employ other tools designed to deliver high-quality drug benefits while bringing down costs.[41] For many brand drugs, PBMs negotiate directly with drug manufacturers who compete for formulary placement by offering rebates.[42] For drugs on a preferred tier of a plan's formulary, patients typically have lower cost sharing.[43]

---

[40] US Food and Drug Administration (FDA). Generic Drugs. February 5, 2021. Available at https://www.fda.gov/drugs/buying-using-medicine-safely/generic-drugs.

[41] Pharmacy Benefit Management Institute (PBMI). Solving America's High Drug Cost Problem: Prevent Drug Company Tactics that Increase Costs and Undermine Clinical Quality. 2020. Available at https://www.pcmanet.org/wp-content/uploads/2021/01/Solving-America%E2%80%99s-High-Drug-Cost-Problem_white paper_FINAL2.pdf. Pharmacy Benefit Management Institute (PBMI). 2017 Trends in Specialty Drug Benefits. 2017. Available at www.pbmi.com/research. Pharmacy Benefit Management Institute (PBMI). 2016 Trends in Drug Benefit Design. 2016. Available at www.pbmi.com/research.

[42] Foley Hoag. The History of Rebates in the Drug Supply Chain and HHS' Proposed Rule to Change Safe Harbor Protection for Manufacturer Rebates. April 2, 2019. Available at https://foleyhoag.com/publications/ebooks-and-white-papers/2019/march/the-history-of-rebates-in-the-drug-supply-chain.

[43] Congressional Budget Office (CBO). Prescription Drugs: Spending, Use, and Prices. January 17, 2020. Available at https://www.cbo.gov/system/files/2022-01/57050-Rx-Spending.pdf.

As competing products enter the market, PBMs gain the flexibility to leverage competitor products to negotiate deeper drug discounts for patients and employers.[44]

PBMs have also led the industry in creating contracts that account for the value of specialty and high-cost medications.[45] Value-based arrangements are at the forefront of new drug payment designs and will be critical to managing the costs of next-generation therapies such as cell and gene therapies, orphan drugs, and ultra-expensive specialty drugs. Value-based contracts will better allow plans to manage these high costs, and plan sponsors will need broad flexibility to craft and employ value-based contracts.

The Medicare Part D program, where older Americans and those living with disabilities can choose among private plans to get their drug benefits, is a great example of how PBMs' support for plans impacts patients. PBMs support Part D plans by negotiating rebates and discounts and promoting better pharmacy quality, passing 99.6 percent of the savings from those negotiations to the Part D plans, which in turn use them to enhance drug benefits and keep premium costs reliably low for beneficiaries.[46] We applaud the introduction of H.R. 2666, the *Medicaid VBPs for Patients (MVP) Act,* which could reduce the barriers to innovative contracting models in Medicaid, hopefully allowing Medicaid programs to better control program costs.

Savings from PBMs benefit health plans, employers, retirees, and patients directly. Prescriptions cost health plans and employers an average of $1,040 per person per year, with patients paying an average of $166 for their prescriptions, or 12 percent.[47] Without PBMs and the savings they generate, drug costs could be over $2,300 per person per year.[48]

Conclusion

Thank you for inviting me to appear before the Committee today. PBMs exist to reduce drug costs for plan sponsors and, most importantly, for the patients for whom those health plan sponsors provide coverage. In doing this work, PBMs generate tremendous value, estimated at $145 billion annually for society,[49] and, when taking Medicare savings into account as well as other programs and the commercial market, save payers and patients an average of $1,040 per person per year.[50] Much of this value is generated by the savings PBMs negotiate with

[44] Congressional Budget Office (CBO). Prescription Drugs: Spending, Use, and Prices. January 17, 2020. Available at https://www.cbo.gov/system/files/2022-01/57050-Rx-Spending.pdf.

[45] Pharmacy Benefit Management Institute. Solving America's High Drug Cost Problem: Prevent Drug Company Tactics that Increase Costs and Undermine Clinical Quality. January 2021. Available https://www.pcmanet.org/wp-content/uploads/2021/01/Solving-America%E2%80%99s-High-Drug-Cost-Problem_whitepaper_FINAL 2.pdf.

[46] Government Accountability Office (GAO). Medicare Part D: Use of Pharmacy Benefit Managers and Efforts to Manage Drug Expenditures and Utilization. August 13, 2019. Available at https://www.gao. gov/products/gao-19-498.

[47] Visante. The Return on Investment (ROI) on PBM Services. January 2023. An analysis prepared by Visante on behalf of PCMA Available athttps://www.pcmanet.org/wp-content/uploads/2023/01/The-Return-on-Investment-ROI- on-PBM-Services-January-2023.pdf.

[48] Visante. The Return on Investment (ROI) on PBM Services. January 2023. An analysis prepared by Visante on behalf of PCMA Available athttps://www.pcmanet.org/wp-content/uploads/2023/01/The-Return-on-Investment-ROI- on-PBM-Services-January-2023.pdf.

[49] National Bureau of Economic Research. 2022. https://www.nber.org/papers/w30231.

[50] Visante. 2023. https://www.pcmanet.org/wp-content/uploads/2023/01/Pharmacy-Benefit-Managers-PBMs-Generating-Savings- for-Plan-Sponsors-and-Consumers-January-2023.pdf.

pharmaceutical manufacturers and pharmacies. PBMs also lower prescription drug costs by promoting the use of generic medications, encouraging better pharmacy quality, and offering things like home delivery of medications. Through their work, PBMs lower the cost of health coverage, reduce drug costs, and support better and more affordable prescription drug access for patients, which means more people can get on and stay on the medications they need. For many years, evidence has shown a return of 10:1 on investments in PBM services for their private sector and government partners.[51] As a result, PBMs will lower the cost of health care by $1 trillion this year alone.[52]

PCMA looks forward to working collaboratively with Congress and other stakeholders to build on the existing private market framework to address prescription drug affordability challenges and improve functionality for patients. As this process moves forward, we would be happy to work with you to minimize unintended consequences that would lead to higher costs for employers, patients, and taxpayers.

Mr. GUTHRIE. Thank you.

Mr. Connell, you are now recognized for 5 minutes for your opening statement.

Statement of Brian Connell

Mr. CONNELL. Thank you, Chairman Guthrie and Ranking Member Eshoo, and members of the committee. My name is Brian Connell, and I serve as the executive director of Federal affairs at the Leukemia & Lymphoma Society, where our mission is to cure blood cancer and to improve the quality of life for patients and their families.

We were founded by 2 parents who had suffered the unimaginable loss of their 16-year-old son to leukemia. In the nearly 75 years since our founding, the nonprofit started by that one couple has invested $1.6 billion in research aimed at creating a world in which cancer patients survive their blood cancer and thrive after treatment.

The good news is that we have made incredible progress. Several cancers considered death sentences not long ago, including the leukemia that sparked our founding, are now highly survivable. The bad news is that we have much more work to do, and it goes far beyond medical research. The work ahead includes both ensuring that every patient can access the care that they need and relieving patients of the terrible financial burden that comes with that care. The work is urgent. This year alone, more than 180,000 Americans will receive the life-changing news that they have a blood cancer. Each of these individuals and their families will be thrust into an overwhelming, impersonal maze of provider institutions and insurance rules with potentially ruinous out-of-pocket costs around every corner.

For a patient with private insurance, a diagnosis of acute leukemia will rack up an average of more than $800,000 in treatment costs in the first year alone. The costs that are not borne directly by patients in the form of deductibles and copays are often foisted upon consumers and public insurance programs. Too often, those insurance companies and public officials then

---

[51] Visante. 2023. https://www.pcmanet.org/wp-content/uploads/2023/01/The-Return-on-Investment-ROI-on-PBM-Services- January-2023.pdf.

[52] Visante. The Return on Investment (ROI) on PBM Services. An analysis prepared by Visante on behalf of PCMA. January 2023. Available athttps://www.pcmanet.org/wp-content/uploads/2023/01/The-Return-on-Investment-ROI-on- PBM-Services-January-2023.pdf.

respond by inventing new ways to shift costs back onto patients. We see higher deductibles, additional noncovered care, increased coinsurance, rising premiums, more red tape, stricter eligibility criteria for insurance. The list goes on.

And this is why patients need bold action to make sure that the system is sustainable for patients today and into the future. We are encouraged that many of the proposals that the committee is considering today to promote—will promote healthcare competition and encourage meaningful transparency. We share these goals because we believe that increased competition and transparency have real potential to realign incentives to achieve the improved outcomes—health outcomes that we are looking for while lowering costs for patients, consumers, employers, and taxpayers.

The system is riddled with perverse incentives and a frustrating lack of transparency, so the opportunities are plentiful. I will just give two quick examples.

First, the disparity in Medicare's reimbursement for the same service across provider settings is one of the incentives that has led to a dramatic rise in hospital acquisitions of physician practices. Hospitals acquiring physician offices leads to the result that we have seen in the past few years of the share of cancer drug infusions happening in hospital outpatient facilities has increased nearly 300 percent. And when a hospital purchases a physician practice, the shift in reimbursement increases the patient's out-of-pocket costs without corresponding improvement to the quality of their care. Cancer patients should not pay more simply because the nameplate on the clinic door says "Hospital" rather than "Physician Office."

Second, the lack of transparency in the pharmacy supply chain has led to the proliferation of so-called spread pricing. Spread pricing is a practice in which the PBM administering a drug's plan charges the plan far more for a drug than the acquisition cost. One study found that PBMs administering Medicaid pharmacy benefits across the country paid roughly $84 per tablet for a critical cancer drug called Imatinib while charging the State Medicaid programs as much as $296 per tablet for the same drug. And this difference adds up. The State of Ohio reported that its Medicaid program had lost more than $233 million in potential savings due to spread pricing in a single year.

These are big problems, but we are encouraged by this committee's bipartisan work to take on these tough issues. Reforming these incentives will make a meaningful and lasting impact on the lives of patients with cancer. So we look forward to continuing to partner with you to promote transparency and competition across every area of the healthcare system. Thank you.

[The prepared statement of Mr. Connell follows:]

Testimony of Mr. Brian Connell
Executive Director of Federal Affairs, The Leukemia & Lymphoma Society
House Energy & Commerce Committee Subcommittee on Health
Hearing on "Lowering Unaffordable Costs: Legislative Solutions to Increase Transparency and Competition in Health Care"
Wednesday, April 26, 2023

Thank you, Chairman Guthrie, Ranking Member Eshoo, and members of the Committee, for the honor of participating in today's hearing and discussing the important issues you are considering today. My name is Brian Connell, and I serve as Executive Director of Federal

Affairs at The Leukemia & Lymphoma Society (LLS), where our mission is to cure blood cancers and improve the quality of life of patients and their families.

Cancer is always personal. LLS was founded by two parents who had suffered the unimaginable loss of their 16-year-old son to leukemia. They sought to spare others their pain. In the nearly 75 years since our founding, the nonprofit started by that one couple has invested more than $1.6 billion in research aimed at creating a world in which cancer patients survive their blood cancer and thrive after treatment.

The good news is that we have made incredible progress, transforming many blood cancers from a death sentence to a daunting but surmountable diagnosis. Indeed, several cancers historically associated with near certain death–including the leukemia that sparked our founding–are now highly survivable.

The bad news is that we have much more work ahead. This work certainly involves the research needed to uncover the next generation of cancer breakthroughs that will lead to more survivors and fewer side effects. But it's much more than that. The work ahead also includes ensuring that every patient can access the care they need–when they need it–and relieving patients and their families of the terrible financial burden of cancer.

This work is urgent. This year alone more than 180,000 Americans will receive the life-changing news that they have a blood cancer.[53] In total, nearly two million people across the United States will be newly diagnosed with cancer in 2023.[54] Each of these individuals and their families will be thrust into an overwhelming, impersonal maze of provider institutions and insurance rules, with potentially ruinous out-of-pocket costs around every corner.

The Unsustainable Cost of Cancer Care

Cancer patients in America now pay over $16 billion in out-of-pocket costs for their healthcare each year.[55] For a patient with private insurance, a diagnosis of acute leukemia will rack up an average of more than $800,000 in treatment costs in the first year alone, with $117,000 billed in just the first 30 days.[56] For a patient with Medicare, while the gross bills are lower, average out-of-pocket costs are astronomical: A newly-diagnosed blood cancer patient on traditional Medicare pays on average more than $25,000 in out-of-pocket costs in the first two years after their diagnosis.[57] And, while recent advances in treatment have turned several cancers into chronic conditions that can be controlled with daily treatments and regular follow-ups, these breakthroughs come with the reality that most cancer patients will encounter higher health costs for the rest of their lives.

Costs this high have tangible consequences. The costs not borne directly by patients in the form of deductibles and copays are foisted upon consumers and taxpayers in the form of higher premiums or ballooning budgets for public insurance programs. Too often, insurance

[53] LLS (2021) "Facts 2020-2021: Updated Data on Blood Cancers," The Leukemia & Lymphoma Society, Accessed at: https://www.lls.org/sites/default/files/2021-08/PS80%20FactsBook_2020_2021_FINAL.pdf.

[54] Siegal, R. L. (2023) "Cancer statistics, 2023," CA: A Cancer Journal for Clinicians, 73(1), pp. 17-48.

[55] Yabroff, K.R. (2021) "Annual Report to the Nation on the Status of Cancer, Part 2: Patient Economic Burden Associated with Cancer Care," JNCI, the Journal of the National Cancer Institute, 113(12), pp. 1670-1682.

[56] Dieguez, G. (2018) "The cost burden of blood cancer care," Milliman. Accessed at: https://us.milliman.com/en/insight/the-cost-burden-of-blood-cancer-care.

[57] Fitch, K. (2019) "The cost burden of blood cancer care in Medicare," Milliman. Accessed at: https://us.milliman.com/en/insight/the-cost-burden-of-blood-cancer-care-in-medicare.

companies and public officials respond by inventing new ways to shift costs back onto the patients receiving care: higher deductibles, additional "non-covered" care, increased co-insurance, rising premiums, more red tape, stricter eligibility criteria for insurance. The list goes on.

For cancer patients, this cycle has produced terrible results. Patients often exhaust their life savings.

Many are forced into bankruptcy. Many more walk away without the care they need because they simply can't afford even lifesaving care when it comes at so high a cost. These are the decisions people are forced to make across our country each and every day.

What good is a medical breakthrough—even a cure for cancer—if a patient can't access it?

As an organization that works with patients every day, we at LLS know the situation has only gotten worse in recent years. It's no longer tenable to ignore the unsustainable growth in the cost of cancer care. We need policymakers to stand up for patients, survivors, and caregivers by advancing solutions that bend the cost curve without sacrificing patient care. We need bold action in order to make the system sustainable for patients, today and in the future.

At LLS, we are passionate that every stakeholder in healthcare bears responsibility for realigning the system's broken incentives and replacing them with new incentives that reward the behavior we want to see. We need incentives that reward the delivery of quality healthcare at a lower cost. We need incentives that reinforce the kind of transparency that allows patients and consumers to find the insurance and the care that fits their needs.

We are encouraged by many of the proposals the Committee is considering today to promote healthcare competition and encourage meaningful transparency. We share these goals because we believe that improved competition and transparency have the potential to realign incentives to achieve improved health outcomes while lowering costs for patients, consumers, employers, and taxpayers.

Re-Assessing Payment Incentives that Promote Provider Consolidation

We appreciate the proposals before the Committee that would make progress toward the goal of aligning the payment incentives that today encourage the type of provider consolidation that increases costs without improving quality. Some of these proposals would expand existing site-neutral payments to additional locations, while others would create a comprehensive process for adding codes to the list of services that could be appropriate for site-neutral payment. Other reforms proposed today would provide Medicare and the public with additional information to inform the expansion of site-neutral payments or other payment changes intended to address the ways in which consolidation negatively impacts patients.

The disparity in Medicare's reimbursement for the same service across various provider settings has led to a dramatic rise in hospital mergers and hospital acquisitions of physician practices in recent years.

Between 2007 and 2013, the number of vertically consolidated hospitals increased by more than 20%, from nearly 1,400 to 1,700, and the number of vertically consolidated physicians nearly doubled from about 96,000 to 182,000.[58]6 This trend has shifted how Medicare pays for

[58] GAO (2015) "Increasing Hospital-Physician Consolidation highlights Need for Payment Reform," Accessed at: https://www.gao.gov/products/gao-16-189.

cancer care. For example, the portion of chemotherapy infusions delivered to Medicare enrollees in hospital outpatient settings increased from 15.8 percent in 2004 to 45.9 percent in 2014.[59]

Indeed, this shift has a significant impact on cancer patients, as the consolidation of providers into settings reimbursed under the Medicare hospital outpatient payment system increases patient out-of- pocket costs. For example, a cancer patient can see their chemotherapy cost-sharing increase significantly when the infusion clinic associated with their physician's office is acquired by a hospital system during the course of their treatment. Despite the patient going to the same office, being treated by the same staff, and receiving the same medication, the shift in underlying reimbursement—from the lower physician fee schedule to the higher hospital outpatient payment system—increases the patient's out-of-pocket costs without any corresponding improvement to the quality of their care. Cancer patients shouldn't pay more simply because the nameplate on the clinic's front door now says "hospital" rather than "physician office."

In short, in the situation described above, realigning reimbursement incentives through site-neutral payments for certain services can help ensure that unequal reimbursements don't drive consolidation decisions and that consolidations don't increase patient and system costs.

Experts have repeatedly identified site-neutral payments as an opportunity to save money for Medicare, reduce cost sharing for beneficiaries, and limit non-clinical incentives to provide services in more expensive settings—all without compromising beneficiary access to care or health outcomes. Indeed, Medicare has implemented a modest site-neutral payment policy for certain office visits, and patients have not experienced a deterioration of their care. Meanwhile, a recent analysis found that further expanding site-neutral payments would have reduced Medicare enrollee cost-sharing in 2019 by $1.7 billion and Medicare program spending by $6.6 billion.[60] In addition to saving taxpayer dollars and reducing patient out-of-pocket costs, equalizing payments between these sites of service would weaken the incentive for provider consolidation, which would also produce long-term cost savings across insurance types and give patients additional options for their care.

Bringing Transparency to Pharmacy Benefit Managers (PBMs)

Given the nature of blood cancers, many patients rely on prescription drugs as their primary form of therapy. As a result, blood cancer patients often access their cancer therapy via their insurance plan's pharmacy benefit—typically managed by their plan's contracted pharmacy benefit manager (PBM). Reforms are needed to ensure greater transparency, oversight, and appropriate guardrails in order to align PBMs' financial incentives with the goals of both plans and patients.

We are encouraged by the proposals being considered today that would empower insurers, employers, and insurance regulators with the information they need to ascertain the extent to

---

[59] Fitch, K (2016) "Cost Drivers of Cancer Care: A Retrospective Analysis of Medicare and Commercially Insured Population Claim Data 2004-2014." Accessed at: https://www.milliman.com/en/insight/cost-drivers-of-cancer-care-a-retrospective-analysis-of-medicare-and-commercially-insured.

[60] MedPAC (2022) "June 2022 Report to Congress, Chapter 6: Aligning fee-for-service payment rates across ambulatory setting," Accessed at: https://www.medpac.gov/wp-content/uploads/2022/06/Jun22_Ch6_MedPAC_Report_to_Congress_SEC.pdf.

which PBM financial incentives are aligned with lowering plan costs and promoting access to appropriate care.

LLS continues to advocate for comprehensive, routine reporting by PBMs to plan sponsors, including details about the list and net prices for drugs accessed through the pharmacy benefit as well as comprehensive rebate information for each drug. Additionally, PBMs should be required to provide important information related to the inflated out-of-pocket costs paid by plan enrollees utilizing a drug whose enrollee cost-sharing is based on its list price rather than net price. Plan sponsors should be aware of the impact on enrollees of choosing to base cost-sharing on an inflated list price, which dramatically increases the cost burden for patients who rely on drugs with high list prices, in order to provide a small amount of savings either to plan cost or enrollee premiums. This trade-off has significant consequences for plan enrollees with blood cancer and other chronic and/or life-threatening conditions, and plan sponsors should be aware of the impact on these enrollees.

LLS is also encouraged by the Committee's consideration of provisions that would rein in so-called 'spread pricing'—a practice that positions a PBM's financial incentives in opposition to the incentives of the plan sponsor for whom they are managing the prescription benefit. Spread pricing describes the practice of PBMs administering a plan's drug benefits charging a plan sponsor far more for a drug than the drug's pharmacy acquisition cost, with the potentially vast difference between the two costs going to the PBM's bottom line.

One study found the generic drug imatinib, a treatment for chronic myeloid leukemia, provides one of the starkest examples of this practice. In 2018, PBMs administering Medicaid pharmacy benefits paid roughly $84/tablet for imatinib, while charging state Medicaid programs as much as $296/tablet.[61] The same study notes that the imatinib case study reflects a broader trend that was highlighted when the state of Ohio reported that PBMs operating pharmacy benefits for the state's Medicaid program had lost more than $233 million in potential savings due to spread pricing in 2017 alone.

The practice of spread pricing prevents public and private plan sponsors from experiencing the financial benefits of generic competition, and it serves no purpose other than to reward PBMs for behavior contrary to the interests of the entities on whose behalf they are contracted to work.

Promoting Transparency in Prices and Ownership

We appreciate the Committee's consideration of provisions aimed at improving the ability of plan sponsors, consumers, and patients to understand the price of healthcare services and therefore get a better deal for their healthcare dollar. A common point of frustration for patients is the inability to know ahead of a healthcare service exactly how much that service will cost. Even with the protections of the No Surprises Act, patients are still often unsure of whether or the extent to which they should expect a facility fee or other unexpected charges. This information could also empower plan sponsors to better negotiate payments and thereby lower costs for their plan enrollees.

---

[61] Pachman, E. (2018). "The Cancerous Design of the US Drug Pricing System," Brooklyn46 Research. Accessed at: https://www.46brooklyn.com/research/2018/7/23/the-cancerous-design-of-the-us-drug-pricing-system.

We also appreciate the proposal under consideration to require providers to report regularly on their ownership structure and other details that may inform healthcare stakeholders as they make decisions. Patients have the right to know the financial model under which their providers—or prospective providers—are operating. While some patients may not value this information, others may consider it valuable in choosing between providers or better understanding a provider's treatment recommendations.

Facilitating Competition Through Consumer-Friendly Plan Transparency

When shopping for coverage during enrollment periods, consumers do not have access to clear and transparent information about key aspects of their plan options. For example, consumers are often unable to ascertain the amount they would be required to pay as their share of the cost of a medication. This is due largely to the prevalence of coinsurance, a cost-sharing technique that requires consumers to pay a percentage of a drug's total cost. Plan formularies typically represent coinsurance as a percentage only – such as "30%" or "45%" – with no accompanying information that consumers can use to translate that percentage to an actual dollar amount.

As a result, consumers must select and enroll in a plan without a full understanding of the affordability of one plan's drug benefit versus another. This lack of transparency poses a real threat to patient well- being: patients are more likely to abandon treatment when the cost of their care is high, a dynamic that is exacerbated when patients are unable to anticipate and plan for the precise out-of-pocket cost of their care. This lack of transparency is harmful to the marketplace as well, as it diminishes competition among plans.

In order to facilitate greater transparency regarding cost-sharing for medications, we urge the Committee to consider requiring CMS to improve Medicare Plan Finder to convey important information on out-of-pocket drug costs so that consumers can judge their health care options based on complete information about the impact of their decision on their financial and physical health. In addition, we urge the Committee to require qualified health plans (QHPs) to provide transparency regarding the plan's prescription drug formulary, including meaningful cost-sharing information, to consumers during the open enrollment process. At a minimum, QHPs should be required to include for every covered drug a range of out-of-pocket spending for the prescription (e.g. $-$$$$ OR $0-10, $11-25…$500+, etc.).

Developing Patient-Centered Value-Based Payment Models

Innovative, value-driven payment models can have the potential to improve health outcomes and promote the development of new and better treatments. To incentivize patient-centered innovation, prescription drugs that significantly improve important patient outcomes should be rewarded generously, in comparison to new therapies that bring limited or no benefit over existing options. For example, a new, curative therapy should be deemed "higher value" than a new brand drug with a clinical value comparable to that of one or more existing drugs.

We are encouraged that the Committee is considering legislation aimed at promoting flexibility for Medicaid programs to engage with drugmakers on value-based payment (VBP) agreements. LLS agrees that there is potential for VBP agreements to achieve important goals for patients and the healthcare system. Unfortunately, there are barriers to developing VBP arrangements. To address a key barrier, we recommend the Committee consider modernizing certain federal rules to facilitate innovative models. Specifically, we recommend reforming the Medicaid best-price regulations and federal anti-kickback protections to better facilitate contracting arrangements that include financial adjustments based on patient outcomes.

Furthermore, we encourage the Committee to consider how to promote the development of long-term financing models that could have a positive impact in promoting patient access to new, innovative treatments. Such models could reduce the upfront burden on the healthcare system, which has the potential to improve access to high-cost, potentially curative treatments for patients. However, these models must be structured in a way that protects patients from undue cost burdens. For example, curative and/or breakthrough treatments are typically associated with major upfront costs, but, over time, can result in significant savings and improve patient outcomes. LLS believes that innovative, long- term financing mechanisms can potentially make it easier for payers to cover high-cost drugs, which could lead to fewer barriers to access for patients.

Encouraging a Better Understanding of the 340B Program

While the 340B program plays an important role in lowering the cost of drugs to participating facilities, we are encouraged that the Committee is considering program reforms aimed at understanding how patients receiving care at 340B facilities are benefiting from the significant drug discounts provided to those facilities. Today, the Committee is considering legislation to require participating providers to report data related to 340B drugs dispensed at each facility and how the facility applies the net savings achieved due to 340B discounts.

We agree that the 340B program should be the subject of additional scrutiny to better determine how to best achieve its goals of promoting patient access to necessary treatments. We urge the Committee to continue to consider 340B program reforms that would improve transparency around how covered entities utilize the significant discounts they receive under the program, in order to promote the sharing of these discounts with patients served by these facilities.

Conclusion

We are encouraged by this Committee's bipartisan work to take on these tough issues. Of course, finding savings in healthcare is never easy: Every dollar goes to someone. And folks who have grown accustomed to those dollars are not going to give them up quietly. But if you have the courage to take on those interests and respond to the urgent need to act, you will have a meaningful and lasting impact on the lives of patients with cancer and their families.

We at The Leukemia & Lymphoma Society look forward to continuing to partner with you to accomplish these goals and consider additional opportunities to promote transparency and competition across every area of the healthcare system.

Thank you.

Mr. GUTHRIE. Thank you. The Chair now recognizes Mr. Cavanaugh for 5 minutes for questions.

Mr. CAVANAUGH. Thank you, Mr. Chairman.

Mr. GUTHRIE. I mean for—excuse me—to—your opening statement.

Statement of Sean Cavanaugh

Mr. CAVANAUGH. Thank you, Mr. Chairman, and I thank the subcommittee for inviting me today to discuss strategies for increasing transparency and competition in healthcare.

My name is Sean Cavanaugh. I am the chief policy officer at Alidade. We help independent primary care practices deliver better care to their patients and thrive in value-based care. Previous to Alidade, I was at CMS Innovation Center and also served as director of the Center for Medicare. I am proud to continue the movement to better care at lower cost in the private sector.

Alidade works with more than 1,500 independent primary care practices, including 200 FQHCs and rural health centers across 45 States to make them successful in value-based care. These practices care for 2.2 million beneficiaries in value-based care contracts. More than half of the practices have fewer than 10 clinicians. Sixty percent of them are in primary care shortage areas. And Alidade is now what is called a public benefit corporation. That means explicitly our mission is to improve healthcare in a way that is good for patients, good for practices, and good for society.

And Alidade is producing meaningful results. Our estimates are that in 2022 our Medicare ACOs are projected to save Medicare more than $535 million. Prior-year data from CMS, official data, in 2021 Alidade sponsored 4 of the top 10 performing ACOs in the United States. And one of those four, our Mississippi ACO, was an FQHC-only ACO, was the fourth-highest saver in the United States.

And these savings were generated through real improvements in the care for Medicare beneficiaries: more primary care delivering better diabetes control, more blood pressure screening leading to fewer hospitalizations and emergency room visits. The data clearly show that ACOs grounded in advanced primary care can deliver better care at lower cost. But that approach is under threat from consolidation and anticompetitive forces.

And let's be clear: The evidence is overwhelming. Hospital mergers are steadily increasing. Horizontal consolidation leads to higher prices. Vertical consolidation leads to higher prices. And there is no clear evidence that consolidation leads to higher quality. Provider concentration increases the bargaining power of large health systems, which allows them to demand higher prices from health plans. And unfortunately, COVID may have accelerated these trends. Small physician practices and safety net hospitals entered the pandemic with vulnerable financial positions and were less likely to access emergency relief funding.

This committee has an opportunity to take meaningful action to promote competition and transparency in this country. First and foremost, we need to invest more in primary care. That means both Community Health Centers but also independent practices. And I thank this committee for its work recently in looking at workforce, which is critical.

Second, we need to put an end to unnecessary facility fees and move to site-neutral payments. Facility fees are part of the financial engine that hospitals rely on to acquire independent practices and reduce competition in their markets. Independent practices and Community Health Centers struggle to recruit new physicians because they cannot compete with hospitals that are receiving higher payments. And these facility fees, of course, also raise out- of-pocket costs to Medicare beneficiaries. Congress and CMS have taken some actions toward site neutrality, but the overwhelming majority of services are still receiving higher payments when they are in the hospital—provider-based clinics.

I would also note there are other policies not in front of the committee today that the Congress should consider, including prohibiting anticompetitive contracting by healthcare providers such as gag clauses, antitiering, antisteering clauses, as well as all-or-noth- ing clauses.

There are—we could optimize some of the incentives in the Medicare shared savings program. We have been talking to CMS about this, especially for rural providers. We could improve access to capital for independent practices, reform CON rules in States, reinvigorate antitrust enforcement, and regulate anticompetitive data sharing practices.

Thank you again for the opportunity to testify, and I look forward to working with this committee on this bipartisan work.

[The prepared statement of Mr. Cavanaugh follows:]

United States House of Representatives
Committee on Energy and Commerce
Subcommittee on Health
"Lowering Unaffordable Costs: Legislative Solutions to Increase Transparency and Competition in Health Care"

April 26, 2023

Sean Cavanaugh
Chief Policy Officer, Aledade
[redacted]

Chairman Guthrie, Ranking Member Eshoo and members of the Committee, thank you for inviting me to discuss strategies for increasing transparency and competition in health care.

My name is Sean Cavanaugh, Chief Policy Officer for Aledade, a health care company that helps independent primary care practices, health centers, and clinics deliver better care to their patients and thrive in value-based care. Previously, I served at the Centers for Medicare & Medicaid Services (CMS) for six years, as the Deputy Director of the Center for Medicare and Medicaid Innovation (CMMI) and then as Director of the Center for Medicare. In those capacities, I supported the movement toward value-based payment and service delivery models in Medicare and Medicaid, and I'm proud to continue that work in the private sector.

Aledade was founded in 2014 to help independent primary care practices thrive in value-based programs. We bring together independent primary care practices that are committed to value-based care, join the Medicare Shared Savings Program, and negotiate similar accountable care organization (ACO) arrangements with Medicare Advantage, Medicaid, and commercial health plans. We provide population health workflow tools and integrated data analytics, and we transform how practices that join our nationwide network deliver care.

Today, Aledade is the largest network of independent primary care in the country. This year, Aledade is partnering with more than 1,500 independent physician practices, including 200 Rural Health Centers and Federally Qualified Health Centers. Organized into 45 MSSP ACOs across 45 states and Washington, DC, these practices are accountable for more than 2.2 million patients; this includes 1 million Medicare beneficiaries through the Medicare Shared Savings Program, and more than 1.2 million patients through ACO arrangements with Medicare Advantage plans, commercial insurers and other payers (Figure 1).

We have committed to our mission to bring the benefits of value-based care to communities all across the country - and to do so the right way. More than half of our primary care providers are in practices with fewer than ten clinicians; 60 percent of our practices are in Primary Care Shortage Areas and 50 percent in Medically Underserved Areas. And by becoming a public benefit corporation, Aledade has committed to a corporate structure that requires weighing the interests of our primary care practice partners, their patients, our employees, and those who bear the burden of rising health care costs, alongside those of our shareholders, when we make decisions.

Figure 1 Map of Aledade's Network of Primary Care Partners

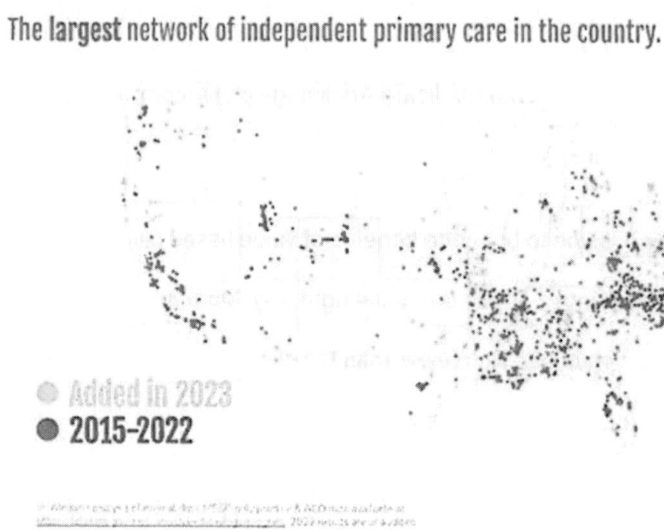

Most importantly, Aledade is producing meaningful results. In 2022, our ACOs are projected to save Medicare more than $535 million. In 2021, four of the top ten performing ACOs in MSSP were Aledade ACOs (measured by per-beneficiary savings), and the top-performing MSSP ACO in the entire country was an Aledade ACO. The fourth-ranked ACO in the nation was also an Aledade ACO, the Mississippi MSSP Community Health Center ACO, which faces some of the most challenging health care headwinds in the entire country. This ACO, composed entirely of community health centers, outperformed many of our nation's top hospitals and health systems in terms of savings for taxpayers through better patient care.

We are not alone in succeeding in the Medicare Shared Savings Program. Our analysis of CMS data shows that physician-sponsored ACOs are generating outstanding results (Figure 2).

Figure 2 Medicare Shared Savings Programs Net Savings by ACO Type

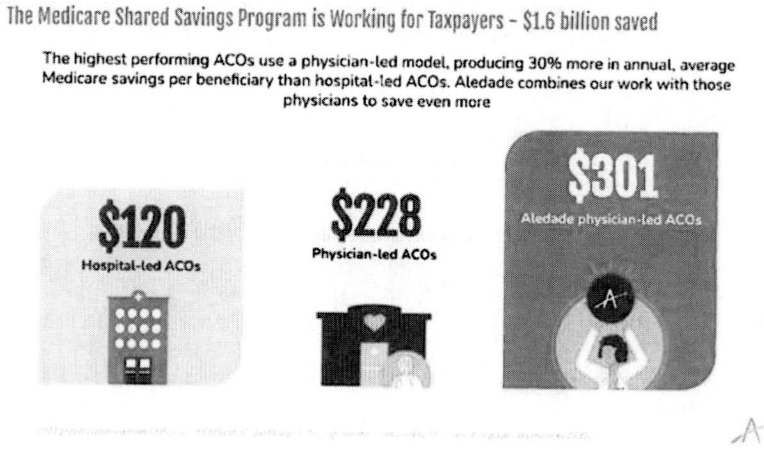

These savings were generated through real improvements in the care primary care practices delivered to Medicare beneficiaries. In 2021, the most recent data released by Medicare, practices in Aledade ACOs helped their patients avoid more than 24,000 unnecessary hospitalizations and more than 120,000 unnecessary visits to the emergency room.

This happened because patients in Aledade's network had better blood pressure screening, A1C control, and cancer screening rates. In MSSP specifically, Aledade had three ACOs in the top ten percent of all ACOs for blood pressure control and statin therapy. An Aledade ACO was also the top performer for diabetes control. We have empowered our practices to deliver more primary care and reduce unnecessary hospitalizations and post-acute care stays, and our results improve the longer our practices work with us (Figure 3).

Figure 3 Aledade's Results from our Longest Running ACOs

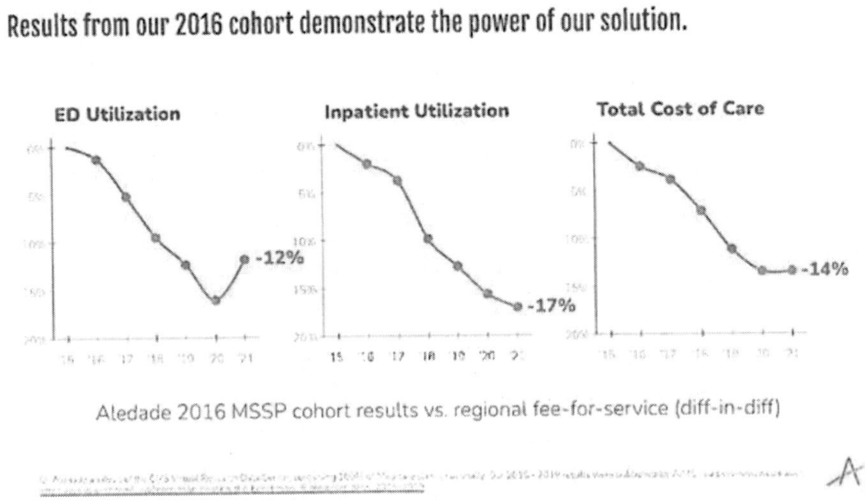

We are committed to outcome-based approaches to improve the value of health care. We are committed to using technology, data, practice transformation expertise and, most important, the relationship between a person and their primary care physician (PCP).

We are pleased to see the Committee's attention to lowering health care costs and believe that increasing provider competition is central to doing so. My testimony focuses on the encouraging pro-competitive provisions included in several of the bills under consideration today. I also offer several additional ideas for the Committee to consider as it continues to assess next steps.

Competition

As a nation, we need to make a fundamental decision about how to drive more efficiency and higher quality in our health care system. In simple terms, this choice is between a competitive approach and a regulatory approach. I have extensive experience as a regulator: I set all-payer prices for Maryland hospitals and established provider and health plan payment rates at CMS, which guide more than $600 billion in spending a year. But, we should rely on regulation only when market competition isn't feasible, or when it has failed. To give markets a chance to work, we have to establish an environment that fosters competition. Unfortunately, our current health care system has a number of market failures, including payer and provider consolidation, and our laws permit practices that undermine competition.

It is well known that hospital consolidation is a growing impediment to a high-value health care system. The Kaiser Family Foundation published a summary[1] of the academic literature on the effects of provider consolidation and they concluded:

[1] https://www.kff.org/health-costs/issue-brief/what-we-know-about-provider-consolidation/

- Hospital mergers have been steadily rising since 2005
- Horizontal consolidation among hospitals and among physician practices leads to higher prices
- Vertical consolidation also leads to higher prices
- There is no clear evidence that consolidation leads to higher quality care

Provider concentration increases the local bargaining power of large health systems, which allows them to demand higher prices for services from health plans. And without alternative providers to generate competition, there is little incentive to provide higher quality care. Further, we see the most aggressive actors exert their market dominance with anti-competitive contracting practices that entrench their position in the market. Hospitals have argued that consolidation will lead to greater efficiencies and more coordinated care, but the evidence shows the opposite is true.

Unfortunately, COVID may have accelerated these trends. Some providers, such as smaller practices and safety net hospitals, entered the pandemic with vulnerable financial positions and were less likely to access emergency relief funding.[2] I worry that the several decade trend of consolidation has accelerated over the past three years.

Reversing these trends and establishing the framework for a high performance health system will require more than legislation, but this Committee has an opportunity to take meaningful action to promote competition and transparency in this country.

---

[2] https://jamanetwork.com/journals/jama-health-forum/fullarticle/2771582

First and foremost, everything we have learned in the recent history of Medicare is that true transformation starts with a robust investment in primary care. This committee should continue to support greater investments in primary care, including community health centers and independent practices. These organizations are the foundation of true health care transformation. I thank the Committee for holding a hearing recently on workforce needs, and recognizing the need to bring more primary care physicians and mental health providers to rural areas.

Second, the Committee should eliminate existing Medicare policies that inhibit competition in health care. Several bills before the committee would move Medicare toward site neutral payments, which is an important first step. Facility fees paid to hospital outpatient departments for services that can be provided in physician offices are part of the financial engine that hospitals rely on to acquire independent practices and reduce competition in their markets. Independent practices and community health centers struggle to recruit new physicians because they cannot compete with hospitals that are receiving higher payments. Congress passed legislation in 2015 to put an end to extra Medicare payments to new hospital sites but "grandfathering" allowed sites acquired before 2017 to continue billing and receiving facility fees. Additionally, CMS imposed site-neutral payments for a limited number of services. However, the vast majority of services in provider-based clinics continue to receive higher payments for services from Medicare and from the many payers that utilize similar payment mechanisms, such as Medicare Advantage and commercial insurance plans. In addition to exacerbating consolidation and increasing costs to the health care system, these facility fees raise out of pocket costs to Medicare beneficiaries. We should not support this whenever these services can be provided safely and at high quality in a physician office or ambulatory surgery center.

Additional Recommendations to Improve Competition

As the Committee continues its work to improve transparency and competition in health care, there are other ideas it should consider as well. The following ideas are drawn from the work of Dr. Farzad Mostashari (CEO of Aledade), Dr. Martin Gaynor and Dr. Paul Ginsburg, writing with the support of the Brookings Institution.[3]

- **Anti competitive contracting.** Congress needs to address some of the current contracting abuses and market failures to chart a path towards true competition. Gag clauses, anti-tiering, anti-steering, as well as all-or-nothing clauses, are prime examples of excess market power enabling anti-competitive behavior. By banning gag clauses, Congress can prohibit dominant providers from concealing the price and quality of the care delivered by health systems; this is information about the people's health care that patients and their representatives, such as employers, need to know. A similar abuse arises when health systems demand

[3] Gaynor, M; Mostashari, F; Ginsburg P (2017) Making Health Care Markets Work: Competition Policy for Health Care. Brookings Institution. https://www.brookings.edu/research/making-health-care-markets-work-competition-policy-for-health-care/

that insurance companies do not "tier," or rank, their providers based on the cost and quality of the care that patients receive. Anti-steering clauses prohibit health plans from encouraging patients to receive care with higher value providers. And finally, "all or nothing" clauses are coercive to health plans; they state that "if you're going to contract with any providers of our system, you must contract with all of them." This allows a monopoly in one area to diminish competition in a completely different market.

Together, these practices are anti-competitive and hurt patients. They stand in direct opposition to the movement to value-based care, asserting that cost and quality don't matter if dominance in the market is great enough.

- **Optimize MSSP for Rural Providers.** Some have claimed that banning these market distorting practices could limit the power of health systems to negotiate higher rates that support some rural hospitals. (Similar claims have been made about site neutral payments.) But in both cases, the solution to inadequate funding is not to promote anti-competitive behavior and opaque cross-subsidies. Where rural hospitals and physicians need greater support, direct subsidies would be a more efficient and transparent mechanism.

In addition, there are other ideas to promote rural health while advancing value-based care competition. As Congress considers updating the 2015

Medicare Access and CHIP Reauthorization Act (MACRA), members can refine the Medicare Shared Savings Program to use cost setting principles, or benchmarking, that creates an enduring opportunity for rural health to succeed in value based care. We urge Congress to direct CMS to set benchmarks that do not decrease as accountable care organizations reduce costs. By doing so, Congress establishes a long term future for rural health based on better care and better health for rural Amercians.

- **Improve access to capital for independent practices.** Independent physician practices, especially primary care physicians, perform better in value-based models, but their financial status is often weak. Congress could expand loan repayment programs to providers who serve in rural areas, even if they work at private practices. Congress could also focus on Small Business Administration loans targeted at rural private practices.

- **Reform Certificate of Need (CON) rules.** When a state strictly limits the number of hospitals that can receive a CON for a particular service, the state is often granting monopoly power for that service in those markets with no corresponding mechanism to control costs or improve quality. Congress could establish federal grants for states that commit to pro-competitive policies, such as repealing or reforming CON laws.

- **Reinvigorate antitrust enforcement.** The FTC, which can oversee mergers of nonprofit hospitals, does not have the ability to review other potentially anti-competitive behavior by hospitals. While this legislation would outlaw many of the contracting abuses that FTC would potentially monitor, we believe that the agency should be better equipped moving forward.

- **Regulating Anti Competitive Data-Sharing Practices.** No one should be able to limit competition by limiting access to patient data. The Office of the National Coordinator of Health IT (ONC) has defined information blocking as required by the 21st Century Cures Act. Since April 2021, ONC has received more than 300 reports of information blocking, yet the Office of the Inspector General (OIG) still has to finalize its rule regarding penalties for networks found to be information blocking.[4] CMS must also propose a framework for "appropriate disincentives" for providers. Access to data leads to better patient care and a more competitive marketplace for health care services. For example, medical and economic literature demonstrates that patients have fewer readmissions and other adverse outcomes when they see their PCP after discharge from the hospital. Aledade practices avoid one hospital readmission for every eight transitional care visits they provide. But independent physicians can provide this care only when they receive timely notification of the patient discharge. Aledade has encountered resistance from some hospitals in providing these data -- even when our company bears the cost of the interfacing and there is no technological barrier. CMS has rules requiring hospitals to share this information for patient safety.

[4]https://www.healthcaredive.com/news/onc-micky-tripathi-information-blocking-enforcement-complaints/637500/#:~:text=The%20OIG%20has%20the%20statutory,the%20size%20of%20any%20penalties.

ONC has rules requiring hospitals not to block information. Yet, health systems and other actors can still prioritize their information-sharing practices in anti-competitive and unsafe ways. OIG should finalize its penalty regulations as soon as possible to ensure that information follows the patient and is not confined to a closed health network, and CMS should take the next step to formalize provider disincentives.

Thank you again for this opportunity to testify on these important bills and I commend the committee for its bipartisan work. Thank you for the opportunity to share Aledade's experiences with you, and I look forward to continuing to engage with Members of the Committee as you consider this legislation.

Mr. GUTHRIE. I thank you for your testimony. The Chair now recognizes Ms. Schuman for 5 minutes for your opening statement.

Statement of Ilyse Schuman

Ms. SCHUMAN. Thank you. Chair Guthrie, Ranking Member Eshoo, and distinguished subcommittee members. Thank you for the opportunity to testify on behalf of the American Benefits Council.

The council represents over 220 of the world's largest corporations advocating on a full range of employee benefit issues. Employ- ers play a critical role in the healthcare system and have a vested interest in securing the health and well-being of their employees. Employers are also deeply concerned about rising healthcare costs and are increasingly frustrated by fundamental failures in the healthcare marketplace that stifle competition, cloud line of sight into price and quality information, impede innovation, and ultimately increase costs.

The only way to truly make healthcare more affordable for working families is to understand and address these root causes of rising healthcare costs by increasing transparency and competition.

Hospital price increases are key drivers of recent spending growth among the privately insured. The most important driver of higher hospital prices is, in turn, the rise of hospital monopolies that use their market power to demand higher and higher prices. And at the same time, many hospital systems are becoming vertically integrated, with physician organizations raising prices. These higher hospital prices are coming without an improvement in the quality of care. In fact, provider consolidation leads to less bang for the buck.

The Council strongly supports legislation to expand site-neutral payment reforms. Often physician offices are being purchased by hospitals and simply rebranded as part of a hospital's outpatient department in order to collect the resulting higher payments. Such legislation, by aligning payment differentials across sites of service, removes a powerful incentive for provider consolidation and corrects a significant distortion leading patients to higher-care settings.

Employers recognize that hospitals are an essential component of the Nation's health system, particularly during the pandemic, and understand that some hospitals are facing financial challenges. A recent Health Affairs article examined the financial performance of large, nonprofit hospital systems in the post-COVID era and revealed a more complex financial picture. Investment losses accounted for approximately 85 percent of overall financial losses. This analysis suggests that investment losses are actually the primary driver of these losses, not increased labor and supply costs. Employers, patients, and taxpayers should not have to foot the bill for a hospital's risky financial position.

Hospitals are also able to use a billing practice which is fueling acquisition of physician practices because they are not required to specify where services are provided. The Council strongly supports legislation that will promote honest billing practices by helping patients—payers to distinguish between sites of care.

The Council also strongly supports the bipartisan Transparent Price Act. A competitive and value-driven healthcare market is predicated on transparency. Effective transparency tools in the hands of employers and consumers can be transformative, making healthcare both simpler and more affordable. Unfortunately, far too many hospitals across the country remain out of compliance, or meaningful compliance, with the hospital transparency rule. Codifying and strengthening the rule, including through increased maximum penalties, is essential to realizing its objective.

The Council also strongly supports the PBM Accountability Act. The current rebate structure is complex and opaque, and employers continue to encounter barriers to PBM pricing transparency. With the three largest PBMs controlling 80 percent of the market, employers—even very large employers—are not going to have the leverage in contract negotiations that they need. Federal legislation requiring strong transparency and accountability for PBMs to employers, their primary clients, is essential to employer efforts to manage prescription drug costs.

While employers continue innovating and exploring strategies to lower costs, Federal legislative solutions are needed to create a more competitive and transparent healthcare marketplace. This hearing and the solutions under review today, therefore, represent a critical step towards making healthcare more affordable.

I appreciate the opportunity to testify, and look forward to answering any questions.

[The prepared statement of Ms. Schuman follows:]

Testimony of Ilyse Schuman, Senior Vice President, Health Policy American Benefits Council Before the United States House of Representatives Committee On energy and commerce, Subcommittee on Health, Hearing on "Lowering Unaffordable Costs: Legislative Solutions to Increase Transparency and Competition in Health Care" April 26, 2023

Chairs Rodgers and Guthrie, Ranking Members Pallone and Eshoo and distinguished subcommittee members:

Thank you for the opportunity to testify on behalf of the American Benefits Council ("the Council") at this important hearing about legislative solutions to lower unaffordable health care costs by increasing transparency and competition. I am Ilyse Schuman, the Council's senior vice president, health policy.

The Council is a national nonprofit organization dedicated to protecting employer-sponsored benefit plans. The Council represents more major employers – over 220 of the world's largest corporations – than any other association that exclusively advocates on the full range of employee benefit issues. Members also include organizations supporting employers of all sizes. Collectively, Council members directly sponsor or support health and retirement plans covering virtually all Americans participating in employer-sponsored programs.

Providing health coverage to more than 178 million Americans,[62] employers play a critical role in the health care system and drive innovations from which the entire health system benefits. With a vested interest in securing the health and well-being of their employees, employers have been at the forefront of initiatives to lower health care costs and improve quality through various value-based strategies. However, employers are deeply concerned about rising health care costs. Employers are increasingly frustrated by fundamental failures in the health care marketplace that stifle competition, cloud line of sight to price and quality information, impede innovation – and, ultimately, increase costs.

The only way to truly make health care more affordable for working families is to understand and address the root causes of rising health care spending, namely a lack of transparency and misaligned incentives that drive market consolidation. This hearing and the legislative solutions under consideration today represent a critical step forward in combatting the nation's health care affordability crisis. The Council applauds the subcommittee's willingness to take action to unleash the power of employer innovation by addressing the drivers of rising health care costs at their core.

The national health expenditure grew to $4.3 trillion in 2021, representing almost one-fifth (18.3%) of the U.S. gross domestic product.[63] The annual growth in national health spending is expected to average 5.1% over 2021-2030 and reach nearly $6.8 trillion by 2030.[64] During this same period, private health insurance spending growth is projected to average 5.7%. According to a study by the Kaiser Family Foundation, annual premiums for employer-sponsored family health coverage reached $22,463 for family coverage in 2022, with workers on average paying $6,106 toward the cost of their coverage.[65] The average premium for family coverage has increased 20% over the last five years and 43% over the last ten years. This trajectory is unsustainable for employers, employees and their families and it is being fueled by hospital consolidation and vertical integration of hospital -acquired physician practices and a lack of transparency in the health care system.

Top executives at nearly 87% of large employers surveyed in a 2021 poll believed the cost of providing health benefits to employees will become unsustainable in the next five-to-10 years.[66] The cost of health care is a top concern for voters as well. According to a Morning Consult poll for the Alliance to Fight for Health Care, 83% of insured adults say they are concerned about costs (with 44% saying they are very concerned.) Reducing health care costs

---

[62] U.S. Census Bureau, *Health Insurance Coverage in the United States: 2021* (September 2022), Table 1.

[63] U.S. Centers for Medicare and Medicaid Services (CMS), *NHE Fact Sheet* (Updated December 14, 2022).

[64] CMS news release, "CMS Office of the Actuary Releases 2021-2030 Projections of National Health Expenditures" (March 28, 2022).

[65] Kaiser Family Foundation, *2022 Employer Health Benefits Survey* (October 27, 2022)

[66] Kaiser Family Foundation news release, "Vast Majority of Large Employers Surveyed Say Broader Government Role Will Be Necessary to Control Health Costs and Provide Coverage, Survey Finds" (April 29, 2021).

was cited as the top health care reform priority for a majority (57%) of insured adults, topping covering more people (19%) and covering more health care services (24%). And almost 80% of voters want Congress to work to lower health care costs for all Americans, no matter how or where they get their health coverage.[67]

With the legislative solutions under review today, the subcommittee is responding to the concerns of employers, employees and voters and helping ensure a healthy and affordable future for America's workers. It's time to pull back the curtain on health care costs and prices. It's time to see and to stem unchecked hospital pricing increases enabled and accelerated by the consolidation of hospital systems that have eliminated competition and by the proliferation of hospital-owned physician practices. It's time to shine a light on the prescription drug pricing system and require greater transparency for pharmacy benefit managers (PBMs).

In the Council's February 27 letter to Congress sharing our health policy priorities for the 118th Congress,[68] we urged congressional action on key policies to improve health care affordability and value by increasing transparency and competition. We are very pleased to see that a number of these important policies are among the proposals discussed today. I will focus my remarks on these proposals that:

- expand site neutral payment reforms;
- restrict hospital billing practices that fuel consolidation and mask what should be the appropriate payment amounts;
- support greater price transparency in the health care system; and

Expand Site Neutral Payment Reforms

The Council strongly supports:

- H.R. __, To amend title XVIII of the Social Security Act to provide for site neutral payments under the Medicare program for certain services furnished in ambulatory settings;
- H.R. __, To amend title XVIII of the Social Security Act to require payment for all hospital-owned physician offices located off-campus be paid in accordance with the applicable payment system for the items and services, and
- H.R. _, To amend title XVII of the Social Security Act to provide for parity in Medicare payments for hospital outpatient department services furnished off- campus.

Hospital spending is the largest health spending category in the United States, accounting for almost one-third of all expenditures. In 2021, according to the Centers for Medicare & Medicaid Services (CMS), hospital spending totaled $1.3 trillion.[69] Spending on hospital services accounts for 44% of total personal health care spending for the privately insured and

---

[67] Alliance to Fight for Health Care & Morning Consult, *Coverage and Reforming the System* (February 21, 2023).
[68] American Benefits Council, "Health Policy Priorities for the 118th Congress" (February 27, 2023).
[69] CMS Office of the Actuary Press Release, "National Health Spending Grew Slightly in 2021" (December 14, 2022).

hospital price increases are key drivers of recent growth in per capita spending among the privately insured.[70]

Employer health plans already pay much higher prices for health care goods and services than public plans. According to a Rand Corporation report, in 2020, across all hospital inpatient and outpatient services, employers and private insurers paid hospitals 224%of what Medicare would have paid for the same services.[71] According to an analysis by the Congressional Budget Office (CBO),[72]

The main reason for the growth of per-person spending by commercial insurers—and for the difference from the growth of per-person spending by Medicare [fee-for-service (FFS)]—has been rapid increases in the prices that commercial insurers pay for hospitals' and physicians' services.

Moreover, providers' market power is a key reason for variation in the prices that commercial insurers pay for hospitals' and physicians' services across the United States.[73]

Consolidation corrodes the competitive market forces needed to align health care cost with value, resulting in higher costs for plans and patients alike. As the 2020 report "Affordable Hospital Care Through Competition and Price Transparency" highlighted:

> One of the greatest challenges to affordable health care is the high cost of American hospitals. The most important driver of higher prices for hospital care, in turn, is the rise of regional hospital monopolies. Hospitals are merging into large hospital systems, and using their market power to demand higher and higher prices from the privately insured and the uninsured.[74]

An estimated 117 million Americans under age 65 live in a concentrated hospital market whereas 160 million reside in a competitive hospital market.[75] According to the Kaiser Family Foundation, between 2010 and 2017, there were 778 hospital mergers.[76] As a result of such consolidation, many local areas are now dominated by one large, powerful health system. By 2017, two thirds (66%) of all hospitals were part of a larger system, as compared to 53% in 2005[77] and, in most markets, a single hospital system had more than a 50% market share of discharges.[78]

In concentrated markets, prices do not flow from competitive market negotiations, but from the outsized leverage that market concentration affords. Substantial evidence links hospital consolidation to higher prices. The Medicare Payment Advisory Commission (MedPAC)

---

70 Rand Corporation, Nationwide Evaluation of Health Care Prices Paid by Private Health Plans (2020).

71 Rand Corporation, Prices Paid to Hospitals by Private Health Plans: Findings from Round 4 of an Employer-Led Transparency Initiative (2022).

72 Congressional Budget Office, The Prices That Commercial Health Insurers and Medicare Pay for Hospitals' and Physicians' Services (January 20, 2022).

73 Congressional Budget Office (CBO), *Policy Approaches to Reduce What Commercial Insurers Pay for Hospitals' and Physicians' Services* (September 29, 2022).

74 The Foundation for Research on Equal Opportunity, Affordable Hospital Care Through Competition and Price Transparency (January 31, 2020).

75 Urban Institute, *Introducing a Public Option or Capped Provider Payment Rates into Concentrated Insurer and Hospital Markets* (March 2021).

76 Martin Gaynor. "Examining the Impact of Health Care Consolidation," Committee on Energy and Commerce Oversight and Investigations Subcommittee (2018).

77 Kaiser Family Foundation (KFF), *What We Know About Provider Consolidation* (September 2, 2020), citing American Hospital Association, *TrendWatch Chartbook* (2018).

78 Medicare Payment Advisory Commission (MedPAC), *Report to Congress: Medicare Payment Policy* (March 2020).

reviewed the published research on hospital consolidation and concluded that the "preponderance of evidence suggests that hospital consolidation leads to higher prices for commercially insured patients."[79] For example, one analysis looking at 25 metropolitan areas with the highest rates of hospital consolidation from 2010 through 2013 found that the price private insurance paid for the average hospital stay increased in most areas between 11% and 54% in the subsequent years.[80] Prices at monopoly hospitals are 12% higher than those in markets with four or more rivals.[81] Moreover, consolidation has not come with demonstrated improvement in the quality of care.[82] Substantial economic literature has demonstrated that provider consolidation leads (on average) to "less bang for the buck"— in other words, higher prices without higher quality or access.[83]

At the same time, many private hospital systems are becoming vertically integrated with physician organizations. Hospitals and corporate entities owned half of America's physician practices and employed nearly 70% of physicians by the end of 2020.[84] Such integration can direct patient referrals to higher-priced hospitals within the system and away from lower-priced community providers. Basic market dynamics are at play.

When monopolistic hospital systems buy competing hospitals and physician practices, the resulting dominance in the local market allows them to raise their prices because plans and patients now have nowhere else to go. Addressing hospital and provider consolidation, restoring competition and better aligning incentives with value are essential to lowering health care costs.

Ending Medicare payment policies that provide incentives for consolidation is a key action Congress can take to increase competition and, thereby, lower health care costs. One such incentive results from differences in Medicare payment rates for the same or similar services at different sites of outpatient care -hospital outpatient departments (HOPDs), ambulatory surgical centers (ASCs) and freestanding physician offices.

Medicare (and private health insurance) generally pay the highest rates for services provided in HOPDs and the lowest rates for services performed in freestanding physician offices. For services provided in freestanding clinician offices, Medicare makes a single payment to the practitioner under the physician fee schedule. For services provided in HOPDs or ASCs, Medicare makes two payments: one for the clinician's professional fee and one for the HOPD or ASC facility fee under the relevant payment system. For example, in 2022, *Medicare paid 141% more in an HOPD than in a freestanding office for the first hour of chemotherapy infusion* (counting both the professional fee and facility fee).

---

[79] *Id.* at pp. 468.

[80] KFF, citing Reed Abelson, "When Hospitals Merge to Save Money, Patients Often Pay More," New York Times (November 18, 2018).

[81] Zack Cooper, Stuart V Craig, Martin Gaynor and John Van Reenen, "The Price Ain't Right? Hospital Prices and Health Spending on the Privately Insured," *Quarterly Journal of Economics, vol. 134, no. 1* (February 2019), pp. 51–107.

[82] As noted in Rand Corporation, *Impact of Policy Options for Reducing Hospital Prices Paid by Private Health Plans* (2021), pp. 2, "A review of all hospital mergers between 2009 and 2013 found that hospital mergers do not lead to improvements in quality (Beaulieu et al., 2020). Likewise, research has found that vertical integration does not lead to increases in the quality of care (Short and Ho, 2019; Post, Buchmueller and Ryan, 2018; Machta et al., 2019). See also Kaiser Family Foundation, *What We Know About Provider Consolidation* (September 2, 2020).

[83] The Hamilton Project, *A Proposal to Cap Provider Prices and Price Growth in the Commercial Health-Care Market* (March 2020), pp 7.

[84] Physicians Advocacy Institute, COVID-19's Impact On Acquisitions of Physician Practices and Physician Employment 2019-2020 [Prepared by Avalere Health] (June 2021).

According to MedPAC, this payment disparity incentivizes consolidation of physician practices with hospitals—that result in care being provided in settings with the highest payment rates. *Often physician offices are being purchased by hospitals and simply rebranded as part of the hospital's outpatient department (HOPD) in order to collect the resulting higher payments.* This increases costs on the overall health care system without significant improvements in patient outcomes. [85]

An important way to decrease incentives for consolidation is for Congress to expand implementation of site-neutral payment reform which aligns payment rates for certain services across the three main sites where patients receive outpatient care. According to CBO, policies that reduce providers' incentive to consolidate would "deter some hospitals and physicians from merging with or acquiring rival firms, which would slow the consolidation of markets."[86]

The Council strongly supports legislation to provide for site neutral payments under the Medicare program for certain services furnished in ambulatory settings as MedPAC recommends. The Council also strongly supports legislation to eliminate the "grandfathering" exception from site-neutral payments for HOPDs billing Medicare before 2015 and for cancer hospitals and notes that the legislation would maintain the exception for dedicated emergency departments. The Council also strongly supports legislation creating parity in Medicare payments for hospital outpatient department services furnished off-campus by requiring that drug administration out-patient department services furnished off-campus will be subject to the ASC rate rather than the HOPD rate. By aligning payment differentials across sites of service, such legislation removes a powerful incentive for hospitals to purchase physicians' practices in order to receive the higher reimbursement rates of HOPDs. In so doing, such legislation will help stem the tide of hospital-physician consolidation and correct a significant distortion driving patients to higher cost care settings.

The potential savings that would be generated to the government, to employers and patients is significant. For example, MedPAC's recommendations to align payment rates across the different ambulatory settings for a greater number of services would have resulted in an estimated $6.6 billion savings to Medicare in 2019 as well as a $1.7 billion reduction in beneficiary cost-sharing. Effects for the commercial market are likely even greater. New research by University of Minnesota economist Steve Parente estimates that expanding site-neutral payment reform could result in nearly $60 billion in savings annually if adopted in the commercial market.[87] Another report estimated the "spillover" effect on the commercial market of MedPAC's recommendations to expand Medicare's site-neutral policies. Site-neutral payments were estimated to yield a reduction in costs and premiums for private insurance plans of $117 billion over 10 years – which amounts to a cut in costs and premiums of about three-quarters of 1%, relative to this paper's projections under current law.[88]

We anticipate that the savings generated from site-neutral polices may be characterized by hospitals as detrimentally impacting their bottom line in a time of ongoing economic pressure. Though these policies may well impact the profit margins of hospitals, it is important to bear in

[85] Medicare Payment Advisory Commission (MedPAC), Report to Congress: Medicare Payment Policy (June 2021).

[86] CBO at pp 16.

[87] Alliance to Fight for Health Care briefing presentation, *The Untapped Potential of Site-Neutral Payment Reform* (February 1, 2023), pp 27.

[88] Blue Cross Blue Shield Association, "Savings estimates for options to reduce spending on health care and private insurance premiums" (January 24, 2023).

mind the misaligned practices that are generating those profits as well and the true source of losses hospitals may be experiencing.

Employers recognize that hospitals are an essential component of the nation's health system, providing care to communities across the country, particularly during the pandemic. Employers have a vested interest in ensuring that employees and families have access to the care they need. Employers also have a vested interest in ensuring that the care their employees receive is affordable and high quality. But the he reality of the hospital financial picture is that in 2021, hospitals' all-payer operating margin reached a record high of 8.7% with federal relief funds and to 7.2%without federal relief funds, both of which were higher than the prior all-time high in 2019.[89]

A recent *Health Affairs* article examined the financial performance of large nonprofit hospitals systems in the post-COVID-19 era.[90] Average overall profit margin fell from 9% in 2021 to -6% in 2022. However, a closer look at financial measures for 10 selected large nonprofit hospital systems revealed a more complex picture. Patient care revenue, revenue obtained from providing hospital services, slightly increased, by just below 1% in relative terms from 2021 to 2022. However, investment income, revenue from financial investments, declined by 185% between 2021 and 2022. Investment losses accounted for approximately 85% of overall financial losses. While other sources may attribute hospital financial losses to increased labor costs, particularly for nurses and health professionals, and increased supply costs, this analysis suggests that investment losses are actually the primary driver of these nonprofit health systems' overall losses. If hospitals now find themselves facing certain investment losses as a result of their risky or aggressive financial investment strategies, employers, patients and taxpayers should not have to foot the bill for hospitals' risky financial positions.

Restrict Hospital Billing Practices that Fuel Consolidation and Mask What Should Be the Appropriate Payment Amounts

The Council strongly supports:

- H.R. , To amend titles XI and XVIII of the Social Security Act to require each outpatient department of a provider to include a unique identification number on claims for services, and to require hospitals with an outpatient department of a provider to submit to the Centers for Medicare & Medicaid Services an attestation with respect to each outpatient department.

A long-standing patient returns to her physician's office for a check-up. She receives the same service from the same doctor, but she gets a very different and more costly bill this time. The only thing that has changed from her prior visit is that her doctor's practice was acquired by a hospital. The appointment was billed as being performed in a hospital-based setting with a hefty facility fee attached rather than in an office-based practice.

---

[89] Medicare Payment Advisory Commission (MedPAC), *Report to Congress: Medicare Payment Policy* (March 2023).

[90] Christopher M. Whaley, Sebahattin Demirkan and Ge Bai, "What's Behind Losses At Large Nonprofit Health Systems?" *Health Affairs Forefront* (March 24, 2023).

After hospitals acquire physician practices, the prices for the services provided by acquired physicians increase by an average of 14.1%.[91] A contributing factor to this increase is the use by hospitals of billing practices that portray services delivered at these sites as 'hospital services' as opposed to 'professional services' in order to receive the higher facility reimbursement fee. Hospitals have leveraged the acquisition of physician practices to unfairly bill payers – including employer-sponsored group health plans – higher rates by portraying non-hospital-based professional services as if they were delivered in a hospital. This unfair and opaque billing practice serves to incentivize vertical hospital-physician consolidation and increase costs for employers and patients.

Hospitals are able to use this billing practice because they are not required to specify where services are provided when they bill to Medicare or other health care payers. The Council strongly supports legislation requiring each outpatient department of a provider to include a unique identification number on claims for services. This important legislation will promote "honest billing" practices by helping payors to distinguish between sites of service in order to apply the appropriate payment amount.

Support Greater Price Transparency in the Health Care System

The Council strongly supports:

- H.R. 2691, the Transparent PRICE Act

Competition and transparency in the health care market are inextricably linked.

Indeed, a competitive health care market is predicated on transparency. Conversely, the ability of hospitals to cloak the underlying price of health care services works hand-in- hand with consolidation to give hospitals free rein to increase prices. Transparency is not an end in itself. It is, however, a means to fuel competition, check price increases, and make health care more value-driven.

Many employers that have had success decreasing the rate of health care spending have done so by analyzing their plan data to better understand how much is being spent on specific services and then using plan design features to promote higher-value, relatively lower-cost providers. Harnessing the promise of technology, effective transparency tools in the hands of employers and consumers can be transformative, making health care both simpler and more affordable.

Despite important legislative and regulatory action to advance health care transparency, impediments remain to meaningful access and utilization of health pricing data. Removing barriers to accessing and using price information is foundational to unleashing the power of transparency to help employers drive lower cost and higher value health care.

Codifying and strengthening the U.S. Department of Health and Human Services (HHS) regulations requiring hospitals to make public standard charges, including negotiated rates, is critical to these efforts. We have urged HHS to undertake vigorous enforcement and to further

[91] Cory Capps, David Dranove and Christopher Ody, "The effect of hospital acquisitions of physician practices on prices and spending," *Journal of Health Economics* (May 2018).

increase the penalties for noncompliance. However, the fact remains that far too many hospitals across the country remain out of compliance - or meaningful compliance - with the rule.[92]

A report by Families USA noted recent estimates suggesting up to 45% of hospitals are not in full compliance with the rule, while other studies estimate that as few as one in five hospitals are in full compliance with the rule.[93] The Families USA report concluded that: "Hospitals are deploying various tactics to either buck the requirements outright or make the information they disclose very hard to understand." While many hospitals have posted no information on negotiated rates at all, the report notes that other hospitals post incomplete required information. The report includes one example of a hospital data file that discloses prices in multiple different formats in one file, making it nearly impossible to interpret. This report cites another example of a hospital data file that fails to display the required pricing information in a usable way, failing to break down the negotiated rates by payer and plan as required. These depictions of the myriad tactics hospitals are using to thwart the letter if not the spirit of the rule means that more is needed to ensure meaning compliance. It is time for Congress to step in to codify and strengthen the hospital transparency rule. Accordingly, we applaud the bipartisan Transparent PRICE Act for increasing the maximum penalty, directing HHS to implement a uniform method and format for hospitals to post data and regularly monitor and publicly report on hospital compliance.

Our plan sponsor members are doing their part to support increased transparency.

They recognize that access to pricing data is critical to unleashing the power of employers to drive lower cost and higher value health care. As such, we support the regulations implementing the transparency in coverage provisions under Section 2715A of the Public Health Service Act, and employers have made great efforts to comply with the full range of requirements. We want to ensure the optimal utility of these requirements to support those employer efforts and that this important transparency tool will not be rolled back by future administrations, while minimizing disruption to plan sponsors.

We appreciate that the legislation provides that the machine-readable file submission requirements shall ensure that such files are limited to an appropriate size and are made available in a widely available format that allows for information contained in such files to be compared across health plans. We hope that will allow employers meaningful and actionable access to the data that can be used to truly analyze how their health care dollars are spent, and take action to direct those resources to high-quality, cost-effective providers.

The Council recognizes that price is just one piece of the puzzle and that, in terms of value, the price of the health care service does not always correlate with the quality of care. Transparency with respect to both price and quality are the foundation for employer's innovative payment reforms. Price transparency will be most effective when coupled with quality, and we urge Congress to support quality transparency and meaningful, harmonized metrics. Yet, price transparency initiatives should proceed apace even if quality transparency will take additional time to realize.

---

92 Families USA, The Power of Price Transparency: Unveiling Health Care Prices to Promote Accountability and Lower Costs (April 19, 2023)

93 Id.

Require Greater Transparency and Oversight of PBMs:

The Council strongly supports:

- H.R. 2769, the PBM Accountability Act

The Council strongly supports legislation to require greater transparency and accountability with respect to PBMs. Employers appreciate that pharmaceutical drug therapies have played a significant role in treating and curing injury, illness and disease. They allow millions of Americans to overcome debilitating conditions, return to work and live longer, healthier, more productive lives. Moreover, money spent wisely on drugs can reduce hospital, physician and other medical expenditures.

Nonetheless, prescription drug costs continue to represent a considerable portion of overall plan costs. In an effort to manage drug costs, employers have implemented innovative strategies while ensuring that employees and families have access to needed drugs and services. Many of these strategies have been developed by, or in concert with, PBMs. However, employers remain deeply concerned about prescription drug costs, particularly the cost of specialty drugs, and the absence of appropriate price – and cost – transparency across the entire drug pricing system.

The current rebate structure is complex and opaque for many employers, making it hard for them and plan participants and beneficiaries to understand the true prices and value of drugs. One of our main goals has been to support initiatives that increase transparency throughout the pharmaceutical distribution system. This includes increased transparency with respect to rebates paid by manufacturers to PBMs.

Increased transparency and accountability could help employers and employees make better informed purchasing decisions and lead to higher value pharmacy expenditures.

Employers continue to encounter barriers to PBM pricing transparency. Federal legislation requiring strong transparency and accountability by PBMs to employers – their primary clients - is essential to employer efforts to manage prescription drug costs. Employers cannot effectively manage prescription drug costs unless they can see the full picture of rebates, fees and other renumeration generated from manufacturers and other parties, drug definition criteria, and amounts charged to pharmacies. This important legislation ensuring greater transparency and accountability for PBMs is critical to employer efforts to make prescription drugs more affordable for employees and their families.

* * * * *

Something must be done to change the trajectory of rising health care costs.

While employers continue innovating and experimenting with solutions to lower costs, federal legislative solutions are needed to create a more competitive and transparent health care marketplace. By addressing the root causes of rising health care costs, legislation that increases transparency and competition empowers employers to lower the cost and improve the quality of health care for employees and their families.

While I focused on several bills in my testimony, other legislation the subcommittee is reviewing today are also positive and important steps toward lowering health care costs by increasing transparency and competition. Individually, these bills represent an important piece in solving the health care cost puzzle. Taken together, they can help transform the health care marketplace, lowering the cost and improving the value of health care for working families in communities throughout the country.

I appreciate the opportunity to testify and the Council looks forward to working with this subcommittee, and all the members of the Energy and Commerce Committee, to advance these proposals.

Mr. GUTHRIE. Thank you. I thank you for your testimony.

The Chair now recognizes Mr. Adler for 5 minutes for your opening statement.

Statement of Loren Adler

Mr. ADLER. Thank you, Chairman Guthrie and Ranking Member Eshoo and members of the subcommittee. Thank you for the opportunity to testify today on the crucial topic of increasing transparency and competition in healthcare.

My name is Loren Adler. I am a fellow and associate director at the USC-Brookings Schaeffer Initiative for Health Policy at the Brookings Institution here in DC. I study a wide range of topics, including healthcare market competition, provider payments, and prescription drug policy. And relevant to today's hearing, much of my current research is focused on private equity and health plan acquisitions of physician practices.

The healthcare industry has experienced significant consolidation over the last decades. Horizontal consolidation, such as the merging of hospitals or physician groups within the same geographic market, unambiguously leads to higher prices for consumers, lower wages for workers, and seemingly actually diminished quality of care. With a greater market power as an employer locally, there is also evidence that hospital mergers reduce the wages paid to nurses and other hospital staff with industry-specific skills.

And vertical consolidation involving hospitals and physician groups has also accelerated. Today about two in five doctors now work for a hospital or a practice that is at least partially owned by a hospital. And more and more evidence suggests that this vertical consolidation appears to drive up costs for consumers with unclear impacts on the quality of care.

And now we are seeing growing vertical consolidation between health plans and physician groups, PBMs, and specialty pharmacies. And we have strong evidence that insurer-provider integration is being leveraged to accelerate coding of their Medicare Advantage enrollees to generate higher government payments than were intended, costing taxpayers billions.

Fundamentally, I want to leave members of the subcommittee with one key message: We need to stop digging the hole deeper. Even with overwhelming evidence of the harms caused by provider consolidation, too little is done to just stop digging the hole deeper. We need to cut it out with policies that encourage consolidation, and we need better data to get a full picture of what is going on to better limit anticompetitive conduct.

There are a wide array of policy options that could enhance competition in healthcare markets, you know, from greater antitrust oversight to Medicare Advantage reform to changes in Medicare payment policies. Today I will try to narrow my focus on two main points relevant to proposals that are under consideration by this subcommittee today.

One, Medicare rates are intended to reflect the costs of providing services for an efficient provider. As such, Medicare should not be paying more for the same exact service when it is delivered in a hospital outpatient department rather than a physician's office, provided that the physician's office setting is safe and clinically effective for most patients. This policy change has widespread bipartisan support in the policy community, across—basically, any think tank you talk to supports this policy. Lobbyists are pretty much the only opposition, really, to this policy.

Number two, increased transparency can both facilitate stronger research and oversight and, in certain circumstances, drive price competition by helping patients select lower-cost, higher-quality providers.

With respect to site-neutral payments, to illustrate this issue I want to consider the example of a Medicare patient receiving a level two nerve injection, as I think one of the congressmen brought up earlier, because it is the example in a MedPAC report, so—right?

Let's take this. If the patient receives this injection at a physician's office, she would owe $51 in coinsurance on a $256 total cost. Now, let's say that a hospital buys that physician's practice and converts it into a hospital outpatient department. The care remains the same. It is the same doctor providing the care, but now that same patient receiving the same service will owe nearly three times as much. They would owe $148 in coinsurance on a total payment of $741. This payment disparity not only increases costs for beneficiaries and taxpayers but encourages hospitals to buy up physician practices, leading to market consolidation and increased healthcare costs that spill over to the commercial market as well. Small efforts have been made to move toward site-neutral payments, but more work is needed. Legislative proposals under consideration today to eliminate this payment disparity for low-complexity services would result in substantial savings for beneficiaries and taxpayers while fostering greater competition in physician markets.

And it is important to note here today that we are focused on lower-complexity services where we are saying to equalize payments. We are primarily here talking about office visits, imaging, and drug administration.

And lastly, for transparency, that is also crucial. Specifically with systematic data about provider ownership arrangements and commercial market prices and volumes, researchers could better identify the effects of various forms of healthcare consolidation and elucidate solutions. The opacity of payment flows between specific actors in the drug supply chain similarly inhibits quality research, and evidence suggests that patients can make use of transparent pricing information for more shoppable services.

The committee's focus on bipartisan policies to improve healthcare, competition, and transparency is a welcome sight. And thank you again for the opportunity to testify today.

[The prepared statement of Mr. Adler follows:]

Testimony of Loren Adler, MS
Associate Director and Fellow, USC-Brookings Schaeffer Initiative for Health Policy Economic Studies, Brookings Institution

Before the United States House of Representatives Committee on Energy and Commerce Subcommittee on Health

Lowering Unaffordable Costs: Legislative Solutions to Increase Transparency and Competition in Health Care
April 26, 2023

Chairman Guthrie, Ranking Member Eshoo, members of the Subcommittee, thank you for the opportunity to testify today on this crucial topic. My name is Loren Adler and I am a Fellow and Associate Director of the USC-Brookings Schaeffer Initiative for Health Policy. My research focuses on health care market competition, provider payments, and prescription drug policy. Prior to joining Brookings, I worked for the Committee for a Responsible Federal Budget and the Bipartisan Policy Center.

Relevant to today's hearing, much of my current research aims to decipher the effects of private equity, payer, and hospital acquisitions of physician practices, as well as develop policy responses.

I have previously written on a broad array of policy options to reduce costs by increasing transparency and competition in health care – most recently in a policy brief with Benedic Ippolito at the American Enterprise Institute.[94] This testimony focuses more narrowly on two main points:

1) Medicare rates are intended to reflect the costs of providing services for an efficient provider. As such, Medicare should not pay more for the same service performed in a hospital outpatient department versus a physician's office, provided that the physician's office setting is safe and clinically effective for most patients. Implementing this policy change would result in substantial savings for beneficiaries and taxpayers, while fostering greater competition in physician markets by reducing incentives for hospitals to acquire physician practices.
2) Increased transparency can both facilitate stronger research and oversight and, in certain circumstances, steer patient volume to lower-cost providers. Specifically, with systematic data about provider ownership arrangements and commercial market prices and volumes, researchers could better identify the effects of various forms of health care consolidation and elucidate solutions. The opacity of payment flows between specific actors in the drug supply chain similarly inhibits research. And evidence suggests that patients can make use of transparent pricing information for more "shoppable" services.

---

[94] Adler, Loren and Benedic Ippolito. "Procompetitive Health Care Reform Options for a Divided Congress." Brookings Institution, March 2023, https://www.brookings.edu/blog/health360/2023/04/25/procompetitive-health-care-reform-options-for-a-divided-congress/.

Background

In 2021, the U.S. devoted 18.3% of its economy to pay for health care, a higher share than any other country.[95] These high costs stem not only by a higher willingness to pay for care, but also insufficient competition in many markets and other market inefficiencies. Elevated health care costs have far- reaching consequences, straining government budgets, hindering wage growth, and affecting individual finances.[96]

The health care industry has experienced significant increases in consolidation, both horizontal and vertical. Horizontal consolidation, such as the merging of hospitals or physician groups within the same geographic market, leads to higher prices for consumers and potentially diminished quality of care.[97] These increased costs, in turn, appear to commensurately reduce employee wages.[98] With greater market power as an employer locally, there is also evidence that hospital mergers reduce the wages paid to hospital staff with industry-specific skills such as nurses.[99]

Private equity firms have also driven substantial horizontal consolidation in many physician specialty markets (Exhibit 1), often focused in specialties that have seen fewer hospital acquisitions. As expected, empirical evidence suggests that these acquisitions have substantially increased health care costs.[100]

"Vertical" consolidation involving hospitals and physician groups (Exhibit 2) also appears to drive up costs, but the impact on the quality of care remains unclear.[101,102] These effects likely operate through multiple channels. Hospital-physician integration directly increases Medicare spending because the program pays substantially more money for the same service

---

95 Centers for Medicare & Medicaid Services. "National Health Expenditures - Historical and Projected Data." CMS.gov. Accessed April 24, 2023. https://www.cms.gov/Research-Statistics-Data-and-Systems/Statistics-Trends- and-Reports/NationalHealthExpendData/NationalHealthAccountsHistorical.

96 Arnold, Daniel and Christopher M. Whaley. "Who Pays for Health Care Costs? The Effects of Health Care Prices on Wages." Santa Monica, CA: RAND Corporation, 2020. https://doi.org/10.7249/WRA621-2.

97 Cooper, Zack et al. "The Price Ain't Right? Hospital Prices and Health Spending on the Privately Insured." The Quarterly Journal of Economics 134, no. 1 (February 1, 2019): 51–107. https://doi.org/10.1093/qje/qjy020; Beaulieu, Nancy D. et al. "Changes in Quality of Care after Hospital Mergers and Acquisitions." New England Journal of Medicine 382, no. 1 (January 2, 2020): 51–59. https://doi.org/10.1056/NEJMsa1901383; Koch, Thomas, Brett Wendling, and Nathan E. Wilson. "Physician Market Structure, Patient Outcomes, and Spending: An Examination of Medicare Beneficiaries." Health Services Research 53, no. 5 (October 2018): 3549–68. https://doi.org/10.1111/1475-6773.12825.

98 Arnold and Whaley, 2020.

99 Prager, Elena, and Matt Schmitt. 2021. "Employer Consolidation and Wages: Evidence from Hospitals." *American Economic Review,* 111 (2): 397-427. DOI: 10.1257/aer.20190690.

100 See, e.g., Singh, Yashaswini, Zirui Song, Daniel Polsky, Joseph D. Bruch, and Jane M. Zhu. "Association of Private Equity Acquisition of Physician Practices With Changes in Health Care Spending and Utilization." *JAMA Health Forum* 3, no. 9 (2022): e222886. https://doi.org/10.1001/jamahealthforum.2022.2886; La Forgia, Ambar, Amelia M. Bond, Robert Tyler Braun, Leah Z. Yao, Klaus Kjaer, Manyao Zhang, and Lawrence P. Casalino. "Association of Physician Management Companies and Private Equity Investment With Commercial Health Care Prices Paid to Anesthesia Practitioners." *JAMA Internal Medicine* 182, no. 4 (2022): 396-404. https://doi.org/10.1001/jamainternmed.2022.0004.

101 See, e.g., Post, Brady, Tom Buchmueller, and Andrew M. Ryan. "Vertical Integration of Hospitals and Physicians: Economic Theory and Empirical Evidence on Spending and Quality." *Medical Care Research and Review* 75, no. 4 (August 2018): 399–433. https://doi.org/10.1177/1077558717727834. Capps, Cory, David Dranove, and Christopher Ody. "The Effect of Hospital Acquisitions of Physician Practices on Prices and Spending." *Journal of Health Economics* 59 (2018): 139-152. https://doi.org/10.1016/j.jhealeco.2018.04.001.

102 Koch, Thomas G., Brett W. Wendling, and Nathan E. Wilson. "The Effects of Physician and Hospital Integration on Medicare Beneficiaries' Health Outcomes." *The Review of Economics and Statistics*, August 16, 2021, 1–15. https://doi.org/10.1162/rest_a_00924.

when performed in a hospital outpatient department rather than an independent physician's office. Bringing together multiple physician practices in the same specialty under a hospital can effectively increase horizontal consolidation, increasing the joint entity's bargaining power. There is also strong evidence that hospital-owned physician practices are more likely to refer patients to their own hospitals and away from lower intensity sites of care, effectively strengthening the hospital's bargaining power vis a vis insurers.[103],[104]

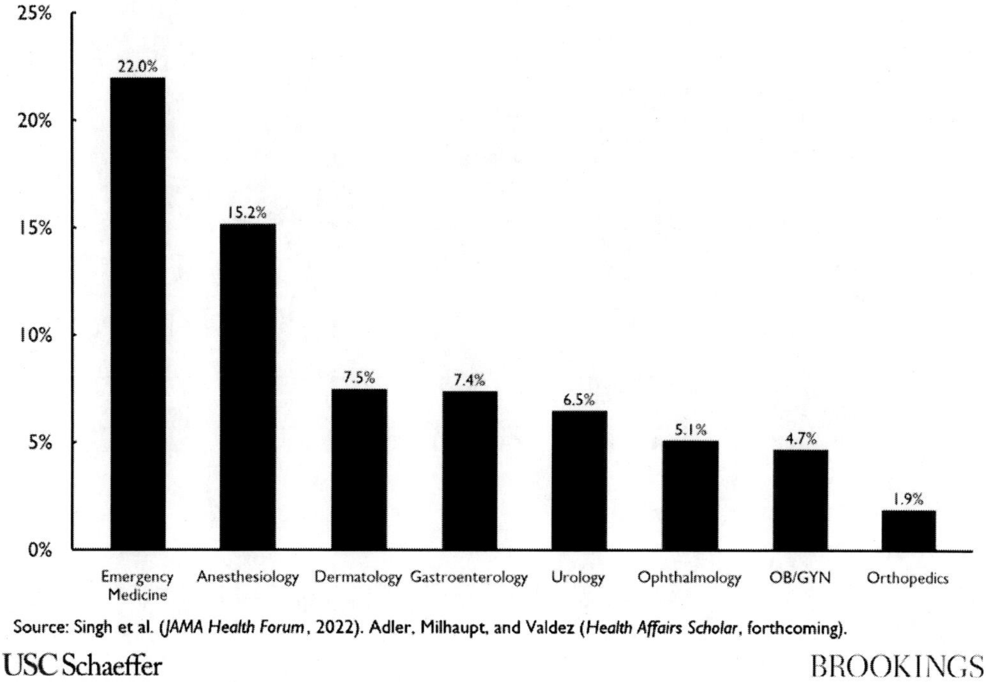

Exhibit 1. Ntional private equity penetration in 2019, by specialty.

Despite evidence pointing to potential antitrust concerns, glaringly so in the case of horizontal consolidation, many acquisitions proceed unchallenged due to factors including insufficient pre-merger notification requirements, data limitations, and resource constraints faced by federal antitrust agencies.

Site-Neutral Payments

Many health care services can be delivered either through a physician's office, an ambulatory surgery center (ASC), or a hospital outpatient department (HOPD). For some services, such as

---

[103] See, e.g., Baker, Laurence C., M. Kate Bundorf, and Daniel P. Kessler. "The Effect of Hospital/Physician Integration on Hospital Choice." *Journal of Health Economics* 50 (December 2016): 1-8. https://doi.org/10.1016/j.jhealeco.2016.08.006; Whaley, Christopher M., Xiaoxi Zhao, Michael Richards, and Cheryl L. Damberg. "Higher Medicare Spending On Imaging And Lab Services After Primary Care Physician Group Vertical Integration." *Health Affairs* 40, no. 5 (May 2021): 811-818. https://doi.org/10.1377/ hlthaff.2020.01006.

[104] Richards MR, Seward JA, Whaley CM. Treatment consolidation after vertical integration: Evidence from outpatient procedure markets. J Health Econ. 2022 Jan; 81:102569. doi: https://10.1016/j.jhealeco.2021.102569.

medical emergencies or complex surgeries, there may be safety and quality benefits to receiving care at a HOPD, where there exists emergency standby capacity and other specialists in the case of complications. But for lower-complexity services such as office visits, imaging, and drug administration, it is typically safe and clinically effective to receive care at a physician's office.[105]

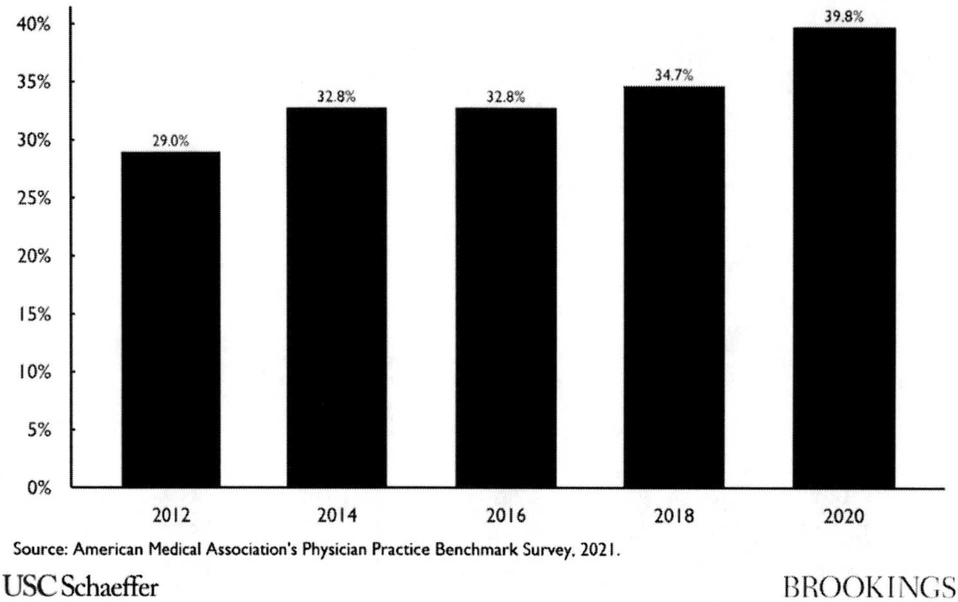

Exhibit 2. Percentage of physicians working directly for a hospital or apractice at least partially owned by a hospital or health system, 2012-2020.

Yet Medicare pays substantially more – typically between two and three times more – even for low complexity services when delivered in a HOPD rather than a physician's office. Similarly, Medicare pays more for the same service in a HOPD compared to an ASC, and (to a lesser extent) in an ASC versus a physician's office. For instance, in their June 2022 report, the Medicare Payment Advisory Commission (MedPAC) notes that "Medicare pays 141 percent more in an HOPD than in a freestanding office for the first hour of chemotherapy infusion … [and] 105 percent more in on-campus HOPDs than in freestanding offices for a midlevel office visit."[106]

When Medicare pays more, Medicare beneficiaries also pay more, both because they are generally responsible for coinsurance equal to 20% of the Medicare rate and because Medicare Part B premiums and deductibles are tied to a percentage of program costs.[107]

Using the example presented by MedPAC in their March 2023 meeting, a Medicare patient receiving a Level 2 nerve injection at a physician's office in 2023 would owe $51 in coinsurance

---

[105] Medicare Payment Advisory Commission. *June 2022 Report to the Congress: Medicare and the Health Care Delivery System*. Washington, DC: MedPAC, 2022. https://www.medpac.gov/document/june-2022-report-to-the-congress-medicare-and-the-health-care-delivery-system/.

[106] Ibid.

[107] For beneficiaries with supplemental coverage who are shielded at least in part from the higher coinsurance, those additional costs translate to higher Medigap premiums, costs to their employer, or higher state Medicaid program costs.

on the total Medicare rate of $256. If that same patient instead received the same service at a HOPD, they would owe nearly three times as much – $148 in coinsurance on a total Medicare payment of $741.[108]

This market distortion created by Medicare policy also incentivizes hospital acquisitions of physician practices. This financial incentive can be quite large. For an independent physician in 2016, integrating with a hospital would have increased total annual Medicare payments for their services by $141,000, on average (or nearly $180,000 in today's dollars).[109] While not the only factor driving vertical consolidation between hospitals and physicians, evidence suggests that Medicare's policy of paying more for the same service when performed in a HOPD has played a substantial role.[110]

As discussed earlier, this vertical consolidation then also has the knock-on effect of increasing health care costs for employers and individuals in the commercial market.

Medicare has taken small steps toward site-neutral payments, first with the Bipartisan Budget Act of 2015 (BBA). That law reduced Medicare payments to off-campus HOPDs to align with physician fee schedule rates, but excepted (or grandfathered) any off-campus HOPD established before November 2, 2015 (the exception was subsequently expanded to protect any off-campus HOPD under construction by that time). The Trump Administration, through rulemaking, then expanded site-neutral payments to office visits at grandfathered off-campus HOPDs.[111]

The justification for paying more for the same service delivered at an off-campus HOPD is particularly weak. Often a hospital would acquire a physician practice and rebrand it as a HOPD with little to no noticeable difference to patients. For example, Dranove an Ody (2019) note how an acquired physician group assured its patients that "our diagnostic testing services will still be provided at the same office locations but will be billed as outpatient hospital procedures. Our staff members caring for you in these areas and the services rendered will remain the same."

But less than 1% of hospital outpatient spending occurs at HOPDs subject to the BBA 2015 changes, and "only one-third of the office visits provided in HOPDs occur in off-campus [HOPDs]."[112] There are also relatively few limits on expanding grandfathered off-campus HOPDs.

Therefore, while modest improvements have been made, Medicare payment policy continues to encourage vertical consolidation by offering higher payments for the same service when performed at grandfathered off-campus HOPDs (other than office visits), on-campus HOPDs, ASCs, freestanding emergency departments, and cancer hospitals, compared to at a physician's office.

---

[108] Zabinski, Dan. "Aligning fee-for-service payment rates across ambulatory settings." MedPAC, Mar. 2023, https://www.medpac.gov/wp-content/uploads/2022/07/Site-neutral-March-2023-SEC.pdf.

[109] Post, Brady, Edward C. Norton, Brent Hollenbeck, Thomas Buchmueller, and Andrew M. Ryan. "Hospital-Physician Integration and Medicare's Site-Based Outpatient Payments." *Health Services Research* (2019). https://doi.org/10.1111/1475-6773.13613.

[110] Dranove, David, and Christopher Ody. "Employed for Higher Pay? How Medicare Payment Rules Affect Hospital Employment of Physicians." *American Economic Journal: Economic Policy* 11, no. 4 (2019): 249-271. https://doi.org/10.1257/pol.20170020.

[111] Adler, Loren, Andrés de Loera-Brust, Matthew Fiedler, Paul B. Ginsburg, and Will Palmisano. "CMS' Positive Step on Site-Neutral Payments and the Case for Going Further." *Brookings Institution*, August 10, 2018. https://www.brookings.edu/blog/usc-brookings-schaeffer-on-health-policy/2018/08/10/cms-positive-step-on-site-neutral-payments-and-the-case-for-going-further/.

[112] MedPAC June 2022.

MedPAC has recommended and this Subcommittee is considering legislation that would end the exception for off-campus HOPDs established before 2015 for all services and align payments between on-campus HOPDs and independent physician offices for a set of low complexity services. These proposals would also align payments between ASCs and HOPDs for certain services that can be safely delivered in an ASC.[113] Office visits, imaging, and drug administration comprise two-thirds of the services, by program spending, that MedPAC identifies where it is safe and clinically effective to deliver care at a physician's office (Exhibit 3).

APC description	Program spending (in millions)	Beneficiary cost sharing (in millions)	Volume (in thousands)
Clinic visits	$ 3,029	$ 757	32,685
Imaging w/o contrast	$ 2,587	$ 647	22,694
Drug administration	$ 2,086	$ 521	24,094
Level 3 nuclear medicine	$ 685	$ 171	696
Skin procedures	$ 673	$ 168	2,418
Nerve injections	$ 663	$ 165	1,888
Diagnostic tests & related services	$ 583	$ 145	1,927
Urology and related services	$ 376	$ 94	518
Other	$ 946	$ 252	11,510
Total	**$ 11,628**	**$ 2,920**	**98,430**

Notes: OPPS stands for Outpatient Prospective Payment System. PFS stands for Physician Fee Schedule. Data is drawn from the MedPAC June 2022 report, Table 6-2, with Ambulatory Payment Classifications (APCs) categorized by the author.

Exhibit 3. Medicare spending, cost-sharing, and volume for services that MedPAC recommends alignment of OPPS and PFS payment rates, 2019.

Taken together, the Congressional Budget Office (CBO) estimated that a similar combination of policies proposed by the Trump Administration would reduce Medicare spending by $140 billion over 10 years.[114] And MedPAC estimated that their June 2022 proposal would have reduced aggregate beneficiary cost- sharing by $1.7 billion in just the year 2019 had it been in place.[115]

Some hospital groups have argued that their payment rates should be higher for the same service because they treat sicker patients. While it is true that HOPD patients tend to have higher risk scores than those treated in physician offices, on average, the policy changes under consideration are focused on low complexity services where the cost of providing care does not

---

[113] Ibid.

[114] Congressional Budget Office. "Proposals Affecting Medicare—CBO's Estimate of the President's Fiscal Year 2021 Budget." March 2020. Accessed April 27, 2023. https://www.cbo.gov/system/files?file=2020-03/56245-2020-03- medicare.pdf.

[115] MedPAC June2022.

appear to differ by patient health status. Hospital outpatient departments can also still bill for additional services for patients requiring more intensive care.[116]

Moving toward site-neutral payments for services that can be safely delivered in a physician's office offers an opportunity to substantially reduce costs for taxpayers and beneficiaries while removing one of the most glaring incentives for consolidation. Similar policies have been proposed in both Obama and Trump budgets,[117] and generate widespread bipartisan support from think tanks and other policy experts.[118]

Transparency

Many of the proposals under consideration by the Subcommittee today would enhance transparency for researchers, patients, and employers.

The data necessary to best understand health care market dynamics and how new policies will affect the system are often difficult or impossible to access, in many cases controlled by private actors who benefit from opacity. Tracking and analyzing growing trends such as private equity and payer acquisitions of physician practices are hampered by a lack of systematic data on the parent companies and ownership structures of physician group owners.

Two transparency proposals, in particular, would provide better tools for research and oversight:

1) Requiring entity-level reporting on the parent company name, address, and ownership structure (e.g., private equity, health plan, hospital) of physician practices and making this data publicly-available. At present, my attempts (and those of collaborators) to compile this sort of information requires a painstaking amount of manual effort on top of purchasing access to privately-held data resources, and is inevitably subject to some level of imprecision given the manual steps involved. Instead, if such information was reported to the government, the Centers for Medicare and Medicaid Studies could make available a longitudinal dataset that identifies the parent company and ownership structure of physician groups matched to identifiers for each clinician who treats Medicare patients.
2) Codifying and standardizing reporting by insurers under the Transparency in Coverage rules. The Transparency in Coverage rules require that health insurance plans and issuers make public a treasure trove of data on contracted prices for health care services and amounts paid for out- of-network services. These data offer an opportunity to get

[116] Zabinski, MedPAC, 2023.

[117] The White House. "Budget of the U.S. Government: Fiscal Year 2016." February 2, 2015. Accessed April 25, 2023. https://www.govinfo.gov/content/pkg/BUDGET-2016-BUD/pdf/BUDGET-2016-BUD.pdf; The White House. "Budget of the U.S. Government: Fiscal Year 2021." February 10, 2020. Accessed April 25, 2023. https://www.govinfo.gov/content/pkg/BUDGET-2021-BUD/pdf/BUDGET-2021-BUD.pdf.

[118] See, e.g., Americans for Prosperity. "Bipartisan Support for Site-Neutral Payment Reform." Sign-on letter to Congress. April 2023. Accessed April 28, 2023. https://americansforprosperity.org/wp- content/uploads/2023/04/Bipartisan-Support-For-Site-Neutral-Payment-Reform.pdf; Van de Water, Paul N. "Strengthening Medicare Financing." *Center on Budget and Policy Priorities*, December 14, 2020. https://www.cbpp.org/research/health/strengthening-medicare-financing; Blase, Brian and Joe Albanese. "Turning the Tide on Red Ink: Commonsense Policies to Make Federal Health Programs More Sustainable." Paragon Institute, March 2023. https://paragoninstitute.org/wp-content/uploads/2023/03/Turning-the-Tide-on-Red-Ink_Brian-Blase_Joe-Alabanese_FINAL_202303072031.pdf.

a more complete picture of our health care system and examine heterogenous effects across payers. The size and varied reporting structures, however, limit the data's usability. The proposal under discussion by this Subcommittee would helpfully require some standardization in the way the data is reported. The most valuable addition for researchers would be to also require reporting on the volume of each service paid for by the health plan.

For consumers, evidence suggests that meaningful price transparency can place modest downward pressure on health care prices, at least for "shoppable" services such as imaging.[119] The proposed codification and standardization of both the hospital and insurer transparency rules, including the requirement for patient-facing tools that provide real-time information, likely offer the greatest benefits in this respect.

Lastly, there is likely value to increasing transparency into the role of pharmacy benefit managers (PBMs) and payment flows between specific actors throughout the pharmaceutical supply chain. CBO, for instance, estimates that transparency about PBM rebates and other fees can help some plan sponsors negotiate better deals, although such savings are expected to dissipate over time as private actors modify the structure of their contracts.[120] Transparency of drug rebates, payment flows in the drug supply chain, and ownership arrangements can also help foster research to better understand prescription drug markets. For instance, such transparency could make it easier to identify whether vertically-integrated PBMs or pharmacies give worse deals to competing insurers.

Conclusion

The Committee's focus on bipartisan policies to improve health care competition and transparency is a welcome sight. Thank you again for the opportunity to testify.

Mr. GUTHRIE. Thank you. We thank you for your testimony, all the witnesses' testimony. We will now move into Members' questions, and I will recognize myself for 5 minutes for questions.

So, Ms. Bass, we were talking earlier that we had some of the same professors. You probably studied harder than I, so I appreciate that, and look forward to your responses on some of these questions that I have.

But on the rebate model—so we are interested in the rebate model—and the, I guess, concern is that it incentivizes brand manufacturers to deliver higher rebates to ensure their products land on the formularies. And I know there is the opposite side that says the brand manufacturers choose to set up prices high. But the reality is that the rebate model seems, in our research, to incent manufacturers to keep prices high to get rebates to get on the formulary. And that affects somebody's paying out of pocket at the counter.

---

[119] Brown, Zach Y. "Equilibrium Effects of Health Care Price Information." *The Review of Economics and Statistics* 101, no. 4 (2019): 699-712. https://doi.org/10.1162/rest_a_00765.

[120] Congressional Budget Office. "Cost Estimate: S.1895, Lower Health Care Costs Act." Washington, D.C.: Congressional Budget Office, July 16, 2019. Accessed April 29, 2023. https://www.cbo.gov/system/files/2019-07/s1895_0.pdf.

So if the manufacturers could just lower their prices to get on the formulary, rather than give rebates, why wouldn't they?

Ms. BASS. Thanks for that—the talk button helps, doesn't it?

Thank you so much for that question. So you are asking about why manufacturers don't just lower their price. And I think we have seen recently that, in fact, manufacturers do sometimes lower their prices. We know that rebates are not correlated with pricing. Medicare Part B gets no rebates, and prices go up at virtually the same amount that is happening on the Medicare Part D side.

The insulin example shows you that manufacturers will, in fact, lower their prices, and only manufacturers can control how the prices are set. So I think we just fundamentally disagree with the premise that rebates have anything to do with driving up prices.

Mr. GUTHRIE. That is kind of the point. You know, we did have some—we had a hearing, and it the was oversight committee, actually, the oversight committee that Mr. Griffith now chairs. And we had all the manufacturers, we had the PBMs, we had all the group, and we really kind of focused on insulin prices. And coming out of that hearing is when, all of a sudden, the prices started dropping.

So it just didn't seem like until we exposed the price, that it was—I mean, this is kind of the concern, is that —what we want, what kind of came out of this, and kind of the genesis for a lot of this work for everybody—I am not just talking to you, Ms. Bass— is that people will react different if they know the price. And if it is inefficient, then the market is going to demand that it change and move forward.

And so, Ms. Schuman, I have a kind of a conglomerate business in my area who have several businesses, but grocery stores and they have supplier retail pharmacy. And they came to me and says, "Look, we are paying this amount of money for our employees to go to the pharmacy," and very few employers have this information because they pay for their employers to go the pharmacy benefit. But since they also own the pharmacy, they don't know what the pharmacy is getting reimbursed. And they sit down, and sit down with their insurance company, and the insurance company, "Well, we will give you a break," because they were going to say we are not going to let you negotiate on our behalf anymore, because we don't—this is—look at the spread between what we are paying and what we are receiving. And so it gets back to making sure people have access to prices, and prices information, and how they react to that.

And so my question: Do employers readily have access to information related to the prices that—so the PBMs will receive for their drug that they are selling it to you differently, do they have access to that information?

Ms. SCHUMAN. Employers don't know what they don't know. And I think that is the issue.

And I think the definitions keep changing about whether something, a rebate, whether it is another fee. And as I mentioned in my testimony, trying to interject all of this transparency, which is, again, foundational for employer efforts to try to manage drug costs, you know, they don't necessarily have the leverage in those contract negotiations to make sure they have the specificity of definitions. And they are shapeshifting, perhaps, on the part of different revenue streams.

And that is why I think this is a really critical market-based solution to require transparency, to require sunshine and daylight, so employers truly know where that money trail is so they can make sure that they are spending their resources wisely.

Mr. GUTHRIE. So it is just difficult to get information.

And I guess what I am trying to get at, so the other argument would be—somebody has made this argument to me—is that, well, employers have the information, and they get to decide do they want to pay a lower monthly premium or do they want higher rebates and—a lower monthly premium and higher rebates, or they are going to have a higher monthly premium. Are you guys seeing that kind of information and making those kind of negotiations?

Ms. SCHUMAN. Well, you know, that is—even large employers, even very large employers have significant challenges, have run up to significant challenges just getting a hold of that information. And that information is so critical to have in hand for employers so they can decide what is the best way to make healthcare for their employees more affordable.

Mr. GUTHRIE. OK, thank you.

Well, I wish I had more time to ask questions. I only have 5 more seconds, so I will yield back to myself and I will recognize the ranking member for 5 minutes for questions.

Ms. ESHOO. Thank you, Mr. Chairman, and thank you to all of the witnesses. I have a few comments to make before I get to my questions.

On PBMs, Ms. Bass, I am pleased to hear that you support getting generics and biosimilars to market, but I find it hypocritical when I hear time and time and time again that plans are often blocked by PBMs from offering the lowest-priced generic. Let me give you an example. The nonprofit Civica Rx in California has manufactured a prostate cancer drug for $160, but PBMs are not letting that cheap drug on insurers' formularies. Instead, the $160 drug is being blocked from the market so that PBMs can take a larger cut, and the larger cut is priced at $3,000.

So I hope our committee really stands up to what needs to be done relative to PBMs, because there is a lot of work to do there.

To the hospitals, on the whole issue of site neutral, we need to get a clear explanation from hospitals on why, after hospitals acquire physician practices, the prices for the services provided by the acquired physicians increases by 14 percent. It is the same doctor, it is the same service, it is the same site, but 14 percent more really doesn't make sense.

So I think that we are going to need more from the hospitals, and I say that really respectfully. Obviously, I love all the hospitals in my district, i.e., you have to love all the hospitals. Look what they have been through with their teams during the pandemic.

To Ms. Schuman, thank you for the written testimony. I just want to highlight something, because hospitals are telling us about—so much about their losses that in—investment losses accounted for approximately 85 percent of overall financial losses.

Now, there is some background in that, but for the large ones to have lost that kind of money because of what they invested in the stock market, I think that the committee needs to take that into consideration.

So to Brian Connell, thank you for the work that you have done, your testimony today, and for working with us on spreading out the costs, which are capped, thank God, for Medicare beneficiaries and out of pocket, being able to spread that. I want to talk to you about the MVP.

Can you explain why this new definition of best price is needed to allow for more value-based payment models?

And in your testimony you recommend that value-based models need to protect patients from undue cost burdens. Do you have suggestions in that area for us, as we really hone the legislation and tailor it really well?

Mr. CONNELL. Yes, thank you for the question, and thank you again for your work and many folks on this committee's work on lowering Part D costs. As you are referencing, this is incredibly important progress made last year.

But to your question on Medicaid best price and its impact on value-based purchasing, we think value-based agreements have a lot of potential. In cancer care, where we have, you know, some potentially curative therapies, some therapies that, you know, might add a little bit of benefit, some that people question the benefit, there is no reason to pay the same for all of those different therapies. There should be rewards for innovation and for making a real impact on patient quality.

And so what we see with the best price rules that we have today is that there is a challenge where, if you have an agreement between a manufacturer and a Medicaid program to pay less for a patient where the drug did not work for them, they didn't respond and it had no clinical benefit, right now that lower price that the— that would be reimbursed for that patient where there was no benefit, even if it is just 5 percent of patients did not respond, low— if you have a reduced cost, that cost could become—that price for the drug could become the price for all Medicaid patients because it is the lower price being paid by Medicaid.

And so, without the flexibility to make sure that lower price can be allowed without drawing down the price for every patient—because there could be some patients that are responding perfectly to that, and really need a better price. So——

Ms. ESHOO. That is——

Mr. CONNELL. I think reforms are necessary there.

Ms. ESHOO. That is helpful. Thank you for everything that you do.

Mr. Loren, real quickly on the transparency for PBMs, I think it is a critical first step to their practices. It drives up drug prices, allows God knows what. What would you add to that?

Mr. ADLER. Sure. So——

Ms. ESHOO. How would you address this?

Mr. ADLER. Yes, thank you for the question. So—sure, so I think you are right, and the Congressional Budget Office has said that they think there are some savings, if sort of temporary, to kind of giving some more information to employers so they know what is going on.

I actually also think there is a lot of value that would be gained from transparency more broadly, and making available all of the various payment flows that go between actors, specific actors in the pharmaceutical supply chain, so we can really get at some basic questions in drug pricing that we just don't have the data for at the moment.

Ms. ESHOO. Great, thank you.

Mr. GUTHRIE. Thank you.

Ms. ESHOO. Thank you to all the witnesses.

Mr. GUTHRIE. The gentlelady——

Ms. ESHOO. I yield back.

Mr. GUTHRIE. Thank you. The gentlelady yields back. The Chair now recognizes Dr. Burgess from Texas for 5 minutes.

Mr. BURGESS. Thank you, Mr. Chairman, and I do want to thank all of our witnesses for being here today.

You can see how extremely important this is. And for all of the discussion that Congress never works together, I think you see the interest is genuine, and it is bipartisan.

Ms. Thompson, let me start with you. We had a press release in September 2022 by the American Hospital Association that stated that 136 rural hospitals closed from 2010 to 2021. Obviously, we have got the pandemic in there, and a record 19 closed in 2020 alone. We continue to receive requests for expanding payments to these hospitals. Many of those expanded payment requests are granted. And yet the closures continue to be reported or threatened.

So the question I would have, is it possible that permitting a new type of entrepreneurial hospital, such as those built and owned by physicians, could be given a chance in rural—other areas, and it would not be risking existing hospitals at all because they are already closing in those areas?

Ms. THOMPSON. Thank you very much for that question, Congressman Burgess, and thank you for your support of the Medicaid DSH bill. We really appreciate what that will do for vulnerable patients in vulnerable communities.

Physician-owned hospitals are very different than freestanding community hospitals. Data has shown that physician hospitals can pick and choose the patients that they see, and those patients are- typically wealthier and less complex to treat. The OIG, the GAO, MedPAC have had some studies in this space.

And so additionally, some of these physician-owned hospitals don't have emergency rooms or backup services. And that means that patients, if something goes wrong, they rely on their community hospital. I think we would be concerned if physician-owned hospitals, given the workforce shortage, were to grow in rural areas such that they would pull workforce from the freestanding emergency—from the freestanding community hospital, and thus they might not be able to fulfill their mission of 24/7 backup services. Mr. BURGESS. We are talking about areas where the existing hospitals have already closed, and we are trying to provide access for patients.

Again, I do not understand why a fundamentally different model could not be entertained, even as a demonstration project. I have already referenced earlier in the previous panel, a hospital down on the Rio Grande Valley was doing an excellent job of providing serv- ice to uninsured and underinsured patients. They do that every day of the week down there. I mean, that is their business model.

And I will just tell you, and I have shared with the committee before, a brilliant paper written in Health Affairs—now it has probably been 10 years ago, I may have even been the one who wrote it—but look, as a physician, I want to go where my time is going to be maximized. And in a physician-owned hospital, a physician- owned-hospital-run operating room, I will just tell you they are much more efficient. There is the pride of ownership. Doctors care about how their patients are taken care of.

And again, I know you have heard me say it over and over and over today, and you all have emphasized, as well, the vertical integration that is occurring where hospitals are buying doctors, and yet doctors can't buy hospitals. I mean, it just fundamentally makes no sense.

Do you think that CMS appropriately adjusts payments to hospitals according to the risk of the patient?

And if not, can you suggest how CMS could improve its risk adjustment methodology to prevent hospitals from cherry-picking sicker patients?

Ms. THOMPSON. So I think that there is a lot to explore in terms of the risk adjustment. I think that different settings of care have different costs associated with them. The fact that freestanding community hospitals have the 24/7 emergency room and backup and standby services is more expensive. I know that we are held to higher regulatory requirements and conditions of participation, et cetera.

Mr. BURGESS. Well, let me ask you this. When an insurance company acquires a hospital and a hospital acquires a medical practice, do they require the doctors to use that hospital?

Ms. THOMPSON. Depending on their insurance, my guess is yes.

Mr. BURGESS. Yes. The answer is yes.

Thank you, Mr. Chairman. I yield back.

Mr. GUTHRIE. Thank you. The gentleman yields back. The Chair now recognizes Mr. Ca´ rdenas from California for 5 minutes.

Mr. CA´RDENAS. Thank you very much, Mr. Chairman. I would like to thank the witnesses for joining us and providing your exper tise on these important issues, and also providing that not only to us but to the American people who are watching.

At the last hearing we had on transparency in this committee, I asked about the use of non-English languages in both the insurance and hospital transparency rules. I am concerned that these rules do not take into consideration constituencies like the majority of the constituents in my district that primarily speak Spanish as their first language.

Mr. Adler, do you have any idea how many hospitals and insurers post information in Spanish and other non-English languages? And how can requiring a greater range of languages improve access to critical care and information?

Mr. ADLER. Sure, thank you for the question, Congressman Ca´ rdenas.

So I don't know that I have a concrete answer to exactly what share of hospitals or insurers have posted this information in Spanish or other languages. Certainly, it is some. I have seen, you know, some of these tools on insurer websites, where you can access this information in Spanish.

I think you are kind of really focused on the consumer-facing tools here, right? These sort of data have kind of the researcher side for people like me, and then the—right? And then the sort of consumer-facing angle here.

I do think, you know, especially on sort of the insurer-facing tools that are under consideration by this subcommittee today, to sort of expand upon, it would be useful to require, right? I mean, it is a very common language in this country to speak Spanish. So I think it is important to require that, right, that these data are available both in English——

Mr. CA´RDENAS. Would providing this important information in

multiple languages, would that help with healthcare, or would it be not important?

Mr. ADLER. I think it would help. I think transparency can help. Transparent data on prices, particularly for folks who are in their deductible, so they are kind of bearing the full cost of these services—we have evidence that, on net, it does seem to lead to sort of better shopping, at least for a subset of services here—you know, imaging, for instance—and that it can lead to lower prices.

I don't think this is, like, changing the whole healthcare system here——

Mr. CA´RDENAS. Sure.

Mr. ADLER. But I think it is—you know, modest steps in the right direction are important here.

Mr. CA´RDENAS. I think it would be an added benefit to everyone and to healthcare overall. So thank you.

And also, as it relates to access, I am worried about the impact of hospital consolidation on access to care in medically underserved communities. Mr. Cavanaugh, in your testimony you note that consolidation has accelerated, and smaller providers and safety net hospitals are among the most likely to need the resources that bigger systems can provide. So, Mr. Cavanaugh, can you describe the impact of these consolidations?

And also, would you expect there to be implications for access quality and affordability for patients because of accelerated consolidation?

Mr. CAVANAUGH. Certainly. Thank you for that question. Yes. As I said, we work with independent practices in 45 States. And if a practice is independent today, it is fiercely independent. It has had multiple opportunities to sell to an insurer, to a hospital system. So we have seen the impact of anticompetitive—when the hospitals do consolidate, and if a practice stays outside of that consolidation, we have seen difficulties in remaining in the hospital's own self-insured network.

So literally we have had hospital systems say to our practices, "If you want to see our employees, you need to join—either you sell your practice or join our CIN." So I think that impacts access. Certainly, as we have all documented on the Medicare side and other places, the facility fees raise the costs. Anytime costs go up, you need to be concerned about access, particularly for lower-income communities.

So I think those are all legitimate concerns that flow from consolidation.

Mr. CA´RDENAS. Thank you.

Ms. Schuman, I want to talk about transparency and PBMs. How would requiring reporting of certain drug pricing information held by the PBMs benefit employers and plan sponsors who provide health insurance coverage?

Ms. SCHUMAN. Well, first of all, they need to know where the money is going. They need to understand what the true cost of drugs are. They need to understand where these different revenue streams are going. Are they flowing back to the plan sponsor to the employer to share those savings with employees?

And the fact remains that, as I said before, they don't know what they don't know. So having this transparency is really foundational to restoring, I think, competition in—with respect to drug pricing and, ultimately, enabling employers to have the tools they need to better manage those costs.

Mr. CA´RDENAS. Can you give an example of what this committee can do to help with that transparency and pricing issue?

Ms. SCHUMAN. Well, the PBM transparency legislation, for one, is just so critical to these efforts, again, to enshrine in legislation so there is this certainty that employers have, that they know that they are going to be able to have access to this information, to be able to have——

Mr. CA´RDENAS. Thank you.

Ms. SCHUMAN [continuing]. The definitional specificity——

Mr. CA´RDENAS. Thank you.

Ms. SCHUMAN [continuing]. About what is going to be covered.

So, yes, that is a very important piece of legislation.

Mr. CA´RDENAS. Thank you. I yield back, Mr. Chairman.

Mr. GUTHRIE. Thank you. The gentleman yields back. The Chair recognizes Mr. Griffith for 5 minutes for questions.

Mr. GRIFFITH. Thank you very much, Mr. Chairman.

Mr. Adler, site-neutral payments, the examples that you gave in your oral testimony, I think it all makes sense. If you are getting, you know, a shot, outpatient, it doesn't matter whether it is in the doctor's office or at the hospital or a facility owned by the hospital. But on Ms.

Thompson's side of the ledger—and this is what we have to try to sort out—you have a patient who is in the hospital. It may be the same procedure or the same shot that could, if that patient were in better health, be done outpatient. But they are not outpatient, they are in the hospital.

So I noticed that you talked about outpatient in your oral testimony. You said outpatient comparisons. Is that because you recognize that if the patient has other issues and is already in the hos- pital, there is going to be more cost with having round-the-clock care?

Mr. ADLER. Sure. So thank you for that question, Congressman Griffith.

So certainly, for—once the patient is on an inpatient basis—for instance, this is actually not—this doesn't apply, so there is a whole different Medicare payment system for inpatient. For—you know, if this is a drug administration, you know, billing on the outpatient side, even on the hospital's campus, right, I think it is an important—the argument that the—Ms. Thompson was making here, right, is important for why we might not want to equalize payments for more complex surgeries, like a—for a complex surgery or an emergency room visit.

But the services that we are talking about today, or that the subcommittee bills are focused on today, are very—we are talking about low-complexity services, where we have not seen—the data shows there aren't—don't seem to be any cost differences between providing that service to a——

Mr. GRIFFITH. Right.

Mr. ADLER [continuing]. Between a sicker patient or a less sick patient.

Mr. GRIFFITH. My next set of questions will be both to you and to Mr. Cavanaugh. And I don't—I am uncomfortable with all the consolidations. I agree with that.

On the other side of the coin, in my district, particularly in the historical coal fields of southwest Virginia, is one of the most economically stressed regions in the country. None of us like the fact that we no longer have any competition. But we had two hospital chains a number of years ago. They looked at it. One of them was looking for a partner from outside the area so they could keep competition going. We couldn't keep our hospitals open if we didn't do something. And the two chains in east Tennessee, in Mrs. Harshbarger's district and in my district, they merged to form one. Is it ideal? No.

But can you each recognize that sometimes in particularly economically stressed areas we may need that consolidation? I know it is a completely different animal when large hospital chains are buying up doctors' practices, but this is a little bit different animal. If you could each speak to that.

Mr. ADLER. Yes, I will jump in quickly. So, yes, I mean, I think fundamentally you are correct, that this is—I think you do need to think about it differently when you are talking about an area with lower population, and, you know, especially lower population and lower-income folks there, where there are inevitably going to be some rural areas in America that can just only really support one hospital.

I want to say what I am sort of focusing on here is the sort of, you know, where a lot of people live, but in the bigger urban markets or suburban markets, where I think that competition——

Mr. GRIFFITH. And because I have time limitations, would that pretty much be your answer, as well, Mr. Cavanaugh, or do you have a different twist?

Mr. CONNELL. Similar, except I would say, yes, rural hospitals, safety net hospitals—certainly don't want to hurt them financially. So if you wanted to do site neutral and then funnel some of that money back to those facilities through some other mechanism that doesn't incentivize consolidation, I think that would be fine.

Mr. GRIFFITH. All right. I appreciate that.

PBMs, a lot of attention here today on that. My experience talking with constituents is there are occasions, Mr. Adler, where the PBMs, for whatever reasons, actually end up—if you use your insurance, which buys through the PBM, you are paying more than you would have paid if you just paid cash. Is that still the case?

Mr. ADLER. Yes, that is—in certain circumstances, yes.

Mr. GRIFFITH. Ms. Bass, how can that possibly be? I mean, if you all are looking out for the consumers, and you keep talking about how you are trying to save money, how can it possibly be that the consumer has to pay more if they use an insurance company that uses one of your affiliates, one of your corporate PBMs?

Ms. BASS. Thank you for the question, Congressman. That is an unusual situation. Our companies are cognizant of it. Some of it has to do with the benefit design chosen by the employers. And as we have learned more about that, our companies have developed programs to address it.

Mr. GRIFFITH. So you wouldn't oppose our bill that says we are not going to let that happen anymore. I have got to move on.

Ms. Schuman, you raised an issue on transparency earlier, and I do support transparency. And if you were—not that you had to, but if you were listening to my testimony earlier—or my questioning earlier when the witness was in front of us, I talked about a disrupter.

This company allows you to get whatever drugs approved by the FDA, but you, based on transparency, can find where you can get it the cheapest. And if you get it below the median price, you get to put that money on account or hit a button that says send me the check. Do you like that concept, at least in principle?

Ms. SCHUMAN. Well, what I like the concept of is making sure you know that you are paying for value. And that is, ultimately, what we are talking about. And that is ultimately why transparency is so important to make sure employers and also patients and consumers are paying for value. And without transparency, they don't know that.

Mr. GRIFFITH. I appreciate it. My time is up. I yield back.

Mr. GUTHRIE. Thank you. The gentleman yields back. The Chair now recognizes Ms. Blunt Rochester for 5 minutes for questions.

Ms. BLUNT ROCHESTER. Thank you, Mr. Chairman, and thank you to our witnesses for being here today.

I am pleased that we are holding this hearing so we can better understand how transparency can lead to lower cost for patients, particularly with respect to drug prices. And I would like to discuss the role of pharmacy benefit managers and the role that they play in the drug supply chain.

We know that PBMs play a dual role in managing negotiations with pharmaceutical manufacturers to determine the price a plan will pay for drugs on their formulary, while at the same time working with insurance plans to determine how drugs for their enrollees will be covered.

PBMs also manage relationships with pharmacies. My understanding is that many of these arrangements are opaque and hard to decipher, not only for patients but also for plan sponsors and other participants in the drug supply chain.

Mr. Adler, can you clearly explain the role PBMs play in the drug supply chain and why the practices utilized by PBMs often lack transparency?

Mr. ADLER. Sure, thank you for the question. So, I mean, I think you described the sort of role well of PBMs, right? The—fundamentally, the PBM's role is to negotiate lower drug prices on behalf of purchasers. And, certainly—right—and plans wouldn't hire them if they weren't getting them lower prices, right? I think that part is fundamental.

Why there is a lack of transparency, fundamentally, because it is not in their competitive interest to have that data be transparent. They think it is in their—each PBM thinks it is in their interest to have that data be secret. And that is sort of why I think, you know, employers, for instance, very much want to see that data, and I think, from my researcher-biased perspective, I think I would very much like to see that data.

Ms. BLUNT ROCHESTER. I think—you go right into my next question, which is do PBMs take advantage of misaligned incentives that allow them to retain profit instead of effectively lowering prices for patients at the pharmacy counter?

Mr. ADLER. Sure. So to some degree. But I do want to—right— I think it is still worth noting that PBMs are generating lower costs than—and drug prices than they would be without them.

But yes, I mean, I—to me, sort of the core issue in the PBM industry is just high levels of consolidation. There are three PBMs that dominate the market, and other insurers have to contract with those PBMs, for instance. Some of them have their own PBMs but often still have to use them. And I think one of the fears, from a sort of antitrust perspective here, is that those big PBMs might not give as good deals to the other insurers, and sort of entrench their market position there.

Ms. BLUNT ROCHESTER. And I think this also goes without saying, because we have talked a lot about transparency, but do you believe increasing transparency related to PBM practices will provide plan sponsors with better tools to leverage power prices for— lower prices for patients?

Mr. ADLER. Sure. So on the margin, yes. So I do think, again, this is up—I agree with the Congressional Budget Office here, who has made this sort of point here, that there are some subset of purchasers here where having this information probably gives them information to lower prices. I don't know how long-term of a thing that is going to be, because there will be sort of—these are private actors, and they will try to renegotiate contracts and stuff like that. But there is always a little bit of a game of Whac-a-mole. But I do think there are benefits.

Ms. BLUNT ROCHESTER. And my last question to you is how might comprehensive pharmacy DIR fee reform or clawbacks be an important element of the strategy to manage the rising drug costs for Americans?

Mr. ADLER. I think it could help. I mean, I will just sort of turn to—I think, when you are talking about drug prices, you know, the bigger picture issues are, you know, competition in the drug industry on the pharmaceutical, you know, manufacturer side of things, or price regulation in the form of, you know, provisions like in the Inflation Reduction Act.

Ms. BLUNT ROCHESTER. OK. Thank you, Mr. Adler. I agree that increasing transparency is also an important tool to rein in PBM practices and reduce costs. And while these are important first steps, much more work, as you have said, will need to be done to address the role of PBMs in increasing patient out-of-pocket costs. I am really pleased to be working with my colleague Congressman Buddy Carter on additional reforms, and I look forward to more discussions about PBMs, DIR fees, and insurance plan practices that keep patient costs from going higher and that really deal with making sure that the quality of care, the value of the care is what is our priority.

Thank you, and I yield back.

Mr. GUTHRIE. Thank you. The gentlelady yields back. The Chair now recognizes Mr. Latta of Ohio for 5 minutes for questions.

Mr. LATTA. Well, thanks, Mr. Chairman, and also thanks to our panel.

Ms. Thompson, if I could start my questions with you. Currently over 62 percent of hospitals in the State of Ohio are operating in a loss, resulting in cuts to services within maternity wards and behavioral health clinics. And in my district, the 5th, which has many rural areas, tight budgets, staff burnout, and overregulation are often cited as the main contributing factors for reduction in care and facility closures. For example, over 50 percent of doctors and nurses say they spend more time in front of a screen fulfilling compliance requirements than they do treating patients.

Would you discuss in detail any regulatory barriers or requirements that are hindering the workforce and provision of care?

And what ideas would you have to fix it? Because I—the question I ask them every time I met one of our facilities in my district, because I look around and I go, you know, who is practicing medicine sometimes? But——

Ms. THOMPSON. Thank you for that question. There are a number of regulatory burdens that are facing our hospitals and, really, our caregivers in those hospitals today.

I think one of the biggest areas is prior authorization delays and denials, where physicians and others are spending more time on the phone, trying to get their patients into a new setting of care. You might be aware that it has been very difficult over the past year-plus for hospitals to discharge patients to the next level of care, whether that is a postacute care setting or whether it is a skilled nursing facility, mainly because it is hard to get patients out of the hospital due to workforce issues in other places, but also because of these delays and denials in care. So I think that one of the biggest areas where we might be able to find savings is there. And there's also just a lot of administrative expenses that I think can be streamlined and processed, so that we can both save some money in the system, make it more efficient, and then also to free up time for our clinicians so that they can see their patients.

Mr. LATTA. And just out of curiosity, a followup on that, because when, you know, you are on the phone and you are trying to get some procedure done, how often is it then that it finally does come through, they say, "OK, you can go ahead and do it, you can get that procedure?"

Ms. THOMPSON. You know, that is interesting. I don't have the exact statistic for you, but I do know that a lot of payment denials are overturned after—let me see, the OIG report, I think, said that there were 13 percent of payment denials or prior authorization denials, and maybe 18 percent of payment denials that were overturned because they actually adhered to Medicare fee-for-service requirements. So MA plans were putting on greater restrictions under fee-for-service.

But how many times or how long it takes for those denials to get overturned, I don't even know. But it is an interesting statistic that we can try to find for you.

Mr. LATTA. Well, thank you very much.

Ms. Schuman, you mentioned in your testimony that the national healthcare costs are expected to grow at an annual rate of 5.1 percent from 2021 to 2030. You know, in your opinion, how can Congress get more employers involved so that the burden of covering this increase does not fall on the Federal Government?

Ms. SCHUMAN. Yes, so absolutely. I mean, employers are, you know, as I said, deeply concerned about rising healthcare costs. And I think that is what is so critical for employers who ultimately are looking at ways to offer higher-quality, more affordable care to their employees about addressing the root causes of rising healthcare costs.

And again, that is why the proposals that we are talking about today around transparency and competition are really handing tools to employers to be able to deliver higher-quality, more equitable care to their employees. And I think, really, you know, taking aim at those payment policies, even in, you know, the Medicare space that really drive the broader market and broader distortions, and certainly Medicare payment policies that drive more consolidations impact not just Medicare patients but all patients.

Mr. LATTA. Well, you know, from the—from what you have heard here today, you know, are there any other proposals that you would have that might not be on the table today that would help?

Ms. SCHUMAN. Absolutely. I think just following up on the vein of really taking aim at some of these anticompetitive contracting clauses, for example, and I think that is something that Mr. Cavanaugh mentioned. What are hospitals able to do? Why are they taking advantage of this monopoly power? It is simple market dynamics. When you are a larger hospital system, you bought up the competitors, you bought up the rivals, you have more leverage, and you can charge higher prices.

And you can also, with that leverage, enter into contracts with plans, with health plans that restrict their ability to try to promote higher-value care, to direct through plan design, to incentivize their employees to go to a different hospital, to a different practice that maybe is less expensive and higher quality.

So I think, also, proposals that take aim at those anticompetitive contracting clauses that tie the hands of employers from pursuing these value-based designs is also really critical.

Mr. LATTA. Well, thank you very much.

And Mr. Chair, my time is expired, and I yield back.

Mr. GUTHRIE. Thank you. The gentleman yields back. The Chair just wants to make everybody aware there is a vote on the floor. So we are probably going to see where we can go, but probably get at least one more question in, and then we have to break and come back afterwards.

So the Chair now recognizes the Chair of the full committee, Chair Rodgers, for 5 minutes.

Mrs. RODGERS. Thank you, Mr. Chairman. I too have concerns about prior authorization and denials within Medicare. I just want everyone to be aware there is a bill in this package—it is one that I am leading—that would address the vertical integration and transparency.

So we have heard in our previous hearings from experts, patients, and employers about how transparent prices can lower healthcare costs. And this morning Administrator Brooks-LaSure reaffirmed this administration's belief in price transparency. I wanted to ask each one of you, yes or no, do you believe that price transparency will put downward pressure on costs?

Ms. THOMPSON. Yes.

Ms. BASS. Price transparency that doesn't expose competitive data to competitors PBMs support.

Mrs. RODGERS. Thank you.

Mr. CONNELL. Yes.

Mr. CAVANAUGH. Yes.

Ms. SCHUMAN. Yes.

Mr. ADLER. Yes.

Mrs. RODGERS. Thank you.

Just as a followup, then, Ms. Bass, the overwhelming opinion from experts, including CBO, is that price transparency lowers cost. In virtually every other part of our economy, consumers know the price they pay. So just—I would like to hear some more about why you think PBMs should be treated specially and not required to be transparent.

Ms. BASS. Thank you for that question. PBMs fully agree that data that will help lead to lower costs—that people can actually use to lower costs—should be transparent. We have no disagreement about that.

But where we have a slight quibble is, for example, in Federal bidding for contracts, you don't have those bidders bid openly so that every competitor knows what the competitor's best price is. You don't do that. You make those sealed bids so that people will be incented to bid as low as possible to get the business. That is the kind of thing that we are concerned about. We think that if every drug manufacturer knew what the other's best deal was, they wouldn't be as willing to go as deep as they are currently going. That is the one quibble we have.

Beyond that, we—our companies make tools available so that, at the prescribing point of prescription, doctors can just know what the cost sharing is going to be for a given patient, and that the patients know what is going to be on their formulary. Our companies are very transparent in their contracts with employers, and respond to employers' requests for information, and put that in contracts.

So we respectfully think that, just with respect to competitors knowing what their competition's best bid is, that would be the problem.

Mrs. RODGERS. OK, I appreciate that. Would—could you cite specific examples where price transparency has resulted in increased prices, cost?

Ms. BASS. There have been cases in the past—there is a concrete case, and we have promised to get that information to your staff. The Justice Department, in a recent case, went through why it thought it was a bad idea to put competitors' information out. The FTC in the past has said that putting out competitors' information leads to tacit collusion. We strongly believe that this is basic economic theory and that when competitors know each other's data, prices go up.

Mrs. RODGERS. Well, I understand that we have heard this before, that we have cited this concrete case. I will just say that this is based upon a study of Danish concrete in the 1990s that CBO's own words said "was based on a small sample of plants over a short period," and how that is comparable to 2023 American healthcare system I am not sure really applies, and I just encourage all of the stakeholders to bring constructive feedback to these proposals.

Simply saying no to price transparency is unacceptable. And I think what you are hearing today is that both Republicans and Democrats are—believe that this is fundamental, that we must address the price transparency, and just—we are anxious to get your feedback and want to have future engagements that reflect that.

Mr. Connell, the Leukemia & Lymphoma Society advocates on behalf of over 1.5 million Americans living with or in remission from blood cancers. Between 2015 and 2019, chemotherapy in freestanding provider offices fell by 5.4 percent, while the volume of chemotherapy delivered for outpatients increased by 27.8 percent. What do seniors pay if they get chemotherapy in a provider's office, compared to a hospital outpatient setting?

Mr. CONNELL. Significantly more is the short answer. It depends on the drug. But provider—or patients who are going to get their chemo at an outpatient facility, whether that is attached to a hospital or off campus, are paying significantly more than they would pay in out-of-pocket costs, which are astronomical, I will say, at the baseline.

So when you start to multiply those, it gets really, really burdensome for patients, and it pays a lot more if you are at a hospital setting than if you are at the physician office——

Mrs. RODGERS. So are there any reasons they should get the chemotherapy in a hospital outpatient setting?

Mr. CONNELL. You know, there is—every clinical case is different. There are some patients who do need to get their care closer to a hospital, but there is no need at the baseline to say that a patient with the same risk score should be getting the same drug at a different price at a different setting.

Mrs. RODGERS. OK. Thank you very much. Thank you, Mr. Chairman. I yield back.

Mr. GUTHRIE. Thank you. The Chair yields back. We do have two more that are present we just sent to vote, so they showed up to do their questions, so we are going to have to adjourn and come back.

However, we are going to do one more question. You have one on your side, and then we will return after votes. So we have a vice chair of the committee, Dr. Bucshon, 5 minutes.

Mr. BUCSHON. Thank you, Mr. Chairman. I thank the witnesses and everyone in the audience and everyone watching.

You know, the ground has shifted on a lot of these issues, and I would encourage all the witnesses to recognize the shifting of the ground in a bipartisan way. I have been working on some of these issues for the 12 years I have been in Congress, talking to stakeholders, trying to find common ground. And by some of the testimony here today, it is pretty clear that that is not going to be possible, maybe, and that disappoints me.

But I want to emphasize the resolve of Congress to address these issues on behalf of the people we represent. We are being—we are—every day, when I am in Indiana, people are demanding that we address these issues. And that is where this is coming from. And it is going to happen.

Ms. Thompson, everybody here supports hospitals, but the fact of the matter is hospital expenses from 2019 to 2022 increased by less than overall inflation. So did they go up? Yes, but inflation was higher overall. And the labor cost surges that many hospitals were experiencing during COVID, those were real. Every hospital had to have traveling nurses. Things like that are beginning to subside, and contract labor costs were down 20 percent year over year, in one recent report from HCA.

In 2021, operating margins went up to a record high, despite COVID relief going down. And that is according to MedPAC. It is not my opinion.

And in 2022, many hospitals said they have lost money, but— and that is probably true for the rural hospitals, and some that I represent, but the reality is there are serious questions in the larger hospitals. In fact, one study which has already been quoted a couple of times today of the—of 10 large nonprofits found that 85 percent of the losses were isolated to the hospitals' investment portfolios, and actual patient revenues year over year were slightly positive.

Of course, the S&P 500 grew by nearly 90 percent from 2019 to 2021. So yes, in 2022 we all lost money in the market, including hospitals.

So I guess my question is, are nonprofit hospitals able to cover their investment losses with the gain, the market gains, they achieved prior to the market softening?

I mean, what is the balance, what is on their balance sheet?

Ms. THOMPSON. Well, thank you, Congressman Bucshon, for that question, and thank you for sponsoring the SAVE Act to protect our healthcare workers.

Mr. BUCSHON. You are welcome.

Ms. THOMPSON. We appreciate that.

Hospitals don't rely on—well, let me take that back. Because investments change every year, plus or minus, we really look at our patient care margins. And yes, MedPAC found a positive patient care margin. But when MedPAC looked at Medicare margins, they were down at negative 8-something percent in 2021, moving to negative 10 percent in 2023.

So right now, Medicare is not covering the cost of its care. Because of that, it is important for hospitals to have financial reserves to cover such things like——

Mr. BUCSHON. OK, fair enough.

Ms. THOMPSON [continuing]. A once-a-year pandemic.

Mr. BUCSHON. Fair enough. I have got other things.

So, I mean, I just want to say Federal Government shouldn't be subsidizing losses in the stock market to some of the largest health systems in the country. And that is where transparency comes in. Honestly, I didn't even know myself the extent of the investment portfolios of some of the largest health systems in the country. It is in the billions and billions of dollars, as they come out and tell the public they are losing money. That is just not right. I mean, OK, you could be losing money on the patient volume, I understand, and on Medicare. But overall, I mean, come on.

I mean—and so my goal is to reduce the—honestly, overall, it is to reduce incentives for hospitals to monopolize healthcare markets, which can increase costs for everyone. And I feel strongly about this because in 2005 my medical practice, in which I was a partner, was purchased by a hospital system in Evansville, Indiana, Ascension Hospital. And that was based essentially on neutral site building. It was based on the fact that we—the reimbursement had gone to where we couldn't recruit doctors, we just couldn't afford it because we were getting paid a third of what the hospital three blocks away would be for the same tests. The hospitals acquired the primary care doctors, forced them to send their ancillary services to the hospital. So not only were we getting paid less, but we didn't have the patients.

So, I mean, I have been involved in this for 25 years, and the argument from the hospitals about their cost of care is totally valid. And I think I have told you that, some of the cases you make about complexity of care, and I am empathetic.

But please, again, everybody, including the PBMs, work with this committee to find commonsense solutions to prevent consolidation and get the cost down. That is what I am asking.

I yield back.

Mr. GUTHRIE. Thank you. The gentleman yields back, so the committee will stand at recess and just be close by. And all you people here, that—if you haven't testified before, you know where to be, but just be close by. And as soon as the third—we have three votes, and as soon as the third vote is conducted, we will——

Mr. BUCSHON. Mr. Chairman?

Mr. GUTHRIE [continuing]. Come straight back.

Mr. BUCSHON. Can I submit two things for the record real quickly, prior to the recess?

Mr. GUTHRIE. Any objection to his submission to the record?

Mr. BUCSHON. One is a letter that Mr. Adler actually signed on to regarding reforms in neutral site billing, and one is a hot-off-the-presses article about how health system Kaiser Permanente is to combine with hospital operator Geisinger, and Kaiser is creating a new subsidiary called Risant Health, and their aim is to acquire four or five more hospital systems across the country, further evidence of consolidation.

Mr. GUTHRIE. Without objection, so ordered.

[The information appears at the conclusion of the hearing.]

Mr. GUTHRIE. So the committee will stand at recess until the call of the Chair following the third vote.

[Recess.]

Mr. BUCSHON [presiding]. The committee will come to order.

I now recognize the gentleman from Ohio for 5 minutes for his questioning.

Mr. JOHNSON. Well, thank you, Mr. Chairman, and thank you to our panelists for being here this afternoon for this very important hearing.

As this subcommittee looks at a number of proposed pieces of legislation to address staggering healthcare costs Americans face every day, it is crucially important to hear from all ends of the spectrum, from patients to hospitals. So thank you all, all of you witnesses here today, for engaging in this conversation.

Like many of my colleagues, I am a believer in the power of the free market. Business will flow to quality and availability, and supply will dictate the demand when you have those. But for that to happen, all involved must have access to the necessary information to make informed decisions. Consumers must be able to know that they are buying—what they are buying, and patients must be able to know what the cost of care is to make those informed decisions.

Now, I have heard from many in the healthcare space that the cost of implementing and complying with some of the proposed transparency legislation at issue today, legislation I believe is critically important, is too much of a burden. So my first question to Ashley Thompson—I don't—my glasses—there you are, way down at the end. Thank you, Ashley. Could you explain the impact of reporting requirements for hospitals, particularly those hospitals participating in the 340B program?

Ms. THOMPSON. Yes, thank you for that question. The 340B program is of immense value to the patients and the communities we serve. And right now, hospitals are reporting—were reporting to CMS on the Medicare cost report, were reporting to the IRS on schedule H, and were reporting to HRSA right now, who audits the program and annually recertifies the ability for hospitals to participate. So there's a number of reporting requirements going on today.

I understand that the bill that is before this committee would have additional reporting requirements, and I think that we would welcome the opportunity to discuss them. I think that they are metrics that are being gathered, that we have some concerns that they might not show the true value of the program. So collecting the metrics, you might not, for example, understand that hospitals are using the program to purchase or to hire——

Mr. JOHNSON. Right.

Ms. THOMPSON [continuing]. Two new behavioral health nurses for a clinic.

Mr. JOHNSON. Right. Well, you know, I am a big fan of 340B. It is something I constantly hear about when I am talking to hospitals in my district. It is a very rural district. It is a lifeline to them. My district, like many other rural areas, relies on the 340B program to help healthcare—to make healthcare more affordable for patients. So I want the program to succeed in the long term, but I am getting increasingly concerned that some nonprofit 340B hospitals are abusing the program rules to actually deprive patients of the types of support that 340B was intended to provide. For example, many of our largest hospital systems, beneficiaries of the 340B program, complain about the cost of price transparency compliance, yet they have signed an HHS Health Sector Climate Pledge to, among other things, designate an executive-level lead for their work on reducing emissions by 2023 and conduct an inventory of scope 3 emissions by the end of next year. Now, I am not sure how this relates to delivering affordable, quality healthcare, but it sounds awfully expensive to me.

Mr. Chair, I ask to consent to put into the record the HHS list of hospitals that have signed that pledge.

Mr. BUCSHON. Without objection.

[The information appears at the conclusion of the hearing.]

Mr. JOHNSON. So, Ms. Thompson, back to you again. I find it hard to believe that some hospitals complain that they are unable to shoulder the burden of transparency—they say it costs too much—yet they can afford the not-so-little cost of climate-resilient infrastructure. Are hospitals taking advantage of the 340B program and, rather than ensuring the savings are being passed onto patients, are instead using these savings to further their liberal ESG agenda?

Ms. THOMPSON. No, the hospitals that are participating in 340B use those savings in a number of ways for their communities, whether it is to provide free and discounted drugs to those in need, whether it is mobile——

Mr. JOHNSON. Well, that is what they are supposed to use them for. But how can they say that the cost of price transparency is too expensive when they are spending money—and they are a 340B hospital, they get money through the 340B program—price transparency is too expensive, but they have got the money to spend on ESG and climate change. Can you help me deconflict that?

Ms. THOMPSON. I know that our hospitals are very supportive of price transparency. And as you heard earlier this morning, we are at 70 percent compliance with the rule. I know that those hospitals that are having the most problem with—— Mr. JOHNSON. Well, compliant with the rule, but a lot of those hospitals are putting "N/A" and blanks and spaces in the data rather than putting the actual price. And we see that—we can see that because we are getting the prices from the insurance companies. So though we know that they have got the prices, they are just not putting them in the database.

So I am just not sure there is not abuse here, Mr. Chairman. I yield back.

Mr. BUCSHON. The gentleman yields back. I now recognize Dr. Schrier for 5 minutes.

Ms. SCHRIER. Thank you, Mr. Chairman, and thank you to all of the witnesses for coming today for this discussion about how we can increase transparency and lower costs and foster more competition and improve care for patients.

Mr. Cavanaugh, I am going to start, and then my first question will be directed to you. I just wanted to talk a little bit about innovation and competition and creative ideas that we are getting ideas about all around the country on how to improve care and decrease cost, because our country spends a tremendous amount of money on healthcare with lackluster outcomes.

I am a big supporter of the Innovation Center and CMS, CMMI, and there are lots of pilot projects out there. Not every model deployed is successful, but they are taking a stab at it. And so much work has gone on at the State level and State Medicare and Medicaid systems, thanks to flexibility for States to partner with local entities and just try out new ideas and see what works.

Direct primary care is one example of that, and employers around the country are reporting up to 20 percent savings on the total cost of care for their employees by providing better healthcare up front, sort of loading more on the primary care provider in that setting, reducing unnecessary ER visits, hospital visits, specialty care, and drastically reducing expenses. So I am excited to be working with my colleague Dan Crenshaw on this—these efforts.

Of course, direct primary care can also incentivize worse outcomes, right? It could discourage patients from coming in. It could mean that expensive tests just don't happen. And so it is really important to track outcomes. And what I haven't really seen is a larger effort to track what works and what doesn't, and where the successes are and what we should roll out in other States and around the country.

And so I was just wondering, Mr. Cavanaugh, what has your experience been, even particularly with direct primary care, and what can Congress and industry do together to improve this work being done and roll it out elsewhere?

Mr. CAVANAUGH. Sure. Thank you for that question. Alidade practices are not direct primary care practices in the way that you mean, but there are some analogies, which is we are—our practices are going to Medicare, to Medicare Advantage plans, to Blue Cross plans, to—even to Medicaid plans and saying we will accept accountability for the total cost of care for your line beneficiaries.

And importantly, and this is—gets to your question about skimping on care—also taking accountability for the quality of care that is delivered and the access, because you are—there's two ways to save money, a bad way and the right way, which is focusing on pre vention, wellness, transitions. And that is what, I think, actually has been proven over and over again through the Medicare Shared Savings Program.

There have been not just—Alidade is probably the biggest, but there are other organizations that have used this primary care approach, held accountable by Medicare and others on the quality measures, and been very successful in reducing costs. That is one of the reasons I am here today, which is we can't get everybody to do this because, if systems consolidate, there is no impetus for them to do this, right? If they are going to be able to consolidate and negotiate higher fee-for-service rates, why do the hard work of learning population health, preventive care? And trust me, it is hard work, and it is different from the way the health system was oriented in the past.

So I would love to look at the bill you are developing. We are not a primary care—excuse me, we are not direct primary care. But I do see analogies of focusing on better care at lower cost through, primarily, primary care.

Ms. SCHRIER. Thank you for mentioning consolidation, because that is another one of my concerns, and I am hearing a lot of echoes of that today with my colleagues.

And you are right. When employers have a choice in who to contract with, their health insurance companies, they are looking at who can give the best bang for the buck, the best care. And when there is consolidation, there is no competition, prices go up, and care potentially can go down because there is no competition.

Thank you, and I will—unless anybody else has a comment on direct primary care.

Ms. SCHUMAN. I just wanted to weigh in from the employer perspective, because you mentioned employers and really looking to get the best bang for their buck for their employees. And that means cost, and it means quality.

And employers are really incubators of innovation, and have really looked to models like primary care as ways to drive a healthier workforce later on and saving healthcare costs later on. So we would love to just follow up with you on your efforts. Thank you.

Ms. SCHRIER. Thank you. Perfect timing. I yield back.

Mr. BUCSHON. The gentlelady yields back. I now recognize the gentleman from Florida, Mr. Bilirakis, for 5 minutes.

Mr. BILIRAKIS. Thank you, Doctor, I appreciate it.

Mr. Cavanaugh, the Providers and Payers Compete Act draft would ensure HHS is taking into account the effect of regulatory changes to Medicare payment systems on provider and payer consolidation, both horizontally and vertically. I have been an advocate of ensuring that policies within the Medicare physician fee schedule, for example, work best for patients access—patient access and don't adversely cause local providers to close their doors and join a larger health system.

You say in your testimony that both types of consolidation have led to higher prices for patients. Can you provide insight into this trend and perspective on whether HHS should be taking these considerations into account as it conducts annual payment rulemaking under Medicare?

Mr. CAVANAUGH. Certainly anything that gets policymakers to think longer and harder about whether public policy is contributing to consolidation is something that deserves support.

I would just say, in the meantime, we know there are specific— rather than—I mean, in addition to focusing on future policies, we should look at existing policies that we know are part of the problem.

This committee, to its credit, has site-neutral bills before it. I would encourage you to look there. But I agree that, if there's ways to get policymakers—and I was formerly one myself—to focus more on this—because I do think it is the major challenge before us in getting our health system to pivot to one that is focused on value and not just focused on price and consolidation.

Mr. BILIRAKIS. Very good, thank you. As cochair of the Congressional Rare Disease Caucus, I know the challenges that rare disease patients face in terms of getting treatments to market in the first place.

Despite the FDA regulatory challenges, we have seen some incredible advances in cell and gene therapies. Yet even after approval, unfortunately, the current pricing structure in place causes additional barriers, unfortunately, to access for these patients. That is why I am grateful for Chairman Guthrie's bill, the Medicaid VBPs for Patients, or the MVP Act, is on the docket.

So, Mr. Connell, can you speak to the potential that reducing payment barriers can have, such as following for more value-based payment arrangements on blood cancer and other rare diseases?

And how can we also ensure the innovation pipeline is strong to give hope to so many patients that currently don't have approved treatments or cures?

If you could answer those questions, I would appreciate it. Elaborate, please.

Mr. CONNELL. Yes, I appreciate that. You know, we—there is a truism that we get what we reward, and so we should be rewarding quality. We should be rewarding improved outcomes. We want patients to have better outcomes. That is what we should be paying for. So we want more value-based agreements.

We want more ways that we can reimburse, whether it is to physicians or for drugs, in ways that actually do promote what we want, which is more investment in the type of innovation, the type of new therapies that are going to be really life-changing for patients. Because you mentioned it is a challenge on the rare disease space, and blood cancers are largely rare diseases, a whole collection of them. Under the mantles of just, you know, three or four names are hundreds of diseases.

And so the market is not there necessarily for any one disease in a way that really creates market problems now in terms of bringing products to patients. And so we see tremendous potential in trying to come up with value-based agreements that do reward that patient-centered innovation, that really make a difference for patients, and use that as a way forward to really get the type of drugs that are most valuable for cancer patients.

Mr. BILIRAKIS. Thank you very much.

And Mr. Chairman, I yield back the rest of my time.

Mr. BUCSHON. The gentleman yields back. I now yield to Dr. Joyce for 5 minutes.

Mr. JOYCE. Thank you for yielding, Dr. Bucshon. This hearing today is incredibly apropos because of the timing. I just received notification that Kaiser Permanente is acquiring Geisinger Health System in my home State of Pennsylvania.

Let's start with addressing, first of all, though, H.R. 977. We all know that our society is full of experts, each owning their own workplace. We know that lawyers own law firms. We know that auto mechanics own auto garages. We know that chefs own restaurants. Yet we stop doctors like myself from owning a hospital because they have earned a medical degree. I would like to add my voice to those who are supporting H.R. 977, which would repeal this incredibly misguided restriction.

One of the most disturbing trends that we see in healthcare that defies logic is the prices that insurers pay for medicines that have been broadly flat or declining. Yet patients continue to pay higher prices. In 2021 the net price for medicines, the price after all rebates are paid to PBMs, grew just 1 percent. Meanwhile, insurers and middlemen continue to increase their profits while pocketing the rebates and pocketing the discounts from patients.

Mr. Connell, do you think it is fair that patients could pay more for their medicine than the insurer or the PBM paid? Does that not defeat the entire point of what insurance is for?

Mr. CONNELL. I don't think it is fair. I think that we should try to make sure that patients pay the lowest amount possible, because we know that for every dollar you increase in someone's cost sharing, that patient is less likely to actually get the care that they need. And so we should be getting those copays as low as possible.

Mr. JOYCE. Thank you.

Ms. Schuman, if prescription drug prices were more transparent, do you think that this would happen?

Ms. SCHUMAN. I think that prescription drug prices being more transparent is the only way for this to happen. It may not be the last step, but it has to be the first step.

Mr. JOYCE. And I agree that that first step must be taken, and I think that is one of the points of this hearing today.

Currently, PBM compensation is, quote, ''linked'' to a percentage of the list price of a drug, which incentivizes higher list prices and more rebates that the insurers and PBMs pocket rather than passing it on to the patient.

Do you believe, Ms. Schuman, that we should delink this compensation based on list price through the supply chain to encourage lower list price?

Ms. SCHUMAN. Well, I think we need to look at the entire ecosystem, the drug pricing ecosystem, and have more transparency throughout the entire drug pricing system.

And why transparency is such a critical first step is you are able to see those links, you are able to see whether—what those incentives are, and what—and how that is really translating into, ultimately, lower costs for employers and, ultimately, employees too. So I think that is why I said transparency is, I think, the necessary first step, so employers have line of sight into whether or not they and their employees are actually benefiting from that.

Mr. JOYCE. And I agree, transparency is ultimately important, but the next step has to be de-linking the compensation based on the price list.

On another subject, Mr. Connell, I understand that in 2022 Medicare paid 141 percent more in a hospital outpatient setting than in a freestanding provider office for the first hour of chemotherapy infusion, including both the professional and the facility fees. Mr. Connell, what does this 141 percent premium for the hospital setting mean for cancer patients and the costs that they face at this incredibly important time of their lives?

Mr. CONNELL. Yes, it means that they pay more. Right now, patients pay, essentially, 20 percent in Medicare Part B of whatever the cost, the underlying cost, of the service is. And so, if you have that higher underlying cost—so if you have that markup that happens when someone is getting that chemo at the hospital setting— then you have a patient who is paying more because they are paying a higher amount from their 20 percent.

And there are some ways to help patients deal with that. Medigap is one, but if you are a blood cancer patient you can't get a Medigap plan. If you get diagnosed, they will not sell you a Medigap plan. And so there are patients who are paying that full 20 percent, and they really feel it when the cost goes up like it does if you go to a hospital——

Mr. JOYCE. It certainly seems unfair at such a critical stage of their lives, as they are battling for the life that they want to lead. Mr. Adler, according to MedPAC, in 2022 Medicare paid 105 percent more in on-campus hospital outpatient departments than in freestanding offices for a midlevel office visit. Can you please elaborate on the economic incentives such a payment disparity creates for consolidation and the acquisition of physician practices?

And do you feel that there is a way to move to site-neutral payments for these visits without risking patient outcomes?

Mr. ADLER. Sure. So I think that is very important to move in that direction, right?

I think the financial incentive created by this market distortion that you are describing is very large. So for an independent physician in 2016, integrating with a hospital would have increased the total annual Medicare payments for their services by $141,000. This is, like, per year, per physician, that is how much money is on the table. And as Mr. Cavanaugh was saying earlier, right, this is just a very big incentive for hospitals to buy out practices and for physicians to go work for hospitals because they just have a lot more money to deal with for the exact same set of services.

I think if—just moving to site-neutral payments, where we are focused here on lower complexity services, right—it is imaging, drug administration, office visits, as you were just describing—it is hard to imagine there would be any adverse effects on patients, and we have not seen that from the steps that Congress took in this direction in 2015.

Mr. JOYCE. My time has expired, but I want to reiterate from the onset that any action this committee takes must carefully balance maintaining access to care across all communities, especially in rural settings.

Thank you, Mr. Chairman, and I yield.

Mr. BUCSHON. The gentleman yields back now. I now recognize Mrs. Harshbarger for 5 minutes for her questions.

Mrs. HARSHBARGER. Thank you, Mr. Chairman.

Thank you all for being here. You know, I am glad to be talking about transparency. And, you know, I looked up the definition of "transparency," and it says it is the quality of being easy to see through. That makes no sense about healthcare.

But Ms. Schuman, this week I introduced a bipartisan bill, along with colleagues Reps. Spanberger and Miller-Meeks and Krishnamoorthi, and it is called the PBM Sunshine and Accountability Act. And what this bill does, it requires public reporting of PBM financial information that the HHS Secretary—he already gets that, and—under current law—but it will enhance the reporting to include other things like the rebates, the fees that PBMs and its financial affiliates receive from drug manufacturers and health insurers.

Would it be helpful to employers if group health plans were able to view publicly reported data on PBM aggregate rebates, including those captured by GPOs, or Group Purchasing Organizations?

Ms. SCHUMAN. I do believe that it would indeed be helpful to employers if they were able to view this publicly reported data on PBM aggregate rebates, including those by these Group Purchasing Organizations. Only with more fulsome transparency around the extent of drug manufacturer rebates received by PBMs can employers begin to understand the value that PBMs are generating from administering their drug benefit for their employer-sponsored plan. And with this increased information, employers will be better positioned to negotiate for reduced administrative fees from their PBMs.

Mrs. HARSHBARGER. Yes, especially self-funded employers.

Would it be helpful for employers to know the highest and lowest retained rebate percentages across all contracts, so employees could see where they fall?

Ms. SCHUMAN. Yes, absolutely. That also would be very helpful information for employers. It will help employers understand where their contract falls relative to other employers and whether they may have an opportunity to negotiate for additional pass-through rebate revenue.

So again, I think it is really important to have this information to help manage a plan's—

Mrs. HARSHBARGER. Yes.

Ms. SCHUMAN [continuing]. Overall drug spend and also ensure that there is no overcompensation.

Mrs. HARSHBARGER. You know, we have—the biggest employer in Tennessee is in the city I live in, and if I went to tell their benefits manager about the discrepancy in payment from specific PBMs they had contracted with, do you know it would negate my contract? I could not tell them, because that was a stranglehold on me, and I think that is unacceptable, to try to save somebody's money and they tell you you can't do it.

Mr. Connell, in your view, does it make sense that, if hospitals have to post laboratory test prices, that retail labs should be required to as well?

Mr. CONNELL. Yes, yes, it does make sense. I know patients like patients with blood cancer get a lot of lab tests, and they get very frustrated by the lack of transparency we see today.

Mrs. HARSHBARGER. Yes, because they are totally different, aren't they?

Mr. CONNELL. Yes.

Mrs. HARSHBARGER. Do you think patients would be able to compare cash prices, or should be able to compare cash prices for tests at retail labs versus hospital labs?

Mr. CONNELL. Yes.

Mrs. HARSHBARGER. Do you think competition makes everything better, Mr. Connell?

[Laughter.]

Mr. CONNELL. I think so, yes.

Mrs. HARSHBARGER. I believe so.

Mr. CONNELL. I think so.

Mrs. HARSHBARGER. I think I agree with you.

You know, something interesting, I know that in the healthcare world NPIs—if you have two different offices, physicians are required to have two NPIs, just like pharmacies are. And I have been reading some things about, you know, when hospitals buy provider practices, and the same provider practices then change your billing methods, you know, generally to generate higher reimbursement for their services. These providers, when they are purchased by hospitals, they can use that hospital's NPI. And I don't think that is—you know, there has to be some kind of differentiation. And there were three things that, you know, we have researched that looks like may help with that.

If you require—do you think that if these—and this goes to Mr. Adler—do you think that if these hospitals or these off-campus facilities were required to get a different NPI, that that would fix a lot of this issue?

Mr. ADLER. Sure. So I think in the commercial market, which is where this would be meaningful—so I think it would help. I don't think it fixes everything, but certainly you talk to insurers, and sometimes they will say, "We have a contract with the hospital that says we do not pay more for an off-campus outpatient department visit," for instance, but they literally cannot figure out whether it is an off-campus facility or an on-campus facility.

Mrs. HARSHBARGER. I know. How can you, if you have got the same NPI?

Mr. ADLER. Yes, exactly. And it is hard to do that.

I mean, I think the Medicare policy is still where more of the money is, but I do think that is an important step.

Mrs. HARSHBARGER. And Mr. Connell, we had the CMS Administrator here earlier talking about how it was a Stark law violation if, like, for example, Tennessee Oncology mailed to their patients in rural areas if they were too sick to pick the drug up, or if they didn't have transportation because it was a couple of weeks ago, and they interpreted an FAQ to do that. What do you think about that?

Mr. CONNELL. I think there are so many ways in which things like Stark—and we talked about Medicaid best price—things that do have an important role also have unintended consequences that definitely need to be addressed.

Mrs. HARSHBARGER. I think it was pretty ludicrous, and even the HHS Secretary told us he would work with our committee to change that, and negate that particular FAQ.

And I guess, with that, I have asked the important questions, and so, Mr. Chairman, I yield back.

Mr. BUCSHON. The gentlelady yields back. I recognize Dr. Miller-Meeks, 5 minutes.

Mrs. MILLER-MEEKS. Thank you, Mr. Chair, and thank you to all of our witnesses that—who are here today, testifying.

Mr. Adler and—or Mr. Loren Adler, excuse me, thank you for testifying before the committee. As you know, we are considering multiple site-neutral payment bills, and I understand that you have written about this topic before.

And let me also state that I am a physician who has done both military medicine, private practice, academic medicine, and then been a hospital employee.

You stated specifically that site-neutral payments should ultimately be applied to a much broader set of clinical services, and then in the 2014 MedPAC recommendations at both off-campus and on-campus HOPDs as well as ambulatory surgery centers.

Furthermore, you stated that increased hospital ownership of physician practices can also drive up costs for private payers by increasing the prices they pay for physician services and the possible hospital services as well. Can you detail how not having site-neutral payments harms our healthcare system and how vertical integration leads to increased costs for patients?

Mr. ADLER. Sure, and thank you for the question, Congresswoman.

So, yes, I mean, I think fundamentally, not having site-neutral payments creates a very large financial incentive to go—for a doctor to go work for the hospital, or for the hospital to go out and buy up physician practices. And as you are saying, right, that has effects on commercial markets, as well, right?

We have more and more evidence now that this vertical consolidation, when the hospital goes and buys up a bunch of physician practices, has—tends to increase costs. And some of that is—it is straight arbitrage, right? This is taking advantage of a Medicare policy where—said earlier, it is basically—it is $140,000 more per year per physician that you get if you do the same set of services in a hospital outpatient department rather than an independent office. That is 2016 numbers, so probably multiply that by a bit to get to modern dollars.

Mrs. MILLER-MEEKS. It was one of the things that myself and others talked about during the debates on the Affordable Care Act, and we were very concerned about that amount of consolidation. And in 2010 there were 50 percent of physician practices that were independent, and now there is 20 percent. So thank you.

Mr. Connell, Congress has always tried to make healthcare more affordable for patients as well as more accessible. But health plans and PBMs continue to increase deductibles, use more coinsurance than copays, and are making patients pay based on the list price of medicine. With ever-increasing insurance costs, millions of hardworking Americans are having to choose between affording, you know, lifesaving medicines or putting food on the table for their families.

On top of that, PBMs have adopted schemes like accumulators and maximizers that force patients to pay even more out of pocket for their drugs, while PBMs, which lack transparency, pocket the money for their own profits.

As a State senator in 2019, I actually passed PBM transparency in the State of Iowa. I was not able to get the rebates through, but we are still working on getting that transparent data all this time later.

I also worked in a bipartisan manner to introduce HELP Copays Act with my colleagues Representative Carter, DeGette, Clarke, and others. This is a bipartisan bill that would prevent PBMs from enacting these schemes, and I am disappointed that it is not included in the hearing today, but I think that it will in the near future.

Do you agree that PBMs and insurers should let cost-sharing assistance count towards patients' out-of-pocket costs and deductibles?

Mr. CONNELL. Yes, it is a great question, and you are dealing with an enormous challenge that is really, really important for patients.

I mean, we see patients, you know, get caught in the middle of a fight between payers and manufacturers of drugs. And so you have, you know, high costs that are dealt with with high cost sharing, and then you have manufacturer assistance, which is certainly an imperfect solution but to a real problem. And then you have copay accumulators, copay maximizers, these solutions that have tried to again continue this fight that happens with, really, industries with patients caught in the middle.

And so we have heard situations where you have patients who have been caught, where their assistance goes away as a result of this back and forth between industries. And that is an enormous problem for patients, because if they are left holding the bag, if they are left with $5,000, $6,000 of out-of-pocket costs, that is prohibitive for a lot of people in this country. A lot of people cannot afford even a cancer medication if it is going to come with a cost so high.

And so we do have patients—we have data patients will walk away from the pharmacy counter. I think Mr. Carter mentioned this earlier in his experience, and many people in healthcare have the same experience of working with folks who have a treatment, the good—the bad news is you get a cancer diagnosis, the good news is maybe you have a treatment that they think will work. You go to the pharmacy counter. Right now we have data that shows that that cost is over $2,000. Then you have 40 percent of patients walking away from the counter without that therapy.

Mrs. MILLER-MEEKS. Thank you.

And Mr. Loren Adler, does the current system ever expose patients to a situation where they might pay more than the net price of the drug?

Mr. ADLER. Sure. So there are certainly situations where that happens.

Mrs. MILLER-MEEKS. Thank you. I yield back.

Mr. BUCSHON. The gentlelady yields back. I recognize Mr. Carter from Georgia for 5 minutes.

Mr. CARTER. Thank you, Mr. Chairman. I am going to jump right into it. You know where I am on this issue, so I don't think anybody needs to be prepped with it. Three companies controlling 80 percent of the market, the vertical integration that exists where the insurance company that owns the PBM that owns the pharmacy, and many times employees to provider, you are all aware of the FTC and the study they are doing, something I asked for 8 years ago. Finally, 71⁄2 years later, it happens. Well, I am glad it is happening.

You know, one of the most egregious practices that I ever witnessed in anything was the gag clause that I was able to get passed in legislation to do away with—where we and—as the pharmacists weren't able to tell—and the gentleman just mentioned— about sometimes the copay is more than the actual cost of the medication. But if we were to tell that, we would be kicked out of the network by the PBMs, another egregious practice of the PBMs. Ms. Bass, how—let me ask you, and Representative Miller-Meeks just mentioned the HELPs copay bill, helping ensure lower patient copays, and how the accumulators are being used and not being used, and the fact that the patient assistance, the cost-sharing assistance to patients aren't being credited to their copay or to their deductible.

Why is that? What is the justification that the PBMs use not to do that? Why am I having to introduce this legislation that would force them to do that?

Ms. BASS. [Inaudible.]

Mr. CARTER. I can't hear you, I am sorry. Ms. BASS. I keep forgetting to push the talk.

Mr. CARTER. That is OK.

Ms. BASS. I apologize. I appreciate the question.

Coupons are a marketing device by drug manufacturers who set high prices for their products. They are considered an illegal kick-back in Medicare, and they are used by manufacturers to get around formularies.

Formularies are designed by independent expert clinicians. And our company's view is that the plan sponsor has chosen a formulary, and that the cost-sharing——

Mr. CARTER. And what do you base that formulary on?

Ms. BASS. The formulary is based on clinical evidence, inde- pendent clinical——

Mr. CARTER. Clinical evidence, and not ever on price. Price never enters into it?

Ms. BASS. The P&T committees tell the PBM, "These are the drugs you have to have on the formulary," and when there are drugs that are——

Mr. CARTER. They tell them that specific drug, or that class of drug?

Ms. BASS. Sometimes specific drugs. And when there are drugs that compete with each other, they say, "These are drugs that you can go out into the market and get to compete on"—

Mr. CARTER. And you base it purely on therapeutics, and not on price at all?

Ms. BASS. The must-haves are purely on therapeutics, and the must-not-haves, because of safety issues.

Mr. CARTER. So you are saying, yes, you base it all on therapeutics, and never on price.

Ms. BASS. I am saying——

Mr. CARTER. Mr. Connell, let me ask you. What kind of financial burdens in the—financial burdens, let's start with that first—does it create for patients when they are not able to use these cost-sharing cards for their deductible or for their copay?

Mr. CONNELL. Well, benefit designs really foist a lot of expense onto patients, so deductibles are getting larger. A lot of times there is no separate deductible for pharmacy. And so, as a result, if you have a $5,000 deductible in your plan, then when you go to that pharmacy for the first time to fill that drug for the first time that year, you are going to pay $5,000——

Mr. CARTER. So we can really question whether or—excuse me, what the intent is of that cost sharing. It may be so that the patient can get the drug because they can't afford their copay, or they can't afford their deductible, and not that there is some marketing ploy, as was described.

You know, let me ask you this—and, you know, never ask a question you don't know the answer to. What about adherence? What does it do to adherence?

Mr. CONNELL. It has a tremendous impact on adherence. I think you mentioned the study that talks about $2,000, which is in Medicare Part D, and the same study also has information on commercial claims. And we see patients—over 30 percent, I think, and Part D, certainly over 40 percent—where, if they faced $2,000 for that first script—and you certainly face that with a high deductible— then if you face $2,000, you are—40 percent of those patients are walking away from the pharmacy counter without it.

Mr. CARTER. Absolutely. And I can tell you, again, from experience as a pharmacist, that they don't it—that it decreases adherence, because they don't come back. They don't get their medication because they can't afford it. And I have witnessed that firsthand. Finally, Mr. Connell, let me ask you, do you agree that these cost-sharing plans should go toward the deductible and toward the cost-sharing?

Mr. CONNELL. I think we should look at all the solutions. I am excited that you all have a solution out there that would try to, like, apply as much assistance as possible to patients who need it. You know, we have at LLS a copay assistance program. There's lots of nonprofits out there. Manufacturers——

Mr. CARTER. Absolutely, absolutely. And that is why we had to introduce this legislation. Again, as Representative Miller-Meeks indicated, it is not on the—not in the markup right now, but I hope it will be, and I think it will be.

And, Mr. Chairman, I thank you, and I yield back.

Mr. BUCSHON. The gentleman yields back.

Ms. Bass, with all due respect, we know for a fact that PBMs keep drugs off of formularies because of cost.

The gentleman has yielded, and I now yield to Ms. Schakowsky for 5 minutes.

Ms. SCHAKOWSKY. Thank you so much, and I really appreciate the opportunity to waive on to this wonderful committee.

So, you know, I have throughout my career been so concerned about the cost and accessibility of healthcare, and we have seen the cost continuing to get higher and higher. The, you know, higher premiums, higher out-of-pocket costs. And we know that right now over 40 percent of Americans face medical debt right now, and half of all Americans have difficulty affording their healthcare costs. Half of all Americans.

And meanwhile we have seen hospital mergers, and acquisitions are growing. And there is plenty of evidence that are saying that, when that happens, studies have shown that it can also raise the cost. So Mr. Adler, you said—where are you? I am sorry, just walked in. There you go.

Mr. Adler, in your testimony you do discuss the significant increase in consolidation and how it can lead to higher prices. I wonder—you have probably gone over that already, but I wonder if you could just say something about that, and if you think that there are any things that the Congress can actually do to address this issue.

Mr. ADLER. Sure. Thank you for the question, Congresswoman. So fundamentally, yes, you are 100 percent correct. The consolidation that we have seen, particularly of hospitals, two hospitals merging, one hospital acquiring another, has been very clear evidence at this point that that increases costs and tends to decrease quality, actually, right?

Those costs then flow through to—right—we keep talking about kind of people paying a lot of money in their deductible. Fundamentally, that is because we have high healthcare prices, drug prices, or hospital prices. That is really kind of the crux of why folks are paying a lot of money here. And now we have a lot of evidence, there is new evidence that has come out that very clearly ties hospital mergers to reductions in employee wages. That— right—when hospitals merge——

Ms. SCHAKOWSKY. Yes.

Mr. ADLER [continuing]. It means workers in the area get paid less.

Ms. SCHAKOWSKY. So the workers have paid a price as well, you are saying.

Mr. ADLER. Correct.

Ms. SCHAKOWSKY. Private equity has gotten involved. You know, we are talking about reimbursement to these companies, often from the Federal Government, because this is healthcare costs, and I wonder if you could talk a little bit about the role of private equity.

Mr. ADLER. Sure. So that is a—very happy to talk, this is where a lot of my research is nowadays.

So, yes, we have seen—I think private equity has come in, particularly in the last decade or so, and been a very big accelerator of these consolidation trends we have seen, and also sort of picking out some areas where hospitals sort of hadn't done the consolidation already. So they got into dermatology or ophthalmology, where there wasn't a lot of hospital ownership, and really sort of drove things there such that you see, you know, 10 percent of docs and a lot of specialties work for a private equity company or—in research we have coming out soon—that more than 20 percent of emergency physicians work for a private equity company right now.

Ms. SCHAKOWSKY. Oh, no. I have been fighting for lower healthcare costs and Medicare for All kinds of policies, and it just seems like now the Big Money people are getting in.

Mr. Cavanaugh—let me see my time—you have also discussed in your testimony how consolidation is leading to higher costs, and I wonder if you could discuss ways that you think—if you think— that Congress can address this.

Mr. CAVANAUGH. Certainly. Thank you for the question. Yes, I think I would summarize it by saying consolidation is sort of the antithesis of value-based care.

So we are all trying to do better care at lower cost. Medicare has programs through the Medicare shared savings program, and there has been success. But consolidation allows providers to avoid the need to move to value-based care, because it allows them to bargain more aggressively with insurers and get higher prices and not engage in the activities that would lead to better care at lower cost. So I think that is the real problem. Some of the bills get at some of the things that are feeding it, but ultimately that is the problem we need to address.

Ms. SCHAKOWSKY. So let me just end with this. You know, I really support efforts to strengthen transparency so that we are even requiring that we get reports on ownership, we know who is owning, including private equity. I am not so sure that everyone is really aware of who is making the decisions, who is owning this maybe on the sidelines. And I really think that we ought to have transparency requirements. What do you think about that? Either one of you, anyone.

Mr. ADLER. I will just say that it is very difficult, as a researcher who has tried to do this, to nail down what sort of entities own physician practices, for instance. There really is not good data out there. And one of the bills before the subcommittee today would require entity-level reporting. So physician group and hospital-level reporting on the parent company name, the address, and the ownership structure of those physician practices, and make that data publicly available. I think that would do a huge service to being able to understand the effects of private equity and other corporate forms of ownership.

Ms. SCHAKOWSKY. I really agree, Mr. Adler, and hopefully we can do something about it.

Thank you, I yield back.

Mr. BUCSHON. The gentlelady——

Ms. SCHAKOWSKY. Thank you so much.

Mr. BUCSHON [continuing]. Yields back. I now recognize Ms. Matsui for 5 minutes.

Ms. MATSUI. Thank you, Mr. Chairman and Ranking Member Eshoo, for holding this hearing and allowing us to waive on to— allowing me to waive on to join this important conversation. I would like to discuss the 340B drug pricing program, which is the subject of one of the transparency bills before the committee today.

For years, I have worked to strengthen this program on a bipartisan basis. This includes transparency and accountability. While some of these bills are ostensibly about transparency, in reality I think they would disincentivize participation in 340B. I know HRSA has requested the authority to audit how entities use their savings, and I want to support their work. But this bill adds a number of burdensome reporting requirements that are unrelated to how 340B operates.

Ms. Thompson, help us to understand why the reporting requirements in this bill do not actually reflect the true value of the true—of the 340B program.

Ms. THOMPSON. Thank you for this question. As you know, hospitals already report quite a bit on the 340B program to CMS and its cost report to the IRS in Schedule H and as well to HRSA, as you mentioned.

The provisions in the bill are metrics, and I think that those metrics, looking at payer mix and looking at every single clinic that receives 340B payment, I think that the metrics will mask all the good work that is being done from the program. It will be very difficult to identify, for example, that a hospital is using the savings to purchase or—sorry, I should say to hire a couple of behavioral health specialists to work in an opioid clinic, or to provide the amount of free or discounted drugs to needy patients or the mobile mammography unit that is out in the community finding breast cancer. I am not sure that those metrics will really be able to show the good works that are being done.

Ms. MATSUI. Right, thank you. You know, I support measures to strengthen program integrity, as we all should.

In addition, I know there is already a movement towards transparency around 340B savings. For example, in your testimony you mentioned the good stewardship principles. Some hospitals in my district have adopted these to help them share how 340B benefits their communities. Ms. Thompson, is it possible to craft reporting requirements that demonstrate the true value of 340B?

Ms. THOMPSON. Well, we would be very interested in working with you on that. I think that the good steward principles have been a good step forward, and we have been working with our hospitals to encourage them to share with their communities what they are doing with those savings as well. So we would be—welcome the opportunity to work with you here.

Ms. MATSUI. OK. So what kind of activities could we support that would not be captured by the requirements in this bill?

Ms. THOMPSON. I think that we would really need to reflect on additional reporting requirements, because there are so many already upon hospitals. And I really do feel that HRSA has the authority to make sure that the program is being implemented as intended and that it audits hospitals to make sure that they are conforming to the program as written. So I am just not sure additional reporting requirements are needed at this time, but happy to speak with you and others on the committee to discuss further.

Ms. MATSUI. Thank you. At the last hearing on transparency, we heard from a witness from Pullman Regional Hospital. He explained how burdensome it already is for entities to participate in 340B. From certifying eligibility every year to preparing for audits to simply administering the program, it is a lot of work. And I am really concerned that some of these new requirements proposed would be near impossible for some entities to comply with.

Ms. Thompson, would these requirements even be workable for hospitals, especially rural hospitals and others with limited resources?

Ms. THOMPSON. I think that you are absolutely right. We have heard from many of our small, rural hospitals that are so grateful for this program, because out of everywhere, I think, the 340B savings in rural communities has really provided a lifeline for these hospitals.

They have limited staff. You know, in many of the critical access hospitals, the CEO is also the COO——

Ms. MATSUI. Right.

Ms. THOMPSON [continuing]. And the CFO and the janitor who changes the light bulb. So any additional requirements that's necessary, you hope that they are not so high a barrier that it decreases the ability of providers to access the funds that might be available. And for 340B, we all have to say that these are no additional costs to taxpayers or the Government. It is really savings on drugs.

Ms. MATSUI. Thank you very much, Ms. Thompson, and I look forward to working with you. Thank you.

I yield back.

Mr. BUCSHON. The gentlelady yields back.

Mr. Pence is going to—Mr. Pence, are you ready for your 5 minutes?

I now recognize the gentleman from Indiana, Mr. Pence, for his 5 minutes.

Mr. PENCE. Thank you, Chairs McMorris Rodgers, Guthrie, and Ranking Member Pallone and Eshoo for holding this hearing, and thank you to the witnesses today.

Hoosiers and all Americans are facing higher medical costs and fewer options for care, particularly in rural communities. Complex medical fee structures, surprise billing, and confusing coverage plans have further eroded patient trust in our healthcare system. Improving healthcare price transparency, however, could inject needed competition for healthcare facilities and, ultimately, lower costs for patients. This is especially needed in the Hoosier State, which consistently ranks among having some of the highest hospital prices in the country.

Across southern Indiana, rural facilities are closing at an alarming rate, going bankrupt, lowering access to care for vulnerable communities. Lack of competition has left patients with fewer alternatives to access care, particularly in rural communities across Indiana's 6th District, often an hour or more drive.

These issues are exasperated by unsustainable workforce shortages and skyrocketing labor costs. There have been recent efforts to improve transparency, such as the Pence-Trump administration's 2019 HHS rule requiring hospitals to disclose standard charges, as well as the transparency and coverage requirements for health insurers. However, it is clear there is still more that needs to be done so that Hoosiers and all Americans can make the best medical decisions for themselves and their families.

Mr. Adler, several years ago Congress took steps to harmonize Medicare payments between various sites of care for the same services provided through a site-neutral payment model for certain services. However, many outpatient facilities were grandfathered in by the legislation, making the services covered under the new policy a relatively small portion of outpatient services. If this policy were to be expanded, do you think there are ways to ensure rural hospitals continue to receive sufficient support and provide healthcare access to rural patients?

Mr. ADLER. Thank you, Congressman. So, yes, I think, as you say, right, this was a pretty small-step policy that was passed in 2015 that tried to move in this direction. Basically, it grandfathered anyone who was—even had their outpatient department under construction at the time back then. You know, the data is basically less than 1 percent of outpatient services were covered by that bill.

I think moving towards getting rid of that grandfathering entirely would, right, save money for taxpayers and patients, reduce incentives to consolidate. And I don't—do not see that there would be—right? We are talking about pretty low-complexity services here. To think that this would sort of have issues on access seems unlikely. And if you do, if you are concerned about that, this isn't the policy to sort of toy with that, right?

I think Mr. Cavanaugh was saying this earlier, but if that is the issue, one, right, there is another bill that is, for instance, getting rid of the—or delaying the DSH cuts. Or you could increase the physician fee schedule or, you know, other hospital payment rates, right? Even if you did this without saving a ton of money, you would at least be still reducing the incentive for hospitals to consolidate and buy up all the physician practices in an area.

I just think there are other policies that, if you want to kind of deal with that issue, that are better uses.

Mr. PENCE. All right, then, kind of from there, do you think it makes more sense to further explore transparent and accountable methods of directly supporting rural and medically underserved hospitals than an opaque and complicated network of cross-subsidies?

Mr. ADLER. Sure, right? I fundamentally think that if the goal is to support rural hospitals, I think directly doing that is the best way. Right now we have all of these policies that kind of do that, kind of don't do it perfectly. I think sort of directly funding that is a much better sense than having, oh, you get to—you know, when, you know, the hospital buys up your physician practice, all of a sudden you owe three times more money on the service you were getting a week ago.

Mr. PENCE. Yes, I—you know, just kind of as we are sitting here and I am wrapping up, you know, I have a number of rural hospitals. I will tell you that two of them are probably in the red right now in a big way. And one of them went bankrupt about 3 years ago, and if it hadn't been some of the bailout or relief that was provided during COVID, they—some of them would be closed today.

So I think we really have to figure out ways to kind of separate rural from some of the other conversations we have, and with that I yield back.

Mr. BUCSHON. The gentleman yields back. I now recognize Mr. Allen from Georgia for 5 minutes.

Mr. ALLEN. Well, thank you, Mr. Chairman, and thank you for allowing me to waive on to this important hearing.

Well, you know, we are going to repeat it again. What we are here today is to address costs by increasing transparency and com- petition rather than price setting that we have seen happen with some drug prices, or with this Medicare for All business. But—and that is where I come from, the business world, very competitive, very transparent. Our clients, our contracts provided for audits and things like that so that, you know, we hid nothing from them. And that is kind of the way the free market works out there. And what we have here is a little different.

Mr. Adler, a bill that I cointroduced that we are discussing today, the Drug Price Transparency and Medicaid Act, would stop the harmful spread pricing practices some pharmacy benefit managers use, where they underreimburse pharmacies while overbilling State Medicaid programs.

Last Congress the Congressional Budget Office estimated a version of this legislation would save approximately 1 billion in Federal dollars. Can you speak to the implications that the practice of spread pricing has on businesses, and the benefit that the healthcare markets would see if we were to implement a ban on spread pricing across the board?

Mr. ADLER. Sure, thank you for the question, Congressman.

I think it is—honestly, I think it is hard to perfectly game things out, in part because these are private actors who will just come— try to come up with other ways to do very similar things. And you have already seen a lot of the big PBMs already kind of move away from spread pricing.

I think an important thing just to keep in mind here is that, right, employers also often want maybe not spread pricing, but they are—right? — cost-sharing is part of the thing, right? There are two sides of this negotiation here. So often the employer sort of wants part of the benefit design as well here.

I do think transparency is useful here to know exactly what money is flowing where, and I think that can be useful. But I think that is sort of where more of the sort of benefits are.

Mr. ALLEN. Ms. Schuman, I have long been concerned with the lack of transparency in the healthcare industry, particularly as it relates to healthcare middlemen like pharmacy benefit managers. Can you talk more about PBM transparency and how we can restructure the current rebate system to be more easily understood by employers, plan participants, and beneficiaries?

Ms. SCHUMAN. Well, let me just thank you very much for that question, and let me just start off by saying that employers, even very large employers, are frustrated by the complexity and opaqueness of the rebate structure, and they need to have the information. They don't know what they don't know. I have repeatedly said that. But that is the issue. And that is why it is so critical for them to be able to have reporting from the PBMs about the revenue streams to be able to find out that, really, they are paying for value, that their patients, that their workers are paying for value.

And I think it is so important to enshrine this in legislation because, number one, employers need the certainty of knowing that this is there. They also need to know that there's the clear definitions in statute about what needs to be reported. And I think, most importantly, the transparency needs to be robust enough that it captures the PBM business model not just today but how it is going to evolve tomorrow as well.

Mr. ALLEN. Well, I served on the Healthy Future Task Force, and I couldn't have any of those experts that we talked to—could tell me how to peel the onion back and find out where all the money is going.

I recently took a trip to Israel, and pretty much I talked to folks about their healthcare, and they were pretty happy with it. Currently, Israel spends less than 8 percent of their GDP on healthcare. We are close to 20 percent. Obviously, we are in a worldwide competition here. We need to be looking where—at where our healthcare dollars are being spent.

Many attribute our increased healthcare prices in part to consolidating by merging hospitals and to—consolidation by merging hospitals and pharmaceutical groups. Health Subcommittee, can you speak to how the hospital consolidation and acquisition of physician practices impacts employers, and why this is such an important issue to them?

Ms. SCHUMAN. Yes. Well, thank you. Thank you so much.

And it impacts employers because it impacts employees. It impacts costs. I mean, ultimately, that is what we are here today, is figuring out what those root causes of higher healthcare costs are and to address them. And consolidation, overwhelmingly, is fueling higher healthcare costs.

So if we are going to really tackle lower healthcare costs at their core, which is what employers want to be able to deliver—high value, affordable care for their employees—they care about consolidation, they care about Medicare policies that are fueling consolidation.

Mr. ALLEN. Exactly, and the Federal Government. Yes. Thank you.

Mr. Chairman, I am out of time, and I yield back.

Mr. GUTHRIE [presiding]. Thank you. The gentleman yields back. Seeing no other Members present for questions, the first thing I will do is ask unanimous consent to insert in the record the documents included on the staff hearing documents list.

Without objection, so ordered.

[The information appears at the conclusion of the hearing.]

Mr. GUTHRIE. You want to comment here? You are sitting here, do you have a final comment? You would just like a couple of minutes?

Ms. ESHOO. I would just like to thank you, Mr. Chairman, all the members of the committee, most especially all of the witnesses. Whether I agree or disagree with you, it is very important that you are here. I think that, you know, to a person—well, maybe not to a—well, just—I am getting myself in a little trouble here.

[Laughter.]

Ms. ESHOO. You did a great job, and I think that you answered— with your answers you were highly instructive to all of the members of the committee. So I truly thank you.

You heard Members complimenting the panel, and we usually do in a very nice way, but it was effusive today on both sides. So know that you are helping to move the needle, and it is so important for the people of our country. They are so hungry and so in need of these changes.

And I often say to my constituents most people don't know who I am, they don't know what I am doing, but the words that we write walk into people's lives. So, Congress willing, we will write very good words to walk into people's lives. So thank you.

Thank you, Mr. Chairman.

Mr. GUTHRIE. Thank you. And I just want to sum up as well. Thanks for everybody being here. It has been a long day, very informative.

We are going to be working together, because we want to deliver the world-class care that you all deliver at the price that—Ms. Schuman, representing the employer-based plans and the individuals who buy their own coverage that have the price that we can afford to pay, and then people know what the prices are so they can make decisions for themselves. So we really appreciate you being here.

I will remind Members that they have 10 business days to submit questions for the record, and I ask the witnesses to respond to the questions promptly. Members should submit their questions by the close of business on May the 10th, so you should have questions before May the 10th, and I ask for your prompt consideration and responses.

And without objection—I see no objection—the committee is— subcommittee is adjourned.

[Whereupon, at 3:27 p.m., the subcommittee was adjourned.] [Material submitted for inclusion in the record follows:]

Questions for the Record for CMS Administrator Chiquita Brooks-LaSure

House Energy & Commerce Committee, Subcommittee on Health Hearing on April 26, 2023
"Lowering Unaffordable Costs: Legislative Solutions to Increase Transparency and Competition in Health Care"

The Honorable Cathy McMorris Rodgers

The Inflation Reduction Act included a new program that requires every Medicare Part D plan to allow enrollees to opt in to a maximum monthly cap on their Part D out-of-pocket costs.

1) What steps is CMS taking to ensure Medicare enrollees are aware of this benefit ahead of 2025 open enrollment?
2) What steps is CMS taking to ensure enrollees who do not enroll in this "smoothing option" prior to January 1, 2025 are able to enroll throughout the year, including at the point of sale of their prescription?

Answer 1-2

Thanks to the Inflation Reduction Act of 2022 (P.L. 117-169), beginning in 2025, Part D enrollees will be able to choose to pay their out-of-pocket Part D costs in monthly amounts spread over the plan year. CMS will engage in education, communications, and outreach to inform people with Medicare about this important new option to spread out-of-pocket Part D costs over the plan year. CMS is committed to engaging with the public throughout the policymaking and implementation processes for the Inflation Reduction Act of 2022. CMS welcomes feedback on the best ways to effectively educate people with Medicare about the new option.

Medicaid Eligibility Rule and Access Rule

In the Office of the Actuary's analysis of the proposed rule titled "Streamlining the Medicaid, Children's Health Insurance Program, and Basic Health Program Application, Eligibility Determination, Enrollment, and Renewal Processes", your agency said that the rule could cost as much as $62 billion in the first five years. Other analysis says that this cost could be as much as $200 billion over 10 years for the federal government.

This increase in federal spending could trigger tens of billions in additional state spending over the next decade as well, due to the state match in Medicaid.

We hear every day about the implications of state budget crunches on Medicaid reimbursement rates, and I can't possibly imagine that putting additional stress on states like this will meaningfully improve access to care.

In regards to this rule,

1) What does CMS estimate will be the increased costs for states over the 10 year window from this rule? Does CMS anticipate changes in reimbursement rates, as a consequence of this rule?
2) What, if anything, in the proposed rule or through other efforts by the Administration would help alleviate the costs being imposed on States?

Similarly, your agency just released two sets of regulations in Medicaid regarding access and Medicaid managed care organizations.

1) What does CMS estimate will be the increased costs for states over the 10 year window from this rule? Does CMS anticipate changes in reimbursement rates, as a consequence of this rule?
2) What, if anything, in the proposed rules or through other efforts by the Administration would help alleviate the costs being imposed on States?

Across the eligibility rule, the access rule, the MCO rule, and the current Medicaid unwinding underway, States are being overwhelmed by unprecedented burdens.

1) When added together, what is the expected, cumulative burden analysis for all of these processes occurring in tandem?

Answers 3-7

Medicaid is an important lifeline for many American families. The partnership between states and the federal government is central to Medicaid, and this Administration is committed to working with states to strengthen this vital program. The Medicaid statute gives states significant flexibility to tailor their programs to meet the unique needs of their residents, within broad national guidelines established by Federal statutes, regulations, and policies. CMS works closely with states to ensure they have access to the tools and resources they need to successfully meet federal requirements.

On September 7, 2022, CMS published a proposed rule[121] to simplify the processes for eligible individuals to enroll and retain eligibility in Medicaid, the Children's Health Insurance Program (CHIP), and the Basic Health Program. In this rulemaking, we seek to streamline the Medicaid and CHIP eligibility and enrollment processes, reducing administrative burden on States and enrollees, and increasing enrollment and retention of eligible individuals. The aggregate economic impact of this proposed rule is estimated to be $61.93 billion (in real FY 2023 dollars) over 5 years. This represents additional health care spending made by the Medicaid and CHIP programs on behalf of Medicaid and CHIP beneficiaries, with $41.41 billion paid by the Federal government and $20.52 billion paid by the States.

CMS is examining ways to help states build stronger programs to better meet the needs of the Medicaid and CHIP populations by improving access to and quality of care provided to Medicaid and CHIP managed care enrollees. CMS is also examining ways to improve access

---

121 "Streamlining the Medicaid, Children's Health Insurance Program, and Basic Health Program Application, Eligibility Determination, Enrollment, and Renewal Processes" (CMS-2421-P).

to care, quality and health outcomes, and better address health equity issues in the Medicaid program across fee-for-service (FFS), managed care delivery systems, and in home and community-based services (HCBS) programs. CMS looks forward to working with stakeholders on these issues, and will take their feedback, including any on administrative burden and costs, into account when finalizing any policy changes. In developing any policy changes, CMS will also seek to mitigate operational concerns by limiting the number of proposals to the most impactful, limiting the scope of some proposals, providing reasonably long timeframes for implementation, and proposing to phase-in certain requirements. We will continue to work with states to ensure that they are able to move these important protections forward without negatively impacting their operations.

The Honorable Gus Bilirakis

1) Administrator Brooks-LaSure, I've previously asked Secretary Becerra about CMS's role in considering coverage determinations for FDA-approved drugs and CMS' chilling effects on innovation. Unfortunately your agency has stood in the way of potential treatments for early-stage Alzheimer's when it doubled-down on its coverage determination restricting access to the drug lecanemab, which has been shown to reduce cognitive decline by up to 27% in patients. Despite being approved for Alzheimer's, CMS has determined that it's not "reasonable and necessary" for seniors. The VA has determined that it is appropriate for Veterans, and yet somehow you've decided it's not appropriate for Medicare patients. Why is that?
2) We've heard repeatedly from your agency that should the FDA approve Leqembi under the traditional approval pathway this summer, your agency "will provide broader coverage using the framework we announced last year, under CED on the same day." The CED framework is still severely restrictive and will make it so many of my constituents in rural and underserved areas won't be able to gain access to the treatment, as well as the 73 percent of individuals living with Alzheimer's disease age 65 and older and, as such, eligible for Medicare. Will you commit that your agency will reconsider the severe restrictions if this new treatment is approved under traditional approval?
3) Leaders in my state of Florida have asked you to reconsider this decision and consider the effects it's having on patients. Do you plan to respond to their concerns?
4) If lecanemab receives traditional full FDA approval in the summer, will CMS still mandate Medicare beneficiaries participate in a registry in order to receive access to the drug?

Answer 8-11

The FDA and CMS have different authorities and requirements when it comes to the approval and coverage of drugs (and devices). The FDA determines whether to approve a new medical product based on a careful evaluation of the available data and a determination that the medical product is safe and effective for its intended use but does not consider the specific needs of the Medicare patient populations. Under Medicare statute in section 1862(a)(1)(A) of the Social Security Act, Medicare coverage is determined whether items and services are reasonable and necessary to diagnose or treat an illness or injury or to improve the functioning of a malformed body member for an individual with Medicare. CMS looks to the evidence supporting FDA decision-making for evidence generalizable to the Medicare population, data on improvement in health outcomes, and durability of those outcomes. If there are no data on those elements, it is difficult for CMS to make an evidence-based decision whether a product is reasonable and necessary for the Medicare population.

In determining the generalizability of the results of the body of evidence to the Medicare population, CMS considers, at minimum, the age, race and gender of the study participants. When making NCDs, CMS conducts its own independent review to determine whether an item or service is reasonable and necessary for use in the Medicare population and should be covered nationally by Medicare. To date, there has not been an antiamyloid monoclonal antibody that has been approved by the FDA for the treatment of Alzheimer's disease based upon evidence of efficacy from a direct measure of clinical benefit. CMS reviews all relevant evidence and weighs the potential benefits and unknowns, and generally evaluates whether the drug is clinically beneficial to Medicare patients.

The final national coverage decision on FDA approved monoclonal antibodies (mAbs) directed against amyloid for the treatment of Alzheimer's disease allows for flexibility in a less rigorous study design for mAbs that receive FDA approval for the treatment of Alzheimer's disease based on a direct measure of clinical benefit. In addition, based on public comment, we did not finalize the patient exclusion criteria in order to allow appropriate access to patient subpopulations that may need treatment based on ongoing research. The final decision also does not restrict the setting of approved clinical trials to ensure that anti-amyloid mAbs that receive FDA approval based upon evidence of efficacy from a direct measure of clinical benefit may be given to a broader patient population.

1) Do you support the use of value-based payment arrangements in Medicaid which can help ensure a robust innovation pipeline for cell and gene therapy companies?

Answer 12

The CMS Innovation Center recently announced a new model[122] to test whether a CMS-led approach for administering outcomes-based agreements (OBAs) for cell and gene therapies (CGTs) can improve beneficiary access and outcomes and reduce health care costs. The model would establish a partnership among CMS, manufacturers and state Medicaid agencies, and would test a new approach for administering OBAs to help Medicaid beneficiaries gain access to potentially life changing, high-cost specialty drugs. In lieu of state Medicaid agencies pursuing manufacturer agreements individually, state Medicaid agencies would have the option of assigning CMS to structure and coordinate multi-state OBAs with participating manufacturers. CMS would also take on the responsibility of implementing, monitoring, reconciling, and evaluating the financial and clinical outcomes outlined in the OBAs. This Model would target CGTs for illnesses like sickle cell disease and cancer.

A national approach for supporting OBAs related to CGTs could offer: better access to treatment for beneficiaries with rare and severe diseases, stability to payers, and payment certainty to providers who are hesitant to acquire and deliver these high-cost treatments. The use of OBAs could enable manufacturers to be compensated based on the clinical impact of

[122] A Report in Response to the Executive Order on Lowering Prescription Drug Costs for Americans: https://innovation.cms.gov/data-and-reports/2023/eo-rx-drug-cost-response-report.

CGTs, therefore increasing accountability of the manufacturer to deliver treatments that improve quality at a more sustainable cost.

1) Given the Inflation Reduction Act has had a chilling effect on the industry, what is your agency doing to promote innovation in the marketplace?

Answer 13

The law requires that at least seven years, for drugs, or 11 years, for biologicals, must have elapsed between the selected drug publication date and the FDA approval or licensure, as applicable. We are implementing the Negotiation Program in accordance with the law.

CMS has been regularly engaging with members of the public to get their feedback so that we are implementing the Negotiation Program in a thoughtful way that balances the goal of improving drug affordability and accessibility for people with Medicare while supporting innovation. We plan to get public input throughout the implementation of the Negotiation Program to make sure that we know what is occurring in the market.

The Honorable Larry Bucshon

1) The paper "Hospital Competition and Restrictions on Physician-Owned Hospitals" discusses the explosive growth in hospital and physician practice mergers over the past few years: "There were 1,412 hospital mergers from 1998 to 2015, with 561 occurring from 2010 to 2015. In 2010, 28 percent of primary physicians were employed by hospitals. By 2016, that number had risen to 44 percent. Large physician practices have been growing larger while smaller practices have been growing smaller. According to recent data, over 90% of metropolitan statistical areas have been estimated as consolidated for hospitals, 65% for specialist physicians, and 39% for primary care physicians." o Source: *https://physiciansled.com/health-policy-thought-leaders-call-for-immediate-reversal-of-physician-led-hospital-ban-house-and-senate-bills-introduced/.*

Do you believe letting physician-owned facilities grow as we did before 2010 would or would not increase healthcare competition?

Answer 14

In the Affordable Care Act, Congress limited the ability of physician-owned hospitals to expand. Section 6001 of the Affordable Care Act of 2010 amended section 1877 of the Social Security Act to impose additional requirements for physician-owned hospitals to qualify for the whole hospital and rural provider exceptions. A physician-owned hospital is now generally prohibited from expanding facility capacity. CMS, in implementing this provision, established in regulations (42 CFR §411.362(c)) a process for physician-owned hospitals to apply for an exception from the expansion prohibition. For example, a physician-owned hospital that qualifies as an applicable hospital or high Medicaid facility may request an exception to the prohibition from the Secretary. CMS is examining ways to improve that process. CMS welcomes feedback and can work with your staff to provide technical assistance on legislation you draft related to this issue.

1) You testified that CMS considers accelerated approval to be in a "different category." However, when Congress codified the accelerated approval pathway in 2012 it affirmed FDA's previous conclusion that accelerated approval did not create a different standard for drug approval, stating that accelerated approval "may result in fewer, smaller, or shorter clinical trials…without compromising or altering the high standards of the FDA for the approval of drugs." (See 158 Cong. Rec. H3825-01, H3848 (2012)).

Please explain why CMS is putting accelerated approval drugs into a "different category," and what precisely that means.

Answer 15

The FDA performs a vital and an important role. CMS recognizes the important and related – but different – roles of the respective agencies. The FDA determines whether to approve a new medical product based on a careful evaluation of the available data and a determination that the medical product is safe and effective for its intended use but does not consider the specific needs of the Medicare patient populations. Under Medicare statute in section 1862(a)(1)(A) of the Social Security Act, Medicare coverage is determined whether items and services are reasonable and necessary to diagnose or treat an illness or injury or to improve the functioning of a malformed body member for an individual with Medicare. CMS looks to the evidence supporting FDA decision-making for evidence generalizable to the Medicare population, data on improvement in health outcomes, and durability of those outcomes. If there are no data on those elements, it is difficult for CMS to make an evidence-based decision whether a product is reasonable and necessary for the Medicare population. In determining the generalizability of the results of the body of evidence to the Medicare population, we consider, at minimum, the age, race and gender of the study participants.

CMS conducts its own independent review to determine whether an item or service is reasonable and necessary for use in the Medicare population and should be covered nationally by Medicare. To date, there has not been an antiamyloid mAb that has been approved by the FDA for the treatment of Alzheimer's disease based upon evidence of efficacy from a direct measure of clinical benefit.

The Honorable Ann Kuster

Northeast Passage

1) The University of New Hampshire is home to Northeast Passage, a national leader in recreational therapy and adaptive sports. Recreational therapy promotes the physical, cognitive, emotional and social functioning of individuals with disabilities to help them achieve independence, productivity, and wellbeing. However, CMS does not currently include coverage of recreational therapy services under Medicare or Medicaid, limiting the breadth of services available to beneficiaries. Would CMS consider expanding Medicare and Medicaid coverage to include recreation therapy services, and if not, what barriers are preventing CMS from doing so?

Answer 16

Medicare coverage is limited to items and services that are reasonable and necessary for the diagnosis or treatment of an illness or injury and within the scope of a Medicare benefit category as defined in the Medicare statute. For example, in an inpatient rehabilitation facility, the statute requires Medicare to cover skilled nursing care or other skilled rehabilitation services.

Recreation therapy services may be provided in an inpatient rehabilitation facility if the medical necessity is well documented by the rehabilitation physician in the medical record and is ordered by the rehabilitation physician as part of the overall plan of care for the patient. Another example is in inpatient psychiatric settings, where recreational therapy services may be covered so long as the services are designated as active treatment and the therapeutic activities are expected to result in improvement in the patient's condition.

With respect to Medicaid, states establish and administer their own Medicaid programs and determine the type, amount, duration, and scope of services within broad federal guidelines. Federal law requires states to provide certain mandatory benefits and allows states the choice of covering other optional benefits. Mandatory benefits include inpatient and outpatient hospital services, physician services, laboratory and x-ray services, home health services, and the Early and Periodic Screening, Diagnostic, and Treatment benefit for children under age 21, among others. Optional benefits include services including prescription drugs, case management, physical therapy, and occupational therapy. States also have the option to provide home and community-based services (HCBS) to allow older adults and people with disabilities to live in the community, instead of institutions. HCBS are optional benefits and may include habilitation services and other services requested by the State and approved by CMS as cost effective and necessary to avoid institutionalization, so long as they are not purely for recreational purposes.

Over the Counter Narcan

According to the CDC – between November 2021 and November 2022 - over 103,000 Americans died as a result of overdose deaths. While I applaud the Administration's efforts on combatting the opioid crisis, more must be done. I was heartened to see the first approval by FDA of over-the-counter naloxone earlier this year. I do have concerns though about how patients – particularly within CMS's purview - will understand the changes.

1) In reference to Medicaid, will CMS issue guidance to ensure practitioners and patients understand that they need an Rx in order for Medicaid patients to access OTC naloxone (in states where there is OTC coverage)?
2) For Medicare beneficiaries, will CMS be taking any steps to address the access gap that will be created with this shift?

Answer 17-18

Over the past year, the Biden-Harris Administration took unprecedented steps to expand access to naloxone and other harm reduction interventions, and CMS is working within the confines of the law to ensure individuals enrolled in our programs have affordable access to this life-saving medication.

In Medicaid, state Medicaid programs are not required to cover OTC drugs and federal financial participation (FFP) is not available for OTC drugs dispensed without a prescription. However, states may cover and receive FFP for OTC drugs when prescribed by professionals authorized to do so under state laws and regulations. Currently all states cover some form of prescription naloxone, and many states have implemented strategies to facilitate easier access, such as allowing pharmacists to dispense drugs prescribed independently, or under collaborative practice agreements, standing orders, or other predetermined protocols. CMS has been keeping states informed about naloxone's OTC status and will continue to provide technical assistance to aid states in updating their State Plan Amendments, if they choose to cover OTC naloxone when dispensed with a prescription.

By law, Medicare Fee-for-Service does not generally cover OTC services and tests.

With respect to Part D, by statute, OTC products do not meet the definition of a covered Part D drug because they are not dispensed only upon a prescription. Part D sponsors do have the flexibility, however, to provide OTCs as part of their administrative cost structure with no cost sharing at point of sale (POS) either as (1) part of general drug utilization management or (2) as part of a step therapy protocol. CMS has taken steps to ensure that Part D sponsors are aware of this flexibility.

In addition, CMS promotes improved access to prescription naloxone by requiring that the antidote appear on all Medicare Part D formularies, and by encouraging sponsors to include at least one naloxone product on a generic or Select Care Tier. Select Care Tiers provide for $0 or low cost-sharing for those plans that utilize such a tier model. CMS encourages Part D plan sponsors to ensure coverage for beneficiaries at risk and recommends targeted education of prescribers and enrollees on co-prescribing of naloxone to prevent accidental overdoses and to sensitively address the needs of beneficiaries with OUD.

Rural Hospitals/Rural Health Care

192 rural hospitals throughout the US have closed their doors since 2005. Moreover, a recent Center for Healthcare Quality and Payment Reform report found that more than 200 hospitals are at immediate risk of closing in 2023 alone because of financial losses and lack of reserves to sustain their operations. Many of these hospitals are located in isolated rural communities across the US, forcing residents to travel a long distance for emergency services or inpatient care. Rural hospitals in many small communities are often the only place where residents can access primary care services.

1) How is CMS ensuring access to care in rural communities given the rise in hospital closures?
2) How is CMS ensuring continuity of care in rural communities? Supporting access to emergency medical services, specialist, and primary care?

Answer 19-20

CMS is committed to ensuring access to care in rural communities and is implementing a range of policies to help secure that access. One such program is Rural Emergency Hospitals (REHs), a new provider type established by the Consolidated Appropriations Act, 2021 to address the growing concern over closures of rural hospitals. On November 23, 2022, CMS published a final rule (CMS-1772-FC) establishing REHs as a new Medicare provider effective January 1, 2023.[123] Eligible hospitals include Critical Access Hospitals (CAHs) and rural hospital (or one treated as such under section 1886(d)(8)(E) of the Social Security Act) with less than 50 beds, and that do not provide acute care inpatient services with the exception of skilled nursing facility services furnished in a distinct part unit. In our final rule, CMS estimated that 68 eligible hospitals could convert to an REH. Conversion to an REH allows rural hospitals to continue providing emergency services, observation care, and additional medical and health outpatient services, if elected by the REH, that do not exceed an annual per patient average of 24 hours. In addition to a monthly facility payment, REHs will receive an additional 5% payment for each covered outpatient department service of the Hospital Outpatient Prospective Payment System rate. The CY 2023 additional monthly REH facility payment is $272,866. For 2024 and each year after, this additional payment will increase by the hospital market basket percentage increase. The REH designation provides an opportunity for rural hospitals to avert potential closure, promote health equity, and continue to provide essential services for the communities they serve. Eligible hospitals can submit their applications to convert to an REH to their Medicare Administrative Contractor, at which point they will be screened for eligibility and to ensure compliance with all Medicare enrollment requirements.

The Honorable Doris Matsui

1) In 2018, I secured a bipartisan provision in the SUPPORT Act that encouraged the Center for Medicaid and Medicare Innovation (CMMI) to initiate a behavioral health information technology demonstration. However, CMMI has still not taken action to initiate this demonstration, while MACPAC reports that fewer than half of psychiatric hospitals operate health information technology systems and roughly 30 percent of Community Mental Health Centers have an IT system capable of exchanging patient information. Can you provide an update on the status of the CMMI behavioral health IT demonstration included in the SUPPORT Act?
2) Do you think that additional financial assistance would increase providers' uptake of interoperable health information systems that comply with ONC certification standards? In turn, how would this impact integrated care delivery and patient outcomes?

Answer 21-22

CMS is committed to reducing administrative burden and advancing interoperability and national standards, and its Office of Burden Reduction & Health Informatics serves as a focal point and champion for burden reduction, national standards and interoperability, and to engage our stakeholders to inform solutions. CMS has continued to seek public input on barriers to accessing health care and related challenges to inform our work and better support the

[123] "Medicare Program: Hospital Outpatient Prospective Payment and Ambulatory Surgical Center Payment Systems and Quality Reporting Programs; Organ Acquisition; Rural Emergency Hospitals: Payment Policies, Conditions of Participation, Provider Enrollment, Physician Self-Referral; New Service Category for Hospital Outpatient Department Prior Authorization Process; Overall Hospital Quality Star Rating; COVID-19"; https://www.federalregister.gov/documents/2022/11/23/2022-23918/medicare-program-hospital-outpatient-prospective-payment-and-ambulatory-surgical-center-payment#footnote-237-p72137.

populations we serve. In the December 2022 Advancing Interoperability and Improving Prior Authorization Processes proposed rule (87 FR 76323), CMS included a Request for Information that acknowledged this provision of the SUPPORT Act and sought feedback from the public on innovative approaches to addressing the need to facilitate the electronic exchange of behavioral health information, as well as approaches to support the exchange of health information to behavioral health providers to inform care and provision of behavioral health services.

In addition to these CMS activities, the Office of the National Coordinator for Health IT (ONC) is working to better enable providers to interact with health care plans and other payers for the automated, electronic completion of prior authorization tasks. More information is available here: https://www.healthit.gov/topic/laws-regulation-and-policy/request-information-electronic- prior-authorization-standards-implementation-specifications. Further, ONC recently proposed rulemaking to advance interoperability, improve transparency, support the access, exchange, and use of electronic health information, enhance health IT certification, and reduce burden and costs. More information is available here: https://www.govinfo.gov/content/pkg/FR-2023-04- 18/pdf/2023-07229.pdf.

In 2020, HHS released a comprehensive strategy to reduce the regulatory and administrative burden related to the use of health IT, including EHRs. Reflective of public comment, the *Strategy on Reducing Regulatory and Administrative Burdens Relating to the Use of Health IT and EHRs* targets burdens tied to regulatory and administrative requirements that HHS can directly impact through the rulemaking process. The report's strategies, recommendations, and policy shifts aim to give clinicians more time to focus on what matters – caring for their patients. This report was developed as a collaborative effort between ONC and CMS. ONC, CMS, and HHS as a whole are working to implement strategies identified within the report to reduce burden and advance interoperable health IT.

1) Last summer, with bipartisan support, the Congress incorporated my Excellence in Mental Health and Addiction Treatment Expansion Act into legislation signed by President Biden that expanded the Medicaid Certified Community Behavioral Health Clinic (CCBHC) demonstration nationwide. I understand that HHS selected fifteen (15) states to receive planning grants. When will the first ten (10) states be selected to participate in the expanded demonstration?
2) How have the mental health and substance use crises impacted the utilization of CCBHCs and the level of acuity of patients seen at CCBHCs?

Answer 23-24

CMS recognizes CCBHCs' critical role in providing crisis services that are available 24 hours a day, 7 days a week and serve anyone who requests care for mental health or substance use, regardless of their ability to pay. The expansion of CCBHCs builds on the Administration's previous work to launch the 988 Suicide & Crisis Lifeline and further builds the crisis continuum of care and addresses the ongoing mental health crisis.

Up to ten states that received planning grants will be able to join the CCBHC demonstration program in 2024 after a separate application process. While up to 10 states can join the Medicaid demonstration in 2024, states will have another chance to join the CCBHC demonstration in 2026, and every two years thereafter. The CCBHC planning phase assists states in certifying clinics as CCBHCs, establishing prospective payment systems for Medicaid reimbursable services, and preparing an application to participate in a four-year demonstration program.

The CCBHC demonstration program provides reimbursement through Medicaid for the full cost of services that CCBHCs provide, at higher, more competitive rates than community mental health centers previously received. This sustainable funding also ensures they can provide a more comprehensive range of services rather than fragmented services driven by billing codes. The President's FY24 budget proposes to make this demonstration model permanent, thereby expanding access to behavioral health services for all Americans and calls for historic funding to support the expansion of mental health and substance use care.

1) CMS currently provides several waiver options for states to increase provider capacity for substance use disorder (SUD) and for serious mental illness (SMI) in adults or serious emotional disturbance (SED) in children by amending the IMD exclusion policy. Can you provide an update on how successful these waivers have been in achieving their goals of increasing provider capacity, reducing ER utilization among Medicaid beneficiaries with SUD/SMI/SED, and improving the continuum of care for Medicaid beneficiaries?

Answer 25

Through section 1115 demonstrations, CMS is partnering with states to test means of increasing access to the full continuum of care for SUD, including medication assisted treatment, and residential treatment, as advocated by leading SUD treatment experts. In November 2022, CMS issued a report entitled "Medicaid Section 1115 Substance Use Disorder (SUD) Demonstrations: An In-Depth Look Into Pre-demonstration Measures of SUD Need, Treatment Use, Availability, and Outcomes Across States."[124] This report is part of a series of rapid cycle reports intended to share findings and insights about section 1115 SUD demonstrations. This report focuses on the pre-demonstration measures of SUD treatment need, treatment use, treatment availability, and health outcomes for Medicaid section 1115 SUD demonstration states that had demonstrations approved by June 1, 2020. The report also provides analogous findings for states without an approved section 1115 SUD demonstration by June 1, 2020. Understanding the pre- demonstration levels of SUD treatment need, treatment use, treatment availability, and SUD- related health and mortality outcomes among Medicaid beneficiaries in section 1115 SUD demonstration states, and how these differ from measures in states that did not have an approved section 1115 SUD demonstration by June 2020, will help ensure estimates of the impact of SUD demonstrations are valid. Rigorous impact estimates for the section 1115 SUD demonstration states support CMS's goal of improving beneficiary outcomes and reducing mortality rates among the Medicaid SUD population. This report, as well as additional evaluations of 1115 demonstrations, can be found at: https://www.medicaid.gov/medicaid/section-1115-demonstrations/1115-demonstration-monitoring-evaluation/1115-demonstration-federal- evaluation-meta-analysis/index.html.

---

[124] "Medicaid Section 1115 Substance Use Disorder (SUD) Demonstrations: An In-Depth Look Into Pre-demonstration Measures of SUD Need, Treatment Use, Availability, and Outcomes Across States" https://www.medicaid.gov/medicaid/section-1115-demonstrations/downloads/sud-115-rcr-baseline.pdf.

1) Patient access to off-label, medically necessary cancer therapeutics has been dramatically increased by the change to allow Medicare coverage if the drug is recognized in certain compendia or supported by two peer-reviewed articles in journals identified by Medicare. Rare disease patients now face the same struggles that cancer patients once did in terms of accessing off-label treatments. In the absence of a compendia for rare disease patients (like the National Comprehensive Cancer Network for oncology), what would be the risks and benefits of using the two-article approach to determine CMS coverage for rare disease therapeutics?

Answer 26

In addition to coverage for off-label use of drugs and biologicals in an anti-cancer chemotherapeutic regimen, FDA-approved drugs and biologicals may also be considered for use in the determination of medically accepted indications for off-label use if determined by the Medicare Administrative Contractor (MAC) to be reasonable and necessary. Drugs used for indications other than those in the approved labeling may be covered under Medicare if it is determined that the use is medically accepted, taking into consideration the major drug compendia, authoritative medical literatures and/or accepted standards of medical practice. In determining whether there is supportive clinical evidence for a particular use of a drug, the quality of the published evidence must be considered. If a use is identified as not indicated by the Centers for Medicare & Medicaid Services (CMS) or the FDA, or if a use is specifically identified as not indicated in one or more of the compendia listed, or if the MAC determines, based on peer-reviewed medical literature, that a particular use of a drug is not safe and effective, the off-label usage is not supported and, therefore, the drug is not covered.

Questions for the Record

Ashley Thompson, Senior Vice President, Public Policy Analysis and Development, American Hospital Association
U.S. House Energy and Commerce Committee Subcommittee on Health
"Lowering Unaffordable Costs: Legislative Solutions to Increase Transparency and Competition in Health Care."
April 26, 2023

In response to The Honorable Richard Hudson's questions

1) Iqvia, a leading pharmacoeconomic and health information vendor, recently examined how patients benefit from the 340B program. In its conclusion it stated: "The 340B Drug Discount Program as it exists today is a complex system of arbitrage involving multiple stakeholders, each of which profits from 340B revenue. It's a drug discount program in which most vulnerable patients at contract pharmacies often do not get the drug discounts." Source. How do hospitals ensure that the drug benefits provided by the 340B program impact the patients to which they apply its discounts?

The 340B program is structured in such a way that it gives hospitals flexibility to use the savings that it achieves from participation in the program to address the unique needs of the patients and communities they serve. This flexibility is extremely important, as the needs of a rural 340B hospitals' patients may be different than those of an urban 340B hospitals' patients.

For example, a rural hospital may use its 340B savings to provide access to labor and delivery services in their local community so that patients do not have to travel long distances to receive that care. On the other hand, an urban hospital may decide to use its savings to support a diabetes counseling and education program to target the city's underserved population. In each of these examples, the hospital's 340B savings are being directly applied in a way that improves access to care and ultimately the health and well-being of the patients they serve. One of the many ways that hospitals use their 340B savings is to discount the cost of drugs directly to their patients. In some cases, hospitals can offset the cost entirely for these medications. Together, 340B hospitals alone provide approximately $68 billion in community benefits, due in large part, to these hospitals' 340B savings.[125]1 In addition, 340B hospitals are responsible for 77% of the inpatient care provided to Medicaid patients.[126]2

Finally, the savings 340B hospitals achieve through the program — whether at the main hospital location, an offsite clinic in the local community or a community pharmacy with which the hospital contracts with — are not limited to use only for the patients at that site of care. The savings are used across the hospital to benefit all as stated in the purpose of the program and spelled out in the 340B statute: to stretch scarce resources and provide more comprehensive services to more patients.

1) The 340B drug discount program has grown dramatically over the past several years. Total program drug purchases grew 15 percent alone in 2021. Among all of the hospital and grantee covered entities, one grew over 54 percent: Sexually Transmitted Disease Clinics (source). Interestingly, the CDC reported that STDs during this time period grew at rates of ~7-10 percent (source). Are you aware of any medical trends that could explain this rapid growth of 340B STD clinic drug purchases? Are you aware of any 340B scheme that could explain this rapid growth of 340B STD clinic drug purchases?

One of the primary factors that influences the amount of drug purchases made by 340B covered entities are the prices of the drugs themselves — which are set by drug companies alone. These drug prices are also constantly and arbitrarily increased by drug companies. This is an unfortunate and challenging situation that all 340B entities must manage. As the prices of the drugs rise, the amount 340B entities spend to acquire those drugs also increases, especially as demand for care also grows.

One factor that may be influencing the growth in drug purchases for 340B STD clinics is the growth in drug prices to treat conditions like Hepatitis C. Drugs like Epclusa, Harvoni and Sovaldi used to treat Hepatitis C can cost anywhere from $22,000 to over $80,000 for a standard 12-week treatment. Even with 340B discounts, these drugs are extremely expensive for 340B entities to acquire and provide to their patients.

---

[125] https://www.aha.org/2022-06-07-2022-340b-hospital-community-benefit-analysis.

[126] https://www.healthaffairs.org/content/forefront/30-years-340b-preserving-health-care-safety-net.

In response to the Honorable Yvette Clarke's questions

2) Starting on October 1st, safety net hospitals will face an $8 billion annual cut this year and continuing through fiscal year 2027 for a total of $32 billion. This represents OVER two-thirds of the federal share of the program and would be a devastating blow to the health care safety net. That is why I introduced, H.R. 2665, the Supporting Safety Net Hospitals Act. Which would eliminate Medicaid Disproportionate Share Hospital (or DSH) cuts in fiscal years 2024 and 2025 – cuts that, as I said, Represent TWO-THIRDS of all federal Medicaid DSH funding.

If the proposed cuts go into effect, rural and urban safety net hospitals will lose critical funding that enables them to keep their doors open and provide care to the most vulnerable Americans.

My first question is intended for Ms. Thompson. Could you describe the impact of these cuts on U.S. hospitals that serve a safety net role, if they were to go in effect? How does this legislation alleviate concerns?

Should these cuts go into effect, it would have a devastating impact on the hospitals that receive Medicaid DSH payments, as well as the patients they serve. We anticipate that hospitals would have to reduce services in their communities to adjust to state allotment cuts that, according to the Medicaid and CHIP Payment and Access Commission, vary from a 10% reduction to as much as a 90% reduction, depending on how a state's DSH program is structured.[127]3 H.R. 2665 would alleviate these concerns by eliminating the pending cuts for the next two fiscal years — a time when our members are still facing financial challenges coming out of the pandemic, as well as the potential of caring for additional uninsured patients who may be losing their Medicaid coverage in the next year as the redetermination process continues.

1) You all may remember, at the beginning of the COVID-19 pandemic, my state, specifically, New York City was hit the hardest and frontline hospital workers were extremely crucial to addressing the ever-evolving needs of the pandemic.

Ms. Thompson, do you believe these cuts would affect the magnitude of hospitals responding to any future pandemics or health crises?

The short answer to your question is yes — any reduction to hospital funding could impact a facility's ability to respond to a future crisis. Hospitals serve as anchors in their communities, providing care to everyone, regardless of insurance status, 24/7. Any cut to their funding could have consequences for hospitals as they prepare to face the next challenge, whether that is a health care pandemic or natural disaster. The investment hospitals make in stand-by capacity is essential to ensuring they have the staff available to serve patients during both daily emergencies as well as more sustained crises.

---

[127] https://www.macpac.gov/wp-content/uploads/2023/03/Chapter-4-Annual-Analysis-of-Medicaid-DSH- Allotments-to-States.pdf.

PCMA

May 31, 2023

The Honorable Brett Guthrie Chairman
Subcommittee on Health
U.S. House Committee on Energy and Commerce 2125 Rayburn House Office Building
Washington, DC, 20515 Dear Chairman Guthrie:

Thank you for the opportunity to testify before the House Committee on Energy and Commerce Subcommittee on Health at your April 26 hearing on behalf of the Pharmaceutical Care Management Association (PCMA). Our responses to Representative Bilirakis's questions for the record are below.

1) What is the PBM industry doing to stop the use of Alternative Funding Venders, also known as, Alternative Funding Programs from taking advantage of compassionate care programs and funding that is intended to provide access and relief for economically challenged patients?

As the industry's trade association, we are not privy to the details of member companies' actions with respect to alternative funding vendors; however, the use of these vendors bypasses formularies and incentives intended to encourage patients to use the most cost-effective and clinically appropriate drugs to treat their condition. PBMs administer formularies on behalf of their health plan sponsor clients to help lower drug costs. Further, PBMs have tools in place to monitor utilization to avoid negative drug interactions and encourage adherence, and alternative funding programs interfere with pharmacy benefit companies' ability to do those things in support of better patient outcomes.

In the United States, pharmacy benefit companies provide affordable access to prescription drugs for 275 million people, who fill more than 3.6 billion prescriptions annually. PBMs support efforts to address high out-of-pocket costs for patients and offer health plan sponsors a variety of programs in the commercial market to lower patient cost sharing. These include benefit design options that allow up to full rebate pass-through at the point of sale and programs for zero or low cost sharing for preventive and chronic medications ahead of meeting a deductible. Through advocacy, pharmacy benefit companies encouraged the U.S. Department of Treasury to expand the list of preventive care for health savings account (HSA) participants to include a wider range of drugs used to treat chronic conditions, such as diabetes, asthma, and heart disease. The U.S. Department of Treasury now allows certain chronic and preventive careprescriptions, including insulin, to be covered at no or low cost sharing ahead of an enrollee meeting the deductible in high deductible health plans.

In addition to offering programs to lower out-of-pocket costs, PBMs work with those providing insurance to encourage patients through formulary design and cost-sharing incentives to use the most affordable drugs, which are usually generics. Generic dispensing has grown over the past decade as more generics have entered the market and patients have responded to health plan designs encouraging their use.[128] PBMs also employ other tools designed to deliver high- quality drug benefits while bringing down costs.[129] For many brand drugs, PBMs negotiate directly with drug manufacturers who compete for formulary placement by offering rebates.[130] For drugs on a preferred tier of a plan's formulary, patients typically have lower cost sharing.[131] As competing products enter the market, PBMs gain the flexibility to leverage competitor products to negotiate deeper drug discounts for patients, plans and employers.[132]

PBMs have also led the industry in creating arrangements that account for the value of specialty and high-cost medications.[133] Value-based arrangements will be critical to managing the costs of next-generation therapies such as cell and gene therapies, orphan drugs, and ultra-expensive specialty drugs. Value-based contracts will better allow plans to manage these high costs, and plan sponsors will need broad flexibility to craft and employ value-based contracts.

2) We've heard concerning stories about patients not gaining access to treatments due to PBM narrow networks with plans. What is the industry doing to ensure patients are not denied access to important medications for serious chronic diseases because of Exclusion Lists?

A formulary is a continually updated list of prescription drugs approved for reimbursement by the pharmacy benefit company's plan sponsor clients. In coordination with independent clinical experts on a pharmacy and therapeutics (P&T) committee, pharmacy benefit companies typically develop a recommended formulary for plan sponsors, who may customize it.

Prescription drug formularies give patients financial incentives to use the most clinically effective and cost-effective generic and brand drugs. When there are multiple drug options that are equally effective at treating a medical condition, pharmacy benefit companies encourage drug companies to compete for formulary placement by offering price concessions. In turn, plan enrollees typically have lower cost sharing for the less expensive drug to encourage its use over costlier drugs that provide no meaningful additional clinical benefit.

With regard to an exclusion list, plan sponsors provide an appeals process for members to utilize for prescription drugs that may be excluded from coverage for a given plan.

Additionally, plan sponsors design pharmacy networks to ensure that patients have access to the medications they need and often must meet network adequacy standards set by federal

---

[128] US Food and Drug Administration (FDA). Generic Drugs. February 5, 2021. Available at https://www.fda.gov/drugs/buying-using-medicine-safely/generic-drugs.

[129] Pharmacy Benefit Management Institute (PBMI). Solving America's High Drug Cost Problem: Prevent Drug Company Tactics that Increase Costs and Undermine Clinical Quality. 2020. Available at https://www.pcmanet.org/wp-content/uploads/2021/01/Solving-America%E2%80%99s-High-Drug-Cost-Problem_whitepaper_FINAL2.pdf. Pharmacy Benefit Management Institute (PBMI). Trends in Specialty Drug Benefits. 2017. Available at www.pbmi.com/research. Pharmacy Benefit Management Institute (PBMI). 2016 Trends in Drug Benefit Design. 2016. Available at www.pbmi.com/research.

[130] Foley Hoag. The History of Rebates in the Drug Supply Chain and HHS' Proposed Rule to Change Safe Harbor Protection for Manufacturer Rebates. April 2, 2019. Available at https://foleyhoag.com/publications/ebooks-and-white- papers/2019/march/the-history-of-rebates-in-the-drug-supply-chain.

[131] Congressional Budget Office (CBO). Prescription Drugs: Spending, Use, and Prices. January 17, 2020. Available at https://www.cbo.gov/system/files/2022-01/57050-Rx-Spending.pdf.

[132] Congressional Budget Office (CBO). Prescription Drugs: Spending, Use, and Prices. January 17, 2020. Available at https://www.cbo.gov/system/files/2022-01/57050-Rx-Spending.pdf.

[133] Pharmacy Benefit Management Institute. Solving America's High Drug Cost Problem: Prevent Drug Company Tactics that Increase Costs and Undermine Clinical Quality. January 2021. Available https://www.pcmanet.org/wp-content/uploads/2021/01/Solving-America%E2%80%99s-High-Drug-Cost-Problem_whitepaper_FINAL2.pdf.

and/or state law. They also include pharmacies that are high quality, ensure patient safety, and are often lower cost for their members. These preferred pharmacies provide a higher standar of care, and some specialize in handling patients who have serious illnesses. Plan sponsors select these specially qualified pharmacies to help manage a member's serious chronic disease, ensure adherence, and lower overall costs.

Again, I appreciate the opportunity to testify and submit answers to the questions for the record. If you have any questions, please do not hesitate to contact me directly at kbass@pcmanet.org.

Sincerely,

Kristin Bass
Chief Policy and External Affairs Officer

USC Schaeffer | BROOKINGS
USC-BROOKINGS SCHAEFFER
INITIATIVE FOR HEALTH POLICY

Economic Studies
The Brookings Institution
1775 Massachusetts Ave NW
Washington, DC 20036

Responses to Questions for the Record Loren Adler, MS
Associate Director and Fellow, USC-Brookings Schaeffer Initiative for Health Policy Economic Studies, Brookings Institution Before the United States House of Representatives Committee on Energy and Commerce Subcommittee on Health
Lowering Unaffordable Costs: Legislative Solutions to Increase Transparency and Competition in Health Care
May 31, 2023

Honorable Gus Bilirakis

1) When we talk about competition, we have to think about it holistically. We can't just talk about hospitals, we have to talk about payers as well. I am a strong supporter of the Medicare Advantage program and believe in it as a long-term part of making Medicare solvent. But we know the landscape is rapidly changing as the health care system vertically consolidates beneath payers. And policymakers need to understand what that means for seniors and taxpayers What incentives are created when the same entity owns the insurance company responsible for paying for care, the doctor responsible for providing care, the pharmacy that dispenses medication, and the PBM that decides how much patients pay for that medication?

There has indeed been a growing trend toward insurer ownership of physician practices, pharmacy benefit managers (PBMs), and pharmacies. These arrangements create multiple incentives.

On the one hand, insurer integration with physicians or pharmacies may enhance incentives to reduce costs. For instance, a primary care physician aligned with an insurer may be more likely to refer a patient needing specialist or hospital care to lower-priced alternatives because the same entity is now responsible for those specialist or hospital costs. These arrangements also increase the incentive to reduce premiums because added enrollees now create provider-level, insurer-level, PBM-level, and pharmacy-level profit margins for the payer.

On the other hand, some payer acquisitions will directly increase horizontal consolidation in physician, ambulatory surgery center (ASC), PBM, or pharmacy markets, which may lead to higher prices. This vertical integration may also generate incentives to raise the price of the insurer-owned physician services to competing insurers (or refuse to contract with them altogether). For example, an acquired physician group might terminate contracts with competing insurers or demand higher prices to remain contracted, thereby making competing insurance plans less attractive to consumers and increasing enrollment in the vertically integrated insurer's plans. Financial integration between payers and physicians will also tend to enhance incentives for the aligned physicians to code patients more intensely in order to generate higher payments to the payer's Medicare Advantage products and larger Affordable Care Act risk adjustment transfers from other plans.

2) What behavior does this vertical consolidation drive?

In the previous answer, I discuss the incentives that are likely created. We have limited evidence to date, however, about the effects of this vertical consolidation on behavior. One area where we do have strong evidence is that Medicare Advantage plans with vertically-integrated providers generated patient risk scores 16% higher than would have resulted in traditional Medicare, whereas non-integrated plans generated risk scores that were 6% higher.[134]

3) Is it driving competition in the health system or does it cause anticompetitive behavior?

To the extent insurer acquisitions of physician practices, PBMs, and pharmacies are horizontally consolidating those markets, it will likely drive anticompetitive behavior. The vertical relationships may also lead to anticompetitive behavior in the form of efforts to raise competing insurers' costs.

On the other hand, payer ownership of primary care practices and ASCs may enhance competition in hospital and outpatient service markets.

4) In many cases there are efficiencies to be gained from integrating care. But these arrangements, which in many cases are novel and growing rapidly, demand transparency into how they are affecting patient care and health costs. Do you support

---

[134] Geruso, Michael, and Timothy Layton. "Upcoding: Evidence from Medicare on Squishy Risk Adjustment." *The Journal of Political Economy*, U.S. National Library of Medicine, Mar. 2020, https://www.ncbi.nlm.nih.gov/pmc/articles/PMC7384673/.

the discussion draft that would gather information on these vertically-integrated arrangements in Medicare Parts C and D, and if so can you speak to why?

5) Do you have any recommendations for the Committee as we attempt to get more information on the topic of vertically-integrated arrangements and consolidation among providers?

Taking questions 4 and 5 together, I agree that more transparency into these vertical arrangements could be immensely valuable. At present, it is difficult to identify which physician groups are owned by payers and there are gaps in the Medicare Advantage data that is made available to researchers.

Along with Matthew Fiedler and Benedic Ippolito, we wrote extensively on these questions in a piece titled "Assessing recent health care proposals from the House Committee on Energy and Commerce", excerpted below:

> Perhaps the most potentially impactful transparency bill put forward by the subcommittee would generate publicly-available data on the parent company and ownership structure of health care providers. Specifically, the proposal would require certain providers—physician groups, hospitals, ASCs, and freestanding emergency departments—to report this information to the Department of Health and Human Services (HHS), along with any mergers, acquisitions, or changes in ownership over the prior year. HHS would then be required to make these data publicly available.
>
> Data like these would facilitate several types of important analyses. For example, by making available information on each entity's ultimate parent company, it would allow agencies and researchers to more easily and accurately track horizontal consolidation in physician and facility markets and trace its effects. Information on ownership structure would also provide an up-to-date snapshot of emerging trends in different forms of corporate ownership of health care providers, as well as allow for stronger analysis of the effects of private equity, hospital, and payer acquisitions of physician practices.
>
> Some similar data are already being reported to the Centers for Medicare and Medicaid Services (CMS), but the bill would greatly improve what is readily available to researchers, especially with respect to physician groups. In particular, there currently is no comprehensive source of data that makes it possible to identify which physician groups share a common owner or determine the ownership structure of the entity with a controlling ownership interest in the group (e.g., private equity, insurer, or hospital).
>
> In detail, physician groups are identified in Medicare claims data by their tax identification number (TIN). But in many cases, large parent companies own and operate many TINs. For instance, Envision, owned by private equity firm Kohlberg Kravis Roberts (KKR), operates more than 100 TINs in its emergency medicine staffing business. Moreover, matching TINs to their parent company and the ownership structure of that parent company is often complex and difficult to automate. The best starting point at present is the Medicare Data on Provider Practice and Specialty (MD-PPAS) data extract, which researchers can purchase from CMS. These data include the legal name associated with physician group TINs, from the Medicare Provider Enrollment, Chain, and Ownership System (PECOS) data, and some information on the geographic location where a clinician delivers most of his or her Medicare services.
>
> But that information is often inadequate to identify a practice's parent company. Researchers are therefore forced to identify parent companies by piecing together additional information on ownership from various sources, which make this type of research very resource-intensive and thus limits how much can be done. This manual work also inevitably ends up incomplete, which can result in researchers underestimating the level of market

concentration, among other potential problems. Ideally, this proposed legislation would lead to CMS releasing a more robust version of the MD-PPAS data extract that additionally includes the parent company and ownership structure of each physician group TIN (or otherwise link TINs to the relevant parent company and its ownership structure).

Another bill considered by the subcommittee also aims to increase the transparency of health care ownership arrangements, with a focus on vertical integration between health plans and providers and in-home medical assessment entities. The bill requires Medicare Advantage Organizations (MAOs) to disclose certain data, including about average enrollee utilization, diagnoses, risk scores, and spending, broken out by whether enrollees' had received services from a provider integrated with the MAO. (The bill would also require certain reporting by prescription drug plan sponsors, pharmacy benefit managers, and pharmacies, which we discuss in a later section.)

As discussed above, we believe that greater disclosure of information about ownership arrangements has high value. If those data can be linked with health care claims data, researchers can then answer a wide range of questions about the behavior of, in this case, vertically integrated entities. In the case that no such linkage is feasible, collecting certain aggregated data—as envisioned in this bill—can also be useful if the data offer insight into business practices and are not otherwise attainable. However, many of the comparisons that could be made using aggregate data requested in this bill would be quite vulnerable to confounding from unobserved differences in patient characteristics, which makes us question whether it is worth bearing the (modest) administrative burdens required to collect them.

As an alternative, we suggest pursuing the enhanced reporting on provider ownership discussed earlier in this section in tandem with improvements to the Medicare Advantage (MA) encounter data available to researchers. Most importantly, CMS should release payment and cost-sharing information it collects with the encounter data, which it currently withholds. It should also begin collecting information on plans' non-fee-for-service payments to providers (e.g., shared savings or shared loss payment), which are not captured in traditional claims data. To facilitate analysis of how vertical integration affects the intensity of diagnosis coding, CMS could also give researchers access to enrollee-level risk scores for years other than 2014.

6) As we know, the trust fund that supports Medicare hospital coverage runs out in 6 years. Research shows physician-led hospitals produce savings for Medicare and are more cost- effective than other hospitals. Physician-led hospitals participated in one of the DRGs for the Center for Medicare & Medicaid Innovation's joint replacement demonstration. 72% of participating physician-led hospitals produced savings – much more than the 52% of other hospitals achieving this goal. If we are serious about addressing Medicare solvency, can you think of a reason why we shouldn't look at physician-owned hospitals to help bring down costs.

I do not know of strong evidence that speaks to effects of allowing physician-owned hospitals, but the case for disallowing them appears weak. Even if the effects of allowing physician-owned hospitals would be small, the bar should be high to limit competition in health care markets.

Index

E

F

G

H

I

K

L

M

N

O

P

Q

R

S

T

P

Q

R

U

V

W

Y